The Ministry

of PETER,

the Chief Apostle

The Ministry
of PETER,
the Chief Apostle

edited by
Frank F. Judd Jr.
Eric D. Huntsman
Shon D. Hopkin

THE 43RD ANNUAL

BRIGHAM YOUNG UNIVERSITY

SIDNEY B. SPERRY SYMPOSIUM

RSC
B Y U

DESERET
BOOK

The Sperry Symposium is sponsored annually by Brigham Young University and the Church Educational System in honor of Sidney B. Sperry. In the course of his forty-five-year career as a religious educator, Dr. Sperry earned a reputation for outstanding teaching and scholarship. The symposium seeks to perpetuate his memory by fostering continuing research on gospel topics.

Copublished by the Religious Studies Center, Brigham Young University, Provo, Utah, and Deseret Book Company, Salt Lake City, Utah.

Library of Congress Cataloging-in-Publication Data

Sperry Symposium (43rd : 2014 : Brigham Young University), author
    The ministry of Peter, the chief apostle / edited by Frank F. Judd Jr., Eric D. Huntsman, and Shon D. Hopkin.
        pages cm
    The 43rd Annual Brigham Young University Sidney B. Sperry Symposium.
    Includes bibliographical references and index.
    ISBN 978-1-60907-922-2 (hardbound : alk. paper) 1. Peter, the Apostle, Saint.—Congresses. 2. Church history—Primitive and early church, ca. 30–600.—Congresses. 3. The Church of Jesus Christ of Latter-day Saints—Doctrines.—Congresses. 4. Mormon Church—Doctrines.—Congresses. I. Judd, Frank F., editor. II. Huntsman, Eric D., 1965– editor. III. Hopkin, Shon, editor.
    BS2515.S65 2014
    225.9'2—dc23   2014012985

Printed in the United States of America
R. R. Donnelley, Harrisonburg, VA

10   9   8   7   6   5   4   3   2   1

Contents

Introduction

This year's Sidney B. Sperry Symposium honors the example, teachings, and legacy of Peter, the chief Apostle, who served as one of Jesus' closest companions during his mortal ministry and then led his church after his Ascension. Of the original Twelve, the New Testament portrait of Peter is the one that is most fully drawn: the Gospels, for instance, provide glimpses of his personality and furnish a view of his strengths, his weaknesses, and, above all, his faithful devotion to his Master and friend, whose gospel Peter preached to the very end of his life. As a fallible but faithful disciple, Peter is a great example for Latter-day Saints and all followers of Christ, not because he perfectly followed the Lord and never made a mistake, but precisely because although he made mistakes and was chastised by the Lord, he repented, humbled himself, and showed us how the grace of Christ can make our weaknesses strengths, enabling us to serve powerfully and endure to the end. As President Gordon B. Hinckley has written, "Draw comfort and resolution from the example of Peter who, though he had walked daily with Jesus, in an hour of extremity denied both the Lord and the testimony which he carried in his own heart. But he rose above this, and became a mighty defender and a powerful advocate. So too, there is a way for you to turn about, and add your strength and faith to the strength and faith of others in building the kingdom of God."[1]

In the tradition of Sidney B. Sperry, a noted latter-day scholar who served as an influential religious educator from 1932 to 1969, papers selected for this volume seek to combine scholarly and theological insights in ways that are both devotional and thoughtful, particularly through careful examination of scriptural texts and religious history. Accordingly, as this year's contributions consider the figure of Peter and his teachings, they reaffirm fundamental doctrines and precepts while bringing new insights to our Latter-day Saint audience. In regard to Peter the man, some papers deal broadly with Peter's ministry and example, considering him as a fallible but faithful disciple and as a powerful witness of Jesus Christ. To supplement these treatments, this volume has reprinted as an appendix the pivotal Brigham Young University address "Peter, My Brother" by Spencer W. Kimball. Other papers explore particular incidents from his life such as Jesus' declaration to Peter about his being "the rock," the nature of the keys that Peter received, his problematic denial on the night of Jesus' arrest, his later ability to heal even as the Savior had, and his relationship with his fellow Apostle Paul. Two additional papers bring to light the contributions of Peter in a wider historical context by reviewing what current archaeology tells us about the setting of his life and about exploring his use in later Christian art and iconography.

Another set of papers deals specifically with texts written by or otherwise associated with Peter. Two papers examine the New Testament letters attributed to Peter, considering the issues that have been raised about the authorship of 1 Peter and the particular genre of 2 Peter, which as an example of testamentary literature serves as a type of "farewell address." While Peter did not write any of the canonical Gospels, one of this year's papers seeks to determine to what extent Peter's preaching may have lain behind the composition of the Gospel of Mark, while another paper considers accounts of Peter in the New Testament apocrypha.

Other papers deal specifically with doctrines that Peter taught and church practices that he established. These include his revelation concerning the extension of the gospel to the Gentiles, the doctrine of calling and election, the importance of preaching and vicarious work for the dead, and the importance of loyalty to civil authority. Finally, another study highlights Peter's importance to the Restoration.

Beyond those whose contributions appear in this volume as written works, we are grateful to those whose efforts helped produce this year's symposium and this collection. These include Thomas R. Valletta of Seminaries and Institutes, Patty Smith and support staff of the College of Religious Education, and the blind reviewers who carefully vetted each submission and made helpful suggestions for all of the papers. Thomas Wayment, Devan Jensen, and the staff of BYU's Religious Studies Center deserve particular mention for bringing a new level of professionalism and scholarship to this volume. In addition, we express appreciation to Elder Bruce C. Hafen, who delivered the keynote address, "Peter, the Melchizedek Priesthood, the Temple, and the Atonement," at the symposium itself.

Finally, we are grateful for what Peter has taught us in both word and deed. Besides teaching vital truths and providing a powerful example in both weakness and strength, above all he is worth honoring for how he served as a witness of the Lord Jesus Christ. As Peter assumed active leadership of the church in the first days after the Savior's Ascension, he led the way in choosing a successor to the fallen Judas Iscariot by laying out the qualifications of one who could serve as an Apostle. He should, Peter declared, be one who had "companied with us all the time that the Lord Jesus went in and out among us, beginning from the baptism of John, unto that same day that he was taken up from us, must one be ordained to be a witness with us of his resurrection" (Acts 1:21–22). These were, of course, the qualifications that Peter himself held. After receiving an early testimony from his brother Andrew (1:40–42) and then being the first, with Andrew, to be formally called (see Mark 1:16–18; parallels Matthew 4:18–20; Luke 5:1–11), Peter witnessed the entirety of Jesus' formal ministry. But above all, he was a witness of the risen and living Lord (see Mark 16:7, 14; Matthew 28:16–18; Luke 24:9, 12, 34, 36–48; John 20:2–10, 19–20; 1 Corinthians 15:4–5).

The power with which Peter would bear testimony of the Resurrection throughout the remainder of his life is perhaps best anticipated by his hope and eagerness at the mere prospect of Jesus living again—his excitement that was exhibited at the news from Mary Magdalene that the tomb was empty.

Indeed, it is the image of Peter running to the tomb that perhaps best encapsulates the wonderful zeal, and at times impulsiveness, that so characterized the personality of this wonderful, yet so human, chief Apostle known affectionately to his Master as "the rock." It is a fervor and passion for Christ that we, as similarly fallible disciples, all strive to emulate as we seek to establish our own testimonies ever more firmly on the foundation that is our Savior.

Frank F. Judd Jr.
Eric D. Huntsman
Shon D. Hopkin
Patty Smith
Sperry Symposium Committee

Note

1. Gordon B. Hinckley, "And Peter Went Out and Wept Bitterly," *Ensign*, May 1979, 67.

1

Fallible but Faithful

HOW SIMON THE FISHERMAN
BECAME PETER THE ROCK

Brent L. Top

Brent L. Top is dean of Religious Education at Brigham Young University.

It is particularly gratifying to me that the focus of this symposium is the life, ministry, message, and enduring contributions to our faith of the Apostle Peter. He is one of my heroes—not in some superficial "hero worship" sort of way, but rather in what I consider to be the truest meaning of the word. A hero is one "who, in the face of danger and adversity or from a position of weakness, display[s] faith, courage, and the will for self-sacrifice . . . for some greater good."[1] Unfortunately, in today's celebrity-centric pop culture, few of those who are viewed as heroes to millions exhibit the virtues of faith, courage, or self-sacrifice. They are most often the sports stars, movie stars, rock stars, stars of reality TV (which is an oxymoron in my estimation), and stars who have become stars for really nothing whatsoever. No wonder worship of such "heroes" is like chasing a mirage—it looks like something, but it really isn't.

My heroes are not perfect, Jesus Christ excepted. They have faults and foibles, frailty and fallibility—like me. That endears them to me. They have faith *and* faithfulness. That inspires me. Their faithfulness *with* fallibility, devotion *despite* deficiencies, gives me hope.

Unfortunately, Latter-day Saints are not immune to unhealthy hero worship. Some expect perfection from their heroes, whether they are prophets, apostles, bishops, or even religion professors. There is a tendency to view past and present church leaders and historical events through the sanitizing lens of a church video, portraying characters who never have a hair out of place, who always say and do the right thing, and who speak in soft, hushed tones. But that is not reality, and sometimes it does more harm than good. Recognizing, and even appreciating, the fallibility of church leaders can help us to avoid unrealistic and unhealthy hero worship, which has led some to lose their faith when their hero inevitably shows his or her fallible and fallen nature, despite also demonstrating great faith and devotion. Of this, President Dieter F. Uchtdorf recently reminded us:

> Some struggle with unanswered questions about things that have been done or said in the past. We openly acknowledge that in nearly 200 years of Church history—along with an uninterrupted line of inspired, honorable and divine events—there have been some things said and done that could cause people to question. . . .
>
> And, to be perfectly frank, there have been times when members or leaders in the Church have simply made mistakes. There have been things said or done that were not in harmony with our values, principles, or doctrine. I suppose the Church would be perfect only if it were run by perfect beings. God is perfect, and His doctrine is pure. But He works through us—His imperfect children—and imperfect people make mistakes. . . .
>
> It is unfortunate that some have stumbled because of mistakes made by men. But in spite of this, the eternal truth of the restored gospel found in The Church of Jesus Christ of Latter-day Saints is not tarnished, diminished, or destroyed.[2]

The Prophet Joseph Smith often worried about unrealistic hero worship among new converts to the church who, upon immigrating to Nauvoo, would have their first encounter with a *real* prophet. William Clayton recorded that on October 29, 1842, the Prophet "went over to the store where a number of brethren and sisters were assembled who had arrived this morning. . . . He said that he was but a man and they must not expect him to be perfect; if they expected perfection from him, he should expect it from them; but if they would bear with his infirmities and the infirmities of the brethren, he would likewise bear with their infirmities."[3] In a sermon preached a little over a month before he was martyred, Joseph declared, "I never told you I was perfect—but there is no error in the revelations which I have taught."[4]

My testimony of the Prophet Joseph Smith is not weakened in the least by the fact that he was not perfect—that he, like each of us, had infirmities and fallibilities, even made mistakes along the way. In fact, it strengthens my testimony to know that God can do his work and perform mighty miracles through fallible but faithful disciples. "A man may have a wart on his cheek and still have a face of beauty and strength," President Gordon B. Hinckley taught, "but if the wart is emphasized unduly in relation to his other features, the portrait is lacking in integrity. There was only one perfect man who ever walked the earth. The Lord has used imperfect people in the process of building his perfect society. If some of them occasionally stumbled, or if their characters may have been slightly flawed in one way or another, the wonder is the greater that they accomplished so much."[5]

So it is with Peter. He was not perfect. As a mortal, he had his full share of weaknesses. There is no record of his *directly* admitting, like Joseph Smith said, "I never told you that I was perfect," but the New Testament record is an *indirect* admission. In the Gospels his shortcomings seem to be deliberately on display. The Gospel of Mark, a book that many scholars characterize as the "memoirs" of Peter, clearly has his "fingerprints" throughout it, and it may very well be the primary source material for the records of Luke and Matthew that were later written. "It has long been debated," wrote Richard Bauckham, a Bible scholar not of the Latter-day Saint faith, "whether Mark's predominantly negative portrayal of Peter, as the foolishly self-confident disciple who misunderstands Jesus and fails him, could plausibly derive from Peter's own self-depiction.... A remarkable feature of this characterization of Peter is that it remains constant through all four canonical Gospels. Petrine material in the other Gospels that is not parallel to Mark's displays the same character traits in Peter: impetuosity, self-confidence, outspokenness, and extravagant devotion to Jesus (Matthew 14:28–33; Luke 5:8; 22:33; John 6:68–69; 13:6–10; 20:2–10; 21:7, 15–19)."[6]

As a primary source for the Gospels, Peter may be consciously highlighting—even overstating—his weaknesses and failures while downplaying his accomplishments and understating his incredible faith in and devotion to the Master. We see his fallibility and imperfections "up close and personal," but we also witness the remarkable transformation from Simon the fisherman to Peter the rock—the chief Apostle. As Bauckham concludes, "Thus the full and nuanced characterization of Peter has the effect of encouraging readers or hearers to sympathize and identify with him."[7] It is this notion upon which I wish to focus.

I do not profess to be a New Testament scholar. I was not trained in biblical studies or classical Greek. Neither do I have much background in first-century Judaism or what life was like in ancient Roman times. This paper is not intended to be a scholarly, in-depth cultural or linguistic examination of the texts associated with Peter's life and ministry. It is neither an examination of the chief Apostle's achievements nor a discussion of the doctrinal contributions of his teachings. Others more qualified than I will address those topics in the chapters that follow. This chapter is, however, my personal observation and testimony of Peter's faithfulness despite his fallibility and the transforming power of the grace of Christ.

I don't just sympathize with Peter. I empathize with him because I see myself in him in many ways. I can relate to him. Like Peter, I have been known to impetuously do or say something that I regret within minutes. Like Peter, I say things that I think are profound or clever only to realize that they fall flat, are inappropriate, or diminish the significance of the moment at hand. A couple of examples from the life of Peter illustrate this dimension of human nature (at least my human nature).

After the transcendent events that occurred on the Mount of Transfiguration—being ministered to and instructed by heavenly beings, beholding unspeakable visions of glory, and witnessing the remarkable Transfiguration of the Lord himself—Peter, in his enthusiasm, blurted out, "Master, it is good for us to be here: and let us make three tabernacles; one for thee, and one for Moses, and one for Elias." Much could be written on what Peter perhaps meant, but suffice it to say, as Luke editorialized, he spoke *not knowing what he said* (Luke 9:33; emphasis added). Luke was in essence telling us that what Simon had stated, though well intended, was a feeble attempt, at best, to capture the significance of the moment. It would be like Joseph Smith saying, as the First Vision concluded, "Wow! That was awesome!" I can imagine that as soon as the words escaped his mouth, Peter was hoping to reel them back in. Yet, despite this, he received under the hands of angelic ministrants the keys of the kingdom and the divine charge to lead the Savior's church after his Resurrection. The Master heard Peter's feeble, fallible—perhaps even foolish—words, yet looked into his heart and saw faithfulness and a future.

On another occasion Jesus taught the Apostles, as Mark records, "that the Son of man must suffer many things, and be rejected of the elders, and of the chief priests, and scribes, and be killed, and after three days rise again" (Mark 8:31). According to Mark, the Savior spoke of his death three times on the road to Jerusalem (see Mark 8:31; 9:31–32; 10:32–34). The first time, Peter "took him, and began to rebuke him" (Mark 8:32). Clearly he didn't understand all the implications of what the Master was teaching. Not wanting to hear that Jesus would soon die, Peter declared, "Be it far from thee, Lord: this shall not be" (Matthew 16:22). Though speaking from his heart, Peter's "rebuking" words to the Son of God were ignorant and inappropriate. Who did he think he was to correct or rebuke the Lord? Peter's words resulted in a sharp rebuke from Jesus: "Get thee behind me, Satan: thou art an offence unto me: for thou savourest not the things that be of God, but those that be of man" (Matthew 16:23). This is a harsh rebuke! What had Peter said or done that warranted such a strong reaction? Was there some form of pride in his heart that needed to be subdued and replaced with humility and submission? Was he proud of his devotion to and protection of the Master? Was it that he valued Jesus' life more than he, at that moment, valued what Christ's death would mean? It may be that Jesus, in his rebuke, is reminding Peter that there are some things worth dying for. Did his words demonstrate that he had zeal without knowledge, courage without comprehension? Whatever the case, Simon's words were not what he would wish they had been. No doubt he felt bad for his foolishness. Yet the Savior loved him and saw in him more *future* strength than *present* weakness.

Peter's words, at times, showed his mortal fallibility in all its glory—insensitivity, impetuousness, and even ignorance. Yet those words, even when they didn't come out right, also showed faithfulness—his love for and devotion to the Savior, albeit without full comprehension of what that love and devotion would require. Two such examples are seen in John's account of the Last Supper:

> [Jesus] riseth from supper, and laid aside his garments; and took a towel, and girded himself.
>
> After that he poureth water into a bason, and began to wash the disciples' feet, and to wipe them with the towel wherewith he was girded.
>
> Then cometh he to Simon Peter: and Peter saith unto him, Lord, dost thou wash my feet?
>
> Jesus answered and said unto him, What I do thou knowest not now; but thou shalt know hereafter.
>
> Peter saith unto him, Thou shalt never wash my feet. (John 13:4–7)

To Peter, having the Savior girded in a towel—the symbol of a household servant or common slave—doing a most menial and unpleasant task seemed as the utmost humiliation. He would have no part of it. He saw the towel, the basin of water, the Master on hands and knees, but he did not see the symbolism: "Thou shalt never wash my feet." Peter's words were aimed to protect the Savior from humiliation.

Or could it be a glimpse of Peter's own prejudice—a feeling that one in a position of importance need not and should not lower himself to such servitude? In the next moments, however, he would once again wish that he hadn't been so quick to speak. His words, though uttered with noble intent, would once again miss the mark as he began to realize that the Master spoke not of physical cleansing, but of becoming clean from sin through his Atonement. "Jesus answered him, If I wash thee not, thou hast no part with me" (John 13:8).

Beginning to understand the deeper meaning, Simon Peter said to him with typical passion and overstatement, "Lord, not my feet only, but also my hands and my head. Jesus saith to him, He that is washed needeth not save to wash his feet, but is clean every whit" (John 13:9–10).

The Savior's words served to tamp down Peter's overzealousness. Zeal can be a virtue, but to a point. Thereafter it becomes a vice. This was a challenge that at times plagued Peter. Another example illustrates this.

During the Last Supper, Jesus once again plainly taught the Apostles of his imminent death: "Now is the Son of man glorified, and God is glorified in him. . . . Little children, yet a little while I am with you. . . . Whither I go, ye cannot come" (John 13:31, 33). Like at the Mount of Transfiguration, the real meaning of the Savior's words went right past Peter, sticking neither in his head nor heart.

> Simon Peter said unto him, Lord, whither goest thou? Jesus answered him, Whither I go, thou canst not follow me now; but thou shalt follow me afterwards.
>
> Peter said unto him, Lord, why cannot I follow thee now? I will lay down my life for thy sake. (John 13:36–37)

From the lips of Simon came another bold declaration of dying devotion and steadfast faith—at least for the moment, for the mortal fallibilities of fatigue and fear would dramatically manifest themselves before the sun rose and the cock crowed. His zeal and courage would surely be tested. As much as I hate to admit it, I see myself much like Simon Peter at that moment. There have been times when my actions haven't exactly squared with my words—my behavior hasn't matched my beliefs. Like Peter, I have at times declared, "Thou art the Christ, the Son of the living God" (Matthew 16:16), and have covenanted to take his name upon me and keep his commandments, yet, spiritually speaking, I fall asleep when he needs me most. "Could ye not watch with me one hour?" (Matthew 26:40), Jesus asks me today as he did Peter that night in Gethsemane. Like Simon, there have been times when, in my own unique way, I have said, "I go a fishing" (John 21:3) when the Savior has invited me to "feed [his] lambs," "feed [his] sheep," "feed [his] sheep" (John 21:15–17). And I am not alone. "So many of us are so much like [Peter]," President Gordon B. Hinckley taught.

> We pledge our loyalty; we affirm our determination to be of good courage; we declare, sometimes even publicly, that come what may we will do the right thing, that we will stand for the right cause, that we will be true to ourselves and to others.
>
> Then the pressures begin to build. Sometimes there are social pressures. Sometimes they are personal appetites. Sometimes they are false ambitions. There is a weakening of the will. There is a softening of discipline. There is capitulation. And then there is remorse, self-accusation, and bitter tears of regret.[8]

In the end, however, Simon's faithfulness overcomes his fallen, foolish, impetuous, speaking-without-thinking nature. He did what he said he would—lay down his life for the Savior's cause. Will my faith be greater than my foibles? Will I allow my mortal selfishness to be consumed by charity, service, and sacrifice, as it was for Peter?

In a way Simon Peter, like Adam, is a type not only of prophets, but for all of us. We see both the effects of the Fall and the Atonement in him—fallibility and faithfulness, the natural man and the Saint (see Mosiah 3:19). There is one scriptural account where this is most evident. It is the account of Peter's walking on water and the events associated with that miracle.

> But the ship was now in the midst of the sea, tossed with waves: for the wind was contrary.
>
> And in the fourth watch of the night Jesus went unto them, walking on the sea.
>
> And when the disciples saw him walking on the sea, they were troubled, saying, It is a spirit; and they cried out for fear.
>
> But straightway Jesus spake unto them, saying, Be of good cheer, it is I; be not afraid. (Matthew 14:24–27)

It is in the next few verses where we see so clearly in Peter both faith and fallibility.

> And Peter answered him and said, Lord, *if it be thou*, bid me come unto thee on the water. (v. 28; emphasis added.)

I have thought a lot about this one verse and have wondered what Peter's words really meant. At first glance, it appears that fearful Simon—the simple Galilean fisherman who had fished those very waters and had experienced many storms on the lake—was calling out to the ghostly figure approaching them. "Who goes there?" I can almost hear him yelling. Upon hearing those words, "Be of good cheer, it is I; be not afraid," undoubtedly Peter felt a sense of relief. At that point, both his and the other disciples' hearts were lifted with hope for rescue from a sinking ship. But could there have been some doubt in their minds? They had never seen another man walking effortlessly on the top of crashing waves. Could their minds be playing tricks on them? Was it a ghost? Was it really the Master? If so, how could that be? How could any mortal man comprehend that miracle, at that moment, under those frightening circumstances? Could it really be?

None of us can know what was going on in Simon's head. We can only speculate why he said what he did. Was it just typical Peter impetuousness—speaking without thinking through what his words could mean? Was it just another example of Peter's zeal or bravado? Or could it be something more? I do not know the answer, but there is a possibility that, at least to me, gives special meaning to the events that follow.

Could it have been that when Peter declared "*If* it be thou," he was throwing down the gauntlet, as it were—challenging or testing the person walking on the water and claiming to be Jesus, the Son of God, to prove his identity? He was not sure at that moment. If it is a ghost, there is fear. If it is merely a figment of Peter's imagination, then there is false hope, no promise of rescue. However, if it truly is the Christ, then there is hope—then Peter can have faith and confidence. But what if it isn't him? *If thou be the Son of God? If?* Peter's "challenge" at that moment—whatever his intentions—is reminiscent of another such "challenge"— clearly not uttered in faith or devotion. "*If thou be the Son of God*, command that these stones be made bread" (Matthew 4:3; emphasis added). "*If thou be the Son of God*, cast thyself down" from the pinnacle of the temple and give the angels charge that "in their hands they shall bear thee up, lest at any time thou dash thy foot against a stone" (Matthew 4:6; emphasis added). *If thou be the Son of God*, "fall down and worship me" (Matthew 4:9).

Please do not misunderstand. I am not equating what Lucifer says to Jesus with what Peter says. Satan was taunting, tempting, and desirous to destroy. Peter, in a moment of desperation, worries and wonders aloud, faith wavering, perhaps a nagging doubt adding to the terror of the night. Lucifer was rebuked and summarily dismissed by Jesus. Simon Peter, however, received an invitation: "Come" (Matthew 14:29).

And when Peter was come down out of the ship, he walked on the water, to go to Jesus.

But when he saw the wind boisterous, he was afraid; and beginning to sink, he cried, saying, Lord, save me.

And immediately Jesus stretched forth his hand, and caught him, and said unto him, O thou of little faith, *wherefore didst thou doubt?*

And when they were come into the ship, the wind ceased.

Then they that were in the ship came and worshipped him, saying; *Of a truth thou art the Son of God.* (Matthew 14:29–33; emphasis added)

Faith and fallibility are on full display in this scriptural account. Much has been said and written about this account through the years. Most often the focus has been on either Peter's faltering, "little faith" that caused him to sink when the waves crashed against him, or his miraculous, supernatural ability to actually walk on water. Both perspectives accurately reflect the scriptural account. But to me, there is another message—symbolism, types, and shadows, if you will—that testifies of Christ's saving and enabling power—divine grace that snatches⁹ fallen man from the depths of despair and certain death (see 2 Nephi 9:10).

Whether Peter momentarily doubted Jesus' divinity, couldn't comprehend what he was seeing and experiencing, feared for his life, temporarily lost his focus, or any combination of these factors became irrelevant when he stepped out of the boat. Simon could have easily cowered in the back of the boat with the others. He could have ignored the Savior's invitation to walk to him. Yet, despite some understandable doubt and fear, he had sufficient faith to step out of the boat and take some steps toward the Savior. As remarkable as it was that he walked on water a step or two or more (which was dramatically more than had been or would ever be done by any other mortal), what he and the other disciples experienced after he sunk into the sea was infinitely more remarkable and life-changing.

To me, this is a story of triumph and transformation more than of failure or lack of faith. The focus should not be on Simon's sinking but on Jesus' lifting—not on Peter's human *fallibility*, but Christ's divine *ability*. I am convinced that Peter's faith became stronger and his leadership more tempered from sinking than had he continued to walk on water. If he had walked to the Savior and then back to the boat, no doubt the other disciples would have been in awe of that miracle, and perhaps of Peter. But that is not what he and the other disciples needed. The chief Apostle's triumph, however, came later—in a different way, in *what he learned* from the Master and in *what he became* because of this experience—a transformation that resulted from sinking and then being rescued by the Lord.

"And when they were come into the ship, the wind ceased" (Matthew 14:32). That is a short and simple verse, but it raises many questions. How far were Jesus and Peter away from the boat? How did Jesus lift Peter out of the water? How did they get back into the boat? The scriptural record is silent with regard to those things, but perhaps in that silence we can see the message of the miracle. I believe that Simon the fisherman, despite his experience and skill as fisherman on that very lake, thought he was going to drown in that very moment. In terror, he cried out, saying, "Lord, save me" (Matthew 14:30). Have you ever felt like you were sinking—drowning, as it were—and called out to the Savior for rescue and relief? Peter's anguished cry for physical rescue mirrors those of the Book of Mormon prophet Alma, who cried out to the Lord for spiritual rescue, "O Jesus, thou Son of God, have mercy on me, who am in the gall of bitterness, and am encircled about by the everlasting chains of death" (Alma 36:18).

Returning to Peter's story, Jesus "immediately stretched forth his hand, and caught him" by the hand and lifted him back to the surface, like a father would lift a fallen child back to his feet (Matthew 14:31). To me the miracle is not so much that Peter may have taken a step or two on the surface of the water at first but rather, as he cried out, "Lord, save me," and caught hold of the Savior's outstretched hand, that he walked back to the boat on the water—*with the Savior.*

As a young missionary in Denmark, I gained a greater appreciation for this miracle as I read the Bible in the Danish language. The word that is translated as "come" in English is "kom" in Danish. It sounds the same and means the same—mostly. But there is an additional meaning in Danish that isn't necessarily found in English. The Savior's invitation to "come unto me" (*"kom til mig"*) can be translated "walk to me" or "walk *with* me." Jesus beckoned Peter to "come"—not just walk *to* him, but walk *with* him. That is the great miracle!

"Of a truth thou art the Son of God," the disciples cried out in amazement (Matthew 14:33). "What manner of man is this, that even the winds and the sea obey him!" (Matthew 8:27). What manner of man indeed! No wonder Peter and the other Apostles glorified God! Not only did Jesus walk on water and silence the storms by his very word, but he *enabled* Peter to do the same. What a great learning experience for Peter, who would be expected to lead the kingdom at the Savior's death, and each of us, whatever our own roles and responsibilities: when "walking on water" by yourself, you will always sink. That is a fact of life for fallen, fallible man. But when you take hold of the Savior's outstretched hand of grace and walk *with* him, you cannot fail. "And if men come unto me I will show unto them their weakness. I give unto men weakness that they may be humble; and my grace is sufficient for all men that humble themselves before me; for if they humble themselves before me, and have faith in me, then will I make weak things become strong unto them" (Ether 12:27).

Simon the fisherman—with all his faults, failings, and fallibility that come with mortality—became Peter the rock only through the grace of Christ. It is his grace that enables and transforms. "The enabling power of the Atonement of Christ strengthens us to do things we could never do on our own," Elder David A. Bednar explained.[10] "[This] enabling and strengthening aspect of the Atonement helps us to *see* and to *do* and to *become good* in ways that we could never recognize or accomplish with our limited mortal capacity. I testify and witness that the enabling power of the Savior's Atonement is real."[11]

Peter is my hero because, like me, he had his share of weaknesses, he sometimes said dumb things, acted impetuously, faltered, failed, doubted, denied, and even stepped on some toes and cut off an ear along his way. I can relate to all that (except the cutting-off-an-ear part). He is my hero not because of those fallibilities, but in spite of them. He is my hero because of what he became— not what he made of himself, but what Christ made of him. He was a simple fisherman who tried to do good, but didn't always. He was well intentioned but, like Joseph Smith, was a "rough stone" that needed some refining to become "a smooth and polished shaft in the quiver of the Almighty."[12] He was a natural man who, through the Master's touch, was transformed into a mighty man of God in whose very shadow the sick and afflicted, the fallible and fallen, were also healed by the grace of Christ (see Acts 5:14–16). "When the Savior sought a man of faith," President Thomas S. Monson explained, "he did not select him from the throng of the self-righteous who were found regularly in the synagogue. Rather, he called him from among the fishermen of Capernaum." When Peter heard the call, "Follow me, and I will make you fishers of men," he followed (Matthew 4:19). President Monson testified that "doubting, disbelieving, unschooled, untrained, impetuous Simon did not find the way of the Lord a highway of ease nor a path free from pain. . . . Simon, man of doubt, had become Peter, apostle of faith."[13]

Peter is my hero—in the truest sense of the word. I don't worship him, but I am inspired by him. Although I can empathize, I don't need to emulate his foibles and fallibilities. I have plenty of my own. But I am inspired by what he became through the grace of Christ. I can only hope that, just as Jesus could make something of Simon the fisherman, he will do the same for me.

Notes

1. "Hero," *Wikipedia, The Free Encyclopedia*, http://en.wikipedia.org/wiki/Hero (accessed March 18, 2014).

2. Dieter F. Uchtdorf, "Come, Join with Us," *Ensign*, November 2013, 22–23.

3. Andrew H. Hedges, Alex D. Smith, and Richard Lloyd Anderson, eds., *The Joseph Smith Papers: Journals, Volume 2: December 1841–April 1843*, vol. 2 of the Journals series of *The Joseph Smith Papers*, ed. Dean C. Jessee, Ronald K. Esplin, and Richard Lyman Bushman (Salt Lake City: Church Historian's Press, 2011), 164.

4. *The Words of Joseph Smith*, ed. Andrew F. Ehat and Lyndon W. Cook (Provo, UT: Religious Studies Center, 1980), 369.

5. Gordon B. Hinckley, "The Continuing Pursuit of Truth," *Ensign*, April 1986, 5.

6. Richard Bauckham, *Jesus and the Eyewitnesses: The Gospels as Eyewitness Testimony* (Grand Rapids, MI: Eerdmans, 2006), 177.

7. Bauckham, *Jesus and the Eyewitnesses*, 177.

8. Gordon B. Hinckley, "And Peter Went Out and Wept Bitterly," *Ensign*, May 1979, 65.

9. See footnote *d* for Mosiah 27:29; see also Alma 26:17.

10. David A. Bednar, "In the Strength of the Lord," *Brigham Young University 2001–2002 Speeches* (Provo, UT: Brigham Young University, 2002), 127.

11. David A. Bednar, "In the Strength of the Lord," *Ensign*, November 2004, 77; emphasis added.

12. *Personal Writings of Joseph Smith*, comp. and ed. Dean C. Jessee, rev. ed. (Salt Lake City: Deseret Book, 2002), 100.

13. Thomas S. Monson, *Pathways to Perfection: Discourses of Thomas S. Monson* (Salt Lake City: Deseret Book, 1980), 83–84.

2

"Whom Say Ye That I Am?"

PETER'S WITNESS OF CHRIST

Terry B. Ball

Terry B. Ball is a former dean of Religious Education and a professor of ancient
scripture at Brigham Young University.

The Apostle Peter is beloved by believers—perhaps because he seems so authentic and approachable to us. We can understand him. We can empathize with him. We admire his courage as he forsook all, "straightway" leaving
his nets as the Master beckoned, "Follow me, and I will make you fishers of
men" (Matthew 4:18–20; see also Luke 5:1–11). We understand his confusion
over the meaning and message of parables (see Matthew 15:15–16). We feel the
desperation in his cry, "Lord, save me," as his feet and faith faltered on the
turbulent waters that night on the Sea of Galilee (Matthew 14:22–33). We
appreciate his awe at the Transfiguration (see Matthew 17:1–13; Mark 9:2–9;
Luke 9:28–36). We weep with him for the shame of his thrice-made denial (see
Matthew 26:69–75; Mark 14:66–72; Luke 22:54–62; John 18:15–27), grieve
with him at Gethsemane (see Matthew 26:36–46; Mark 33–37), and join in his
joy and wonder at the empty tomb (see John 20:1–10).

Perhaps the Gospel writers want us to make this personal connection with
Peter. In their accounts they appear to purposely preserve more of his experiences
and conversations with Jesus than with any of the other original Twelve.[1] Many
of us assume that so much attention is given to Peter in the Gospels because he

became the spokesman and chief among the Apostles. But perhaps Matthew, Mark, Luke, and John also speak so often and intimately of Peter's association with Christ because they hoped that as we come to love and understand Peter, we will be more ready and able to accept his special witness of Christ—a testimony that he seems to have been carefully prepared to bear.

Peter's Preparation

As Peter accompanied Jesus through his mortal ministry, the Apostle's witness and testimony that the Master was the Messiah seems to have been acquired through the intellectual, practical, and revelatory experiences afforded him. That is to say his testimony, like ours today, came through his head, his hands, and his heart.

Reason alone could have provided ample intellectual evidence to Peter that Jesus of Nazareth was more than a mere man, for if he were an imposter, if he were not the very Messiah, how then could he give sight to the blind, cleanse the leper, cause the lame to walk, or raise the dead (see Matthew 11:4–5; see also John 2:11; 10:25; 20:30–31)?

His logical affirmation that Jesus was the Christ would have been regularly bolstered by what he learned as he acted upon the Master's directions. He learned that if he cast his net as the Savior directed, he would gather a great multitude of fishes (see Luke 5:1–9; John 21:5–7), that if he stepped forward with faith when the Savior bid him "come," he too could walk on water (Matthew 14:22–33), and that if he passed the meager loaves and fishes to the multitude as the Savior instructed, the miracle of multiplication would happen under his very hands (see John 6:1–14).

Those witnesses to his head and his hands would have significantly supplemented the most powerful witness provided Peter—the witness revealed to his heart. Jesus helped the humble fisherman recognize the source of that witness. As he questioned his disciples, "Whom do men say that I the Son of man am?" (Matthew 16:13), they rehearsed the common conclusions of their contemporaries. "Some say that thou art John the Baptist: some, Elias [Elijah]; and others, Jeremias [Jeremiah], or one of the prophets" (16:14). Personalizing the query, the Savior then asked, "But whom say ye that I am?" (16:15). Without hesitation, Peter avowed, "Thou art the Christ, the Son of the living God. And Jesus answered and said unto him, Blessed art thou, Simon Bar-jona: for flesh and blood hath not revealed it unto thee, but my Father which is in heaven" (16:16–17). The Savior may have been employing an instructive play on words by using Peter's full Aramaic name on that occasion. "Simon Bar-jona" means "Simon son of Jona" or "Simon begotten of Jona." Jona can be understood to be the Aramaic form of the Hebrew name "Jonah" and appears to be the actual name of Peter's father. In Hebrew, the word "Jonah" literally means a dove.[2] Thus, in using the name Bar-jona, Christ may have been not only speaking of Peter's biological parentage but also further explaining how his testimony had been conceived—not revealed through "flesh and blood," but through the Spirit of God, born of the dove, the very sign in which the Spirit of God descended at Jesus' baptism (see Matthew 3:13–17).[3]

On another occasion, Peter bore a similar Spirit-inspired testimony. Many who had followed Christ were confused, shocked, and even offended by his bread of life sermon given at the synagogue in Capernaum (see John 6:48–65). John records that "from that time many of his disciples went back, and walked no more with him" (6:66). Testing the depth of their conviction, Jesus there turned to the Twelve and asked, "Will ye also go away?" (6:67). Speaking for all, Peter faithfully reasoned, "Lord, to whom shall we go? thou hast the words of eternal life. And we believe and are sure that thou art the Christ, the Son of the living God" (6:68–69).

Peter's preparation to be a special witness of Christ included several somewhat private experiences with Jesus. Only he and one other disciple, likely John, followed the multitude taking the Savior from Gethsemane to Caiaphas's palace so that they might witness and know what would happen to the Master (see Matthew 26:58; Mark 14:15; Luke 22:54; John 18:15).[4] With James and John alone he was brought by the Savior to witness the raising of the daughter of Jairus from the dead (see Luke 8:49–56; Mark 5:35–43) and to the Mount of Transfiguration, there to receive special priesthood power and keys (see Matthew 17:1–13; Mark 9:2–9; Luke 9:28–36).[5] These same three Apostles were asked to "watch with" Jesus as he bore the atoning sorrow and suffering at Gethsemane (see Matthew 26:36–46; see also Mark 14:33–37). In answer to their questions, the three, joined by Andrew, also received privileged instruction from Jesus concerning the signs that would precede the Second Coming (see Mark 13:1–37).

Peter's testimony was often informed by such personalized counsel and direction when he approached the Savior with questions or whenever Christ perceived this Apostle needed further training. When Peter asked how often he should forgive his brother, Christ taught him that there should be no limit to our forgiveness of others, and that as we forgive, we can expect to be forgiven (see Matthew 18:21–35).[6] When he asked Jesus what reward he could expect for faithfully following him, the Savior promised him a great reward but then told the parable of the laborers hired throughout the day, in part perhaps to help the Apostle understand that he should focus more on the privilege of laboring for the Master than on the reward, lest he end up offended or disappointed (see Matthew 19:27–20:26).[7]

When Peter asked if the parable of the well-prepared servants was meant just for the disciples or all, Jesus taught him that anyone wishing to be a servant of the Master should be ever prepared for his coming (see Luke 12:31–49).[8] Once, recognizing a lack of understanding in the disciple, Jesus taught Peter that as the Son of God he was not obligated to pay the annual tribute to the temple collected to maintain his Father's house, but lest they offend those who likewise lacked understanding, he had Peter catch the fish carrying the coin (see Matthew 17:24–27).[9] At the Last Supper when Peter protested the Savior's condescending to wash his feet, he learned of the cleansing power of the ordinance and then willingly offered his all to the Master's will (see John 13:6–19).

Although Peter's witness of Christ grew as he accompanied Jesus day by day through his ministry, the disciple seems to have struggled to comprehend the fullness of the Messiah's mortal mission of which he was to be a witness. Near the end of his ministry, Christ attempted to help the disciples understand the sacrifice he was to make, clearly warning that "the Son of man must suffer many things, and be rejected of the elders, and of the chief priests, and scribes, and be killed, and after three days rise again" (Mark 8:31). Peter panicked at the thought of Jesus being killed and tried to dissuade him, for which he received a not-too-gentle rebuke from the Master: "Get thee behind me, Satan: for thou savourest not the things that be of God" (Mark 8:32–33). Peter was perhaps the most reprimanded of all Christ's disciples. The Savior chided Peter for doubting as he rescued him while walking on the water (see Matthew 14:31), reproved Peter for not understanding the meaning of a parable (see Matthew 15:15–16), assured Peter he was not as strong as he professed when he claimed he would never be offended (see Matthew 26:33–34; Mark 14:29–30; Luke 22:33–34; John 13:36–38), upbraided him for succumbing to sleep at Gethsemane (see Matthew 26:40), and scolded him for smiting off the ear of the high priest's servant (see John 18:10–11). Remarkably, in spite of the regular reprimands he received from Jesus, Peter chose not to be affronted, but rather continued following the Master, daily adding to his witness and learning of him.[10]

Peter's preparation to be a special witness of Christ neared completion through what he saw, felt, and experienced during the final days of Jesus' life. During those last days, he would have seen Lazarus raised from the dead (see John 11:1–46). He also would have joined in the celebration of the triumphal entry (see Matthew 21:1–11; Mark 11:1–11; Luke 19:29–40; John 12:12–19). He was sent to prepare the Passover and received the sacred ordinances, teachings, and commandments given at that Last Supper (see Matthew 26:17–35; Mark 14:12–25; Luke 22:7–38; John 13–17). He felt some of Gethsemane's sorrow, stood by Christ at the arrest, and followed him to the trial (see Matthew 26:36–75; Mark 14:32–72; Luke 22:40–62; John 18:1–27).

The Galilean fisherman's preparation culminated in what he witnessed following the Crucifixion, beginning on the morning of the first day of the week. Upon hearing of the empty tomb, Peter rushed to see for himself and left "wondering in himself at that which was come to pass" (Luke 24:1–12; see also John 20:1–9).[11] Luke records that sometime that same day the resurrected Savior appeared privately to Peter, though we know little of that event (see Luke 24:34; 1 Corinthians 15:3–8).[12] Later that evening, when Peter with the other Apostles and some disciples were met in a closed room, the risen Lord appeared unto them all. To allay their fears and to affirm the reality of the Resurrection of his tangible body, he invited them to feel the wounds in his body and ate with them. He then opened their understanding of how his Resurrection fulfilled the prophecies written in the law of Moses and the scriptures, declaring, "Ye are witnesses of these things" (Luke 24:36–48; see also Mark 16:14; John 20:19–23).[13] The eleven disciples later traveled to Galilee, as the Savior had instructed them, and there on "a mountain where Jesus had appointed them," he assured them, "All power is given unto me in heaven and in earth" (Matthew 28:7, 10, 16–20).

Through it all, Peter's head, hands, and heart were further tutored to be a witness of the resurrected Christ, for he saw the risen Lord with his eyes, heard him with his ears, felt him with his hands, and surely, like the disciples on the road to Emmaus, felt again the Spirit's confirmation in his heart (see Luke 24:13–32).

Peter's Commission

Just as it took time, teaching, and experience for Peter to fully understand the atoning mission of the Messiah, comprehending his mission as a special witness of Christ was a gradual process. When Jesus first called Peter and his brother Andrew from their nets, he clearly communicated his plans to make them "fishers of men" (Matthew 4:18–20; see also Luke 5:1–11). Later, when Peter and the other eleven were selected to be special witnesses, Jesus gave them power to minister and perform miracles and sent them forth to declare that "the kingdom of heaven is at hand" (Matthew 10:1–42). Yet after all this, and indeed after having followed Jesus throughout his three-year ministry, the Savior perceived that his chief Apostle still needed help in understanding his calling. In the solemn chamber of the upper room, shortly before descending to the agony of Gethsemane, Jesus warned, assured, and commanded Peter, "Simon, Simon, behold, Satan hath desired to have you, that he may sift you as wheat: but I have prayed for thee, that thy faith fail not: and when thou art converted, strengthen thy brethren" (Luke 22:31–32).[14]

It seems the full realization of what was to be required of him came to Peter as the Lord taught him on the shores of the Sea of Galilee. Peter and some of the other Apostles had traveled to Galilee, surely with the memory of having twice felt the wounds of crucifixion on the resurrected body of their Master fresh on their minds.[15] Apparently still wondering what to do with themselves, Peter announced to his brethren, "I go a fishing" (John 21:3). He had been a fisherman before forsaking his nets to follow Christ, but now that Jesus was no longer with them, Peter seemed resigned to returning to his old life and livelihood. His brethren followed.

Toiling through the night, they caught nothing. Nearing the shore, likely exhausted and discouraged, they saw someone standing there whom they did not recognize bidding them to cast their nets again. Perhaps recalling an earlier occasion when obedience to similar advice had yielded a great catch, they complied, this time without protest or question (see John 21:3–6; Luke 5:1–9). As they drew in their nets teeming once again with a multitude of fish, recognition came to John. "It is the Lord," he exclaimed to Peter (John 21:7). Too anxious to wait for the boat to reach the shore, Peter "cast himself into the sea" to reach the Master sooner (John 21:7). When the others arrived, they found a meal of fish and bread awaiting them. As they dined with Jesus, John reminisced, "And none of the disciples durst ask him, Who art thou? knowing that it was the Lord" (John 21:12–13).

Following the meal, Jesus turned to Peter and, most likely pointing to the very fish Peter had chosen to pursue, asked of his Apostle, "Simon, son of Jonas, lovest thou me more than these?" (John 21:15).[16] Surely Peter thought this question strange. Of course he loved the Savior more than fish—or fishing. Perhaps there was a touch of incredulity in his answer to such an absurd question. "Yea, Lord; thou knowest that I love thee," to which Christ responded, "Feed my lambs" (John 21:15). Again the Savior put the question to Peter, and Peter again avowed his love for Christ, and Christ again commanded, "Feed my sheep" (John 21:16). Peter was grieved as Jesus asked a third time for the disciple to affirm his love. We can feel the pathos and passion in Peter's third witness, "Lord, thou knowest all things; thou knowest that I love thee" (John 21:17). Once again Jesus commanded, "Feed my sheep" (John 21:17).[17] How could the message to Peter be any clearer? If he truly loved the Lord, then Peter was no longer to be a fisherman, but rather a shepherd, caring for the Master's flock.[18] Peter's actions and ministry from that time forward affirm that he at last understood his commission and mission to be a special servant and witness of Christ.[19]

Peter's Witness

Following that day in Galilee, Peter went forth to fulfill his commission from Christ with remarkable faith, courage, and rigor. As a leading Apostle, he stepped forward to conduct and preside over the first order of business in the young church, that of replacing Judas. As he described the credentials the first new Apostle was to have, Peter made it clear that he must be one who had a witness of Christ, from the Savior's baptism even through to his Resurrection (see Acts 1:15–26). When Phillip had successfully taken the gospel to Samaria, Peter took John with him to give, by the laying on of hands, the gift of Holy Ghost to the new converts there, and subsequently to discipline and correct the misunderstanding of Simon the sorcerer (see Acts 8:14–25). As the lead Apostle, Peter later received the revelation that opened the door for the gospel to be taken to the Gentiles, and he initiated the work by teaching and baptizing the household of Cornelius (see Acts 10). It was subsequently his duty and privilege to declare and explain to his brethren in Jerusalem that "God [hath] also to the Gentiles granted repentance unto life" (Acts 11:1–18). Earlier he had presided over the trial of Ananias and Sapphira (see Acts 5:1–11), and later he led out in the Jerusalem council that met to discuss what was to be expected of Gentile converts (see Acts 15:6–22).

While being occupied with these duties and likely many others not recorded in Acts, Peter did not neglect his responsibility to ever be a witness of Christ. On the day of Pentecost, when thousands had assembled to witness the wonders of the outpouring of the Holy Ghost and began speculating, "What meaneth this?" (Acts 2:12), Peter seized upon the moment to teach of Christ (see Acts 2:1–40). Lifting his voice to the curious crowd, he declared that the outpouring of spiritual manifestations they were witnessing was a fulfillment of "that which was spoken by the prophet Joel" (Acts 2:16–21). He then spoke of Jesus, reminding them of his ministry and miracles among them, of how they rejected and crucified him and of how his Resurrection fulfilled a prophecy of their beloved David. He concluded his witness with a confirming and condemning testimony. "Therefore let all the house of Israel know assuredly, that God hath made that same Jesus, whom ye have crucified, both Lord and Christ" (Acts 2:22–36). Peter's words "pricked" their hearts, causing them to petition, "Men and brethren, what shall we do?" (Acts 2:37), to which Peter readily responded, "Repent, and be baptized every one of you in the name of Jesus Christ for the remission of sins, and ye shall receive the gift of the Holy Ghost" (Acts 2:38). About "three thousand souls" that "gladly received" Peter's words and invitation were added to the church that day (Acts 2:41).

Not long after, Peter again bore witness of Christ to an astonished multitude, this time gathered at the temple on Solomon's porch. At "the hour of prayer," Peter and John had come to the Beautiful Gate of the temple, where a well-known man, "lame from his mother's womb," asked alms of them (Acts 3:1–2, 10). Peter invited the man to look on them, and as he expectantly complied, Peter, on behalf of the Savior, granted him much more than alms. "Silver and gold have I none; but such as I have give I thee: In the name of Jesus Christ of Nazareth rise up and walk" (Acts 3:6). As the man took Peter's hand, with faith sufficient to be healed, his feet and ankles received the strength to be lifted and even leap (see Acts 3:7, 16). As he went through the temple "walking, and leaping, and praising God," an amazed crowd apparently began to follow him, wondering how the miracle was done. The exuberant man returned to Peter and John and "held" them. As the marveling crowd assembled, Peter once again raised his voice to witness of Christ. He testified to them that the lame had been healed in the name and by the power of Jesus. As on the day of Pentecost, he reminded the listeners that they had denied, rejected, and "killed the Prince of life" and testified that in fulfillment of prophecy God raised him from the dead. Peter then implored the multitude, "Repent ye therefore, and be converted, that your sins may be blotted out," and he taught them that as "children of the prophets" they had been especially privileged to have Christ first sent to them (see Acts 3:19–26). About five thousand more believers were added from the miracle performed and the witness given by Peter on that day (see Acts 4:4).

We can imagine the disappointment and dismay of "the priests, and the captain of the temple, and the Sadducees" when they learned that Jesus' followers were performing miracles in his name and preaching "through Jesus the resurrection from the dead" (Acts 4:1–2).[20] We suppose that they had thought that the execution of Jesus would have put an end to his work and ministry. In a desperate attempt to once again quench the fire of faith in Jesus, they arrested Peter and John that day in the temple and held them in prison overnight. The next day, as their council "examined" Peter and John, they provided the Apostles another opportunity to bear witness of Christ. Peter, filled with the Holy Ghost, caused them to marvel as he boldly testified that the miracle of healing for which they were arrested was done in the name of Jesus Christ of Nazareth, whom they had crucified and whom God had raised from the dead, even the "stone" which they the "builders" had "set at nought" but which is to become "the head of the corner" and the only name whereby "we must be saved" (Acts 4:9–12). Frustrated by the undeniable and well-known evidence before them, the council could only release them, but not before threatening them, "that they speak henceforth to no man" in the name of Jesus (Acts 4:13–18). Unfazed by the threats and fully understanding their call as Apostles and of whom they had received that call, Peter and John responded, "Whether it be right in the sight of God to hearken unto you more than unto God, judge ye. For we cannot but speak the things which we have seen and heard" (Acts 4:19–20).

This confrontation with the council of Jewish leaders who wanted Peter to cease witnessing of Christ was not Peter's last. His next arrest was again precipitated by performing miracles of healing. As believers in Christ were daily added to the church, they brought their sick to Peter to be healed, hoping that at least the shadow of Peter might touch them as he passed by, and "they were healed every one" (Acts 5:14–16).[21] Filled with indignation at Peter's refusal to yield to their threats, the council rose up and put Peter with other Apostles in the common prison, but during the night the angel of the Lord opened the prison doors and commanded them to "go, stand and speak in the temple to the people all the words of this life" (Acts 5:20).

When the council gathered the next morning to once again examine Peter, they must have been surprised to learn that not only had the Apostles escaped through a locked and guarded door, but also that they were at that very moment teaching in the temple (see Acts 5:21–25). They immediately dispatched the captain and officers to once again arrest the Apostles and bring them before the council, which they did "without violence" for fear of causing an uprising (Acts 5:26–27). The council sternly reminded the Apostles that they had been commanded to not teach in the name of Christ and accused the Apostles of "filling Jerusalem" with doctrine that was intended to bring Christ's blood upon the council. Peter and the other Apostles once again retorted, "We ought to obey God rather than men," and further testified that Jesus, whom they had indeed slain, had been resurrected and exalted to be a "Prince and a Savior, for to give repentance to Israel, and forgiveness of sins" (Acts 5:29–32). The angry and guilt-ridden council at that moment determined to slay them all, and would have, had not the wise Pharisee Gamaliel reasoned with them that if the Apostles' work was not of God, it would die away of its own accord, but if it was of God, the council was in danger of engaging in a surely futile fight with God (see Acts 5:33–39). Somewhat softened, or perhaps frightened, by Gamaliel's reasoning, the council chose rather to beat the Apostles, commanded them again to not speak in the name of Jesus, and let them go (see Acts 5:40). Peter and the other Apostles "departed from the presence of the council, rejoicing that they were counted worthy to suffer shame for his name. And daily in the temple, and in every house, they ceased not to teach and preach Jesus Christ" (Acts 5:41–42).

As the book of Acts turns its agenda to chronicling Paul's ministry, we read less and less of Peter. We know that he was arrested yet again when Herod "stretched forth his hands to vex certain of the church" (Acts 12:1–3). To prevent Peter's escape, Herod assigned four squads of soldiers to guard him in prison, yet one night, while sleeping chained between two soldiers, the angel of the Lord again delivered him from prison (see Acts 12:1–19).[22] We read that Peter subsequently made his home in Caesarea for a time (see Acts 12:19). The last mention of Peter in the book of Acts finds him at the council in Jerusalem in which the church's expectations for Gentile converts were discussed. At that council, ever true to his mission, Peter witnessed to all that Gentile and Jew alike would be saved "through the grace of the Lord Jesus Christ" (Acts 15:6–11).

While New Testament historical narrative grows relatively silent about Peter after Acts 15,[23] we are fortunate to have two epistles from the Apostle.[24] Peter's witness of Christ permeates those epistles. In the letters Peter teaches us that we can become elect through the blood of Christ and have "a lively hope" by his Resurrection (1 Peter 1:2–3). He reminds us that Christ's sufferings and glory fulfilled prophecy and that the trial of our own faith will be rewarded with praise, honor, glory, and grace at the "appearing" and "revelation" of Christ (1 Peter 1:7, 10–11, 13). He testifies that our "spiritual sacrifices" are made acceptable to God by Christ and that Christ suffered for our sins "that he might bring us to God" (1 Peter 2:5, 3:18). He speaks of Christ's ministry to the "spirits in prison" that they too might be justly judged (1 Peter 3:19, 4:6; see also D&C 138:18–21, 30). He exhorts us to endure suffering in the flesh "with the same mind" with which Christ suffered and encourages us to rejoice should we "be reproached for the name of Christ" (1 Peter 4:1, 13–14). He prays that we might receive grace and peace through knowledge of Christ and teaches that acquiring Christlike virtues helps us obtain that knowledge as well as "an entrance" into his kingdom (see 2 Peter 1:2, 4–11). He warns that if we return to the pollutions of the world after having once escaped through Christ, then our "latter end" will be "worse . . . than the beginning" (2 Peter 2:20). He reflects on his personal witness of Christ's sufferings and expresses his hope to be "a partaker of the glory that shall be revealed" (1 Peter 5:1). Towards the end he resolutely acknowledges that he too must "shortly . . . put off this my tabernacle, even as our Lord Jesus Christ hath shewed me" (2 Peter 1:14).

In making this solemn observation, perhaps Peter was reflecting on the words Jesus spoke to him so many years earlier on the shores of Galilee. There, after commanding Peter to feed his sheep, the Savior gave him a glimpse of the future, declaring, "When thou wast young, thou girdedst thyself, and walkedst whither thou wouldest: but when thou shalt be old, thou shalt stretch forth thy hands, and another shall gird thee, and carry thee whither thou wouldest not" (John 21:18). John saw martyrdom for Peter in these words of Christ, explaining, "This spake [Jesus], signifying by what death [Peter] should glorify God. And when he had spoken this, he saith unto [Peter], Follow me" (John 21:19).[25] Surely in his old age as he contemplated death, Peter could find peace and joy in knowing that he had indeed followed Christ in life and was ready to follow him in death.

Conclusion

We wish more of Peter's activities and writings were preserved in the New Testament.[26] What has been preserved is a treasure and endears us to this faithful fisherman. The record, small as it is, shows us how Peter was carefully and personally prepared by Christ to be a special witness of him. As we read the account, we can discover our faith and understanding of Christ growing along with Peter's. That growth can give us hope and perspective in our personal journeys to faith. As we watch what Christ expected of Peter become clear to him and then see the courage and dedication with which he labored to fulfill his commission from the Savior, we are led to ponder "What does Christ expect of me?" and "Am I doing enough?" As we study Peter's witness of Christ, we find ourselves anxious to echo his words "We believe and are sure that thou art that Christ, the Son of the living God" (John 6:69).

Notes

1. While the witness, experiences, and teachings of the Apostle Paul are more thoroughly chronicled in the New Testament than those of Peter, Paul was not one of the original Twelve and not mentioned in the four Gospels.

2. Francis Brown, "יוֹנָה," "הוֹנָה," *The New Brown-Driver-Briggs-Gesenius Hebrew and English Lexicon* (LaFayette, IN: Christian Copyrights, 1983), 401–2.

3. The Prophet Joseph Smith taught that the Holy Ghost is a personage and did not "confine itself to [the] form of a dove" at the baptism of Jesus. "President Joseph Smith's Journal," Journal, 4 vols., December 1842–June 1844, 161. http://josephsmithpapers.org/paperSummary/journal-december-1842-june-1844-book-1-21-december-1842-10-march-1843?locale=eng&p=161 (accessed March 4, 2014). Thus Latter-day Saints typically understand the sign of the dove to be a witness of the Holy Ghost's presence rather than the actual embodiment of the Holy Ghost on that occasion.

4. The other disciple is only mentioned in John's account and is not named. Because John is reluctant to refer to himself by name throughout his Gospel, many speculate that he was the other disciple. See John 18:15.

5. While the Gospel accounts describe Peter, James, and John more as simple observers at the Transfiguration, Latter-day Saints understand that these three Apostles were likewise transfigured and there received special priesthood authority. Joseph Smith taught, "the Savior, Moses, and Elias, gave the Keys to Peter, James and John on the mount when they were transfigured before him." Joseph Smith, History, volume C-1 [2 November 1838–31 July 1842], 546. http://josephsmithpapers.org/paperSummary/history-1838-1856-volume-c-1-2-november-1838-31-july-1842?p=546 (accessed February 26, 2014). Joseph Fielding Smith suggested that these three Apostles received their temple endowments and other keys associated with those ordinances on the mount at the same time. Bruce R. McConkie, comp., *Doctrines of Salvation* (Salt Lake City: Bookcraft, 1954–56), 2:165.

6. Christ's instruction to Peter that he should forgive seven times seventy (see Matthew 18:22) is not meant to mean 490 times. Since God created the world in six days and rested on the seventh, the number seven came to mean completeness or wholeness in Hebrew culture. Thus if one does something seven times, he does it completely or entirely (e.g., Joshua 6:16; Leviticus 14:7; Daniel 4:16). Accordingly, in instructing Peter to forgive seven times seventy, Christ is telling the Apostle to forgive completely and entirely. The parable of the unmerciful servant that follows appears to be given to further teach that we are forgiven as we forgive (see Matthew 18:23–35).

7. In the parable of the laborers who were hired throughout the day, Peter would have certainly identified himself with those who had labored all day long but ended up unhappy because they felt shortchanged in some way. The message would have been clear to Peter—be thankful for the privilege of working and let the Master be concerned about the reward.

8. Joseph Smith Translation, Luke 12:38–57, makes this point more clearly than the KJV.

9. For an interesting discussion on this event, see Bruce R. McConkie, *Doctrinal New Testament Commentary*, 3 vols. (Salt Lake City: Bookcraft, 1965), 1:412.

10. Of Peter and the frequent reproofs he received from Christ, President Spencer W. Kimball observed, "He reproved Peter at times because he loved him, and Peter, being a great man, was able to grow from this reproof. There is a wonderful verse in the book of Proverbs all of us need to remember: 'The ear that heareth the reproof of life abideth among the wise. He that refuseth instruction despiseth his own soul: but he that heareth reproof getteth understanding.' (Prov. 15:31–32.) It is a wise leader or a wise follower who can cope with the 'reproof of life.' Peter could do this because he knew that Jesus loved him, and thus Jesus was able to groom Peter for a very high place or responsibility in the kingdom." "Jesus: The Perfect Leader," *Ensign*, August 1979, 5.

11. There is some confusion among the Gospel writers about how soon the disciples understood that Christ had been resurrected. While John and Luke suggest that initially they did not know why the tomb was empty, Matthew and Mark record that the angel explained to Mary that Christ had risen from the dead and told her to report such to the disciples (see Matthew 28:1–8; Mark 16:1–8). Mark further reports that when told by Mary that Jesus had risen and had been seen by her, they did not believe her (see Mark 16:9–11).

12. Luke is the only Gospel writer to refer to this private visit to Peter. Paul seems to affirm it in his first epistle to the Corinthians (see 1 Corinthians 15:3–8).

13. All the Gospel writers but Matthew give some version of this appearance. Luke's is the most detailed. John records that the experience was repeated eight days later when the still unbelieving Thomas, who was absent at the first appearance, was present and made a witness as well (see John 20:24–29).

14. For more on this exchange between Christ and Peter and the principles that can be learned from it, see Joseph B. Wirthlin, "Spiritual Bonfires of Testimony," *Ensign*, November 1992, 34–36; L. Tom Perry, "When Thou Art Converted, Strengthen Thy Brethren," *Ensign*, November 1974, 16–18.

15. Matthew and Mark both report that when Jesus first appeared to Mary after the Resurrection, he told her to tell the disciples that he would meet them in Galilee, perhaps to facilitate the teaching moment that occurred there (see Matthew 28:7; Mark 16:7). John indicates that Peter, James, John, Nathaniel, Thomas, and two other disciples made the journey. It is not clear if the unnamed disciples were part of the Twelve (see John 21:2).

16. Some understand the antecedent of *these* in this verse to be the other disciples dining with them, but the message is clearer if we understand *these* as a reference to the fish.

17. Some observe that by thrice allowing Peter to affirm his love for him, Christ was giving Peter a chance to amend for his thrice-made denial that desperate night of the trial. See, for example, James E. Talmage, *Jesus the Christ* (Salt Lake City: Deseret Book, 1916, repr. 1982), 693; Jeffrey R. Holland, "The First Great Commandment," *Ensign*, November 2012, 83–84. For a discussion of the denial and lessons to be learned from it, see Gordon B. Hinckley, "And Peter Went Out and Wept Bitterly," *Ensign*, May 1979, 65–67; Neal A. Maxwell, "A Brother Offended," *Ensign*, May 1982, 37–38. Other commentators, noting the subtle differences in the Greek of the text, suggest that the three questions were each asked to teach Peter different aspects and duties of his calling. Accordingly the Savior twice asked Peter "lovest thou me" using the Greek *agapao* for love, meaning a social or moral kind of love, often thought of as godly or unconditional love and elsewhere trans-lated as "charity" (e.g., 1 Corinthians 13:1–4; 2 Peter 1:7; Revelations 2:19). The third time Jesus asked Peter, "Lovest thou me," he used the term *phileo* for love, meaning friendship, affection, or brotherly love. Interestingly, in answer to each of the three questions Peter affirmed his love using *phileo*. To the first affirmation of Peter's love, Christ commanded him to "feed" from the Greek *bosko*, meaning to pasture, graze, or nourish, his "lambs," from the Greek *arnion*, meaning a young or baby sheep. To the second affirmation of Peter's love, Christ commanded him to "feed," from the Greek *poimaino*, meaning to tend or shepherd, his "sheep," from the Greek *probaton*, meaning an adult sheep. In response to Peter's third affirmation of love for Christ, he was to *bosko* his *probaton*. Thus by asking the question three times in three ways the Savior asked the disciple if he had both charity and brotherly love for him, and in his subsequent commandments the Savior taught Peter that he was to not only nourish but also shepherd both the young and old of his flock. For Latter-day Saint commentaries of this type, see Anthon H. Lund, in Conference Report, October 1908, 119, and Robert C. Webb, "Truth Seeking: Its Symptoms and After Effects," *Improvement Era*, September 1913, 1075–91.

18. For more discussion on this event and the principles that can be learned from it, see Robert D. Hales, "When Thou Art Converted, Strengthen Thy Brethren," *Ensign*, May 1997, 80–83.

19. The Apostles appear to have been commissioned by the resurrected Christ to be witnesses to the world on two other occasions. Matthew records that on that day in Galilee when Jesus assured the eleven that all power in heaven and earth had been given him, he commanded the eleven to go and "teach all nations, baptizing them in the name of the father, and of the Son, and of the Holy Ghost; Teaching them to observe all things whatsoever I have commanded you" (Matthew 28:16–20; see also Mark 16:15–18; Luke 24:46–47). A similar commission is recorded in Acts. After the Savior commanded the Apostles to stay in Jerusalem until they "receive power, after that the Holy Ghost is come upon" them, then they were to "be witnesses" of Christ "in Jerusalem, and in all Judea, and in Samaria, and unto the uttermost part of the earth" (Acts 1:4–11).

20. The teaching of the resurrection of the dead would have been especially distressing to the unbelieving Sadducees, for it was a point of contention between them and the Pharisees (see Matthew 22:23; Acts 23:6–8).

21. Two other specific accounts of healing by Peter are found in Acts. One is the healing in the name of Christ of Æneas, who "had kept his bed eight years, and was sick of the palsy," and the other the raising from the dead of the beloved seamstress Dorcas (see Acts 9:43).

22. The account of the damsel Rhoda, who in her surprise and excitement to hear the escaped Peter's voice at the door left him knocking while she awakened the household to share the good news, adds a personal and humorous touch to the account (see Acts 12:12–19).

23. There are two additional references to Peter's activities found in Paul's epistle to the Galatians. One speaks of Paul spending fifteen days with Peter in Jerusalem three years after his conversion, and the other describes a confrontation Paul had with Peter over the propriety of eating with Gentiles (see Galatians 1:18; 2:7–12).

24. While the authorship of the Petrine epistles is a topic of debate among biblical scholars, I accept Peter's authorship. For a recent defense of Peter's authorship, see Larry R. Helyer, *The Life and Witness of Peter* (Downers Grove, IL: InterVarsity Press, 2012), 107–13, 207–14.

25. Some see another prophecy of Peter's martyrdom given at the Last Supper. That night as Jesus explained to his disciples, "Whither I go, ye cannot come" (John 13:33), "Peter inquired, Lord, whither goest thou? Jesus answered him, Whither I go, thou canst not follow me now: but thou shalt follow me afterwards" (John 13:36). For a discussion of this as a prophecy of Peter's martyrdom, see McConkie, *Doctrinal New Testament Commentary*, 1:769, 863–64.

26. Some Christian writers of the second through fourth centuries AD apparently decided to satisfy our want for more writings from or about Peter by composing apocryphal works such as *The Acts of Peter*, *The Acts of Peter and Andrew*, *The Acts of Peter and the Twelve*, and *The Acts of Peter and Paul*.

3

Simon Peter in Capernaum
AN ARCHAEOLOGICAL SURVEY OF
THE FIRST-CENTURY VILLAGE

Matthew J. Grey

Matthew J. Grey is an assistant professor of ancient scripture at
Brigham Young University.

During the last several decades, scholars have researched the life and ministry of Simon Peter to understand how Jesus' most famous disciple—a Galilean fisherman called to "fish for people" (Matthew 4:19)[1]—became the "rock" upon which the Christian church was built (see Matthew 16:18).[2] In particular, studies on the historical Peter have raised a number of important questions regarding his personal background and development, including his original social context (would he have been poor or financially comfortable?), the extent of his literacy (would he have been illiterate or well educated?), and his cultural familiarities (in addition to being Jewish, would he have been inherently sympathetic to Gentile concerns?). These issues are significant for understanding Peter's missionary activities among Jews (see Galatians 2:7–8), traditions of his scriptural authorship (see 1 Peter 1:1–2; 2 Peter 1:1), and his role as chief Apostle whose revelations led to the inclusion of Gentiles within the Christian community (see Acts 10:1–48).

In an attempt to answer these questions, scholars have painted two very different pictures of Peter's background and cultural proclivities. Traditionally, many scholars have claimed that Peter was a fisherman of modest means who left his occupation to follow Jesus at a great personal cost. Peter likely spoke Aramaic, lacked formal education, and did not have a sufficient knowledge of Greek to write the New Testament letters ascribed to him. As an inherently conservative Jew, Peter would have had to overcome his natural religious sensitivities to bring the gospel to the Gentiles.[3] Recently, however, other scholars have challenged this portrayal by arguing instead that Peter was a successful, multicultural, and bilingual businessman, whose Greek proficiency and intellectual sophistication enabled him to write polished letters, whose temporal resources afforded him the luxury to follow Jesus, and whose early exposure to Hellenistic culture uniquely positioned him to teach Gentiles.[4]

While most of this debate has focused on the relevant literary sources (such as the New Testament), some scholars are beginning to recognize the potential of archaeology to illuminate Peter's early life and ministry.[5] No first-century artifacts linked to Peter himself have been found,[6] but the broader study of material culture—especially in his native region of Galilee—can offer valuable insights into the cultural, religious, and economic environment in which he lived. For example, recent studies have examined the site of et-Tell/"Bethsaida," a town in the predominantly Gentile tetrarchy of Herod Philip to the northeast of the Sea of Galilee that might have been Peter's birthplace. This village had a mixed population of Jews and non-Jews (shown by the presence of pig and nonkosher fish bones[7]) and was highly Hellenized (reflected by the existence of a Roman temple[8]), suggesting to some scholars that Peter's cultural upbringing required him to speak fluent Greek as well as Aramaic, and naturally prepared him to work with Gentiles as well as Jews.[9]

Despite this intriguing possibility, however, the emphasis on Bethsaida suffers from two major difficulties. First, the identification of Bethsaida as Peter's hometown rests on one ambiguous reference in the Gospel of John and has little corroborating support.[10] Second, the identification of Bethsaida with the site of et-Tell is debated among scholars, making its relevance to Peter's life uncertain.[11] In light of this uncertainty, I believe that a more important and reliable site to examine is Capernaum—a Jewish fishing village on the Sea of Galilee in which, according to the synoptic Gospels, Peter lived with extended family (see Mark 1:29–30), worked as a fisherman (see Matthew 4:18), witnessed many of Jesus' miracles (see Matthew 8:1–17), and began his life of discipleship (see Mark 1:16–20). Curiously, few scholars have effectively incorporated the archaeology of this site into their study of the historical Peter. Therefore, in an attempt to illuminate Peter's formative cultural environment, I will provide an archaeological survey of first-century Capernaum, Simon Peter's ostensible hometown.[12]

A survey of Capernaum provides a very different picture of Peter's origins than the remains of et-Tell/"Bethsaida." Unlike Bethsaida, Capernaum (a modest Jewish village whose population appeared to be religiously conservative) left no discernable trace of Gentile presence or influence and did not enjoy the amenities of larger towns and cities. Neither being completely destitute nor economically prosperous, Capernaum's inhabitants secured a stable living through their labors in fishing and agriculture. This assessment supports the more traditional view of Peter as a common fisherman who came from a conservative Jewish background and who likely possessed little or no formal education. To illustrate this observation, I will provide a brief overview of Capernaum's history and excavations, and will then consider three aspects of the first-century village that relate to Peter's experience there: Capernaum's relationship to the Galilean fishing industry, the nature of Capernaum's civic and domestic life, and the presence of a synagogue.

The History and Excavations of Capernaum

Before beginning an archaeological survey of Capernaum, it is helpful to provide a brief overview of the ancient history and modern exploration of the village. For centuries scholars have known of the existence of Capernaum (Kefar Nahum, the "Village of Nahum"[13]) from references in ancient literary sources.[14] The village is not mentioned in the Old Testament,[15] but it is mentioned in Jewish texts from the late Second Temple period. It appears that Capernaum was settled as a small Jewish fishing village along the north shore of the Sea of Galilee sometime in the second century BC, likely during the Hasmonean colonization of the region.[16] By the time of Jesus and Peter in the early first century AD, Capernaum was situated on the border of two realms: the Jewish tetrarchy of Herod Antipas to the west (in which Capernaum was located) and the predominantly Gentile tetrarchy of Herod Philip to the east. Because of its new status as a border town, Capernaum's fishing and farming population expanded to include officials from Antipas' administration, such as toll/tax collectors (see Mark 2:13–17; Matthew 9:9–13; Luke 5:27–32) and military officers (see Matthew 8:5–13; Luke 7:1–10). The growing village's proximity to the lake and a local trade route also brought interregional traffic and may have attracted less reputable elements of society, such as prostitutes and beggars.[17]

Despite its potentially strategic situation, Capernaum is best known in ancient sources as a central location for the early Jesus movement. The synoptic Gospels regularly refer to Capernaum as the residence of Jesus' earliest disciples (including Peter, Andrew, James, John, and Matthew/Levi; see Mark 1:16–31; Matthew 9:10–13), the adopted home base of Jesus' Galilean ministry (see Matthew 4:13–17;

9:1), the location of numerous healings and exorcisms performed by Jesus (see Mark 1:23–34; 2:1–12), and the site of a synagogue in which Jesus taught (see Mark 1:21–22). Outside of the New Testament, however, Capernaum receives little attention in ancient Jewish texts; Josephus briefly mentioned it as a village with limited medical resources,[18] and later rabbinic literature decried some "unorthodox" Jews who lived there in the second and third centuries.[19]

Following the two Jewish revolts against Rome (AD 66–73 and 132–135), Capernaum experienced significant development and expansion with the presence of a Roman military unit in the village. Its population continued to be predominantly Jewish,[20] but Capernaum's traditional associations with Jesus and the "house of Peter" made it a popular site for Christian pilgrimage during the Byzantine period.[21] Following the Muslim conquest of the Galilee region in the seventh century, Capernaum's Jewish population became outnumbered by Christians and Muslims.[22] For an unknown reason, the village was abandoned in the eleventh century and was never reinhabited.[23] Following centuries of abandonment, Capernaum's precise location was forgotten, but by the early twentieth century most scholars agreed that Capernaum should be identified with the ruins at Tel Hum along the northern shore of the Sea of Galilee.[24] There, early explorations uncovered the remains of a monumental synagogue and an octagonal church shrine thought to commemorate the location of Peter's house.[25]

Beginning in the late 1960s, extensive archaeological excavations have been conducted at the site. The first were carried out between 1968 and 1986 by Stanislao Loffreda and Virgilio Corbo (on behalf of the Studium Biblicum Franciscanum) in the western part of the village. Their excavations focused on the octagonal church, the monumental synagogue, and some of the surrounding dwellings. Between 1978 and 1987, the neighboring Greek Orthodox Church conducted additional excavations (directed by Vassilios Tzaferis) of the site's eastern ruins that uncovered domestic structures and portions of the village's harbor facilities. These projects produced valuable material from the ancient village and greatly clarified its historical development.[26] Their findings also led to numerous speculations regarding the relationship between remains at the site and the stories of the New Testament.

More recent studies of Capernaum have attempted to contextualize the village within its surrounding Galilean culture. As Galilee's ancient cities (Sepphoris and Tiberias) and other villages (e.g., Cana, et-Tell/"Bethsaida," and Magdala) have been excavated, scholars have gained increasing insight into the religious, economic, and cultural dynamics of the entire region at the time of Jesus and Peter.[27] As a result, new questions about the region have arisen which have not yet been resolved:

Was first-century Galilee sharply divided between the urban elites and rural peasants?[28] Or was there an economic symbiosis between the cities and villages that resulted in financial prosperity for many?[29] Was Galilee thoroughly Hellenized, mostly Jewish, or a synthetic mixture of both?[30] These regional questions are still being debated and have recently been applied to Capernaum in particular: Was the residence of Jesus and Peter a poor village of illiterate subsistence-level fishermen,[31] or was it a prosperous town of successful, multicultural businessmen that benefited from a bustling trade network?[32]

The answers, of course, impact the way we view the historical Jesus and his earliest followers, including Peter. Unfortunately, our ability to reconstruct first-century Capernaum and definitively answer these questions is limited by a number of factors. First, portions of the site remain unexcavated, currently leaving us with an incomplete picture of the ancient village. Second, many of the published excavation reports are inaccessible and inadequate by modern standards, making it difficult to date its remains with precision and often forcing researchers to rely on secondary or anecdotal evidence.[33] Therefore, any reconstruction of the first-century village must be tentative. Despite these limitations, however, historical sources and the excavation reports allow us to make some observations about Peter's hometown with relative confidence.

For example, it appears that in the first century Capernaum was a modest, unwalled village that extended in a thin strip along the lakeshore and had a population of between 1,000 and 1,500.[34] Excavations have shown that Capernaum was more prominent than small rural hamlets like Nazareth, but its lack of monumental public architecture, paved streets, sewage systems, and Roman luxuries ranked it far below Galilee's major cities: Sepphoris and Tiberias.[35] Capernaum's material culture indicates that its inhabitants in this period were mostly conservative (non-Hellenized) Jews who relied on fishing, agriculture, and commerce for their living, and who were neither wealthy nor completely impoverished. The population of the first-century village included many families that were living modestly above subsistence level, a few that may have enjoyed additional affluence, and some that were destitute. In other words, support exists for both sides of the current debate over Capernaum's socioeconomic status, with the cumulative evidence pointing to a Jewish village that was mostly lower to "middle" class.

Since this assessment has significant implications for Peter's early life and the beginnings of the Jesus movement, it is important to examine the archaeological remains of Capernaum and compare them to the scriptural accounts of Peter's experience there. In the following sections I will consider three aspects of the first-century village that elucidate Peter's formative cultural environment—its fishing industry, its civic and domestic life, and the presence of a synagogue.

Capernaum and the Galilean Fishing Economy

The ancient literary sources and archaeological evidence confirm that Capernaum's location on the north shore of the Sea of Galilee led to its natural involvement with the Galilean fishing economy. This, of course, is the vocational context for Peter, his extended family, and his associates, who were fishermen based in the village. By the first century, the fishing industry had become a major source of revenue in Galilee, with fish and fish products (including a popular fish sauce called garum) serving both as staples of the local diet and as exportable commodities.[36] While this activity resulted in economic prosperity in some areas—particularly in the larger lakeside towns and cities—the remains at Capernaum suggest that its inhabitants benefited from the fishing industry to a lesser degree.

Since the late Hellenistic period, local administrators sought to enhance the regional economy by taking advantage of the Galilee's natural freshwater resources. By the Roman period, over a dozen ports and harbors were constructed around the lake to accommodate fishing and other maritime activities.[37] These harbors reveal much about the local fishing industry, as well as the relative importance of the port cities, towns, and villages. For example, explorations have shown that the more prosperous cities and towns around the lake built large and well-constructed ports for fishing and for docking military and transport vessels. On the east side of the lake, the Greco-Roman Decapolis cities of Hippos and Gadara both possessed impressive harbors, the latter consisting of a three-acre enclosed basin, a breakwater and promenade made of finely chiseled stone, a large tower, and administrative buildings around the harbor's gate.[38]

On the west side of the lake, the Hasmoneans established the port town of Magdala/Tarichaeae (the home of Mary "Magdalene"; see Luke 8:2) as a location for the processing and selling of fish. Josephus describes the many maritime vessels, shipyard workers, and wood supplies associated with Magdala's harbor,[39] and excavations have uncovered its promenade, a sheltered basin, basalt moorings, a colonnaded springhouse, a tower for processing fish, and nearby buildings (one containing a mosaic depicting a fishing boat).[40] In the first century, Herod Antipas built Tiberias, one of his two regional capitals, just south of Magdala. Unfortunately, little of its ancient harbor survives under the modern city, but large numbers of mooring stones, stone anchors, and hundreds of stone net sinkers found along the shore attest to the significant fishing activity of this city.[41] Both ports encouraged a vibrant fishing economy in the lake's western district.[42]

Capernaum, like other villages around the lake, had its own harbor facilities, but they were much more modest than those found in the more prosperous towns and cities. Most of the exposed harbor facilities at Capernaum have been uncovered on the east side of the site, but the precise dating and extent of these features are debated.[43] At some point in the Roman period, Capernaum had a basalt breakwater that stretched along its shore to protect the village from the lake and to provide an anchorage for fishing boats.[44] This breakwater created a promenade between the shore and the closest dwellings, providing an open space in which fishermen could unload their catches, wash and repair their equipment, and possibly sell their fish to others in the village.[45] The harbors along the promenade were constructed with unworked basalt fieldstones and were built in various shapes and sizes, having curved piers, triangular piers, or straight docks. Some of these extended about a hundred feet into the lake.[46] Onshore near the largest harbor, excavators discovered artificial storage pools built to keep fish fresh after being caught.[47]

Unfortunately, it is difficult to date Capernaum's extant harbor features with precision. Some scholars claim that they date to the first century, and are thus contemporary with Jesus and Peter.[48] It is much more likely, however, that they were not built until the second or third century as a part of Capernaum's expansion in the Late Roman period, and that prior to their construction the village's shoreline was largely unprotected, consisting of only a few smaller jetties made of stacked basalt fieldstones.[49] Therefore, Capernaum's harbor facilities in the first century were quite modest in comparison to those serving the Decapolis cities, Tiberias, and Magdala. They do, however, provide a sense of Capernaum's ancient fishing activities and paint an approximate picture of important New Testament scenes, such as the disciples washing their nets on the shore (see Luke 5:2), Jesus' calling of Peter and Andrew along the shore to "fish for people" (see Mark 1:16–18), and Jesus' calling of James and John to leave their boat in the harbor (see Mark 1:19–20).

It is possible that near Capernaum's harbor there was a small customs office for the collection of tolls and taxes on catches of fish and other interregional trade.[50] Administrative buildings likely related to these activities have been found next to the harbors at other sites such as Kursi, where the foundations of a public building (adorned with a mosaic floor) survive north of the pier and were surrounded by hundreds of lead net weights.[51] However, at Capernaum no such structures have yet been discovered from the first century.[52] The Gospels do record the existence of a "tax booth" (*telonion*) from which Jesus called Matthew/Levi to a life of discipleship (see Matthew 9:9; Mark 2:13–14),[53] but the size and

An artistic reconstruction of Capernaum's ancient shoreline, including its modest jetties made of stacked basalt fieldstones, typical first-century boats, and activities of local fishermen. Painting by Balage Balogh, used by permission.

nature of this facility are not certain.[54] If Matthew's "tax booth" was an actual building, it may have been a modest structure that is not easily recognizable as an administrative office.

Small finds at Capernaum and nearby villages also illuminate Peter's occupation, attest to fishing activities around the Sea of Galilee, and help us to identify the various methods of fishing used in the first century.[55] It appears that the most common method was net fishing. This included the use of large dragnets spread into the lake by men on a boat and handled by two teams of workers on the shore. Once the net was spread, lead or stone weights attached to the bottom of the net would sink the net into the water, creating a wall to catch anything in its path. After the men on shore pulled in the net, they would separate the kosher fish (mostly tilapia) from the nonkosher fish (such as scaleless catfish; Leviticus 11:9–12) and send the catch to be processed.[56] Another method of net fishing used small, circular throw nets (or "cast nets") worked by one or two individuals either on shore or from a boat. These nets also required weights to sink them low enough into the lake to catch the fish (mostly smaller freshwater sardines).[57] A third method—typically used from boats in deeper waters—was with a trammel net, which used several layers of weighted netting to create underwater walls designed to trap the fish.[58]

Archaeological evidence exists for net fishing around the Galilee during the first century. We would not expect the rope or linen nets themselves to survive long in Galilee's humid climate, although one such net was found preserved in the arid Judean desert.[59] The small lead and stone net weights, however, do survive in significant quantities in villages around the lake.[60] These finds illustrate Jesus' parable of the dragnet, which caught both the good (kosher) and bad (nonkosher) fish, requiring them to be separated (see Matthew 13:47–50); Peter and Andrew throwing a small cast net from the shore when they were called by Jesus (see Matthew 4:18; Mark 1:16); and episodes in which the disciples were told to let down their trammel "nets" in deep water fishing (see Luke 5:3–6; John 21:6). Other small finds that survive include needles for mending nets (see Mark 1:19–20),[61] small metal hooks for line fishing (see Matthew 17:24–27),[62] and stone anchors for docking boats.[63]

One remarkable discovery that helps us to understand the work of Jesus' fishermen-disciples is the hull of a small wood boat from the first century that was submerged in the Sea of Galilee until its recovery in 1986 off the coast between Capernaum and Magdala.[64] Through creative conservation work, the boat has been carefully excavated, preserved, and studied. Despite its popular name ("the Jesus boat"), there is no evidence that the boat belonged to Jesus or his disciples, but it represents the type of vessel they likely would have used on a regular basis. The boat was made of low-quality timber (often patched together with different types of wood), was smeared on its underside with bitumen pitch, and contained a small mast and sail.[65] Based on the size of the vessel, archaeologists estimate that between five and seven grown men could work in the boat comfortably, but that up to fifteen men could fit within it if necessary.

Small groups of men would go out on the lake in such a boat and would work through the night (typically without clothing; see John 21:7). This boat vividly illustrates New Testament accounts of Jesus teaching in a small boat offshore (see Mark 4:1–2; Matthew 13:1–3), the offshore fishing activities of Jesus' disciples (see Luke 5:1–11; John 21:1–11), and the moments when Jesus and his disciples traveled in a single boat across the Sea of Galilee (see Mark 4:35–41; 6:32; Matthew 8:23–27; 14:13; Luke 8:22–25). It also reflects the likely professional limitations of Jesus' fishermen-disciples; not being a large or expensive fishing vessel, the boat's construction and traces of frequent repair reflect the work of skilled craftsmen who had only modest resources at their disposal.[66]

These maritime discoveries from the Capernaum region not only illustrate important episodes from the New Testament, but they help us in assessing Peter's occupational pursuits and the context in which he operated. Recent research on the Galilean fishing industry has led to a debate over the socioeconomic status of fishermen in Capernaum. Fishing businesses had the potential to prosper in the larger ports like Tiberias or Magdala, but what about those in the smaller villages?

Some scholars have argued that to afford supplies (boats, weights, anchors, and nets), obtain an imperial fishing license, and operate a successful fishing operation, Peter and his associates must have been savvy and bilingual businessmen who possessed significant capital.[67] Others have contended that the multilayered bureaucracy of the Galilean economy, high overhead costs, the need to have fish processed (dried, smoked, and salted) in Magdala, and heavy taxation would have left those doing the actual fishing (like Peter) with extremely limited income.[68] As is often the case, reality might have been somewhere in between, with some fishing families receiving more "take home" revenue than others.

The New Testament leaves only a few hints of Peter's status in this economy, but those few hints might be telling. Interestingly, different Gospels give different impressions of Peter's work as a fisherman. According to Mark and Matthew (the earliest Gospels written),[69] Peter and his brother Andrew were called by Jesus as they were casting small throw-nets into the lake from the shore (see Mark 1:16–18; Matthew 4:18–20), and Peter occasionally fished with a line and hook (see Matthew 17:27). Both of these methods were typically employed by lower-class fishermen with no better resources at their disposal. In contrast, James and John left a larger fishing operation with boats and hired day laborers (see Mark 1:19–20; Matthew 4:21–22), suggesting a higher level of resources and income among the Zebedee family.[70] Peter owned his own home and seemed able to pay his taxes (see Mark 1:29), showing that he was not destitute, but he does not appear to have had the same resources (boats and hired help) as some of the other disciples.[71]

The Gospel of Luke, on the other hand, rewrites the narrative of Peter's calling by describing Peter as owning his own boats and being a full business partner with James and John (see Luke 5:1–11; also see John 21:1–3), implying a more prosperous status for Peter.[72] It is not clear why Luke gives this different portrayal, but his personal inexperience with Galilee and his consistent effort to elevate stories of Jesus and Peter for his urban Greek audience might help explain his anomalous account.[73] In any case, Gospel accounts provide two slightly different pictures of Peter's economic status, with the fisherman either living at subsistence level (the impression given in Mark and Matthew) or well above subsistence level (the impression given in Luke). As will be seen in the following section, the civic and domestic life of first-century Capernaum suggests an economic status for Peter's family that may have been somewhere in between.

Civic and Domestic Life at Capernaum

In addition to viewing Peter's vocation in the context of the local fishing economy, an examination of the civic and domestic life of Peter's village can provide further evidence for his socioeconomic and religious background. The excavations of Capernaum's western remains can be particularly helpful in this regard, as Loffreda and Corbo uncovered numerous houses, streets, alleyways, and other finds that illuminate the cultural dynamics of the ancient village. Unfortunately, as with so much at the site, it is often difficult to determine the precise dating and original appearance of these features. Nevertheless, the remains provide glimpses into Peter's hometown and allow for comparisons with other sites in the region. They suggest that fishing, agriculture, and commerce were secure sources of income for Capernaum's inhabitants, but that these professions were not as lucrative in the village as they might have been in other locations.

Recent excavations at other sites in Galilee have given evidence for prosperity and centralized urban planning in some parts of the region. For example, excavations at the cities of Sepphoris and Tiberias—and to a more limited degree at the walled town of Yodefat and the port town of Magdala—have shown that some Galilean sites possessed such amenities as stone-paved streets and plazas, sewage systems provided by aqueducts and drainage channels, monumental public buildings used for administrative purposes, and even entertainment facilities. Upper-class domestic structures at these sites also incorporated Roman-style luxuries, such as private baths and interior decoration (mosaic and opus sectile floors, stucco work, and Pompeian wall frescoes). Although the inhabitants of these sites were primarily Jewish, the material culture displays their Hellenistic proclivities and their financial means to support an aristocratic lifestyle.[74]

In contrast, excavations at Capernaum revealed no evidence for Roman amenities, central planning, or a Hellenized upper class in the first century. Capernaum's streets and alleys were not originally laid out on a grid system, leaving them to evolve with the organic growth of the village's domestic structures.[75] These streets and alleys were not paved with stone, but were mostly packed dirt and pebbles, making Capernaum dusty during the dry season and muddy during the rainy season. With no aqueducts, drainage channels, private bathrooms, public latrines, or any other form of sewage system,[76] inhabitants likely relieved themselves outdoors or tossed the contents of chamber pots into the alleyways between houses, producing a malodorous environment typical of ancient villages.[77] Furthermore, aside from the likely presence of a modest synagogue (see below), there is no evidence at Capernaum for public building projects—basilicas, theaters, paved plazas, etc.—thus contrasting the village's economic status with the cities and more prosperous towns in the region.

Based on the excavated groups of houses at the site, it appears that the average inhabitants of Capernaum were neither destitute nor wealthy. The dwellings in this village were typical of first-century villages in the Galilee region. These were modest structures consisting of three or four single-story rooms surrounding a central courtyard, with walls made of various-sized basalt fieldstones.[78] Unlike the well-dressed blocks used at more prosperous sites, the irregular stones used at Capernaum were not chiseled to fit into place, but were held together by a mixture of pebbles and "mortar."[79] The walls contained no traces of interior plaster or decoration.[80] As noted by the excavators, this style of wall construction was not able to support a second story or heavy roof. Instead, the dwellings at Capernaum were covered with thatched roofs supported by wood beams and reeds bound together with a thick mud mortar.[81] The thatching and mortar was smoothed out with stone roof rollers and subsequently dried, providing a sufficiently sturdy roof that could be used for light work, sleeping, storage, and drying produce.[82]

This style of roof construction nicely illustrates Mark's account of four men from the village who "removed the roof" of a house by "having dug through" (*ezoryzantees*) the dried mud, straw, and reeds to lower a paralytic into the crowded room so he could be healed by Jesus (see Mark 2:1–12). The excavators and other scholars have observed that Mark's details accurately reflect an average home in Capernaum.[83] Luke's version of the story, however, differs from Mark by claiming that the men removed the house's "ceramic roof tiles" (*keramōn*; see Luke 5:17–26). In Roman Galilee, ceramic roof tiles are mostly found in an urban context associated with monumental structures or upper-class dwellings. They are extremely rare in village domestic architecture, where walls were not designed to support their weight and where the flat roofs provided valuable work space.[84] At Capernaum, no roof tiles were discovered in any first-century domestic context.[85] Therefore, it appears that Luke's account assumed the Roman-style villas familiar to his urban Gentile audience rather than accurately describing a home in a Galilean village.[86]

Inside Capernaum's domestic structures, the small living rooms around the courtyard had uncovered openings for windows, but these were located high on the wall to serve for lighting and ventilation rather than to provide a view of the outside.[87] Most of the living rooms left no traces of a permanent door, suggesting that the rooms opened to the shared courtyard with only a mat or curtain covering.[88] The floors of these rooms were made of either packed dirt or a basalt cobblestone pavement with thin spaces (interstices) between the cobbles, which often contained broken pottery or an occasional dropped coin.[89] Both styles of flooring can illustrate Jesus' parable of the lost coin in the house—a story of a woman who swept all day over the packed dirt or basalt cobbles to find the precious coin that would feed her family (see Luke 15:8–10).[90]

An artistic reconstruction of the first-century "house of Peter" (Insula I) nicely illustrates the typical domestic structures in Capernaum, including the modest walls made of basalt fieldstones, the roofs made of wood beams and reeds bound together with a mud mortar, and the shared courtyard space which allowed members of the extended family to live and work in close proximity. Painting by Balage Balogh, used by permission.

As was typical for a Galilean village, each housing complex in Capernaum consisted of three or four rooms clustered around an open courtyard. This arrangement allowed numerous members of an extended family to live and work together in the same shared space. These housing complexes were accessed from the street through doorways with thresholds, doorjambs, and a wooden door equipped with a locking mechanism that opened into the courtyard.[91] Courtyards in Capernaum were paved with basalt cobblestone and often contained small presses for crushing olives, hand-operated grinding stones for wheat, small ovens for baking bread and other meals, and loom weights for making clothing, reflecting the daily routine of women in the family.[92] Courtyards often contained areas for housing animals and crude stone staircases that led to the roofs of the living rooms.[93] Some courtyards also included a small shop that opened to the street so that the family could sell their produce or fish to neighbors.[94]

Most of the dwellings at Capernaum contained common household pottery such as cooking pots, "casseroles," wine jugs, cups, and bowls, almost all of which were low-quality locally produced wares.[95] This pottery assemblage suggests that villagers ate modest meals of soups and thin stews (surely supplemented with local staples such as bread, fish, and olives) out of shared dishes,[96] likely as they sat close together in a living room upon mats placed over the packed dirt floor.[97] In addition, an ostracon and the absence of imported amphorae at Capernaum suggest that villagers drank local wine.[98] These observations illustrate stories in the synoptic Gospels in which Jesus, his disciples, and "sinners" gathered for meals within various homes (see Mark 2:15–17; Matthew 9:9–13).

Other finds in Capernaum's domestic structures indicate that the village's inhabitants were mostly conservative and religiously observant Jews. Unlike at nearby Hellenistic sites (including the Decapolis cities and et-Tell/"Bethsaida"),[99] no pig or nonkosher fish bones were found in the excavations at Capernaum, showing that the villagers maintained a diet in accordance with the law of Moses (see Leviticus 11). In addition, each of the excavated houses contained stone vessels (mostly cups) used for ritual purity washings, such as the washing of hands before eating meals according to Jewish custom (see Mark 7:1–4; Matthew 15:1–2).[100] Most of these stone vessels were of a low quality, either carved by hand or made on a small lathe.[101] No ritual baths (*miqva'ot*) were found in the village, but the lake likely provided the means for ritual bathing.[102]

These finds point to a high level of observance of the Jewish purity and food laws in Peter's hometown. This aligns with the impression of Capernaum given in the New Testament, which contrasts the Jewish village with nearby Gentile cities (e.g., Matthew 11:20–24). The stone vessels and absence of pig bones at Capernaum might also reflect Peter's initial discomfort over Jesus' apparent indifference toward ritual hand washings (see Matthew 15:1–20; Mark 7:1–23)[103] and Peter's later anxiety over his vision of the unkosher foods, in which he exclaimed, "I have never eaten anything that is profane or unclean" (Acts 10:9–16). Even after his vision, Peter's inherent cultural tendencies manifested themselves in Antioch, as he naturally preferred dining with Jewish-Christians rather than with Paul's Gentile converts (see Galatians 2:11–14). In short, Peter seems to have been comfortable in and influenced by the conservative Jewish culture of his home village.

In light of these observations, it is interesting to note that the New Testament does record the presence of a few Gentiles at Capernaum. This includes a Gentile "centurion," whose servant was paralyzed (see Matthew 8:5–13),[104] and a "royal official" (presumably a Gentile), whose son was ill "at the point of death" (see John 4:46–54), both of whom sought Jesus' help.[105] Unfortunately, there is no archaeological trace of a Gentile presence at Capernaum—no pig bones, Greek inscriptions, or Roman art—leaving the impression that the village was entirely inhabited by conservative Jews.[106] Therefore, it is difficult to know how the Gentiles in these stories would have interacted with Capernaum's majority Jewish population. Matthew implies a high degree of tension between the "centurion" and his Jewish neighbors (see Matthew 8:5–13), whereas Luke claims that there was a mutual affection between him and the local elders (see Luke 7:1–5). In light of Capernaum's material culture and Luke's tendency to present Gentiles in the best possible light, the impression given in Matthew may more accurately reflect the village's cultural dynamics.[107]

Although there is no archaeological evidence for a Gentile minority at Capernaum, there are indications that some families in the villages were more affluent than others. Most of the domestic structures, pottery, and small finds suggest that the average family at Capernaum lived at or slightly above subsistence level. However, some families may have enjoyed modest surplus income. For example, some dwellings in Capernaum contained higher quality household vessels than were found in most of the residential area. These include a small collection of glassware,[108] limited quantities of imitation Roman pottery (Eastern Terra Sigillata A),[109] and a few fragments of large lathe-turned stone vessels.[110] The presence of such finds does not point to an elite upper class,[111] but they might reflect the presence of individuals, such as the small contingent of Herodian customs and military officers, who enjoyed more affluence than others. Yet, despite their presence, Capernaum was still very much a lower to "middle" class village.

An important example of an average first-century dwelling at Capernaum that reflects the domestic profile described in this section is a structure identified by early Christians as the "house of Peter" (Insula I). The remains of this house were uncovered in the late 1960s as the Franciscans excavated an octagonal chapel built in the Byzantine period to memorialize the location.[112] In the process of excavating the shrine, Loffreda and Corbo discovered that the earliest structure underneath was a typical domestic complex built around the first century BC. They also found that its subsequent history lent plausibility to the tradition that the house once belonged to Jesus' most famous disciple. Excavations showed that by the late first or early second century AD, the largest room of the complex (room 1) was renovated with a plastered floor, a feature unattested elsewhere at Capernaum.[113] At this same time, the pottery assemblage in the room shifted from common household wares to oil lamps and storage jars, suggesting that the room began to be used for communal gatherings rather than daily living. Loffreda and Corbo interpreted these developments as evidence that Jewish-Christians in Capernaum treated the room as having special value and held assemblies there.[114]

By the fourth century, the entire housing complex was identified by Christian pilgrims as the "house of Peter" and was converted into a *domus ecclesia*—a church building that incorporated elements of the private dwelling for worship purposes. At that time the walls of room 1 were plastered and decorated with painted images of paradise scenes, buildings, and possibly floral crosses.[115]

Throughout the next century, pilgrims etched Greek, Syriac, Hebrew, and Latin inscriptions into the plaster walls that included their own names, pleas for Jesus to save them, and the name of Peter.[116] Sometime in the fifth century, this house church was demolished and replaced by a domed octagonal shrine built over room 1, complete with mosaics, an eastern apse, and a small baptismal font. Thus the first-century "house of Peter" was enshrined for Christian pilgrims within a memorial chapel for the remainder of the Byzantine period.

Based on the history of this building, its excavators claimed that Capernaum's Jewish-Christian population accurately preserved the memory of the site and that the dwelling below the shrine did indeed belong to Peter. This claim has received varying levels of acceptance over the last forty years. Recently, however, scholars have challenged the notion that an established Jewish-Christian community existed in Capernaum in the first three centuries, casting doubt on the claim that a continuous memory of the location of Peter's house was accurately transmitted.[117] Therefore, while identifying Insula I as Peter's house is an intriguing possibility—especially considering the site's long tradition of Christian veneration—it is ultimately impossible to prove.

Regardless, the first-century dwelling on the site fits the profile of other domestic structures in the village, and its features resemble the New Testament stories regarding Peter's house. For example, the original complex contains four or five rooms clustered around a central L-shaped courtyard, suitable to accommodate an extended family.[118] This is similar to the Gospels' description of Peter, Andrew, and Peter's in-laws all living together in a shared residence (see Mark 1:29–31; Matthew 8:14–17).[119] The courtyard had a spacious entryway from the street at the northeast corner,[120] and both the courtyard and the entryway were large enough for crowds to gather to see Jesus teach and perform miracles within the house (see Mark 1:32–34; 3:20–21, 31–35).

So while we cannot be certain that this building was the actual house of Peter, it does reflect the type of dwelling in which Peter and his family likely lived. The quality and material profile of the building also support the impression that Peter's family lived as average villagers, perhaps above subsistence level but without wealth, affluence, or Hellenistic tastes. By all accounts it appears that Peter and his family fit in with their religiously conservative Jewish surroundings and that their fishing activities were not lucrative, but were sufficient to support an extended family.

The "Synagogue of the Centurion"

A final issue that sheds light on the social, economic, and religious dynamics of first-century Capernaum is the presence of a synagogue within the village. The

New Testament indicates that a synagogue was at the center of Capernaum's village life and that Jesus frequently taught and performed exorcisms in that setting (see Mark 1:21–27; Luke 4:31–37; John 6:24–59). The existence of this institution in Peter's hometown supports the observation that Capernaum's inhabitants were religiously conservative Jews, whose regular routine included Sabbath observance, the study of scripture, and some form of communal prayer. This was likely the setting in which Peter and his family learned the Torah and the writings of the prophets (through Aramaic translations of the Hebrew texts), as well as gathered for holy days and performed many of their other religious obligations.[121]

Any reconstruction of first-century Capernaum must acknowledge this synagogue and its place on the village landscape. However, there are two important issues that must be considered when doing so. First, it is necessary to note the multifaceted yet modest nature of synagogues in Judea and Galilee during this period. Second, for Capernaum it is necessary to evaluate the relevance of the extant synagogue remains at the site for the time of Jesus and Peter. Space will not allow for a full discussion of these issues, but a brief overview will provide some final observations on Peter's hometown.

In recent years, numerous studies have shed light on the nature and function of synagogues during the late Second Temple period (ca. 200 BC–AD 70), which is when this institution began to grow and develop.[122] Even though the law of Moses did not require congregational assembly outside of a temple setting, Jewish communities by the first century regularly met together for a variety of reasons, and synagogues became the settings for these meetings. In its earliest uses, the word "synagogue" (synagōgē) simply referred to "a gathering" of people for a single purpose. These "gatherings" could occur in various settings, including in a building specifically made for assembly, in a private home, or in an open public space (such as a town square). Furthermore, the purpose for the "gathering" could be religious worship, but it could also be to discuss local politics, conduct legal proceedings, or facilitate limited educational activities. In short, the earliest "synagogues" were multipurpose community centers.[123]

Scores of synagogue buildings have been found in Galilee from late antiquity (ca. AD 300–600), showing that by those centuries most Jewish communities built large structures specifically for the purpose of religious worship. These buildings contained assembly halls, shrines for housing sacred scrolls, and religious iconography (such as menorahs or biblical mosaics) to accompany the liturgy. Synagogues in the first century, however, are not as consistent, defined, or prominent. In comparison to later periods, very few first-century synagogue buildings have been discovered in Galilee, with structures at Gamla, Magdala, and Khirbet Cana as rare examples.[124] With the exception of the large hall in the densely populated town of Gamla, these are small buildings that contain no religious iconography or liturgical features,[125] but that were designed as general public meeting places.[126]

Because there was no set template for synagogue architecture in this period, different locations could have had different types of "synagogues"; some cities and towns may have had the means to build modest structures, while Jews in other locations (often including the villages) could have held their "gatherings" in any space conducive for meeting. In the case of Capernaum, most New Testament references do not elaborate on the precise nature of the village's synagogue, but one passage in the Gospel of Luke specifically mentions the building of a physical structure:

> A centurion [in Capernaum] had a slave whom he valued highly, and who was ill and close to death.
> When he heard about Jesus, he sent some Jewish elders to him, asking him to come and heal his slave.
> When they came to Jesus, they appealed to him earnestly, saying, "He is worthy of having you do this for him,
> For he loves our people, and it is he who built our synagogue for us." (Luke 7:2–5)

Unfortunately, Luke does not describe its size or layout, but his account has led many to refer to Capernaum's first-century synagogue as the "synagogue of the centurion."[127]

Luke's mention of a synagogue building in Capernaum has created significant interest in the monumental synagogue remains that now dominate the site. This imposing structure, built with imported limestone ashlars, is one of the largest synagogues in Israel. It features a main prayer hall (with benches along two walls, Corinthian columns on three sides, and a second story), a large open courtyard to its east (with colonnaded porticoes on three sides), and a porch entryway along its south side.[128] Soon after these ruins were uncovered and partially reconstructed in the early 1900s, some scholars began to wonder if this was the "synagogue of the centurion" mentioned in Luke.[129] Most, however, came to believe based on its architectural style that the building dated to the second or third century, long after the time of Jesus and Peter.[130]

This second conclusion was almost universally accepted until the Franciscans excavated the building in the late 1960s, removed portions of the synagogue's pavement, and cut trenches underneath its main features.[131] In every trench they dug—in the prayer hall, the courtyard, and the porch—Loffreda and Corbo discovered

The monumental limestone synagogue at Capernaum, built during the Byzantine period, rests on a basalt foundation and included a large prayer hall, courtyard, and porch entryway. Photo courtesy of Kent P. Jackson.

pottery and thousands of coins dating to the fourth and fifth century sealed under the stone pavement (in both the mortar bedding and the fill below), showing that the synagogue could not have been constructed before the Byzantine period.[132] Most scholars now agree that Capernaum's monumental limestone synagogue was built around the fifth century,[133] but some claim that this building was built on an earlier basalt synagogue that stood on the site in the first century.[134] If this claim is correct, the limestone synagogue may have preserved and incorporated portions of the "synagogue of the centurion" known to Jesus and Peter.

Those who make this claim point to three main observations: (1) Religious buildings are often built on the location of earlier religious buildings, thus preserving the sanctity of the site. Therefore, it is reasonable to suggest that Capernaum's Byzantine synagogue marked the location of its first-century synagogue. (2) The monumental limestone synagogue at Capernaum rests upon a basalt foundation. However, in the southwest corner of the prayer hall, the basalt foundation and the limestone wall are misaligned by about 10 centimeters, suggesting that the foundation represents portions of an earlier building on which a later structure was constructed.[135] (3) Deep under the limestone pavement of the synagogue's nave, Loffreda and Corbo discovered a basalt cobblestone pavement dating to the Early

In the southwest corner of Capernaum's synagogue, the basalt foundation and limestone wall are slightly misaligned. This has led some scholars to argue that the basalt foundation represents an earlier synagogue building from the time of Jesus and Peter, but numerous factors controvert this proposal. Photo courtesy of Kent P. Jackson.

Roman period.[136] Since the area covered by this lower basalt pavement seemed too large for a domestic structure, the pavement must have been the floor of an earlier public building, such as a synagogue.[137]

Based on these observations, some scholars believe that the basalt foundations of the prayer hall were originally the lower courses of the walls belonging to the first-century "synagogue of the centurion."[138] No other features of this building have been found, but proponents claim that it was a rectangular, single-story structure constructed and paved with basalt. Proposed reconstructions include two rows of columns that run north-south through the hall and rest on stylobates (low foundation walls designed to support the colonnades), three to four rows of benches along its west wall, and entrances on the east and west of the building.[139] Since its dimensions were the same as the prayer hall of the later synagogue, the first-century synagogue would have measured approximately 24.2 x 18.5 meters (covering an area of 448 square meters), making it by far the largest first-century synagogue building ever discovered.[140]

As intriguing as this possibility may be, however, such a large public structure seems incongruent with the nature of the first-century remains at

Capernaum. Would the small population of a fishing and farming village, most of whom (like Peter) lived at or modestly above subsistence level, have had the means to construct the largest synagogue in the region? Even if a "centurion" built the synagogue for the estimated 1,000 to 1,500 Jewish inhabitants of Capernaum, would he have built an assembly hall almost 50 percent larger than the hall at Gamla, with its estimated population of 3,000 to 4,000?[141] If so, the massive basalt synagogue at Capernaum could significantly impact our assessment of financial resources within Peter's village. In light of this potential significance, it is important to note that some scholars point to archaeological reasons why the basalt foundation of the limestone synagogue likely did not belong to an earlier structure, making it irrelevant to an evaluation of first-century Capernaum.

First, the proposed reconstruction of the first-century synagogue has a number of key weaknesses: no evidence for its benches have been discovered;[142] traces of its other building materials are either absent or not adequately published for examination;[143] an architectural connection between the basalt cobblestone pavement and the basalt "walls" of this synagogue has not been demonstrated;[144] the extant basalt "walls" rise four feet above the basalt pavement and extend the entire length of the limestone synagogue, but contain no openings for doors;[145] the proposed "stylobates" of the synagogue (which run almost the entire length of the hall) rise unusually high above the main floor, which would make movement in the hall extremely difficult;[146] and it would be the only known synagogue from this period paved with a cobblestone floor (other first-century synagogue floors consist of pavement stones and/or packed earth covered with mats).[147]

Second, the difference in building materials and alignment between the basalt foundation and the limestone walls of the Byzantine synagogue does not need to indicate two separate buildings: the construction technique of using basalt courses as the foundation for a monumental limestone building is attested in contemporary nearby architecture, reflecting the benefits of basalt (which is harder than limestone) as a foundation;[148] the misalignment between the basalt foundation and limestone wall in the southwest corner of the building could easily be explained as an unfortunate result of the area's sloping topography;[149] and, if the misalignment reflects the adjustment of a later building, why is this misalignment only reflected in the southwest corner and not in all areas of the building? (The basalt and limestone features are perfectly aligned in every other corner and under both stylobates. Was the original building asymmetrical?)

Finally, and most convincingly, it is clear from the excavation reports that the entire fifth-century synagogue building—including its basalt foundation—cut through and demolished residential structures that were built

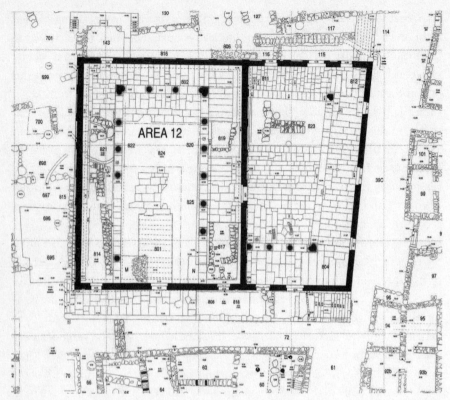

Top plans of the excavations of Capernaum's synagogue (outlined in bold) show the remains of walls and other features from earlier domestic structures that were demolished when the synagogue was constructed (see the drawings of numerous walls running beneath the synagogue's prayer hall, courtyard, and porch). The presence of these Hellenistic and Roman period homes undermine claims that a first-century synagogue existed at this location. Top plan adapted from the map of the site in Stanislao Loffreda, *Cafarnao V* (Jerusalem: Franciscan Printing Press, 2005).

between the first century BC and first century AD, and which appear to have been occupied into the third or fourth century.[150] These late Hellenistic and Early Roman period domestic complexes are represented by remains of their walls,[151] basalt pavement,[152] and other features which were covered by the synagogue's prayer hall, courtyard, and porch.[153] Within these earlier dwellings, excavators found evidence for domestic life including ovens, grinding stones, and household pottery such as cooking pots, jugs, storage jars, bowls, and cups.[154] We would not expect to find these items in a public space such as a synagogue, but rather in the courtyards and rooms of private dwellings.[155] The coins and pottery found on the floors showed that these dwellings were likely inhabited into the fourth century,[156] leaving no place for an earlier synagogue to exist at this location.

Together, these observations make a strong case against the proposal that a first-century basalt synagogue stood at the site. Instead, the basalt "walls" appear to have been originally built as the foundations for the fifth-century synagogue and not as the walls of an earlier structure. As a result, many current synagogue scholars either reject this proposal or remain agnostic on the issue.[157] Since the site was the location of common residential dwellings at the time of Peter and for centuries afterward, it is theoretically possible that this residential structure was the location of a "house synagogue,"[158] but there is no positive evidence for this usage or for the building having been built by a Gentile benefactor such as the "centurion."

So, while the New Testament indicates that a synagogue existed in Capernaum when Jesus and Peter lived there, no reliable evidence survives for its construction, size, layout, or location. Assuming a synagogue building did exist in the first-century village, it likely resembled other known village synagogues (e.g., Qiyrat Sefer and Khirbet Cana), which were small, modestly constructed buildings with no Jewish iconography and no liturgical furniture.[159] In short, the New Testament references to a synagogue in Capernaum confirm that Peter's hometown was inhabited by religious Jews, but the extant synagogue remains at the site cannot be used as evidence for wealth in the first-century village and likely have no bearing on reconstructing Peter's social context.

Conclusion: Peter in Capernaum

In providing this archaeological survey of first-century Capernaum, I have attempted to elucidate the socioeconomic, religious, and cultural setting of Peter's early life and ministry. As mentioned previously, scholars debate the extent of Peter's financial status, education, and inherent sympathies to Gentile customs in order to evaluate the scriptural traditions about his missionary efforts, his leadership in the early church, and the authorship of the New Testament books associated with his name. Could Peter have been wealthy enough to leave his fishing business unharmed while he followed Jesus, or did his discipleship come at great financial cost to his family? Did his cultural upbringing naturally incline him to fellowship with Gentiles, or did he need to overcome his cultural tendencies to bring them the gospel? Was Peter educated enough to write letters in polished Greek using sophisticated rhetoric and citations from the Septuagint, or would he have needed to rely on more educated scribes to do so?

While archaeology cannot answer these questions directly, the excavations of Capernaum can establish a valuable context for understanding Peter's early life. This survey has shown that first-century Capernaum was a lower to "middle" class Jewish fishing village. At the time of Jesus and Peter, it was not one of the poorest villages in the region (such as Nazareth), but it was also not a wealthy city like Tiberias or Sepphoris, or even a prosperous port town like Magdala. Most of the village's population, it seems, lived at or modestly above subsistence level. Within this environment, it appears that Peter and his brother Andrew were able to support their families, own a courtyard house, and pay their taxes through their work as fishermen (even if they might not have been as successful as James and John), but likely enjoyed little additional revenue or affluence.

The archaeological evidence also indicates that Capernaum's inhabitants were religiously conservative Jews who had no Hellenistic leanings, explaining Peter's natural interest in ritual purity laws and observance of a kosher diet. Therefore, if Peter was eventually sympathetic toward Gentiles, he likely did not develop these sympathies in his home village. While Peter and his Jewish associates may have had some interaction with Gentiles in the village through a few local military officers, interregional traffic, or travels around the lake, there is no indication that the average Aramaic-speaking Jew in Capernaum knew much Greek beyond, perhaps, the vocabulary necessary to do business. With no multicultural educational institution in Capernaum, anyone who reached a higher Greek proficiency than this must have acquired it elsewhere.

As for his level of cultural sophistication, descriptions of Peter in the New Testament accord with what we know of his life in Capernaum—Peter and the other disciples were astonished by Jerusalem's monumental architecture (see Matthew 24:1), Peter's unpolished accent betrayed his rural Galilean origins (see Matthew 26:73), and Jerusalem elites viewed Peter as a "common uneducated" man (see Acts 2:7–8; 4:13). These descriptions confirm that Peter was very much a product of his upbringing in a modest village on the north shore of the Sea of Galilee. Therefore, while there are many questions that archaeology cannot answer directly, the archaeological evidence from first-century Capernaum is an important source of information in our study of the early life, work, and ministry of Jesus' most famous disciple.

Notes

1. All biblical translations in this paper have been taken from the New Revised Standard Version.

2. For recent studies on the historical Peter, see Pheme Perkins, *Peter: Apostle for the Whole Church* (Minneapolis: Fortress Press, 2000); Martin Hengel, *Saint Peter: The Underestimated Apostle* (Grand Rapids, MI: Eerdmans, 2010); and Markus Bockmuehl, *Simon Peter in Scripture and Memory: The New Testament Apostle in the Early Church* (Grand Rapids, MI: Baker Academic, 2012).

3. See John H. Elliott, *1 Peter: A New Translation with Introduction and Commentary* (New York: Doubleday, 2000), 120; Bart D. Ehrman, *The New Testament: A Historical Introduction to the Early Christian Writings*, 4th ed. (Oxford: Oxford University Press, 2008), 443–44.

4. See Jerome Murphy-O'Connor, "Fishers of Fish, Fishers of Men: What We Know of the First Disciples from their Profession," *Bible Review* 15, no. 3 (June 1999): 22–27, 48–49.

5. The early use of archaeology in research on Peter was limited, focusing mainly on the identification of the "house of Peter" at Capernaum and the location of Peter's burial in Rome; see Perkins, *Peter*, 38–39.

6. Sensational claims have been made that Peter's bones were discovered in the necropolis under St. Peter's Basilica in Rome (see John Evangelist Walsh, *The Bones of St. Peter: The First Full Account of the Search for the Apostle's Body* [Garden City, NY: Image Books, 1985]), but these claims are impossible to substantiate and are not typically incorporated into serious scholarship on the historical Peter.

7. Rami Arav, "New Testament Archaeology and the Case of Bethsaida," in *Das Ende der Tage und die Gegenwart des Heils: Begegnungen mit dem Neuen Testament und seiner Umwelt*, ed. M. Becker and W. Fenske (Leiden, Netherlands: Brill, 1999), 84.

8. Rami Arav, "Bethsaida Excavations: Preliminary Report, 1994–1996," in *Bethsaida: A City by the North Shore of the Sea of Galilee*, vol. 2, ed. Rami Arav and Richard A. Freund (Kirksville, MO: Truman State University, 1999), 18–24, 32–44.

9. See Mark Appold, "Peter in Profile: From Bethsaida to Rome," in *Bethsaida: A City by the North Shore of the Sea of Galilee*, vol. 3, ed. Rami Arav and Richard A. Freund (Kirksville, MO: Truman State University, 2004), 133–45; Markus Bockmuehl, "Simon Peter and Bethsaida," in *The Missions of James, Peter, and Paul: Tensions in Early Christianity*, ed. Bruce Chilton and Craig Evans (Leiden, Netherlands: Brill, 2005), 53–90, and Markus Bockmuehl, *Simon Peter*, 165–76.

10. In John 1:44, Bethsaida is called "the city of . . . Peter" without any further reference to Peter's life there. The synoptic Gospels, on the other hand, do not mention any relationship between Peter and Bethsaida. Instead, they consistently indicate that Peter's family lived in Capernaum. Some scholars have attempted to harmonize these accounts by speculating that Peter was born in Bethsaida but later moved to Capernaum for tax purposes (see Murphy-O'Connor, "Fishers of Fish," 25–27, and Appold, "Peter in Profile," 141). Others point out the lack of historical support for a connection between Peter and Bethsaida and claim that there existed competing traditions among early Christians over Peter's residence. See Peter Richardson, "What Has Cana to Do with Capernaum?," in *Building Jewish in the Roman East* (Waco, TX: Baylor University Press, 2004), 91–107, and Fred Strickert, *Philip's City: From Bethsaida to Julias* (Collegeville, MN: Liturgical Press, 2011), 47–59.

11. See Mendel Nun, "Has Bethsaida Finally Been Found?," *Jerusalem Perspective* 54, no. 3 (1998): 12–31 and R. Steven Notley, "Et-Tell Is Not Bethsaida," *Near Eastern Archaeology* 70, no. 4 (December 2007): 220–30.

12. In referring to Capernaum as Peter's "hometown," I recognize that none of the Gospels specify the location of Peter's birthplace. However, the synoptic Gospels consistently present Capernaum as the residence of Peter's family, the location of Peter's home, the setting of Peter's livelihood, and the location of his early interactions with Jesus.

13. The identity of the "Nahum" after whom the village was named is not known, but a relationship with the Old Testament prophet Nahum is unlikely. Because of the different transliterations of the village's name from Hebrew into Greek, some early Christian writers translated it as the "Village of Consolation." See Stanislao Loffreda, *Recovering Capharnaum*, 2nd ed. (Jerusalem: Franciscan Printing Press, 1993), 14–15. Despite its name referring to a "village," New Testament writers often identify Capernaum as a "city" (*polis*; e.g., Luke 4:31). However, there is no evidence that Capernaum was ever raised to the official status of a polis, and it shared none of the features (walls, public architecture, political importance, or substantial population) that characterized contemporary cities, such as Sepphoris, Tiberias, Caesarea, or Jerusalem. Since the Gospel authors also refer to small hamlets like Nazareth and Nain as "cities" (e.g., Luke 2:4; 7:11), their use of this term is likely an attempt to highlight the importance of Jesus' activities (e.g., Acts 26:26) without intending to provide precise nomenclature. See Jonathan L. Reed, *Archaeology and the Galilean Jesus: A Re-Examination of the Evidence* (Harrisburg, PA: Trinity Press International, 2000), 166–69. Josephus seems to be more technically correct when he refers to Capernaum as "a village" (κωμη; *Life* 403). See Steve Mason, *Flavius Josephus: Life of Josephus* (Leiden, Netherlands: Brill, 2003), 160. For discussions on the differentiations between cities, towns, villages, and hamlets in Galilee, see Martin Goodman, *State and Society in Roman Galilee, AD 132–212*, 2nd ed. (London: Valentine Mitchell, 2000), 27–40; and Ze'ev Safrai, *The Economy of Roman Palestine* (London: Routledge, 1994), 17–103.

14. See Joseph Blenkinsopp, "The Literary Evidence," in *Excavations at Capernaum Volume 1: 1978–1982*, ed. Vassilios Tzaferis (Winona Lake, IN: Eisenbrauns, 1989), 201–10.

15. Although it is not mentioned in the Old Testament, archaeological excavations showed that the site was inhabited in the Bronze Age, abandoned in the Iron Age, and possibly reoccupied on a limited scale during the Persian period. See Loffreda, *Recovering Capharnaum*, 27.

16. See Mordechai Aviam, "People, Land, Economy, and Belief in First-Century Galilee and Its Origins: A Comprehensive Archaeological Synthesis," in *The Galilean Economy in the Time of Jesus*, ed. David A. Fiensy and Ralph K. Hawkins (Atlanta: Society of Biblical Literature, 2013), 11–20.

17. For the debate over Capernaum's proximity to a local trade route in the first century, see Reed, *Archaeology and the Galilean Jesus*, 146–48. It is well known that Jesus dined with "tax collectors and sinners" while in Capernaum (see Matthew 9:10–11; also see Luke 7:36–50), and his parables to the indignant Pharisees on these occasions often included references to prostitutes and beggars (e.g., Luke 15:1–2, 30; 16:3, 19–31).

18. Josephus, *Life* 403–4 (see *War* 3.519–20). At a skirmish near Bethsaida/Julias during the first Jewish revolt against Rome (ca. AD 66–67), Josephus fell off his horse and fractured his wrist. He was taken to Capernaum, but since that village had such limited resources, he was transported to better medical facilities at Magdala/Tarichaea. See Mason, *Life of Josephus*, 160.

19. *Ecclesiastes Rabbah* 1:8§4. Previous generations of scholars argued that the "heretics" (minim) in Capernaum were Jewish-Christians, but more recent scholars have challenged this claim; for overviews of this debate, see Joan E. Taylor, *Christians and the Holy Places: The Myth of Jewish-Christian Origins* (Oxford: Clarendon, 1993), 25–31, 276–77,

and Stuart S. Miller, "The Minim of Sepphoris Reconsidered," *Harvard Theological Review* 86 (1993): 377–402.

20. Epiphanius, *Haer* 30, no. 11, reported that Capernaum was exclusively Jewish until the fourth century.

21. See the fourth-century pilgrimage itinerary of Egeria in John Wilkinson, *Egeria's Travels*, 3rd ed. (Oxford: Aris & Philipps, 2006), 97–98.

22. For the occupation of Capernaum in the early Islamic period, see Blenkinsopp, "Literary Evidence," 206. Although the Franciscan excavations of western Capernaum suggested a decline and abandonment of the site in the early seventh century, the Greek excavations of eastern Capernaum showed that the village expanded to the east and north during the seventh century and was inhabited until its abandonment in the eleventh century, just prior to the first crusade. See Tzaferis, "Historical Summary," *Capernaum* 1, 213–21.

23. Burchardus wrote in 1283 that Capernaum was by then a poor village containing only seven dilapidated houses belonging to fishermen. See Stanislao Loffreda and Vassilios Tzaferis, "Capernaum," *The New Encyclopedia of Archaeological Excavations in the Holy Land*, ed. Ephraim Stern (Jerusalem: The Israel Exploration Society, 1993), 292.

24. By the late nineteenth century, American and European explorers debated Capernaum's precise location. Edward Robinson, Eli Smith, and Heinrich Kiepert, *Biblical Researches in Palestine and the Adjacent Regions* (Boston: Crocker and Brewster, 1856), 346–58, identified it with the ruins at Khirbet el-Minyeh, while Charles W. Wilson, *The Recovery of Jerusalem* (New York: D. Appleton, 1872), 266, 292–301, and *The Survey of Western Palestine* (London: Palestine Exploration Fund, 1881), 298–99, identified it with the ruins at Tel Hum. This debate is reflected in James E. Talmage, *Jesus the Christ* (Salt Lake City: The Church of Jesus Christ of Latter-day Saints, 1981), 186–87 n. 5, who cites Charles F. Deems, *The Light of the Nations* (New York: Gay Brothers, 1884), 167–68, as saying that ancient Capernaum's exact location will probably never be known. For the arguments that ultimately convinced scholars that the ruins of Tel Hum were ancient Capernaum, see John C. H. Laughlin, "The Identification of the Site," in *Capernaum* 1, 191–99.

25. The synagogue was first excavated in 1905 by the Deutsche Orient–Gesellschaft. See Heinrich Kohl and Carl Watzinger, *Antike Synagogen in Galiläa* (Leipzig: J. C. Hinrichs, 1916), 4–40. Shortly thereafter, the church shrine was uncovered by the Franciscan Custody of the Holy Land. See Gaudence Orfali, *Capharnaüm et ses Ruines* (Paris: A. Picard, 1922).

26. Summaries of these excavations and their findings can be found in Loffreda, *Recovering Capharnaum*, 7–12, and Loffreda and Tzaferis, "Capernaum," 291–96.

27. For examples of recent studies, see Douglas R. Edwards and C. Thomas McCollough, *Archaeology and the Galilee: Texts and Contexts in the Greco-Roman and Byzantine Periods* (Atlanta: Scholars Press, 1997), and Jürgen Zangenberg, Harold W. Attridge, and Dale B. Martin, eds., *Religion, Ethnicity, and Identity in Ancient Galilee: A Region in Transition* (Tübingen: Mohr Seibeck, 2007).

28. See John Dominic Crossan and Jonathan L. Reed, *Excavating Jesus: Beneath the Stones, behind the Texts* (New York: HarperCollins, 2002), 51–97, and Douglas E. Oakman, "Execrating? or Execrable Peasants!," in *Galilean Economy in the Time of Jesus*, 139–64.

29. See Douglas R. Edwards, "Identity and Social Location in Roman Galilean Villages," in *Religion, Ethnicity, and Identity*, 357–74, and Aviam, "People, Land, Economy," 5–48.

30. Mark A. Chancey, *The Myth of a Gentile Galilee* (Cambridge: Cambridge University Press, 2002), and Mark A. Chancey, *Greco-Roman Culture and the Galilee of Jesus* (Cambridge: Cambridge University Press, 2005), provide a helpful overview of this debate and demonstrate that the evidence favors a traditional Jewish atmosphere in first-century Galilee, with little support for extensive Hellenization in the region before the revolts.

31. Reed, *Archaeology and the Galilean Jesus*, 139–69; Crossan and Reed, *Excavating Jesus*, 51–97.

32. Sharon Lea Mattila, "Revisiting Jesus' Capernaum: A Village of Only Subsistence-Level Fishers and Farmers?," in *Galilean Economy in the Time of Jesus*, 75–138.

33. To their credit, Loffreda and Corbo published final reports of their finds in western Capernaum, but these were published in Italian and do not contain all of the necessary data pertaining to the site's architecture, ceramics, coins, and inscriptions. The small finds have yet to be published, and the reports are often lacking in stratigraphic analysis. See Virgilio C. Corbo, *Cafarnao I: Gli edifici della citta* (Jerusalem: Franciscan Printing Press, 1975); Stanislao Loffreda, *Cafarnao II: La Ceramica* (Jerusalem: Franciscan Printing Press, 1974); Augusto Spijkerman, *Cafarnao III: Catalogo Delle Monete della Citta* (Jerusalem: Franciscan Printing Press, 1975); Emmanuele Testa, *Cafarnao IV: I graffiti della casa di S. Pietro* (Jerusalem: Franciscan Printing Press, 1972). Critical reviews of these reports can be found in James F. Strange, "Review: The Capernaum and Herodium Publications," *BASOR* 226 (April 1977), 65–73; James F. Strange, "Review: The Capernaum and Herodium Publications, Part 2," *BASOR* 233 (Winter 1979), 63–69; and L. Michael White, *The Social Origins of Christian Architecture, Volume II* (Valley Forge, PA: Trinity Press International, 1997), 153–54. Tzaferis published a preliminary report ("New Archaeological Evidence on Ancient Capernaum," *Biblical Archaeologist* 46, no. 4 [1983]: 198–204) and a high-quality final report (*Capernaum 1*) of finds on the east side of the site, but these reports only contain descriptions of the Muslim-era remains (long after the time of the first-century village). Promised reports on the earlier periods have not yet appeared. Currently, the only preliminary report of the Roman period remains on the east side of the site is in John C. H. Laughlin, "Capernaum: From Jesus' Time and After," *Biblical Archaeology Review* 19, no. 5 (1993): 55–61, 90.

34. Because of ancient sensitivities against placing burials inside an inhabited area, the presence of several sarcophagi in a Late Roman mausoleum about 300 meters north of the shore marks the northernmost boundary of the village. Although a (later?) promenade appears to extend east-west along the shore for about 800 meters, ruins from the Early Roman period have only been found along 300–500 meters of the shoreline, leaving Capernaum's first-century borders to extend a maximum of 300 x 500 meters. The site's excavators estimated that the inhabited area of 10–12 acres could accommodate a population of no more than 1,500 inhabitants, causing them to refer to Capernaum as "a relatively small village." These calculations can be found (with slight variation) in Loffreda and Tzaferis, "Capernaum," 292; Tzaferis, "Historical Summary," 216; and Reed, *Archaeology and the Galilean Jesus*, 149–52.

35. See the comparisons between Capernaum and the cities in Crossan and Reed, *Excavating Jesus*, 51–97.

36. A thorough examination of Galilee's fishing industry in the first century can be found in K. C. Hanson, "The Galilean Fishing Economy and the Jesus Tradition," *Biblical Theology Bulletin* 27 (1997): 99–111.

37. With the receding of the lake in recent decades, archaeologists have been able to explore the remains of ports and harbor facilities in various locations around the lake. See Mendel Nun, "Ports of Galilee," *Biblical Archaeology Review* 25, no. 4 (July/August 1999): 18–31, 64. Since most of these have not been systematically excavated, however, their precise date is often difficult to determine with certainty.

38. Second-century coins indicate that Gadara's harbor was sufficiently large to host naval battle games. See Nun, "Ports of Galilee," 29–31, 64.

39. Josephus, *War* 3.462–542; Nun, "Ports of Galilee," 27–29.

40. See Hershel Shanks, "Excavation Planned for Mary Magdalene's Hometown," *Biblical Archaeology Review* 33, no. 5 (September/October 2007): 52–55, and Nun, "Ports of Galilee," 27–29. Aviam, "People, Land, Economy," 13–15, considers Magdala's impressive harbor built by the Hasmoneans and expanded by Herod Antipas to be "the first evidence for the royal investment in the Galilee."

41. Nun, "Ports of Galilee," 27–29.

42. Murphy-O'Connor, "Fishers of Fish," 25–27, speculated that Peter moved from Bethsaida (in Philip's territory) to Capernaum (in Antipas' territory) to take advantage of the flourishing fishing industry in the tetrarchy of Antipas, and also to avoid double taxation incurred by sending fish across political borders to Magdala. This is an interesting possibility, but there is no direct evidence for this suggestion and no reason to believe that there were no fish-processing facilities on Philip's side of the lake.

43. Nun, "Ports of Galilee," 24–25, shows that harbor remains survived on the western side of the site as well, but that the Franciscan excavators did not recognize them as such and unknowingly dumped their excavation debris into the ancient harbor.

44. Loffreda and Tzaferis, "Capernaum," 296. See Tzaferis, *Capernaum 1*, 2–3.

45. Capernaum's promenade appears to extend about 800 meters along the lakeshore. See Nun, "Ports of Galilee," 24–25. However, the excavation reports show that the extent of the Early Roman period village was much shorter, with buildings extending only -300–500 meters. See Loffreda and Tzaferis, "Capernaum," 292; Tzaferis, "Historical Summary," 216; and Reed, *Archaeology and the Galilean Jesus*, 149–52.

46. Nun, "Ports of Galilee," 24–27.

47. Loffreda and Tzaferis, "Capernaum," 295; Tzaferis, "Ancient Capernaum," 201; Tzaferis, *Capernaum 1*, 2–3, 218, suggests that these pools may have belonged to an ancient fish market. Similar storage pools have been found at the nearby sites of Kursi and Magdala. See Nun, "Ports of Galilee," 21, and Dina Avshalom-Gorni, "Migdal—Preliminary Report," *Hadashot Arkeologiyot*, 125.

48. Nun, "Ports of Galilee," 24–27, seems to prefer this position.

49. In the one preliminary report of the Roman period remains from eastern Capernaum, Laughlin, "Capernaum," 58–59, states that the extant port features date to the Late Roman period (i.e., the second and third centuries). See also Crossan and Reed, *Excavating Jesus*, 85.

50. Appold, "Peter in Profile," 141, claims that Antipas' administration taxed 25–40 percent of the income from daily catches, thus necessitating administrative buildings and officers to document business and collect taxes near the harbors. See Hanson, "Galilean Fishing Economy," 99–111.

51. Nun, "Ports of Galilee," 21, describes this structure, but does not provide a precise date for it.

52. Some public buildings (including a bathhouse and storerooms) were excavated along the eastern portion of the promenade, but these date to the second or third centuries. See Laughlin, "Capernaum," 58–59.

53. K. C. Hanson and Douglas E. Oakman, *Palestine in the Time of Jesus: Social Structures and Social Conflicts*, 2nd ed. (Minneapolis: Fortress Press, 2008), 99, identifies Matthew/Levi the "tax collector" as working for Antipas' administration providing fishing licenses and collecting tolls on catches.

54. Based on the diminutive form of the word, Gerhard Friedrich, ed., *Theological Dictionary of the New Testament* (Grand Rapids, MI: Eerdmans, 2006), 7:97 n. 93, states that "the τελώνιον at which Levi (Mt.) sat was probably a simple exchange table on which receipts were written and payments received . . . The tax collector could get up and go away without ado." In contrast, the term *baythamekes* used in b. Sukk. 30a likely referred to "a proper building." If this assessment is correct, Matthew/Levi may not have required an actual structure from which to conduct his business.

55. For small finds relating to the Galilean fishing industry, see Sandra Fortner, "The Fishing Implements and Maritime Activities of Bethsaida-Julias (et-Tell)," in *Bethsaida: Volume 2*, 269–80. For overviews of ancient Galilean fishing methods, see Mendel Nun, *The Sea of Galilee and Its Fishermen in the New Testament* (Israel: Kibbutz Ein Gev, 1989) and Mendel Nun, "Cast Your Nets Upon the Waters: Fish and Fishermen in Jesus' Time," *Biblical Archaeology Review* 19, no. 6 (November/December 1993): 46–56.

56. Nun, *Galilee and Its Fishermen*, 16–22.

57. Nun, *Galilee and Its Fishermen*, 23–27, claims that these were the small fish (*opsaria*) referred to in the New Testament accounts of the multiplication of the fish and loaves (see John 6:9).

58. Nun, "Cast Your Nets," 53–56.

59. The net was discovered in a cave near Ein Gedi used during the Bar Kokhba revolt (AD 132–35). Yigael Yadin, *Bar-Kokhba: The Rediscovery of the Legendary Hero of the Second Jewish Revolt against Rome* (New York: Random House, 1971), 194–97, claimed that the net was for trapping fowl, but Nun, *Galilee and Its Fishermen*, 26, argued that it was a fishing net.

60. For the different kinds of stone and lead weights found at et-Tell/"Bethsaida," see Fortner, "Fishing Implements," 270–76. Since the small finds from Capernaum have not been published, there is no record of weights from the first-century village, although they certainly were used there. Such weights were found on the east side of Capernaum in domestic structures from later periods. See Tzaferis, *Capernaum 1*, 131–35 (fig. 72, nos. 15–21).

61. Fortner, "Fishing Implements," 272, reports seven needles for mending sails and nets found at et-Tell/"Bethsaida." A similar needle was found at Magdala. Nun, *Galilee and Its Fishermen*, 31.

62. Fortner, "Fishing Implements," 271; Nun, *Galilee and Its Fishermen*, 45–46. As for Capernaum, Crossan and Reed, *Excavating Jesus*, 84, states that "fish-hooks and net weights [were] strewn around" Capernaum's courtyards (see Reed, *Archaeology and the Galilean Jesus*, 157). However, as far as I can determine, only two fishhooks have been published by the excavators. These were found in the "house of Peter" embedded within a fourth-century floor (Corbo, *Cafarnao I*, 75, table, 80, photo, 32). While they may be evidence for the occupation of the home's earliest inhabitants, Taylor, *Christians and the Holy Places*, 278, suggests that the two hooks were deposited by later Christian pilgrims to commemorate Peter.

63. Fortner, "Fishing Implements," 278, discusses the irregular shapes and sizes of stone anchors from et-Tell/"Bethsaida." Tzaferis, *Capernaum 1*, 132–33 (fig. 72, no. 31) reports the discovery of a stone anchor on the east side of Capernaum from a later context.

64. Shelley Wachsmann, *The Sea of Galilee Boat: A 2000-Year-Old Discovery from the Sea of Legends* (Cambridge, MA: Perseus Publishing, 2000).

65. See John J. Rousseau and Rami Arav, *Jesus and His World: An Archaeological and Cultural Dictionary* (Minneapolis: Fortress Press, 1995), 25–30; Crossan and Reed, *Excavating Jesus*, 86.

66. Appold, "Peter in Profile," 141.

67. Murphy-O'Connor, "Fishers of Fish," 22–27, 48–49.

68. Hanson, "Galilean Fishing Economy," 99–111.

69. Scholars typically locate the Matthean community in Syria, but arguments have been made that Matthew's Gospel was written in Galilee, highlighting Matthew's ties and familiarity with the region. See Anthony J. Saldarini, "The Gospel of Matthew and Jewish-Christian Conflict in the Galilee," in *The Galilee in Late Antiquity*, ed. Lee I. Levine (New York: Jewish Theological Seminary of America, 1992), 23–38. Similar, though weaker, arguments have been made for locating the composition of Mark in Galilee. See Raymond E. Brown, *An Introduction to the New Testament* (New York: Doubleday, 1997), 127, 162, and Cilliers Breytenbach, "Mark and Galilee: Text World and Historical World," in *Galilee through the Centuries: Confluence of Cultures*, ed. Eric M. Meyers (Winona Lake, IN: Eisenbrauns, 1999), 75–85.

70. Nun, *Galilee and Its Fishermen*, 23–27.

71. Appold, "Peter in Profile," 141.

72. However, Hanson, "Galilean Fishing Economy," 105, points out that even if Peter, James, and John owned their own boats and were able to hire day laborers to assist in their work, they should not necessarily be considered "wealthy," especially in comparison with the urban elites of Tiberias. This caution is supported by the modest nature of the "Galilee boat" discussed previously, which shows that fishermen with very limited resources could own their own boats.

73. For the Lucan account of Peter's calling (including Luke's reworking of Mark and incorporation of additional details), see François Bovon, *Luke 1: A Commentary on the Gospel of Luke 1:1–9:50* (Minneapolis: Fortress Press, 2002), 166–72. Hanson, "Galilean Fishing Economy," 105, points out that fishing "cooperatives" (*koinōnoi*) are attested in Egypt and Asia Minor during the first century, but not in Palestine until the fourth century. Therefore, Luke's account of Peter's fishing business "may be due to [Luke's] own experiences or interests rather than those of the [Galilean] fisherman."

74. See the descriptions and analyses of these sites in Morten Horning Jensen, *Herod Antipas in Galilee* (Tübingen: Mohr Siebeck, 2006), 126–86; Aviam, "People, Land, Economy," 5–48; Reed, *Archaeology and the Galilean Jesus*, 62–138; and Avshalom-Gorni, "Migdal."

75. Loffreda and Tzaferis, "Capernaum," 292, claim that the "planning of the village was organic and orderly," with main streets dividing the village into quarters and small neighborhoods. However, other scholars point out that the semblance of order at the current excavation site was imposed on the village by the building of the monumental synagogue in the Byzantine period. In the first century, Capernaum's streets did not intersect at right angles. There was no cardo or decumanus, and the blocks of buildings do not appear to have been arranged along axes. See Reed, *Archaeology and the Galilean Jesus*, 152–53; Chancey, *Greco-Roman Culture*, 111 n. 89; and Jensen, *Herod Antipas*, 171–72.

76. Loffreda, *Recovering Capharnaum*, 21, 24.

77. Reed, *Archaeology and the Galilean Jesus*, 153; Katharina Galor, "Domestic Architecture," in *The Oxford Handbook of Jewish Daily Life in Roman Palestine*, ed. Catherine Hezser (Oxford: Oxford University Press, 2010), 434; Barry Hobson, *Latrinae et Foricae: Toilets in the Roman World* (London: Duckworth, 2009), 129–30. Jodi Magness, *Stone and Dung, Oil and Spit: Jewish Daily Life in the Time of Jesus* (Grand Rapids, MI: Eerdmans, 2011), 130–44, also discusses these conditions, the lack of toilet privacy in ancient villages, and the work of manure merchants who often removed accruing human and animal waste to sell as fertilizer. The Torah required the Israelites of the desert wanderings to bury their excrement outside the camp to ensure ritual (not hygienic) purity in the vicinity of the Tabernacle (see Deuteronomy 23:12–14), but in the Second Temple period this practice was only a concern to sectarians who sought to extend the purity laws of the temple into daily life. For example, Josephus (*War* 2.147–49) notes that the Essenes were unusual among Jews for their concern over toilet privacy and their literal observance of Deuteronomy's injunction. In contrast, later rabbis did not consider excrement to be ritually impure in a daily context, and were thus less concerned about its visible presence in the community. See also Jodi Magness, "What's the Poop on Ancient Toilets and Toilet Habits?," *Near Eastern Archaeology* 75, no. 2 (June 2012): 80–87.

78. For a more complete study on ancient domestic architecture, see Yizhar Hirschfeld, *The Palestinian Dwelling in the Roman-Byzantine Period* (Jerusalem: Israel Exploration Society, 1995) (For domestic architecture in Capernaum specifically, see pages 68–69, 254); Loffreda, *Recovering Capharnaum*, 20–24; Reed, *Archaeology and the Galilean Jesus*, 157–60. Appold, "Peter in Profile," 141–42, discusses the similarities between the average dwelling at Capernaum and the domestic architecture at other nearby villages.

79. Katharina Galor, "Domestic Architecture in Roman and Byzantine Galilee and Golan," *Near Eastern Archaeology* 66, nos. 1–2 (March/June 2003): 48, 54, considers the quality and dressing of building stones as reflections of the inhabitants' relative wealth and prosperity. At less prosperous villages like Capernaum, the irregular fieldstones used for construction were bound by a "mortar" mixed of marly soil, water, and straw. See also Galor, "Domestic Architecture" (2010), 432.

80. V. Corbo, *The House of Saint Peter at Capharnaum* (Jerusalem: Franciscan Printing Press, 1969), 37.

81. See Corbo, *House of Saint Peter*, 37. Some dwellings in the region used basalt pilasters, vaulting, arches, and beams to support roofs of heavy stone slabs (as seen at nearby Chorazin), but this technique is not attested in Galilee until the third century AD and was not popular until the Byzantine period. During the Early Roman period, the wood, reed, and mud thatched roofs used at Capernaum were much more common in Galilean villages. See Hirschfeld, *Palestinian Dwelling*, 237–43, and Galor, "Domestic Architecture" (2010), 430–32. For the absence of stone beams, arches, or roof slabs in Capernaum's domestic structures, see Laughlin, "Capernaum," 60, and Galor, "Domestic Architecture" (2003), 49–55.

82. Hirschfeld, *Palestinian Dwelling*, 243–46, describes this common style of roof construction and the effort required to maintain it during the rainy season. See also Galor, "Domestic Architecture" (2010), 433.

83. Corbo, *House of St. Peter*, 37; Loffreda, *Recovering Capharnaum*, 72.

84. See Hirschfeld, *Palestinian Dwelling*, 243, and Galor, "Domestic Architecture" (2010), 430.

85. The only published report of ceramic tiles at Capernaum is in Laughlin, "Capernaum," 61, which indicated that tiles were found in association with a Byzantine-period public fountain on the northeast side of the site.

86. See Crossan and Reed, *Excavating Jesus*, 83–84; Hirschfeld, *Palestinian Dwelling*, 243; and Galor, "Domestic Architecture" (2010), 430.

87. See Galor, "Domestic Architecture" (2010), 431, and Reed, *Archaeology and the Galilean Jesus*, 157.

88. Evidence for stone thresholds, door posts, and locking mechanisms were found at the courtyard entrances, but not in association with the living rooms. See Mattila, "Revisiting Jesus' Capernaum," 115; Reed, *Archaeology and the Galilean Jesus*, 159; and Hirschfeld, *Palestinian Dwelling*, 254–55.

89. Galor, "Domestic Architecture" (2010), 432, also considers a structure's flooring as an indication of the prosperity of its inhabitants. In contrast to more wealthy homes with floors of hewn or polished stone, simple homes with floors of compact dirt or basalt cobbles typically indicate more limited means.

90. Corbo, *House of St. Peter*, 39.

91. Corbo, *House of St. Peter*, 37–39; Hirschfeld, *Palestinian Dwelling*, 254–55; Reed, *Archaeology and the Galilean Jesus*, 159; Mattila, "Revisiting Jesus' Capernaum," 115.

92. Corbo, *House of St. Peter*, 40–50, describes the fireplaces and ash deposits in the courtyard of Insula I (the "house of Peter"). For the multifaceted uses of courtyards, see Galor, "Domestic Architecture" (2010), 433; Loffreda, *Recovering Capharnaum*, 20; and Reed, *Archaeology and the Galilean Jesus*, 157.

93. Hirschfeld, *Palestinian Dwelling*, 245.

94. Loffreda, *Recovering Capharnaum*, 24; Mattila, "Revisiting Jesus' Capernaum," 117.

95. For an official report on the pottery at Capernaum, see Loffreda, *Cafarnao II*. Unfortunately, this report does not include a full tally of household vessels, but a description and evaluation of the assemblage can be found in Andrea M. Berlin, "Romanization and anti-Romanization in pre-Revolt Galilee," in *The First Jewish Revolt: Archaeology,*

History, and Ideology, ed. Andrea M. Berlin and J. Andrew Overman (London: Routledge, 2002), 60–64; see also Crossan and Reed, *Excavating Jesus*, 85.

96.   Andrea Berlin's analysis of Galilean household pottery has shown that cooking pots (with rounded bodies and narrow mouths) were well designed for preparing soups, beans, and other long-simmering meals, while "casseroles" (with wide bodies and broad mouths) were well designed for preparing thin stews containing chunks of meat and vegetables. Furthermore, the relatively small number of serving vessels per household indicates that Galilean families shared two to three common platters or bowls while they dined; see Andrea Berlin, *Gamla I: The Pottery of the Second Temple Period* (Jerusalem: Israel Antiquities Authority, 2006), 140–51, and "Jewish Life before the Revolt: The Archaeological Evidence," *Journal for the Study of Judaism* 36, no. 4 (2005): 437–45; see also Crossan and Reed, *Excavating Jesus*, 96.

97.   Berlin, *Gamla I*, 137–38, supports this suggestion by pointing out that domestic space in Galilean villages was rarely large enough to accommodate family dining at a table; see also Magness, *Stone and Dung*, 77–84.

98.   Mattila, "Revisiting Jesus' Capernaum," 90, points to a small number of Rhodian wine jars as evidence for imported wine at Capernaum (see Loffreda, *Cafarnao II*, 65, 209–10), but these date to the second century BC, when such wine was distributed throughout Galilee (see Chancey, *Greco-Roman Culture*, 134). Evidence for local wine production and consumption at Capernaum in the Roman period is found on a Hebrew ostracon from Insula I, which reads: "N the wine maker/wine which he squeezed/may it be for good." Strange, "Review," 69, argues against Corbo's claims that the inscription refers to the Eucharist practices of Jewish-Christians (Corbo, *Cafarnao I*, 107–11).

99.   For example, see Arav, "New Testament Archaeology," 84.

100.   Stone is not in the list of materials susceptible to impurity in Leviticus 11, so stone vessels were seen as acceptable for the purposes of ritual hand washings (m. Kelim 10:1). For the use of stone vessels in early Judaism, see Yithak Magen, *The Stone Vessel Industry in the Second Temple Period: Excavations at Hizma and the Jerusalem Temple Mount* (Jerusalem: Israel Antiquities Authority, 2002). Orfali, *Capharnaüm*, 64, fig. 115, reports stone vessels being found in the areas around Capernaum's synagogue. Reed, *Archaeology and the Galilean Jesus*, 160, reports stone mugs, cups, and basins found elsewhere at the site.

101.   Jonathan Reed, "Stone Vessels and Gospel Texts: Purity and Socio-Economics in John 2," in *Zeichen aus Text und Stein: Studien auf dem Weg zu einer Archäologie d es Neuen Testaments*, ed. Stefan Alkier and Jürgen Zangenberg (Tübingen: A. Francke, 2003), 381–401, especially pages 385, 395–96. Although Capernaum's stone vessels were never published, Reed claims to have personally examined 150 fragments recovered in the excavations.

102.   Reed, *Archaeology and the Galilean Jesus*, 157–58.

103.   In this account, the Pharisees criticize Jesus' disciples because "they break the tradition of the elders, for they do not wash their hands before they eat" (Matthew 15:2). In response, Jesus rebukes them for emphasizing traditional practices (see Matthew 15:3–9) and focusing on outer ritual purity at the expense of inner ethical purity (see Matthew 15:10–11, 17–20; see also Matthew 23:25–26). Peter's initial discomfort at this exchange is reflected in the disciples' concern that Jesus offended the Pharisees (see Matthew 15:12)

and in his request for Jesus to clarify his unpopular teaching on ritual purity (see Matthew 15:15). For a technical consideration of Jesus' relationship to the ritual purity laws in this episode, see Thomas Kazen, *Jesus and Purity Halakhah: Was Jesus Indifferent to Impurity?* (Winona Lake, IN: Eisenbrauns, 2010), 60–88.

104. The nature of this man's position as a "centurion" is uncertain. It implies a Roman military presence in Capernaum during the time of Jesus and Peter, but historical sources indicate that Roman military units had no permanent presence in Galilee until after the Jewish revolts, when Galilee was stripped of its relative auton-omy and placed under the administrative control of the Roman legate in Syria. The excavations at Capernaum support this picture, with the only traces of a Roman military presence—a bathhouse, mausoleum, and milestone—dating to the second century (Loffreda, *Recovering Capharnaum*, 81; Laughlin, "Capernaum," 55–61, 90; Reed, *Archaeology and the Galilean Jesus*, 155–56). Therefore, the "centurion" of the synoptic Gospels must have been a Herodian military officer who was given a title adopted from the Roman army. See Chancey, *Myth of a Gentile Galilee*, 102, and *Greco-Roman Culture*, 50–55.

105. The desperation of the royal official to find a cure for his sick son recalls the limited medical resources Josephus found in the village. See Josephus, *Life* 403–4; Mason, *Life of Josephus*, 160.

106. A small number of imported Rhodian wine jars stamped with Greek letters were found in Capernaum from the second century BC (Loffreda, *Cafarnao II*, 65, 209–10), and Hasmonean coins with Greek legends circulated in the region up to the first century AD. However, none of these items were produced in Capernaum and are thus not evi-dence for a Greek-speaking population in the village. See Chancey, *Greco-Roman Culture*, 133–41. The only known inscription produced in Capernaum in the Roman period was a Hebrew ostracon mentioning a local winemaker. See Strange, "Review," 69, and Corbo, *Cafarnao I*, 107–11.

107. Bovon, *Luke 1*, 257–65, suggests that Luke's redacted version of this story was meant to emphasize the kindness and benefaction of a "pious centurion" toward the lo-cal Jewish community, a trend manifested elsewhere in Luke's writings (e.g., Acts 10:1–11:18). For the actual tensions between Jews and Roman culture in first-century Galilean villages, see Berlin, "Romanization and anti-Romanization," 57–73.

108. A full set of first- or second-century glass vessels—including plates, bowls, goblets, and flasks—were discovered at Capernaum in Insula II (between the synagogue and "house of Peter"). See Stanislao Loffreda, "Vasi in vetro e in argilla trovati a Cafarnao nel 1984. Rapporto preliminare," *Liber Annuus* 34 (1984): 385–408, and *Holy Land Pottery at the Time of Jesus: Early Roman Period, 63 BC–70 AD* (Jerusalem: Franciscan Printing Press, 2002), 103–4. Mattila, "Revisiting Jesus' Capernaum," 94–95, points to this collection as evidence for moderate wealth at Capernaum (contra Crossan and Reed, *Excavating Jesus*, 85, which denies the existence of even the simplest glass forms). However, Mattila recognizes that this elegant-looking glassware is free blown, making it the least expensive glass available.

109. Loffreda, *Cafarnao II*, 66, 210, and *Holy Land Pottery*, 70–72; Mattila, "Revisiting Jesus' Capernaum," 91–92. Berlin, "Romanization and anti-Romanization," 57–73, shows that this type of pottery was present at Capernaum (and other Galilean sites) in

the first century BC but not after, suggesting that its subsequent absence reflects anti-Roman attitudes among Jewish villagers at the time of Jesus and Peter.

110. Reed, "Stone Vessels and Gospel Texts," 385, 395–96, shows that these represent 2 percent of Capernaum's stone vessels, a slight indicator of modest wealth; see also Mattila, "Revisiting Jesus' Capernaum," 98.

111. Jensen, *Herod Antipas*, 172.

112. For the excavations and assessment of the site, see Corbo, *House of St. Peter*; Corbo, *Cafarnao I*, 25–111; Loffreda and Tzaferis, "Capernaum," 295; and James F. Strange and Hershel Shanks, "Has the House Where Jesus Stayed in Capernaum Been Found?," *Biblical Archaeology Review* 8, no. 6 (1982): 26–39. For a critique of the excavators' interpretations, see Taylor, *Christians and the Holy Places*, 273–90.

113. Anders Runesson, "Architecture, Conflict, and Identity Formation: Jews and Christians in Capernaum from the First to the Sixth Century," in *Religion, Ethnicity, and Identity*, 240–42.

114. Loffreda, *Recovering Capharnaum*, 57. Breytenbach, "Mark and Galilee," 84, points out that Mark (written in the 60s AD) identifies the house of Peter in Capernaum as a spiritual center of the early Jesus movement around the same time Room 1 was renovated.

115. For the original report of the painted and decorated plaster, see Testa, *Cafarnao IV*, 13–48. Strange, "Review, Part 2," 64–65, offers a summary and critique of the excavators' interpretation of the images.

116. Testa, *Cafarnao IV*, 51–182; Jack Finegan, *The Archaeology of the New Testament: The Life of Jesus and the Beginning of the Early Church* (Princeton, NJ: Princeton University Press, 1992), 108–9. Based on the official publication reports, inscriptions included the following: ΠΕΤΡΟ(C or Υ) ΒΕΡΕΝΙ(ΚΗ)("Peter" or "of Peter Bereni(ce)"); (Ι)ΧΘΥС ("fish"); (ΧΡΙ)СΤΕ ΕΛΕΗС(ΟΝ) ("Christ have mercy"); (ΚΕ ΙС ΧΕ ΒΟΗΘΙ ("Lord Jesus Christ Help"); RO M AE BO PETR US ("Peter, Helper of Rome"?). Strange, "Review, Part 2," 66–68, evaluates Testa's readings and, in some cases, offers a devastating critique.

117. For example, see the assessment of Taylor, *Christians and the Holy Places*, 273–77, 293–94.

118. Loffreda, *Recovering Capharnaum*, 52, 71.

119. Appold, "Peter in Profile," 140.

120. Loffreda, *Recovering Capharnaum*, 54, 71.

121. For a discussion of common religious activities in first-century synagogues, see Lee I. Levine, *The Ancient Synagogue: The First Thousand Years*, 2nd ed. (New Haven, CT: Yale University Press, 2005), 145–69.

122. For example, see Howard Clark Kee, "Defining the First-Century C.E. Synagogue: Problems and Progress," *New Testament Studies* 41 (1995): 481–500, and Levine, *Ancient Synagogue*, 21–44, 135–73.

123. Chad S. Spigel, *Ancient Synagogue Seating Capacities: Methodology, Analysis and Limits* (Tübingen: Mohr Siebeck, 2012), 1–6; Levine, *Ancient Synagogue*, 135–45; Richard A. Horsley, *Archaeology, History, and Society in Galilee: The Social Context of Jesus and the Rabbis* (Harrisburg, PA: Trinity Press International, 1996), 131–53.

124. Anders Runesson et al., *The Ancient Synagogue from Its Origins to 200 C.E.: A Source Book* (Leiden, Netherlands: Brill, 2008), 22–25, 33.

125. A stone table decorated with a menorah found in the synagogue at Magdala (dating to the 60s AD) is the lone example of religious iconography in a pre–AD 70 synagogue. See Avshalom-Gorni, "Migdal."

126. Levine, *Ancient Synagogue*, 45–55; Jodi Magness, *The Archaeology of the Holy Land* (Cambridge: Cambridge University Press, 2012), 286–92.

127. Recalling this account, there is epigraphical evidence from the late first century that a synagogue in the Diaspora (Acmonia) was built for a Jewish community by a Gentile benefactor (Julia Severa, a high priestess of the imperial cult in the city). See Runesson et al., *Ancient Synagogue*, 134–35.

128. The initial excavation report for this building is found in Corbo, *Cafarnao I*, 113–69.

129. For example, see Orfali, *Capharnaüm*, 74–86.

130. Kohl and Watzinger, *Antike Synagogen*, 218, were the first to make this argument.

131. For descriptions of these excavations, see Loffreda and Tzaferis, "Capernaum," 292–95.

132. Over 20,000 of these coins were discovered in a single locus (Trench 12; L812) in the northeast corner of the courtyard. See Ermanno A. Arslan, "The L812 Trench Deposit inside the Synagogue and the Isolated Finds of Coins in Capernaum, Israel: A Comparison of Two Groups," *Israel Numismatic Research* 6 (2011): 147–62. Thousands of coins from the fourth and fifth century were also found in other trenches under the courtyard, prayer hall, and porch. The complete collection has not been published, but examples of coins and pottery from each trench can be seen in Virgilio Corbo, Stanislao Loffreda, and Augusto Spijkerman, *La Sinagoga di Cafarnao* (Jerusalem: Franciscan Printing Press, 1970), 61–139; S. Loffreda, "Potsherds from a Sealed Level of the Synagogue at Capharnaum," *Liber Annuus* 29 (1979): 215–20; and "Coins from the Synagogue at Capharnaum," *Liber Annuus* 47 (1997): 223–44.

133. See David Milson, *Art and Architecture of the Synagogue in Late Antique Palestine* (Leiden, Netherlands: Brill, 2007), 335–36; Levine, *Ancient Synagogue*, 77; Spigel, *Ancient Synagogue*, 173–77. Jodi Magness, "The Question of the Synagogue: The Problem of Typology," in *Judaism in Late Antiquity*, ed. Alan Avery-Peck and Jacob Neusner (Leiden, Netherlands: Brill 2001), 18–26, argues that the synagogue was built in the early sixth century. A small number of Israeli scholars still hold to a second- or third-century date for the building based on its architectural style. E.g., Gideon Foerster, "The Ancient Synagogues of the Galilee," 289–319 (esp. 300) in *Galilee in Late Antiquity*. They claim that the fourth- and fifth-century coins and pottery were deposited under the pavement during later repairs or renovations, but this is now a minority position.

134. The first to make this claim was one of the synagogue's excavators, Virgilio Corbo. Although he and Loffreda had previously shown that residential buildings existed under the fifth-century synagogue, they later reinterpreted the evidence and argued that an earlier first-century synagogue stood on the site. See Virgilio Corbo, "Resti della sinagoga del primo secolo a Cafarnao," in *Studia Hierosolymitana III*, ed. Giovanni Claudio Botini (Jerusalem: Franciscan Printing Press, 1982), 313–57; Stanislao Loffreda, "Ceramica ellenistico-romana nel sottosuolo della sinagoga di Cafarnao," in *Studia Hierosolymitana III*, 273–312; see also James F. Strange and Hershel Shanks, "Synagogue Where Jesus Preached

Found at Capernaum," *Biblical Archaeology Review* 9, no. 6 (1983): 24–31; Loffreda, *Recovering Capharnaum*, 43–49.

135. Similar basalt foundations were found under the other limestone walls and stylobates of the prayer hall. See Strange and Shanks, "Synagogue," 30, and Loffreda, *Recovering Capharnaum*, 45–49.

136. Pottery found in and under this basalt cobblestone dates to the first century AD, indicating that the pavement must have been laid during or after that century. See Strange and Shanks, "Synagogue," 29.

137. Loffreda, *Recovering Capharnaum*, 45–49; Loffreda and Tzaferis, "Capernaum," 294–95.

138. Some believe that the basalt foundation represents the walls of a synagogue renovated in the second or third century. See Loffreda, *Recovering Capharnaum*, 45–49, and Runesson, "Architecture," 239 n. 30.

139. For proposed reconstructions, see Runesson et al., *Ancient Synagogue*, 29–32; Runesson, "Architecture," 237–39; Donald D. Binder, *Into the Temple Courts: The Place of the Synagogues in the Second Temple Period* (Atlanta: Society of Biblical Literature, 1999), 186–92; Strange and Shanks, "Synagogue," 28–31.

140. These measurements are given in Strange and Shanks, "Synagogue," 30. According to their calculations, the large hall at Gamla measured 19.4 x 15.4 meters (covering an area of 299 square meters), making the proposed first-century synagogue at Capernaum significantly larger than the Gamla synagogue. For slight variations on the measurements of both buildings, see Spigel, *Ancient Synagogue*, 76–78, 173–77, 326–27. Based on his calculations, Lee Levine estimates that the proposed first-century synagogue at Capernaum would have been "about 50 percent larger than the one at Gamla and more than twice the size of the Masada and Herodium buildings." Levine, *Ancient Synagogue*, 71; see also Binder, *Into Temple Courts*, 192–93.

141. According to Spigel, *Ancient Synagogue*, 173–77, 326–27, the prayer hall at Capernaum could hold over 700 individuals, which, for the site's first-century population, could be over half of the village. In contrast, the much more prosperous, densely populated, and partially walled town of Gamla had a synagogue that could fit around 500 (between one-sixth and one-eighth of the community).

142. Levine, *Ancient Synagogue*, 71.

143. As far as I can determine, no reliable evidence has been found for the roof, columns, or other building materials of this building. Corbo, "Resti della sinagoga," 339, and Strange and Shanks, "Synagogue," 31, claim that column drums—one made of gray granite—and fragments of cornice molding were discovered in the fill under the pavement of the limestone synagogue, but they do not provide the necessary illustrations or stratigraphic data to demonstrate a connection between this material and a first-century synagogue.

144. Yoram Tsafrir, "The Synagogues at Capernaum and Meroth and the Dating of the Galilean Synagogue," in *The Roman and Byzantine Near East: Some Recent Archaeological Research*, ed. John Humphrey (Ann Arbor, MI: Journal of Roman Archaeology, 1995), 154–56; Levine, *Ancient Synagogue*, 71.

145. Tsafrir, "Synagogues," 155; Levine, *Ancient Synagogue*, 71. Corbo, "Resti della sinagoga," 339, and Strange and Shanks, "Synagogue," 28, 30, acknowledge this problem and

speculate that an elevated entrance existed along the west wall (above the extant courses of the basalt wall), which must have been accessed by stairs. However, no evidence for a door or stairs in this area has been discovered.

146. According to their reconstructions, Strange and Shanks, "Synagogue," 28, and Runesson et al., *Ancient Synagogue*, 29–32, draw in the west stylobate as extending the full length of the hall, but postulate a small gap to the south of the east stylobate. For an image of the unusually high eastern "stylobate" (MB5), see Binder, *Into Temple Courts*, 189, fig. 9.

147. For the synagogue floors at Gamla, Magdala, and Khirbet Cana, see Runesson et al., *Ancient Synagogue*, 23–25, 33; Avshalom-Gorni, "Migdal."

148. For example, the seventh-century palace at Khirbet el-Minyeh is a limestone structure with a basalt foundation. See K. Creswell, *Early Muslim Architecture* (Oxford: Oxford University Press, 1969), 2:381–89.

149. Magness, "Question of the Synagogue," 19–20; Tsafrir, "Synagogues," 155–56, points out that the misalignment in the southwest corner is so slight (ca. 10 cm) that, given the sloping topography of the site, the architect likely left room for minimal corrections as he laid the basalt foundations.

150. Stanislao Loffreda, "The Late Chronology of the Synagogue of Capernaum," *Israel Exploration Journal* 23 (1973): 37–42; Kee, "Defining," 495–96; Magness, "Question of the Synagogue," 20–22.

151. Walls of earlier domestic structures were found in numerous areas under and around the synagogue: Trench 6 (outside the northeast corner of the prayer hall) contained a wall belonging to a house whose pavement extended into Trench 2 (inside the northeast corner of the prayer hall); Trench 9 (outside the southwestern section of the porch) contained a north-south wall which originated from a group of private houses to the south of the synagogue and continued under the foundations of the porch; outside the northern face of the prayer hall, a long wall ran parallel to the synagogue and continued under the stepped structure on the synagogue's northwest corner; the street built between the synagogue and private houses to the south blocked a corridor used by one of these houses (Room 66); the northeast stairway of the synagogue courtyard was also built against the wall of a private house; finally, a long north-south wall from a Hellenistic structure was found in Trench 14 (the southwest portion of the prayer hall), and remains of that building continued outside the synagogue in Trench 15. For a description and top plan of these features, see Loffreda, "Late Chronology," 38–40, and Tsafrir, "Synagogues," 156. The presence of these walls both under and continuing outside the synagogue shows that they could not have been internal rooms of the proposed first-century synagogue, which was supposedly confined to the space of the prayer hall.

152. Basalt pavements belonging to domestic structures were also found under and around the synagogue. Sections extend from under the southern part of the nave (Trench 1) to under the southern façade, under the foundations of the northern wall and stylobate of the prayer hall (Trench 2) to under the northwest corner of the courtyard (Trench 11), under the foundations of the west wall of the prayer hall (Trench 3), and beyond the northwest corner of the prayer hall (Trench 7). See Loffreda, "Late Chronology," 38–40. Like many of the walls, these pavements also extend well beyond the proposed boundary of the first-century synagogue.

153.   For example, a small channel to the north of the synagogue was put out of use with the synagogue's construction (Trench 12). See Loffreda, "Late Chronology," 38–40. Chancey, *Myth of a Gentile Galilee*, 103, claims that stairs from these early domestic structures were also found under the synagogue, but it is not clear from his description where these were located.

154.   Loffreda, "Late Chronology," 40.

155.   For a comparison between the basalt cobblestone under the synagogue and other courtyard pavements at the site, see S. Loffreda, "A Reply to the Editor," *Israel Exploration Journal* 23 (1973): 184.

156.   According to the excavators, fourth-century coins found in the occupational levels of some of the domestic structures under the synagogue demonstrate that "the private houses . . . were in use until the second half of the fourth century AD." See Loffreda, "Late Chronology," 40, and Spijkerman, "La moneta della sinagoga di Cafarnao," in *La Sinagoga di Cafarnao*, 125–39. Tsafrir, "Synagogues," 156, also points out that in the fill above the basalt pavements, the layers closest to the pavement only contained coins dating through the third and early fourth centuries (likely representing the accumulations on the residential floors), whereas the upper layers of the fill contained all of the late-fourth- and early-fifth-century coins (likely representing the fill brought in to support the synagogue pavement); see also Magness, "Question of the Synagogue," 22, and Loffreda, "Coins," 230, 240–41.

157.   Those who reject the presence of a first-century synagogue at Capernaum include Kee, "Defining," Tsafrir, "Synagogues," and Magness, "Question of the Synagogue." Those who omit it from their work on ancient synagogues include Milson, *Art and Architecture*, 335–36, and Spigel, *Ancient Synagogues*, 173–77. Levine, *Ancient Synagogue*, 71, simply states that "given the meager remains, there is little to be learned about the overall plan of this building and its identification as a synagogue is at present rather tenuous."

158.   Strange and Shanks, "House Where Jesus Stayed," 29–30, recognized this possibility, and suggested that the remains of a home were eventually converted into a synagogue.

159.   See Runesson et al., *Ancient Synagogue*, 22–25, 65–66.

4

Stand Down and See the End

PETER'S CHARACTERIZATION IN THE GOSPELS

Jared W. Ludlow

Jared W. Ludlow is an associate professor of ancient scripture at
Brigham Young University.

Peter's bold, passionate, and zealous personality is readily grasped from the New Testament text. At times Peter's eagerness lands him in trouble as Jesus has to restrain and redirect him. Peter's denial of Christ[1] at the high priest's house is one of the most well-known episodes of the Gospels, but it seems to contradict the portrayal of Peter's zealousness that we grow accustomed to from other Gospel episodes. This paper will examine Peter's denial by applying narrative methodology to the depiction of Peter in the Gospels. While we cannot know exactly what was in Peter's mind that night, we can benefit from closely examining the New Testament text and the interactions between Jesus and Peter leading up to this pivotal moment. Several times Jesus had to tell Peter in effect to "stand down." By the time of the trial at the high priest's residence, Peter was simply following behind to "see the end" (Matthew 26:58). Peter was no longer ready to engage others in defense of his Master, but he still followed to see what would happen (while most of the other Apostles fled from the Garden of Gethsemane and temporarily abandoned their Master). Through the narrative study of earlier episodes, it becomes apparent that Peter often acted out of fear, ignorance, and impulsiveness—characteristics also revealed in the denial scene.

Narrative approaches, previously common in the field of literature, spread to biblical studies in the 1970s. Although biblical narrative critics commonly focus on the *creation* of the biblical stories, treating them as they would a work of fiction,[2] a narrative approach can still be used from a faith perspective. Rather than focusing so much on the creativity of the author (assuming the author mostly made up the stories), the emphasis can be on the *selection* of material in the portrayal of episodes and characters.[3] The Evangelist John, for example, clearly explains that there were many other stories that could have been told about Jesus, but he selected the ones he did to help the reader or listener come to believe that Jesus is the Christ, the Son of God (see John 20:30–31; 21:25). Thus each Evangelist had a pool of stories from which to select, arrange, shape, and proclaim his witness of Jesus Christ. Each had a different audience which affected the choices he made and the themes he developed. They did not make up these events and characters ex nihilo, but they fashioned powerful stories from either their own experiences or the experiences of others preserved in oral and written sources.

An example of producing a narrative critical study on the figure of Peter in the Gospels was done by Richard J. Cassidy in 2007.[4] Cassidy highlights three major aspects of narrative criticism: (1) analysis of the various elements that serve as building blocks of the overall story, (2) analysis of the literary techniques used by the author to present the narrative in a coherent and engaging way, and (3) investigation of the author's assumptions about the readers [or listeners] of the original audience.[5] One of the primary narrative building blocks alluded to in number one above is characterization (along with plot, time, and setting). This study focuses on the characterization of Peter and how he was portrayed in the various episodes selected by each Gospel writer.

Characterization

Characterization is a term narrative critics use for how a figure is developed through the course of a story. This term seems out of place in the usual devotional reading of scripture, but how the characters are depicted may give us insights into what we should learn from their experiences. Some questions one can ask about the characterization of Peter include details about his personal life, his qualities, his relationship with Jesus, and his development over time. There is a hierarchy in the disclosure of information about characters in the Bible: a ranking of the best sources to learn what a character is thinking or why he or she is acting a certain way. Robert Alter, a well-known Hebrew Bible narrative scholar, outlined this hierarchy from least to greatest reliability based on who or what is revealing details about characters.

> There is a scale of means, in ascending order of explicitness and certainty, for conveying information about the motives, the attitudes, the moral nature of characters. Character can be revealed [1] through the report of actions; [2] through appearance, [3] gestures, [4] posture, [5] costume; [6] through one character's comments on another; [7] through direct speech by the character; [8] through inward speech, either summarized or quoted as interior monologue; [9] or through statements by the narrator about the attitudes and intentions of the personages, which may come either as flat assertions or motivated explanations.[6]

On the lower end of the scale, the reader must infer things about the figures based on their actions and appearance. In the middle categories, we can weigh the statements from the characters themselves and from others. The top categories are most reliable because we are told the character's own thoughts, and thus motives, or these aspects are revealed by the narrator[7] without leaving it to the reader's inference. In the case of Peter, most of his characterization is in the lower categories—his actions—or on inference from his dialogues with others. Occasionally the narrator will make overt statements about Peter's feelings or thoughts, but unfortunately not about Peter's denial. Thus, when we try to deduce why Peter denied Jesus the night of Jesus' trial, we lack Peter's own explanation and instead rely on interpretation from how this event is portrayed by each Gospel writer. But rather than relying on the interpretation of only this one episode, it may be useful to examine some earlier episodes in the Gospels leading up to the denial to see how Peter is portrayed. In this way, we discover what each Evangelist wants us to learn about him and particularly his relationship with Jesus. To look at the development of the relationship between Jesus and Peter leading up to his denial, we will analyze the characterization of Peter in several Gospel episodes separately and draw comparisons across the Gospels.[8] We will first look at his initial introduction in each Gospel and then at those episodes that reveal characteristics relevant to Peter's denial.

Initial Introduction of Peter

The Gospels are extremely brief in their introduction and description of Peter. What Alter has stated about the Hebrew Bible seems to pertain to the Gospels as well (and to many other narrative sections of scripture since they are not usual biographies or histories):

> How does the Bible manage to evoke such a sense of depth and com-
> plexity in its representation of character with what would seem to
> be such sparse, even rudimentary means? Biblical narrative offers
> us, after all, nothing in the way of minute analysis of motive or de-
> tailed rendering of mental processes; whatever indications we may
> be vouchsafed of feeling, attitude, or intention are rather minimal;
> and we are given only the barest hints about the physical appearance,
> the tics and gestures, the dress and implements of the characters, the
> material milieu in which they enact their destinies. In short, all the
> indicators of nuanced individuality to which the Western literary
> tradition has accustomed us—preeminently in the novel, but ulti-
> mately going back to the Greek epics and romances—would appear
> to be absent from the Bible.[9]

Yet, despite the lack of details and the inner thoughts and feelings of biblical characters, they have become vivid individuals and models to countless readers over the centuries. The paucity of Peter's background at the beginning of the Gospels is at first surprising, yet consistent with biblical narrative.[10] Peter simply enters the story as if the reader should already know who he is. For example, in the Gospel of Luke, which gives a little more initial information about Peter than the other synoptic Gospels, Simon Peter's first introduction is not focused on him but Jesus going into "Simon's house," where "Simon's wife's mother" was ill with a fever. Those in the house summoned Jesus for her, and he "rebuked the fever; and it left her" (Luke 4:38–39).[11] When Luke then recounts Peter's call to follow Christ, Jesus asks to borrow Simon Peter's boat so he could preach from it to the audience on the shore. The boat is simply identified as "Simon's" without any explanation of who Simon is (see Luke 5:3), similar to the previous healing episode of Peter's mother-in-law in Luke.

When Jesus finishes teaching, he tells Simon to let his nets out in the deep. Simon first explains that they had toiled unsuccessfully all night, "nevertheless at thy word I will let down the net" (Luke 5:5). Peter's immediate obedience—despite poor results earlier, but perhaps with some faith from the previous healing of his mother-in-law—is rewarded with a net-breaking multitude of fish. Simon Peter was overwhelmed with the haul and "fell down at Jesus' knees, saying, Depart from me; for I am a sinful man, O Lord. . . . And Jesus said unto Simon,

Fear not; from henceforth thou shalt catch men. And when they had brought their ships to land, they forsook all, and followed him" (Luke 5:8, 10–11).

Peter's occupation sets up Jesus' call to abandon that livelihood for bringing new spiritual life to others through becoming a fisher of men. But most importantly, Luke's narrative includes miraculous encounters between Jesus and Peter—both in the healing of Peter's mother-in-law and with the abundant catch of fish. Jesus' command to cast down their nets elicits Peter's acknowledgment of him as the Master[12] and his faith in Jesus' word in that Peter would try fishing again. The results led to Peter's acknowledgment of Jesus as "Lord" and a feeling of sinfulness in the presence of the divine. Yet Peter's initial fear is allayed by the Savior's command to "fear not" and his invitation to discipleship.

Matthew and Mark lack a miraculous introduction between Jesus and Peter; they merely state Jesus' invitation to follow him and become a fisher of men and Peter's immediate obedience to that command (see Matthew 4:18–20; Mark 1:16–18).[13] The reader is left wondering what, if any, previous contact Jesus and Peter had such that from a brief invitation, Peter would be willing to give up his livelihood. Similar to Luke, the emphasis is on Peter's immediate obedience to the call of the Master,[14] but the experiential element is left unexplained in Matthew and Mark—what did he feel or know when Jesus summoned him which led him to immediately follow him?

The Gospel of John gives an introduction of Jesus to Peter, but again gives little description of who Peter is. Here Peter first hears about Jesus from his brother Andrew, who had become a follower of John the Baptist. When John the Baptist identified Jesus as the Lamb of God to Andrew and another disciple, they followed after Jesus (see John 1:35–37). Andrew then sought out his brother Peter and announced, "We have found the Messias" (1:41).[15] Andrew then brought Peter to Jesus, "and when Jesus beheld him, he said, Thou art Simon the son of Jona: thou shalt be called Cephas, which is by interpretation, A stone" (1:42). Cephas is an Aramaic equivalent of the Greek *Petros*, "rock." The Joseph Smith Translation adds an additional meaning to *Cephas* with Peter and Andrew's response to Jesus' invitation: "Thou shalt be called Cephas, which is, by interpretation, a seer, or a stone. And they were fishermen. And they straightway left all, and followed Jesus" (Joseph Smith Translation, John 1:42). Jesus does not explain here *why* he is giving this name to Peter. The other Gospels will begin using the name *Petros* for Simon (or occasionally combined—Simon Peter) but without an explanation of what it means or where it came from except that Jesus gave him the name (e.g., Mark 3:16—"surnamed Peter"; Luke 6:14—"Simon, (whom he also named Peter)"; Matthew 4:18 says

"Simon called Peter" without acknowledging Jesus giving him this name, however, Matthew is the only one to record the actual occasion of Jesus giving the name "Peter" to Simon later on in his Gospel). It may be that Peter's later denial is ironically juxtaposed with his nickname Peter, calling into question Peter's rocklike characteristic.

When comparing the initial introduction of Peter in the four Gospels, we see that Matthew and Mark are the simplest and do not reveal much about Peter except his willingness to follow Jesus' invitation. John includes information on how Peter first learned about Jesus and Jesus' giving of the name Cephas to Peter, but there is little description of Peter except in the Joseph Smith Translation that relates Peter's willingness to leave everything and follow Jesus. Luke certainly is the most revealing of Peter's initial characterization in that he has a miraculous experience with Jesus and progresses from doubt (recounting their unsuccessful fishing efforts), to faith ("nevertheless at thy word"), to fear ("Depart from me; for I am a sinful man"). This progression is a glimpse into Peter's complex characterization, revealed through Peter's own words (no. 7 on scale). On the one hand Peter shows a normal human perspective of doubt and fear, yet on the other hand he manifests tremendous faith.

Ordination of the Twelve— Peter as the Chief Apostle

The synoptic Gospels portray Peter at the time of his ordination as an Apostle. (The Gospel of John omits this episode. In fact, Peter is only mentioned in the Gospel of John in one episode between his call and the Last Supper, that of the Bread of Life sermon). Mark 3:13 describes Jesus going up into a mountain (praying all night according to Luke 6:12) and calling his disciples unto him. From this group, Jesus ordained twelve ("whom also he named apostles"; Luke 6:13) who should be with him so that he might send them forth to preach and have power to heal sicknesses and cast out unclean spirits (see Matthew 10:1; Mark 3:14). The names and their ordering are different in each list, but what is consistent is Peter's place at the head of the list, in fact Matthew explicitly states, "the first" (protos). From this episode we see the power and authority bestowed upon Peter in his new calling as an Apostle and his placement at the head of the Twelve. This preeminence of Peter will be common in many other group settings.[16] This experience solidifies the beginning of Peter's ministry to follow Christ and to be sent out by him to teach and heal others while being distinguished as a leader among the Twelve.

Walking on Water

The Gospel of Matthew is the only one to share Peter's participation in Jesus' miracle of walking on the Sea of Galilee. When Jesus appeared near the disciples' boat in the middle of the sea, the disciples (including Peter) "were *troubled*, saying, It is a spirit; and they *cried out for fear*" (Matthew 14:26; emphasis added). The last phrase gives insight from the narrator about what the disciples were feeling—fear—and why: they thought it was a spirit walking on the water towards them. After Jesus' reassurance that it was him and they did not need to be afraid, Peter was the only one to ask if he could walk on water too (see Matthew 14:28). "And when Peter was come down out of the ship, he walked on the water, to go to Jesus" (Matthew 14:29). According to the text, Peter was initially successful in walking on the water, but when his attention was diverted to the billowing wind and waves surrounding him, he began to sink: "When he saw the wind boisterous, *he was afraid*; and beginning to sink, he cried, saying, Lord, save me" (Matthew 14:30; emphasis added). Jesus was there with his stretched forth hand to catch Peter, rescuing him. Jesus then chastised Peter, "O thou of *little faith*, wherefore didst thou doubt?" (Matthew 14:31; emphasis added). It was as if Jesus were saying, "You were doing it, Peter, why did you start to doubt yourself?"

This incident is a rare example of the narrator revealing Peter's emotion: he was afraid. It also includes Jesus' assessment of Peter as having "little faith." Based on the scale of reliability of the exposition of character given above, we have examples of characterization through other characters' comments (in this case the main character, Jesus; no. 6 in scale) and characterization through the narrator's statement about attitude (no. 9), and both could be considered negative traits: fearful and lacking faith. Yet these are juxtaposed with Peter's eager personality: a man of action wanting to participate in this incredible miracle rather than merely observing it from a distance. This episode reveals that Peter's faith and understanding still needed further development, but Jesus was there to admonish and instruct him.[17]

Clarification of a Parable

Another episode that reveals Peter's limited understanding was shared next in the Gospel of Matthew. After Jesus taught a parable about the Pharisees, Peter stepped forward and asked Jesus to declare unto the disciples this parable (see Matthew 15:15). Jesus scolded, "Are ye also yet without understanding?" (Matthew 15:16). Still, Jesus proceeded to explain the meaning of the parable to Peter and the others. Luke also records an instance when Peter asked for clarification regarding a parable. After Jesus told the parable of the diligent and lax servants, Peter questioned, "Lord, speakest thou this parable unto us, or even to all?" (Luke 12:41).

Jesus did not reproach Peter; nor did he directly answer his question, but further elaborated on the significance of the parable, especially in the context of the last days. In a similar vein but in reverse order, Matthew records an instance when Peter asked him for clarification about forgiveness, which then led to Jesus teaching through a parable. "Then came Peter to him, and said, Lord, how oft shall my brother sin against me, and I forgive him? till seven times? Jesus saith unto him, I say not unto thee, Until seven times: but, Until seventy times seven" (Matthew 18:21–22). Jesus then broadened Peter's understanding of forgiveness through the telling of the parable of the unforgiving servant (see Matthew 18:23–35).[18] Thus there were many instances when Peter did not understand Jesus' teachings, and he sought for further clarification, which is understandable considering his role as chief Apostle who presumably would be expected to teach these things to others.

Confession of Faith

Peter next shows up in the synoptic Gospels in an episode that shows the height of his spirituality, but is then followed by a strong rebuke from the Savior.[19] When Jesus asked his Apostles, "Whom do men say that I am?," various answers were given (see Matthew 16:13–14; Mark 8:27–28; Luke 9:18–19). When Jesus asked more specifically, "But whom say ye that I am?" (Matthew 16:15), Peter, taking the lead as spokesman,[20] gave the memorable response "Thou art the Christ, the Son of the living God" (Matthew 16:16).[21] In each of the synoptic Gospels, Jesus commanded them not to tell anyone about him yet (see Matthew 16:20; Mark 8:30; Luke 9:21), but in Matthew, before he gives this command, he has additional dialogue with Peter.

In Matthew, Jesus first commends Peter for his declaration, "Blessed art thou, Simon Bar-jona:[22] for flesh and blood hath not revealed it unto thee, but my Father which is in heaven" (Matthew 16:17). Then he gives Simon the appellation "Peter" and promises keys of authority: "And I say also unto thee, That thou art Peter, and upon this rock I will build my church; and the gates of hell shall not prevail against it. And I will give unto thee the keys of the kingdom of heaven: and whatsoever thou shalt bind on earth shall be bound in heaven: and whatsoever thou shalt loose on earth shall be loosed in heaven" (Matthew 16:18–19). Volumes have been written on this passage and its significance in Christianity. For our purposes here, we see that Jesus is playing off of the meaning of Peter's nickname—rock—with a likely reference to himself (the subject of Peter's confession) as the stone or cornerstone of Israel and the church.[23] We also see that Peter will have the authority to bind things here on earth and have it recognized in heaven and he will need to serve as a "rock" for the emerging church. Matthew's inclusion of this additional dialogue may point towards his purpose in showing a Jewish audience that not only did Jesus have authority as the Messiah, but he passed on this authority to Peter.

Jesus' Prophecy of His Suffering and Death

When Jesus later[24] prophesied that the Son of Man would suffer many things, be rejected by Jewish leaders and killed, but after three days would rise again (see Matthew 16:21; Mark 8:31; Luke 9:22), Peter took Jesus aside and began to rebuke him, saying, "Be it far from thee, Lord: this shall not be unto thee" (Matthew 16:22; see also Mark 8:32). Peter's actions (ranked lowest in scale of characterization above) and dialogue (ranked high, no. 7, in scale) are very forceful for a disciple to a master and again disclose Peter's impulsive nature and lack of understanding of Jesus' true purpose (a sacrificial Messiah).[25] The Greek word translated "rebuke" here and everywhere else in the New Testament is ἐπιτιμάω (epitimaō).[26] It is used in many situations such as to describe Jesus rebuking storms and evil spirits (see Matthew 8:26; 17:18), the Apostles rebuking people bringing children to Jesus (see Matthew 19:13), the multitude rebuking a blind man calling after Jesus (see Matthew 20:31), and one thief rebuking the other while hanging on a cross (see Luke 23:40). The Greek term is also used in some situations without a negative connotation of reprimanding someone, but where Jesus admonished or charged others not to tell about his messiahship or miracles (see Matthew 12:16; Mark 3:12; Luke 9:21).

After Peter rebuked Jesus, Jesus returned Peter's rebuke, saying, "Get thee behind me,[27] Satan: thou art an offence[28] unto me: for thou savourest not the things that be of God, but those that be of men" (Matthew 16:23; Mark 8:31–33 has a similar dialogue; curiously Luke does not include Peter's rebuke or, consequently, Jesus' response). The harsh term "Satan" used by Jesus has the meaning of *adversary* and is a strong example of character exposition (no. 6 in scale) by the main character towards Peter;[29] Peter was not fulfilling his call as a witness of Christ, but instead was opposing Jesus' need to fulfill a divine mission of suffering and death.[30] This is the first of several times Jesus announces his impending death only to have Peter try to thwart it presumably out of his love and loyalty for his Master, whom he would not allow to be taken and killed. Jesus' rebuke reminded Peter that Jesus was only following God's plan and that Peter should consider that before his personal feelings or agenda.[31] Peter should rely on revelation from the Father and not his own "flesh and blood" understanding.

Mount of Transfiguration

The Mount of Transfiguration episode affords an opportunity for Jesus to separate Peter, James, and John from the other disciples to participate in a special spiritual experience.[32] Jesus' invitation to Peter indicates that the earlier episode of rebuke was pardoned and Peter was once again given an opportunity to participate in a choice event, thereby prefiguring Jesus' later exoneration of Peter after his denial.

From a narrative perspective this pericope has some of the greatest differences among the Gospels in the retelling of an experience related to Peter. According to Mark, Peter suggested making three tabernacles because "*he wist not* [did not know] *what to say*; for they were *sore afraid*" (Mark 9:6; emphasis added). This is another rare direct statement from the narrator about Peter's inner feelings (no. 9 in scale)—uncertainty and fear. In Matthew and Luke, however, the fear resulted from the next stage of the Apostles' experience as a cloud overshadowed them and they heard the voice of the Father bearing witness of the Son. According to Matthew, "when the disciples heard it, they fell on their face, and were *sore afraid*" (Matthew 17:6; emphasis added).[33] According to Luke's account, after the cloud overshadowed them, "they *feared* as they entered into the cloud" (Luke 9:34; emphasis added) and then heard the voice of the Father.[34] So all three Gospels agree that Peter (and James and John) was afraid, but in Mark the cause of fear was the appearance of Elijah and Moses; in Luke it was the cloud that suddenly overshadowed them; and in Matthew it was the voice of the Father.[35] In all three cases, a manifestation of spiritual power was the source of fear similar to earlier episodes discussed above, and that fear was divulged by the narrator.

Rich Young Man

Following the encounter between Jesus and the rich young man, Jesus told his disciples how hard it was for those that trust in riches to enter into the kingdom of God (see Matthew 19:23–24; Mark 10:23–25; Luke 18:24–25). The disciples were astonished wondering who would be saved, but Jesus assured them that with God all things are possible (Matthew 19:25–26; Mark 10:26–27; Luke 18:26–27). Peter then remarked, "Behold, we have forsaken all, and followed thee; what shall we have therefore?" (Matthew 19:27; Mark and Luke are very similar: "Lo, we have left all, and have followed thee"—Mark 10:28; see also Luke 18:28). Jesus acknowledges Peter's sacrifice and says that anyone who has given up family and possession for the gospel's sake will be blessed an hundredfold now ("manifold" in Luke) and shall obtain eternal life in the world to come (Mark 10:29–30). Matthew also adds an additional future blessing for the Twelve: after the Second Coming, they will "sit upon twelve thrones, judging the twelve tribes of Israel" (Matthew 19:28), another instance of Matthew focusing on the authority of Peter and the other Apostles. But according to the Joseph Smith Translation in Mark, Peter's eagerness to vocalize his sacrifice is met with a rebuke from Jesus: "But there are many who make themselves first that shall be last; and the last first. *This he said rebuking Peter*" (Joseph Smith Translation, Mark 10:31–32; emphasis added). This clarification by Joseph Smith is a narrator's statement (no. 9 in scale) giving the motive behind Jesus' dialogue with Peter.[36] This is another example of Jesus correcting Peter about his misunderstanding of the gospel and specifically in this case of the need for humility in leading others.

Washing of Feet

John is the only Gospel that includes the report of Jesus washing the feet of the Apostles. When Jesus came to Peter, Peter questioned why Jesus, the Master, should be doing this menial task. Jesus replied, "What I do thou knowest not now; but thou shalt know hereafter" (John 13:7), indicating another instance when Peter did not yet understand Jesus' purpose. Peter continues his protest in a dialogue with the Savior, "Thou needest not to wash my feet. Jesus answered him, If I wash thee not, thou hast no part with me" (Joseph Smith Translation, John 13:8). Then Peter, to declare his loyal discipleship and desire to remain with Jesus, swings completely in the other direction, requesting his entire body be washed: "Lord, not my feet only, but also my hands and my head" (John 13:9). Jesus reassures him that this foot washing would be sufficient and pronounces the group clean (except Judas). Peter's tendency to speak first and understand later is yet again exposed, this time through his speech and Jesus' responses (nos. 6 and 7).

Jesus' Prediction of Peter's Denial

All four Gospels contain Jesus' prediction of Peter's denial, although there are some differences in each Gospel leading up to it. Matthew and Mark closely parallel each other as they describe Jesus and his Apostles walking toward the Mount of Olives after the Last Supper. As they proceeded, Jesus told them, "All ye shall be offended because of me this night: for it is written, I will smite the shepherd, and the sheep shall be scattered. But after that I am risen, I will go before you into Galilee" (Mark 14:27–28; see also Matthew 26:31–32). Peter disagreed, saying, "Although all shall be offended, yet will not I" (Mark 14:29; see also Matthew 26:33), seemingly setting himself up as stronger or more loyal than the others. Perhaps to humble his chief Apostle, Jesus prophesied that even that night before the rooster would crow twice, Peter would deny him three times (see Mark 14:30; Matthew 26:34). "But [Peter] spake the *more vehemently*, If I should die with thee, I will not deny thee in any wise. Likewise also said they all" (Mark 14:31; emphasis added; see also Matthew 26:35).[37] Mark includes this slight description by the narrator (no. 9) of Peter's second response—more vehemently—which bluntly reveals that Peter's objection is growing stronger. Peter is also taking the lead among the other ten Apostles present to be the first to refuse Jesus' prediction and is revealing a strong sense of loyalty by twice using the pronoun "thee" in his vehement response. The ten Apostles all interpret Jesus' statement as saying they lack commitment, but Peter places himself as the "chief" Apostle in loyalty to Jesus. However, he again reveals his ignorance of Christ's true mission and of his own actions in the face of the impending opposition. Peter will be severely humbled before the next dawn.

In Luke and John, the dialogue is between Jesus and Peter instead of to the broader group of Apostles, despite their presence in the same setting. At the end of the Last Supper and the institution of the sacrament in the Gospel of Luke, Jesus directly addresses Peter: "Simon, Simon,[38] behold, Satan hath desired to have you, that he may sift you as wheat: But I have prayed for thee, that thy faith fail not: and when thou art converted, strengthen thy brethren" (Luke 22:31–32). Jesus' point-blank warning about Satan's intention must have been shocking, but he immediately followed it up with reassurance that he had prayed for Peter's welfare (the only time in Luke that Jesus prays as an intercessor for an individual). Jesus' concluding statement, "when thou art converted," implies that Peter's full conversion is still a future experience; so he still has more to learn and develop. When Peter then declared, "Lord, I am ready to go with thee, both into prison, and to death" (Luke 22:33), Jesus instead predicted his denial.[39] Conspicuously, Peter gives no response to Jesus' prediction in Luke. Despite Peter's earlier claim of commitment, his denials will reveal that he is not yet ready to fully go with Christ (but later in his ministry he will be ready to face many prisons and even death).

John's dialogue begins with Peter's question about Jesus' earlier statement "Little children, yet a little while I am with you. Ye shall seek me: and as I said unto the Jews, Whither I go, ye cannot come; so now I say to you" (John 13:33). Peter queried where the Lord was going. Jesus responded, "Whither I go, thou canst not follow me now; but thou shalt follow me afterwards" (John 13:36). Note the presence of both a proximate following ("canst not follow me *now*") and a future following ("shalt follow me *afterwards*"). In the short term, Peter will be unable to follow Jesus to his death, but he will later follow Christ to his own death as a martyr, foreshadowing Jesus' later prophecy for Peter in John 21:22 discussed below.[40] Peter would not let it end at that but asked and proclaimed, "Lord, why cannot I follow thee now? I will lay down my life for thy sake" (John 13:37).[41] Jesus' response cast some doubt on Peter's awareness and led to Jesus' piercing prediction of Peter's proximate denial: "Wilt thou lay down thy life for my sake? Verily, verily, I say unto thee, The cock shall not crow, till thou hast denied me thrice" (John 13:38).

Despite having three different versions of Jesus' prediction of Peter's denial (Matthew and Mark seem to be sharing the same version), they all contain the same narrative elements: (1) Jesus' statement regarding the future; (2) Peter's rejection of Jesus' statement and proclamation of his enduring loyalty; and (3) Jesus' prediction of Peter's denial that night. Thus, in all cases, Peter's brash, overconfident rejoinder reveals his ignorance of Jesus' mission and his own capability and sets up Jesus' foreknowledge of how Peter will react later that night. One significant difference among the Gospel accounts is that Peter continues protesting against Jesus' prediction in Matthew and Mark, but any response to Jesus' prediction is absent in the other two Gospels.

Garden of Gethsemane

Shortly after Jesus' prediction of Peter's denial, they arrived at the Garden of Gethsemane. Jesus began to feel sorrowful and very heavy (Matthew 26:37). The Joseph Smith Translation in Mark makes an interesting change to the text here, putting some of the emotions on the Apostles, not on Jesus:

> And the disciples began to be sore amazed, and to be very heavy, and to complain in their hearts, wondering if this be the Messiah.
>
> And Jesus knowing their hearts, said to his disciples, Sit ye here, while I shall pray.
>
> And he taketh with him, Peter, and James, and John, and rebuked them, and said unto them, My soul is exceeding sorrowful, even unto death; tarry ye here and watch. (Joseph Smith Translation, Mark 14:36–38)

Like elsewhere, Peter, James, and John are separated from the others, but here to receive a rebuke because of the complaining feelings wondering if Jesus was the Messiah. It is not clear in the text which of the disciples had this doubtful attitude towards Jesus' messiahship, but perhaps Jesus rebuked these three Apostles because they were considered the leaders of the others and either did not understand Jesus' mission themselves or had not taught the others sufficiently. Following his prayer to the Father, Jesus came and found them sleeping and said to Peter, "Simon,[42] sleepest thou? couldest not thou watch one hour?" (Mark 14:37; see also Matthew 26:40). It is not clear why Peter was singled out here, perhaps because of his leadership status or in response to his strong declaration of loyalty in the preceding episode that already seems to be eroding here in the garden with his lack of watching out for Jesus. Jesus encouraged them to watch and pray, lest they enter into temptation, and then he returned to pray more to the Father (Luke does not record multiple prayers; see Luke 22:46). After returning, Jesus found them sleeping again and the narrator explains why (no. 9): their eyes were heavy (see Matthew 26:43; Mark 14:40).[43] The narrator in Mark also adds that they did not know what to say to Jesus after he found them sleeping the second time (see Mark 14:40). Jesus prayed a third time and then told them they could sleep on (see Matthew 26:45; Mark 14:41).[44] This episode includes some censure from the Savior for his three chief Apostles and their fatigue from everything they had been experiencing. Peter is also the point person in Matthew and Mark for Jesus' questions. Despite Peter's earlier protestations that he would do anything for the Savior, even die for him, he cannot stay awake and watch for Christ now.

Jesus' Arrest

When Judas came with armed officers to betray Jesus, Peter tried to intervene (although only the Gospel of John identifies him by name). As recorded in all four Gospels, Peter drew his sword and cut off the ear of a servant of the high priest (see Matthew 26:51; Mark 14:47; Luke 22:50; John 18:10). In the Gospel of Matthew, Jesus essentially tells Peter to stand down. "Put up again thy sword into his place: for all they that take the sword shall perish with the sword. Thinkest thou that I cannot now pray to my Father, and he shall presently give me more than twelve legions of angels? But how then shall the scriptures be fulfilled, that thus it must be?" (Matthew 26:52–54).[45] Even in this intensely charged moment, Jesus is teaching his chief Apostle the divine nature of his mission and that if it did not need to happen this way, he could call down heavenly forces to protect himself. Similarly, John records Jesus' admonition to Peter to allow him to fulfill his mission: "Put up thy sword into the sheath: the cup which my Father hath given me, shall I not drink it?" (John 18:11). In Luke, Jesus simply said, "Suffer ye thus far" and healed the injured man's ear (Luke 22:51). (The Gospel of Mark omits any healing of the severed ear or any reaction to Peter's rash action). In this moment, even with armed soldiers around him, Peter had no qualms about fighting to defend his Master, but Jesus had to restrain his ardent Apostle and teach about the higher purpose for which he was there.

As they dragged Jesus away, all four Gospels single out Peter as following the group to the high priest's house (John includes another unnamed disciple who was able to gain them access into the high priest's complex—John 18:15–16). In Matthew, it gives the plain motive for Peter's actions—"to see the end" (Matthew 26:58). All of Jesus' other followers scattered like sheep from the Garden of

Gethsemane upon Jesus' arrest, but Peter remained to mutely witness what would come next in his Master's mission.

Peter's Denial

At the courtyard of the high priest's palace, Peter remained outside among servants and officers and warmed himself at the fire. As the trial of Jesus proceeded inside the palace of the high priest, Peter was approached consecutively by three people claiming that he was with Jesus of Nazareth. The Gospel of John identifies the first accuser as the person watching the gate and letting Peter gain entrance into the complex before he warms himself by the fire. The third accuser is specifically identified as a kinsman of the high priest's servant, Malchus, whose ear Peter had cut off in the Garden of Gethsemane (see John 18:26), a justifiable reason for Peter fearing for his life as retribution for his actions in the garden.[46] Mark's account captures the rising emotion that built up inside Peter:

> And when she saw Peter warming himself, she looked upon him, and said, And thou also wast with Jesus of Nazareth.
>
> But he denied, saying, I know not, neither understand I what thou sayest. And he went out into the porch; and the cock crew.
>
> And a maid saw him again, and began to say to them that stood by, This is one of them.
>
> And he denied it again. And a little after, they that stood by said again to Peter, Surely thou art one of them: for thou art a Galilean, and thy speech agreeth thereto.
>
> But he began to curse and to swear, saying, I know not this man of whom ye speak.
>
> And the second time the cock crew. And Peter called to mind the word that Jesus said unto him, Before the cock crow twice, thou shalt deny me thrice. And when he thought thereon, he wept. (Mark 14:67–72)

The charge of being "with Jesus" echoes earlier Markan texts, including Peter's former willingness to die "with Jesus" (14:31). But now Peter is denying being "with Jesus." By the third denial, Peter has reached the low point of his discipleship. "Only a few hours earlier he proclaimed his willingness to die with Jesus. Now he affirms that he has no ties with Jesus. He does not even know him!"[47] Reflecting back on Jesus' words in Mark 8:34–38 when Jesus referred to Peter as Satan, Jesus counseled that any who would come after him should deny himself and take up his cross. In this instance, Peter did not deny himself to follow Christ, but he denied knowing Jesus; haunting last words for Peter in each of the synoptic Gospels. Luke adds a poignant aspect to Peter's denial—a brief mention of the Savior's presence at the scene as "the Lord turned, and looked upon Peter" (Luke 22:61). Then Peter remembered Jesus' prediction and "went out, and wept *bitterly*" (Luke 22:62; emphasis added). The narrator's use of the adjective *bitterly* (no. 9; found also in Matthew 26:75) provides a subtle glimpse into Peter's horror and sorrow when he realized he had fulfilled Jesus' prediction of his denial. It also is likely an indication that Peter has begun the repentance process for his denials. Because Peter's internal thought is not revealed in this episode, nor does the narrator explicate why Peter acted the way he did (the narrator only described his rising emotions during the denials and his sorrowful feelings afterwards), a close narrative examination does not disclose exactly why Peter denied knowing Jesus. However, we can compare his actions in this moment with how he was portrayed in earlier episodes to try to draw some conclusions.

Conclusions

This narrative study of Peter leading up to the denial is not meant to criticize him nor condemn him as a failure. Instead, it is to remind us that Peter was mortal and as such had fears and made mistakes, but also grew, developed, and accomplished great things. He was not so high above other mortals that we cannot possibly relate to him. It is refreshing and inspiring that he seems more normal and more like us in our uncertain and often unsteady walk through life. It is this eager, yet often misguided, Apostle that the Gospel writers want us to examine and relate to. Thus a narrative presentation helps uncover the facets of Peter's characterization that can instruct us along our own paths of discipleship.

Despite the Gospels' brevity of description about Peter, a many-sided picture of Peter emerges from their portrayals of him in various settings. Despite a relatively humble background, he became recognized as the chief Apostle by Jesus, outsiders, and the Gospel writers. Peter came to learn through faith, miraculous events, and revelation that Jesus was the very Christ and the Son of God. Yet Peter, like the other disciples, was slow to grasp the divine purpose of Jesus' mission of suffering and death, so he continually proclaimed his eagerness to protect Jesus at all costs, even sacrificing his own life if necessary. Perhaps Peter thought he knew Jesus' mission better—something akin to Jewish messianic views of a triumphant, world-changing Messiah—not a Messiah handed over to human hands for punishment and death.[48] Peter's impetuous actions and his tendency to speak before understanding are consistent across the Gospels. Consequently,

Jesus needed to continually rebuke, refine, and rein him in. By the time of Jesus' trial, it seems Peter was resigned to the fact that Jesus must suffer, so he followed along to see the end.[49]

While one may think that Peter would be courageous in any setting, as demonstrated in the Garden of Gethsemane and in his rebukes of his Master, the narrator of each Gospel reveals moments when Peter was afraid and unsure of what to do. In fact, before Peter's denial the only descriptions by narrators about Peter's feelings and emotions were fear and uncertainty.[50] In addition, Jesus' reprimands included statements of Peter's lack of faith and understanding, a high level of exposition about a character from the main character in the narrative. Could not these characteristics have carried over to the pivotal moments of accusation—"thou art one of them"—and led him to his three denials? Between knowing that Jesus did not want him to prevent what was happening, and Peter's fear and uncertainty of what to say in some circumstances, Peter denied. Upon recognition of his weakness, Peter wept bitterly.

When briefly comparing the portrayal of Peter in each of the Gospels, a few insights can be gleaned. First, despite having four different accounts of Peter in the four Gospels, they are remarkably similar in their characterization of the chief Apostle: very powerful and positive at moments, then shockingly candid and critical in the next moment.[51] Even within unique episodes of a Gospel or in the Gospel of John, which includes very little about Peter during Jesus' ministry, similar characterization of Peter is portrayed. However, despite having these shared elements, Luke consistently softens the treatment of Peter. For example, in Luke, Peter did not rebuke his Master, nor was he called "Satan." In the prediction of Jesus' denial, Luke moderates the exchange by highlighting Satan's role in the initial sifting of the disciples rather than focusing on a character flaw. When Peter denies Christ three times, his words are much softer: "I know him not" (22:27); he denied he was one of them (Jesus' Galilean followers) (22:28); and he claimed to not understand the question (22:60). The Gospel of Matthew has some unique incidents related to Peter, probably to emphasize the authority to lead the church being passed down from Jesus to Peter. Mark possibly had the most critical characterization of Peter with its repeated emphasis on Peter's rising emotions and ignorance (twice the narrator explicitly states that Peter did not know what to say in certain situations). If Mark's Gospel was heavily influenced by Peter himself, as traditionally ascribed, then this critical examination of Peter is quite surprising. It may indicate that Peter shared with others that he did not know what to say or do in certain situations, which may have relevance for his actions and speech in the denial episode, and he was very forthright about the emotions he felt in these episodes.

It is also interesting to note how several times the Joseph Smith Translation adds to the characterization of Peter. It begins in the Joseph Smith Translation of John with Peter receiving an invitation to discipleship and with defining Cephas (see Joseph Smith Translation, John 1:42). It continues in the Joseph Smith Translation of Mark with Jesus rebuking Peter for his self-important statement that he had given up much in following Jesus (see Joseph Smith Translation, Mark 10:31–32). Near the end, the Joseph Smith Translation of Mark adds another rebuke by Jesus in the Garden of Gethsemane towards Peter (and James and John) for doubting feelings among the Apostles towards Jesus' messiahship (see Joseph Smith Translation, Mark 14:32–33). The Joseph Smith Translation additions in Mark are consistent with the more critical view of Peter that the Gospel of Mark gives.

If that were the end of the story, it would be a sad ending indeed. But the good news of the gospel brings restoration to Peter as well. Although he "disappears" from the story in the synoptics,[52] John relates a glorious reunion between the Master and his chief Apostle (see John 21). As part of that experience, Peter received the opportunity to redeem his threefold denial with a threefold declaration of his love.[53] Yet, even in this redemptive moment, Peter was grieved because Jesus had to ask him three times if he loved him, and Jesus made an ominous prophecy of Peter's future martyrdom (John 21:17–19).[54] But before that martyrdom would take place, Peter was obedient to Jesus' invitations to follow him[55] and became an indefatigable force for good in the early Christian church; a true shepherd (rather than a fleeing hireling) following in the steps of the Good Shepherd. Peter would love Christ's sheep and willingly give up his life for them.

Whatever one may say about his denial, Peter became a model of one overcoming a failing or weakness to rise to new heights through the strength of the Holy Ghost and a firm commitment to follow Jesus Christ. President Spencer W. Kimball stated: "If we admit that he was cowardly and denied the Lord through timidity, we can still find a great lesson. Has anyone more completely overcome mortal selfishness and weakness? Has anyone repented more sincerely? Peter has been accused of being harsh, indiscreet, impetuous, and fearful. If all these were true, then we still ask, Has any man ever more completely triumphed over his weaknesses?"[56] President Gordon B. Hinckley exhorted, "If there be those throughout the Church who by word or act have denied the faith, I pray that you may draw comfort and resolution from the example of Peter, who, though he had walked daily with Jesus, in an hour of extremity momentarily denied the Lord and also the testimony which he carried in his own heart. But he rose above this and became a mighty defender and a powerful advocate. So, too, there is a way for any person to turn about and add his or her strength and faith to the strength and faith of others in building the kingdom of God."[57]

We are fortunate that despite our failures, mercy is constantly extended and restoration provided. There are times in life when we can think we know God's plan for ourselves better than he does, so we try to pursue our own agenda. May we learn from Peter's example, who despite imperfections allowed himself to be refined until he ultimately fulfilled the mission given him by the Savior to feed his sheep until the end of his life.

Notes

1. Many have pointed out that Peter did not deny his testimony of Jesus as the Christ, but denied knowing Jesus or his association with Jesus. See, for example, Spencer W. Kimball, "Peter, My Brother," *BYU Speeches of the Year* (Provo, UT: BYU Press, 1971), 3.

2. E.g., Mary Ann Tolbert, *Sowing the Gospel: Mark's World in Literary-Historical Perspective* (Minneapolis: Fortress Press, 1989), 25–26.

3. Some scholars use a narrative approach to understand Peter during his own time (versus understanding the Gospel accounts as basically nonhistorical and reflecting a time of composition in the early church). For a helpful review of these works, see Timothy Wiarda, *Peter in the Gospels: Pattern, Personality, and Relationship* (Tubingen: Mohr Siebeck, 2000), 12–17.

4. Richard J. Cassidy, *Four Times Peter: Portrayals of Peter in the Four Gospels and at Philippi* (Collegeville, MN: Liturgical Press, 2007).

5. Cassidy, *Four Times Peter*, 1.

6. Robert Alter, *The Art of Biblical Narrative* (San Francisco: HarperCollins, 1981), 116–17. Wiarda uses a similar schema when approaching a characterization study of Peter, but he classifies these elements under two broad categories: direct shaping (the higher numbers in Alter's schema) and indirect shaping (the lower numbers). See *Peter in the Gospels*, 66–68.

7. A note on the use of the term "narrator": Many stories are told by a narrator who moves the story along through descriptions of events, dialogue, and transitions between episodes. Sometimes the narrator is explicitly revealed, such as when the story is told through the eyes and voice of a main character. Often the author plays the role of the narrator. In the case of the Gospels, the four evangelists are the narrators even though they do not identify themselves in the text (the Gospel of John comes the closest when the writer is identified as "the disciple whom Jesus loved" [see John 21:20, 24]). Except in the case of Luke, each evangelist is a "public narrator" addressing a general audience (whether that be Jews, Greeks, or members of the church) rather than a specific individual or an audience at a particular telling. Luke addresses his Gospel to Theophilus—likely an actual person or a general audience of those who love (or want to love) God (Luke 3:3; see also LDS Bible Dictionary, "Theophilus," 785, and Joseph Smith Translation, Luke 3:19–20).

8. Timothy Wiarda also argues for the value of viewing narrative development in episodes across the Gospels because patterns and threads can be observed that probably point to earlier traditions. See *Peter in the Gospels*, 1, 6–8. Cassidy, on the other hand, decided to look at each Gospel individually to determine how Peter's characterization was developed within each particular Gospel irrespective of the other accounts. See *Four Times Peter*, 5. This approach ignores any possible literary dependence among the four Gospels.

9. Alter, *The Art of Biblical Narrative*, 114.

10. Cassidy sees the paucity of character development in the Gospels as a result of each Gospel being more plot-driven than interested in developing characters. *Four Times Peter*, 2.

11. Luke has switched the order from Matthew and Mark of this healing episode with Peter's call. In each of the synoptic Gospels, this healing episode lacks any dialogue or action from Peter, but does reveal some facts about him: Peter is married and has a house in Capernaum (living with his brother Andrew).

12. The Greek term here (*epistatēs*) only occurs in the New Testament in the vocative and is unique to Luke. Luke seems to be translating rabbi rather than transcribing it like the other Evangelists.

13. The case of the Gospel of Mark may take on another interesting layer since it is traditionally held that Peter himself is the primary source for much of the material in this Gospel. What did Peter relate about his experiences that were preserved here? It is perhaps also worth noting that it is Jesus who chooses his disciples, and then they decide to follow him, rather than the disciples first choosing to follow Jesus.

14. "Mark's characteristic phrase, 'and immediately,' underscores that Peter accepted Jesus' call without any hesitation." Cassidy, *Four Times Peter*, 22.

15. In the Gospel of Mark, Peter is the first mortal to identify Jesus as the Christ, but in John it is his brother Andrew (although Andrew is identified in relation to Peter: "Simon Peter's brother").

16. For example, Peter is singled out in Luke's recounting of the healing of the woman with an issue of blood when Jesus asked who touched him out of the multitude and "Peter and they that were with him said . . . " (Luke 8:45). Peter is the only one mentioned and is thus treated as the leader of the group. Very early in Mark, Jesus departed to a solitary place away from the crowds (see Mark 1:35). Simon and others later found Jesus there and told him that everyone was looking for him (1:36–37). What little this tells us about Peter is that he is the only one specifically named among a group following after Jesus. Since Peter is the only named follower in this brief pericope, it may indicate the beginning of his leadership over Jesus' disciples. In another episode (only found in Matthew), outsiders recognized Peter as the leader among Jesus' followers and approached him to ask about his Master's tribute-paying habits. When tax collectors approached Peter in Capernaum and asked him whether his Master paid tribute, Peter replied in the affirmative (see Matthew 17:24–25). When Peter then went to enter the house (presumably his own house), Jesus asked Peter a question about whether royal children or strangers pay custom or tribute, then told Peter to catch a fish which would have a piece of money in its mouth (see Matthew 17:25–27). The story does not relate the fulfillment of this miracle, but Christian tradition presumes it occurred. As such, it is another demonstration of Jesus' miraculous power to Peter and another example of his leadership among the Apostles.

17. Another example of Jesus teaching his Apostles that they need more faith occurred after Jesus cursed the barren fig tree. According to the Gospel of Mark, Peter was the one who first noticed the withering of the fig tree the day after Jesus cursed it (11:21). Jesus' response: "have faith in God" (11:22).

18. Another example of the Apostles, including Peter, approaching Jesus for further insights came after his prophecy about the destruction of the temple. Following Jesus' foretelling that not a single stone of the temple would be left standing on another, Peter was among four of the Apostles who asked Jesus privately when these things would happen (see Mark 13:3). In one instance in the Gospel of John, Peter asks John to question the Lord who it was who was going to betray him (see John 13:24). There's nothing in the text to explain why Peter went through John to ask his question except maybe John's physical proximity to Jesus. In both these cases, there is no reproof from Jesus for lack of understanding.

19. Arlo Nau sees this portrayal as following "a known rhetorical pattern in the ancient world, that of an encomium containing both praise and dispraise. Nau discerns repeated instances in which Peter moves from an action or attitude which can be compared with that of Jesus to one which stands in contrast to Jesus." As quoted in Wiarda, *Peter in the Gospels*, 22–23. Wiarda shows an observable pattern of positive intention-reversed expectation where Peter had positive intentions with respect to Jesus, but then those intentions were reversed. See *Peter in the Gospels*, 34–40.

20. Timothy Wiarda spends considerable effort distinguishing between terms like "spokesman," "representative," and "opinion leader." He argues that Peter should be seen as an "opinion leader" in this episode in the Gospel of Mark (the focus of his study) because Mark does not use a spokesman in other episodes with the disciples, and in this one the other disciples are only able to report what others are saying about Jesus (see Mark 8:28), while Peter says the truth (8:29). See "Peter as Peter in the Gospel of Mark," *Journal of New Testament Studies* 45 (1999): 28–29. Cassidy notes the significance of the location of this episode in the Gospel of Mark where many see a two-part division in Mark's Gospel. Part I ends at 8:30 with Jesus' pronouncement and height of popularity among the multitudes. Part II begins at 8:31 and relates Jesus' path to suffering and death; commencing with a prophecy of his impending death (followed by two others in 9:31 and 10:33–34). See *Four Times Peter*, 15–16.

21. Mark gives a shorter form: "thou art the Christ" (8:29); and Luke states, "The Christ of God" (9:20). The Gospel of John includes a similar declaration of faith by Peter, but in a different context: after Jesus gave his Bread of Life discourse. When many of the hearers of that sermon forsook Jesus, Jesus asked the Twelve if they would go away also. Peter again took the lead and answered, "Lord, to whom shall we go? thou hast the words of eternal life. And we believe and are sure that thou art that Christ, the Son of the living God" (John 6:68–69). Note the use of plural "we," which indicates Peter is not only speaking for himself but for the entire group. They not only believe in Jesus, but are choosing to remain with him because he has the words of eternal life.

22. Jesus' use of Peter's full name, "Simon bar-Jona," sets up the fact that Jesus is about to rename him.

23. *Petros* is the Greek word for Peter, and *Petra* is the "stone" or "bedrock" that Jesus said the church will be built upon. In 1 Corinthians 10:4, Paul uses *Petra* in reference to

Jesus: "for they drank of that spiritual Rock [*Petras*] that followed them: and that Rock [*Petra*] was Christ."

24. It is unclear from the text in Matthew ("from that time forth . . .") how much time expired between Jesus' blessing of Peter and his first prediction of his death. Mark and Luke make it seem that it came immediately after Peter's confession of faith (see Mark 8:31; Luke 9:22).

25. Joseph Ratzinger, *Called to Communion* (San Francisco: Ignatius Press, 1996), 61, "contrasts Peter's answer (by divine revelation and not by 'flesh and blood') in this passage with his response in the next passage when he attempts to dissuade Jesus from following the path to suffering and execution. In the latter passage Peter's answer *is* by 'flesh and blood.'" Cited in Cassidy, *Four Times Peter*, 138 n. 17.

26. Interestingly, the Gospel of John never uses this term, and Jesus is never described as rebuking anyone in his account. Thanks to Andy Mickelson for noting this fact.

27. Perhaps Jesus' command is a reminder to Peter of his initial call to *follow* Christ.

28. The Greek word *skandalon* can also be translated "stumbling-block;" impeding Jesus to fulfill his mission. Note the irony in the contrast with the "foundation rock" for Jesus' church mentioned in the earlier passage (v. 17).

29. "Formerly he merited the new name of 'Peter.' Now he bears the name of 'Satan.'" From Cassidy, *Four Times Peter*, 77. "Human beings, allied with Satan, would consider the suffering Son of Man a contradiction to Jesus' role as Messiah. But he has just told the disciples that the Passion and Resurrection of the Son of Man is God's plan. Peter has proven unable to hear that word." Pheme Perkins, *Peter: Apostle for the Whole Church* (Columbia: University of South Carolina Press, 1994), 62.

30. It is ironic that Jesus' enemies actually advance Jesus' mission by making him suffer and killing him, while his disciples, especially Peter, try to stop his mission because they do not fully understand the need for Jesus to suffer. "The disciples are 'insiders' who remain 'outsiders' in their understanding." Perkins, *Peter: Apostle for the Whole Church*, 57, 76 n. 29.

31. There is nothing in the text to indicate Peter's response or feelings from this upbraiding.

32. This is the second time Jesus has separated out these three Apostles; the earlier episode was when Jesus raised Jairus' daughter from the dead (Mark 5:37—note the purposeful use of "no one" and "except" to separate out these particular Apostles; Luke 8:51; curiously Matthew completely omits the singling out of Peter, James, and John from this episode). In Jairus' daughter's healing, Peter plays only the role as a witness of the miraculous deed.

33. Only Matthew relates how Jesus comforted his fearful Apostles: "Jesus came and touched them, and said, Arise, and be not afraid" (Matthew 17:7).

34. Luke earlier recorded that initially "Peter and they that were with him were heavy with sleep," similar to their future fatigue in the Garden of Gethsemane, so they saw Jesus' glory after they awoke (Luke 9:32).

35. The aftermath of their experience on the mount also differs among the three Gospels. After the divine manifestation, Matthew and Mark relate that Jesus "charged them that they should tell no man what things they had seen, till the Son of man were risen from the dead" (Mark 9:9; see also Matthew 17:9). Luke omits the charge from the

Savior to not share the experience, but states that the three Apostles "kept it close, and told no man in those days any of those things which they had seen" (Luke 9:36). Mark and Matthew then add some details about their questions related to that experience, which led to further questions about Elias and Christ's coming: "They kept that saying with themselves, questioning one with another what the rising from the dead should mean" (Mark 9:10). Peter was thus commanded in Matthew and Mark to refrain from sharing anything from this very powerful experience until after the Resurrection, a promise he kept (he later shared his feelings about it in 2 Peter 1:16–18). This experience also led to further questioning as Peter and his two companions tried to understand more about Jesus' mission and figures related to it.

36. In the Gospel of Matthew, Jesus expanded on the statement "the first shall be last and the last shall be first" by giving the parable of the laborers in the vineyard, which was another occasion when Jesus used a parable to teach Peter (and the other Apostles) more about a principle (see Matthew 20:1–16).

37. Richard Cassidy sees Peter's response as "the moment of Peter's highest standing within the Gospel narrative. He is now so personally committed in his allegiance to Jesus that he will readily die *with you*." *Four Times Peter*, 30. Peter also tacitly accepts the possibility of Jesus' future death by no longer disputing Jesus' prediction of his death.

38. "At other places in Luke's Gospel in which he repeats the name of the addressee, Jesus' usage implies a degree of solicitude or compassion for the person or entity to whom he speaks." Cassidy, *Four Times Peter*, 51.

39. Jesus addresses Peter for the only time in the Gospel of Luke as "Peter" in this prediction of his denials. Jesus' earlier exhortation to Peter to "strengthen thy brethren" may be the reason for using this name at this time. There would be a future need for Peter's rock-solid assistance to the other disciples (which may have come as early as Luke 24:34, when Peter and others could bear witness that the Lord had risen because he had appeared to Simon). "Given the phenomenon of Peter's denials, there may also be a dimension of irony in Jesus' use of this name. In the events that will immediately unfold Peter will not be able to live up to his name: he will not be a 'rock' when he denies Jesus three times. Nevertheless, even though Peter's behavior in the next hours will be decidedly 'unrocklike,' Jesus still looks to a future in which Peter's renewed strength will enable him to be a source of strength for others." Cassidy, *Four Times Peter*, 51.

40. See Cassidy, *Four Times Peter*, 98.

41. "Peter will die 'for' Jesus not merely 'with' him as in Luke 22:33. The reader of the Fourth Gospel knows that Jesus is the shepherd who lays down his life 'for' the sheep (10:15)." Perkins, *Peter: Apostle for the Whole Church*, 106 n. 56.

42. It is noteworthy that once Simon is named "Peter" by Jesus in the Gospel of Mark (3:16), Jesus always refers to him by Peter until this episode. "Jesus seemingly underscores Simon's failure by electing not to address him with the 'disciple's name' (Peter) he earlier bestowed on him." "Peter's behavior is far from 'rocklike.'" Cassidy, *Four Times Peter*, 21, 23.

43. Luke later on says they were sleeping because "they were filled with sorrow"— Joseph Smith Translation, Luke 22:45.

44. The three failed attempts at watching out for Jesus "can be regarded as a narrative anticipation of the far more serious three denials that are still to come. In reporting this sequence, at 26:43b, Matthew offers the slightly exculpatory comment: 'for their eyes

were heavy.' There will be no such exonerating reference when Peter makes his denials."
Cassidy, *Four Times Peter*, 80.

45. This sentiment is also behind Jesus' later statement to Pilate in John 18:36 when he stated that if his kingdom were of this world, then his disciples would fight, but since it is not, they do not need to fight.

46. Cassidy sees a literary parallel between Jesus' Good Shepherd identification (see John 10) and the denial scene. The same Greek word is used for both the "sheepfold" and "the courtyard," enclosed spaces accessible through a guarded gate. Instead of Jesus' I Am identification, Peter responds to his accusers, "I am *not*." *Four Times Peter*, 100. Peter's actions are like the hireling fleeing from the Good Shepherd's sheep when he sees danger approaching.

47. Cassidy, *Four Times Peter*, 31.

48. See Frank F. Judd Jr., "The Parables of Matthew 13: Revealing and Concealing the Kingdom of God," in *The Life and Teachings of Jesus Christ, Volume 2: From the Transfiguration through the Triumphal Entry*, ed. Richard Neitzel Holzapfel and Thomas A. Wayment (Salt Lake City: Deseret Book, 2006), 88–94.

49. See Kimball, "Peter, My Brother," 4.

50. It is interesting that the Joseph Smith Translation follows two of the narrator's tendencies in the Gospels in relation to Peter: descriptions of Peter's emotions of fear and uncertainty and Jesus' rebuking of Peter.

51. Note Wiarda's assessment: "A remarkable consistency of characterization across four streams of gospel tradition is to be observed." In *Peter in the Gospels*, 119.

52. Matthew makes no mention of Peter after his denial. Mark makes brief mention of him in the invitation by the angels to the women to tell Peter and the disciples that Jesus is going before them to Galilee (Joseph Smith Translation, Mark 16:7). When the women's message was delivered to Peter, it must have been a relief for Peter to know the Savior was willing to see him even after his denial. Luke mentions a post-Resurrection appearance to Peter without any details of that encounter (see Luke 24:34). The post-Resurrection reunion between Jesus and Peter alluded to by Mark and Luke indicates Jesus' willingness to pardon Peter for his denials. Peter was *with Jesus* once again.

53. Another narrative link between these two episodes is the use of the Greek word *anthrakia* (charcoal fire), which is only found in the New Testament in these two settings. Another parallel is "in that previous scene Peter faced a threefold interrogation *about Jesus*. Now he faces a threefold interrogation *by Jesus*. In both cases, it is Peter's *relationship* to Jesus that is at issue." See Cassidy, *Four Times Peter*, 103.

54. Compare with Jesus' earlier prophecy that Peter would follow in his steps to martyrdom (see John 13:36).

55. The risen Lord twice reinvited Peter to follow him on the shores of the Sea of Galilee (see John 21:19, 22).

56. Kimball, "Peter, My Brother," 2.

57. "And Peter Went Out and Wept Bitterly," *Ensign*, March 1995, 6.

5

Peter's Keys

S. Kent Brown

S. Kent Brown is a professor emeritus of ancient scripture at
Brigham Young University.

Somewhere near the base of Mount Hermon, within sight of its towering prominences and sheer cliffs, Jesus speaks words to his Apostle Peter that find no correspondence in ancient scripture:[1] "I will give unto thee the keys of the kingdom of heaven" (Matthew 16:19). What are we to make of Jesus' promise? What are these keys? Latter-day Saints usually think of keys as the divinely bestowed, authorizing powers that allow a priesthood holder to exercise priesthood authority when performing an ordinance such as a baptism, a setting apart, or a sealing in a temple. Standing beside this Latter-day Saint understanding of such priesthood and temple keys are colors and contours that illuminate how people in the New Testament world may have understood the nature of Peter's keys. To begin to understand, we first turn to a scene recorded in the book of Isaiah and then look at the promise of keys made to Peter at Caesarea Philippi. Along the way, it will become clear that the promised keys bear a relationship to "the gates of hell" (Matthew 16:18), to the next world, and to a greater knowledge of God.

The Key of the House

Isaiah's record offers the one instance of an Old Testament person receiving keys. This man is named Eliakim, son of Hilkiah, and otherwise remains unknown. He is called by the Lord through Isaiah his prophet to serve as the royal treasurer. He succeeds an unreliable man named Shebna who has held responsibility "over the house," that is, over the royal household (Isaiah 22:15). In evocative language, the Lord hands the duty to Eliakim with the words, "the key of the house of David will I lay upon his shoulder; so he shall open, and none shall shut; and he shall shut, and none shall open" (Isaiah 22:22). It appears that, among his duties, this man is to hold the key to the main door of the palace.[2]

The New Testament picks up the language addressed to Hilkiah and places it in a totally different context. According to the book of Revelation, it is the Resurrected Christ who holds "the key of David." Moreover, like Eliakim, he is the one who "openeth, and no man shutteth; and shutteth, and no man openeth" (Revelation 3:7). Obviously, in this passage the Risen Jesus is not in charge of the door to an earthly palace as Eliakim evidently is. Rather, he has responsibility for access into and out of the abode of God—that is, the heavenly palace[3]—or alternatively, into and out of the new city of David, or the New Jerusalem.[4] By extension, he controls the door or gate that leads into heaven. Further, this responsibility also has to do with access to heaven at the end-time when access means everything (see 2 Nephi 9:41).

What does this key of David, now held by the Savior, have to do with the keys promised to Peter? On one level, they appear to exhibit close ties to one another. How so? To answer, it is important to examine the scene wherein Peter receives keys. As a first step, we notice that commentators generally agree that Matthew's record of Jesus' words to Peter is Semitic in character. Generally, these Semitic touches are seen to include the Aramaic name "Bar-jona," the expression "flesh and blood" for mortality, the term "the gates of [Hades]," the expression "shall be bound . . . shall be loosed," and the play on the Aramaic word *kephā* that underlies both the Greek name Peter and the word "rock" (Matthew 16:17–19).[5] Why are these elements important? Because the presence of Semitic characteristics demonstrates that the story belongs to the early strata of Christian memory about Jesus' ministry. For some scholars, much in the gospels derives from a generation following the Apostles and is therefore suspect. But the Semitic coloring of the account of Peter and the keys puts the memory of this scene among Aramaic-speaking eyewitnesses, the earliest of Jesus' followers.[6]

At Caesarea Philippi

The earliest followers, of course, include the Twelve and others (see Acts 1:21–22). The narrative of the keys occurs when they and Jesus are traveling in the area of Caesarea Philippi, a Gentile city that lies some twenty-six miles north of the Sea of Galilee. The ruins of the city sit at the base of Mount Hermon where an enormous spring emerges. Of the three Gospels that report the event, Matthew alone recounts that Jesus entrusts keys to Peter (see Matthew 16:13–20; Mark 8:27–30; Luke 9:18–21). In an attempt to encourage his disciples to express what they now know about him after months of traveling with him,[7] Jesus asks them, "Whom do men say that I am?" (Mark 8:27). The disciples repeat back opinions that they have heard, all of which tie to the dead: John the Baptist, or Elijah, or one of the prophets, or perhaps Jeremiah (see Matthew 16:14). At this moment, Jesus addresses the disciples and springs the question, "But whom say ye that I am?" (Matthew 16:15; Mark 8:29). Speaking for the others, Peter says, "Thou art the Christ, the Son of the living God" (Matthew 16:16).[8]

In the next part of the story, Jesus congratulates Peter and points to the source of Peter's testimony by saying, "Blessed art thou, Simon Bar-jona: for flesh and blood hath not revealed it unto thee, but my Father which is in heaven" (Matthew 16:17). But Jesus does not leave matters here. He now gives to Peter the first hint about keys: "I say also unto thee, That thou art Peter, and upon this rock I will build my church;[9] and the gates of hell shall not prevail against it" (16:18). Plainly, the term *gates* (Greek *pylai*) hints at the need for keys to open them.

Hades

Before going further, we need to say a word about the prominent term translated "hell" in this passage. It is the Greek term *hadēs* or, as we say in English, Hades. In the Septuagint, the Greek word *hadēs* generally bears the meaning of a permanent, dark underworld where departed spirits are confined (see LXX Job 7:9–10; 10:21–22). Later, the New Testament adjusts this view: here, *hadēs* is a temporary abode where the spirits of the dead await the Resurrection and Judgment (see Acts 2:27, 31; Revelation 20:13) and where Jesus preaches during the time that his body lies in the tomb (see 1 Peter 3:19–20; 4:6).[10] A similar notion appears in the Book of Mormon where we read that the "souls of the wicked [shall be] . . . in darkness, . . . as well as the righteous in paradise, *until the time of their resurrection*" (Alma 40:14; emphasis added). Similarly, the Prophet Joseph

Smith taught that "hell . . . is annother modern term [that] is taken from hades the greek, or shaole, the (hebrew) & the true signification is a world of spirits."[11]

But Hades has another meaning. In some passages, Hades is a name or title held by an individual in the underworld who has charge of the spirit prison. We find a hint of this meaning when the Risen Savior affirms, "I am he that liveth, and was dead . . . and have the keys of hell and of death" (Revelation 1:18). The clear implication is that he has taken possession of those keys and now holds them in his hand. How do we know this? Behind such a notion stands the view that, when Jesus descends into the world of spirits after his death on the cross, he faces closed gates that keep the departed spirits inside a prison. Meeting resistance from those who hold the keys—death and hell (see Revelation 6:8; 20:13–14; 2 Nephi 9:12; Doctrine and Covenants 121:4)—he takes control of the keys from them and opens the closed gates. In the language of Isaiah, after this confrontation, he opens "the prison to them that are bound" and proclaims "liberty to the captives" (Isaiah 61:1).

Importantly, at the beginning of his earthly ministry, Jesus virtually quotes these lines and applies them to his future activities: "The Spirit of the Lord is upon me, because he hath anointed me . . . to preach deliverance to the captives, and . . . to set at liberty them that are bruised" (Luke 4:18). These words from Isaiah are both metaphorical and real. On a metaphorical level, Jesus offers liberty to those held captive by their sins and opens doors to them to escape the prison of their worst selves (see 3 Nephi 20:26). On the physical level, in coming to earth, Jesus invades the domain of Satan and engages in a contest for souls (see Isaiah 49:25; 53:12; 2 Nephi 2:29).[12] In a way, this contest persists into the afterlife because there he deals with those who have fallen under the sway of Satan's powers. But he must first gain access to these individuals. And that means taking physical control of "the gates of hell" by holding the keys.[13] As we are reminded when we sing the hymn "We Sing All Hail to Jesus' Name,"

> He seized the keys of death and hell
> And bruised the serpent's head;
> He bid the prison doors unfold,
> The grave yield up her dead.[14]

In the end, of course, according to John's revelation, the triumphant Christ will see to it that the twin evils "death and hell [are] cast into the lake of fire" (Revelation 20:14; see also Acts 2:24; Romans 6:9). This set of observations about Jesus' postmortal ministry leads to hell's gates.

The Gates of Hell

What do the gates of hell have to do with Peter's keys? A lot, I suggest, especially because just before Peter is promised keys Jesus tells him that "the gates of hell shall not prevail against [the church]" (Matthew 16:18). The church in this passage points to the Savior's future church for which the Twelve and other disciples will form the core.[15] Inside of that church will be its members, all of whom face the prospect of ending up in the spirit prison unless Jesus has control of the keys to its gates.[16] Thus Jesus' promise that "the gates of hell shall not prevail" against the church and its members because, as the keeper of the keys, he will free them from hell, has everything to do with "the keys of the kingdom of heaven" (Matthew 16:18–19). The same person holds both sets of keys, one that allows departed spirits out of Hades and the other that allows entry from prison into God's kingdom. It is the latter set of keys that Jesus promises to entrust to Peter.

What does it mean that the gates of hell will not "prevail" against the church and, by extension, its members? The Greek verb *katischyō* carries the sense "to overpower," "to prevail," "to overcome."[17] But these meanings do not help us understand how gates overpower individuals, almost as if the gates attack and overcome a person. Although this imagery is possible,[18] it seems instead that the gates exercise power over individuals by keeping them inside Hades. That is, the gates prevent persons from gaining access to the saving power of the Atonement by keeping them inside the spirit prison. But because of Jesus' Atonement and because he has taken possession of the prison's keys, all will be released from this prison and be reunited with their bodies in the Resurrection (see Doctrine and Covenants 17:8; 18:5; 21:6).[19]

Departed Spirits

Relevant here is the disciples' response to Jesus' first question, "Whom do men say that I am?" (Mark 8:27). Significantly and probably unwittingly, they answer by pointing to some who are already dead: John the Baptist, Elijah, Jeremiah, "or one of the prophets" (Matthew 16:14). Their answer, in effect, spreads out a context for what follows in the conversation between Jesus and the disciples. Even though the keys that Jesus promises to Peter concern this life—"whatsoever thou shalt bind on earth . . . whatsoever thou shalt loose on earth"—they also have to do with the heavenly world and what will persist there to the end of time. That is one of the points of the clauses "shall be bound in heaven: and . . . shall be loosed in heaven" (Matthew 16:19; see also Doctrine and Covenants 132:46, "eternally bound in the heavens").

The then-future roles of these three deceased individuals makes this conclusion even firmer. Latter-day Saints are well aware of the task of John the
Baptist in the latter days—to restore the Aaronic Priesthood and its keys—and
are aware of Elijah's role in bringing back the keys of the sealing powers (see
Doctrine and Covenants 13; Doctrine and Covenants 110:13–16). What is less
known are the tasks entrusted to Jeremiah. In Jewish literature, the prophet
Jeremiah is seen as the person who has charge of the sacred tent and ark of
the covenant until the end of time (see 2 Maccabees 2:4–7). According to the
pseudepigraphical book of 4 Ezra, also known as 2 Esdras, among others God
will send his servant Jeremiah at the end of days to make his people prosperous (see 4 Ezra 2:18). Hence, these three personalities perform tasks associated
with the latter days whose effects last into the end of time. Thus, the effect of
the disciples mentioning the names of these earlier individuals prepares the
reader for an important element tied to keys that reaches into the next world,
including the world of the dead.

The Keys of the Kingdom of Heaven

Concern for the next world, of course, is plainly present in the expression "the
keys of the kingdom of heaven" (Matthew 16:19). Five related but differing points
are important here. First, possession of these keys does not mean that the holder is
a mere doorkeeper, a person who checks the identity of those entering and leaving.
By being entrusted with keys, Peter stands as Jesus' fully authorized representative. This dimension appears in the verb "I will give." On one level, the verb stands
as a simple future tense and is to be understood as a promise that surely will later
be fulfilled. That is, Jesus will give the keys to Peter at an undisclosed date in
the future. In addition, the Greek future tense here is equivalent to the Aramaic
imperfect tense and can bear a voluntative sense. That is, the verb may also carry
the meaning "I will (or am determined) to give." In this light, Jesus may be subtly
emphasizing that the promised conferral of keys on Peter forms a key moment
in his ministry among his disciples, a fulfillment that we see occurring at least in
part on the Mount of Transfiguration.[20]

Second, we observe that the Greek term translated "heaven" (*ouranos*) is plural. Hence, it could be rendered "heavens" throughout verse 19—"kingdom of the
heavens . . .," "bound in the heavens . . .," and "loosed in the heavens." Although
this kind of translation possesses intriguing possibilities for Latter-day Saints, the
singular translation "heaven" is most likely correct. Why? Because the plural is
simply a Semitism. It is the way that a person refers to heaven in Semitic languages
(for example, *shāmayim* in Hebrew).[21]

Third, it is evident that the keys establish Peter's authority over earthly church matters. This observation is buttressed by Jesus' words "bind on earth" and "loose on earth." Effectively, Jesus is handing to Peter the chief responsibility for leading his church. But Peter does not have to carry this responsibility by himself. As a matter of fact, the keys come to be held jointly among the Twelve, as Jesus later implies: "Verily I say unto you [Twelve],[22] Whatsoever ye shall bind on earth shall be bound in heaven: and whatsoever ye shall loose on earth shall be loosed in heaven" (Matthew 18:18).[23] A revelation that the Prophet Joseph Smith received in January 1841 confirms this observation: "[The] Twelve hold the keys to open up the authority of my kingdom upon the four corners of the earth" (Doctrine and Covenants 124:128; see also John 20:23; Doctrine and Covenants 90:6; 112:16).

Fourth, certain earthly church matters now come under Peter's authority. In rabbinic law, "to bind" and "to loose" mean "to forbid" and "to permit," that is, to forbid or permit activities under the strictures of the law of Moses.[24] But Jesus' words about keys and their associated authority carry a much broader sense because, from now on, Peter will carry the same powers over followers that Jesus does. These powers include remitting sins (see 1 John 3:5; Doctrine and Covenants 132:46),[25] withholding remission of sins (see John 20:23),[26] establishing doctrine (see Luke 11:52; Doctrine and Covenants 84:19),[27] excommunicating and reinstating to full membership (see Doctrine and Covenants 132:46–48),[28] and overseeing ordinances and keeping them pure (see Doctrine and Covenants 124:33–36; 132:7).

Fifth, turning to the celestial realm, it is clear that what Peter does on earth carries with full effect into heaven and into the next life. This is where the true power of the keys lies. What Peter and his fellow members of the Twelve offer is a link to God's kingdom and a grand future beyond death. This link is underlined by the passive voice "shall be bound in heaven" and "shall be loosed in heaven" (Matthew 16:19). Almost consistently in scripture, passive verbs without a subject point directly to the actions of God. The binding in heaven and the loosing in heaven are not done by Peter and the Twelve but by the Father.[29] Hence, the earthly actions taken in the church such as baptizing, remitting sins, and reinstating to full church membership are fully effective in heaven and in the next life.[30] As the Lord reminds Joseph Smith, who possessed the keys of the kingdom in modern times, "whatsoever you seal on earth shall be sealed in heaven; and whatsoever you bind on earth, in my name and by my word, saith the Lord, it shall be eternally bound in the heavens; and whosesoever sins you remit on earth shall be remitted eternally in the heavens" (Doctrine and Covenants 132:46).

We now come full circle to the passage from Isaiah's book that we cited at the beginning. There we find Eliakim the son of Hilkiah charged with keeping the door that leads into and out of the palace. With "the key of the house of David," he "shall open, and none shall shut; and he shall shut, and none shall open" (Isaiah 22:22). Clearly, he controls entry. Similarly, "the keys of the kingdom of heaven" that are held by Peter and his fellow members of the Twelve control entry, in this case entry into God's kingdom. That kingdom has been brought to earth by the Savior. As his authorized representatives, Peter and his fellow Apostles allow entry into the earthly manifestation of that kingdom— namely, the church. Notably, entry into the church is also entry into the heavenly congregation. Why? Because they are one and the same and are inextricably linked (see Doctrine and Covenants 42:69).

The Key of Knowledge

But this is not the end of the matter. The "keys of the kingdom" also embrace "the key of knowledge," specifically, the knowledge of God (Doctrine and Covenants 128:14; also 84:19). The first appearance of this expression in the New Testament, in Luke's Gospel, indicates that this key is one of celestial entry. On an occasion when Jesus confronts his opponents and, in a strong rebuke of the scribes, or specialists in the law of Moses, we hear him almost shout, "Woe unto you, lawyers! for ye have taken away the key of knowledge: ye entered not in yourselves, and them that were entering in ye hindered" (Luke 11:52). Plainly, Jesus' words indicate that "the key of knowledge" allows access or entry, exactly what the "keys of the kingdom of heaven" allow. This observation receives support from adjustments in the Joseph Smith Translation to these words of Jesus where we read, "Ye enter not in yourselves into the kingdom; and those who were entering in, ye hindered" (Joseph Smith Translation, Luke 11:53). More than this, in his condemning statement, Jesus seems to hold up not only the scripture but also the sacred rites that scribes fence off as too holy to share with common people, including the nature and meaning of sacred ceremonies, covenants, and laws.[31] The Joseph Smith Translation buttresses this observation too by calling "the key of knowledge, the fullness of the scriptures" (JST, Luke 11:53). Such a key, of course, opens a door to heavenly knowledge (see Luke 24:31–32 where, implicitly by a key, eyes and scriptures are "opened" by the Resurrected Jesus).[32]

According to modern scripture, the key of knowledge is equivalent to the "key of the mysteries of the kingdom" (Doctrine and Covenants 84:19). Broadly speaking, these mysteries include "obtaining a knowledge of facts in relation to the salvation of the children of men, both as well for the dead as for the living" (Doctrine and Covenants 128:11). In this light, the key of knowledge has to do with gaining a full and correct grasp of salvation and all of its parts. That knowledge, then, allows us to enter properly into the church and into the kingdom of heaven.

Conclusions

To conclude, the scene that takes place in the neighborhood of Caesarea Philippi brims with terrestrial and celestial meaning. Disparate elements such as keys and foundation, rock and gates, and the next world intersect in a stunning revelation to Peter and his fellow disciples. Jesus appears to be drawing out of his disciples what they have learned about him during their months of travel with him when he asks, "Whom do men say that I am?" (Mark 8:27). But he will enrich the conversation in unexpected ways beyond Peter's affirmation that he is the Christ.

The disciples seemingly do not know that they are fixing the nature of the discussion that follows by pointing to prominent persons who have died yet will play important roles in the last days: John the Baptist, Elijah, and Jeremiah. On this occasion, they surely do not expect Jesus to promise to grant full power to them inside his kingdom, beginning by promising the keys of the kingdom to Peter. But he does, making an astonishing promise of power, a dimension that he later reinforces when he assures them that eventually they will "sit upon twelve thrones, judging the twelve tribes of Israel" (Matthew 19:28). This promise, with celestial and terrestrial dimensions, points to a framework that what Peter and his fellow Apostles will do in the earthly church carries with full force into the next world. This remarkable aspect is made possible by Jesus' actions during the hours that his body lies in the tomb, wherein he takes control of the gates of the spirit prison and offers an escape for the imprisoned spirits that have departed this life. Effectively, through the power of his Atonement, Jesus provides not only an escape from the prison but also an entry into his heavenly kingdom, an entry that he places in the hands of Peter and the Twelve by transmitting keys to them. Finally, it becomes clear that Jesus guides the whole experience so that his future earthly church becomes the repository of celestial power whose reach extends into the heavenly world. Thus Peter, along with his fellow members of the Twelve, become the administrators of the house of God (see Doctrine and Covenants 112:16; 124:128).[33]

Notes

1. Outside of scripture, similar scenes appear with Michael the Archangel as keyholder; see 3 Baruch 11:2, translated by H. E. Gaylord Jr., and 4 Baruch 9:5, translated by

Stephen E. Robinson, in *The Old Testament Pseudepigrapha*, ed. James H. Charlesworth, 2 vols. (Garden City, NY: Doubleday, 1983 and 1985), 1:674 and 2:424.

2. R. B. Y. Scott and G. D. Kilpatrick, "The Book of Isaiah: Chapters 1–39," *The Interpreter's Bible: A Commentary in Twelve Volumes*, ed. George Arthur Buttrick (Nashville: Abingdon Press, 1980), 5:293; Joachim Jeremias, "*kleis*," in *Theological Dictionary of the New Testament*, ed. Gerhard Kittel and Gerhard Friedrich, 9 vol., trans. Geoffrey W. Bromiley (Grand Rapids, MI: Eerdmans, 1964–74), 3:750 (hereafter *TDNT*).

3. Jeremias, "*kleis*," in *TDNT*, 3:748.

4. R. H. Charles, *A Critical and Exegetical Commentary on the Revelation of St. John*, 2 vols. (Edinburgh: T&T Clark, 1971), 1:86; Richard D. Draper and Michael D. Rhodes, *The Revelation of John the Apostle* (Provo, UT: BYU Studies e-Book, 2013), 93.

5. Oscar Cullmann, *Peter: Disciple, Apostle, Martyr*, 2nd ed., trans. Floyd V. Filson (London: SCM Press, 1962), 192–93; Jeremias, "*kleis*," in *TDNT*, 3:749–50; Karl Ludwig Schmidt, "*kaleō*," in *TDNT*, 3:520; Jeremias, "*pylē*," in *TDNT*, 6:924; W. D. Davies and Dale C. Allison Jr., *A Critical and Exegetical Commentary on the Gospel of Saint Matthew, Volume II* (Edinburgh: T&T Clark, 1991), 605, 627; Donald A. Hagner, *Matthew 14–28*, Word Biblical Commentary, vol. 33B (Dallas, TX: Word Books, 1995), 466, 469–71.

6. Colin Brown, "The Gates of Hell and the Church," in *Church, Word and Spirit: Historical and Theological Essays in Honor of Geoffrey W. Bromiley*, ed. James E. Bradley and Richard A. Muller (Grand Rapids, MI: Eerdmans, 1987), 33; Hagner, *Matthew 14–28*, 465–66.

7. Hagner, *Matthew 14–28*, 463; John Nolland, *The Gospel of Matthew: A Commentary on the Greek Text* (Grand Rapids, MI: Eerdmans, 2005), 657.

8. A number of scholars hold that this scene is out of place, likely belonging to a post-resurrection event or to the last supper; see, for example, Rudolph Bultmann, *The History of the Synoptic Tradition*, 2nd ed., trans. John Marsh (New York: Harper & Row, 1968), 259; Cullmann, *Peter: Disciple, Apostle, Martyr*, 176–91.

9. An enormous literature exists on the genuineness of Jesus' saying because of the presence of the term "church" (Greek *ekklēsia)* in this passage, a word that many hold to be an addition by a later generation of Christians into the text. See, for instance, Schmidt, "*kaleō*," in *TDNT*, 3:501–31, especially 504, 518–26; Cullmann, *Peter: Disciple, Apostle, Martyr*, 193–204.

10. Alfred Plummer, *A Critical and Exegetical Commentary on the Gospel According to Luke*, The International Critical Commentary, 5th ed. (Edinburgh: T&T Clark, 1989), 397–98; Jeremias, "*hadēs*," *TDNT*, 1:146–49; Walter Grundmann, "*ischyō*," in *TDNT*, 3:399–401; Draper and Rhodes, *The Revelation of John the Apostle*, 57.

11. Wilford Woodruff Journal, June 11, 1843; quoted in Andrew F. Ehat and Lyndon W. Cook, *The Words of Joseph Smith* (Provo, UT: Religious Studies Center, 1980), 213; spelling in original preserved.

12. Walter Grundmann, "*ischyō*," in *TDNT*, 3:399–401; S. Kent Brown, Richard Neitzel Holzapfel, and Dawn Pheysey, with Nicole Cannariato, *Beholding Salvation: The Life of Christ in Word and Image* (Salt Lake City: Deseret Book; Provo, UT: BYU Museum of Art, 2006), 90–93.

13. Jeremias, "*hadēs*," in *TDNT*, 1:146–49. Hugh Nibley holds that Jesus already possesses the keys and therefore only has to open the gates to the spirit prison; see Nibley,

Mormonism and Early Christianity, ed. Stephen D. Ricks and Todd M. Compton (Salt Lake City: Deseret Book; Provo, UT: FARMS, 1987), 107–9.

14. Richard Alldridge, "We'll Sing All Hail to Jesus' Name," *Hymns* (Salt Lake City: The Church of Jesus Christ of Latter-day Saints, 1985), no. 182.

15. The Greek pronoun "it" in the expression "the gates of hell shall not prevail against it" is the feminine *autēs* and could agree with either the feminine term for "rock" (Greek *petra*) or the feminine word for church *(ekklēsia)*. But it stands closer to "church" in the statement and is therefore the natural antecedent of this noun; also see Jeremias, *"pylē,"* *TDNT*, in 6:927; Hagner, *Matthew 14–28*, 472.

16. Jeremias, *"hadēs,"* in *TDNT*, 1:148–49; Grundmann, *"ischyō,"* in *TDNT*, 3:398; Jeremias, *"pylē,"* in *TDNT*, 6:924–28.

17. Walter Bauer, *A Greek-English Lexicon of the New Testament and Other Early Christian Literature*, trans. William F. Arndt and F. Wilbur Gingrich (Chicago: University of Chicago Press, 1957), 425; Grundmann, *"ischyō,"* in *TDNT*, 3:397–98.

18. Jeremias, *"pylē,"* in *TDNT*, 6:927.

19. Joseph Fielding McConkie and Craig J. Ostler, *Revelations of the Restoration: A Commentary on the Doctrine and Covenants and Other Modern Revelations* (Salt Lake City: Deseret Book, 2000), 177, 1029; Stephen E. Robinson and H. Dean Garrett, *A Commentary on the Doctrine and Covenants*, 4 vols. (Salt Lake City: Deseret Book, 2000–2005), 1:151–52.

20. Jeremias, *"kleis,"* in *TDNT*, 3:749–50; Nibley, *Mormonism and Early Christianity*, 104–5; D. Kelly Ogden and Andrew C. Skinner, *Verse by Verse: The Four Gospels* (Salt Lake City: Deseret Book, 2006), 340–41; S. Kent Brown, "The Twelve," in *The Life and Teachings of Jesus Christ: From the Transfiguration through the Triumphal Entry*, ed. Richard Neitzel Holzapfel and Thomas A. Wayment (Salt Lake City: Deseret Book, 2006), 119.

21. Helmut Traub and Gerhard von Rad, *"ouranos,"* in *TDNT*, 5:513; Friedrich Blass and Albert Debrunner, *A Greek Grammar of the New Testament and Other Early Christian Literature*, trans. Robert W. Funk (Chicago: University of Chicago Press, 1961), §141(1); G. Bartelmus, *"šāmayim,"* *Theological Dictionary of the Old Testament*, ed. G. Johannes Botterweck, Helmer Ringgren and Heinz-Josef Fabry, 15 vols. (Grand Rapids, MI: Eerdmans, 1974–2006), 15:205.

22. According to Matthew 18:1, "the disciples" are the hearers of Jesus' words in the first half of chapter 18 (v. 2–20). The expression "the disciples" is in some cases limited to the Twelve, as implied in Matthew 18:18, and, in other cases, includes other followers; see Karl Heinrich Rengstorf, *"apostellō,"* in *TDNT*, 1:424–27; Schmidt, *"kaleō,"* in *TDNT*, 3:517–18.

23. Jeremias, *"kleis,"* in *TDNT*, 3:752; Cullmann, *Peter: Disciple, Apostle, Martyr*, 211.

24. Friedrich Büchsel, *"deō (lyō),"* in *TDNT*, 2:61–62; Cullmann, *Peter: Disciple, Apostle, Martyr*, 210–11.

25. Büchsel, *"lyō,"* in *TDNT*, 4:335–37; Cullmann, *Peter: Disciple, Apostle, Martyr*, 211.

26. Büchsel, *"katara,"* in *TDNT*, 1:449.

27. Cullmann, *Peter: Disciple, Apostle, Martyr*, 211; William Barclay, *The First Three Gospels* (Philadelphia: Westminster Press, 1966), 94–95.

28. Büchsel, *"deō (lyō),"* in *TDNT*, 2:61; Cullmann, *Peter: Disciple, Apostle, Martyr*, 211; Raymond E. Brown, Karl P. Donfried, and John Reumann, eds., *Peter in the New Testament* (Minneapolis: Augsburg Publishing House, 1973), 97, 99.

29. Jeremias, "*kleis*," in *TDNT*, 3:751, 753 n. 86; examples are numerous.

30. Traub and von Rad, "*ouranos*," in *TDNT*, 5:519.

31. Jeremias, *Jerusalem in the Time of Jesus* (Philadelphia: Fortress Press, 1969), 239–42.

32. Jeremias, "*kleis*," in *TDNT*, 3:744–48.

33. Cullmann, *Peter: Disciple, Apostle, Martyr*, 209–10.

6

Peter, Stones, and Seers

Shon D. Hopkin

Shon D. Hopkin is an assistant professor of ancient scripture at
Brigham Young University.

Peter's stirring affirmation of Christ's messianic role found in Matthew 16:15–19 has been dear to Latter-day Saints since the days of Joseph Smith. His heartfelt testimony and the Lord's response to him have served as the seedbed for numerous discourses on gospel principles that have been particularly emphasized in the restored gospel.[1] This paper will first provide a close reading of these famous verses and will propose that Jesus' words "upon this rock I will build my church" (Matthew 16:18) equates Peter himself with the rock upon which the church would be built. A full discussion of how Jesus' disciples would have understood this statement connects Peter with the role of the high priest. One of the implications of this understanding points to a further connection, strengthened by Joseph Smith Translation, John 1:42, between Peter, the role of a seer, and the high priest's use of the Urim and Thummim. The last portion of this paper will explore these connections in order to demonstrate possible links between Peter, Joseph Smith, and Latter-day Saints today. The textual analysis that begins with Matthew 16:13–19 will lead back to the scriptural witness of 1 and 2 Peter at the close of this paper.

Peter's Witness in the Gospels

The account of Peter's testimony of Jesus as the Messiah that is familiar to most Christians is found in Matthew 16:

> When Jesus came into the coasts of Caesarea Philippi [meaning the environs surrounding Caesarea Philippi, or its towns, as stated in Mark 8:27], he asked his disciples, saying, Whom do men say that I the Son of man am?
>
> And they said, Some say that thou art John the Baptist: some, Elias [Greek for Elijah, the Old Testament prophet]; and others, Jeremias, or one of the prophets.
>
> He saith unto them, But whom say ye that I am?
>
> And Simon Peter answered and said, Thou art the Christ, the Son of the living God.
>
> And Jesus answered and said unto him, Blessed art thou, Simon Bar-jona: for flesh and blood hath not revealed it unto thee, but my Father which is in heaven.
>
> And I say also unto thee, That thou art Peter, and upon this rock I will build my church; and the gates of hell shall not prevail against it.
>
> And I will give unto thee the keys of the kingdom of heaven: and whatsoever thou shalt bind on earth shall be bound in heaven: and whatsoever thou shalt loose on earth shall be loosed in heaven.
>
> Then charged he his disciples that they should tell no man that he was Jesus the Christ. (16:13–20)

This passage is structured in layers of three, with three statements by Jesus (vv. 13, 15, 17–19). The last statement contains three parts, each in the form of a triplet with an initial proposition that is developed by two antithetical statements. The first part declares Simon blessed, the second part promises to build the church upon Peter, and the third part promises him the keys of the kingdom.[2]

A comparison with other versions of this account in the synoptic Gospels shows that Matthew's record—which likely built upon the Gospel of Mark[3]—contains important details lacking elsewhere, while the other accounts add little to Matthew's version. Luke 9:18 does provide the important element that one of Jesus' purposes in taking the disciples to Caesarea Philippi was to find time and space for prayer. Jesus' declaration that Peter's witness was revealed to him by his Father in Heaven connects well with Luke's description of prayer as one of the primary antecedents to that witness. Building on the teachings of Moroni at the end of the Book of Mormon, Latter-day Saints also see prayer as a primary precursor to obtaining a witness of the central truths of the gospel (see Moroni 10:4–5).

Verse 13

The location of Caesarea Philippi approximately twenty miles north of the Galilee served as a useful backdrop for Peter's conversation with the Lord. The city had been built up by the tetrarch Philip, one of the sons of Herod the Great. It was named after the Roman emperor Tiberius Caesar, with the added title of "Philippi" to distinguish it from the great city of Caesarea built by Herod the Great in the south along the Mediterranean. Today the area is known as Banias, an Arabic permutation of the Roman name Paneas, named in honor of the Greek deity Pan. Remains of Roman worship of Pan can still be seen carved as niches into the cliffs found there. Situated far away from the religious center of the Israelites at the base of Mount Hermon, the area had apparently been a location of idolatrous worship since Old Testament times and was known alternatively as Baal Gad (see Joshua 11:17) and Baal Hermon (see Judges 3:3), in honor of the Canaanite worship of Baal. By the time that the Gospel of Matthew was written, its readers would also have associated the location with the deaths of several Jewish prisoners who were thrown to wild animals there by Titus to celebrate his victory over Jerusalem and the Jews.[4]

As noted by Elder James E. Talmage in *Jesus the Christ*, the location was away from the regular environs of Jesus' teachings and required travel that would have afforded Jesus time to provide special instruction to his disciples away from the crowds that often followed him in other areas of Galilee.[5] Caesarea Philippi is the location of the primary source waters of the Jordan River, which spring from the base of the majestic Mount Hermon and rapidly become a strong river, leading to powerful waterfalls a short distance away. The combination of idolatrous worship, nationalistic pride, the immense "rock" of Mount Hermon, and the flowing streams of the Jordan each would have come together to highlight the truths that were communicated in this passage, that Jesus himself, not the false religions of the Canaanites, Greeks, or Romans, was the Messiah, the Son of God, and that from God sprang the knowledge of Jesus' role to Peter as the river sprang from the "rock" of the great mountain. Jesus' designation of Peter as the rock as he stood in front of the imposing Mount Hermon would likely have been a surprise to Peter and his companions, since Peter's behavior had clearly demonstrated courage and faith, but not necessarily the kind of consistency typically connected with mountains. Jesus' rebuke of Peter immediately following this commandment serves to further highlight that the designation of Peter as the rock was in some senses a prophetic call rather than a statement of current fact (see Matthew 16:21–23).

Verses 14–16

In verse 16, Peter's identification of Jesus as the Messiah, with the added phrase "the Son of the Living God" that is not included in Mark or in Luke, stands in contrast to the opinions of the Jews. These viewpoints connected Jesus with famous prophets such as Elijah, whose return was anticipated by the Jewish people (see Malachi 3:1; 4:5–6).[6] Matthew's witness not only saw Jesus as the Messiah who would come to save God's people, but proclaimed the much more profound sentiment that Jesus was of heavenly origin, the Son of God as compared with the ambiguous designation, "Son of Man," in verse 13.[7] This understanding is found clearly from the beginning of the Gospel of John but develops more gradually among Christ's Apostles in the Gospel of Matthew. Shortly before Peter's testimony, the disciples were constrained to exclaim, "Of a truth thou art the Son of God" (Matthew 14:33) after Jesus had calmed the storm. Peter's declaration and his subsequent experience on the Mount of Transfiguration allow for the culmination of this growing awareness of the disciples, albeit still without a full understanding of the necessary suffering and death that will be required of their Messiah. As will be shown below, the phrase "Son of God" did not just designate Jesus as of heavenly origin but also connected him with biblical expectations of the Davidic Messiah.

Verse 17

In Jesus' response to Peter, he calls him Simon bar-Jona, "or son of Jona" (Greek *Bariōna*). However, since John 1:42 and 21:15 both identify Simon Peter as the son of John (*Iōannou*),[8] it is difficult to know what his father's real name was.[9] The Greek designation of Jonah may have simply been the way in which the Aramaic name for John was transliterated into Greek.[10] The designation of bar-Jona in Matthew 16, however, could also have been an intentional redaction with several possible purposes. First, the name "Jonah" serves to remind the reader of the sign of Jonah that had earlier been introduced as a prophecy of Christ's death and Resurrection (see Matthew 12:38–41). Second, the identification of Peter with Jonah points to the similarity of these two figures as those who were reluctant to take the gospel to the Gentiles but did so at God's command. Third, the name Jonah, which means "dove" in Hebrew, could connect with the presence or witness of the Spirit of God, as it did at Christ's baptism in Matthew 3:16. In light of this interpretation, Jesus' statement could identify Peter as one who has been born of the Spirit, becoming, in a sense, the son of the dove. A related way of reading this passage is that Christ is the new Jonah (because of his three days in the grave) and that Simon has become a child of Christ.[11]

Verses 18–19

These verses have been more hotly debated by biblical commentators than any other statements of Jesus.[12] Some scholars have seen this entire passage as created decades later at the time of the composition of the Gospel of Matthew, most likely in Antioch of Syria, an area where Peter spent much time and where his leading role in the Christian church would have been an important point.[13] Notwithstanding the likelihood that Matthew was composed many decades after the life of Jesus in Antioch, there are a number of clues—accepted by many scholars today—that point to an earlier, Aramaic foundation for the statement. Certain phrases appear to be connected much more closely to a Semitic/Aramaic linguistic background rather than a Greek linguistic background: "gates of hell," "bind and loose," "flesh and blood," possibly "bar-Jona," and others.[14] In other words, these concepts would not have been phrased in the same way unless they were first spoken in a Semitic language such as Aramaic.[15] If the Aramaic origins of the statement are accepted, various arguments have been proposed to explain why the statement is only included in Matthew, the most prevalent of which suggests that it was originally connected to a Resurrection setting.[16] This paper will proceed on the premise that the original Aramaic speaker of this statement was Jesus and that his words were included in Matthew because of the unique timing and audience of that Gospel's audience, Jewish Christians, as will be explained below. Mark's and Luke's presumed primary audience of Gentiles[17] would have been less concerned with the implications of Jesus' words.

An approach at appropriately interpreting the identity of the "rock" upon which the church would be built is only possible via an analysis of the meanings and interconnections of the following key words from the passage: "Peter" (Greek *petros*), "rock" (*petra*), "church" (*ekklēsian*), "keys" (*kleidas*), "bind . . . loose" (*dēsēs . . . lysēs*), and "gates of hell" (*pylai hadou*).

Rock

If Jesus is accepted as the source of the "rock" statement, then that statement would have first been made in Aramaic and the only viable interpretation of the rock upon which the church would be built is Peter. When Jesus told Simon that he (Simon) was the rock, he was playing upon a name—Kephas (Aramaic *kêpā[s]*)[18]—that the Gospel of John records had first been given to Peter when Jesus called him to become a disciple: "When Jesus beheld [Peter], he said, Thou art Simon the son of [John]: thou shalt be called Cephas (pronounced Kephas), which is by interpretation, A stone" (John 1:42).[19] Protestant commentators have often emphasized the difference between the Greek for Peter—*petros*, or a stone— and the *petra*, or bedrock/foundation upon which Jesus says that the church would be built: "Thou art Peter (*petros*), and upon this rock (*petra*) I will build my church."[20] For many of these commentators, Jesus was not saying that the community or church would be built upon Peter, since Peter was only a "stone," not a "bedrock," but was merely using Peter's name as a wordplay to distinguish him from the greater bedrock of Christ on which the church would be built. Because of Roman Catholic claims of authority based on their direct descent from Peter's authority, this Protestant interpretation of *petros* vs. *petra* became one of the most important ways to refute the authority of that church.

If, however, as is likely, Peter's name in the Gospel of Matthew is based on the Aramaic for rock—*kepha* (*kêpā*)—then this argument breaks down. In Aramaic there is no designation for *kepha* that would differentiate the *petros* from the *petra*. Both words would have been the same in Aramaic. Only when placed in the Greek do these terms of necessity differ. Although that difference could be understood as a purposeful one in the Greek of the Gospel of Matthew, it is much more likely that the Aramaic was translated into Greek in the only way possible. When used as a name for the male figure of Peter, the word *petra* was necessarily altered to its male form of *petros*, creating the differing forms in this verse.

The view that Peter is the rock does not eliminate the significance of other biblical images that picture Jesus or the gospel of Christ as the rock. Scriptural symbols are not mutually exclusive and often build on each other. Thus biblical and restoration-scripture references to Jesus or the gospel as the rock provide the supporting imagery that will be discussed below. Paul's statement "For other foundation can no man lay than that is laid, which is Jesus Christ" (1 Corinthians 3:11) builds on Old Testament witnesses (see Isaiah 28:16; also 1 Peter 2:6–8; Romans 9:33) and is supported by Book of Mormon prophets such as Helaman: "Remember that it is upon the rock of our Redeemer, who is Christ, the Son of God, that ye must build your foundation" (Helaman 5:12). Joseph Smith also understood Christ as the rock, stating that "Christ was the head of the church, the chief cornerstone, the spiritual rock upon which the church was built, and the gates of hell shall not prevail against it."[21] Other biblical and restoration verses refer to Jesus' gospel using similar imagery (see Matthew 7:24; 3 Nephi 27:8; Doctrine and Covenants 11:25, 18:17, 39:5). Peter, of course, had just borne witness of the same concept that these verses are teaching: that Jesus was the Messiah, the one with true heavenly authority to build a church, a concept he had learned through direct revelation.

The proposal that Peter was the rock to which Jesus referred fits well with literary themes developed in the Gospel of Matthew. Peter alternates between strength and weakness—walking on water, being called "Satan" by Jesus, denying Christ, and more—but is consistently seen as the spokesman for the other Apostles (see Matthew 15:15, 19:27, 18:18).[22] After his glorious Ascension, Christ would leave the management of his new community in the hands of imperfect humans, but he would endow those leaders with great power to effectively support the church, as shown by Peter's strength in the book of Acts. Doctrine and Covenants 1:17–20 connects the imagery of Peter as the weak one called to lead the church with the role of Joseph Smith: "I, the Lord . . . called upon my servant Joseph Smith, Jun., and spake unto him from heaven, . . . The weak things of the world shall come forth [that] . . . every man might speak in the name of God the Lord."

The view of Peter as the first bishop in Rome, who subsequently handed down authority and primacy to that office continuing to the present day, has in the past been a central holding pin of the Catholic claim to apostolic authority through direct succession. The view that Jesus named Peter the rock upon which his church would be built does not of necessity, however, serve as a complete support for the Roman Catholic claims to authority, since scholars from all backgrounds have demonstrated that this understanding of Peter did not develop in the Roman Catholic Church until many centuries later.[23]

Latter-day Saints, of course, also claim a direct connection to Peter, who descended from the heavens in order to bestow priesthood authority upon the heads of Joseph Smith and Oliver Cowdery, who subsequently passed that authority on to others. Each possessor of the Melchizedek Priesthood in the church traces his priesthood lineage back to the rock or foundation of Peter. As Doctrine and Covenants 27:12–13 describes it, "Peter, and James, and John, whom I have sent unto you, by whom I have ordained you and confirmed you to be apostles, and especial witnesses of my name, and bear the keys of your ministry and of the same things which I revealed unto them; unto whom I have committed the keys of my kingdom." From the Latter-day Saint point of view, the gates of death and hell did not prevail against the early church or against Peter, who was resurrected through the power of the Messiah of whom he bore testimony, in order to come forth in the last days to restore the keys of apostolic power and authority. In order to understand the full implications of the church or community, the keys, and the powers that Jesus was describing to Peter, those terms need to first be viewed in connection with the concept of Peter as the rock.

Church

With the understanding of the rock described above, Jesus was stating that the church would be built upon Peter. Paul later offered related imagery when he called Peter, James, and John "pillars" that held up the church of God (Galatians 2:9).[24] Jesus' statement can be seen as the declaration of a new covenant community, built upon the rock of Peter, just as his ancient covenant community was hewn from the rock of Abraham: "Look unto the rock whence ye are hewn . . . Look unto Abraham your father, and unto Sarah that bare you: for I called him alone, and blessed him, and increased him" (Isaiah 51:1–2). One scholar has suggested that prophetic figures such as Abraham (and, by extension, Peter) typically received new names when God gave them a people to lead.[25]

But how would Jesus' listeners have understood this reference to a church or community (ekklēsia)? Since Jesus' statement was prophetic, it was also anachronistic.[26] Later on, at the time of the composition of Matthew, ekklēsia would have more specific connotations for the Christian community, but in Jesus' day it could refer to any called assembly or gathering, and in Roman usage referred to a civil institution: the citizens were the ekklēsia who were called together by the herald.[27] In light of the Aramaic foundation of the statement, the original was most likely qāhāl, a word translated as ekklēsia more than one hundred times in the LXX (i.e., the Septuagint).[28]

Seen through the lens of Matthew's Jewish expectations, this assembly, or qāhāl, can most likely be understood as the fulfillment of the hope that the Davidic Messiah would usher in a new community, and that new community would be centered on the temple.[29] Many biblical scriptures speak of building a community,[30] and a text at Qumran has textual connections to this passage: "My soul went down to the gates of death . . . it is thou who will set the foundation upon rock . . . in order to build a stout building."[31] Peter had just proclaimed Jesus to be the Messiah, an identification that had connotations to temple building for Matthew's primary audience, connections that would have been missed by a primarily Gentile audience (possibly explaining why this passage was not included in Mark or Luke). Not only did messianic expectations in 2 Samuel 7:12–13 and 1 Chronicles 17:7–10 refer to the future temple builder—particularly Solomon, but with pointed messianic undertones as well—as a son of God, as Peter had just called him, but many other biblical verses prophesied of the role that the Messiah would take in building a renewed temple.[32]

The allusion to the "Son of God" scriptures that talk of Solomon with messianic undertones is further strengthened by the allusion to building in Matthew 7:24, in which Jesus says that the "wise man" (a potential allusion to Solomon or the Messiah) "built" his house upon "the rock." Who was the wise man? Solomon or Jesus the Messiah. What would the house be that both Solomon and the future Messiah would build? A temple. Upon what would Jesus the Messiah, the "wise man," build his house or his temple? Upon Peter, the rock.[33] Matthew accordingly shows Jesus speaking in positive terms about temple worship (see Matthew 5:23–24), and even shows him quoting a scripture that was seen as prophetically anticipating a renewed temple at the end of times (see Isaiah 56:7 and Matthew 21:12). The text of Matthew is picturing Jesus as the messianic temple builder, the Son of God, and Jesus is designating Peter as the rock upon which this community, centered on the temple or as a temple itself, would be built.[34]

As mentioned above, Paul picks up the imagery of temple building when he calls Peter, James, and John pillars, pointing many in his audience to the famous pillars of the temple known as Boaz and Jachin (see 2 Chronicles 3:17). The designation of Peter primarily as a rock upon which the future temple community would be built makes him the foundation stone of that temple,[35] an image Paul also uses in Ephesians 2:20: "[The household of God is] built upon the foundation of the apostles and prophets." Since the foundation of the temple would not have been the only temple stone important to Jesus' audience, other connections with the rock and the temple will be discussed further below.

Keys: Bind and Loose

After identifying Simon as Peter and indicating that he would build his church upon "this rock," Jesus went on to promise, "I will give unto thee the keys [Greek *kleidas*] of the kingdom of heaven: and whatsoever thou shalt bind [*dēsēs*] on earth shall be bound in heaven: and whatsoever thou shalt loose [*lysēs*] on earth shall be loosed in heaven" (Matthew 16:19). This assurance connects with a statement about palace authority in Isaiah 22:22, in which a figure known as Eliakim is given the authority of a viceroy: "the key of the house of David [Hebrew *maptēaḥ bêt-dāwiḏ*] will I lay upon his shoulder; so he shall open, and none shall shut; and he shall shut, and none shall open." In Isaiah 22:24, Isaiah prophesies that "they shall hang on [Eliakim] all the glory [or "weight" (Hebrew *kĕḇôḏ*)] of his father's house," a possible connection with the weight of the church being placed upon Peter. Although this statement could simply be interpreted as indicating that Eliakim, a servant of Hezekiah, would be promoted and given authority in the palace that would allow him to determine who would enter before the king, most have understood the Eliakim "prophecy" as having messianic undertones, especially in light of his possession of the key of the "house of David" and the reference to "his father's house."[36] Peter, then, was being promised the keys that would first be held by the Messiah.

In light of other elements of apostolic authority connected to the new community, or the "kingdom of heaven," these keys may give the ability to forgive sins (as mentioned in Matthew 18:18–22). Others have claimed that they included the ability to decide what behaviors were appropriate or inappropriate in the new church, since rabbinic teachers used the terms "bind" and "loose" to refer to things that were bound by law or those that were loosed or freed from legal regulations.[37] The power could also refer to the right to determine to whom permission to enter the new community would be granted and to whom it would be denied (such as first only allowing the gospel to go to the Jews and later extending that right to the Gentiles).[38] It should be noted that all of these rights were connected to priestly roles: the priests were the teachers of the law, they were those who granted access to the temple rites, and they were those who would have to approve entrance into the community, since they had authority over the rites that allowed that entrance.

The keys offered to Peter are understood by Latter-day Saints as the right to preside in the priesthood (see Doctrine and Covenants 107:8). According to Joseph Smith, they were given to Peter, James, and John when they ascended the Mount of Transfiguration with Jesus as recorded in Matthew 17:1–12. "The Savior, Moses, and Elias gave the Keys to Peter, James and John on the Mount when they were transfigured before him."[39] The keys of apostleship were then given in modern times to Joseph Smith and Oliver Cowdery by Peter, James, and John according to Docrine and Covenants 27.[40] Additional keys were also provided in the last dispensation to Joseph and Oliver in the Kirtland Temple by figures similar to those who appeared upon the mount: "The heavens were again opened unto us; and Moses appeared before us, and committed unto us the keys of the gathering of Israel . . . [and] after this, Elias appeared . . . [and] Elijah the prophet, who was taken to heaven without tasting death, stood before us . . . [and] . . . Therefore, the keys of this dispensation are committed into your hands" (Doctrine and Covenants 110:11–16).

President Boyd K. Packer has recounted a stirring experience in which President Spencer W. Kimball, visiting in Copenhagen, Denmark, testified that he, as the current prophet, was currently in possession of those Petrine keys:

> We were standing near the statue of Peter, whom the sculptor depicted holding keys in his hand, symbolic of the keys of the kingdom. President Kimball said, "We hold the real keys, as Peter did, and we use them every day." Then came an experience I will never forget. President Kimball, this gentle prophet, turned to President

Johan H. Benthin, of the Copenhagen Stake, and in a commanding voice said, "I want you to tell every prelate in Denmark that they do not hold the keys! I hold the keys!" There came to me that witness known to Latter-day Saints but difficult to describe to one who has not experienced it—a light, a power coursing through one's very soul—and I knew that, in very fact, here stood the living prophet who held the keys.[41]

The Gates of Hell

One element of the Eliakim prophecy that has often been missed by biblical scholars when discussing how Jesus' disciples would have understood his statement is that the imagery in the remainder of the prophecy pictures Eliakim not only as one connected to the Messiah and his kingly authority, but also provides clear connections to the sacred vestments of the high priest. In Isaiah 22:21, Eliakim is clothed with a "robe" (Hebrew *kuttānēṯ*; see Leviticus 8:7) that is circled by a "girdle" or sash (*'aḇnēṭ*; see Leviticus 8:7, 13), and the government is placed "in his hand" (*bĕyāḏô*; see Leviticus 8:33). Along with the "filling of the hand," a Hebrew phrase referring to the ordination of priests in Exodus 28:41, Leviticus 8:33, and many other places,[42] Eliakim is also "called" in verse 20. He is told that he will act as a "father" "to the house of Judah" in verse 21.[43] Other phrases in Isaiah 22:22–25 that refer to "his father's house" may also have either palace or temple connotations, such as "a nail in a sure place," the "throne of his father's house" (23), referring either to a kingly throne or to the mercy seat of the Holy of Holies, and the "vessels" (24).[44] All of these images appear to purposefully point to the role of the high priest and the temple, and Jesus uses language designed to connect Peter with that role.[45] In fact, a Jewish explanation or midrash of this passage identifies Shebna, the man that Eliakim will replace, as the high priest.[46] Numerous references in later Jewish literature discuss the role of the priests as holders of the "keys" to the temple.[47]

With this understanding of Peter's role as connected to the temple, the reference to the "gates of Hell" (Greek *pylai hadou*; see Matthew 16:18) suggests an additional understanding for the "rock" upon which the church would be built and the "keys" that Peter would hold. In addition to Jewish connotations with the foundation stone of the temple, the giant rock found in the Holy of Holies (possibly where the "throne" or mercy seat sat) was understood by Jews as the foundation stone of the world, and as the gate to the world of the dead (Greek *Hades* or Hebrew *šĕ'ôl*). Many Christians have understood Jesus' promise that "the gates of Hell shall not prevail" as an assurance that the power of the devil would not prevail against the church in a way that would cause a general apostasy.[48] Biblical commentators, however, have understood the reference to *Hades* or *She'ol* as indicating an assurance that death itself would not triumph over the church. In other words, even if the leaders and members of the new community should die or be killed, the kingdom of God would still survive.[49]

For Latter-day Saints, a belief in a general apostasy would not necessarily contradict Jesus' promise, considering the Restoration of the gospel in the last days and the fact that the very person to whom this promise was made conquered death through the power of the Resurrection in order to return in resurrected form and provide priesthood authority to Christ's church. Rather, from a Latter-day Saint viewpoint, the promise would provide hope during the difficult days of martyrdom and apostasy ahead. When the church was organized in 1830, the Lord used language connected to this promise in Matthew 16: "Wherefore, meaning the church, thou shalt give heed unto all [Joseph Smith's] words and commandments which he shall give unto you as he receiveth them, . . . for by doing these things the gates of hell shall not prevail against you; yea, and the Lord God will disperse the powers of darkness from before you, and cause the heavens to shake for your good, and his name's glory" (Doctrine and Covenants 21:4–6).

Another fascinating connection for Latter-day Saints may be derived from the identification in Jewish literature of the foundation rock of the world, located at the center of the Holy of Holies, as a gateway to the world of departed spirits,[50] indicating that Peter would be given keys or authority to overcome the power or the claims of the world of spirits. Latter-day Saint views of the importance of keys given in the temple (see Doctrine and Covenants 110:11–16) to open or shut the gates of spirit prison and let the prisoners go free as a result of vicarious work for the dead are an interesting modern-day corollary to this promise. The connection becomes even more interesting in light of the existence of passages referring to Christ's descent to the prisoners in the world of the spirits in 1 Peter 3:18–20 and 1 Peter 4:6. The reference to Jonah, one who descended into the waters of death and was lifted out of those waters three days later, also supports this connection between Peter and the foundation rock of the world, since Jews understood the primordial ocean as connected to *Hades* and kept at bay by the stone in the Holy of Holies that served as a gateway to that world.

An additional implication of Peter's priestly role with the rock found in the Holy of Holies could also point to the high priest's ability to pass through the veil of the temple on the Day of Atonement, symbolically representing all of Israel and providing them the opportunity through him to enter into the presence of the Lord (see Leviticus 16:15). Joseph Smith referred to "keys" when he taught that encouraging God's people to enter into God's presence was one of the roles of Moses, and, by extension, of modern-day prophets:

> Moses sought to bring the children of Israel into the presence of God through the power of the Priesthood but he could not. In the first ages of the world they tried to establish the same thing... but did not obtain them but they prop[h]ecied of a day when this glory would be revealed. Paul spoke of the Dispensation of the fulness of times when God would gather together all things in one &c and those men to whom these Keys have been given will have to be there.[51]

Peter, "a Seer, or a Stone"

The Gospel of John indicates that Jesus gave Peter his name early on, as recorded in John 1:42. The Joseph Smith Translation for this verse suggests one more "rock" with which the disciples might have connected Peter's new, high-priestly role in connection with the temple: "Thou art Simon the son of Jona: thou shalt be called Cephas, which is by interpretation, *a seer, or* a stone" (italics indicate Joseph Smith Translation addition).[52] In what sense would the Jews of Jesus' day have connected Peter, the rock or stone, with a seer, one who would receive the knowledge of Jesus through "revelation"?

Multiple passages in the Hebrew Bible indicate that the high priest, the leading priesthood authority in Israelite society (and as such in at least one sense an equivalent to the Latter-day Saint prophet in the church), received precious rocks called Urim and Thummim (typically translated as "lights and perfections") as part of his priesthood calling. Aaron, the first high priest under the law of Moses, was given Urim and Thummim that he bore on or in the "breastplate of judgment" (see Exodus 28:30; Leviticus 8:8). He was to always wear the Urim and Thummim when he went in before the Lord. The Urim and Thummim appear to represent in some way "the judgment [Hebrew *mišpāṭ*] of the children of Israel" (Exodus 28:30). This description fits well with the possible functions of Peter's keys as described above. The concept of Aaron bearing the Urim and Thummim "before the Lord" would be particularly true on the Day of Atonement, the only officially designated time when the high priest entered into the Holy of Holies "before the Lord" to obtain forgiveness of Israel's sins. From a Latter-day Saint and Christian perspective, this passage connects the Urim and Thummim with the presiding priesthood authority in the land and his role as a type of Christ in representing all of Israel.

Moses' prayer in Deuteronomy 33:8 indicates a desire that the tribe of Levi would continue to be a possessor of the Urim and Thummim in the future, demonstrating a connection between the Urim and Thummim and the authority and power of the office of the Israelite high priest. The Urim and Thummim held by the high priest are closely connected with receiving revelation in other Old Testament passages. Numbers 27:21 indicates that Eleazar the priest should ask "after the judgment of Urim before the Lord" in order to determine the will of the Lord concerning Joshua and all of Israel. In this case "judgment" appears more closely connected to the decisions of the Lord regarding his people. First Samuel 28:6 makes reference to how the Urim and Thummim had been used in the past, indicating that it was one of the ways (including dreams and revelation to prophets) in which the Lord had provided answers and direction to kings of Israel through the high priest. The Lord's unwillingness to answer Saul through the Urim and Thummim (presumably in the hands of the high priest) demonstrates the Lord's rejection of him as king. Ezra 2:63 and Nehemiah 7:65 indicate that the lack of Urim and Thummim in the hands of the high priest demonstrated a lack of priesthood authority and that full priesthood authority would not be recognized again until a priest with Urim and Thummim once again arose. Each of these references loosely connects with Peter's role as one with authority, or "keys," given him by Christ to fully lead the church and to receive revelation on its behalf. The Aramaic *kepha* appears to allow this interpretation, since the Aramaic word can be understood as a foundation stone but was also used to describe a precious stone.[53]

Multiple scriptural references to the importance of stones through which a presiding authority could gain revelation are also found in restoration scriptures. In the Book of Mormon, Mosiah 8:13–19 discusses the ability of King Mosiah to look into stones or "interpreters" in order to gain knowledge. They were also given to the brother of Jared as two stones that he was to seal up with his account so that the one who received them would be able to translate or interpret his writings (see Ether 3:23; 4:5). These were the stones that Joseph Smith found with the Book of Mormon record when he first obtained the plates. In the 1835 manuscript prepared for the Doctrine and Covenants, he referred to them as the Urim and Thummim[54] (see Doctrine and Covenants 17:1; Ether 4:6–7; Joseph Smith—History 1:52), providing a textual link between the interpreters and the biblical Urim and Thummim.

The description of two stones in the possession of the brother of Jared is found in close proximity to another account of sacred stones that are not explicitly described as interpreters. When the brother of Jared sought a way for the Jaredites to travel in their eight boats without light, the Lord touched sixteen stones—two stones per boat. Later these stones are described in a manner that places them as symbolic lessons for God's way of leading all his children through the challenges of life: "And thus the Lord caused stones to shine in darkness, to give light unto men, women, and children, that they might not cross the great waters in darkness" (Ether 6:3). The description of those affected by the stones as including "men, women, and children" (rather than just the Jaredite voyagers) demonstrates that Moroni is describing a broader pattern in which God prepares stones such as the Urim and Thummim, or interpreters, in order to give mankind access to the light of revelation. This pattern certainly fits the sacred stones, but it seems to fit even better the pattern that God has followed of using prophets in order to lead his people through darkness through the power of inspiration. The description provides a link between the role of the stones and that of the seer, such as the link regarding Peter as a stone, or in other words a seer, in Joseph Smith Translation, John 1:42.[55]

References to the Urim and Thummim also exist in the Book of Abraham, in which they are used by Abraham to receive revelation (3:1), including an overarching vision of God's creations and the history of the world. Providing another link with Peter, keys, and the Urim and Thummim, Doctrine and Covenants 63:20–21 implies that a magnificent vision of the future of the world was opened to Peter, James, and John on the Mount of Transfiguration, similar to that had by Abraham, Moses, the brother of Jared, Nephi, John the Revelator, and others. Since Herod's temple operated under the Levitical Priesthood of the law of Moses, President Joseph Fielding Smith suggested that the Mount of Transfiguration functioned as a location where Melchizedek Priesthood temple ordinances could be revealed to Peter.[56] Indeed, Doctrine and Covenants 132:59 connects the keys of the priesthood with a sacred endowment of power from God. Through this lens, when Peter was given the keys of the priesthood promised in Matthew 16 and received the endowment of priesthood power, he had a vision of the future of the earth and became himself a seer, or a stone, one through whom the Lord would reveal truth to the world.

Joseph Smith, of course, also received the Urim and Thummim. Although the phrase was first added for the 1835 Doctrine and Covenants and does not exist in the 1833 Book of Commandments passage, Doctrine and Covenants 10:1 states that Joseph translated the Book of Mormon "by means of the Urim and Thummim."[57] Joseph had also found another stone, often referred to either as a seer stone or as the Urim and Thummim, that he used at times in his translation of the plates.[58] Some uncertainty still exists as to how Joseph used the Urim and Thummim and the seer stone to translate the plates. One of the methods he employed, according to some witnesses, included placing the stone (either the seer stone or Urim and Thummim) in a hat in order to exclude outside light, and then placing his face into the hat so that he could see the information that would appear in light by means of the Urim and Thummim.[59] Much like the Old Testament high priest, Joseph Smith was also known to inquire before God for revelation using the Urim and Thummim. At one point while seeking an answer to a biblical question, Joseph and Oliver "mutually agreed to settle it by the Urim and Thummim." Orson Pratt also describes Joseph using a seer stone to inquire of the Lord when Orson went to Joseph with a question.[60]

From the perspective detailed above, Jesus' designation of Peter as the rock right after he told Peter that he had learned of Jesus' messianic role through revelation was in part referring to Peter's role as the high-priestly possessor of the Urim and Thummim. Joseph Smith stated very clearly what has become a very important view for Latter-day Saints: "Peter obtained his knowledge through revelation, and if they could not know him they did not build upon him; they could not be his church; . . . whenever the church is built upon that rock, and have the revelation of heaven for their guide, as Peter had, the gates of hell cannot prevail against it."[61] Interestingly, early church fathers such as Origen, Ambrose, and Chrysostom also understood that it was Peter's testimony of and faith in Jesus that were commended in Matthew 16:18. According to them, the church was to be built on the type of experience Peter had.[62] Revelation 19:10 connects thematically with Peter's prophetic witness of Christ and supports the view that it is the testimony of Christ that stands at the center of the prophetic gift: "The testimony of Jesus is the spirit of prophecy." The wording of Doctrine and Covenants 21:4–6 relies upon language found in the famous promise to Peter, "[The prophet's] word ye shall receive, as if from mine own mouth. . . . For by doing these things the gates of hell shall not prevail against you." President Kimball has forcefully declared the constant existence of revelation to every presiding prophet from the time of Joseph Smith until the present: "I say, in the deepest of humility, but also by the power and force of a burning testimony in my soul, that from the prophet of the Restoration to the prophet of our own year, the communication line is unbroken, the authority is continuous, a light, brilliant and penetrating, continues to shine. The sound of the voice of the Lord is a continuous melody and a thunderous appeal."[63]

The writings of 1 and 2 Peter also support the connection of Peter with the high-priestly role that received revelation for the community of the church. Second Peter 1:19 states, "We have also a more sure *word of prophecy*; whereunto ye do well that ye take heed, *as unto a light that shineth in a dark place*" (emphasis added). Earlier in the same text it was made clear that this word of prophecy that "shineth in a dark place" is connected to the knowledge of Jesus (just as Revelation 19:10 connects the spirit of prophecy with the testimony of Jesus), "For if [the attributes of godliness] be in you, and abound, they make you that ye shall neither be barren nor unfruitful in the knowledge of our Lord Jesus Christ" (2 Peter 1:8). Peter's description of the "light that shineth in a dark place" is linguistically connected to Alma's description of Gazelem, "a stone, which shall shine forth in darkness unto light" (Alma 37:23).

Second Peter 1:20–21 goes on to further discuss the process of revelation through the Holy Ghost, affirming that prophets (or seers) have the right to provide or interpret scripture: "Knowing this first, that no *prophecy of the scripture* is of any private interpretation. For the *prophecy* came not in old time by the will of man: but holy men of God spake *as they were moved by the Holy Ghost*" (2 Peter 1:20–21; emphasis added). Having just introduced the concept that the "word of prophecy" is "as a light that shineth in a dark place" (2 Peter 1:19), the immediately following detail that the text is specifically referring to the "prophecy of scripture" by "holy men . . . moved upon by the Holy Ghost" links well with the claims of Joseph Smith regarding the Book of Mormon and the description of the translation process provided by others. Interestingly, this description is located in an epistle bearing the name of Peter, who was designated a seer and a stone in Joseph Smith Translation, John 1:42.

The First Epistle of Peter encourages true disciples to come unto Christ as a precious, living stone: "To whom coming, as unto a living stone [Greek *zonta lithon*], disallowed indeed of men, but chosen of God, and precious" (1 Peter 2:4). He follows this concept by indicating that as they come unto Christ they themselves will become "as lively stones [*zontes lithoi*] . . . an holy priesthood" (1 Peter 2:5). This democratic ideal in which all have the ability to become stones—similar to Joseph Smith's and Moses' desire that all would learn the spirit of prophecy—is so pronounced in this section of 1 Peter that the text became one of the primary points used in support of the Protestant view known as the "priesthood of all believers," the belief that all can hold the priesthood simply by exercising faith in Christ.[64] While Joseph Smith and Latter-day Saints do not interpret this concept in exactly the same way as Protestant Christians, the encouragement in 1 Peter is clear. Terms reserved for Abraham or Peter elsewhere are used here to describe the entire church. The same pericope in 1 Peter later employs language reminiscent of imagery that 2 Peter 1:19 uses to describe "the word of prophecy": "But ye are a chosen generation . . . that ye should shew forth the praises of him who hath called you out of darkness into his marvellous light" (1 Peter 2:9). The people were to become rocks of revelation themselves, seers or stones that would shine with light.

Joseph Smith did not simply serve as a type of seer stone for his people. Like 1 and 2 Peter, his revelations also show a willingness of the Lord to help others become seers as well. Joseph appears to have echoed the feelings of Moses in Numbers 11:29: "Would God that all the Lord's people were prophets, and that the Lord would put his spirit upon them!" Both prophets desired that all would learn the spirit of prophecy, which is "the testimony of Jesus" (Revelation 19:10). The Doctrine and Covenants also extends the role of a seer, one who can use a seer stone, beyond the high priest. According to Doctrine and Covenants 130:10–11, "The white stone mentioned in Revelation 2:17, will become a Urim and Thummim to each individual who receives one, whereby things pertaining to a higher order of kingdoms will be made known; And a white stone is given to each of those who come into the celestial kingdom, whereon is a new name written, which no man knoweth save he that receiveth it." In Doctrine and Covenants 130:11, the name of the possessor of the stone is also inscribed upon the stone, so that both the individual and the stone bear the same name. This connects well with Peter's experience, who was called a seer, or a rock. Elder David A. Bednar has recently repeated this interpretation of the "rock": "As is evidenced in Peter's reply and the Savior's instruction, a testimony is personal knowledge of spiritual truth obtained by revelation. A testimony is a gift from God and is available to all of His children."[65] In many respects, it is the testimony of Christ found in individual members of the church that keeps the "gates of hell" from prevailing against the restored church. As has been noted by President Henry B. Eyring, the church is "always one generation away from extinction."[66] When members of the church cease to have a burning witness of the gospel, the strength of the church will rapidly fade.

Conclusion

As has been shown, Jesus' own disciples would likely have connected his designation of Peter as the rock on whom the church would be built with Davidic, messianic expectations centered on the temple. Jesus was appointing Peter as the leader or high priest of his new community, one with temple authority over the gates of death, one with authority to use the Urim and Thummim to gain revelation for God's community, and possibly one with authority to help that community receive their own revelation and symbolically enter into the presence of God. If this understanding of Jesus' words is correct, it connects in remarkable ways with the witness of the Book of Mormon and other restoration scriptures, and with the modern-day experiences and teachings of Joseph Smith. Like Peter, the presiding high priest today holds the keys of temple work for the living and the dead. One of his greatest desires is to help the Latter-day Saints learn to gain revelation for themselves and return to God's presence, where they will dwell upon the glorified earth, which "will be a Urim and Thummim [i.e., a rock] to the inhabitants who dwell thereon" (Doctrine and Covenants 130:9).

Notes

1. A review of general conference talks, talks recorded in *Journal of Discourses*, and the teachings of Joseph Smith reveals 325 times that these verses have been quoted or referenced. These references, of course, are only the smallest fraction of the talks that have been given by General Authorities and individual members of the church since the days of Joseph Smith. See http://scriptures.byu.edu.

2. Stanley Hauerwas, *Matthew* (London: SCM Press, 2006), 402.

3. Other possibilities exist, including that Mark was the last of the three synoptic Gospels to be written and that it relied on Matthew and Luke. See M. J. Brown, "Matthew, Gospel of," in *The New Interpreter's Dictionary of the Bible*, ed. K. D. Sakenfeld (Nashville: Abingdon Press, 2008), 3:841–42; and E. B. Powery, "Synoptic Problem," in *The New Interpreter's Dictionary*, 5:429–34.

4. For information regarding Banias/Paneas, see Leander E. Keck, *The New Interpreter's Bible*, vol. 8 (Nashville: Abingdon Press, 1995), 343; and Tremper Longman III and D. Garland, eds., *The Expositor's Bible Commentary: Matthew–Mark* (Grand Rapids, MI: Zondervan, 2010), 9:415. Josephus recorded the death of the Jewish prisoners in William Whiston, trans., *The Works of Flavius Josephus: A History of the Jewish Wars* (Philadelphia: Kregel Publications, 1971), 3:9:7, 443–44.

5. James E. Talmage, *Jesus the Christ: A Study of the Messiah and His Mission According to Holy Scriptures Both Ancient and Modern*, Missionary Reference Library (Salt Lake City: Deseret Book, 1988), 334.

6. Although texts indicating a return of Jeremiah in the last days may be later than Jesus' time, Jeremiah's role as one who preached strongly against the people and the temple may have led to his identification in verse 14, and Jeremiah was often considered a representative of the entire group of the prophets. For reference to an eschatological appearance of Jeremiah along with Isaiah, see 2 Esdras 2:18. For Jeremiah as representative of all biblical prophets, see the list of Hebrew prophets found in *baraita B. Bat. 14b*. The *baraitot* are Jewish oral traditions that were not included in the Mishnah, but were compiled afterward and are relied on by the Talmud in assessing the validity of arguments. Jews maintained beliefs that many of the prophets would return before the end of the world, particularly those such as Enoch and Elijah for whom no death was recorded. See Donald Alfred Hagner, *Matthew 14–28*, Word Biblical Commentary (Dallas: Word Books, 1995), 467. The belief of the return of all prophets before the end of the world fits well with the Latter-day Saint concept of the great meeting at Adam-ondi-Ahman, described in D&C 27:5–14.

7. Matthew provides the title "Son of Man" in verse 13 to Jesus' question, "Whom do men say that I, the Son of Man, am?" Mark and Luke leave this title out, possibly because its ambiguous nature might have raised questions for their primarily Gentile

audiences. Although Bible references use the title in different ways (for example, in numerous designations of Ezekiel as a son of man), a Jewish audience would have been aware of its potential messianic implications as given in Daniel 7:13. See *Expositor's Bible Commentary*, 9:247.

8. Although the King James Version names Peter as bar-Jona[s] in both John 1:42 and John 21:15, the Greek clearly names him as the son of John in those places.

9. See D. J. Harrington, *The Gospel of Matthew* (Collegeville, MN: Liturgical Press, 1991), 247. For a full discussion of the issue, see Joachim Jeremias, in *Theological Dictionary of the New Testament*, ed. Gerhard Kittel, trans. and ed. Geoffrey W. Bromiley (Grand Rapids, MI: Eerdmans, 1965), 3:407–8; hereafter *TDNT*.

10. For this possibility, see the Lucianic Septuagint's similar designation for John in Nehemiah 6:18, 2 Kings 25:23, and 1 Chronicles 3:24.

11. Although the designation of Jonah could be a textual corruption, considering the other wordplay employed with Peter's name in these verses strengthens the possibility that the use of a similar literary technique in this case was intentional.

12. W. F. Albright and C. S. Mann, The Anchor Bible: Matthew (New York: Doubleday, 1971), 197.

13. See Geoffrey W. Bromiley, ed., "Peter," in *Encyclopedia of Christianity* (Grand Rapids, MI: Eerdmans, 2005), 4:170. See also John P. Meier, "Matthew," in *Anchor Bible Dictionary*, ed. David Noel Freedman (New York: Doubleday, 1992), 4:626. For a discussion of the importance of Antioch in the developing understanding of Christianity and for the provenance of the Gospel of Matthew, see Raymond E. Brown and John P. Meier, *Antioch and Rome* (New York: Paulist Press, 1983), 15–27.

14. See Jeremias, "*kleis*," in *TDNT*, 3:749–50; Karl Ludwig Schmidt, "*kaleō*," in *TDNT*, 3:520; Jeremias, "*pylē*," in *TDNT*, 6:924. See also Karl P. Donfried, "Peter," in *TDNT*, 5:257; W. D. Davies and Dale C. Allison Jr., *A Critical and Exegetical Commentary on the Gospel of Saint Matthew* (Edinburgh: T&T Clark, 1991), 2:605, 627; Hagner, *Matthew 14–28*, 465–66, 469–71.

15. I am not arguing here that the Gospel of Matthew was first written in Aramaic, but rather that this passage shows evidence that it was originally spoken in Aramaic and then translated to Greek. For a discussion of a possible Aramaic/Hebrew Gospel of Matthew that was then translated into Greek—a concept that I do not support—see Joseph A. Fitzmyer, *The Semitic Background of the New Testament* (Grand Rapids, MI: Eerdmans, 1987), 63–64; and Matthew Black, *An Aramaic Approach to the Gospels and Acts* (Peabody, MA: Hendrickson, 1998), 15–17.

16. For a summary, see Hagner, *Matthew 14–28*, 471; and Harrington, *The Gospel of Matthew*, 250.

17. Paul J. Achtemeier, "Mark, Gospel of," *Anchor Bible Dictionary*, 542–44; and L. T. Johnson, "Luke–Acts, Book of," *Anchor Bible Dictionary*, 404–8.

18. This chapter uses SBL academic style throughout. The style has been modified in the Hebrew and Aramaic transliterations to show spirantization (softening) of certain consonants for a general audience. Consonants that have a line beneath them received a "soft" or spirantized pronunciation anciently. Thus *b*=v, *p*=ph, *t*=th, and so forth.

19. This early naming of Peter may be supported by a similar identification in Mark 3:16.

20. Gundry, *A Survey of the New Testament*, 4th ed., 185; Meier, "Matthew," 623–24. For an ecumenical statement that encompasses the arguments in this paragraph, see Raymond E. Brown, Karl P. Donfried, and John Reumann, *Peter in the New Testament* (Minneapolis: Augsburg, 1973).

21. Joseph Smith to Isaac Galland, 22 March 1839; *Times and Seasons*, February 1840, 53; http://josephsmithpapers.org/paperSummary/letter-to-isaac-galland-22-march-1839?p=3.

22. The depiction of Peter as the spokesman for the other Apostles becomes less clear in the view of some biblical scholars who believe—based on their reading of certain passages in Acts—that James became the leader of the church at some point after Jesus' death. See Donfried, "Peter," 253–54.

23. See Erwin Fahlbusch and Geoffrey William Bromiley, *The Encyclopedia of Christianity* (Grand Rapids, MI: Eerdmans 1999), 171. Cyprian, in the third century AD, appears to have been the first of the church fathers to identify Peter as the first bishop of Rome, who subsequently passed his authority down to others.

24. Paul's imagery also relies on the concept of the church as God's temple, a view connected to Jeremiah 1:18. This concept is discussed extensively in Michael Patrick Barber, "Jesus as the Davidic Temple Builder and Peter's Priestly Role in Matthew 16:15–19," *Journal of Biblical Literature* 132, no. 4 (2013): 935–53.

25. Hagner, *Matthew 14–28*, 470. Schmidt sees a different *ekklēsia* as connected to a different word. See Schmidt, *TDNT* 3:525.

26. There have been numerous proposals for how to understand the community that is suggested in the Gospel of Matthew. For an excellent summary of six influential viewpoints, see Paul Foster, *Community, Law, and Mission in Matthew's Gospel* (Tubingen: Mohr Siebeck, 2004), 22–79.

27. David L. Turner, *Matthew* (Grand Rapids, MI: Baker, 2008), 404; Schmidt, *TDNT*, 1:518–26.

28. Even though ʿêdā was the word most frequently used for assembly or congregation in Jesus' day, Matthew used that word to refer to the Jewish assemblies at the synagogue. See Turner, *Matthew* 404; *New Interpreter's Bible* (Nashville: Abingdon Press, 1995), 346; Hagner, *Matthew 14–28*, 471; Harrington, *The Gospel of Matthew*, 251.

29. For discussions of Matthew's Davidic messianic expectations, see Lidija Novakovic, *Messiah, The Healer of the Sick: A Study of Jesus as the Son of David in the Gospel of Matthew* (Tubingen: Mohr Siebeck, 2003), 152–83; Young S. Chae, *Jesus as the Eschatological Davidic Shepherd* (Tubingen, Mohr Siebeck, 2006); and Joel Willitz, *Matthew's Messianic Shepherd-King* (Berlin: de Guyter, 2007).

30. Jeremiah 12:16, 18:9, 31:4, 33:7, 42:10; Amos 9:11; 1 Corinthians 3:9–15, 14:4–5,12; Ephesians 2:19–20; 1 Timothy 3:15; Hebrews 3:1–6; 1 Peter 2:5, 4:17; 1QS 5:5–7; 8:4–10; 9:3–6; 1Qp Habbakkuk 12:3; 4Q164. See Turner, Matthew, 405.

31. 1QH 6:24–28.

32. The messianic role was connected with temple building both in connection with its Davidic roots (see 2 Samuel 7:12–13, 1 Chronicles 17:7–10, and 4Q174) and, more importantly, with the anticipation of a renewed temple in the last days. See Isaiah 2:2–3; Ezekiel 37:26–27,40–48; Micah 4:1–2; Psalm 87:5–6; Zechariah 4:7–9; Tobit 14:5; Sirach 36:13–14; 2 Maccabees 1:29; 11Q19 47:1–18. 4Q174 links Nathan's prophecy to David with his messianic hopes for a temple in the end of times.

33. Barber, "Jesus as the Davidic Temple Builder," 942.

34. The Gospel of Matthew again connects the title "Son of God" with building and the temple when Jesus was accused of being the Son of God at his trial and he promises that he will rebuild the temple (see Matthew 26:61, 27:40). See Barber, "Jesus as the Davidic Temple Builder," 941.

35. W. D. Davies and Dale C. Allison, *A Critical and Exegetical Commentary on the Gospel According to Matthew* (Edinburgh: T&T Clark, 1988–97), 2:626–68; R. J. McKelvey, *The New Temple: The Church in the New Testament* (Oxford: Oxford University Press, 1969), 193–94; Tremper Longman III and David E. Garland, *The Expositor's Bible Commentary: Matthew–Mark* (Grand Rapids, MI: Zondervan, 2010), 9:410.

36. For a few scholars who have supported this connection, see H. Benedict Green, *Matthew, Poet of the Beatitudes* (Sheffield, England: Sheffield Academic Press, 2001), 135; J. A. Emerton, "Binding and Loosing—Forgiving and Retaining," in *Journal of Theological Studies* 13 (1962): 325–31; Davies and Allison, 2:640; Craig A. Evans, *Matthew* (Cambridge: Cambridge University Press, 2012), 314; John T. Willis, "An Interpretation of Isaiah 22:15–25 and Its Function in the New Testament," in *Early Christian Interpretations of the Scriptures of Israel: Investigations and Proposals*, ed. Craig A. Evans and James A. Sanders (Sheffield, England: Sheffield Academic Press, 1997), 344–51.

37. See Joel Marcus, "The Gates of Hades and the Keys of the Kingdom (Matthew 16:18–19)," in *Catholic Biblical Quarterly* 50 (1988): 449–52. The *Sipre* on Deuteronomy 32:25 actually speaks of this authority in connection with Eliakim's authority to open and shut, in a direct allusion to Isaiah 22:22.

38. Hagner, *Matthew 14–28*, 473; Robert H. Gundry, *A Survey of the New Testatment, Fourth Edition* (Grand Rapids, MI: Zondervan, 2003), 186.

39. Joseph Smith, History, 1838–1856, Volume C-1 [2 November 1838–31 July 1842], 546; http://josephsmithpapers.org/paperSummary/history-1838-1856-volume-c-1-2-november-1838-31-july-1842?p=546.

40. "How have we come at the priesthood in the last days? It came down in regular succession. Peter, James, and John had it given to them and they gave it to others." Smith, History, 1838–1856, Volume C-1, 546.

41. Boyd K. Packer, "The Shield of Faith," *Ensign*, May 1995, 7.

42. See James Hastings, *Encyclopedia of Religion and Ethics* (Edinburgh: T&T Clark, 1914), 12:494.

43. For the priesthood connection with fatherhood, see Judges 17:10.

44. See Exodus 37:16, Numbers 4:7–15, 1 Kings 7:50, 1 Chronicles 28:11–19, and Jeremiah 52:19.

45. Although I am responsible for the specific Hebrew connections, the proposal of Eliakim as a messianic high priest is by Barber, "Jesus as the Davidic Temple Builder," 944.

46. This is from the Midrash Rabbah. See Leviticus Rabbah 5:5.

47. Barber summarizes this literature effectively in "Jesus as the Davidic Temple Builder," 946–47.

48. Neil M. Alexander, ed., *NIB* (Nashville: Abingdom Press, 1995), 8:346.

49. Hagner, *Matthew 14–28*, 472; Albright and Mann, *The Anchor Bible: Matthew*, 196; George Arthur Buttrick, *The Interpreter's Bible*, 12 vols. (New York: Abingdon-Cokesbury Press, 1951), 7:452.

50. Gerhard Friedrich, ed., *Theological Dictionary of the New Testament* (Grand Rapids, MI: Wm. B. Eerdmans, 1985), 6:96.

51. Joseph Smith, History, 1838–1856, Volume C-1–2 [2 November 1838–31 July 1852], 547; http://josephsmithpapers.org/paperSummary/history-1838-1856-volume-c-1-2-november-1838-31-july-1842?p=547.

52. It is not possible for a modern reader to determine whether this addition by Joseph Smith was meant to restore an ancient meaning that had been lost from the text, or whether it was meant as modern prophetic commentary on the role of Peter and the role of prophets.

53. Gerhard Friedrich, ed., *Theological Dictionary of the New Testament*, 6:96.

54. Revelation, June 1829-E [D&C 17]; http://josephsmithpapers.org/paperSummary/revelation-june-1829-e-dc-17. W. W. Phelps appears to be the first to have referred to the interpreters and Joseph's seer stone as "Urim and Thummim," as can be seen in "The Book of Mormon," *The Evening and the Morning Star*, January 1833, 2.

55. A similar connection between seer and stone may be found in Alma 37, in which Alma the Younger asks his son to preserve the Nephite interpreters (see Alma 37:21, 24–25). The Lord states, "I will prepare unto my servant Gazelem, a stone, which shall shine forth in darkness unto light," whose purpose is to assist God's people in obtaining knowledge. The difficulty in distinguishing whether Gazelem refers to the servant or to the stone may indicate that both will "shine forth in darkness unto light."

56. "I am convinced in my own mind that when the Savior took the three disciples up on the mount. . . . He there gave unto them the ordinances that pertain to the house of the Lord and that they were endowed. That was the only place they could go. That place became holy and sacred for the rites of salvation which were performed on that occasion." Bruce R. McConkie, comp., *Doctrines of Salvation: Sermons and Writings of Joseph Fielding Smith* (Salt Lake City: Bookcraft, 1955), 2:170.

57. Revelation, Spring 1829 [D&C 10]; http://josephsmithpapers.org/paperSummary/revelation-spring-1829-dc-10.

58. Michael Hubbard MacKay, ed., *The Joseph Smith Papers: Documents, Volume 1: July 1828–June 1831* (Salt Lake City: The Church Historian's Press), xxx.

59. MacKay, *Documents, Volume 1: July 1828–June 1831*, xxxii.

60. MacKay, *Documents, Volume 1: July 1828–June 1831*, xxxv.

61. Joseph Smith, *Times and Seasons*, 15 February 1842, 693; http://josephsmithpapers.org/paperSummary/times-and-seasons-15-february-1842?p=7.

62. Donfried, "Peter," 257.

63. Spencer W. Kimball, "Revelation: The Word of the Lord to His Prophets," *Ensign*, May 1977, 78.

64. Fahlbusch and Bromiley, *The Encyclopedia of Christianity*, 172.

65. David A. Bednar, "Converted unto the Lord," *Ensign*, November 2012, 106.

66. Henry B. Eyring, "We Must Raise Our Sights," as quoted in *Book of Mormon Seminary Teacher Manual* (Salt Lake City: The Church of Jesus Christ of Latter-day Saints, 2012), 405.

7

The Accounts of Peter's Denial
UNDERSTANDING THE TEXTS AND MOTIFS

Eric D. Huntsman

Eric D. Huntsman is an associate professor of ancient scripture at
Brigham Young University.

*"And Peter remembered the word of Jesus, which said unto him, Before the cock
crow, thou shalt deny me thrice. And he went out, and wept bitterly"
(Matthew 26:75).*

The Passion narratives that chronicle Jesus' suffering and prayer in the Garden
of Gethsemane, his arrest, and the subsequent abuse and false judgment that
followed also include accounts of Peter's actions that night. These include his
overconfident declaration that he would never deny his Lord, his inability to stay
awake during his watch with the Savior in the garden, his impulsive attempt to
defend Jesus by the sword, and his eventual flight. But nothing stands out so poi-
gnantly as his repeated denial that he either knew Jesus or that he was one of his
followers. In many ways Peter's denials stand in glaring contrast with the portrait
of Peter painted elsewhere by the Gospels. Peter had been impulsive before and
would be again even on a few occasions after, but abandoning and, even worse,
denying association with his Lord seems clearly out of character with the disciple
otherwise known as "the rock."

Nevertheless, a memory of Peter's denial was a clear part of the Christian communal memory of what occurred that terrible night. All four of the canonical Gospels contain versions of the same basic story, presumably drawn from some sort of primitive Passion narrative, probably oral but perhaps even written, that was familiar to all of the Evangelists.[1] They each contain accounts of a prediction, in which Jesus announces that before the rooster crows that next morning Peter would deny Jesus three times. Beyond this, however, the Gospels present differences in the circumstances surrounding Jesus' pronouncement and use two different grammatical constructions in quoting it (see Table 1: The Prediction, p. 144). All four Gospels then have accounts of the fulfillment of Jesus' words to Peter, though these differ even more significantly than do the accounts of the prediction, seeming to disagree in the timing of Peter's disavowals, the people to whom he made the denials, and even in the details of where these statements occurred (see Table 2: The Fulfillment, see p. 145). Despite these differences, the attestation of the denials in all four Gospels and the unlikelihood that early Christians would create a story like this about one of their leading figures establishes the historicity of the basic story in the minds of even skeptical biblical scholars.[2]

Despite this, the apparent inconsistencies in the accounts caution against definitive interpretations of exactly what happened that night, let alone *why* Peter acted as he did. As a result, in Peter's case, as in the case of so many others in the scriptural record, we ought to be particularly careful about how we judge the actions and especially the motivations of historical figures about whose circumstances we know so little. Nevertheless, there is a long tradition of using Peter's failing that night first as a criticism of the Apostle himself and then as a model of how believers should *not* act.[3] This prevailing tendency has encountered occasional resistance, however, by some within the Latter-day Saint community, which has a long tradition of respecting leaders and avoiding unnecessary criticism. For instance, in a well-known speech to Brigham Young Univeristy faculty and students in 1971, then-acting President of the Twelve, Spencer W. Kimball, responded to criticisms of Peter. After reviewing several possible motivations for Peter's actions,[4] he concluded, "I do not pretend to know what Peter's mental reactions were nor what compelled him to say what he did that terrible night. But in light of his proven bravery, courage, great devotion, and limitless love for the Master, could we not give him the benefit of the doubt and at least forgive him as his Savior seems to have done so fully."[5]

Nevertheless, while we cannot—and should not—try to judge the motivations of *the historical figure* of Peter, the actions of *the literary character* certainly fit into the clear pattern of betrayal, abandonment, confusion, and fear that permeates the narratives describing Jesus' arrest and condemnation. While this pattern highlights the Savior's suffering and his utter aloneness during his atoning journey that night and the next morning,[6] it also teaches us lessons about ourselves as disciples. Not just Peter but all the disciples present failed Jesus that night, as do we each day as we fail to fully live up to our covenants. In this way the character of Peter helps us see our own weakness and need for Christ's grace.[7]

The Prediction

While Jesus and his disciples presumably spoke Aramaic, all four of the canonical Gospels were written in Greek anywhere from thirty to sixty years after the events that they describe. While two of the Evangelists have traditionally been identified as Apostles who would have been witnesses of many of the events that these Gospels preserve, all four exercise frequent literary license in how they craft their narratives, relating events and teachings truthfully enough but feeling free to sometimes order them differently, present different details, and emphasize particular ideas and themes. This pattern is particularly clear in the Gospels' different accounts of the prediction of Peter's denial. All four preserve the same basic points regarding what Jesus and Peter said to each other, which, presumably, the Evangelists drew from possibly different versions of the earliest primitive Passion narrative that had been circulating since the events of Jesus' death and Resurrection. Either before or just after the Last Supper, Peter expressed a great willingness to be faithful to Jesus. In spite of Peter's confidence, Jesus declared that before morning, signaled by the crowing of a rooster, Peter would, in fact, deny Jesus three times. Beyond this, however, the Gospels differ, though Matthew largely seems to follow Mark (see again Table 1: The Prediction). Despite these differences, however, Raymond Brown notes that "perhaps nowhere else in the [Passion narrative] do the Gospels agree so much in the overall flow of the story as in the denials of Jesus by Peter."[8]

The prevailing consensus of biblical scholarship holds that the Gospel according to Mark was the earliest of the four Gospels to actually be written. If this assumption is correct, then the Marcan version represents the earliest surviving written account of Jesus' prediction of Peter's denial (Mark 14:26–31). This version places Jesus's prediction after the Last Supper, thus framing the institution of the sacrament, by which believers remember and commit themselves to Jesus, with two predictions of betrayal, Judas' at the beginning (Mark 14:18–21) and Peter's after it is over.[9] In the Marcan account, the prediction of Peter's denial occurs on the Mount of Olives, where Jesus declares that all of his disciples would stumble or be caused to fall away [skandalisthēsesthei, KJV, "be offended"] that night.[10] He illustrates their expected behavior with a passage from Zechariah 13:7, using this prophecy about the sheep scattering after the shepherd had been struck to anticipate how the disciples would flee when Jesus was arrested in Gethsemane. Jesus softens how they would fail to stand with him, however, by promising that he would go before them into Galilee, which is later realized when he appears to them there after his Resurrection. Nevertheless, the prophecy of the disciples' flight causes Peter to confidently declare, "Although all shall be offended, yet will not I" (Mark 14:29).

It is this confident assertion that leads Jesus to reply in the Marcan version by saying, "Verily I say unto thee, That this day, even in this night, before the cock crow twice, *thou shalt deny me thrice*" (Mark 14:30; emphasis added). Jesus' prediction does little to daunt Peter's resolve: he emphatically declares that even if it meant that he would need to die, he would never deny Jesus, a sentiment that the other disciples all take up as well. This Marcan account thus establishes all of the basic elements of the prediction: a confident assertion by Peter that is met with a declaration by Jesus that Peter would in fact deny Jesus three times before morning. Mark's account emphasizes that the denials would occur "this day, even in this night," perhaps because Mark's presumed Gentile audience might not be familiar with Jewish methods of reckoning days beginning with sunset on the previous day. Otherwise the only other unique aspect of the Marcan account is the detail that the rooster would crow twice, while the other three Gospels mention the cock crowing once.[11] The reason for this difference remains obscure, though it might have been intended to make Jesus' statement seem proverbial, borrowing the counting figure of "for three . . . and for four" seen in Proverbs 30 and applying it to a rooster crowing twice and Peter denying thrice.[12] For those who give credence to the early Christian tradition that Peter in some way lay behind Mark's Gospel, the fact that the Marcan prediction is, in fact, the most detailed could reflect the possibility that the double cockcrow might preserve a vivid, personal memory of the Apostle himself.[13]

Generally assumed to have been the second Gospel to have been written, Matthew follows the Marcan account of the prediction very closely. The Matthean version (Matthew 26:30–35) similarly places the prediction on the Mount of Olives after the Last Supper and uses the Zechariah quotation in connection with Jesus' prediction that the disciples would all stumble (*skandalisthēsesthe*) in their faith in and devotion to Jesus that night. As is often the case, Matthew improves Mark's Greek grammar and style, which in this passage not only results in smoother Greek (and English for that matter) but also emphasizes Peter's confidence.[14] In the Matthean version, for instance, Mark's "Although all shall be offended, yet not I" is rendered "Though all men shall be offended *because of thee, yet will I never be of-fended*" (Matthew 26:33; emphasis added). Otherwise the prediction in Matthew differs from Mark only in omitting the explanatory reference to that night being part of that "day" and Mark's double crowing by the rooster.

Luke's Gospel, while generally following the basic outline of Mark, also shares much material, usually discourse passages, with Matthew. Luke frequently reworks this common material, however, and in addition, this Gospel contains important unique material, suggesting that it drew upon another independent source or sources. Accordingly, the Lucan version of Jesus' prediction of Peter's denial (Luke 22:31–34) differs significantly from the earlier Marcan and Matthean versions. First, it begins earlier at the site of the Last Supper rather than on the Mount of Olives. Also notable among these differences is Luke's omission of the prophecy of the disciples' being offended and scattered. This omission is in line with the Evangelists' consistently gentler treatment of the disciples, which includes omitting or at least downplaying examples of their failure and mistakes and portraying them in the Passion narrative as those who remain faithful to Jesus and do not flee or fall away.[15]

Instead the prediction episode begins in the Lucan account with Jesus praying for Peter, who is referred to, as is common in Luke, by his original name, "Simon." Jesus' prayer that Peter's faith not fail is followed by the injunction, "and when thou art converted [*epistrepsas*], strengthen thy brethren" (Luke 22:32). This direction may well have had particular meaning in this context, because the Greek *epistrepsas* literally means "to turn back again" and is rendered by the New Jerusalem Bible as "once you have recovered." This may have held out particular hope for Peter when his faith did fail, as was the case with the denials: he could turn back again and, after his recovery, be a greater strength to his brothers.[16] Likewise, Luke softens Peter's response. Rather than the brash, self-referential "I [will] never be offended," the Lucan account has Peter express willingness to follow Jesus: "Lord, I am ready to go with thee, both into prison, and to death," acts of faith that Peter would in fact accomplish later in his own mission.

Despite this generally positive focus on Peter in Luke, Jesus proceeds with his declaration that Peter will yet disown Jesus: "I tell thee, Peter, the cock shall not crow this day, before that thou shalt thrice deny that thou knowest me" (Luke 22:34). Given the general Lucan use of the name "Simon" instead of "Peter," the return to the name more commonly used by the other Gospels (John commonly uses the combined name "Simon Peter") may be significant,[17] suggesting perhaps that this was actually how Jesus addressed Peter in that moment. Since Mark and Matthew do not record Jesus as addressing Peter directly by name in their accounts of the prediction, Luke may have been following another source here, perhaps accounting for the considerably different wording "the cock *shall not crow* this day, *before that* thou shalt thrice deny that thou knowest me" (Luke 22:34; emphasis added). The difference, which is even more apparent in Greek than in the English of the King James Version, is more apparent still in the rendering of the New Revised Standard Version: "the cock will not crow this day, until you have denied three times that you know me" (more on the differences of this verse is discussed in the section "The Grammar of the Denial" below). Only after Jesus' prediction do he and his disciples proceed to the Mount of Olives.

The Johannine account of the prediction (John 13:36–38) is also still set at the place of the Last Supper, and it grows directly out of Jesus' earlier announcement after the meal that he would only be with his friends a little while longer and where he was going they could not come (John 13:33). When Peter asks Jesus to clarify where he is about to go, the Lord tells Peter that he cannot follow now but will later. Peter's response in this Gospel is not at first a self-confident declaration that he will never be offended but a seemingly genuine question: "Peter said unto him, Lord, why cannot I follow thee now?" (John 13:37a). Peter begins his rejoinder with a proclamation that he is ready to go with Jesus in the Lucan account as well (Luke 22:33), and the fact that they had not yet gone to the Mount of Olives in both of these Gospels creates an interesting parallel of David's sad departure from Jerusalem at the time of Absalom's rebellion (see 2 Samuel 15:13–37). As David was going across the Kidron towards the Mount of Olives, Ittai asked him where he was going and whether he could come with him, much as Peter asked Jesus where he was going and whether he could go with him. But the parallel is even stronger with the example of Hushai, whom David sent back to Jerusalem until he could return. Similarly, Peter could not follow Jesus at that time but was of more use to his Lord there.[18]

But in John's account Peter does not stop with a question about following Jesus. Rather, as in Luke, he proclaims, "I will lay down my life for thy sake" (John 13:37b). Here Peter seems to be purposefully echoing the words of Jesus in the Discourse on the Good Shepherd (see John 10:11) as he affirms his willingness to die for Jesus. But as Morris notes, "The exact opposite is true in two ways. In the first place Peter was not really ready, as the sequel would show. And in the second Jesus was about to lay down *his* life for Peter."[19] Perhaps because of Peter's lack of readiness at that point, in the Johannine account Jesus prefaces his prediction by saying, "Wilt thou lay down thy life for my sake?" and then proceeds with a prediction that in Greek is much closer to the Lucan version than that of Mark or Matthew: "Verily, verily, I say unto thee, The cock shall not crow, till thou hast denied me thrice" (John 13:38).

The Grammar of the Denial

Certain aspects of the Greek used to report Jesus' words to Peter could have bearing on how to understand what Jesus was saying to Peter in his prediction. These include the use of *amēn* to begin the pronouncement in three of the four versions and the possible meanings of the word translated as "deny" in each account. While the discussion of these words and their grammatical forms can be somewhat technical, it is important for assessing claims made regarding what Jesus may or may not have intended when he told Peter that he would deny the Savior that night.

In every version except for that of Luke, Jesus begins by saying "Verily [*amēn*] I say unto thee" (Mark 14:30; Matthew 26:30; John 13:38), with John characteristically doubling it to "Verily, verily" as he often does in his Gospel. The Greek transliteration of the Hebrew asseverative particle *'āmēn*, meaning "truly," was commonly used as a word of assent at the end of both Jewish and Christian prayers, becoming a liturgical formula meaning "so let it be."[20] Jesus' use of it, however, seems to have been idiosyncratic, because only he appears to have used it at the *beginning* of statements.[21] As such, this use of *'āmēn* emphasizes the truthfulness and validity of what he is about to say, and the effect of its use at the beginning of all the predictions (except for the one in Luke) emphasizes the solemnity on what Jesus is about to declare.[22] Thus Jesus' statement to Peter was not simply a saying but was a solemn, weighty pronouncement.

All four accounts use forms of the verb *arneomai* for "deny," John in its simple form and the synoptics in a compound form with the preposition *apo*. Meanings of *arneomai* or *aparneomai* range from "refuse or disdain" to "deny something or say that it is not true" and "repudiate, disown, or disclaim association with someone or something."[23] Although generally compound forms are stronger than simple ones, we should probably not see too much significance in the difference between the synoptic *aparnēsē* and the Johannine *arnēsē*, and the shorter, simpler form is used in the fulfillment section of all four texts each time that Peter actually does the denying.[24] Rather, what is more significant is what it meant to "deny" Jesus. Although the Lucan account has Jesus say that Peter will "thrice deny that thou knowest me" (Luke 22:34), the other three accounts have Jesus simply say that Peter will "deny me [*me aparnēsē* or *arnēsē*]" (Mark 14:30; Matthew 26:34; John 13:38). Then again, only once in the four accounts of these three denials does Peter actually "deny him [*ērnēsato auton*]" (Luke 22:57) directly (see the section "The Fulfillment" below). Otherwise Peter never denies anything in particular about Jesus—and, as President Kimball was anxious to emphasize, never denied that he was "the Christ."[25] Nor does he "disdain" Jesus directly. While we shall see that he does, in fact, deny that something is true, such as the charge that he was one of Jesus' disciples, this can only be seen as "denying Jesus" in the sense that Peter was repudiating Jesus by denying that he was his disciple or one of his followers. Consequently, the meaning of *arneomai* that consistently fits both the accounts of Jesus' prediction and the fulfillment is the idea that Peter would repudiate or otherwise disown Jesus.

While it has not been an important or regular feature of analysis outside of Latter-day Saint discussions, the actual grammar of Jesus' prediction has been the focus of some efforts among Latter-day Saints, at least since President Kimball's 1971 talk, which encouraged a few commentators to find another motive that would be less critical of Peter. The possibility that Jesus might have been commanding or directing Peter to deny knowing him is an attractive idea to those desiring to somehow excuse or better understand why Peter acted as he did that night.[26] Such commentators have suggested that Jesus had given such direction to Peter so that the Apostle, otherwise an ardent supporter and defender of his lord, could elude arrest and trial that terrible night, thereby surviving to lead the church.[27] Such attempts are usually rooted in possible meanings of the expression "thou shalt deny" in English, but such efforts require further examination of the Greek texts behind the phrase.

Assuming Marcan priority, the reading "before the cock crow twice, thou shalt deny me thrice [*tris me aparnēsē*]" in Mark 14:30 is the earliest version of Jesus' statement. In this instance, the verb *aparnēsē* appears as a second person singular future deponent indicative form. The natural sense of the future here is a predicative future, meaning that Jesus was foreseeing or prophesying what Peter would do. Some seeking to excuse Peter, however, have wondered whether this future might, as can happen in English, have had in addition the sense of a command. This sense is, in fact, possible in some periods of Greek.[28] For instance, such an imperatival use of the future, though rare, is found in Classical Greek, where it is known as the jussive future. Generally it has a *familiar* tone—as when we say to our children "you *will* go to bed!"—making it a somewhat weak form of the imperative.[29] This imperatival use was adopted and used fairly commonly in the Greek of the Septuagint to render *formal* injunctions and prohibitions, particularly in the case of divine commandments, the most notable example of which is the Ten Commandments (Exodus 20:3–17; Deuteronomy 5:6–21, Septuagint, or LXX).[30] Significantly, while there are cases of positive commands in the jussive future in the LXX (e.g., Leviticus 19:18–19, 22), most commonly it is used in negative prohibitions, and in the Ten Commandments themselves positive injunctions, such as "remember the Sabbath day" and "honor thy father and thy mother," appear in the standard imperative mood. Furthermore, the future imperative often follows a preceding imperative verb (for example, as in Genesis 40:14) rather than occurring in isolation.

Such a usage is rarer in the New Testament itself, but when it appears it is usually quoting the LXX or otherwise imitating the legal language of the Old Testament.[31] As a result, the future imperative appears mostly in Matthew, being uncommon in other New Testament authors.[32] However, because Matthew seems to be following the Marcan account in the prediction of the denial, it is unlikely that "thou shalt deny" in Matthew 26:34 reflects a Matthean jussive future. Moreover, in the Sermon on the Mount the independent injunctions of Jesus (i.e., when he is not quoting the Old Testament) usually appear in the imperative mood rather than in an imperatival future.[33]

Most problematic for the future-command argument, however, is the fact that it is only a possibility in two of the four prediction accounts—and in only one of three if, in fact, Matthew is following Mark. That is because the forms *aparnēsē* and *arnēsē* are grammatically ambiguous: while they can be the form of future indicative of this verb, they also look exactly like another form, the aorist subjunctive, that is required for certain sentence constructions. However, only the construction of Mark 14:30 and Matthew 26:34, which follows it, allows *aparnēsē* to be the future form.[34] These Gospels both begin Jesus' pronouncement with the introductory temporal phrase "before the cock crow [*prin phōnēsai*]" that is followed by the main clause "thou shalt deny me thrice [*tris me aparnēsē*]," clearly making *aparnēsē* a future form.

On the other hand, neither the Lucan nor the Johannine accounts allow the verb to be a future. The NRSV rendition of Luke 22:34 reveals that earlier Greek manuscripts of this account use a very different construction,[35] beginning with a main clause in the future that is followed by a subordinate temporal clause that requires *aparnēsē* to be an aorist subjunctive:[36] "I tell you, Peter, the cock will not crow [*ou phōnēsei*] this day, until you have denied three times [*heōs tris me aparnēsē*] that you know me."[37] This better Lucan reading is close to the Johannine version of Jesus' prediction, "The cock shall not crow [*ou mē phōnēsē*], till thou hast denied [*heōs hou arnēsē*] me thrice" (John 13:38), which differs only in making "shall not crow" more emphatic with a double negative in Greek, adding a relative pronoun after the subordinating conjunction, and using the shorter form *arnēsē*. As a result, the future form, which can be either predicative or imperatival, appears in only two of our four Greek sources (and Matthew may only be following the earlier Marcan version, leaving the future in only one of *three* sources).

While the future form in Mark (and by extension in Matthew) could be an imperatival future, the immediate context of Jesus' pronouncement in even these accounts also favors a prediction over a command. This is because in those two Gospels it is preceded by Jesus' statement that "All ye shall be offended because of me this night" (Mark 14:27; parallel Matthew 26:31), which is almost certainly a prediction because of its tie to the prophecy from Zechariah 13:7 that the sheep will be scattered when the shepherd is struck. If Jesus' saying about the disciples being offended is a predicative future, it follows that the saying about Peter's denial would likewise be predicative.

But in the end, this grammatical possibility in two of our four texts is not conclusive, because Jesus would presumably have been speaking to Peter in Aramaic, not Greek. In other words, arguments based upon the Greek grammar in all probability only represent the understanding of what the Evangelists (or their sources) thought Jesus meant or intended when he originally spoke in Aramaic. Attempts to get close to what his original saying might have been are not only difficult,[38] their results sometimes end up being as ambiguous as the Greek they are trying to clarify. For instance, the reconstructed Salkinson-Ginsburg Hebrew New Testament uses *tkḥš* (תכחש), a form which is imperfect for *aparnēsē*.[39] Perhaps even closer to what Jesus actually said, however, is the translation into Old Syriac, which, though a later dialect, is closest linguistically to Jesus' Palestinian Aramaic. Like modern attempts to translate the Greek back into Hebrew, the Syriac also uses the imperfect, in this case of the root *kpr* (ܬܟܦܘܪ). The imperfect in these Semitic languages can serve as both a future *and* an imperative, much as the Greek future can represent either futurity or in some instances a command.[40] Thus these attempts leave the uncertainty exactly where it was when only looking at the two Greek versions that use the future: Jesus may possibly have intended his pronouncement as a command, but it is just as likely, or more likely, that it was a prediction.

Accordingly, while arguments based upon grammar remain inconclusive, they incline against the possibility that Jesus had issued a command to Peter. As Elder Jeffrey R. Holland has observed, "We don't know all that was going on here, nor do we know of protective counsel which the Savior may have given to His Apostles privately."[41] Nevertheless, the context and a straightforward reading of the texts support the traditional interpretation that Jesus was predicting what Peter would do.

The Fulfillment

Considerable differences in the four Gospel accounts of the fulfillment of Jesus' words to Peter reveal either less certainty about what exactly happened or considerably more liberty on the part of the Evangelists in shaping the material they had to work with. As noted, the accounts diverge on the timing, audience, and even place of Peter's denials (see Table 2: The Fulfillment). The texts resist simple harmonization, and the fact that Matthew and Luke presumably were familiar with Mark's text makes the differences in their accounts even more unexpected.[42] Indeed, they agree only in the broad story that three times Peter was asked whether he was one of Jesus' followers or had at least been with him, and three times Peter denied either associating with or even knowing Jesus.

Once again, Mark's account, apparently the earliest and perhaps based upon Peter's own recollections or upon a tradition attributed to him, provides the basic story. Having followed Jesus and his captors at a distance, Peter joined with a group of the high priest's servants at his palace who were warming themselves by a fire (see Mark 14:54). Following a scene that Mark relates about the inquisition and maltreatment of Jesus at the hands of the Jewish authorities, the fulfillment episode begins when one of the high priest's housemaids (*mia tōn paidiskōn*) sees Peter by a fire in the courtyard and states that he had been with Jesus of Nazareth (Mark 14:66–67). Peter not only denies (*ērnēsato*, an aorist or "past" tense of *arneomai*) that this is true, he claims that he neither knows nor understands what she is talking about. He then retreats from the court into the porch, presumably to get away from his accuser. At this point a rooster crows once, something that only happens in the Marcan account at this point. Because this denial is preceded directly by the chief priest's interrogation of Jesus, the maid is portrayed as interrogating Peter at the same time but with very different results.[43]

While the King James Version reads that "a" maid sees him a bit later, the Greek text of Mark and most modern translations make it clear that this is the maid (*hē paidiskē*) who had seen him earlier (Mark 14:69). She remarks to those who are standing by that Peter was one of those with Jesus, which causes Peter to deny (*ērneito*) again, this time using the imperfect tense that may mean that he *kept* denying Jesus or that he *tried*, unsuccessfully, to disassociate himself from him.[44] The bystanders insist that Peter must be one of Jesus' following because he sounds like a Galilean. At this point "he began to curse and to swear, saying, *I know not this man* of whom ye speak" (Mark 14:71; emphasis added), and at this third denial the cock crows again, causing Peter to weep.

Matthew's account follows the basic line of Mark's, but in addition to generally improving Mark's Greek grammar and style, it also makes a few changes and additions (although some seeming differences, such as the KJV's "damsel" in Matthew instead of "maid" as in Mark, are more apparent than real because both use the same word, *paidiskē*, in Greek).[45] One of the changes is the introduction of "another maid" in Matthew 26:71 because this adds another person to the list of people to whom Peter denies Jesus. This difference, however, may well be explained by an editorial pattern or literary technique often found in Matthew, whereby he doubles the number of people that he found in his original source material,[46] perhaps because of his desire to establish "two witnesses" to fulfill the Old Testament requirement for two or more witnesses (see Deuteronomy 17:6; 19:15).

A more significant Matthean addition, however, is the adding of "with an oath [*meta horkou*]" to Peter's second denial (Matthew 26:72). This second denial is that Peter does not "know the man," something that Mark reserved for the third denial. This renunciation leads into the cursing and swearing (*katathematizein kai omnyein*) that Matthew, like Mark, has accompanying the third denial, when Peter once again denies knowing Jesus. The effect in Matthew is to highlight that Peter's denials progressively become both more public and more serious. Whereas the first denial had been made to the first maid in private and was a general denial, Peter's denial to the second maid is made in front of bystanders and with an oath meant to confirm that he did not know Jesus. The final denial, in which Peter again says that he does not know Jesus, is then in public, made with cursing and swearing that might imply a formal renunciation of his association with Jesus and even possibly numbering himself among those who curse him.[47] This supports the idea that *arnēsē* in this context meant "you will renounce or disown me."

Luke's account differs significantly from that of Mark and Matthew's. While it likewise takes place in the courtyard of the high priest, all three Lucan denials take place beside the fire without Peter withdrawing to the porch. Because Luke does not have a nighttime hearing before the Sanhedrin, Peter's ordeal takes place while Jesus is in the custody of the high priest's men but before the Lord's abuse and own questioning begin, which occurs in Luke only the next morning *after* the cock crows (see Luke 22:63–71). More significantly, however, Luke differs in the order of the denials and in two cases even to whom they are made. While the first denial is made to a maid as in Mark and Matthew, Peter's denial at that time is that he does not know Jesus, which is the last denial in the other two versions (see Luke 22:57).

The second Lucan denial, that Peter is not one of Jesus' followers, is made to "another [*heteros*]," who the Greek makes clear is a man and not another maid as in Matthew (Luke 22:58). The third denial, made to a second man (*allos*, which is also masculine),[48] is, in fact, the softest: it is simply that he does not know what the man is talking about (Luke 22:59–60), which is the first denial in Mark and Matthew, and in Luke this denial does not include any cursing or swearing. The overall effect seems to be a result of Luke's usual efforts to present the disciples in a better light and minimize their failings.[49] That said, the Lucan account nonetheless adds perhaps the most poignant detail to the scene: of the four accounts, only Luke's recounts that after the third denial, and before the rooster crowed, "the Lord turned [*strapheis*], and looked upon Peter" (Luke 22:61). But even in this, Luke may be offering a note of hope, for his portrayal of Jesus turning and looking may recall Jesus' prophecy to Peter that when he "had turned back" (*epistrepsas*; KJV, "art converted") he was to strengthen his brethren (Luke 22:32).[50]

As expected, the Johannine fulfillment account differs considerably from the synoptic accounts. First, rather than following from a distance on his own, Peter is actually accompanied by another, unnamed disciple who is known to the high priest and manages to get admission for both of them to his palace (John 18:15–16). This other disciple is frequently identified with the main source and possible author of the Gospel, the figure of the Beloved Disciple, who has been traditionally identified with John himself.[51] The existence of another informant beside Peter himself may account in part for some of the differences in the Johannine version. One of these differences is that the high priest in this instance is not the current high priest, Caiaphas, but rather his father-in-law, Annas (John 18:13), who had previously held the position but had since been deposed. Another difference is that the maid (*paidiskē*; KJV, "damsel") is specifically identified as a *thyrōros* or doorkeeper, meaning that she was the one through whom the other disciple had gained their admission. When she asks whether Peter was one of Jesus' disciples, his first denial in the Johannine account consists of the single statement, "I am not [*ouk eimi*]" (John 18:17). He then joins a group of men warming themselves by a fire.

Whereas Mark and Matthew placed Jesus' questioning by the Jewish authorities under the direction of Caiaphas *before* Peter's first denial, John places the questioning done by Annas and his associates after the denial (see John 18:19–23). This separates the first denial from the second and third, which only take place after Jesus is sent to Caiaphas, the current high priest, for more questioning. Peter, meanwhile, continues to warm himself by the fire, where those present repeat the doorkeeper's question about his being one of Jesus' disciples, and "he denied it [*ērnēsato*], and said, I am not [*ouk eimi*]" (John 18:25). Peter's third and final denial in John occurs when one of the high priest's servants, the brother of Malchus, whose ear Peter had cut off in Gethsemane, asks whether he had seen Peter in the garden. Peter denied again, and immediately the cock crowed (see John 18:27). As with the Lucan version, John's account of Peter's denials is actually softer, without the progressively more severe denials found in Mark and Matthew, and likewise lacking the accompanying cursing and swearing.[52]

While the words of Peter's third denial are not preserved by John, his response "I am not" in the first and second denials contrast markedly with Jesus' response to the high priest as preserved in Mark: to Caiaphas' question "Art thou the Christ, the Son of the Blessed?" Jesus responded simply, "I am [*egō eimi*]" (Mark 14:61–62; parallel Matthew 26:63–64).[53] While this particular interchange is not included by John, the *egō eimi* formula is a common expression on the lips of Jesus in that Gospel, highlighting the extent of Peter's disassociation from the Lord. John's account leaves the condemnatory crow as the last word, omitting any references to Peter's crying as is found in all three of the synoptic accounts.

Despite the considerable variety in the Gospel accounts, the basic elements of the fulfillment of Jesus' words to Peter are found in all four versions, namely that before the cock crowed near or at dawn the next morning, Peter would in some way deny Jesus three times. Also, while the timing, placement, and even audience of the denials are not always consistent, the usual substance of the denial seems to have been that Peter either denied knowing Jesus or having been one of his disciples, with his claim he simply did not understand the questioner being a less frequent variation. While President Kimball is correct that Peter never denied the revelation he had received at Caesarea Philippi regarding Jesus' divine identity and mission,[54] his denial of Jesus and his association is consonant with the still serious meaning of *arneomai*, which is to repudiate or disown.

The Motif of the Denial

Both the criteria of multiple attestation and embarrassment support the basic historicity of Peter's denial of Jesus, but the wide variation in the accounts suggests that the story was used somewhat freely as a motif by the Evangelists as part of what they were trying to accomplish in their depiction of the larger Passion narrative. Thus, while we ought to reserve judgment on the motivations of the historical Peter, it is worthwhile to see what the Gospel authors may have been trying to illustrate in their depiction of his actions as a literary character.

Indeed, to a certain extent asking why Peter did what he did is the wrong question to ask in the broader context of a Passion narrative, because these narratives focus mainly upon Jesus and what happened to him in the hours leading up to Calvary. In this regard the actions of Peter are part of the larger succession of events where Jesus is first let down by his friends—especially Peter, James, and John—who are not able to keep watch with him in Gethsemane. He is then betrayed by Judas and abandoned by his other disciples, their flight constituting what can be seen as a form of passive betrayal following Judas's more active treachery. In Mark and Matthew, Jesus' betrayal consists in particular in being "given over [*paradidotai*]": first Judas hands Jesus over to the chief priests, who give him over to Pilate, who then delivers him to the soldiers who will crucify him.[55] Peter's denial, then, simply appears as the next in a series of events where Jesus is abandoned by all who know him and handed over from one party to another. With Peter's threefold renunciation, Jesus' prophecy of his denial is fulfilled at the very moment when he is being accused of being a false prophet by the Sanhedrin in Mark and Matthew and by those who are mocking him in Luke.[56]

The net effect of all this is that from Gethsemane to Calvary Jesus walked what Elder Holland has called "the loneliest journey ever made, . . . the Savior's solitary task of shouldering alone the burden of our salvation."[57] Yet it was Peter who impulsively tried to defend Jesus in the garden until directed by Jesus himself to "put up his sword." And it was only Peter—except in John where he is accompanied by the other disciple—who, after his initial flight, tried to follow the Savior. In that sense, from a literary perspective, these efforts at supporting Jesus needed to be counterbalanced by the denial to ensure that, in the end, Jesus was alone throughout the experience. The importance of this lonely atoning journey to us can be seen in the fact that so many people experience, to some degree, aspects of some of the things that Jesus underwent that night as he not only suffered our sins, pains, and sorrows but also experienced the terrible realities of betrayal, false judgment, arrest, and rejection. No wife betrayed by a husband, no child abused by a parent, no friend rejected by another person will fail to resonate with Jesus' being betrayed by the kiss of a friend, abandoned by his disciples, denied by Peter, and falsely accused and condemned.[58]

Yet while the Passion narratives are primarily about Jesus, they also feature other characters, Peter foremost among them. In this regard, Peter is the perfect tragic character, good but not too good so that the audience, in this case the reader, can identify with him. His efforts to defend Jesus and then to follow him even after a temporary moment of terror and flight represent well the inadequate efforts of all of us to love and serve Jesus. This lesson may have had particular meaning for early Christians, particularly for the Marcan Christians who are presumed to have suffered persecution in Rome, when many of them may have failed in their discipleship and even renounced their Christianity.[59] The seriousness of such denial would have been apparent to them in the words of Jesus that "whosoever shall deny me before men, him will I also deny before my Father which is in heaven" (Matthew 10:33; parallel Mark 8:38; Luke 9:26, 12:9),[60] yet there remained hope, for he had also said, "whosoever speaketh a word against the Son of man, it shall be forgiven him" (KJV, Matthew 12:32; parallel Luke 12:10).[61]

The figures of Jesus and Peter are brought together in what has been called the "theology of the cross," most clearly seen in Mark. According to this proposal, Peter and the other disciples are not capable of being truly successful until after Jesus has actually died on the cross—in other words, until Jesus had completed the Atonement for them. Throughout the ministry they consistently failed to understand or act faithfully, and such failings accelerated in the final hours of Jesus' mission. Only when Jesus' atoning sacrifice had been completed did grace sufficient begin to flow, enabling Peter, and us, to be successful and valiant as disciples.[62] After the Resurrection that followed, Peter's rehabilitation is immediately implied in the angel's direction to go tell his disciples *and Peter* (see Mark 16:7; emphasis added), with Peter being singled out. Only then could Peter realize Jesus' other prophecy that night, that when converted, he would strengthen his brethren (Luke 22:32).[63] While the four accounts differ in detail and emphases, they teach the same basic points about Peter and his experience. As the foremost of the disciples, Peter serves as an "everyman" figure, both for the original disciples, the first generation of Christians, and all subsequent believers.

The use of Peter's denial in the Passion narratives of the four Gospels is not the only way the motif of his denial was or can be used. As Jared Ludlow's paper in this volume on the characterization of Peter in the Gospels demonstrates, the denial story was also the part of the portrait that the larger Gospel narratives paint of Peter. Regardless of how historically accurate this "many-sided picture of Peter" was, it certainly presents Peter as a relatable character, both to early Christians and to later believers. Thus the Evangelists emphasize different details about the basic story in order to apply them to teach universally applicable points.

Peter, Our Weakness, and Christ's Grace

Focusing on Peter's weakness that night can produce a distorted portrait of the chief Apostle, detracting from his full redemption and acceptance by Jesus and his subsequent ardent, devoted service to Christ and his kingdom. What should perhaps be the greatest lesson drawn from the denial stories is that Peter, like all of us, could make mistakes, but through Jesus Christ he could be fully redeemed, rehabilitated, and able to serve faithfully. As President Kimball observed, "If we admit that he was cowardly and denied the Lord through timidity, we can still find a great lesson. Has anyone more completely overcome mortal selfishness and weakness? Has anyone repented more sincerely? Peter has been accused of being harsh, indiscreet, impetuous, and fearful. If all these were true, then we will ask, Has any man ever more completely triumphed over his weaknesses?"[64] As has been often noted, Jesus' triple questioning of Peter, asking whether Peter loved him, at the end of John's Gospel provided an opportunity for Peter to proclaim his love three times, compensating for his earlier threefold denial (John 21:15–19). His subsequent faithfulness in feeding Christ's sheep through the course of his faithful ministry thus illustrated his complete rehabilitation.[65]

Ruth Fox, a sister of the Order of St. Benedict, has written: "It is commonly supposed that Peter himself must have painfully revealed his denial to the other disciples, perhaps for their strengthening. No one else [except perhaps the other disciple in John] was there to witness the event, and it is quite unlikely that such a disparaging story of the community's leader would have circulated if it were not true. It is indeed a beautiful and endearing quality for leaders to be able to confess their own weaknesses to those who look to them for guidance and compassion."[66] By showing his own weakness, Peter provided a model to other believers of how they could overcome their own weaknesses. Indeed, regardless of whatever our individual mistakes and failings might be, we all share in the same fundamental weakness, that as fallen men and women we lack both the ability to fully overcome our shortcomings and the strength to do any further good on our own. As Jacob taught in the Book of Mormon, "the Lord God showeth us our weakness that we may know that it is by his grace, and his great condescensions unto the children of men, that we have power to do these things" (Jacob 4:7; see Ether 12:27).

The strong affiliation that many early Christians felt with Peter's experience can be seen by the role of the rooster in Petrine iconography, particularly on graves.[67] Perhaps at the time of death and burial, the model of Peter's failure being overwhelmed by Christ's grace was a comforting one as they pondered the state of their loved ones' souls. His experience can also be encouraging for us. As Sister Fox went on to note, "Opportunities for conversion experiences like Peter's, with all the accompanying pain, often become the best means for one to enter into one's own total dependence upon God."[68] Then, just as the full power of Jesus' grace was manifested in Peter's momentary failure and his later complete redemption, so can it be with us: as we slip and fall, we too can repent and return to the Lord, who will accept our love and then empower us to overcome our weaknesses and press forward in Christ to do greater things in his strength.[69]

Table 1: The Prediction

Mark 14	Matthew 26	Luke 22	John 13	John 18
KJV 26 And when they had sung an hymn, they went out into the mount of Olives. 27 And Jesus saith unto them, All ye shall be offended because of me this night: for it is written, I will smite the shepherd, and the sheep shall be scattered.* 28 But after that I am risen, I will go before you into Galilee. 29 But Peter said unto him, Although all shall be offended, yet will not I. 30 And Jesus saith unto him, Verily I say unto thee, **That this day, even in this night, before the cock crow** [*prin phōnēsai*] **twice, thou shalt deny** [*aparnēsē*] **me thrice.** 31 But he spake the more vehemently, If I should die with thee, I will not deny thee in any wise. Likewise also said they all.	KJV 30 And when they had sung an hymn, they went out into the mount of Olives. 31 Then saith Jesus unto them, All ye shall be offended because of me this night: for it is written, I will smite the shepherd, and the sheep of the flock shall be scattered abroad.* 32 But after I am risen again, I will go before you into Galilee. 33 Peter answered and said unto him, Though all men shall be offended because of thee, yet will I never be offended. 34 Jesus said unto him, Verily I say unto thee, **That this night, before the cock crow** [*prin phōnēsai*] **thou shalt deny** [*aparnēsē*] **me thrice.** 35 Peter said unto him, Though I should die with thee, yet will I not deny thee. Likewise also said all the disciples.	KJV 31 And the Lord said, Simon, Simon, behold, Satan hath desired to have you, that he may sift you as wheat: 33 But I have prayed for thee, that thy faith fail not: and when thou art converted, strengthen thy brethren. 33 And he said unto him, Lord, I am ready to go with thee, both into prison, and to death. [34 And he said, **I tell thee, Peter, the cock shall not crow** [*ou mē phōnēsei*] **this day, before that thou shalt thrice deny** [*prin aparnēsē*] **that thou knowest me.**] NRSV 34 Jesus said, "I tell you, Peter, **the cock will not crow** [*ou mē phōnēsei*] **this day, until you have denied** [*heōs aparnēsē*] **three times that you know me.**" KJV 39 And he came out, and went, as he was wont, to the mount of Olives; and his disciples also followed him.	KJV 36 Simon Peter said unto him, Lord, whither goest thou? Jesus answered him, Whither I go, thou canst not follow me now; but thou shalt follow me afterwards. 37 Peter said unto him, Lord, why cannot I follow thee now? I will lay down my life for thy sake. 38 Jesus answered him, Wilt thou lay down thy life for my sake? Verily, verily, I say unto thee, **The cock shall not crow** [*ou mē phōnēsei*], **till thou hast denied** [*heōs hou arnēsē*] **me thrice.**	KJV 1 When Jesus had spoken these words, he went forth with his disciples over the brook Cedron, where was a garden, into the which he entered, and his disciples.

* Awake, O sword, against my shepherd, and against the man *that is* my fellow, saith the Lord of hosts: smite the shepherd, and the sheep shall be scattered: and I will turn mine hand upon the little ones. (KJV, Zechariah 13:7)

Table 2: The Fulfillment

Mark 14	Matthew 26	Luke 22	John 18
KJV 66 And as Peter was beneath in the palace, there cometh one of the maids of the high priest: 67 And when she saw Peter warming himself, she looked upon him, and said, And thou also wast with Jesus of Nazareth. 68 But **he denied** [*ērnēsato*], saying, I know not, **neither understand I what thou sayest.** And he went out into the porch; and the cock crew. 69 And [the] maid* saw him again, and began to say to them that stood by, This is one of them. 70 And **he denied** [*ērneito*] it again. And a little after, they that stood by said again to Peter, Surely thou art one of them: for thou art a Galilaean, and thy speech agreeth thereto. 71 But **he began to curse and to swear,** saying, I know not this man of whom ye speak. 72 And the second time the cock crew. And Peter called to mind the word that Jesus said unto him, **Before the cock crow** [*prin phōnēsai*] **twice, thou shalt deny** [*aparnēsē*] **me thrice.** And when he thought thereon, he wept.	KJV 69 Now Peter sat without in the palace: and a damsel came unto him, saying, Thou also wast with Jesus of Galilee. 70 But **he denied** [*ērnēsato*] before them all, saying, I know not what thou sayest. 71 And when he was gone out into the porch, another maid saw him, and said unto them that were there, This fellow was also with Jesus of Nazareth. 72 And again **he denied** [*ērnēsato*] **with an oath,** I do not know the man. 73 And after a while came unto him they that stood by, and said to Peter, Surely thou also art one of them; for thy speech bewrayeth thee. 74 Then **began he to curse and to swear,** saying, I know not the man. And immediately the cock crew. 75 And Peter remembered the word of Jesus, which said unto him, **Before the cock crow** [*prin phōnēsai*] **me thrice, thou shalt deny** [*aparnēsē*] **me thrice.** And he went out, and wept bitterly.	KJV 56 But a certain maid beheld him as he sat by the fire, and earnestly looked upon him, and said, This man was also with him. 57 And **he denied** [*ērnēsato*] **him,** saying, Woman, I know him not. 58 And after a little while another saw him, and said, Thou art also of them. And Peter said, Man, **I am not.** 59 And about the space of one hour after another confidently affirmed, saying, Of a truth this fellow also was with him: for he is a Galilaean. 60 And Peter said, Man, I know not what thou sayest. And immediately, while he yet spake, the cock crew. 61 **And the Lord turned, and looked upon Peter.** And Peter remembered the word of the Lord, how he had said unto him, **Before the cock crow** [*prin phōnēsai*], **thou shalt deny** [*aparnēsē*] **me thrice.** 62 And Peter went out, and wept bitterly.	KJV 15 And Simon Peter followed Jesus, and so did another disciple: that disciple was known unto the high priest, and went in with Jesus into the palace of the high priest. 16 But Peter stood at the door without. Then went out that other disciple, which was known unto the high priest, and spake unto her that kept the door, and brought in Peter. 17 Then saith the damsel that kept the door unto Peter, Art not thou also one of this man's disciples? He saith, **I am not.** 18 And the servants and officers stood there, who had made a fire of coals; for it was cold: and they warmed themselves: and Peter stood with them, and warmed himself. KJV 25 And Simon Peter stood and warmed himself. They said therefore unto him, Art not thou also one of his disciples? **He denied** [*ērnēsato*] **it,** and said, **I am not.** 26 One of the servants of the high priest, being his kinsman whose ear Peter cut off, saith, Did not I see thee in the garden with him? 27 **Peter then denied** [*ērnēsato*] **again:** and immediately the cock crew.

---

* While the KJV text reads "a maid," the use of the definite article in *hē paidiskē* makes it clear that this second figure is, in Mark, the same as the first.

Notes

1. Raymond E. Brown, *The Death of the Messiah* (New York: Doubleday, 1994), 51, 53–56, 92–93, 610–11; Eric D. Huntsman, *God So Loved the World: The Final Days of the Savior's Life* (Salt Lake City: Deseret Book, 2011), 127.

2. The story of Peter's denials is thus substantiated by two important criteria used in historical Jesus studies, namely multiple attestations and the so-called "criterion of embarrassment." See Brown, *Death of the Messiah*, 615–17, 620–21.

3. See, for instance, Robert W. Herron, *Mark's Account of Peter's Denial of Jesus: A History of Its Interpretation* (Lanham, MD: University Press of America, 1992).

4. Spencer W. Kimball, "Peter, My Brother," *Speeches of the Year* (Provo, UT: Brigham Young University Press, 1971), 1–8, reprinted pp. 375–86 in this volume. The possible reasons that Kimball reviews include possible cowardice (p. 2), confusion (p. 3), circumstances justifying the denial as an expedient act (p. 3), frustration from being prohibited from trying to stop the arrest and subsequent Crucifixion (p. 4), or reasons that we simply cannot know (p. 5).

5. Kimball, "Peter, My Brother," 5.

6. Jeffrey R. Holland, "None Were with Him," *Ensign*, May 2009, 86, 88; Huntsman, *God So Loved the World* (Salt Lake City: Deseret Book, 2011), 66, 78, 137 n. 2.

7. Huntsman, *God So Loved the World*, 68–69.

8. Brown, *Death of the Messiah*, 610.

9. R. T. France, *The Gospel of Mark: A Commentary on the Greek Text* (Grand Rapids, MI: Eerdmans, 2002), 573–74.

10. Walter Bauer, "skandalizō," *A Greek-English Lexicon of the New Testament*, rev. and ed. Frederick William Danker, 3rd ed. (Chicago: University of Chicago Press, 2000), 926. While the late Byzantine texts (such as A, K, and W) followed by the KJV include "because of me this night" (*en moi en tē nykti*), earlier better manuscripts (including ℵ, B, C*, D, and L) followed by most modern translations simply read, "You will stumble or fall away."

11. The difference in including "twice" (*dis*) is so great that some Greek manuscripts move it within the verse or even omit it altogether in attempt to harmonize Mark with the other Gospels. Nonetheless, the manuscript evidence is strong enough that textual critics are generally confident that this is the original reading. See Metzger, *Textual Commentary of the Greek New Testament* (Stuttgart: Deutsche Bibelgesellschaft, 1998), 96.

12. Brown, *Death of the Messiah*, 137. Other reasons summarized by Brown include the assonance of twice/thrice found in the Greek (*dis/tris*) or the fact that in Greek and Roman writing dawn was associated with the second cock crow.

13. France, *Gospel of Mark*, 579. For the issue of Petrine authority and the Gospel according to Mark, see Richard Bauckham, *Jesus and the Eyewitnesses: The Gospels as Eyewitness Testimony* (Grand Rapids, MI: Eerdmans, 2006), 155–82, as well as my "The Petrine *Kērygma* and the Gospel of Mark" in this volume. Regardless of whether the Marcan account preserves a direct memory from Peter, Thomas E. Boomershine, "Peter's Denial as Polemic or Confession," *Semeia* 39 (1987): 60, makes the case that the denial story could not have become a cornerstone of the early Christian tradition of the Passion unless Peter had originally told it and permitted it to be told about him.

14. John Nolland, *The Gospel of Matthew: A Commentary on the Greek Text* (Grand Rapids, MI: Eerdmans, 2005), 1090–91.

15. I. Howard Marshall, *The Gospel of Luke: A Commentary on the Greek Text* (Grand Rapids, MI: Eerdmans, 1978), 820; Brown, *Death of the Messiah*, 126, 135.

16. Marshall, *Gospel of Luke*, 821.

17. Marshall, *Gospel of Luke*, 818.

18. Brown, *Death of the Messiah*, 135.

19. Leon Morris, *The Gospel according to John*, rev. ed. (Grand Rapids, MI: Eerdmans, 1995), 563–64.

20. Bauer, "*amēn*," in *A Greek-English Lexicon*, 53–54.

21. Schlier, "*amēn*," in *Theological Dictionary of the New Testament*, ed. Gerhard Kittel, trans. Geoffrey W. Bromiley (Grand Rapids, MI: Eerdmans, 1964), 1:335, 337–38.

22. Brown, *Death of the Messiah*, 134, 137.

23. Bauer, "arneomai," in *A Greek-English Lexicon*, 132–33.

24. Brown, *Death of the Messiah*, 137.

25. Kimball, "Peter, My Brother," 3.

26. Although anecdotal evidence exists that President Kimball actually made this suggestion in his 1971 talk, there is nothing in the printed version or in the audio recording of the address corroborating this idea. This perception may arise from the fact that immediately after Kimball discussed expediency as a possible reason for Peter's denial (Kimball, "Peter, My Brother," 3), he noted in his discussion of frustration as a possible motivation that Peter had been "prohibited from resisting the coming crucifixion by the Redeemer himself" (p. 4).

27. For perhaps the best articulation of this possibility, see John F. Hall, *New Testament Witnesses for Christ: Peter, John, James, and Paul* (American Fork, UT: Covenant Communications, 2002), 65–66, and especially Andrew C. Skinner, "Peter— the Chief Apostle," in *Go Ye into All the World: Messages of the New Testament Apostles*, ed. Ray L. Huntington, Thomas A. Wayment, and Jerome M. Perkins (Salt Lake City: Deseret Book, 2002), 208–13, *n.b.* 212; Andrew C. Skinner, *Golgotha* (Salt Lake City: Deseret Book, 2003), 54–59.

28. Hall, *New Testament Witnesses*, 65–66, for instance, notes, "In Greek, a future tense verb in the second person can also be construed to express a command, just as if it were an imperative form of the verb. This usage is given the grammatical term of the 'jussive future.' It occurs not infrequently in both Classical and koine Greek."

29. Herbert W. Smyth, *Greek Grammar* (Cambridge: Harvard University Press, 1984), 428–29 (§1917).

30. F. C. Conybeare and St. George Stock, *Grammar of Septuagint Greek* (Grand Rapids, MI: Baker, 1995), 74 (§72).

31. F. Blass and A. Debrunner, *A Greek Grammar of the New Testament and Other Early Christian Literature*, trans. Robert W. Funk, 3rd ed. (Chicago: University of Chicago Press, 1961), 183 (§362).

32. Daniel B. Wallace, *Greek Grammar Beyond the Basics: An Exegetical Syntax of the New Testament* (Grand Rapids, MI: Zondervan, 1994), 452–53, 569.

33. Blass and Debrunner, *Greek Grammar of the New Testament* 183 (§362).

34. Huntsman, *God So Loved the World*, 68.

35. These include important manuscripts of the Alexandrian text family such as codex Sinaiticus (ℵ) and codex Vaticanus (B).

36. Blass and Debrunner, *Greek Grammar of the New Testament*, 195–96 (§383.2); Wallace, *Greek Grammar*, 479–80. While some may argue that in Classical Greek the subjunctive usually appears with the particle *an*, when *heōs* means "until" and is followed by the indicative, the verb is usually in the imperfect and "the future is very rare." Smyth, *Greek Grammar*, 548 (§2425). In New Testament Greek, on the other hand, the *an* can be omitted after *heōs*, as here in Luke, and is almost always missing after *heōs hou*, as in John 13:38. Blass and Debrunner, *Greek Grammar of the New Testament*, 195 (§383.1); Wallace, *Greek Grammar*, 479 (John 13:38 n. 2).

37. The somewhat awkward "before that thou shalt thrice deny" of the KJV followed the later Byzantine text known as the Textus Receptus, which reads *prin ē tris aparnēsē*, a construction that would require *aparnēsē* to be a future indicative. Nevertheless, the future here is being required for the subordinate temporal clause and could not be an imperatival future.

38. For the methods that can be used, together with some of the challenges associated with this process, see Maurice Casey, *Aramaic Sources of Mark's Gospel* (Cambridge: Cambridge University Press, 1998), especially 73–110.

39. *The New Testament*, Salkinson-Ginsburg Hebrew text, ed. Eric S. Gabe, 3rd ed. (Hitchin, Hertfordshire, England: Society for the Distribution of the Hebrew Scriptures, 2000), 59, 100, 167, 210.

40. J. Weingreen, *A Practical Grammar for Classical Hebrew*, 2nd ed. (Oxford: Clarendon Press, 1959), 75–77 (§39–41) and 88 (§48c); Theodore Nöldeke, *Compendious Syriac Grammar* (London: Williams & Norgate, 1904), 208 (§266).

41. Holland, "None Were with Him," 87.

42. Neil J. McEleney, "Peter's Denials—How Many? To Whom?" *Catholic Biblical Quarterly* 52 (1990): 468.

43. Ruth Fox, "Peter's Denial in Mark's Gospel," *Bible Today* 25 (1987): 298–99.

44. These are the so-called iterative and conative renderings of the Greek imperfect. See France, *Gospel of Mark*, 621.

45. Nolland, *Gospel of Matthew*, 1138, posits that Matthew might, in fact, have had a second source in addition to Mark but otherwise, 1140–43, notes Matthew's deviations from Mark as being stylistic.

46. McEleney, "Peter's Denials," 468, 471; Nolland, *Gospel of Matthew*, 375.

47. Birger Gerhardsson, "Confession and Denial before Men: Observations on Matt. 26:57–27:2," *Journal for the Study of the New Testament* 13 (1981): 52–55. Nolland, *Gospel of Matthew*, 1142, agrees but also notes that Peter could be cursing himself here, and either way he is condemning himself by his act.

48. The separation of the bystanders into the two separate men in Luke is an editorial technique that McEleney, "Peter's Denials," 469, 471, calls "clearing the stage."

49. Marshall, *Gospel of Luke*, 839.

50. Brown, *Death of the Messiah*, 608.

51. Brown, *Death of the Messiah*, 596–97.

52. Brown, *Death of the Messiah*, 623–24, who also notes that Peter here is mostly a foil for the more consistently faithful other disciple.

53. Brown, *Death of the Messiah*, 599, 622.

54. Kimball, "Peter, My Brother," 3.

55. Brown, *Death of the Messiah*, 211–13.

56. Brown, *Death of the Messiah*, 622–23

57. Holland, "None Were with Him," 86.

58. Huntsman, *God So Loved the World*, 66.

59. Brown, *Death of the Messiah*, 141, 625.

60. Brown, *Death of the Messiah*, 608; Gerhardsson, "Confession and Denial before Men," 48–49.

61. Gerhardsson, "Confession and Denial before Men," 62–63.

62. Brown, *Death of the Messiah*, 624–25. See also Martin Hengel, *Saint Peter: The Underestimated Apostle*, trans. Thomas H. Trapp (Grand Rapids, MI: Eerdmans, 2006), 43.

63. Gerhardsson, "Confession and Denial before Men," 62.

64. Kimball, "Peter My Brother," 2.

65. James E. Talmage, *Jesus the Christ* (Salt Lake City: Deseret Book, 1916, repr. 1982), 693; Gerhardsson, "Confession and Denial before Men," 62; F. F. Bruce, *The Gospel of John* (Grand Rapids, MI: Eerdmans, 1983), 404–5; Huntsman, *God So Loved the World*, 69.

66. Fox, "Peter's Denial in Mark's Gospel," 301.

67. D. Gewalt, "Die Verleugnung des Petrus," *Linguistica Biblica* 43 (1978): 114–16; Brown, *Death of the Messiah*, 621 n. 63.

68. Fox, "Peter's Denial in Mark's Gospel," 303.

69. Huntsman, *God So Loved the World*, 69.

8

Healing, Wholeness, and Repentance in Acts 3

Jennifer C. Lane

Jennifer C. Lane is an associate professor of Religious Education at
Brigham Young University–Hawaii.

After Luke's account of the events of Pentecost and the further establishing of Christ's church in Acts chapter 2, we see Peter and John continuing to live and worship in Jerusalem. They go to the temple to pray "at the hour of prayer, being the ninth hour" (Acts 3:1) and encounter a beggar at the gate of the temple that is known as the Beautiful Gate.[1] This would probably have been a commonplace event for the Apostles and for any Jews who worshipped and prayed at the temple. An entry point to sacred space would have been a strategic location for someone like this beggar who, unable to walk from birth, would have contributed to his family finances by begging for alms. We read that he was "laid daily at the gate of the temple" (v. 2).

This ordinary event of being approached by a beggar while going to worship takes on extraordinary layers of meaning as the setting for Peter's first miracle as the leader of the church in the post-Resurrection era. The subsequent healing, as recorded in Acts 3, contains a deeper spiritual message of Christ's power than we may recognize. Symbolic action, like all symbols, can have multiple meanings and great depth. After reviewing the events of the healing and different interpretations of the symbolic action of this healing, I will develop the image of healing and wholeness within the context of intertestamental views about ritual defilement and access to the temple.

One Afternoon at the Temple

The setting for this profound event was commonplace. Lying at the gate of the temple when Peter and John had come for the midafternoon hour of prayer was a man who had not been able to walk since birth. And so, "seeing Peter and John about to go into the temple," the man "asked an alms" (Acts 3:3). Rather than continuing on and ignoring the man, Peter must have felt prompted to engage with the man and to give a gift beyond what silver and gold could buy. After "fastening his eyes upon [the man]" and asking him to "look on us" (v. 4), Peter caught his attention. Luke explains that the man "gave heed unto them, expecting to receive something of them" (v. 5). Of course, based on his life experience the only thing that he could have hoped for would have been a generous financial gift.

Instead, Peter spoke directly of the contrast between the resources of this world and the priceless gifts available by the power of Christ. "Silver and gold have I none; but such as I have give I thee: In the name of Jesus Christ of Nazareth rise up and walk" (v. 6). Peter then "took him by the right hand and lifted him up" (v. 7). We learn that through this intervention in the name of Christ that "immediately his feet and ankle bones received strength. And he leaping up stood, and walked, and entered with them into the temple, walking, and leaping, and praising God" (vv. 7–8).

Peter's response to the man's request for alms begins with a powerful rhetorical contrast between "silver and gold have I none" and "such as I have give I thee." This rhetorical contrast alone makes this a memorable statement to this day, but in this historical setting Peter's focus on Jesus would have been electric. His gift was to say, "In the name of Jesus Christ of Nazareth rise up and walk." We need to remember that it would have likely still just have been months since the death of Jesus of Nazareth, and so this public witness of the power of Jesus and his living reality manifest through his servant Peter is the central message of this healing miracle. Those who watched it in this very public setting, as well as the man healed, were being taught that Jesus was the Messiah and that his messianic power to make the lame walk was still in effect (see Luke 7:19–22).

It is significant that, as the author of both the Gospel of Luke and the Acts of the Apostles, Luke emphasizes Jesus' healings as evidence that he is the Messiah. In the account in Luke 7 we learn of disciples of John who are going to learn of Jesus. They are witnesses of his healing power and thus are able to "tell John what things ye have seen and heard; how that the blind see, the lame walk, the lepers are cleansed, the deaf hear, the dead are raised, to the poor the gospel is preached" (Luke 7:22). These healings echo the passage in Luke 4 where Jesus in the synagogue in Nazareth testifies that he is the Messiah, literally the Anointed One: "The Spirit of the Lord is upon me, because he hath anointed me to preach the gospel to the poor; he hath sent me to heal the brokenhearted, to preach deliverance to the captives, and recovering of sight to the blind, to set at liberty them that are bruised, to preach the acceptable year of the Lord" (Luke 4:18–19).[2]

The Messiah was coming to heal and to include those who had been excluded. Christ had taught: "But when thou makest a feast, call the poor, the maimed, the lame, the blind" (Luke 14:13). Those others who were invited to the feast would not come, making excuses, but the feast of the establishment of the kingdom was designed to be inclusive of those who had hitherto been excluded: "Go out quickly into the streets and lanes of the city, and bring in hither the poor, and the maimed, and the halt, and the blind" (Luke 14:21). The healing power that testified of Jesus as the Messiah during his ministry was a symbol of the universal invitation to the kingdom and that witness continues as Peter heals in the name of Jesus.[3] Joseph Fitzmyer, a prominent New Testament scholar, notes that "for Luke the 'name of Jesus' connotes real and effective representation of Jesus himself."[4] By healing in the name of Jesus, Peter was making Jesus and his messianic power present to all who saw the miracle.[5]

Healing as Symbolic Action

Both the way in which Peter lifted up the lame man and the response of the man who was healed functioned as symbolic actions on multiple levels. These layers of symbolism are part of how Peter used this healing to teach and testify to the people gathered at the temple about the power and mission of Jesus Christ. I will briefly discuss insights into the symbolism of this healing and then develop an additional dimension that I think deserves further attention.

One reflection on the way in which Peter healed the man emphasizes how Peter is becoming more like his master, Jesus Christ, through the echo of the hand reaching out to rescue one who is faltering. Andrew Skinner describes Peter's healing in Acts 3 as a mirror of the Savior reaching out to him when he was sinking on the Sea of Galilee. He comments, "I also wonder if this episode didn't come back into sharp remembrance for Peter on a future occasion when he came across another person years later at the entrance to the Jerusalem temple who was struggling—only with a physical infirmity." Here Skinner emphasizes the healing of the lame man as a physical event. Skinner observes, "The parallel can hardly be missed. The chief Apostle took the floundering man at the temple by the hand and lifted him out of his distress just as Jesus had lifted Peter out of his distress years earlier on the Sea of Galilee [see Matthew 14:28–31]. This shows us just how much Peter was destined to become like his Master when he became the earthly head of the church."[6]

Another insight into the spiritual maturity and discipleship that Peter illustrated in reaching out to the man who needed healing is offered by President Harold B. Lee. President Lee emphasizes the way in which Peter's ministry and awareness of an individual in need mirrored the way the Lord reaches out to each of us and lifts us up. He notes that "Peter just didn't content himself by commanding the man to walk, but he 'took him by the right hand, and lifted him up.' (Acts 3:7)."[7]

President Lee continues, giving us insight into Peter's imitation of Christ, "Will you see that picture now of that noble soul, that chiefest of the apostles, perhaps with his arms around the shoulders of this man, and saying, 'Now, my good man, have courage, I will take a few steps with you. Let's walk together, and I assure you that you can walk, because you have received a blessing by the power and authority that God has given us as men, his servants.' Then the man leaped with joy."[8]

President Lee then applies this experience to us in a classic quote: "You cannot lift another soul until you are standing on higher ground than he is. You must be sure, if you would rescue the man, that you yourself are setting the example of what you would have him be. You cannot light a fire in another soul unless it is burning in your own soul. You teachers, the testimony that you bear, the spirit with which you teach and with which you lead, is one of the most important assets that you can have, as you help to strengthen those who need so much, wherein you have so much to give. Who of us, in whatever station we may have been in, have not needed strengthening?"[9]

Elder Marvin J. Ashton drew similar conclusions as he commented on Peter's noble example of friendship. "'And he took him by the right hand and lifted him up. . . .' (Acts 3:6–7). Peter was a friend. He told the beggar, 'Rise and walk; I'm going to help you.' We too must take the friend by the hand until he sees and finds that he has enough strength to go on his own. Is it not appropriate to conclude that Peter was willing to take the friend the way he was but left him improved?"[10]

More recently, Elder Jeffrey R. Holland has used this story of healing to emphasize not just the Christlike friendship and personal care that Peter illustrated, but also the miraculous blessings that the Lord has for each of us, far exceeding our expectations. He commented: "In this Church, you get a lot more than you bargain for. That man on the steps of the temple that day had no higher hope than that he would get a [coin]. . . . What he got were straightened legs and the chance to walk and leap and sing and praise God and go into the temple." Elder Holland then identified with the man who had been healed: "I testify that I count myself one among you, like the lame man on the steps of the temple, who never dreamed what lay in store."[11]

Fitzmyer observes how this story teaches of the abundance and restoration of blessings that Jesus came to bring. He emphasizes how Luke's description of healing is portrayed as a fulfillment of Isaiah's prophecy. He notes how "Luke describes the complete cure of the beggar and his consequent reaction in almost the same way that Isaiah once proclaimed the restoration of Zion: 'Then shall the lame one leap like a deer' (Isaiah 35:6)."[12] He is referring to the messianic prophecy of divine intervention that we are familiar with from the beautiful oratorio by Handel. Israel is promised: "Your God will come with vengeance; . . . he will come and save you. Then the eyes of the blind shall be opened, and the ears of the deaf shall be unstopped. Then shall the lame man leap as an hart, and the tongue of the dumb sing" (Isaiah 35:4–6). The day of salvation is made visible with the signs of healing associated with the Messiah.

Fitzmyer argues that by describing the lame man "leaping up," the language of Isaiah "makes it clear that Luke sees this miracle as a fulfillment of the prophet's utterance, an event of salvation history. The lame man's praise of God is duly noted. So he passes from paralysis to joyful activity, from begging to praising God within the Temple."[13] The healing of the lame man witnesses that a new day had dawned—that God had come to save.

Richard Pervo connects another symbolic meaning with the Acts 3:8 allusion to the Isaiah 35:6 prophecy of the day in which "the lame man [shall] leap as an hart," noting that this prophecy of the restoration of Israel would be reinforced by the observation that the man had been disabled for at least forty years (see Acts 4:22). Here forty becomes a symbol of alienation and then restoration. Pervo observes that "this healing represents an opportunity for the restoration (see Acts 3:21) of Israel."[14]

While I believe that all of these observations about these dimensions of symbolic action in the healing of the man at the gate of the temple are very important, I would like to suggest that we consider the possibility that Peter's healing illustrates and explains the power of Christ not just to heal bodies, but to reconcile fallen and unclean humanity to the presence of God, something that the law was not able to do (see Acts 13:38–39; Hebrews 10:1).

One detail of the account that has not been fully developed is the description that the man then "entered with them into the temple." The ability of this man to enter with Peter and John into the temple might not just be an additional witness of his physical healing through the power of Christ. It also corresponds with some historians' understanding of the intertestamental attitudes towards disability and defilement and how this healing would have made him whole and thus able to enter sacred space. So Peter's healing of this man through the power of Christ might not have just been about Peter becoming more like Christ by taking him "by the right hand, and lift[ing] him up" or his "leaping up" (v. 8), a witness that a new era in salvation history had been reached. The fact that this man was able to enter the temple may very well take on a spiritual as well as a physical dimension. Being whole through the power of Christ, he was no longer excluded from the sacred space. By associating Christ's ability to heal with access to the temple, this healing symbolically testifies of the spiritually healing power of the Atonement to give us access to the presence of God.

There is not a conclusive answer to the historical question about the status of the lame in this era, but there is strong evidence that this man was at the gate of the temple not merely because it was a strategic location for begging, but because his physical condition would have been seen as excluding him as unclean, having the potential to profane or pollute the sacred space.[15]

This interpretation gives additional insight into Peter's subsequent teaching about repentance after the healing. It is not that the lack of physical wholeness is a sin, but that physical healing can be a symbolic action to teach about Christ's power to heal spiritually, and thus invites us to trust him and to repent. A similar parallel can be found in Luke 5:17–26 with the story of the man with the palsy. The man asks Christ to heal him, who then says to him, "Man, thy sins are forgiven thee." This is not intended to mean that having a physical ailment was something to be repented of, but to show how spiritual and physical healing parallel each other and that Christ has the power to do both. Those listening to Christ tell him that his sins were forgiven thought that proclamation was blasphemous, "but when Jesus perceived their thoughts, he answering said unto them, What reason ye in your hearts? Whether is easier, to say, Thy sins be forgiven thee; or to say, Rise up and walk? But that ye may know that the Son of man hath power upon earth to forgive sins, (he said unto the sick of the palsy,) I say unto thee, Arise, and take up thy couch, and go into thine house. And immediately he rose up before them, and took up that whereon he lay, and departed to his own house, glorifying God" (Luke 5:22–25). Christ's ability to heal physical afflictions testifies of the power that is less visible, but of greater eternal worth: his ability to heal our souls.

Peter's Witness of Christ's Power: Wholeness, Holiness, and "Entering In"

In Acts 3, Peter not only heals "in the name of Jesus Christ" (v. 6) but also explains that "his name through faith in his name hath made this man strong" (v. 16). Peter's actions are a powerful symbolic witness of the gospel message that through Jesus Christ, the separation between unclean, polluted, and profane humanity (represented here by the lame man) and the holiness of God's presence can be overcome.

After the healing, the people at the temple were astonished at what they had seen. Peter had used the symbolic action of this healing as a very public teaching moment. Luke explains that "all the people saw him walking and praising God: and they knew that it was he which sat for alms at the Beautiful gate of the temple" (vv. 9–10), emphasizing again that he would have very likely asked alms of all of them. He was a very public figure, and this was a very public healing. As such the healing got people's attention: "they were filled with wonder and amazement at that which had happened unto him" (v. 10). It seems as though Peter and John accompanied the lame man as he walked in the temple, perhaps helping him make his way. We read that "as the lame man which was healed held Peter and John, all the people ran together unto them in the porch that is called Solomon's, greatly wondering" (v. 11). Just as he had after the events at Pentecost, Peter is about to skillfully use this miraculous event as an opportunity to teach people at a moment when their hearts and minds are open to receive the gospel.

The story here shifts to Peter using the healing as a way to teach of Christ's power to heal and cleanse and thereby invite people to repent. "When Peter saw [the people gathered and wondering], he answered unto the people, Ye men of Israel, why marvel ye at this? or why look ye so earnestly on us, as though by our own power or holiness we had made this man to walk?" (v. 12). Peter then testifies that Jesus was the Son of God and that he was rejected by his listeners, "whom *ye* delivered up, and denied him in the presence of Pilate, when he was determined to let him go. But *ye* denied the Holy One and the Just, and desired a murderer to be granted unto *you*; and killed the Prince of life, whom God has raised from the dead; whereof we are witnesses" (vv. 13–15, emphasis added).[16] Peter's audience will have thought that Jesus died because he was a blasphemous man who posed a threat to the Jewish people (see John 11:48–50; Mark 14:64). In addition, his death on the cross would have been seen as an additional witness that he died cursed of God (see Deuteronomy 21:23; Galatians 3:13). Peter needs to help them reframe their worldview and help them understand that Jesus died as a sinless sacrifice and that he has been raised up by God to provide healing to us all.

Peter is not talking to this audience to condemn them, but to let them know that they are unclean and in need of healing. He begins his explanation by reiterating that the power of Christ performed the miracle: "And his name by faith in his name hath made this man strong, whom ye see and know; yea, the faith which is by him [Christ] hath given him [the lame man] this perfect soundness in the presence of you all" (Acts 3:16). Peter compassionately acknowledges that the audience and the leaders of the Jews acted in ignorance, but emphasizes that Christ's death came as the fulfillment of the words of all the prophets (see vv. 17–18). It is important that his listeners understand that the death of Jesus Christ was foreseen and was part of God's plan of redemption.

Peter then gets to the central point of his address—he extends an invitation to repent and be converted "that your sins may be blotted out" (Acts 3:19).[17] His discussion continues and he finally ends with a witness of why Christ came and died, that "God, having raised up his Son Jesus, sent him to bless you, in turning away every one of you from his iniquities" (Acts 3:26). The access that the man who was healed now had to the temple through the name of Christ can symbolically represent the access that repentant souls have to the presence of God through "his name through faith in his name." The physical wholeness of the man through Christ's power symbolically represented the holiness and spiritual wholeness that is available through faith and repentance.

Wholeness and Holiness in the Torah

The symbolic connection between wholeness and holiness can easily be seen in the regulations about the temple in the law of Moses. This symbolic background from the Old Testament can help us understand Peter's teaching at the temple more fully. The impairment chapters of Leviticus illustrate spiritual principles symbolically by outlining the strict boundaries about who could officiate and approach the presence of God. The message of the holiness of the temple is reinforced with a focus on wholeness, just as the law required that the sacrificial animals be whole and unblemished (see Leviticus 22:20–25). In Leviticus 21 we read very clear prohibitions against physically impaired priests being able to "come nigh to offer the offerings of the Lord made by fire, . . . to offer the bread of his God, . . . [to] go in unto the veil, nor come nigh unto the altar, because he hath a blemish; that he profane not my sanctuaries: for I the Lord do sanctify them" (vv. 21–23). Along with excluding the lame and the blind, the disqualifying blemishes include "he that hath a flat nose, or anything superfluous, or a man that is brokenfooted, or brokenhanded, or crookbackt, or a dwarf, or that hath a blemish in his eye, or be scurvy, or scabbed, or hath his stones broken" (vv. 18–20). Some scholars see in the Levitical regulations about priests needing to be whole the roots of the intertestamental attitudes towards the lame and blind worshippers as also being excluded from the temple. Hector Avalos argues, "By the postexilic period the Priestly code, which may be viewed as an extensive manual on public health that centralizes in the priesthood the power to define illness and health for an entire state, severely restricted access to the temple for the chronically ill (e.g., 'lepers' in Leviticus 13–14; see also 2 Samuel 5:8 on the blind and the lame) because of fear of 'impurity.'"[18]

In addition to the limits on the impaired priests to "draw near" to the holiest places of the temple, in the Torah there is another explicit linking of wholeness and holiness for ordinary worshippers. The way in which some physical deformities would certainly have functioned to exclude worshippers as well as priests can be seen in the commentary on genital deformity or damage in Deuteronomy 23:1: "He that is wounded in the stones, or hath his privy member cut off, shall not enter into the congregation of the Lord."[19] Thus eunuchs or others with genital damage would clearly have been excluded from entering into the temple. Isaiah 56:3–5 is a moving passage that looks forward to the day when the eunuch who might say, "Behold, I am a dry tree" shall hear the Lord's assurance of inheritance and entrance into the temple: "For thus saith the Lord unto the eunuchs that keep my sabbaths, and choose the things that please me, and take hold of my covenant; Even unto them will I give *in mine house and within my walls* a place and a name better than of sons and of daughters: I will give them an everlasting name, that shall not be cut off" (emphasis added). This rejoicing that those formerly excluded shall inherit "in mine house and within my walls" is the spirit in which Peter's healing of the lame man may have been received.

Wholeness and Holiness in the Second Temple Period

The symbolic message of Peter's healing and the man's entrance into the temple is informed by both the specific prohibitions in the Old Testament and also by Old Testament passages that later became influential in shaping ideas about ritual defilement and the temple. Along with the exclusion of physically impaired priests from drawing near the altar in Leviticus 21 and the clear prohibition of all men with genital deformity in Deuteronomy 23, there is also a cryptic comment in 2 Samuel 5:8 that "the blind and the lame shall not come into the house." Some have suggested that this text informed or reflected attitudes towards wholeness and holiness in the Second Temple period. As I mentioned before, the question of the status of the lame in the Second Temple period is a debated issue in the scholarship, and I do not want to definitely claim that they were excluded from the temple during this period. But these insights can help to inform our understanding of the meaning of the events in Acts chapter 3.[20] By briefly exploring this text and the influence it had in the Second Temple Period we gain a clearer picture of how Peter's healing and the entrance of the man who had been healed into the temple would have been understood in its time period.

In its setting in the Old Testament this passage in 2 Samuel 5:8 appears as an authorial aside after a statement by David. "And David said on that day, Whosoever getteth up to the gutter, and smiteth the Jebusites, and the lame and the blind, that are hated of David's soul, he shall be chief and captain. Wherefore they said, The blind and the lame shall not come into the house." The first part of this passage could also be translated: "David had said on that day, 'Whoever strikes down the Jebusites, let him strike at the windpipe, for David hates the lame and the blind.'"[21]

There has been much discussion of the meaning of this text in the context of the Davidic political scene.[22] Clearly the phrase "wherefore they said the blind and the lame shall not come into the house" is a later addition or commentary. It can be seen as an etiological addition, using the past to explain why things are done in a certain way. McCarter argues that this "secondary parenthesis [is] offering an explanation of a practice current in the time of its author on the basis of the events described here."[23]

While the phrase "the house" might have had multiple meanings in the historical context of King David, for our purposes it is significant that by the second century BC, when the text was translated into Greek in the Septuagint, the term "the house," which in the original Hebrew might have some ambiguity referring to political dynasty or even David's palace, was explicitly rendered "the house of Yahweh," making it clear it was understood as the temple.[24] This evidence from the Septuagint means that this phrase may not have had this meaning during the time when 2 Samuel was written, but by the time it was translated into Greek, "the house" was clearly seen as the temple. This intertestamental understanding of the statement that "the blind and the lame shall not come into the house" is a critical piece in the argument that the lame would have been excluded from the temple during the Second Temple period.

While it is hard to be certain from the Greek translation of Samuel 5:8 exactly what the state of affairs was like in the first century, we do have additional support because the idea of excluding the physically impaired also exists in the writings of Qumran and in early rabbinic texts.[25] Olyan notes the influence of the 2 Samuel 5:8 passage on the Temple Scroll (11QT), arguing that the authors of the scroll, recasting "the restriction of 2 Sam 5:8b and elaborating upon it, proscribe the entry of blind persons into the sanctuary-city and associate the presence of such persons with pollution."[26] He argues that this expansion of the prohibition to include all of Jerusalem rather than just the temple is evidence that "in later times, some Jewish interpreters read 2 Sam 5:8b as a text with reference to worshipers," in other words, that they understood maimed or disabled worshippers to be excluded, not just priests. Olyan sees the broadening of the Old Testament restrictions in other Qumran documents beyond the Temple Scroll (11QTa 45:12–14).[27] He sees in this pattern an overarching movement towards a more extreme position towards that which can pollute.[28] So the exclusion of the lame and the blind from the temple in practice in the first century seems more likely when those in the Qumran community are taking this biblical basis and projecting from it the entire city of Jerusalem as off-limits to those who might pollute it. Olyan observes that, in addition to the texts of those associated with the Qumran community, "similarly, several tannaitic texts exclude blind and lame Jewish males from obligations to pilgrimage, probably echoing the concerns of 2 Sam 5:8b."[29] These tannaitic texts were written by Jewish teachers, known as the tannaim, in first and second centuries AD.

Thus I think we can have some confidence that at this time the idea of excluding the lame and the blind from the temple would have been familiar to many people, even if we cannot be certain that it was practiced or enforced. The image of moving from profane lack of wholeness outside the gate of the temple and then, as a whole man, entering into the holy presence of the temple would represent the bridging of a symbolic barrier and would illustrate the message of repentance that Peter was teaching through this symbolic action.

While in our day the idea that people with physical infirmities would be seen as unfit for God's presence seems extraordinarily prejudiced and hard to understand, it is important to remember that under the law of Moses over and over again spiritual truths were taught in symbolic ways, often through ritual impurity and cleansing. And while this particular exclusion, if it did exist in the Second Temple period, was not explicitly a prohibition on general worshippers found in the law, the spirit of the prohibition does makes sense in the symbolic universe of the law. John Pilch explains these ideas in a clear manner: "In the Israelite tradition, no matter how the impairment occurred, limited mobility was not the main concern; impurity was. 'You shall be holy, for I the Lord your God am holy' (Leviticus 11:45, 19:2, 20:26; 1 Peter 1:16). An impaired person was impure, because he or she was not whole or holy (Leviticus 21:18) and was excluded from the holy community (Leviticus 13:46) and its worship. For collectivistic personalities like the ancient Israelites, this consequence of impairment was catastrophic, a type of sociocultural death."[30]

How Can We Become Whole and Clean?

Understanding the lack of wholeness that the lame man may have symbolized can help us appreciate how such a healing in the context of the temple could represent how the spiritual barriers to God that were insurmountable in the law of Moses were able to be overcome through Jesus Christ. It is important to remember that the law of Moses very specifically and consistently reinforced the principles of purity and purification from impurity through the concept of ritual impurity. While these ritually impure states were likely designed as types and shadows to point to how sin makes us unfit for the presence of God, ritual impurity was different than not being worthy to have a temple recommend. It would be inevitable that human beings would become ritually impure through the very processes of mortality. In fact, it was specifically those things tied to the power to procreate and arrival of death that occurred as an ordinary part of human life that would make people ritually impure. Menstrual blood, childbirth, seminal emission, and touching dead bodies all rendered people ritually impure on a temporary basis (see Leviticus 12, 15, 22). But each of these forms of temporary impurity also had a means by which individuals could become clean—often some time needed to elapse, they needed to wash themselves, and perhaps make an offering at the temple. Even leprosy, once healed, had a means appointed within the law by which those formerly afflicted could be brought back to the temple as clean (see Leviticus 13–14). The law had within it the means of reconciling these forms of impurity.

The kind of pollution represented by the lack of wholeness of the eunuch or, possibly, the lame and blind, was not, however, something that would pass or could be cleansed through the means established in the law of Moses. Some people were permanently excluded from the temple and God's presence. In his preaching to the people of Antioch, Paul taught that the things that could not be cleansed or forgiven through the law of Moses could be overcome through Christ: "Be it known unto you therefore, men and brethren, that through this man [Jesus Christ] is preached unto you the forgiveness of sins: and by him all that believe are justified from all things, from which ye could not be justified by the law of Moses" (Acts 13:38–39).

We read the same principle in Hebrews: "For the law having a shadow of good things to come, and not the very image of the things, can never with those sacrifices which they offered year by year continually make the comers thereunto perfect" (Hebrews 10:1). The language of the King James Version obscures some of the power of this declaration that the law cannot make people perfect, even if they come with sacrifices. It is only a shadow of the good things to come in Christ. An alternate translation captures the doctrinal beauty of this passage:

"The Law cannot make whole those who draw near."[31] Wholeness comes only in and through Christ. Simon Horne notes that the Greek term for "drawing near" in this passage refers to the Greek translation of the verses in Leviticus that explain how some priests are forbidden to draw near the holiest places in the temple because of their physical impairments.[32] In other words, the law's restrictions for those who are physically impaired itself illustrates its own limitations to bring people into the presence of God.

In his first epistle Peter taught a similar principle of how Christ's sacrifice transcended the redemption made available by the sacrifices of the law of Moses. It is striking how the language he chooses here echoes his statement to the man in Acts 3:6 "Silver and gold have I none; but such as I have give I thee." In Peter's epistle he compares the redemption made possible by the death of Christ to both the lambs under the law of Moses and to redemption from bondage through the payment of a price. "Forasmuch as ye know that ye were not redeemed with corruptible things, as silver and gold, from your vain conversation received by tradition from your fathers; But with the precious blood of Christ, as of a lamb without blemish and without spot" (1 Peter 1:18–19). The blood of Christ provides reconciliation and redemption that are possible in no other way. Through Peter's symbolic action at the temple he testified that the blood of the Lamb of God was able to offer redemptive cleansing and access to the presence of God.

Peter also tied together the physical and spiritual healing made available through Christ and his atoning sacrifice in the second chapter of his first epistle. He speaks of Christ's death as the means by which we can be healed from sins. "Who his own self bare our sins in his own body on the tree, that we, being dead to sins, should live unto righteousness: by whose stripes ye were healed" (1 Peter 2:24). It is significant that Peter connects Christ's vicarious death with the hope that we have to "live unto righteousness" specifically in the language of Isaiah 53, "by whose stripes ye were healed" (see Isaiah 53:5). Our confidence that we can be healed from spiritual sickness is rooted in our trust in the power of his redeeming blood.

Under the law of Moses permanent impairments kept people from the temple permanently, but in this encounter in Acts 3, Peter taught that through Christ all could be made whole and clean, worthy to enter God's presence. The physical illustration with the healing of the lame man was accompanied by his teaching that Christ was raised up and sent to bless us, "in turning away every one of you from his iniquities" (Acts 3:26). Christ did not come to bring us into God's presence just as we are, but to make us whole and fit for his presence. Just as Peter told the people at the temple that they had killed the Holy One, but also opened up hope of cleansing and having their sins blotted out, we also need to know that Christ is sent to turn "away every one of [us] from [our] iniquities" no matter how seemingly impossible to change.

Like any who were banned from the temple because of their lack of wholeness, we may feel our weakness and sinful nature will permanently keep us from living lives of faithfulness and entering in the presence of the Lord to inherit his glory. But just as "his name through faith in his name hath made this man strong" (v. 16), we too can have confidence that our infirmities can be healed and we can become whole and holy, fit to enter the presence of the Lord. While we might define ourselves by our spiritual infirmities, they are not a barrier if we are willing to have faith on his name and repent. The scope of this healing power is clarified in President Boyd K. Packer's stirring promise: "I repeat, save for the exception of the very few who defect to perdition, there is no habit, no addiction, no rebellion, no transgression, no apostasy, no crime exempted from the promise of complete forgiveness. That is the promise of the Atonement of Christ."[33]

Peter's healing of the lame man who suffered since birth with this infirmity can give us confidence that even the deepest-seated inclinations and proclivities to sin can be removed. With this symbolic action, he gave his apostolic witness of the infinite power of the Atonement of Christ. As we trust in this witness and in the power of Christ's name, we too can receive strength and enter "into the temple, walking, and leaping, and praising God" (v. 8). Like the man who was no longer lame, our lives of wholeness and happiness then stand as witnesses. "and all the people saw him walking and praising God: And they knew that it was he which sat for alms at the Beautiful gate of the temple: and they were filled with wonder and amazement at that which had happened unto him" (vv. 9–10). Our lives of wholeness and holiness will lead us to leap with joy and witness to others of the divinity and power in the name of Jesus Christ of Nazareth.

Notes

1.   For an overview of debate over where the "Beautiful Gate" was located, see Joseph A. Fitzmyer, *The Acts of the Apostles: A New Translation with Introduction and Commentary*, in The Anchor Bible, vol. 31 (New York: Doubleday, 1998), 277–78. Some argue that it was the Shushan Gate located "in east wall of the Temple precincts, which gave access from the outside to the Court of the Gentiles and was located roughly where the modern Golden Gate is." Others see it as the Nicanor Gate, "also called the Corinthian or Bronze Gate, which gave access on the east from the Court of the Gentiles to the Court of the Women," or the gate of rabbinic tradition that "gave access from the Court of the Women to the Court of Israel (the Men)" (277).

2. S. John Roth comments on the connection between Luke 4 and Luke 7: "The importance of the echo of 4.18–19 in 7.18–23 can scarcely be overestimated. It places Jesus' healing and preaching within the context of Isaiah's announcement of the 'acceptable year of the Lord.' The logic of the narrative may now be seen. In 4.18–19, the audience finds a statement in eschatological terms of what to expect of Jesus' ministry. The Sermon on the Plain, healings, and resuscitation show Jesus in the act of carrying out that ministry. The scene with John's disciples (7.18–23) recaps Jesus' ministry to this point and connects it to Jesus' reading in the synagogue. Of course, this narrative logic is available only to Luke's audience, not to characters in the story." *The Blind, the Lame, and the Poor: Character Types in Luke–Acts*, Journal for the Study of the New Testament: Supplemental Series 144 (Sheffield, England: Sheffield Academic Press, 1997), 174–75. He observes, "To Luke's audience, then, Jesus' words and actions towards the blind, the lame, lepers, the deaf mute, the dead, and the poor confirm him to be God's unique eschatological agent of salvation" (177).

3. Roth notes that "the function of 'the dead,' 'the lame,' and 'the blind' in Acts is to assist in characterizing the apostles as prophets who announce Jesus' resurrection from the dead and display the power of God's Spirit and Jesus' name through miraculous deeds." Roth, "The Blind, the Lame, and the Poor," 211. For an overview of Roth's analysis on how Luke uses the character types of the blind, the lame, and the poor, see pages 212–21.

4. Fitzmyer, *Acts of the Apostles*, 266. He notes here that Luke uses the terms "the name of Jesus/Christ/the Lord" or "his name" or "the name" throughout Acts and that his use of the term "echoes the OT use of *šēm*, 'name,' which makes a person present to another: 'For as is his name, so is he' (1 Sam 25:25)."

5. Daniel Marguerat also comments on the importance of healing in the name of Jesus as a witness of the ongoing power of Christ and of his Resurrection: "Therefore, it is to the 'name of the Lord' that the healing power, which manifested itself at the Beautiful Gate of the Temple, is to be traced back. What is this about? The 'name of the Lord' is a concept dear to Luke, one which he has inherited from the Hebrew theology of the divine Name; it designates the sphere of power within which Christ acts in the midst of history. One of the Lukan theological originalities is to trace the miracles back to Christology, via the concept of the Name, and not to pneumatology as Paul and the majority of the early Christianity writings do. The speech of Acts 3 is a nice illustration of this Lukan theological structure: the healing of the lame man is not to be taken as the expression of charismatic power or exceptional piety, be it that of the apostles; *its origin lies in the historical action of the Resurrected One.* Once again, Peter witnesses to the resurrection by discerning the trace of the risen Christ in a historical event." "The Resurrection and Its Witness in the Book of Acts," in *Reading Acts Today: Essays in Honour of Loveday C. A. Alexander*, ed. Steve Walton et al., Library of New Testament Studies, 427 (London: T&T Clark, 2011): 175–76; emphasis in original.

6. Andrew C. Skinner, "Peter, the Chief Apostle," in *Sperry Symposium Classics: The New Testament*, ed. Frank F. Judd Jr. and Gaye Strathearn (Salt Lake City: Deseret Book, 2006), 341.

7. Harold B. Lee, "Stand Ye in Holy Places," *Ensign*, July 1973, 123.

8. Lee, "Stand Ye in Holy Places," 123.

9. Lee, "Stand Ye in Holy Places," 123.

10. Marvin J. Ashton, "What Is a Friend?," *Ensign*, January 1973, 43.

11. Heather W. Wrigley, "Elder Holland Tells Ghanaian Saints to Be Their Best," *Church News*, February 21, 2012.

12. Fitzmyer, *Acts of the Apostles*, 279.

13. Fitzmyer, *Acts of the Apostles*, 279.

14. Richard I. Pervo, *Acts: A Commentary*, Heremenia—A Critical and Historical Commentary on the Bible (Minneapolis: Fortress Press, 2009), 101.

15. For a look at the question of whether the lame and the blind are profaning or polluting, see Saul M. Olyan, *Rites and Rank: Hierarchy in Biblical Representations of Cult* (Princeton: Princeton University Press, 2000), 111.

16. Note the role of the chief priests in advocating Christ's death (see Matthew 27:20). It is significant to contextualize Peter's accusation of his audience at the temple. Here the priests would certainly have been part of the audience given the attention the healing caused.

17. Ravens notes: "One further point that the speech makes is that repentance is required before God will send his Messiah 'appointed for you' (Acts 3:20) and, with the coming of the Messiah, the restoration of all that God has promised. No other NT writer combines the themes of repentance and national restoration as Luke does here, giving them an eschatological impetus. The whole passage is given an even richer Jewish perspective by the use of key figures from Israel's past: Moses' promise of a future prophet and the promise to Abraham of the blessing of all nations in his posterity are both fulfilled in Jesus (3:22–25). The result is that every Israelite shall be blessed in turning from his wickedness." David Ravens, *Luke and the Restoration of Israel*, Journal for the Study of the New Testament Supplement Series 119 (Sheffield, England: Sheffield Academic Press, 1995), 152. Another discussion of Luke's understanding of restoration and blessing through repentance can be found in Max Turner, *Power from on High: The Spirit in Israel's Restoration and Witness in Luke–Acts*, Journal of Pentecostal Theology Supplemental Series 9 (Sheffield, England: Sheffield Academic Press, 2000), 308–12.

18. Hector Avalos, "Illness and Health Care," *Eerdmans Dictionary of the Bible* (Grand Rapids, MI: Eerdmans, 2000), 630.

19. "If 2 Sam 5:8b refers to blind and lame (and probably other blemished) worshipers, as I believe it does, it marginalizes such persons by prohibiting their entry into the sanctuary sphere. As I have noted, Deut 23:2 (Eng., 1) is similar in its treatment of genitally damaged men. Whether because of their power to pollute the sanctuary or profane it, blind and lame worshipers of 2 Sam 5:8b lose access to what texts represent as the prime context for the slaughter and distribution of meat, the prime locus for the realization and communication of hierarchical social relations, and the prime site for the worship of Yhwh. The genitally damaged men of Deut 23:2 are similarly cut off. As is true of all who are excluded from the sanctuary sphere because of long-term pollution, removal because of physical defects, whether they are conceived as polluting or not, stigmatizes those removed. They are marked off as distinct from the unblemished of the community, as persons whose appearance is presumably displeasing to Yhwh in the same way that the appearance of blemished animals is said to be displeasing to him in various texts. Like the excluded alien of

Deut 23:4–9 (Eng., 3–8) and Isa 56:3–7, they do not participate in the rites of the cult and therefore experience social marginalization." Olyan, *Rites and Rank*, 113.

20. For an argument against those like Olyan who see the lame and the blind as excluded in the Second Temple period, see Simon T. Thorne, "Injury and Blessing: A Challenge to Current Readings of Biblical Discourse Concerning Impairment" (PhD diss., University of Birmingham, 1999), 273–75.

21. T. M. Lemos, "Shame and Mutilation of Enemies in the Hebrew Bible," *Journal of Biblical Literature* 125, no. 2 (Summer 2006): 231; McCarter argues, "David's aversion to 'the lame and the blind' is not, we may assume, simply a matter of personal sensibility, still less of callous convenience or lack of charity. Instead, the remark is probably intended to reflect religious scruples against the mutilation of living human beings, a violation of the sanctity of the body to which David finds killing preferable. To this extent, therefore, the annotator responsible for the parenthesis that follows was justified in associating David's remarks with the exclusion of the disfigured from the temple." P. Kyle McCarter, *II Samuel: A New Translation with Introduction, Notes and Commentary*, The Anchor Bible, vol. 9 (Garden City, NY: Doubleday, 1984), 135, 140.

22. For an overview of political implications of this statement for the Davidic dynasty, see Anthony R. Ceresko, "The Identity of 'the Blind and the Lame' (*'iwwēr ûpissēah*) in 2 Samuel 5:8b" *Catholic Biblical Quarterly* 63 (2001): 23–30. For a focus on the time of David and what the imagery of disability meant in this political climate, see Jeremy Schipper, "Reconsidering the Imagery of Disability in 2 Samuel 5:8b," *The Catholic Biblical Quarterly* 67 (2005): 422–34.

23. McCarter, *II Samuel*, 140.

24. "LXX makes it explicit that 'the house' thus referred to is the temple, reading 'the house *of Yahweh*.'" McCarter, *II Samuel*, 136; emphasis in original.

25. For an interesting discussion of the Qumran community's concerns, see Eyal Regev, "Abominated Temple and a Holy Community: The Formation of the Notions of Purity and Impurity in Qumran," *Dead Sea Discoveries* 10, no. 2 (2003): 243–78, and Aharon Shemesh, "'The Holy Angels and in Their Council': The Exclusion of Deformed Persons from Holy Places in Qumranic and Rabbinic Literature," *Dead Sea Discoveries* 4, no. 2 (July 1997): 179–206.

26. Saul M. Olyan, "'Anyone Blind or Lame Shall Not Enter the House': On the Interpretation of Second Samuel 5:8b," *Catholic Biblical Quarterly* 60, no. 2 (April 1998): 223.

27. "According to 1QSa 2:3–9, the blind and the lame, among others with bodily imperfections or impurities, may not present themselves in the congregation of the men of renown. In 1QM 7:4–5, the blind and the lame, along with others having permanent blemishes or polluting conditions, are forbidden from participating in the eschatological war. Each of these proscriptions has its basis in particular biblical texts, yet each reflects exegetical reworking of those texts." Saul M. Olyan, "The Exegetical Dimensions of Restrictions on the Blind and the Lame in Texts from Qumran," *Dead Sea Discoveries* 8, no. 1 (2001): 38. Olvan's article provides an important study of the relationship of the biblical and sectarian texts.

28. He observes that "the relatively severe treatment of the blind and the lame in texts such as 11QTa, 1QSa and 1QM is not unlike the treatment of other individuals who

are to be excluded from community and cult according to these texts and others from Qumran." Olyan, "Exegetical Dimensions," 50.

29. Olyan, "'Anyone Blind or Lame Shall Not Enter the House,'" 222–23.

30. John J. Pilch, "Lame, Lameness," in *The New Interpreter's Dictionary of the Bible*, vol. 3 (Nashville: Abingdon, 2008), 564.

31. Simon Horne, "Injury and Blessing: A Challenge to Current Readings of Biblical Discourse Concerning Impairment" (PhD diss., University of Birmingham, 1999), 283.

32. "The word for drawing near—προσερχομαι—is an allusion to the Septuagint version of the Leviticus impairment chapters." Horne, "Injury and Blessing," 283–84.

33. Boyd K. Packer, "The Brilliant Morning of Forgiveness," *Ensign*, November 1995, 19.

9

The Petrine *Kērygma* and the Gospel according to Mark

Eric D. Huntsman

Eric D. Huntsman is an associate professor of ancient scripture at
Brigham Young University.

"God anointed Jesus of Nazareth with the Holy Ghost and with power: who went about doing good, and healing all that were oppressed of the devil; for God was with him. And we are witnesses of all things which he did both in the land of the Jews, and in Jerusalem; whom they slew and hanged on a tree: him God raised up the third day, and shewed him openly" (Acts 10:38–40).

Besides 1 and 2 Peter, no other canonical documents have been attributed to the Apostle Peter, and even in the case of the Petrine epistles there has been some question about their composition and authorship.[1] Nevertheless, the Lucan versions of speeches put in the mouth of Peter witness the strong tradition of Peter's preaching in the early church, preaching that affected not only the early chapters of Acts but also may have been an important source for the earliest of the New Testament Gospels, Mark. Such proclamation of Jesus and his gospel by those who were his witnesses were of vital importance in the early Christian church, especially in the years between Jesus' ministry and the writing of the Gospels.[2]

Early Christian discussions about the authorship of the Gospel of Mark had already connected it to the authority and figure of the chief Apostle, a connection that is further suggested by the prominence of Peter in that Gospel. This link may be further supported by the influence of Petrine preaching and testimony on the Gospel's structure and content. The technical term for this kind of apostolic testimony is *kērygma*, a Greek term related to the word for "herald," which has the general meaning of "proclamation."[3] As used here, the adjective "Petrine" refers to a range of possibilities: material that originated with Peter himself, either directly or via his students and followers; that bore Peter's authority and approval; that was generally apostolic, for whom Peter was a representative figure; or that was simply believed to have been from Peter. To the extent that Peter's preaching—or at least the tradition of Petrine *kērygma*—can be shown to have influenced the composition, shape, and content of the Gospel according to Mark, Petrine authority may explain not only how Mark attained canonical status but also why it so strongly influenced the other synoptic Gospels.

Marcan Authorship

Like the other canonical gospels, the Gospel according to Mark is formally anonymous, meaning that it does not directly reveal the identity of its author nor make any claims about him or his authority. The titles that now head each of the four Gospels do not seem to be original parts of the texts but began to appear later in the second century AD as attempts to distinguish the different Gospels when they began to be put together into collections.[4] Thus, attempts to identify the author—or to at least begin to know something about him and his original audience—must begin by looking at evidence from within the texts themselves. This evidence generally consists of indirect clues about the evangelists' backgrounds, interests, and target audiences that can be discerned from the use of language and the specific content of each Gospel.

Mark, sometimes referred to as "the second Gospel" because of its position in the canon after Matthew, is written in passable, but not always good, Greek. On the other hand, the evangelist appears have known Aramaic, was knowledgeable about Jewish customs, and frequently used quotations and ideas from the Hebrew Bible. Despite this, he does not appear to have been familiar with or always accurate about the geography of the Holy Land, at least not outside of Jerusalem and its immediate environs,[5] and sometimes his portrayal of certain Jewish practices was broad, perhaps even a bit inaccurate, as in the case of his description of practices regarding washing and the particular custom of *qorbān* (KJV, "Corban," Mark 7:1–13).[6] Nevertheless, of the four Gospels, Mark in many ways most accurately portrays the different Jewish groups and the situation in Jerusalem before its destruction in AD 70. These factors point to an author who was a Jew, perhaps from Jerusalem, where many of the upper classes in the first century were Hellenized to some degree and could have some facility in Greek.[7]

Despite his own origins and background, the Marcan evangelist frequently explains Jewish customs and Aramaic terms, as when he translates the phrase *talitha cumi* (see Mark 5:41) or translates *qorbān* and tries to explain how the practice worked (see Mark 7:11), suggesting that these were not familiar to his readers. Mark also includes Latinisms—Latin words like *legio* (English, "legion," in Mark 5:9) that are transliterated into Greek—and uses other terms suggestive of a Roman audience. Particularly because of this text's emphasis on persecution and failed discipleship, it may have been originally written for Christians in the capital itself, where Christians were persecuted by the emperor Nero after the fire of AD 64, with some of them forsaking the faith under pressure.[8] The dating of the Gospel thus seems to fall between the death of Peter, traditionally placed at the time of the Neronian persecutions in AD 64, and the second phase of the Jewish War, which began after the suicide of Nero (AD 68) and the overthrow of Galba (AD 69).[9]

When titles did begin to appear with some manuscripts later in the second century, they consistently identified the text as *euangelion kata Markon*, or "the Gospel according to Mark." Significantly, none of the titles ever read *euangelion tou Markou*, "the Gospel of Mark" or "Mark's Gospel," the sense being that there was only one proclamation of Jesus Christ and this was simply Mark's version of it. Despite the fact that titles for all of the Gospels were not original, as soon as multiple gospels began to circulate and communities had more than one at hand, there was a need to distinguish between them. The fact that titles became common to each of the Gospels so quickly and were used so consistently is a good indication that there was widespread agreement among the early Christians about their identification.[10]

This consensus is attested by evidence from the writings of early church fathers. The first of these was Papias of Hierapolis, who wrote in the first third of the second century AD, but whose writing only survives in quotations by Eusebius, a church historian writing later in the fourth century. In one of these quotations, Papias cites an "elder" who had asserted the following about the authorship of the second Gospel:

Mark became Peter's interpreter [*hermēneutēs*] and wrote accurately all that he remembered, not, indeed, in order, of the things said or done by the Lord. For he had not heard the Lord, nor had he followed him, but later on, as I said, *followed Peter, who used to give teaching as necessity demanded but not making, as it were, an arrangement* [*syntaxin*] *to the Lord's oracles* [*logion* or "sayings"], so that Mark did nothing wrong in thus writing down single points as he remembered them. For to one thing he gave attention, *to leave out nothing of what he had heard* and to make no false statements in them. (Papias *ap.* Eusebius, *Ecclesiastical History* 3.39.15; emphasis added)[11]

Despite the fact that Papias wrote within two generations of the time that the Gospel was written and claims to have heard from those who knew the Apostles and other eyewitnesses, some scholars have questioned Papias' testimony about both Mark and his connection with Peter.[12] Richard Bauckham, however, has reaffirmed Papias' basic reliability, demonstrating that he drew his information about the Gospels from either eyewitnesses or those who knew them firsthand.[13]

Papias not only identified the author of the Gospel as a "Mark" but also claimed that this Mark was the interpreter of the Apostle Peter, though whether by *hermēneutēs* he meant that Mark interpreted for Peter when he spoke or translated for him as scribe is unclear.[14] Papias' statement also suggests that because Peter preached according to what each situation demanded, Mark's account, too, might not have been in strictly chronological or perhaps literary order (*syntaxin*).[15] Irenaeus, writing in the second half of the first century, confirmed Papias' basic assertions when he wrote, "After [Peter and Paul's deaths], Mark, the disciple and interpreter of Peter, did also hand down to us in writing *what had been preached by Peter*" (*Adversus Haereses* 3.1.1; emphasis added).[16] Another source, the Anti-Marcionite Prologue to Mark (ca. AD 160–180), supports the assertion that Mark wrote down Peter's testimony in Italy only after the Apostle's death.[17] On the other hand, Clement of Alexandria (ca. AD 150–216) wrote that

When Peter had publicly *preached the word* [*kēryxantos to logon*] at Rome, and by the spirit had proclaimed the Gospel, those present, who were many, exhorted Mark, as one who had followed him for a long time and remembered what had been spoken, *to make a record of what was said*; and he did this, and distributed the Gospel among those that asked him. And when the matter came to Peter's knowledge, *he neither strongly forbade it nor urged it forward* (Clement of Alexandria *ap.* Eusebius, *Ecclesiastical History* 6.14.5–7; emphasis added).[18]

The Greek word here translated as "preached," *keryxantos*, is a participial form of the verb *kēryssō*, from which comes the noun *kērygma,* or "proclamation." According to Clement, when Peter learned that his preaching had been recorded by Mark, he neither disclaimed it nor encouraged it. But Eusebius, who preserved this quotation as he did that of Papias, elsewhere in his history "corrected" it, claiming that Peter was actually inspired to authorize Mark's Gospel:

> But a great light of religion shone on the minds of the hearers of Peter, so that they were not satisfied with a single hearing or with *the unwritten teaching of the divine proclamation* [*tē agraphō tou theiou kērygmatos didaskalia*], but with every kind of exhortation besought Mark, whose Gospel is extant, seeing that he was Peter's follower, *to leave them a written statement of the teaching given them verbally,* nor did they cease until they had persuaded him, and so became the cause of the scripture called the Gospel according to Mark. And they say that *the apostle,* knowing by revelation of the spirit to him what had been done, *was pleased at their zeal and ratified the scripture for the study of the churches.* (Eusebius, *Ecclesiastical History* 2.15.2; emphasis added)[19]

Likewise, Origen (ca. AD 184–254) maintained that the second Gospel was written by Mark, "who wrote it following Peter's directives" (Eusebius, *Ecclesiastical History* 6.25.5).[20]

None of these sources clearly associates the Mark who wrote the Gospel with any known biblical figure, but his close association with Peter made the companion of Peter mentioned in 1 Peter 5:13, a Mark whom Peter refers to as if he were his son, a likely candidate. This seems to be the same figure as the John Mark whose mother, Mary, gave Peter refuge after he escaped from prison in Jerusalem (see Acts 12:12). *Yôḥanan* was a Jewish name, and his surname, *Marcus,* was a very common Roman name that was also becoming a Greek name (*Markos*), suggesting a situation perhaps comparable to the Pharisee Saul who, as a Roman citizen, also had the name Paul. If Mary's owning a substantial house in Jerusalem is indicative of her family's status, John Mark could easily

meet many of the characteristics that the Gospel of Mark suggests for its author—namely, a member of the Jerusalem upper class who may have known
some Greek. This Mark is further mentioned in Acts as a missionary companion to Barnabas and Paul (12:25), though he later left the mission (13:13), which
led to a disagreement between Barnabas and Paul and kept Paul from taking
Mark on his next mission (15:36–39). Apparently Paul and Mark were recon-
ciled, since Mark appears in the Pauline correspondence as a "fellow worker"
(see Colossians 4:10; Philemon 1:24).

While giving Mark an association with Peter might have been the result
of early Christian attempts to validate the second Gospel,[21] the prevalence and
relative consistency of such early postapostolic sources on the Petrine connection suggest that this connection was, in fact, based upon an early, probably reliable, tradition.[22] Because Papias received his information from an "elder" who
was part of the second generation of Christians who had known the Apostles,
the tradition connecting the second Gospel with the figures of Mark and Peter
is one that originated within a few decades of its composition. Further, if one
were manufacturing a figure to serve as an anonymous document's author, he is
not likely to have selected as minor a figure as John Mark.[23]

This account of Petrine preaching followed by Marcan composition is
repeated with little variation by other patristic sources, the only significant
discrepancy being whether the evangelist composed the Gospel before or after Peter's death.[24] But this memory of a Petrine connection with Mark and
the second Gospel does not necessarily mean that the evangelist in fact wrote
down directly what he had heard Peter say. In many ways Peter served as a
representative figure for all of the Apostles, in which case the attribution of
Peter as the authority or source for Mark may simply have meant that early
Christians recognized the content of this Gospel as having come from the
apostolic preaching tradition.[25]

Latter-day Saints do not need to assume that restoration scripture or
theology directly supports traditional authorship for the Gospel according to Mark,[26] let alone its direct connection to the Apostle Peter. Not only
are the Joseph Smith Translation changes of the titles of the Gospels from
"Gospel" to "Testimony" of each evangelist not necessarily direct evidence
of authorship,[27] but the original Joseph Smith Translation manuscripts only
changed the titles for Matthew and John, not for Mark or Luke.[28] Further,
it is not clear that Joseph Smith's maintenance of the figures named in the
titles was necessarily a prophetic endorsement of them. As Kent Jackson
has observed: "Neither the New Testament nor modern scripture identifies

Mark as the author of the second Gospel. No scriptural passage says Mark wrote Mark. . . . I do not know of any way in which the restored gospel has anything at stake in whether he did or did not. Thus it seems that this matter—unlike the issue of Jesus' Resurrection—is fair game for continued exploration, interpretation, and examination of the evidence."[29] Nevertheless, as Frank Judd has observed, the early tradition of Petrine authority behind Mark's Gospel might, in fact, reflect the possibility that "in this particular case, the scribe rather than the source of the information received credit for the Gospel. Thus this Gospel might have been called the Gospel of Peter, [even though] it is traditionally called the Gospel of Mark."[30]

Peter in Mark

Mark mentions Peter twenty-five times, so given the length of the Gospel, it mentions the chief Apostle more frequently than the other three texts.[31] Peter is also always the foremost of the Twelve discussed in Mark and the only one with whom Jesus speaks one-on-one and addresses by name.[32] But it is Peter's prominence at the beginning and conclusion of the body of Mark—starting with the call of Peter and Andrew (see Mark 1:16–20) and ending with the angel's directive that the women at the empty tomb go to the disciples and Peter (see Mark 16:7)—that is perhaps the most significant. These references to the chief Apostle frame the body of the Gospel,[33] and because such framing in contemporary popular biographies was used to denote the witnesses behind that material, Bauckham takes this as being a possible sign that Peter's eyewitness is the authority behind much of its content.[34]

Bauckham further notes that an often overlooked narrative device in Mark also suggests that an eyewitness was behind much of the material in the Gospel. This device, the shift from a plural verb to a singular whenever Jesus and his disciples travel around Galilee or arrive at a specific place and Jesus then proceeds to do or say something (see Mark 5:1–2; 8:22; 11:12; 14:32), suggests that the source was traveling with Jesus.[35] Peter is either explicitly mentioned or assumed to be part of the group in most of these instances, but some of Peter's appearances in Mark can be even more clearly explained as personal recollections of Peter.[36] These include his call from his nets (see Mark 1:16), Jesus entering his house after synagogue and then healing his mother-in-law (see Mark 1:29–31), and times when only he or a small group was present to witness something Jesus said or did, such as the raising of Jairus' daughter (see Mark 5:37–43), the Transfiguration (9:2–10), the Olivet Discourse (13:3–37), and Gethsemane (14:33–42). In this regard, the story of Peter's denials stands out, since in the synoptics no other disciple was present (see Mark 14:66–72; parallels Matthew 26:69–75; Luke 22:56–62).

Some, however, maintain that if Mark were truly a "Petrine Gospel," then it should feature Peter even more, noting, for instance, that there are significant traditions about the Apostle in Matthew that are missing in the second Gospel.[37] The Matthean additions, however, may well be explained by that Gospel's Christology, ecclesiology, structure, and even perhaps its author's own deference to Peter. For instance, the expansion of Peter's confession at Caesarea Philippi in Matthew 16:16 can be understood to be a result of Matthew's more developed, or at least more explicit, Christology, and Jesus' further discourse about the rock on which the church would be built and the role of the keys in the kingdom (see Matthew 16:17–19) could have resulted from Matthew's interest in the church as a body, which is unique among the Gospels. Even the inclusion of the rather minor story of tribute (temple tax) and the fish with the coin in its mouth (see Matthew 17:24–27) may have resulted from its serviceability in connecting the previous section of Matthew, Jesus' growing rejection by Israel (see Matthew 13:53–17:27), with the following Sermon on the church (see Matthew 18:1–35).

Another surprising aspect of Marcan passages featuring Peter is the inclusion of episodes that are critical of Peter. These include how the disciples, including Peter, repeatedly fail to understand Jesus (e.g., Mark 8:14–18); Jesus' personal rebuke of Peter after the first passion prediction, when he actually says to Peter, "get thee behind me Satan" (Mark 8:33); and of course the entire denial sequence, coming as it does after Peter's steadfast boast that he will never be offended in Jesus (see Mark 14:29).[38] Rather than being indications of an anti-Peter source, such passages portraying Peter negatively might represent the candid admissions of the Apostle himself, who, until the cross and the empty tomb, could not understand Jesus, adequately follow him, or find forgiveness.[39] If this represents humility on the part of Peter, who might have preferred to focus on proclaiming Jesus and only use himself as a negative example to illustrate how all needed the Lord, this might explain why Matthew, for instance, portrays Peter *better* than Mark does. If Peter, representing not only the Apostles as a group but perhaps also the authority of the church, served as more of a positive example in Matthew's Gospel, this might account for more hagiographic anecdotes, such as the fact that in the Matthean account of Jesus walking on water Peter actually *begins* to walk on water (see Matthew 14:22–33; parallels Mark 6:45–52; John 6:16–21).

In Mark's Gospel, Peter becomes a type for discipleship generally, including negative discipleship. While the original followers of Jesus eagerly gave up all to follow Jesus, they nonetheless frequently failed to understand his teachings or his mission, exhibited improper behavior, and increasingly fell short in their faithfulness—failing to support Jesus adequately during his Passion, abandoning him at his arrest, and, in the case of Peter, even denying knowing him.[40] In this sense, the earliest disciples, foremost represented by Peter, serve as models for the original presumed audience of Roman Christians and the modern reading audience, both of whom are prone to falter in their discipleship. Indeed, Martin Hengel has directly asserted that in these instances, "Mark has a lively witness of Peter as his source, one that is theologically stylized and dramatically described."[41]

The Preaching of Peter

In considering the preaching of Peter as a possible source or influence on the Gospel according to Mark, we must first recognize that the term *kērygma* presents a certain ambiguity: it can indicate both the *act* of preaching and the *content* of such preaching.[42] If, however, the major thrust of the term consists of *what* was preached, particularly about who Jesus was and what he did, it might help account for greater emphasis on the acts of Jesus in the first half of the Gospel and the passion account in the second. Although too much distinction can be made between the terms *kērygma* (proclamation) and *didachē* (teaching),[43] seeing *kērygma* as representing the early preaching of the saving message of Jesus and *didachē* as the body of Christian moral instruction and ethical admonition is still useful.[44] Mark certainly contains teaching in the form of the parables and sayings of Jesus, but the emphasis in this shorter Gospel is in its first half more on the deeds and then, in the second half, on the salvific acts and significance of Jesus. If this is due in part to its being dependent upon the *kērygma* of Peter, it might help account for one of the major differences between Mark on the one hand and Matthew and Luke on the other, inasmuch as these latter two Gospels contain significantly more *didachē* in the form of extended sermons and other teachings of Jesus.

Presuming that the Lucan speeches of Peter reflect to some degree what Peter said on those occasions,[45] it next remains to be considered which of these represent a distinct pattern of apostolic preaching that may be termed kerygmatic and what the content of this *kērygma*, or preaching, was. Forms of the noun *kērygma* itself are actually rare in the New Testament, appearing only once in Matthew and Luke each and six times in the Pauline epistles.[46] The verb *kēryssō*, however, appears much more frequently: nine times in Matthew, fourteen in Mark, nine in Luke, eight in Acts, nineteen in the Pauline epistles, and once in 1 Peter 3:19

and Revelation 5:2 each.[47] Although this preaching may have included historical content, including the deeds of Jesus, its main emphasis in most instances is "proclaiming Christ."[48] Perhaps significantly, *kēryssō* appears most frequently in Mark, even though it is the shortest of the Gospels. In this regard, the apostolic *kērygma* roughly equals *euangelion*, or "good news,"[49] which Mark uses seven times—four times in Jesus' mouth as the pre-Easter good news of the kingdom, but otherwise as the saving story of Jesus.[50]

For Paul, the essence of the gospel message was "Jesus Christ, and him crucified" (see 1 Corinthians 2:2), and presumably this was the heart of the message that he had initially preached not only among the Corinthians but also in each of the cities he visited.[51] Indeed, it is in Paul's discourse on the Resurrection to the Corinthians that we see one of the earliest versions of the *kērygma*:

> Moreover, brethren, I declare unto you the gospel which I preached [*euēngelisamēn*] unto you, which also ye have received, and wherein ye stand;
>
> By which also ye are saved, if ye keep in memory what I preached unto you, unless ye have believed in vain.
>
> For I delivered unto you first of all that which I also received, how that *Christ died for our sins* according to the scriptures;
>
> And that *he was buried, and that he rose again the third day* according to the scriptures:
>
> And that **he was seen of Cephas, then of the twelve**:
>
> After that, he was seen of above five hundred brethren at once; of whom the greater part remain unto this present, but some are fallen asleep.
>
> After that, he was seen of James; then of all the apostles.
>
> And last of all **he was seen of me also**, as of one born out of due time. . . .
>
> Therefore whether it were I or they, so we preach [*kēryssomen*], and so ye believed. (1 Corinthians 15:1–8, 11; emphasis added, with italics representing the main kerygmatic points and bold text emphasizing the role of witnesses in the proclaiming the *kērygma*)

Here, the "good news" that Paul preached to the Corinthians (*euēngelisamēn*) was that Christ died for our sins and rose again, which Peter (Cephas), the Twelve, five hundred other brethren, James, and Paul were all witnesses, each having actually seen the risen Lord. This was the core message that Paul and the other witnesses proclaimed (*kēryssomen*), which led the Corinthians, and others, to believe in Jesus. Other Pauline passages contribute to a slightly fuller view of his *kērygma*: prophecies in the scriptures have been fulfilled in Christ, who was born of the seed of David, died, was buried, rose again, has been exalted to heaven, and will come again as judge.[52]

All of this is part of the Petrine *kērygma* as discerned in Acts, which, however, contains one notable addition in the form of references or allusions to Jesus' acts in his ministry. While the five speeches of Peter in Acts that most clearly reflect the *kērygma* (see Acts 2:14–36, 38–39; 3:12–26; 4:8–12; 5:29–32; 10:34–43) may reflect as much patterns of apostolic preaching familiar to Luke as they do the original preaching of Peter,[53] they were nonetheless accepted as representative of the kind of preaching that Peter and the Apostles proclaimed.[54] F. F. Bruce has identified four elements that characterize them as kerygmatic: the time has come for the fulfilment of God's promises; Old Testament prophecies confirm the good news; this has been done through the ministry, death, and Resurrection of Jesus; and repentance is incumbent upon those who hear the proclamation.[55]

The first of these apostolic proclamations of Jesus occurs at the climax of Peter's sermon at Pentecost. After connecting the events of the good news to the promises made to Joel, Luke has Peter proclaim:

> Ye men of Israel, hear these words; Jesus of Nazareth, *a man approved of God among you by miracles and wonders and signs*, which God did by him in the midst of you, as ye yourselves also know:
> Him, being delivered by the determinate counsel and foreknowledge of God, *ye have taken, and by wicked hands have crucified and slain:*
> *Whom God hath raised up, having loosed the pains of death*: because it was not possible that he should be holden of it. (Acts 2:22–24; emphasis added)

After demonstrating that David had prophesied Jesus' Resurrection and exaltation, Peter continued:

> *This Jesus hath God raised up, **whereof we all are witnesses**.*
> Therefore *being by the right hand of God exalted*, and having received of the Father the promise of the Holy Ghost, he hath shed forth this, which ye now see and hear.
> For David is not ascended into the heavens: but he saith himself, The LORD said unto my Lord, Sit thou on my right hand,

Until I make thy foes thy footstool.

Therefore let all the house of Israel know assuredly, that *God hath made that same Jesus, whom ye have crucified, both Lord and Christ.* (Acts 2:32–36; emphasis added)

When the crowd listening responds to this proclamation by asking what they should do, Peter's call is that they repent and be baptized, which some three thousand do (see Acts 2:37–42).

In this first kerygmatic speech, the only reference to any of the historical actions of Jesus is found in the statement that he was "a man approved of God among you *by miracles and wonders and signs.*" Nevertheless, this is different from Paul, who rarely talks about the actions of the historical Jesus (his institution of the sacrament the night he was betrayed in 1 Corinthians 11 being a notable exception). Presumably this is because Paul himself was not a witness of the mortal ministry of Jesus; Peter was. Nevertheless, in the Petrine *kērygma*, the emphasis is on the Lord's Crucifixion, Resurrection, and exaltation to heaven. As with Paul, Peter and the rest of the Twelve are held up as witnesses, they being the ones who are to proclaim the saving message.

Similar features appear in the other four Petrine kerygmatic speeches. The last of these five speeches, the sermon to Cornelius and his household, serves as perhaps the most comprehensive summation of this apostolic preaching.[56] After introductory verses connecting the immediate situation, the faith of Cornelius and his acceptance by God, to the sermon he is about to preach, Peter then proclaims:

The word which God sent unto the children of Israel, preaching peace [*euangelizomenos eirēnēn*] by Jesus Christ: (he is Lord of all:)

That word, I say, ye know, which was published throughout all Judaea, and began from Galilee, after the baptism which John preached;

How God anointed Jesus of Nazareth with the Holy Ghost and with power: *who went about doing good, and healing all that were oppressed of the devil; for God was with him.*

And *we are witnesses of all things which he did* both in the land of the Jews, and in Jerusalem; *whom they slew and hanged on a tree:*

Him God raised up the third day, and shewed him openly;

Not to all the people, but ***unto witnesses chosen before of God, even to us***, who did eat and drink with him after he rose from the dead.

And *he commanded us to preach* [*kēryxai*] unto the people, and to testify that it is he which was ordained of God to be the Judge of quick and dead.

To him give all the prophets witness, that through his name whosoever believeth in him shall receive remission of sins. (Acts 10:36–43; emphasis added)

The Holy Ghost immediately fell upon all who heard Peter's preaching, and the Gentiles in Cornelius' house received the Holy Ghost and spoke in tongues, leading Peter to command that they be baptized (see Acts 10:44–48).

In this last example of Petrine preaching, the notice that Jesus "went about doing good" represents the ministry of Jesus, in which his healings and exorcisms are seen as confirmation that God was with him. Even more than in previous speeches, the apostolic role as witness is emphasized and linked with the prophetic witness of scripture. In addition, the Apostles are explicitly commanded to preach (*kēryxai*, from the verb *kēryssō*). Still at the heart of Peter's preaching is the crucified and risen Lord, but it is supported by a recollection of the ministry of Jesus (see Acts 10:38; see also 2:22) and the Old Testament prophecies and expectations concerning the Messiah. As O'Grady has observed, "The purpose of this preaching was to effect a religious experience in the listener, a call to repentance, to change his or her way of living, to turn over a new leaf by making an act of faith which was then to be sealed by the acceptance of baptism."[57]

Although there are other slight differences between this Petrine *kērygma* and that of Paul,[58] the most significant unique elements are references to the miracles and teachings of Jesus.[59] Significantly, this very addition is the point of content that most notably separates the narrative Gospel of Mark from the basic Christ message of the Pauline epistles, with the miracles that play such a prominent role in the second Gospel representing the "doing good." Indeed, the deeds of Jesus, including and especially the miracles, receive more emphasis in Mark than do his teachings,[60] as opposed to Matthew, who prioritizes the teachings, and Luke, who balances the teachings and miracles.[61] With the exception of the emphasis on the miracles, and perhaps other deeds, of Jesus, the Lucan speeches and the Gospel according to Mark do not provide enough information to allow us to glean from them a distinctive "Petrine theology," but, as C. H. Dodd observes, "The theme of Mark's Gospel is not simply the succession of events which ended in the crucifixion of Jesus. It is the theme of the *kerygma* as a whole."[62]

Marcan Structure and Content

The outline of Mark is, in fact, parallel to Peter's speech to Cornelius in Acts 10:36–41: it begins with prophecies of Jesus (see Mark 1:1–2) that are followed by the baptizing activity of John the Baptist (1:3–8), God's proclaiming Jesus his Son (1:9–11), narratives that are dominated by Jesus' mighty deeds (1:16–10:52), and then accounts of Jesus' Jerusalem ministry (11–14), which focuses on his death on the cross (15) and finally his Resurrection (16:1–8).[63] A clear dividing point in the Gospel occurs with Peter's declaration at Caesarea Philippi that Jesus was the Christ (see Mark 8:27–30). Immediately thereafter, the text shifts from Jesus the doer of mighty deeds (*dynameis*, or "miracles") to the suffering Son of Man, who three times predicts his coming Passion (see Mark 8:31; 9:31; 10:33–34) and then suffers, dies, and rises again.

With a little more nuance, the second Gospel has also been described as a drama that is divided into a heading (see Mark 1:1), a prologue (1:2–23), and then three distinct acts—Jesus' authoritative mission in Galilee (1:14–18:30), his road to Jerusalem (8:31–10:52), and the Gospel's climax in Jerusalem (11:1–16:8).[64] The first, and to some extent the second, acts of this drama can be seen as extended forms of the historical part of the *kērygma*, consisting of the deeds of Jesus, though this is not separate from the general proclamation.[65] The third act then focuses on the heart of the apostolic preaching: that Jesus suffered, died, and rose again.

Regardless of what structure one adopts in analyzing Mark, it is apparent that it represents a geographic, not a strictly chronological, progression, following Jesus in a path from Galilee to Jerusalem. This is evident in the fact that Mark, followed by Matthew and Luke, only has Jesus go to Jerusalem once at the end of his earthly ministry, when it is more likely that the historical Jesus, as an observant Jew, would have gone to the Holy City frequently for pilgrimage festivals, as is the case in the Gospel according to John. This, perhaps, may be partly what Papias meant when he reported that Mark wrote accurately but not in order, following "Peter, who used to give teaching as necessity demanded but not making, as it were, an arrangement to the Lord's oracles." By asserting that Mark wrote accurately (*akribōs egrapsen*), Papias seems to be defending the accuracy and the correctness of the material in the second Gospel without defending, among other things, its chronology. Further, he seems to attribute the lack of order, at least partly, to the nature of Peter's preaching.[66] This may well have been because the preaching of all the Apostles, including and especially that of Peter, regularly culminated in the salvific acts of Jesus, in which case the progression in the second Gospel is theological as well as geographic, showing that all of his mission led to the cross.

Inasmuch as the kerygmatic function of the Gospel was to get people to respond to the message of Jesus and what he has done, Mark's emphasis on the Passion and his conclusion, focusing on the empty tomb as it does in the short ending, may well have resulted from his intent not so much to inform people about Jesus as to lead them to believe in him and then share that message with others.[67] Thus the words of the angel to the women at the tomb can be seen as summarizing the central message of the *kērygma*, together with an injunction for the listeners to respond to it: "Be not affrighted: Ye seek *Jesus of Nazareth, which was crucified: he is risen; he is not here*: behold the place where they laid him. But go your way, ***tell his disciples and Peter*** that he goeth before you into Galilee: ***there shall ye see him***, as he said unto you" (Mark 16:6–7; emphases added).

Not only the structure but also some of the content of Mark might reflect the preaching of Peter. With the exception of Mark 13, the Olivet Discourse, Jesus' teaching in the second Gospel is rarely lengthy, never occurring in long sermons as in Luke or especially in Matthew. Rather, it consists mostly of short parables and *chreiai*, which are short anecdotes comprised of the words or deeds of a subject chosen to reveal his character or significance.[68] This rhetorical form, in fact, leads Ben Witherington to interpret Papias' statement about Peter's preaching differently: rather than reading it as "Peter, who used to give teaching as necessity demanded [*pros tas chreias*] but not making, as it were, an arrangement to the Lord's oracles," he sees it as meaning "Peter who composed his teachings according to the *chreiai* [revealing anecdotes] and not as a rhetorical arrangement of the Lord's sayings."[69]

While the vivid, fast-moving style of Mark is often attributed to the possibility that it was composed for oral recitation in Christian meetings, the fact that Peter—or whoever the second Evangelist's source was—necessarily only told anecdotes or short stories about Jesus when he preached might help explain why Mark usually only includes short dominical sayings. As R. T. France notes, "If Papias' information is correct, Peter . . . must have been a lively preacher. The vivid narrative style and content of the Marcan stories may well derive as much from the way Peter used to tell them as from Mark's own skill as a raconteur [one skilled in relating stories and anecdotes]."[70]

On the other hand, while Mark is the shortest of the four canonical Gospels, its descriptions of Jesus' actions are often the most fulsome. This is particularly the case in regard to the miracles of Jesus. In total, Mark records nineteen miracles stories, four summaries of miracles, and one miracle report, which together make up a full third of his Gospel.[71] Because of its shorter length, this represents the highest frequency of miracles in the Gospels even though the other synoptics actually record a slightly larger number. These miracles are related very descriptively, with the same miracle story in Mark often being twice long as it is in Matthew or even Luke. Part of this may be the result of the redactional activity of Matthew and Luke, but it may also reflect the proclivity of Mark—or his source.[72]

The Canonical Position of Mark, the Memory of Peter, and the Power of *Kērygma*

Among the criteria that Raymond Brown deduced to determine whether early Christians preserved and eventually accepted texts as canonical includes the idea that "scripture" should have apostolic origin, whether "real or putative."[73] Whereas the authors of Matthew and John were early identified with the Apostles of those names, the Gospels of Mark and Luke did not carry as much inherent authority. The association of the figure of Luke with the Apostle Paul, plus the third Gospel's reference to many (though unnamed) eyewitnesses, helped bolster the credentials of that text. The second Gospel, however, could have been more at risk. Not only did it not make any specific claims about the authority of its source or sources, but so much of its material was successfully reworked and expanded upon by the Gospel according to Matthew that it might have been totally eclipsed by what quickly took pride of place as the "first" Gospel. The connection of Peter with Mark's Gospel, whether real or assumed, may have thus secured for Mark a permanent place in the canon.

Nevertheless, long before such canonical decisions were being made, Petrine authority may well explain the deference of the authors of Matthew and Luke to Mark as those Gospels were being composed.[74] Particularly in the case of Matthew, the fact that a Gospel either written by or held to be so closely associated with one of the Twelve would follow Mark even when his chronology is not likely to have been accurate is striking. And assuming the traditional authorships are correct, why would an Apostle have deferred to a minor figure such as John Mark? This could be either because the other synoptic Evangelists were in fact deferring to the testimony and authority of Peter or simply because the Christology of Mark had already been widely preached and was already accepted.[75] It could also be a testament to the literary genius of the Marcan evangelist, who in setting the Petrine *kērygma* into a narrative form succeeded in telling the story of Jesus in such a powerful and effective way that he effectively created a new genre that subsequent Gospel writers could build and expand upon.[76]

Short of newly discovered materials or revealed insights, the patristic claims of a Petrine connection to the Gospel according to Mark cannot be proven. But the possibility that the second Gospel contains early Petrine memories, perhaps from the Apostle himself, remains intriguing and important. Mark 14 in particular includes features that may be reminiscent of the individual memory of Peter as an eyewitness. These include his being singled out, along with James and John, to be near Jesus in Gethsemane; his individual rebuke for not staying awake; and his being the only disciple (in the synoptics, at least) to follow Jesus after his arrest. But overall, Markus Bockmuehl observes that the Marcan depiction of Peter constitutes "a profile that does not conceal the volatility of a flawed and fallible character but nonetheless assigns immense importance as both confidant of Jesus and authentic point of access to his tradition."[77] Likewise, from the various pieces of evidence found throughout the New Testament, Hengel not only sees Peter as "a theologically powerful thinker, an impressive proclaimer, and a competent organizer" but also sees his preaching as the base of the *kērygma* and the Christian ethos that developed so quickly after Jesus' Resurrection.[78]

Perhaps nowhere else in the extant canon can this be seen than in the assumption of Petrine material in and Peter's authority behind the Gospel according to Mark.[79] Yet regardless of how Petrine either the second Gospel or the Lucan speeches of Peter in Acts ultimately turn out to be, the proclamation of the divinity of Jesus and the power of his salvific acts is something that Peter himself, the Marcan evangelist, the author of Acts, the early Christians, and we, as modern believers, can all accept as truthful, vital, and saving.

Notes

1. Markus Bockmuehl, *Simon Peter in Scripture and Memory* (Grand Rapids, MI: Baker, 2012), 30–32.

2. C. H. Dodd, *The Apostolic Preaching and Its Developments* (New York: Harpers & Brothers, 1960), 7–24.

3. Walter Bauer, "*kērygma*," in *A Greek-English Lexicon of the New Testament and Other Early Christian Literature*, 3rd ed. (Chicago: University of Chicago, 2000), 543.

4. Joel Marcus, *Mark 1–8*, Anchor Bible 27 (New York: Doubleday, 1999), 17; John R. Donahue and Daniel J. Harrington, *The Gospel of Mark*, Sacra Pagina 2 (Collegeville, MN: The Liturgical Press, 2002), 38.

5. Apparent mistakes appear in Mark's descriptions of the northern part of the land, as seen in assumptions about the distances from Gadara (or Gerasa) from the Sea of Galilee (see Mark 5:1–13), the relative positions of Bethsaida and Gennesaret on that same sea (see Mark 6:45–53), or the geographical relationships of Tyre, Sidon, and the Decapolis (see Mark 7:31). See Raymond E. Brown, *Introduction to the New Testament* (New Haven, CT: Yale University Press, 1997), 160, n. 83.

6. R. T. France, *The Gospel of Mark*, The New International Greek Testament Commentary (Grand Rapids, MI: Eerdmans, 2002), 281–83, 286–87.

7. Martin Hengel, *Studies in the Gospel of Mark*, trans. John Bowden (Eugene, OR: Wipf and Stock, 1985), 9–10, 29; Marcus, *Mark 1–8*, 19–21; Donahue and Harrington, *Gospel of Mark*, 38–39.

8. Hengel, *Studies in the Gospel of Mark*, 29.

9. Hengel, *Studies in the Gospel of Mark*, 7–14, 28.

10. Hengel, *Studies in the Gospel of Mark*, 81–84.

11. Eusebius, *The Ecclesiastical History I*, trans. Kirsopp Lake, Loeb Classical Library 153 (Cambridge, MA: Harvard University Press, 1926, repr. 1998), 297.

12. See, for instance, the doubts of Marcus, *Mark 1–8*, 22–23, and, to a lesser extent, the hesitancy to accept or reject Papias. Donahue and Harrington, *Gospel of Mark*, 41. Such suspicion seems, in part, to be a function of a larger trend in historical Jesus studies to be suspicious to varying degrees regarding the reliability of the Gospels, usually by questioning the reliability of their sources. Partly because Papias' own description of how he gathered his information suggests that he preferred what he heard rather than what he could find in books (Papias at. Eusebius, *Ecclesiastical History* 3.39.4; Eusebius, *Ecclesiastical History I*, 293), some have in fact seen Papias as getting his information from a chain of possibly unreliable oral transmission.

13. Richard Bauckham, *Jesus and the Eyewitnesses: The Gospels as Eyewitness Testimony* (Grand Rapids, MI: Eerdmans, 2006), 15–34, 202–4. Bauckham differentiates carefully between oral tradition, which is anonymous and usually spans many generations, and oral history, which is more immediate and includes eyewitnesses.

14. Bauckham, *Jesus and the Eyewitnesses*, 205–14.

15. See Bauckham's discussion as to whether *syntaxin* here refers to chronological order or an aesthetic, literary arrangement. *Jesus and the Eyewitnesses*, 217–21.

16. Irenaeus, *Ante-Nicene Fathers. Volume 1: The Apostolic Fathers, Justin Martyr, Irenaeus* (Peabody, MA, 1885, repr. 2004), 414.

17. R. G. Heard, "The Old Gospel Prologues," *Journal of Theological Studies*, n.s., 6 (1955): 4; Hengel, *Studies in the Gospel of Mark*, 3.

18. Eusebius, *The Ecclesiastical History II*, trans. J. E. L. Oulton, Loeb Classical Library 265 (Cambridge, MA: Harvard University Press, 1932), 49.

19. Eusebius, *The Ecclesiastical History I*, 143, 145.

20. Eusebius, *The Ecclesiastical History II*, 75; see Hengel, *Studies in the Gospel of Mark*, 4.

21. Marcus, *Mark 1–8*, 22–24.

22. Hengel, *Studies in the Gospel of Mark*, 3–4; William L. Lane, *The Gospel according to Mark*, The New International Commentary on the New Testament (Grand Rapids, MI: Eerdmans, 1974), 7–10; Donahue and Harrington, *Gospel of Mark*, 40–41; Bauckham, *Jesus and the Eyewitnesses*, 235–39.

23. Brown, *Introduction to the New Testament*, 159.

24. France, *Gospel of Mark*, 36–38.

25. Brown, *Introduction to the New Testament*, 160. See, however, the recent arguments of Bauckham, *Jesus and the Eyewitnesses*, 210–214.

26. Frank F. Judd Jr., "Who Really Wrote the Gospels?," in *How the New Testament Came to Be*, ed. Kent P. Jackson and Frank F. Judd Jr. (Provo, UT: Religious Studies Center; Salt Lake City: Deseret Book, 2006), 130–32, 135.

27. Kevin L. Barney, "The Joseph Smith Translation and Ancient Texts of the Bible," in *Dialogue: A Journal of Mormon Thought* 19, no. 3 (1987): 88.

28. Barney, "The Joseph Smith Translation and Ancient Texts of the Bible," 88; *Joseph Smith's New Translation of the Bible: Original Manuscripts*, ed. Scott H. Faulring, Kent P. Jackson, and Robert J. Matthews (Provo, UT: Religious Studies Center, 2004), 235, 314, 359, 442; Kent P. Jackson, "Asking Restoration Questions in New Testament Scholarship," in *How the New Testament Came to Be*, 30.

29. Jackson, "Asking Restoration Questions," 29–30.

30. Judd, "Who Really Wrote the Gospels?," 132.

31. Hengel, *Studies in the Gospel of Mark*, 10, 59. Of these times, Mark specifically names Peter (either as Simon or Peter) 20 times: Mark 1:16 (called from nets); 1:29 (Jesus enters his house); 1:36 (follows Jesus out of Capernaum); 3:16 (numbered among the Twelve and surnamed Peter); 5:37 (taken with James and John to witness the raising of the daughter of Jairus); 8:29 (declares Jesus to be the Christ at Caesarea Philippi); 8:32 (rebukes Jesus after the first passion prediction); 8:33 (rebuked by Jesus and told to "get behind him"); 9:2 (Jesus takes onto the Mount of Transfiguration); 9:5 (offers to build "tabernacles" for Jesus, Moses, and Elijah); 10:28 (claims to have left all); 11:21 (recalls Jesus' cursing of the fig tree); 13:3 (with James, John, and Andrew hears the Olivet Discourse); 14:29 (claims he will not be offended in Jesus); 14:33 (taken with James and John into Gethsemane); 14:37 (found sleeping); 14:54 (follows Jesus to the palace of the high priest after his arrest); 14:67 (set up to first denial); 14:70 (set up to third denial); 14:72 (weeps after cock crows); 16:7 (to be told about the empty tomb).

32. Hengel, *Studies in the Gospel of Mark*, 59; Bockmuehl, *Simon Peter in Scripture and Memory*, 132.

33. Pheme Perkins, *Peter: Apostle for the Whole Church* (Minneapolis: Fortress Press, 2000), 57; Bockmuehl, *Simon Peter in Scripture and Memory*, 132.

34. Bauckham, *Jesus and the Eyewitnesses*, 124–27, 132–47. He makes similar arguments for the Beloved Disciple in John (127–129) and the women in Luke (129–32).

35. Bauckham, *Jesus and the Eyewitnesses*, 156–64.

36. Hengel, *Studies in the Gospel of Mark*, 50. See, for instance, Justin, *Dialogue with Trypho*. 106.3 on Mark 3:16 and the renaming of Peter.

37. Marcus, *Mark 1–8*, 24.

38. Hengel, *Studies in the Gospel of Mark*, 51.

39. C. Emden, "St. Mark's Debt to St. Peter," *ChurchQuarterly Review* 154 (1953): 67; Bauckham, *Jesus and the Eyewitnesses*, 177–79. See, however, Marcus, *Mark 1–8*, 24, for the opposite conclusion.

40. Ben Witherington, *The Gospel of Mark: A Socio-Rhetorical Commentary* (Grand Rapids, MI: Eerdmans, 2001), 54–56; Donahue and Harrington, *Gospel of Mark*, 30–34; France, *Gospel of Mark*, 27–29.

41. Martin Hengel, *Saint Peter: The Underestimated Apostle*, trans. Thomas H. Tripp (Grand Rapids, MI: Eerdmans, 2010), 43.

42. James I. H. McDonald, *Kerygma and Didache: The Articulation and Structure of the Earliest Christian Message* (Cambridge: Cambridge University Press, 1980), 1.

43. McDonald, *Kerygma and Didache*, 2–7.

44. Dodd, *The Apostolic Preaching*, 7.

45. Acts 1:16–22 (speech about replacing Judas); 2:14–36, 38–39 (sermon at Pentecost); 3:12–26 (sermon after healing the lame man); 4:8–12 (speech to the Sanhedrin after first arrest); 5:3–4, 8–9 (words to Ananias and Saphira); 5:29–32 (speech to Sanhedrin after second arrest); 10:34–43 (sermon to Cornelius and his household); 11:5–17 (speech to the Judaizers); 15:7–11 (speech at the Jerusalem Council). While sayings of Peter dominate the first part of the book of Acts, it is unclear to what extent these speeches, sermons, and other words of the Apostle reflect what he actually said on the various occasions. In addition to not having been present in any of these instances, Luke, the traditional author of Acts, seems to have largely followed the literary conventions of Classical historiography, which allowed authors to compose speeches for their characters, which, following the method of the Greek historian Thucydides, tried to be as accurate as possible while reflecting what the author himself thought was appropriate for the occasion. See Thucydides, *History of the Peloponnesian War* (Cambridge, MA: Harvard University Press, 1919), 1.22.1–2. See also Ben Witherington, *The Acts of the Apostles: A Socio-Rhetorical Commentary* (Grand Rapids, MI: Eerdmans, 1998), 47, interprets the Thucydides passage slightly differently, suggesting that "what was fitting" (*edokoun*) may in fact be translated as "seems likely" was actually said.

46. Matthew 12:41 and Luke 11:32, both referring to the preaching of Jonah; Romans 16:25 (x2); 1 Corinthians 1:21, 2:4, 15:14; 2 Timothy 4:17; Titus 1:3. See Gerhard Friedrich, "*kēryx, kēryssō, kērygma, prokēryssō*," in *Theological Dictionary of the New Testament*, ed. Gerhard Kittel, trans. Geoffrey W. Bromley (Grand Rapids, MI: Eerdmans, 1965), 704; O. Merk, "*kēryssō*," in *Exegetical Dictionary of the New Testament*, ed. Horst Balz and Gerhard Schneider (Grand Rapids, MI: Eerdmans, 1991), 2.288. It also appears in Mark only in the so-called shorter ending of Mark. See Bruce M. Metzger, *Textual Commentary on the Greek New Testament*, 3rd ed. (Stuttgart, Germany: United Bible Societies, 1975), 122–26, an addition to Mark 6:18 that refers to "the holy and imperishable *proclamation* of eternal salvation" (*to hieron kai aphtarton kērygma tēs aiōniou sōtērias*) that the risen Jesus sent out to the world through Peter and those with him.

47. Merk, "*kēryssō*," 288. With the exception of Revelation 5:2, neither the verb nor the noun appears in the Johannine writings, which prefer *marytreō*, or "witness." See Friedrich, "*kēryx, kēryssō, kērygma, prokēryssō*," 703.

48. Friedrich, "*kēryx, kēryssō, kērygma, prokēryssō*," 711.

49. C.H. Dodd, *The Apostolic Preaching and Its Developments* (New York: Harper & Brothers, 1960), 8.

50. Hengel, *Studies in the Gospel of Mark*, 53–54.

51. Dodd, *The Apostolic Preaching*, 9–17.

52. Dodd, *The Apostolic Preaching*, 17.

53. Perkins, *Peter*, 33–34.

54. See Dodd, *The Apostolic Preaching*, 20, who notes that the speech at 5:29–32 appears in an episode which may well be a doublet of the earlier arrest, and this speech largely recycles the earlier speeches without the telltale Aramaicisms that might suggest that is was based on a Semitic original.

55. F. F. Bruce, *The Book of Acts* (Grand Rapids, MI: Eerdmans, 1988), 63.

56. Hengel, *Studies in the Gospel of Mark*, 54–56; Witherington, *The Gospel of Mark*, 359–68. Perhaps significantly this speech, though written in Greek, contain Semiticisms—constructions and even vocabulary that reflect the influence of Hebrew or Aramaic. In this instance, Luke may have been following a source rather literally, whether oral or written, that may have been quite close to Peter's original words. See F. F. Bruce, *The Book of Acts*, The New International Commentary on the New Testament, rev. ed. (Grand Rapids, MI: Eerdmans, 1988), 213.

57. John F. O'Grady, "The Origins of the Gospels: Mark," in *Biblical Theology Bulletin* 9 (Sage, 1979), 157–58.

58. Dodd, *The Apostolic Preaching*, 25–26.

59. Dodd, *The Apostolic Preaching*, 27.

60. Graham H. Twelftree, *Jesus the Miracle Worker* (Downers Grove, IL: InterVarsity Press, 1999), 57–58, 92–101.

61. Eric D. Huntsman, *The Miracles of Jesus* (Salt Lake City: Deseret Book, 2013), 134–35.

62. Dodd, *The Apostolic Preaching*, 47.

63. C. H. Dodd, "The Framework of the Gospel Narrative," *Expository Times* 43 (1931–32): 399–400; Lane, *The Gospel according to Mark*, 10–11; Bruce, *The Book of Acts*, 212–13. France, *Gospel of Mark*, 8 n. 18, is less convinced by the correspondence, noting that the speech in Acts 10 corresponds to other kerygmatic outlines.

64. France, *Gospel of Mark*, 11–14; see also Marcus, *Mark 1–8*, 63–64; Donahue and Harrington, *Gospel of Mark*, 46–50.

65. Dodd, *The Apostolic Preaching*, 47.

66. While the statement of Papias that Peter preached *pros tas chreias* has traditionally been taken to mean "as necessity demanded" (Eusebius, *Ecclesiastical History*, 3.39.15), *chreiai* may also refer to the types of anecdotes that Peter related (see discussion below).

67. If Mark ended with Mark 16:8, as the earliest and best Greek manuscripts do, the final response of the women to this charge after their initial uncertainty and fear is unknown: they may in fact be types of all readers and potential believers who must make a decision about how to respond to the proclamation. But even with the longer, probably reconstructed, ending (see Mark 16:9–20), the responses of others to the Risen Lord serves the same function. See Eric D. Huntsman, *God So Loved the World: The Final Days of the Savior's Life* (Salt Lake City: Deseret Book, 2011), 111.

68. Witherington, *Gospel of Mark*, 6, 9, 12–15; Donahue and Harrington, *Gospel of Mark*, 7.

69. Witherington, *Gospel of Mark*, 22. See also Bauckham, *Jesus and the Eyewitnesses*, 214–17.

70. France, *Gospel of Mark*, 9.

71. Miracle stories: Mark 1:21–28, 29–31, 40–45; 3:1–6; 4:35–41; 5:1–20, 21–24, 35–43, 25–34; 6:32–44, 45–52; 7:24–30, 31–37; 8:1–10, 22–26; 9:2–8, 14–29; 10:46–52; 11:12–14, 20–26. Summaries: Mark 1:32–34; 3:7–12; 6:2, 5; 53–56; Report: Mark 3:22.

72. Huntsman, *The Miracles of Jesus*, 134.

73. Brown, *Introduction to the New Testament*, 10–11.

74. Hengel, *Studies in the Gospel of Mark*, 52; *St. Peter*, 43–44.

75. Brown, *Introduction to the New Testament*, 156.

76. Hengel, *Studies in the Gospel of Mark*, 83.

77. Bockmuehl, *Simon Peter in Scripture and Memory*, 134–35.

78. Hengel, *Saint Peter*, 101.

79. Lane, *Gospel according to Mark*, 8; France, *Gospel of Mark*, 41.

10

Peter in the House of Tabitha
LATE ANTIQUE SARCOPHAGI AND CHRISTIAN PHILANTHROPY

Catherine C. Taylor

Catherine C. Taylor is adjunct faculty in the Department of Ancient Scripture at Brigham Young University.

In the Acts of the Apostles 9:36–41 are accounts of Peter's miracles in Lydda and Joppa; namely, the healing of Aeneas and the raising of Tabitha prior to the conversion of Cornelius and the opening of the Gentile mission. Luke, the author of Acts, situates Peter's journeys and miracles directly following the conversion of Saul and the subsequent Pauline ministry. Peter's authority is the clear marker for the inauguration of the mission to the Gentile nations[1] and results in kindling faith in Christ and regional conversion. While these broad-ranging themes make the Petrine miracles coherent as a whole, there are very important individual themes that help illuminate early Christian reception of these accounts. The aim of this paper is not to address the overarching and even contextually divisive issue of Gentile conversion, but to focus instead on the single illustration of Peter in Tabitha's house.

The similitude of the Apostle's action to Jesus' own raising of the daughter of Jairus by his command "*Talitha cumi*,"[2] "Damsel, . . . arise" (Mark 5:41), echoes in Peter's familiar and imperative command "Tabitha, arise" (Acts 9:40). Peter's interaction demonstrates the archetypal attentiveness and care for women that Jesus modeled for his followers. This same close attention and interaction was also demonstrated in the memorialization of the lives of late antique Christian women. With regard to this particular miracle, scriptural text and its earliest visual representations reveal how virtuous matronage of late antiquity was a force of public legitimization for the cause of Christianity and the elevation of its philanthropic profile. Latter-day Saint women today carry on this same heritage by relieving suffering wherever it is found and expanding hearts and minds through their spiritual gifts and humanitarian service.

As early as 1989, President Thomas S. Monson called attention to the account of Peter's healing of Tabitha:

> Now there was at Joppa a certain disciple named Tabitha, which by interpretation is called Dorcas: this woman was full of good works and almsdeeds which she did.
>
> And it came to pass in those days, that she was sick, and died: whom when they had washed, they laid her in an upper chamber.
>
> And forasmuch as Lydda was nigh to Joppa, and the disciples had heard that Peter was there, they sent unto him two men, desiring him that he would not delay to come to them.
>
> Then Peter arose and went with them. When he was come, they brought him into the upper chamber: and all the widows stood by him weeping, and shewing the coats and garments which Dorcas made, while she was with them.
>
> But Peter put them all forth, and kneeled down, and prayed; and turning him to the body said, Tabitha, arise. And she opened her eyes: and when she saw Peter, she sat up.
>
> And he gave her his hand, and lifted her up, and when he had called the saints and widows, presented her alive.
>
> And it was known throughout all Joppa; and many believed in the Lord. (Acts 9:36–42)

President Monson asked several poignant questions about the account of Peter and Tabitha that are applicable today: "Would it not be ever so sad if such a window to priesthood power, to faith, to healing, were to be restricted to Joppa alone? Are these sacred and moving accounts recorded only for our uplift and enlightenment? Can we not apply such mighty lessons to our daily lives?"[3] These questions of reception are prophetically the same today as they were for the earliest Christians. The particular focus of this paper remains on this query, "Are these sacred and moving accounts recorded only for our uplift and enlightenment?" The visual iconography and texts that were part of the early church provide us with a clear and didactic answer to that question. Not only was the account of Peter and Tabitha important as part of a larger narrative, it was used to underscore faithful female industriousness and the generosity of their Christian households.

The story of Peter in Tabitha's house has traditionally been used to highlight widows' experiences in the early church or to illustrate charitable love within early Christian communities.[4] However, little attention has been given to the reception of early Christian images and text that address the iconography of Peter and the household of Tabitha. It is worth looking closely at sarcophagi with Christian iconography, including that of Peter raising Tabitha from the dead, because they demonstrate the devotion of late antique Christians, whose faith "was so certain in the face of death that it admitted no doubts and no alternative thoughts and feelings."[5]

One underlying factor that the textual account has in common with the visual representation of Peter raising Tabitha is the rhetorical nature of both. The viewer is asked, in the questioning context of text and image, something very striking about late antique reception of scripture. Namely, how and why were text and image used as points of commemoration and memorialization in the lives of Christian believers? While Peter is most frequently represented in art associated with his apostleship to the Lord Jesus Christ, the account of Peter raising Tabitha illuminates the Apostle's ministry at the very cusp of Christianity's unhindered spread.

Peter in Tabitha's House

Peter's interactions with Aeneas, Tabitha, and Cornelius can be seen as a series of culminating events in which Cornelius's conversion marks that pinnacle moment when Peter establishes the blessings of Israel amongst all faithful Gentiles. For Peter, Cornelius, and the Gentile world, Jesus Christ becomes Lord of all. However, privileging the visit of Peter to Caesarea necessarily overshadows his visits to Lydda and Joppa, without regard for the fact that, literally and figuratively, Peter doesn't make his way to Caesarea unless he traveled the road through Lydda and Joppa.

The second miracle of these three, described in Acts 9:39–41, finds Peter the chief Apostle in the city of Joppa, having been summoned to Tabitha's house. According to Acts 9:31, which directly precedes the trilogy of healing and conversion events, it becomes clear that the churches in Galilee and Judea were established in relative peace, and Luke witnesses the progress of the church under the authority of Peter.[6] The deliberate choice of Peter's journeying is not recorded according to happenstance or to merely provide fodder for his culminating interaction with Cornelius. The author of Acts has necessarily focused attention on this series of three Petrine interactions by specifically choosing to include them, perhaps over others. In a similar gesture, this study will examine Peter's interaction with Tabitha at an interdisciplinary crossroad, where Acts 9 meets the earliest visual representations of Peter in Tabitha's house.

Luke introduces Tabitha, whose Aramaic name translated into Greek is Dorkas, with both names meaning "gazelle." Tabitha's character has been associated with the gazelle as a symbol of a nurturer or life giver.[7] The speed of the gazelle is noted in *The Targum of Canticles* 2:9 and 2:17 as Yahweh "runs like a gazelle" to save Egypt and Abraham, Isaac, and Jacob are "swift in worshiping Him, as a gazelle."[8] It is easy to see how Peter's attentions to Tabitha were useful in expanding Christianity's borders beyond Jewish believers. His miracle was a symbol of love, compassion, service, and graciousness, demonstrated for Jewish Christians or proselytes to emulate as they interacted with new communities of Christian converts. Tabitha's example of Christian acceptance is an important and underlying foundation to charitable acts during the earliest years of the church and its continued historicity during the fourth century.

Tabitha's story is quintessentially the story of faithful women whose actions help establish a model of valiancy meant for emulation in the emerging Christian borderlands. Joppa or Jaffa was an ancient Philistine maritime city conquered by David and ruled over by Solomon. It was set in the Plain of Sharon and had long been associated as a Mediterranean seaport and hub of commerce.[9] Joppa was a crossroads, a borderland, but also a place specifically associated with materials used for the building of the temple. Joppa is twice used in the Old Testament to receive materials for the temple of Jerusalem: first as a port of landing for the cedars of Lebanon (see 2 Chronicles 2:16) and second during the reign of Cyrus, when it was also a landing port for materials intended for the reconstruction of the temple (see Ezra 3:7). During the first century, Joppa was home to Jews, Jewish Christians, and Gentiles. It was also home to Tabitha, whose tomb is still visited as part of Christian pilgrimage.[10] Luke seems to emphasize the geography of the Holy Land,[11] including Joppa, as a way of perhaps setting it apart or making it special from the rest of the world. Tabitha's merit amongst her community is also associated with material goods: coats and garments or tunics and mantles, articles of material substance given to her household, the widows, and the poor are depicted in a series of three sarcophagi from the fourth century.

Art and Artifactual Data

Turning our attention to art, artifacts, and material culture has long been a practice for scholars of late antique Christianity. Art has been used to augment our understanding of the New Testament text with little-known insights occasionally coming to light through the historical reception of artistic representation. The study of sarcophagi has long focused on iconographic categories that aligned across the divide of pagan and Christian subjects. However, the understanding of each category can help illuminate the development of the other.

Elaborate and figural decorated sarcophagi from the end of the second century to the beginning of the fifth century represent a massive oeuvre numbering thousands with even tens of thousands of non-complex designed sarcophagi that remain from the period. These sarcophagi vary in richness and type. Many problems are inherent in the use of sarcophagi for historical references including issues of original site destruction and the loss or absence of epigraphic data. However, there is still much evidence toward visual reception that can be gleaned from patterns of iconography.

Sarcophagi were used, often for multiple family members, reused, and even reappropriated for saintly reliquaries or displayed as *spolia* decoration on the facades of later churches.[12] Sarcophagi were sometimes decorated to represent a type of micro-architectural box used to house one or more bodies of deceased persons,[13] often members of the same familial household. Despite the absence of an integrated context for most sarcophagi, it remains relevant that sarcophagi were meant to house and protect the deceased and were designed for view by the living.[14] Furthermore, sarcophagi provide us with our richest single source of late antique Christian iconography and immediately cross into the realm of the most personal and even private of contexts; death and the memorialization of life.

The space available for visual representation on sarcophagi is inherently limited and literally set in stone with images meant to be read and understood as messages, even for those without literary training. So, when Peter is featured on a sarcophagus in a singular role in a particular narrative, it becomes rather evident that the viewer is to read the story through the lens of its specificity. Peter's association with Tabitha, underscored by his apostleship, legitimizes the Christian household for the late antique audience. His presence and the miracle wrought through the name of Jesus give attention, credence, and validity to the model of matronly virtue, borrowed from Roman social mores and adapted for Christian use.

Only recently have scholars started to revisit the patterns of iconography available on late antique sarcophagi, objects necessarily restricted in spatial field and with a relatively limited repertoire of iconographic types.[15] These types were, however, subject to the varied and creative license of the artisan in their execution. The sarcophagi discussed here are Roman in style and provenance with Christian themes, a dynamic that immediately calls our attention to the issues of the faithful demonstration of piety and Christian apology.

A fourth-century sarcophagus fragment, today in the Musée de L'Arles Antique (fig. 1), features two scenes divided by a fluted Corinthian column; the first scene includes two female figures, one kneeling and one standing. They are both wearing Phrygian-style snood caps, a phenomenon to be discussed later in this paper. In the scene below, the Apostle Peter is shown raising Tabitha from the dead. Her figure fills the picture plane and is elegantly positioned in a seated recline with Peter grasping her wrist with both hands to raise her. She is surrounded by four female figures; two stand behind Tabitha's bed each wearing a snood. The other two wear a traditional palla and stola and are kneeling beneath the raised bed platform. The figures are scaled according to hierarchal proportion and eagerly gesture toward Peter. The woman nearest Peter touches the hem of his garment. The high-relief figures in the scene are framed with an architectural cornice and Corinthian columns. There is no background detail. The sarcophagus front is from Roman Gaul with a likely provenance in Arles prior to the reign of Honorius (AD 395–423).[16]

Another fourth-century sarcophagus (fig. 2), today at Assunta Cathedral in Fermo, Italy, shows a series of five scenes along its frontal frieze, all separated by a series of architectural pediments and arches supported by columns.[17] The central

Fig. 1. Raising of Tabitha, sarcophagus fragment, Musée de L'Arles Antique, 4th century AD. Giuseppe Wilpert. Rome: Pontificio Istituto di Archeologia Cristiana, 1929. Plate CXLV, no. 6.

Fig. 2. Sarcophagus, Assunta Cathedral, Fermo, Italy, 4th century AD. Giuseppe Wilpert. Rome: Pontificio Istituto di Archeologia Cristiana, 1929. Plate CXVI, no. 3.

panel shows Christ flanked by Cain and Abel with their respective offerings of lamb and sheaf.

The vignettes above show a story continuum related to Peter. Each scene relates to the merits of individual offerings, including sacrificial offerings, good works, and the actual life of the Apostle. On the far left we find Peter standing between a disciple and a widow with another widow supplicating him at his feet, symbolic of the widows who show Peter the fruits of Tabitha's generous offerings. The continuous narrative sees the story to its conclusion with Peter grasping Tabitha's arm and raising her. Now on her feet, Tabitha is dressed as a traditional matron, while another male disciple stands witness to the miracle at Peter's left. To the immediate right of Christ in the central panel, we find the narrative sequence describing Peter's miraculous escape from prison as the fully armed soldiers are found sleeping in the fourth panel and Peter is being led away by a wingless angel in the fifth.

The most detailed of our three sarcophagi is the fourth-century Roman-style example today at the Church of Ste. Madeleine in Saint Maximin, France (fig. 3).[18] The columnar sarcophagus is large and elaborate with scenes depicting Christ healing the centurion's servant, healing the man born blind, Christ's Resurrection represented symbolically, Christ prophesying the denial of Peter, and the miracle of the woman with an issue of blood. All of these scenes are Christ-centered along the main frieze of the sarcophagus with the ends being significantly different in subject matter. It was not an uncommon practice for the short ends of a sarcophagus to be carved in lower-relief scenes, perhaps even specified or chosen by the patron. On the left end we find Peter raising Tabitha (fig. 4) in a well-appointed room, complete with draperies, a luxurious bed, an architectural column, and a pipe organ.

Tabitha is depicted here as a type of new philanthropic exemplar as demonstrated in the varied figures she is shown helping. Figures of the poor are diminutively small and kneel or sit near the side of the bed. Two women (widows) are standing behind Tabitha with their gaze and gestures directed toward her. Tabitha is proportionately

Figs. 3, 4. Sarcophagus front and Raising of Tabitha detail, Church of Ste. Madeleine, Saint Maximin, France, 4th century AD. Giuseppe Wilpert. Rome: Pontificio Istituto di Archeologia Cristiana, 1929. Plate CXLV, nos. 5, 7.

large and fills the picture plane. Her dress is a simple stola without the traditional palla to veil her head. Her hair is neatly coiffed, perhaps covered, and prepared for burial. In addition to the two widows standing behind Tabitha's bed, we find three smaller figures representing the poor in the foreground next to Tabitha's bed. Indeed, they are small, according to the standards of hierarchy of scale, precisely because they are poor and are of a distinctively different social class when compared to Tabitha and the stately, matronly widows. Tabitha's left hand rests on the head of the small female figure at her left who supports a seated, naked figure with her hands and right knee. The third kneeling figure is set apart from the others and reaches out to touch the hem of Peter's garment: a gesture similar to that of the woman with an issue of blood touching Christ's garment. This third figure wears a peculiar head covering like the female figures on the sarcophagus from Arles (fig. 1). This pointed snood is akin to the Phrygian cap of the foreign magi who are often shown wearing similar hats in artistic representations of the Adoration of the Magi. The widows and the woman with the naked boy are easy to situate into the Levitical laws regarding the care of the widows and the fatherless.[19] However, the inclusion of the Phrygian capped figures indicates that Tabitha's generosity was considered, within the fourth century, to include the foreign poor as well, a notion that coincides with the nature of diverse port cities like Joppa.

At the opposite end of the sarcophagus, we find an extraordinary depiction of the deceased as a female orant figure posed in a formalized portrait of prayer (fig. 5). She is dressed with matronly finesse and stands in a *contrapposto* pose between two trees with a large scrinium at her feet.

Fig. 5. Sarcophagus detail, Female Orant, Church of Ste. Madeleine, Saint Maximin, France, 4th century AD. Giuseppe Wilpert. Rome: Pontificio Istituto di Archeologia Cristiana, 1929. Plate CCXVII, no. 1.

The choice of detail here may indicate that the deceased was a lettered woman, perhaps with resources to become educated.[20] We can relate the scenes on the ends of the sarcophagus to each other. Both display Christian women of some means, respectively represented for their good works and lauded for their piety. This visual connection between the textual past and the visual present became the new model for female Christian householders.

On the Ste. Maximin sarcophagus, Christian iconography was employed alongside scenes presenting the deceased as an orant, pious believer. This combination served to close the idealized gap between the character and meaning of the biblical scenes and the attributes, idealized though they may be, of the deceased, their associates, and the anonymous viewer. Deceased orant figures could be pictured praying on behalf of their spouse or kinsmen. It is equally valid to argue that she was praying for her own salvation, armed with the example of Tabitha as her guide. If the scene of the deceased is to be read as an individual interpretation, a more general image of devotion and salvific hope is in order. Nevertheless, evoking the notion that Christianity was connected with social status, at least where decorated sarcophagi were concerned, was a popular trend.

Clearly, one of the most divisive issues in the book of Acts was the status of Gentiles amongst Christian communities. By examining this series of fourth-century sarcophagi, produced with Roman provenance, we find that the iconography of Tabitha and her association with varied classes of people and with Peter takes on a particular agenda. It is not hard to imagine that these images moved beyond the mere illustration of Christian storylines to a decisive display of new legitimacy for new converts amongst Jewish communities, Gentiles, and foreigners alike, that aligned themselves with the respectable, honored, and sanctioned household of the faithful, even the household of faithful women.

Although we are only examining three sarcophagi here, they should not be dismissed, regardless of their initial singularity in image or scope. Scenes on sarcophagi act as points of historic reference whether they demonstrate actual events, idealized events, or even imaginary events; they give us insight into the paradigms of their day. These scenes reference real people, typologies of real people, and the ideals and values chosen to commemorate them in death.

Patristic Historicity and Fourth-Century Context

Peter's association with Tabitha, perhaps a widow herself, and the widows within her care is directly related to fourth-century patristic language with regard to widows, their social status, and their official treatment within the early church.

The status of unmarried women, widows in particular, seems to have changed over time. By the beginning of the second century, there was a body of Christian widows large enough to require official statements on how they should be cared for and their role in performing charitable works.[21] Additionally, there was some censure directed at the behavior of indiscreet widows in Polycarp's *Letter to the Philippians*, in which he adjures them to "refrain from all slander, gossip, false witness, love of money."[22] That there is some talk of the inappropriate behavior of widowed women in gossiping, idleness, and meddling would either indicate that it was indeed happening, or that it was perceived as happening by those writing about it, and that this behavior was seen as a threat.

In the third-century treatise *Didascalia Apostolorum*, widows are again censured not only as gossips and chatterers, but also as women who use their circumstances to unfairly profit by it; those who "are no widows, but wallets, and they care for nothing but to be making ready to receive" and "impatient to be running after gain."[23] Widows with means and the ability to make money are addressed as a threat, perhaps without merit. However, the tone of rhetoric towards women in the third century changes dramatically in the fourth century when those same women are lauded for their status as widowed, wealthy ascetic types that have dedicated their lives and fortunes to God. Women like Macrina the Younger and Melania the Elder are lauded as young widows who dispensed of their immense wealth among the poor.[24] One of the most notable women, also not forgotten, was Olympias of Constantinople, who, when widowed at twenty-one, dedicated her wealth to the patronage of a women's community adjacent to Hagia Sophia.[25] The official tone of patristic rhetoric changes from condemnation to commemoration as John Chrysostom, Olympias's friend, will comment on Tabitha's material benevolence. Chrysostom acknowledges Tabitha's house and indirectly comments on its wealth through counterpoint by describing how "it was not her house that proclaimed her wealth, nor the walls, nor the stones, nor the pillars, but the bodies of widows furnished with dress, and their tears that were shed, and death that played the runaway, and life that came back again."[26]

Ambrose (AD 340–97) in his *Concerning Widows*, affirmed that widowhood is very close in status and esteem to that of virginity, and that both are to be preferred over the married state.[27] He uses examples of widows from the Old and New Testaments as bastions of social good and asserts that only idolaters condemn widows.[28] Without condemning second marriages outright, Ambrose encourages those under his stewardship to embrace widowhood as the highest good available to them. In chapter 1 of his commentary, he emphasizes the virtues of widowhood and specifically discusses the expectations of widows' hospitality, that it should not be limited in its scope. To illustrate his point, he exemplifies the widow of Sarepta who gave all she had to Elijah, the prophet of God.[29] From its inception, it was not uncommon for women, especially wealthy widows, to give their wealth to the church.[30]

In his praise of widows, Ambrose elevates the status of widows in a public way by associating them with heavenly honor and virtue. In fact, no more than a century following Ambrose, we find evidence that the Christian elite is being addressed in letters and household manuals, like the *Liber ad Gregoriam in palatio*, written specifically for the Christian *Domina*, who could be encouraged to distribute her independent wealth and property with the aid of her spiritual leaders.[31] There is a direct correlation between the language associated with widowhood and virginity that will ultimately undermine the power of familial social structures, estates, and inheritances through church acquisition of such properties.[32]

Classic acts of charity, providing for widows and orphans, were true religion in the early Christian world and were closely related to ideals of personal perfection. Female patrons had perhaps become so influential in the early Christian world that by the fourth century, the church took decisive action and established a formulaic ideal for female patronage as witnessed in Ambrose's treatises. The church gladly acted as beneficiary to whom a large portion of property as well as liquid assets would eventually come. Ambrose is certainly influenced by the example of his own ascetically minded sister, Marcellina, to whom he dedicates Book III of his *De Virginibus ad Marcellinam* or *On Virgins*. Ambrose's language in his theological treatises reads much like a coercive capital campaign speech directed at wealthy widows and was effective in underpinning Christian ideas regarding true charity and philanthropy.

The Philanthropy of Death and Women's Households

Female family members, in particular widows, were known to be heads of household, a circumstance that was mitigated early by the church. Some of our best evidence for the influence of virtuous matrons whose resources impacted the spread of Christianity comes to us from the New Testament.[33] In a world where patronage was essential to maintaining social mores, it is revealing to find matrons who not only managed a household but also acted as benefactors beyond their immediate family in the pattern of Tabitha. *Matronae* in the early Christian tradition are evidenced in text and image. For example, Anicia Faltonia Proba clearly viewed Christianity as a legacy "to be handed down within families, rather than a call to abandon family life."[34] Furthermore, there are late-fourth-century inscriptions lauding her role as familial matron: "Anicia Faltonia Proba, trustee of the ancient *nobilitas*, pride of the Anician family, a model of the preservation and teaching of wifely virtue, descendant of consuls, mother of consuls."[35] Other women, not quite so conspicuous in their patronage, are visually represented for their charitable guidance toward pious matrons. For example, the Catacombs of Domitilla in Rome are home to a fourth-century lunette fresco depicting Saint Petronilla, the legendary daughter of Peter, leading Veneranda, a matron worthy of veneration for her Christian faith, toward paradise, in a scene complete with a large scrinium.[36]

While female patronage within households and within secular settings has not been adequately documented, we do have a number of sources that identify Imperial Christian women of the fourth century who follow in the footsteps of Constantine's mother Helena in undertaking such a course for the church. Women like Aelia Flavia Flaccilla, Galla Placidia, Eudoxia, and Pulcheria are important examples because they were conspicuous in their patronage of the church—an example not lost on Christian women of various social classes.[37] It is clear that the influence of female householders during the fourth century was anything but an anomaly in late antique Christianity. Part of the reason they were so conspicuous and crucial to the cause of Christianity was precisely because of their ability to provide money, and the substantive resources of their household, if not a church.

Early Christian communities seem to have had some difficulties coming to terms with the complexities of Christian charity. Their primary actions seem to have an eschatological concern over the structures of charitable behavior.[38] Bluntly told, the admonition to "sell that thou hast, and give to the poor" in Matthew 19:21 smacks loudly of ascetic practice, privileging the sanctification of the donor over the benefit to the poor. The emphasis of giving money or goods was closely connected with good works, as was alleviating suffering of all kinds. As Christ had taught the practice, it was to be done in secret, yet the dichotomy remained in which individuals were recognized as charitable by their fruits. For the early Christians, Peter raising Tabitha was in imitation of Jesus' raising the daughter of Jairus, as is evident in the similar iconographic scene from the late-fourth-century Brescia casket with ivory panels (fig. 6). Just as Jesus was concerned over the affairs of women, so Peter is shown administering to Tabitha in recognition of her piety and good works.

Early Christian piety mimicked traditional Jewish piety, functioning through liturgical prayer and good works or benevolent deeds in order to provoke God to gracious action towards the intended supplicant.[39] Peter in Tabitha's house is a fine model of recognizing and empowering women in their charitable

Fig. 6. Brescia casket, Museo di Santa Giulia, Brescia, Italy, 4th century AD. Courtesy of Wikipedia Commons.

capacity to provide for others, not just in physical ways, but also in spiritual ways. Although Peter's interaction with Cornelius is lauded as the inauguration of spiritual rebirth for the Gentile nations, Peter raising Tabitha from the dead is also salvific precisely because her household had already drawn the attention, by love and many almsdeeds, of those who would seek out Peter as the authorized servant of Jesus Christ. For Christians, "good works had no value unless they were motivated by love and were generally subsumed into the normal pattern of daily existence rather than singled out."[40] But here we do have a particular model singled out—the capable household. Again we are presented with an impossible dichotomy and contrasting attitude; charitable gifts are required acts of piety, but a barren household cannot give. In this dichotomy we find the kind of supplicant desired and demonstrated in the rhetorical arrangement of art and text. The sarcophagi discussed here are evidence that up through the third and fourth centuries, late antique Christians chose the story of Tabitha not only as a trope of salvific memorialization, but also as a model for the new Christian household.

The status of widow seems to alleviate some concerns over material needs; it even demands that this group of women be cared for according to Levitical law.[41] Additionally, widows were in a unique position to host the Christian community, visitors, and guests.[42] Widows become distinctive for their acts of service and charity, but also become the focus of some censure precisely because of their influence on their communities. Widows, or more precisely, moneyed and lettered widows of the fourth century, retained a kind of independence that was publicly visible, respectable, and legitimizing, with widowed mothers in particular enjoying full legal status as mistresses of the household.[43]

While it is common to focus on Peter's raising Tabitha from the dead as a miracle with the convenient effect of conversion,[44] commentators have long hesitated in defining the role of Tabitha as a model for late antique Christian women to emulate in performing acts of charity and bestowing goods on the widowed and others less fortunate. There is some discussion that Tabitha was likely a widow herself, but one that had means to maintain her household and expand her philanthropic reach to her community.[45] That Peter goes to Tabitha's house to raise her is not just to demonstrate her ability as a Jewish Christian proselyte to expand the cause of Christianity, but also to normalize a new type of patron within the early church, that of the *Matrona*. The Roman sarcophagus, today in Marseilles, bears out evidence that by the fourth century, Christians have visually interpreted Peter's raising of the deceased Tabitha with the hand of fellowship to a certain type of proselyte: the wealthy, influential, networked matron.

Conclusion

So, what do Christian relief images mean for patrons and viewers of the fourth century? It should be noted that the iconographic themes that we find on sarcophagi are also represented in number on other objects like fresco paintings, mosaics, jewelry, and textiles. As much as Christians were using sculpted relief images on sarcophagi to commemorate the dead, they were also living with these images, making connections with the meaningful representations of scripture in ways that went beyond mere ornament or illustration of Bible stories. Like their pagan counterparts, who largely used myth as an allegorizing feature on their sarcophagi, Christians also use artistic symbolism to celebrate the character and values of the deceased within their communities. Unlike their pagan counterparts, sarcophagi of the late third- and fourth-century take on a kind of seriousness associated with death. The very crossroads of death and tomb, image and text demonstrate that the living were engaged in "assuring themselves of the order of their own world."[46] Furthermore, they speak to hopes, fears, passions, and spiritual aspirations as much as they do to idealized qualities, intellectual values, or virtues.

Like Jonah, saved from the belly of the whale, a certain allusion to the hopes of the deceased in a miraculous resurrection, so too is Tabitha presented amongst scenes of deliverance and miracles in a way that expresses hope in personal salvation for late antique Christians.[47] Paul Zanker, in his discussion of Christian sarcophagi, states, "Gone is any evocation of the achievements and merits of the deceased in the form of mythological allegories."[48] Respectfully, I disagree and counter that a new kind of allegory, a new kind of Christian household, is here introduced and legitimized, in the case of the Tabitha sarcophagi, by Peter himself. We find that just as allegorizing and mythological themes had been indicative of the pagan paradigms of life, so too were Christian sarcophagi concerned with this life, but also necessarily and inextricably tied to salvation in the next life.

This kind of analysis answers the call by President Monson to look further at the scriptural narrative, its representation, and reception; to understand it as more than just an uplifting scripture story or enlightening narrative. This paper contributes new material concerning the memorialization of the late antique Christian dead and focuses our attention on the image of Peter legitimizing the role of the Christian household on sarcophagus images produced during the fourth century. Social standing did not cease to be an important factor for Christian believers. Instead, it became a source of social legitimacy that reinforced the new world of Christian empire with the rule of Constantine.

In Acts, we find Peter and Paul as those authorized to establish communities of believers through priesthood power and the outpouring of the Holy Ghost. For the men of Joppa who seek Peter to come to Tabitha's house after he has healed Aeneas in Lydda, it is necessary that Peter be present as he restores Tabitha to life. Peter will "present" Tabitha as a "living one" to the widows and saints gathered at her house. Peter Strelan has noted that the verb "presented" is used in the same sense that Jesus was presented to the Lord in the temple, with the same impression of dedication and consecration present in the language.[49] Additionally, the Greek translation of *paristano* includes to stand beside, to exhibit, or to recommend. I submit that these defining characteristics were also present in images of Tabitha produced during the fourth century, with special attention focused on Tabitha as a *matrona* type, an able householder of means dedicated and consecrated to the spread of Christianity in all the world. By associating Tabitha visually with widows, the poor, and the foreigner, Luke brings this honored type of female patronage to the fore, all falling under the ultimate sanction of Peter.

Notes

1. Joseph A. Fitzmyer, *The Acts of the Apostles* (New York: Doubleday, 1998), 443.
2. Peter was present when Jesus raised the daughter of Jairus, making the similar imperative language and circumstances even more compelling.
3. Thomas S. Monson, "Windows," *Ensign*, November 1989, 69.
4. Rick Strelan, "Tabitha: The Gazelle of Joppa (Acts 9:36–41)," *Biblical Theology Bulletin* 39, no. 2: 77–86.
5. Paul Zanker and Björn C. Ewald, *Living with Myths: The Imagery of Roman Sarcophagi* (Oxford: Oxford University Press, 2012), 265.
6. A. E. Harvey, *The New English Bible Companion to the New Testament* (Oxford: Oxford University Press; Cambridge: Cambridge University Press, 1970), 434. See Johannes Munck, *The Acts of the Apostles*, The Anchor Bible (Garden City, NY: Doubleday, 1967), 87–88.
7. Asa Strandberg, "The Gazelle in Ancient Egyptian Art: Image and Meaning" (PhD diss., Uppsala University, 2009), 9, 25–32.
8. Philip S. Alexander, *The Targum of Canticles* (Collegeville, MN: The Liturgical Press, 2003), 105, 114; see Strelan, "Tabitha," 80.
9. Joseph A. Fitzmyer, *The Acts of the Apostles* (New York: Doubleday, 1998), 445.
10. Siméon Vailhé, "Jaffa," *The Catholic Encyclopedia*, vol. 8 (New York: Robert Appleton, 1910), 268.
11. Robert M. Grant, "Early Christian Geography," *Vigiliae Christianae* 46, no. 2 (1992): 105.
12. Jaś Elsner, "Introduction," in *Life, Death and Representation: Some New Work on Roman Sarcophagi*, ed. Jaś Elsner and Janet Huskinson (Berlin: De Gruyter, 2011), 4.
13. Edmund Thomas, "'Houses of the Dead': Columnar Sarcophagi as 'Microarchitecture,'" in *Life, Death and Representation*, 387–436.
14. Elsner, "Introduction," 4. Extant historical context is extremely limited and may only be applicable to a few hundred sarcophagi of the many thousand that survive.
15. Jaś Elsner, "Image and Rhetoric in Early Christian Sarcophagi: Reflections on Jesus' Trial," in *Life, Death and Representation*, 359.
16. Fernand Benoit, *Sarcophages Paléochrétiens d'Arles et de Marseille* (Paris: Centre National de la Recherche Scientifique, 1954), 39.
17. Giovanna Maria Gabrielli, *I Sarcophagi Paleocristiani e AltoMedioevali delle Marche* (Ravenna: Edizioni Dante, 1961), 33–41.
18. Brigitte Christern-Briesenick et al., *Repertorium der Christlich-Antiken Sarkophage*, vol. 3 (Mainz am Rhein: Verlag Philipp von Zabern, 2003), 233–35.
19. See Exodus 22:22; Deuteronomy 10:18; Leviticus 19:9–10, 23:22.

20. Jerome's letters are especially rich sources for examples of Christian women who can read and write. Evidence to this end is Jerome's letter to Laeta on the education of her daughter. Jerome, *Epistle* 107. See *Women and Society in Greek and Roman Egypt: A Sourcebook*, ed. Jane Rowlandson (Cambridge: Cambridge University Press, 1998), no. 58, 77–78.

21. Patricia Cox Miller, *Women in Early Christianity* (Washington, DC: The Catholic University of America Press, 2005), 49.

22. Polycarp, *To the Philippians* 4.3, in Miller, *Women in Early Christianity*, 50.

23. *Didascalia apostolorum* 3.6, 3.7, in Miller, *Women in Early Christianity*, 54.

24. Carolinne White, ed. and trans., *Lives of Roman Christian Women* (London: Penguin Books, 2010), 19–48.

25. *The Life of Olympias, Deaconess* (Selections) in Miller, *Women in Early Christianity*, 228–36.

26. John Chrysostom, *Homily XIV on Romans*. From *Nicene and Post-Nicene Fathers, First Series*, vol. 11, ed. Philip Schaff (Grand Rapids, MI: Wm. B. Eerdmans, 1956), 451.

27. Ambrose, *Concerning Widows* 1.1, from *Nicene and Post-Nicene Fathers, Second Series*, vol. 10, ed. Philip Schaff and Henry Wace (Buffalo, NY: Christian Literature, 1896), 391.

28. Ambrose, *Concerning Widows*, 1.3.

29. Ambrose, *Concerning Widows*, 3.14, from *Nicene and Post-Nicene Fathers*, 393.

30. See Luke 8:1–3.

31. Kate Cooper, *Fall of the Roman Household* (Cambridge: Cambridge University Press, 2007), 101–11.

32. Cooper, *Fall of the Roman Household*, 93–143.

33. For example, Luke 8:1–3; Luke 10:38; John 12:2; Acts 16:14–15. See Kate Cooper, *Band of Angels: The Forgotten World of Early Christian Women* (New York: The Overlook Press, 2013).

34. Cooper, *Fall of the Roman Household*, 66.

35. *CIL* 6.1755, trans. in Brian Croke and Jill Harries, *Religious Conflict in Fourth-Century Rome: A Documentary Study* (Sydney: Sydney University Press, 1982), 116, amended by Kate Cooper.

36. Nicola Denzey, *The Bone Gatherers: The Lost World of Early Christian Women* (Boston: Beacon Press, 2007), 125–29.

37. Catherine Taylor, "Allotting the Scarlet and the Purple: Late Antique Images of the Virgin Annunciate Spinning" (PhD diss., University of Manchester, 2012), 206–15.

38. Judith Herrin, *Margins and Metropolis: Authority across the Byzantine Empire* (Princeton: Princeton University Press, 2013), 270–73.

39. Harvey, *The New English Bible Companion to the New Testament*, 436.

40. Herrin, *Margins and Metropolis*, 273.

41. Herrin, *Margins and Metropolis*, 276; see Exodus 22:22; Deuteronomy 10:18; Leviticus 19:9–10, 23:22.

42. Carolyn Osiek and Margaret Y. MacDonald, *A Woman's Place* (Minneapolis: Fortress Press, 2006), 12, 13; see 1 Timothy 5:10.

43. Osiek and MacDonald, *A Woman's Place*, 230.

44. See Fitzmyer, *The Acts of the Apostles*, 445; Munck, *The Acts of the Apostles*, 89.

45. Bonnie Bowman Thurston, *The Widows: A Women's Ministry in the Early Church* (Minneapolis: Fortress Press, 1989), 32–35.

46. Paul Zanker and Björn C. Ewald, *Living with Myths: The Imagery of Roman Sarcophagi* (Oxford: Oxford University Press, 2012), x.

47. Zanker, *Living with Myths*, 264.

48. Zanker, *Living with Myths*, 265.

49. Strelan, "Tabitha," 84.

11

Peter, Cornelius, and Cultural Boundaries

Thomas A. Wayment

Thomas A. Wayment is a professor of ancient scripture at Brigham Young University.

In the second half of the New Testament, the letters of Paul and the book of Acts are particularly and carefully focused on the issue of the church's early missionary efforts among Greek-speaking Gentile communities in Asia Minor, Macedonia, Rome, and Greece.[1] In fact, the interest in and focus on the Gentile mission might be considered a unifying theme in Paul's letters and in Acts. For example, discussions on important doctrinal topics such as grace and foreordination were necessary in light of the increasing numbers of Gentiles joining the church. Some important questions arose in the early church as a result of the Gentile mission: Would God accept Gentiles into heaven, and if he did so, would *they* need grace to enter unlike Jews, who were guaranteed a place in heaven through birthright? Were God's people forever chosen despite the fact that Jews were only infrequently accepting baptism and joining the fledgling Christian church? These questions shaped Paul's letters and forced him to address these topics on multiple occasions. They also direct us to some of the interesting points of discussion that arise out of the letters and histories from the first three decades of the church's existence (AD 30–60).[2]

One particularly perplexing and thematic issue is the resistance that some early Jewish members of the church felt toward teaching the gospel to Gentiles. Additionally, it is possible that some early church leaders may have been culturally conditioned to feel a need to place restraints on the teaching of the gospel to Gentiles. A study of this length cannot consider all of the attitudes that early church members expressed towards Gentiles or whether or not there were even different opinions expressed towards different ethnic groups within the church: Macedonians, Greeks, Romans, Egyptians, or Samaritans. Some would have been more culturally different—Egyptians—while the Samaritans shared many of the same beliefs and practices as ethnic Jews. Despite the limitations of a study such as this, it will be possible to consider briefly how Peter treated Gentiles within the church and how his actions shaped early church policy and practice. Peter is at least emblematic of the wide spectrum of attitudes that existed in early Christianity, and his attitudes and actions are woven into the fabric of an ethnically diverse, multilingual, geographically distant, early Christian church. The modern reader will find in this discussion an important study of how cultural boundaries shaped the growth of the early church and how the Lord guided early church leaders to navigate an ethnically diverse organization.

Ultimately, this paper will seek to establish the thesis that Peter, the church's leader and most recognizable member, was both part of the hesitance in initially limiting the mission to the Gentiles and a significant part of the solution in initiating the mission to the Gentiles after his vision in Joppa. Moreover, this paper will attempt to establish the fact that Peter's actions were representative of the attitudes and opinions of Jewish Christians regarding the evangelization of Gentiles and regarding the early hesitance to permit Gentiles into full fellowship without first requiring them to be circumcised and live the kosher laws (i.e., the *kashrut*). This study will not consider the successes or the failures of the early Gentile mission, nor will it address the doctrinal question of whether a Gentile mission was even permissible. Instead, this paper will focus closely on whether Luke's portrayal of events, particularly those involving Peter, intentionally suggests that Peter had reservations in taking the gospel to the Gentiles.

A Brief Survey of Previous Studies

A number of careful and contemplative studies on the subject of Acts and the Gentile mission have been carried out by Latter-day Saint scholars, all of which appear to be genetically linked to Bruce R. McConkie's seminal series on the books of the New Testament.[3] Each of the subsequent major studies on Acts builds on the position advanced in Elder McConkie's work and argues with minor alterations that Peter was hesitant to accept Gentiles into the church in full fellowship but that he eventually, through revelation, accepted them, thus paving the way for a full-blown Gentile mission.[4] There has been little discussion about the ramifications of Peter's act of hesitation, and almost no discussion of where Peter's attitudes came from and whether they represented those of other members of the early church or whether the Galilean Peter was predisposed to exclude Gentiles. These questions have major ramifications for the development of Christianity because they provide us with an awareness of the outlook of the early disciples and whether or not they had considered taking the gospel beyond Judea and Galilee.

Outside of Latter-day Saint circles of scholarship, the question of attitudes toward Gentiles within early Christianity has been closely considered with emphasis on the chronological development of the question and the social impact of those attitudes.[5] As a general rule, these studies typically assume that early Christian leaders held attitudes that were very similar to or even identical to other first-century Jews who did not convert to Christianity.[6] This is, of course, certainly possible, but upon careful scrutiny of the evidence it is not necessarily certain that early Christians felt the same way about Gentiles that their Jewish counterparts did. In addition to that concern is the question of whether the early disciples shared the common cultural bias that their Jewish counterparts exhibited.

Some of Jesus' teachings in the Gospels clearly point in the direction of an eventual Gentile mission. Following Luke's overall interest in the mission to the Gentiles, he was careful to narrate Simeon's blessing of the infant Jesus: "A light to lighten the Gentiles, and the glory of thy people Israel" (Luke 2:32). Although the disciples would not have heard Simeon speak the prophecy, Luke's recording of the story shows that it was foundational for understanding Jesus and the purpose of his ministry. An additional saying in Matthew 12:21 records a saying of Jesus that points clearly in the direction of the Gentiles coming to accept the gospel: "And in his name shall the Gentiles trust." The quotation itself is derived from Isaiah 42:1–4, but Jesus changed the wording: "He shall bring forth judgment unto truth. He shall not fail nor be discouraged, till he have set judgment in the earth: and the isles shall wait for his law" (Isaiah 42:3–4). By changing Isaiah's "isles" to Gentiles, Jesus unequivocally changed the meaning and helped his disciples see that a Gentile mission was possible.

It is certainly time to relook at the issue of the Gentile mission and to reappraise the evidence. That evidence will help us determine whether Peter was caused to accept Gentiles through visionary prompting after expressing early reluctance to do so or whether Peter and other early Christians were simply anti-Gentile in their attitudes because they had been culturally conditioned via Judaism to be that way.[7]

A Mission to the Gentiles?
The Purpose of Acts

It is important for this study to note that writing and recording history in the first century was fundamentally different than writing history today. For the purposes of this study, it is worthwhile to consider what it might mean to us if Luke wrote with a particular agenda and how he treated his ancient eyewitness sources. Oral history was preferred over written history.[8] The oft-quoted saying of Papias is helpful here and is worth including in full:

> I shall not hesitate also to put into properly ordered form for you everything I learned carefully in the past from the elders and noted down well, for the truth of which I vouch. For unlike most people I did not enjoy those who have a great deal to say, but those who teach the truth. Nor did I enjoy those who recall someone else's commandments, but those who remember the commandments given by the Lord to the faith and proceeding from the truth itself. And if by chance anyone who had been in attendance on the elders should come my way, I inquired about the words of the elders—[that is,] what [according to the elders] Andrew or Peter said, or Philip, or Thomas or James, or John or Matthew or any other of the Lord's disciples, and whatever Aristion and the elder John, the Lord's disciples, were saying. *For I did not think that information from books would profit me as much as information from a living and surviving voice.* (Eusebius, *Historia Ecclesiastica* 3.39.3–4)[9]

This cautionary type of attitude, if representative of the attitudes held by others towards book reading in the early church, should not cause us to question the accuracy of books per se, but to evaluate books that claim to present firsthand experiences differently than we might evaluate an ancient book that was not written by eyewitnesses. That is to say, books that advocate that their information was derived from eyewitnesses were superior, according to Papias, to books where the author has collected written sources and evaluated them. A modern scholarly book would not fare well in ancient Christianity. But additionally it should be pointed out that a book that promotes eyewitness accounts may also be taking advantage of the skepticism of writing history via reading books and promoting its own account as superior to other books on the subject. Two canonical Gospels intentionally promote eyewitnesses as the source of their writing: Luke and John.[10]

Although we cannot take up the discussion of John as an eyewitness, we do have space to consider Luke's eyewitness sources.[11] He, more than any other New Testament writer, established his credentials in writing at the outset of his account: "Forasmuch as many have taken in hand to set forth in order a declaration of those things which are most surely believed among us, *Even as they delivered them unto us, which from the beginning were eyewitnesses,*[12] and ministers of the word; it seemed good to me also, having had perfect understanding of all things from the very first, to write unto thee in order" (Luke 1:1–3; emphasis added).[13] What is useful to this study are two features from this discussion: first, Luke may have intentionally wanted his readers to recognize his *written* gospel as more authoritative than the oral reports circulating in his day, and second, his confidence that his report was based on a "perfect understanding." For the present study, this evidence points in the direction of an author who had something definitive and authoritative to say and that there may also be undertones of a corrective interest. It would appear safe to say that Acts, also written by Luke, bears a similar interest in setting forth the story that was based on eyewitness accounts and was reliant upon a "perfect understanding."[14]

A parallel situation occurs in Joseph Smith's 1838 journal history, where he also records history with an overt purpose, "Owing to the many reports which have been put in circulation by evil-disposed and designing persons, in relation to the rise and progress of The Church of Jesus Christ of Latter-day Saints, all of which have been designed by the authors thereof to militate against its character as a Church and its progress in the world—I have been induced to write this history, to disabuse the public mind, and put all inquirers after truth in possession of the facts, as they have transpired, in relation both to myself and the Church, so far as I have such facts in my possession" (Joseph Smith—History 1:1).

Discovering Luke's Agenda

Building upon the proposition that Luke wrote with a particular agenda in mind and that he intentionally wanted to advertise his account as one that was built upon better eyewitness sources, it should be possible to at least describe the contours of that agenda.[15] Several features of Luke's account reasonably represent at least a portion of his agenda.[16] First, Paul is formally introduced into the story in Acts 9:1 and takes over the narrative almost completely by Acts 13:1. Even though Luke began by retelling the history of Christianity and the early experiences of the Apostles, he no longer does so in a significant way after narrating Paul's first mission. Second, the stories that are told after Paul's introduction are almost exclusively focused on the question of the Gentile mission: Cornelius, Peter's vision at Joppa, the church expanding into Antioch (a Gentile city), and the death of an old nemesis from the Herodian family.[17] Although Luke certainly had additional intentions in writing his Gospel and history, such as the role of women in the church and the plight of the poor, we can be fairly confident that one of the items of central importance was his interest in describing the Gentile mission.

The Gentile mission was arguably the foremost interest driving Luke's narrative: he was searching for causes and solutions.[18] And he may have taken his narrative structure in part from Paul's letter to the Romans, "For I am not ashamed of the gospel of Christ: for it is the power of God unto salvation to every one that believeth; *to the Jew first, and also to the Greek*" (Romans 1:16; emphasis added, see also 2:10).[19] The taking of the gospel to the "Jew first, and also to the Greek" accurately describes Luke's account where he abbreviates the story of taking the gospel to the Jews (Acts 1–8) and then expands the discussion of the gospel to the Gentiles (Acts 9–21).[20] Luke also foreshadowed his greater interest in the Gentile mission when he reported a cautionary statement by a leading Jewish leader of the day that has prophetic hints at the success of the Gentile mission, "Refrain from these men, and let them alone: for if this counsel or this work be of men, it will come to nought: but if it be of God, ye cannot overthrow it; lest haply ye be found even to fight against God" (Acts 5:38–39). Luke went on to demonstrate that the growth of Christianity among the Gentiles was something that could not be overthrown. Having discussed both Luke's agenda in writing as well as his interest in establishing his history as authoritative, we can now look at how Luke's portrayal of Peter fits into this developing narrative.

Peter's Role in the Gentile Mission

Returning directly to the original focus of this paper, it is necessary to consider Peter's part in the unfolding story of the Gentile mission. In the Gospel of Luke, Peter is mentioned by name in eighteen verses, with twelve of those references coming from two stories: the Mount of Transfiguration and Peter's denial (see Luke 5:8; 6:14; 8:51, 45; 9:20, 28, 32–33; 12:41; 18:28; 22:8, 34, 54–55, 58, 60–62). Peter is mentioned fifty-six times in Acts, with fifty-five of those references coming in Acts 1–12 (see also Acts 15:7). Of necessity, Peter is portrayed differently in the two sources: in the Gospel of Luke he is the impetuous disciple who faithfully seeks to testify and demonstrate his faith, whereas in the book of Acts he is the relentless leader of the church who is carefully guided through revelation (see Acts 10) to lead the church in a new age. The two viewpoints are congruous, and in the

Gospel of Luke, Peter can be described as learning to be a disciple, and in Acts he demonstrates that he has learned and is capable of leading.

Some of the features that are characteristic of Peter in the Gospel of Luke are that he is frequently portrayed as asking questions and giving answers (see Luke 8:45; 9:20). He is also the voice for the other disciples and frequently uses the first person plural when speaking, "Then Peter said, Lo, we have left all, and followed thee" (Luke 18:28). In Acts this portrayal of Peter subtly shifts when he asks the disciples, "Men and brethren, what shall we do?" (Acts 2:37). This question is characteristic of Peter as portrayed in the Gospel, but after Pentecost it appears that Peter only asks questions to which he already knows the answer. To be precise, after Acts 2:37 he asks questions on two different occasions: In Acts 5:3, 8, and 9, Peter asks questions of Ananias and Sapphira where he already knew through inspiration what they had done, and in Acts 10:21 he asks Cornelius, "Behold, I am he whom ye seek: what is the cause wherefore ye are come?" Effectively, Peter has become the leading disciple in Acts that is on some level omniscient of the answers he will receive, a contrast that Luke highlights by making the final verse in his Gospel that specifically mentions Peter to say, "And Peter went out, and wept bitterly" (Luke 22:62). In the Gospel he is also human and subtly weak, but the weakness also serves to heighten the contrast of the new Peter in Acts.

In a diachronic retelling of the history of Christianity and the story of Peter and the early Gentile mission, Luke was faced with several challenges of how to incorporate some of the difficulties that arose when ethnic Jews were faced with the possibility of dining with Gentiles in their Christian house-churches where non-kosher foods were offered and where the Gentile members were uncircumcised. The trauma of such an event is recognizable in Paul's description of one such encounter in Antioch, "But when Peter was come to Antioch, I withstood him to the face, because he was to be blamed. For before that certain came from James, he did eat with the Gentiles: but when they were come, he withdrew and separated himself, fearing them which were of the circumcision" (Galatians 2:11–12).[21] In structuring the story, Paul may have supposed that Peter ceased eating with Gentiles because he was afraid of what ethnic Jews might think of him for eating with Gentiles.[22] Luke does not report the story in the way that Paul does and he omits the story of conflict, perhaps because he was more sensitive to Peter's actual motives. What Peter's concerns were is a subject to which we will return.

Part of Luke's narrative in Acts may initially appear to depict Peter as part of the obstacle in taking the gospel to the Gentiles, an important part of the discussion considered in this study. The key verses treating this theme read, "And there came a voice to him, Rise, Peter; kill, and eat. But Peter said, *Not so,*

Lord; for I have never eaten any thing that is common or unclean" (Acts 10:13–14; emphasis added) and later in the chapter, "Ye know how that it is an unlawful thing for a man that is a Jew to keep company, or come unto one of another nation; but God hath shewed me that I should not call any man common or unclean" (Acts 10:28). Both of these passages convey the idea that Peter was in part an obstacle to a Gentile mission because he had never considered the unclean (the Gentiles) and because even after the vision of the sheet and the unclean animals, Peter still maintained that he was a "Jew" (and not a Christian) and that it was "unlawful" for him to come into the home of a Gentile. Both of these obstacles should naturally have been resolved in the Resurrection and the command to take the gospel to all nations, but Luke is here subtly reminding the reader that there were still cultural obstacles to overcome and Peter was pivotal in resolving those obstacles (see Matthew 28:19–20). Assuming that Luke was intentionally retelling this story to help demonstrate to the reader that he was aware of the implications of Peter calling himself a Jew after the Resurrection of Christ, then this story has great meaning in understanding some of the cultural boundaries that existed between Jewish Christians and Gentile Christians.

Simplifying the story in this way, however, misses the opportunity to ask whether or not Luke may have shaped the story in a way to express to his audience the validity—the revelatory foundation—of the Gentile mission. In other words, when Peter expressed his hesitancy to the angel, "I have never eaten any thing that is common or unclean," he may have revealed his deep-seated concerns about a mission to the unclean Gentiles, but Luke may have recorded that particular part of the story because it so adequately described the sentiments of Judean/Jewish Christians. In analyzing the story further, it becomes apparent that Peter may have been savvier to the meaning of the vision than we might have initially assumed. Luke reports, "Peter went up upon the housetop to pray about the sixth hour: and he became very hungry, and would have eaten: but while they made ready, he fell into a trance, and saw heaven opened, and a certain vessel descending unto him, as it had been a great sheet knit at the four corners, and let down to the earth: wherein were all manner of fourfooted beasts of the earth, and wild beasts, and creeping things, and fowls of the air. And there came a voice to him, Rise, Peter; kill, and eat" (Acts 10:9–13). By drawing attention to Peter's concluding statement we overlook two important features: (1) there were clean beasts on the sheet and (2) Peter knew he was being asked to eat the unclean beasts, which is surprising given that observant Jews would certainly assume they were only to eat the clean animals.[23] For an observant

Jew, the command to eat from the sheet would typically be understood as a request to avoid the unclean and to eat only the clean: Peter saw it differently.

It can be stated with some confidence, that on a simple reading of Acts 10, Peter is part of the hesitance in expanding the mission to the Gentiles, but that upon closer inspection, Peter knew the way forward and saw how the Lord was directing him to take the gospel beyond Judea and Galilee. Luke spends more time on this part of the discussion between Peter and Cornelius than he does on any other aspect.[24] He reports Peter's words, "Then Peter opened his mouth, and said, Of a truth I perceive that God is no respecter of persons: But in every nation he that feareth him, and worketh righteousness, is accepted with him" (Acts 10:34–35). Luke is careful to note that Peter's declaration caused some concern for ethnic Jews when they heard his report, "While Peter yet spake these words, the Holy Ghost fell on all them which heard the word. And they of the circumcision which believed were astonished, as many as came with Peter, because that on the Gentiles also was poured out the gift of the Holy Ghost" (Acts 10:44–45). By retelling the story in this way, Luke has helped the reader see that the common attitude that Gentiles could not receive the Holy Ghost had been unequivocally answered through Peter and through revelation.

Peter at the Jerusalem Conference (AD 49)

To fully appreciate the importance of Acts 15 and its account of the Jerusalem Conference that was convened to settle the matter concerning the Gentile needs to be circumcised and to maintain the kosher standards of Judaism, we must first take a closer look at Peter's vision of the sheet and its aftermath. This will be important to the discussion because it will help demonstrate how the early church resolved the issue of the cultural divide between its members.

The most important verse in this discussion will be "When they heard these things, they held their peace, and glorified God, saying, Then hath God also to the Gentiles granted repentance unto life" (Acts 11:18). Because the verse reads as a declaration of the early church's position on Gentile conversion and because of its pivotal nature in this discussion, it will be helpful to scrutinize the translation. In Greek, the passage reads, "ἀκούσαντες δὲ ταῦτα ἡσύχασαν καὶ ἐδόξασαν τὸν θεὸν λέγοντες, Ἄρα καὶ τοῖς ἔθνεσιν ὁ θεὸς τὴν μετάνοιαν εἰς ζωὴν ἔδωκεν," which translated in a very literal way reads, "having heard this thing, they were silent and were glorifying God saying, 'Then God has given to the Gentiles the repentance that leads to life.'"

An important feature of this verse is the statement that they were "silent" and "glorifying," the latter of which is not a particularly silent gesture, which indicates that they were probably silent in their resistance to the Gentile mission but vocal in their praise of God. The "thing" that caused them to rejoice openly was the unequivocal statement "Forasmuch then as God gave them the like gift as he did unto us, who believed on the Lord Jesus Christ; what was I, that I could withstand God?" (Acts 11:17). In other words, they could no longer withstand the will of God. But perhaps most important is the verb translated as "has given" (ἔδωκεν), which conveys a past tense action or an action that had occurred prior to the speech being reported. God "has given" the Gentiles an opportunity to enter the fold and who can "withstand God?"

In looking closer at Peter's experience, another interesting facet of the story catches our attention. By reporting Peter's declaration that being commanded to eat unclean foods helped Peter see that *people* should not be declared unclean (Acts 10:15, 28), Luke has subtly made the connection that people are equal to the unclean food in the vision. Through this connection, Luke is able to draw out the idea that the center of the divide between Gentiles and Jews in early Christianity was an issue of food.[25] At the very heart of the debate was the real-life concern that in giving up the kosher laws of the Old Testament, ethnic Jews were turning their back on their religious identity and uniqueness. And one of the fundamental reasons Gentiles were considered unclean is because they partook of unclean foods. Now Jewish Christians would be unclean in the eyes of their non-Christian countrymen.[26]

This brings us to what appears to be Luke's clearest expression of frustration that the issue continued to divide ethnic Gentiles like Luke and ethnic Jews like Peter. In reporting the Jerusalem Conference, Peter states with authority,

> And when there had been much disputing, Peter rose up, and said unto them, Men and brethren, ye know how that a good while ago God made choice among us, that the Gentiles by my mouth should hear the word of the gospel, and believe.
>
> And God, which knoweth the hearts, bare them witness, giving them the Holy Ghost, even as he did unto us;
>
> And put no difference between us and them, purifying their hearts by faith.
>
> Now therefore why tempt ye God, to put a yoke upon the neck of the disciples, which neither our fathers nor we were able to bear?
>
> But we believe that through the grace of the Lord Jesus Christ we shall be saved, even as they. (Acts 15:7–11)

Peter's redeclaration of God's will in Acts 15 was the second announcement of church policy, and the fact that God had already declared his will on the matter in Acts 11:18 as ἔδωκεν ("hath given") was already sufficiently clear.

Peter, following the direction God had given him, announced the decision on two separate occasions, which is why Acts 15:20 represents a step backwards in the narrative: "But that we write unto them, that they abstain from pollutions of idols, and from fornication, and from things strangled, and from blood." These strictures all relate to the *kashrut*, the kosher requirements of the law of Moses, and they were given despite Peter's clear declaration on the matter. Phrases such as "put no difference between us and them" are in open conflict with "But that we write unto them."

It is to be expected that Luke, Paul's traveling companion, would hold an opinion similar to Paul's regarding the Jerusalem conference (for Paul's view, see Galatians 2:12–13), i.e., that he saw the resolution of the conflict of cultural boundaries as foundational to the success of the Gentile mission. When Paul denounced Peter in Antioch, he perhaps failed to apprehend that though he was commissioned to take the gospel to the Gentiles, Peter was commissioned to take the same message to the Jews so that their hearts could be softened to accept the Gentiles that Paul would convert. Paul appears to have interpreted the situation through its effects on his mission in Antioch and not in light of the larger issue of harmony within the church between Jewish and Gentile Christians. Luke, however, shows some sensitivity in not taking either side in the conflict, but in focusing on the resolution.

Why Joppa?

Finally, it is helpful to see that there may be a larger symbolic undertone to why Peter was at Joppa when he received the revelation that Cornelius was awaiting him. According to the story in Acts, Cornelius was at Caesarea Maritima when he had the vision telling him to send for Peter, while Peter was a short distance away in the coastal city of Joppa (Acts 10:1).[27] Acts reports simply, "And now send men to Joppa, and call for one Simon, whose surname is Peter" (Acts 10:5). The significance of Joppa is easily overlooked in the story, but it may have a connection to an earlier prophet who was similarly called to teach the gospel to Gentiles. In the book of the prophet Jonah, when the Lord commanded Jonah to go to Nineveh, Jonah fled in the opposite direction, "But Jonah rose up to flee unto Tarshish from the presence of the Lord, and went down to Joppa; and he found a ship going to Tarshish: so he paid the fare thereof, and went down into it, to go with them unto Tarshish from the presence of the Lord" (Jonah 1:3). Jonah's starting point for taking the gospel to the Assyrians was the same city where Peter was later praying on his roof.

The symbolic significance is overt: Jonah fled the command to take the gospel to the Gentiles, while Peter in the same city accepted the call of the Lord to take the gospel to the Gentiles. Interestingly, Jonah was originally called upon to deliver a message of doom, "Arise, go to Nineveh, that great city, and cry against it; for their wickedness is come up before me" (Jonah 1:2). Peter was given the command to take a message of peace and of good news.[28] Although the actual occurrence of the vision in Joppa is probably little more than happenstance, given Luke's careful documentation of the Gentile mission, it is possible that he recorded the location with the intent that the reader would see the connection to the mission of Jonah and see the parallel that is mentioned here.

Conclusion

Looking carefully at the New Testament texts and their accounts of the early Gentile mission may raise concerns in the minds of some readers: concern that there was discord in the early church, concern that James and Paul may have handled the issue of kosher requirements very differently, and concern that Peter's revelation was only gradually adopted.[29] But those concerns are really only minor when we compare the issues in the early church with any other dispensation where the faithful have wrestled to accept all of God's words: We have seen that there is at times discord in the way we understand revelation; we have teachings that appear to offer differing opinions; and ultimately we have a prophet who reveals the mind of the Lord that we are obligated to accept. The history of the early church is the history of God's people. Luke's honesty is refreshing and insightful.

Reconstructing what Luke appears to intend, we can conjecture that Peter was initially resistant to accepting Gentiles into the church without the Gentiles previously having committed themselves to live the full law of Moses as he had done. With revelatory prompting, Peter came to see a way forward through grace wherein the Gentiles could enter the church in full fellowship. Some early missionaries, notably not referred to as Apostles in Acts, disagreed on how Peter's revelation should be implemented. And perhaps the most resounding message comes from Peter, who understood fully the impact of what the Lord had revealed to him. The Gentiles were and are the future of the church and Peter opened the door through which they entered. Elder Hales noted the pivotal nature of Jesus' words to Peter when he said, "Brothers and sisters, do we really understand the teachings of the Savior, 'When thou art converted, strengthen thy brethren'?

(Luke 22:32). Feed my lambs. Feed my sheep. Feeding the lambs could well be missionary labors working with newly baptized members, who must be nurtured and given caring warmth and fellowship in the family of Saints. Feeding the sheep could well refer to the mature members of the church, some active and some less active, who need to be cared for and brought back to the flock."[30]

It is the conclusion of this paper that seeing Peter as the resistant disciple is perhaps too simplistic and that the development of the Gentile mission was in fact much more complicated. In the end, there simply is not enough evidence to distinguish Peter's personal views about Gentiles from those of his Judean peers, although I expect that they were different. Ultimately, the church was slow to take the gospel to the Gentiles. A multitude of reasons exists to explain this occurrence, but the most likely reason is that cultural attitudes were the root cause. Luke, a fellow traveling companion of Paul's, saw the need to document the Gentile mission and sought to help the reader see it as part of the larger historical portrait of Christianity.

Notes

1. The New Testament term denoting "Gentile" is ἔθνος (ethnos), which functionally indicates a group of people unified by family or culture. Typically the term is modified by a genitive description of the people, i.e., "the people of the Samaritans" or "the people of the Greeks." Often it is used in the sense of those who have another faith, regardless of their ethnicity (see Matthew 10:18).

2. For example, Paul's teaching that the law of Moses acted like a schoolmaster to bring Israel to Christ in Galatians 3–4 may be understood as a conversation arising out of the Gentile mission. See also Romans 1–3.

3. Bruce R. McConkie, *Doctrinal New Testament Commentary*, 3 vols. (Salt Lake City: Bookcraft, 1965–73). The series is now published by Deseret Book in both electronic and print editions.

4. See Robert J. Matthews, "Unto All Nations," in *Studies in Scripture*, vol. 6, *Acts to Revelation*, ed. Robert L. Millet (Salt Lake City: Deseret Book, 1987), 34–36; Gaye Strathearn, "The Jewish and Gentile Missions: Paul's Role in the Transition," in *The Apostle Paul: His Life and His Testimony* (Salt Lake City: Deseret Book, 1994), 194–96; Gaye Strathearn, "Law and Liberty in Galatians 5–6," in *Go Ye into All the World* (Salt Lake City: Deseret Book, 2002), 62–63; Jared W. Ludlow, "The Book of Acts: A Pattern for Modern Church Growth," in *Shedding Light on the New Testament: Acts–Revelation*, ed. Ray L. Huntington, Frank F. Judd Jr., and David M. Whitchurch (Provo, UT: Religious Studies Center, 2009), 1–29; Eric D. Huntsman, "The Impact of Gentile Conversions in the Greco-Roman World," in *The Life and Teachings of the New Testament Apostles: From the Day of Pentecost through the Apocalypse*, ed. Richard Neitzel Holzapfel and Thomas A. Wayment (Salt Lake City: Deseret Book, 2010), 80–96.

5. An excellent recent study on the question is a collection of essays edited by David C. Sim and James S. McLaren, *Attitudes to Gentiles in Ancient Judaism and Early Christianity* (London and New York: T&T Clark, 2013). A particularly helpful article in the collection is Elizabeth V. Dowling, "'To the Ends of the Earth': Attitudes to Gentiles in Luke–Acts," 191–208. See also James Carleton-Paget, *Jews, Christians and Jewish Christians in Antiquity* (Tübingen: Mohr Siebeck, 2010).

6. D. C. Sim, "Gentiles, God-Fearers and Proselytes," in *Attitudes to Gentiles in Ancient Judaism and Early Christianity*, ed. David C. Sim and James S. McLaren (London and New York: T&T Clark, 2013), 4–8.

7. I recognize that this is a somewhat simplistic dichotomy and is not likely to express all of the nuances in the excellent studies already in print. The dichotomy is admittedly a characterization of the two different sides of the discussion. What is not at issue is the simple fact that both sides accept a certain anti-Gentile attitude in earliest Christianity.

8. See Thomas A. Wayment, "From Jesus to the Written Gospels: The Oral Origins of the Gospel," in *The Life and Teachings of the New Testament Apostles: From the Day of Pentecost through the Apocalypse*, 11–34.

9. I have taken the translation of this passage from Richard Bauckham's excellent study on the topic, *Jesus and the Eyewitnesses: The Gospels as Eyewitness Testimony* (Grand Rapids, MI: Eerdmans, 2006), 15–16: his translation of the passage is the most nuanced and careful of which I am aware.

10. Some will note that Matthew (9:9) was also an eyewitness to the events told in his account, but Matthew as a personal witness to events is not a developed theme in the first Gospel.

11. For John as an eyewitness, see John 1:35–40 and 19:26.

12. The phrase "Even as they delivered them unto us, which from the beginning were eyewitnesses" could be read to imply that Luke was including himself as an eyewitness. In Greek, however, the phrase is not ambiguous and it unquestionably refers to the eyewitnesses, i.e., Luke was stating that the unnamed eyewitnesses passed on things to "us," a group that included Luke.

13. For a discussion of this passage, see Richard Neitzel Holzapfel and Thomas A. Wayment, "Introduction: The World of the New Testament," in *The Life and Teachings of Jesus Christ*, vol. 1: *From Bethlehem through the Sermon on the Mount*, ed. Richard Neitzel Holzapfel and Thomas A. Wayment (Salt Lake City: Deseret Book, 2005), xxii–xxix.

14. Acts 16:10 begins a series of first-person plural passages, the so-called "we" passages, that point to Luke being physically present for the events he is narrating.

15. This approach has often been viewed with skepticism because scholars who seek to determine Luke's method of writing history often use terms such as *myth*, which has been offensive to many Latter-day Saint scholars. In telling a story with an overt agenda, however, the author is not obligated to create a mythical account or an account built upon fabricated sources. Even the act of selecting which stories to tell is an act of writing with an agenda. For a recent discussion of Luke's agenda, see Mikeal C. Parsons, *Luke: Storyteller, Interpreter, Evangelist* (Peabody, MA: Hendrickson, 2007).

16. Adele Berlin, *Poetics and Interpretation of Biblical Narrative*, Bible and Literature 9 (Sheffield: Almond, 1983), 46, details the difficulties in identifying an author's agenda in writing. See also David L. Cowles, "Formalism," in *The Critical Experience: Literary*

Reading, Writing, and Criticism, ed. David L. Cowles, 2nd ed. (Dubuque, IA: Kendall/ Hunt Publishing, 1994), 11–12.

17. Acts 10:45 preserves an allusion to what I will argue is Luke's agenda, "And they of the circumcision which believed were astonished, as many as came with Peter, because that on the Gentiles also was poured out the gift of the Holy Ghost."

18. Luke also expresses a clear interest in the Samaritan mission in the early part of Acts. See Elizabeth V. Dowling, "'To the Ends of the Earth': Attitudes to Gentiles in Luke–Acts," in *Attitudes to Gentiles in Ancient Judaism and Early Christianity*, 191–208.

19. Somewhat surprisingly, two passages from Mark that emphasize Gentile involvement are not retold in Luke (Mark 7:24–30; 8:1–10).

20. This emphasis has been noted by numerous other scholars. See, for example, Jeffrey S. Siker, "'First to the Gentiles': A Literary Analysis of Luke 4:16–30," *Journal of Biblical Literature* 111 (1992): 73–90.

21. James D. G. Dunn, "The Incident at Antioch (Gal 2:11–18)," *Journal for the Study of the New Testament* 18 (1983): 3–57; John G. Gager, "Jews, Gentiles, and Synagogues in the Book of Acts," in *Christians among Jews and Gentiles: Essays in Honor of Krister Stendahl on His Sixty-Fifth Birthday*, ed. George W. E. Nickelsburg and George W. MacRae (Philadelphia: Fortress, 1986), 93. Gager thinks Gentiles were welcome in the synagogues. Most scholars today seem to refute Gager's findings, but it remains a possibility that in diaspora communities Gentiles were frequently in attendance.

22. The participle *foboumenos* (φοβούμενος) in Galatians 2:12 conceptually conveys genuine fear and apprehensiveness. See H. Balz, "φοβέω," in *Theological Dictionary of the New Testament*, ed. Gerhard Kittel and Gerhard Friedrich, trans. G. W. Bromily, 9 vols. (Grand Rapids, MI: Eerdmans, 1978), 208–19.

23. It may be that the instruction to eat the unclean was implied in the injunction "Rise, Peter; kill, and eat." The inference was that Peter was to eat everything on the sheet, clean and unclean. Clinton Wahlen, "Peter's Vision and Conflicting Definitions of Purity," *New Testament Studies* 51 (2005): 515, notes that the impure (κοινόν) and unclean (ἀκάθαρτον) animals symbolized impure (κοινόν) and unclean (ἀκάθαρτον) people, a possible reference to two types of Gentiles: God-fearers and idolaters, respectively.

24. R. W. Wall, "Peter, 'Son' of Jonah: The Conversion of Cornelius in the Context of the Canon," in R. W. Wall and E. Lemcio, eds., *The New Testament as Canon: A Reader in Canonical Criticism*, JSNTSS 76 (Sheffield: JSOT Press, 1992), 129–40, argues that the Cornelius episode has historical foundations in a conversion story of a Gentile household.

25. See Dunn, "The Incident at Antioch (Galatians 2:11–18)," 3–57, who comes to similar conclusions through looking at the incident in Galatians.

26. C. K. Barrett, *Acts: Volume I, I–XIV*, 2 vols. (Edinburgh: T&T Clark, 1998), 494.

27. For an excellent discussion of how Luke wrote with intent, see Walter T. Wilson, "Urban Legends: Acts 10:1–11:18 and the Strategies of Greco-Roman Foundation Narratives," *Journal of Biblical Literature* 120 (2001): 77–99.

28. For a discussion of the mythology associated with Joppa, see Paul B. Harvey, "The Death of Mythology: The Case of Joppa," *Journal of Early Christian Studies* 2 (1994): 1–14.

29. A similar idea is touched upon in Doctrine and Covenants 64:8: "My disciples, in days of old, sought occasion against one another and forgave not one another in their hearts; and for this evil they were afflicted and sorely chastened."

30. Robert D. Hales, "When Thou Art Converted, Strengthen Thy Brethren," *Ensign*, May 1997, 82–83.

12

Peter and Paul in Antioch

Gaye Strathearn

Gaye Strathearn is an associate professor of ancient scripture at
Brigham Young University.

"When Peter was come to Antioch, I withstood him to the face, because he was to be blamed. For before that certain came from James, he did eat with the Gentiles: but when they were come, he withdrew and separated himself, fearing them which were of the circumcision" (Galatians 2:11–12). So wrote the Apostle Paul to the Galatian Saints. This passage is a difficult one. Just as ancient Saints were not comfortable with the public tension between Christianity's most prominent leaders, neither are modern Saints today.

Peter's importance comes from his close association with Jesus during his mortal ministry and his prominence among the Twelve as the chief Apostle. In the synoptic Gospels "he is always spokesperson for and representative of the disciples as a group,"[1] and as Acts opens, after Christ's Ascension, it is clear that Peter is the one leading out and shepherding the church. In contrast, Paul comes on the scene only after the Ascension. Not only does he play no role in Jesus' mortal ministry, but when he does first appear in Acts he is making "havoc of the church, entering into every house, and haling men and women committed them to prison" (Acts 8:3). Luke's decision in Acts to shift focus from Peter's ministry to that of Paul's has undoubtedly impacted the course of early Christian history.

Paul's importance comes from the sheer weight of his writings that were collected into the canon and because he is arguably the one who most shapes the Christian message in a way that is both acceptable and enticing to the Gentile world.

Given the importance of both leaders, it can be difficult to understand what would cause Paul to publicly confront and question Peter's actions. Latter-day Saint commentators on this passage acknowledge the tension. In trying to explain it, sometimes Paul's actions are criticized,[2] but sometimes he is vindicated.[3] Generally, if addressed at all in Latter-day Saint writings, the passage is used to simply explain that leaders in the church can disagree,[4] but rarely is the passage analyzed in its Galatian context.

Frankly, there is no simple explanation for Galatians 2:11–12 because the incident is complicated by many issues, three of which we will try to address in this paper. First, Jesus' command to the Apostles on the Mount of Olives to "be witnesses unto me both in Jerusalem, and in all Judea, and in Samaria, and unto the uttermost part of the earth" (Acts 1:8) exposed deep-seated tensions between Jews and Gentiles, especially with respect to Israel's status as God's covenant people and the place of the law of Moses in the church as it began to expand its missionary work among the Gentiles. The early church struggled to envision a church that proselyted both Jews and Gentiles: how would the law of Moses function in such a church, and how would it impact Israel's calling as God's chosen people?

Second, the issue in Galatians 2:11–12 is further complicated because we only have access to one side of the story. The New Testament does not include Peter's perspective, only Paul's. It might be helpful, for example, if we had more information about questions such as the following: Why had Peter come to Antioch? What was the nature of the gathering? What was Peter thinking as "he withdrew and separated himself"? If we had Peter's side of the story, we might be able to gain a more balanced perspective of the event. Without his perspective we can only postulate possibilities.

Third, the issue is also compounded by the fact that Paul is clearly upset as he writes to the Galatian Saints because both his authority as an Apostle and the gospel that he taught were under attack. This leaves modern readers trying to recreate the events and motives from an account that has a decided agenda, with rhetorical language that is sometimes used to heighten, rather than downplay, the tension.

The purpose of this paper, therefore, is to provide some context for Galatians 2 that may help modern readers better understand the relationship between Peter and Paul and why the issues were so important to them. In doing so we will first briefly overview the historical interaction between Jews and Gentiles to understand the early church's reluctance to widen the scope of its missionary

activities. Then we will discuss the Antioch incident in its larger Galatian context, which includes two other meetings between the two Apostles: Paul's first
visit to Jerusalem after his conversion (see Galatians 1:16–19) and the Jerusalem
Council (see Galatians 2:1–10; Acts 15:1–11). While it is impossible, without
further information, to come to a definitive and comfortable answer to explain
the tension in Antioch, I will argue that the incident took place sometime after
the Jerusalem Council (see Galatians 2:1–10; Acts 15:1–11) but before the apostolic decree described in Acts 15:12–21. Therefore, while the issue of circumcision for Gentiles had been decided by the Jerusalem Council, the issue of table
fellowship, which is at the heart of the Antioch incident, had not been settled
by the church. Therefore, I will argue that what we see in Galatians 2:11–14 is
evidence of a theological debate between Peter and Paul that had not yet been
decided by the church leadership.

Teaching All Nations

The tension in Galatians 2 is broader than the one incident between Peter and
Paul; it is between two fundamentally different ways of interpreting Jesus' command on the Mount of Olives to expand their missionary activities beyond the
house of Israel (see Matthew 28:19; Acts 1:8). This Olivet command must have
raised some questions for the early church leaders and members; especially since
Jesus, on calling the Twelve, had directly instructed them, "Go not into the way
of the Gentiles, and into any city of the Samaritans enter ye not: but go rather to
the lost sheep of the house of Israel" (Matthew 10:5–6). Historically and theologically, Abraham and his descendants, the house of Israel, had been called to
enter into a covenant with God that *they* would be his covenant people. As part
of that covenant, Abraham and his seed were promised two blessings that sometimes stood in tension with each other: that they would become "a great nation"
(Abraham 2:9) and that through them "all the families of the earth [would] be
blessed" (Abraham 2:11; Genesis 12:3).

On the one hand, to make Israel into a great nation God required that Israel
distanced themselves from other nations in order to establish its geographical, political, and religious boundaries. At Mount Sinai, God reiterated that *they* would
"be a peculiar treasure [i.e., a treasured possession; Hebrew *sĕgullāh*] unto me above
all people, . . . a kingdom of priests, and an holy nation" (Exodus 19:5–6; 1 Peter
2:9). They were to be "the people of the Lord" (2 Samuel 1:12; Ezekiel 36:20), distinct from the other nations of the world. As they entered the promised land, God
knew that the nations of Canaan would be a constant threat to the covenantal
integrity of his chosen people (see Deuteronomy 12:1–3, 29–32). Therefore, they

were directed not to marry outside of the covenant: "For they will turn away thy son from following me, that they may serve other gods" (Deuteronomy 7:4) and they were directed to "make no league with the inhabitants of this land" (Judges 2:2). Nevertheless, Israel always struggled with these commands and so the prophets routinely called them to repentance on this account.

Two watershed events heightened Israel's sense of isolation from the other nations: the Exile (ca. 597–538 BC) and the Maccabean Revolt (ca. 167–160 BC). Prior to the exile, "the identity of the people had been shaped and supported by a number of complementary factors—common territory, political loyalty, ethnic continuity, common language, religious observance, and tradition."[5] But during the exile, the people had to find ways to maintain their identity in a Gentile environment. Thus, their "religious tradition and observance assumed an ever greater role in maintaining distinctive identity."[6] They had to learn to "sing the Lord's song in a strange land" (Psalm 137:4). When they returned to Judea, Ezra and Nehemiah focused on establishing the social, religious, and political boundaries that separated the returnees from outsiders in an effort to reestablish a holy people (see Ezra 3–4, 9–10; Nehemiah 3–4; 8:1–8).

The second watershed event was the Maccabean Revolt. Alexander the Great had invaded Palestine militarily and culturally, and one of his successors attempted to unify the Seleucid kingdom under the banner of the worship of Zeus. This highlighted the tension between the desire to be a peculiar people and the yearning for acceptance among the other nations. The Maccabean Revolt championed religious independence, but it did not advocate cultural independence.[7] It did, however, force the Jews to identify what were the core elements that gave them their cultural and religious identity and enabled them to be a peculiar nation: worship at the temple, circumcision as the sign of the covenant, keeping the Sabbath day holy, and table fellowship.[8] The last of these, table fellowship, included not only the dietary restrictions outlined in Leviticus 11, but by the intertestamental period they were expanded to include elements of ritual purity.[9] As we will see, two of these elements, circumcision and table fellowship, will be issues central to the interactions between Peter and Paul. Table fellowship, in particular, created a wall of isolation for some Jews from Gentiles, particularly those living in the diaspora. In a blessing reportedly given by Abraham to his son Jacob recorded in the *Book of Jubilees*, we read, "Separate yourself from the gentiles, and do not eat with them, and do not perform deeds like theirs. And do not become associates of theirs. Because their deeds are defiled, and all of their ways are contaminated, and despicable, and abominable" (22.16). Similarly, in the *Letter of Aristeas*, we read that Moses "surrounded us with unbroken palisades and iron walls to prevent our mixing with any of the other peoples in any matter. . . . So, to prevent our being perverted by contact with others or by mixing with bad influences, he hedged us in on all sides with strict observances connected with meat and drink and touch and hearing and sight, after the manner of the Law" (139, 142). Thus it is not surprising that Cicero, as an outsider, notes that in Rome the Jews stick together as a large, close-knit group (*Flaccus* 28.66).

In the Roman Empire, Jews were generally afforded freedom to practice their religion (Josephus, *Antiquities of the Jews* 19.288–90). But that did not mean that they were exempt from episodes of persecution. The Emperors Tiberius and Claudius both ordered expulsions of Jews from Rome (*Antiquities of the Jews* 18.83–84; Acts 18:2).[10] Philo describes riots that took place in Alexandria in AD 38 because of the destruction of Jewish synagogues (*Flaccus* 41–54; *On the Embassy to Gaius* 132–37).[11] Undoubtedly these attacks from without only served to fuel their sense of religious isolationism, especially when living in the midst of Gentile communities.

But we must not let these issues overshadow the very real efforts that Jews made to bless "all the families of the earth" (Abraham 2:11; Genesis 12:3; 28:14). Although God covenanted with Israel that they would be a peculiar people, the covenant was never intended to be an exclusive affair.[12] Abraham left Haran with "the souls that they had gotten in Haran" (Genesis 12:5), and when Israel left Egypt "a mixed multitude went up also with them" (Exodus 12:38). Ruth, a Moabite, converted to the Abrahamic covenant through Naomi (see Ruth 1:16); Jonah was called to cry repentance to the inhabitants of Ninevah (see Jonah 1–4); and Isaiah prophetically declared that Israel would be "a light to the Gentiles" (49:6), that "the Gentiles shall come to thy light" (60:3), and that "the Gentiles shall see thy righteousness" (62:2).

During the intertestamental period there appears to be a heightened awareness of, and attraction to, Judaism by Gentiles.[13] The antiquity of the religion and the ethical guidelines of the law of Moses were two characteristics that appealed to Gentiles.[14] Two Jewish writers, Josephus and Philo, make significant comments about Jewish proselytes. Josephus records that the Jews welcomed those who wished to adopt their laws (*Against Apion* 2.28) and that "the masses have long since shown a keen desire to adopt our religious observances" (*Against Apion* 2.39). Philo says that those who have chosen to follow a single creator must be looked upon "as our friends and kinsmen" (*On the Virtues* 33.179).[15] In part, this is because "those men . . . have left their country, and their friends, and their relations for the sake of virtue and holiness (Greek *hosiotēs*)" (*The Special*

Laws 1.9.52). What is their motivation for conversion? According to Philo, it was because of their search for "the certainty and clearness of truth, and of the worship of the one true and living God" (*On the Virtues* 20.102).[16] In the New Testament, Jesus confirms that Jews actively proselyted converts. He declares that scribes and Pharisees "compass sea and land to make one proselyte" (Matthew 23:15).[17] Josephus also records the conversion of the royal house of Adiabene in the first century AD (*Antiquities of the Jews* 20.2.3–4).

In addition to proselytes to Judaism, we also find evidence for people who were attracted to Judaism, but who did not convert. Philo mentions proselytes who have not undergone circumcision and insists that they are not true converts (*Questions and Answers on Exodus* 2.2). Josephus, in describing those who sent contributions to the temple, makes a distinction between the "Jews throughout the habitable world" and "those who worshipped God" (Greek *sebomenōn ton theon*; *Antiquities of the Jews* 14.7.2). The same Greek phrase is also found in the New Testament to describe Lydia (see Acts 16:14) and Justus (see Acts 18:7). Another parallel New Testament phrase that seems to also describe Gentiles who participate in Judaism to a limited degree are those who "fear God" (*phoboumenoi ton theon*; see Acts 10:2, 22, 35; 13:16, 26, 43, 50; 17:4, 17). Scholars sometimes identify this group of Jewish sympathizers with the technical term of "God-fearers,"[18] which may help us understand why two Gentiles, the centurion and the Canaanite woman, could appeal to Jesus with such extraordinary faith (see Matthew 8:5–10; 15:21–28). Both the proselytes and the God-fearers seem to have been a fruitful source for early Christian missionary activity.

In summary, the Abrahamic covenant was designed to accomplish two tasks: to create a peculiar and holy people who would become a great nation and to bless all the nations of the earth. This brief sketch of Israelite and Jewish history highlights that there was sometimes a pulsating tension between these two goals. At times an emphasis on the first goal overshadowed the importance of the second, but in the intertestamental period we see the planting of seeds that would mature to harvest in the New Testament. Although there is no evidence for an organized, large-scale Jewish program of proselyting, there is evidence to suggest that missionary work did exist on some level (see Matthew 23:15).[19]

When the resurrected Jesus stood on the Mount of Olives and gave his command to take the gospel to all the world, he initiated a major shift in direction for the early church. Given the evidence in Acts, it is fair to say that the church and its leaders struggled to comprehend and act upon the new direction. The Twelve, as represented by Peter and John, did not immediately respond. Rather they continued to concentrate their missionary work among the Jews, particularly those that they found in and around the temple precinct (see Acts 2; 3:11–26; 4:1–22; 5:12–16, 19–21, 27–42).

Two events seemed to shift the momentum. The first event was Saul's persecution of Christians after the death of Stephen. This persecution forced Christians to be "scattered abroad" and, as a result, they "went every where preaching the word" (Acts 8:4). In particular, Acts represents this expansion with the work of Philip among the Samaritans and with the Ethiopian eunuch (see Acts 8:5–40). The second event was Peter's vision of the unclean animals that he reluctantly received in Joppa and that led to him teaching the Roman centurion Cornelius and his household (see Acts 10:9–48). What is significant about the results of both of these events is that the missionary work only expanded to those who already had a relationship with Israel: the Samaritans who had a connection with Israelite religion and lived the law of Moses (although not the oral law), a eunuch who was probably a proselyte because he was returning home after worshipping in Jerusalem (Acts 8:27–28), and the God-fearer Cornelius, "a devout man, and one that feared God [*phoboumenoi ton theon*] with all his house, which gave much alms to the people, and prayed to God alway" (Acts 10:2). The reaction of the Jerusalem church to these missionary endeavors was mixed. Apparently they approved of Philip's work among the Samaritans, because Peter and John came down and conferred the Holy Ghost upon the converts (see Acts 8:14–17).

Unfortunately, Acts is silent on the reaction of the Jerusalem church to the conversion of the eunuch. However, they react heatedly to the news of Peter's dealings with Cornelius: "And when Peter was come up to Jerusalem, they that were of the circumcision contended with him, saying, thou wentest in to men uncircumcised, and didst eat with them" (Acts 11:2–3). This reaction of the Jerusalem church focuses on two of the four elements that, as we have seen, were identified as the key essentials in Jewish cultural and religious identity. Circumcision and table fellowship are also the two issues that are at the very heart of the tension between Peter and Paul in Antioch and evoked important questions for the early church. For example, not only did the early leaders and members struggle to envision a church that included both Jews and Gentiles, they also struggled with the questions of the doctrinal and practical implications of Gentiles becoming part of the seed of Abraham. The command on the Mount of Olives and in Peter's vision to include Gentiles in the missionary work did not give specific instructions for how it was to be carried out. Paul's missionary work "to bear [Christ's] name before the Gentiles" (Acts 9:15) brought the issue to a head, and Antioch became the test case for two competing approaches.

Peter and Paul in the Epistle to the Galatians

Paul wrote to the Galatians in response to charges against him by Christian missionaries who had come to Galatia with a very different approach to the Gentile mission. Although he never specifically mentions their charges, we can get a pretty good sense of them because of the issues Paul chose to address in his response. The three overarching concerns in the epistle seem to center on the issues of Paul's authority and the gospel, how Gentiles *become* a part of the seed of Abraham, and how they then *live* within the covenant.

Scholars generally identify Paul's opponents in Galatia as a group of Jewish Christians, known as Judaizers, who insisted that Gentiles enter the church through the law of Moses. As we have seen in Acts, the Judaizers' approach probably represents the church's earliest interpretation of the Olivet command. From their perspective they were continuing the established method of proselyting Gentiles who were already attracted to Judaism. Paul's earliest missionary endeavors seem to be situated within this same paradigm: when he entered into a new city at the beginning of his first missionary journey he went and taught in the synagogue. There he was able to address both Jews and those who "fear God" (*phoboumenoi ton theon*; Acts 13:16, 26). But by Acts 13:46–47, Paul shifted his missionary focus to the Gentiles. Acts does not provide us with the specific details of how that shift in focus impacted his preaching. At the end of that first mission, however, Christian missionaries from Jerusalem (probably Judaizers) came to Antioch criticizing him for not requiring the Gentile converts to be circumcised (15:1). The result was "no small dissension and disputation with them" (15:2), meaning that there was major contention over the issue.

Similar conflict over Paul's missionary work with the Gentiles is again a prominent concern underlying his epistle to the Galatians. That there is an added criticism of his apostolic authority seems certain given Paul's opening declaration: "Paul, an apostle, (not of men, neither by man, but by Jesus Christ, and God the Father, who raised him from the dead;)" (Galatians 1:1).[20] In no other epistle does Paul immediately begin with a justification for his apostolic authority. Generally he simply acknowledges that he was "called to be an apostle" (Romans 1:1), sometimes adding the statement "through the will of God" (1 Corinthians 1:1; 2 Corinthians 1:1; Ephesians 1:1; Colossians 1:1; 2 Timothy 1:1). The criticism by Paul's opponents in Galatia, however, is not just about his apostleship. The question of authority is directly tied to the gospel that he taught. With language that is closely tied to the opening verse, Paul also defends the veracity of his gospel message: "But I certify you, brethren, that the gospel which was preached of me is not after man. For I neither received it of man, neither was I taught it, but by the revelation of Jesus Christ" (Galatians 1:11–12).

Paul's feelings about the attack on his authority and the gospel are reflected in his pejorative choice of words to describe the situation in Galatia. He argued that "false brethren" (Galatians 2:4) had "bewitched" (Galatians 3:1) the Galatian churches, and he fears that he has become their enemy (Galatians 4:16). It is therefore not surprising that immediately after his opening salutation he forgoes his usual thanksgiving and immediately writes:

> I marvel that ye are so soon removed from him that called you into the grace of Christ unto another gospel:
> Which is not another; but there be some that trouble you, and would pervert the gospel of Christ.
> But though we, or an angel from heaven, preach any other gospel unto you than that which we have preached unto you, let him be accursed.
> As we said before, so say I now again, If any man preach any other gospel unto you than that ye have received, let him be accursed.
> For do I now persuade men, or God? or do I seek to please men? for if I yet pleased men, I should not be the servant of Christ. (Galatians 1:6–10)

The more specific issues from the law of Moses that the Judaizers seem to be pushing in both Galatia and Antioch, and that Paul is opposing, is that the church, and all who join it, should continue the practices of circumcision and table fellowship. Remember that these practices were two of the four core elements that enabled Jews to live in a Gentile world while still maintaining their religious covenantal identity. From the Judaizers' perspective, Paul's missionary efforts, if unchecked, placed their very identity in jeopardy.

In responding to these accusations, Paul makes reference to three meetings that he had with Peter: two in Jerusalem and one in Antioch. Even though all of these meetings occur outside of Galatia, it is clear that Paul believes that they have a bearing on the argument that he will make to the Galatians. In appealing to these three meetings, it is also clear that there is an underlying tension in the rhetoric of Paul's description of them. On the one hand, he specifically meets with Peter (and James) when he travels to Jerusalem some three years after his conversion (see Galatians 1:17–19); he also acknowledges the importance of Peter, James, and John as pillars of the church (2:9); and he seeks their approval for his missionary activities among the Gentiles (2:9). Yet, on the other hand, he is quick to remind his opponents that "they [Peter, James, and John] . . . added nothing to me" (2:6), and, in fact as we have noted, in Antioch he "withstood [Peter] to the face, because he was to be blamed" (Galatians 2:11).

In recounting Paul's first visit with Peter (Galatians 1:15–19), he seems to be trying to correct "possible misperceptions . . . as to where [he] got his Gospel and how much contact he may have had with the Jerusalem authorities."[21] Paul writes that "it pleased God, who separated me from my mother's womb, and called me by his grace, to reveal his Son in me, that I might preach him among the [Gentiles]" (Greek *ethnoi*; Galatians 1:15–16). Paul addresses the concern about his authority in two ways. First, he uses language that hearkens back to Jeremiah 1:4–5. In doing so, Paul implies that he, like Jeremiah, was foreordained to his call. Second, by referring to his revelatory experience on the road to Damascus, he reminds his audience that his call to preach came directly from the resurrected Jesus.

Paul then insists that "immediately I conferred not with flesh and blood: Neither went I up to Jerusalem to them which were apostles before me; but I went into Arabia, and returned again unto Damascus" (Galatians 1:16–17). His point is that just because his contact with the Jerusalem authorities was limited, it did not weaken his authority to teach the Gentiles because his authority did not come from humans, but from God. In making this claim it is important to note that here Paul is not attacking Peter and the other Apostles. Rather, he acknowledges that there were people in Jerusalem who had been Apostles before him, and as one scholar has noted, "He does not call them so-called or pseudo-apostles (contrast 2 Cor. 11:13), there is no pejorative tone to this mention of these persons. . . . [Rather,] this is a tacit admission of the legitimacy of these persons, and that they had a certain pre-eminence over Paul as authorities having been commissioned before Paul."[22]

In some important ways, however, Paul was not like Peter and the other Apostles; he did not come through the same ranks, so to speak.[23] For example, Paul did not meet all of the requirements that were established in Acts 1:21–22 for a person to fill the vacancy in the Twelve: He had not "companied with [the other disciples] all the time that the Lord Jesus went in and out among us, Beginning from the baptism of John, unto that same day that [Jesus] was taken up from us." His experience on the road to Damascus, however, did qualify him for the second requirement: "one of these must become a witness with us to his resurrection" (NRSV, Acts 1:22).

Since Paul often uses the language of his opponents' rhetoric,[24] perhaps one of their issues that they had against him was that he didn't qualify as an Apostle because he had not been associated with Jesus' ministry from the beginning, and therefore, his brand of missionary work among the Gentiles was invalid. Paul's response is that he received his authority directly from God, not from any human, not even from Peter. When eventually he did go to Jerusalem, not until three years after his conversion, he went to get the "history" (Greek *historeō*) from Peter. The Greek word *historeō* can mean that he went to meet Peter, probably because Paul recognized his status as a pillar in the early church, but the fact that he stayed with him for fifteen days suggests that he also went to get information from him. Perhaps that information included, among other things, Peter's reminiscences of Jesus' ministry. While in Jerusalem, Paul also met with James, the Lord's brother. This visit suggests that Paul also recognized James' importance in the Jerusalem church. But he is quick to note: "But other of the apostles saw I none" (Galatians 1:19). In other words, Paul acknowledges the importance of Peter and James, but his point is that his authority did not come from them; it came because of the revelation that he had experienced on the road to Damascus.

Whereas chapter 1 focuses on Paul's personal credibility, chapter 2 describes his second visit to Jerusalem (Galatians 2:1–10), but this time the focus is on the credibility of his gospel message to the Gentiles.[25] Unfortunately, the nature and timing of this visit is the subject of considerable scholarly debate. Paul writes, "Then fourteen years after I went up again to Jerusalem with Barnabas, and took Titus with me also" (2:1). The text is unclear as to whether this date was fourteen years after his conversion or after his first visit to Jerusalem. In addition, there is considerable debate over whether this account refers to the Jerusalem Council that Luke describes in Acts 15.[26] There are some significant parallels. Both the Jerusalem Council and the meeting described in Galatians 2 are the result of people criticizing Paul's missionary activities among the Gentiles; in both, the issue centers on Paul not requiring Gentiles to be circumcised; both accounts include the same major players: Paul, Barnabas, Peter, James, and the Judaizers; both deal with issues of how Gentiles join the church; both conclude that circumcision is not required for Gentiles to become members of the church; and both agree that this issue involved participation in the Christian church and had nothing to do with "the relationship between non-Christian Jews and Christians"[27] (see Galatians 2:1–10; Acts 15:1–11).

Certainly, there are also some differences in the two accounts,[28] something that we would expect given that Luke and Paul have very different agendas for recording their accounts. Since Galatians 2 reflects a firsthand account of the events, its details should be given priority, when necessary, over Luke's second-hand account. Some of the unique material that Paul includes in Galatians 2, but is missing in Acts 15, is that he and Barnabas took Titus with them to Jerusalem

(Galatians 2:1). Titus becomes an important living witness that a Gentile could be an acceptable member of the church without being circumcised.[29] The passive voice in Galatians 2:3 opens the possibility to infer from this verse that neither Paul nor the Jerusalem authorities required that he be circumcised. In addition, Paul indicates that he went up to Jerusalem by revelation, which again reminds readers that his call in Galatians 1:16 continues to be the undergirding moving force of his missionary work.[30] Such a statement does not need to be, as some have argued, a conflict with the account in Acts that they went because of the dispute with those who "came down from Judea" (15:1).[31]

Paul notes two outcomes of this meeting. First, the conference decided that the church would have two parallel missions: "the gospel of the uncircumcision" over which Paul and Barnabas would have stewardship, and "the gospel of the circumcision" over which Peter was given stewardship (Galatians 2:7). There is nothing in this verse to indicate that Paul considered "the gospel of the circumcision" to be "another gospel" which "would pervert the gospel of Christ" (1:6–7) that he strongly objects to in chapter 1. Rather, Galatians 2:7 indicates that Peter, Paul, and Barnabas were united in their missionary efforts, although they recognized that their approaches would have different emphases according to their audience. In addition, we should note that this verse does not necessarily mean that their responsibilities were exclusive to the mission over which they had stewardship. Paul's commission by the Savior was that he was "a chosen vessel unto me, to bear my name before the Gentiles, and kings, and the children of Israel" (Acts 9:15), and in his letter to the Romans he notes, "Brethren, my heart's desire and prayer to God for Israel is, that they might be saved" (Romans 10:1). Likewise it appears that Peter was active in Gentile locations such as Antioch, where he was eating with Gentile members, and also gained some missionary converts in Corinth (1 Corinthians 1:12).

Second, Paul notes that "James, Cephas [Peter], and John,"[32] who he acknowledges are recognized (Greek *dokeō*) as "pillars, perceived the grace that was given unto me, they gave to me and Barnabas the right hands of fellowship; that we should go unto the Gentiles [Greek *ethnoi*], and they unto the circumcision" (Galatians 2:9). Paul's point in verse 6 that the Jerusalem leadership "added nothing to me," in the context of verse 9, indicates that, unlike the "false brethren" of verse 4, they did not want to change Paul's methods or insist that Gentiles had to do any more than Paul and Barnabas required of them. The only exception was that the Gentiles should remember the poor,[33] which Paul says he was eager to do (Greek *ho kai espoudasa auto touto poiēsai*; 1:10). Instead, James, Peter, and John gave them the "right hands of fellowship" (2:9). Thus Paul's second visit with Peter, like the first, was amicable. Paul recognized the status of Peter as one of the leading Apostles in Jerusalem and came seeking his seal on Paul's missionary work.

The question then remains, if on the Mount of Olives Jesus gave the command to teach the gospel to all the world, why did it take around fifteen years for the church in Jerusalem to come to a decision on how Gentiles were to join the church? The simple answer is that the issue would have had a higher priority for the church in Antioch than it would have for the church in Jerusalem. The evidence in the New Testament suggests that the church in Jerusalem consisted predominantly of Jewish Christians, people who were already living the law of Moses, and who continued to live it even after their conversion to Christianity (Acts 21:20). Christian Jews continued to worship at the temple (21:23–26) and at the synagogue (9:20; 13:5, 14–15; 14:1; 17:1–17; 18:4, 7, 19; 19:8), to participate in the Jewish festivals of Passover (18:21) and Pentecost (Acts 2:1; 20:16; 1 Corinthians 16:8), and to make Jewish vows (Acts 18:18).

For all intents and purposes, Christianity was initially viewed as just another one of the varieties of Judaism.[34] That's certainly how Saul viewed it as he embarked on his persecutions. In Antioch, however, the situation would have quickly become very different. Although the Christian congregation there began within the synagogue, the city was predominantly Gentile, and the converts to the church eventually were attracted from outside the sphere of the synagogue and the Gentile proselytes and God-fearers. But it wasn't until Judaizers came from Jerusalem the first time that the status quo was upset. The Jerusalem Council settled the issue of how Gentiles should *enter* the church: Gentiles did not need to be circumcised, but it did not address the question of how Gentiles should live *in* the church. That issue came to a head when the Judaizers came to Antioch a second time.

Paul now moves to address his third meeting with Peter, this time in Antioch. He claims that the reason that he "withstood [Peter] to the face" was because "before that certain came from James, he did eat with the Gentiles: but when they were come, he withdrew and separated himself, fearing them which were of the circumcision." Even more problematical in Paul's eyes was that "the other Jews [played the hypocrite (Greek *sunupekrithēsan*)] likewise with him; insomuch that Barnabas also was carried away with their [hypocrisy (Greek *hypokrisei*)]" (Galatians 2:11–13). Therefore Paul confronted Peter, "But when I saw that they walked not uprightly according to the truth of the gospel, I said unto Peter before them all, If thou, being a Jew, livest after the manner of Gentiles, and not as do the Jews, why compellest thou the Gentiles to live as do the Jews?" (Galatians 2:14).

At the heart of the tension between Peter and Paul on this occasion was the issue of table fellowship. It seems clear that initially Peter had no reservations about eating with Gentiles, and the imperfect tense of the verb "did eat" (Greek *sunēsthien*) suggests that his actions were not a once-off event but had taken place over a period of time. Such an understanding corresponds with Peter's experience with Cornelius in Acts 10 and the general statement that he gave at the Jerusalem Council, "Now therefore why tempt ye God, to put a yoke [i.e., the law of Moses] upon the neck of the disciples, which neither our fathers nor we were able to bear? But we believe that through the grace of the Lord Jesus Christ we shall be saved, even as they" (Acts 15:10–11). Paul does not tell us what the men from James said or did that caused Peter to withdraw, but it seems certain that they disapproved of his eating with Gentiles, just as the Jerusalem church had when they heard that he had done likewise with Cornelius and his household (see Galatians 2:12; Acts 11:1–3).

Again, we reiterate that any understanding of this incident is limited because we do not have access to Peter's side of the story. Nevertheless, we can say a few things. First, it seems likely that the men from James came to Antioch insisting on a strict separation of "the gospel of the circumcision" and "the gospel of the uncircumcision" that had been established at the Jerusalem Council. Thus they would have argued that Peter should continue to live the law of Moses, as did the Christians in Jerusalem.[35] Peter may have felt that his actions to withdraw from the meal would alleviate the tension, at least on the part of the Judaizers. Perhaps he felt that he needed to do what Paul claimed for himself: "And unto the Jews I became as a Jew, that I might gain the Jews; to them that are under the law, as under the law, that I might gain them that are under the law" (1 Corinthians 9:20).[36] After all, at one point Paul seemed to have done likewise when he had Timothy circumcised "because of the Jews" (Acts 16:1–3).

Second, the imperfect tense of the verbs "withdrew" (Greek *hypestellen*) and "separated himself" (Greek *apōrizen*) indicates that Peter's withdrawal and separation was done over a period of time. Perhaps this indicates that Peter came to the realization that to maintain the unity of the church the separation of the two missions should indeed be maintained and that he should focus on his particular stewardship.

Third, it seems to me that the best way of understanding the account of the Jerusalem Council in both Galatians 2 and Acts 15 is to recognize that the Lukan account conflates two different meetings: the first of which, where Peter presided, dealt with the issue of circumcision of Gentiles, and that the second, where James seems to be in charge, dealt with the issue of table fellowship.[37]

This reading helps a number of issues. For example, it explains why Peter seems to be in charge in Acts 15:6–11 but then falls into the background when James delivers the apostolic decree in Acts 15:13–19. It also helps us understand why Paul makes no reference to the apostolic decree when he confronts Peter in Galatians 2:11–14. Lastly, it also helps us understand James' comment in Acts 15:24, "Forasmuch as we have heard, that certain which went out from us have troubled you with words, subverting your souls, saying, Ye must be circumcised, and keep the law: to whom we gave no such commandment." Acts 15 indicates that Paul's opponents "came down from Judea" (Acts 15:1). There is no mention of their relationship with James; that is found only in Galatians 2. If this reading is correct, then the crisis in Antioch precipitated a return to Jerusalem where the matter would be sorted out by James, since the Judaizers were claiming their authority through him. Therefore Peter's actions in Antioch, Paul's response notwithstanding, would not have been a betrayal of guidelines already established by the church. Rather they would simply be evidence of the ongoing development of the church to understand, line upon line, the practical implications of Jesus' direction to take the gospel to all the world.

So, why was Paul so angered over this incident in Antioch, especially since his two previous meetings with Peter had been both cordial and amicable, with Paul implicitly acknowledging Peter's position? Again, there are a number of factors that we should consider. First, we must recognize the tone of Paul's letter to the Galatians. The lack of any kind of thanksgiving section, which he normally includes after his salutation, suggests that Paul is upset as he pens this epistle.[38] Second, the reason for Paul writing this epistle is that members in the Galatian churches are in a situation where they are returning to a law-observant understanding of the Christian message. Thus Paul implores them, "Stand fast therefore in the liberty wherewith Christ hath made us free, and be not entangled again with the yoke of bondage," which he understands to be the law of Moses (Galatians 5:1). I have argued elsewhere that this situation is best understood if the Galatian churches consist predominantly of Gentile God-fearers who, prior to being taught the gospel by Paul, were already attracted to the law of Moses.[39] These were Paul's converts. He had taught them that the Christian message is founded on Christ's grace, which is now incompatible with the law of Moses. True, the law was indeed a "schoolmaster to bring us unto Christ," but only so that they could be made righteous or justified by faith (3:24). Paul himself had been "more exceedingly zealous of the traditions of my fathers" than "my equals in mine own nation" (1:14). He had lived the law as well as it was possible for a human to do so, but it was God's grace, not the law, that led to his revelation on the road to Damascus and his conversion. In Paul's mind, Peter's actions at Antioch were a type of what the Saints in Galatia were doing: having received the gospel that comes through Christ's grace, they were trying to turn back to their old ways of understanding God, ways that were not consistent with "the truth of the gospel" (2:5). It is possible that Paul's language in describing this incident is so strong because his opponents were using Peter's actions as evidence that the Galatians should also return to a law-observant understanding of the Christian message. The whole message of Galatians is that all people, both Jew and Gentile, are made righteous through the faith of Jesus Christ and not, as the Judaizers argued, through the law of Moses (2:16). According to Paul, the Christian approach to inviting Gentiles into the kingdom of God was meant to be very different from the Jewish approach. Clearly, Paul had strong feelings on this topic, and it may well be that, in an effort to convince his readers that they were headed in the wrong direction, he intentionally employed rhetoric that heightened the tension of the Antioch incident.

Conclusion

Paul's account of the incident at Antioch is part of a larger rhetorical effort to crush the inroads that Judaizers were making in the churches in Galatia. His description has troubled readers who are uncomfortable with such tension between the early church's most influential leaders. While not explicitly referring to the incident at Antioch, the Petrine epistles make a significant effort to emphasize the unity between Peter and Paul. The epilogue of 1 Peter (5:12–13) includes the names of two individuals who are known to be missionary companions of Paul: Silvanus (2 Corinthians 1:19; 1 Thessalonians 1:1; 2 Thessalonians 1:1) and Marcus (see Acts 13:13; 15:37; Colossians 4:10). The inclusion of these two individuals emphasizes the ties (rather than any rift) between the Pauline and Petrine missionary efforts. In 2 Peter 3:15–16, Paul is described as "our beloved brother," and his epistles, although they are described as having "some things [which are] hard to be understood," are judged to be equivalent to scripture.

The incident in Antioch is a reminder that history, even religious or sacred history, is rarely neat and straightforward. Even though the resurrected Jesus directed his Apostles to expand the missionary work to take the gospel to all the world, the early church clearly struggled to grasp and comprehend all of the implications of such a command. Paul's account in Galatians 2 reminds us that leaders of the church, even after receiving revelation, must still wrestle with complex doctrinal issues. As Elder Bruce R. McConkie taught, even though Peter received a revelation and opened the door for missionary work among the Gentiles, "there would yet be difficult doctrinal, administrative, and procedural problems to be solved."[40]

Notes

1. Pheme Perkins, *Peter: Apostle for the Whole Church* (Minneapolis: Fortress Press, 2000), 20.

2. For example, in 1853 Jedediah M. Grant wrote, "But if you pass on in their history to seek for uniformity and beauty, you will find some grand flare-ups among them. Look, for instance, at Paul and Peter, disputing and quarrelling with each other [2 Pet. 3:15–16; Gal. 2:11]; and Paul and Barnabas contending, and parting asunder with angry feelings [Acts 15:36–41]. 'When Peter came to Antioch,' says Paul, 'I withstood him to the face, because he was to be blamed,' [Gal. 2:11] &c. Paul does not gain much credit with the Mormons for taking this course. We know he had no right to rebuke Peter; but some man said he was like Almon Babbit, *he wanted to boast of rebuking Peter.* He thought it was a feather in his cap because he coped with Peter and rebuked him. Had that affair come before a 'Mormon' tribunal, they would have decided in favor of Peter and against Paul. We believe when Paul rebuked Peter, he had in him a spirit of rebellion, and was decidedly wrong in rebelling against the man who held the keys of the kingdom of God on the earth." In *Journal of Discourses*, 26 vols. (London: Latter-day Saints' Book Depot, 1854–86), 1:346.

3. Bruce R. McConkie, *Doctrinal New Testament Commentary*, 3 vols. (Salt Lake City: Bookcraft, 1971), 2:463–64.

4. D. Kelly Ogden and Andrew C. Skinner, *New Testament: Apostles Testify of Christ: A Guide for Acts through Revelation* (Salt Lake City: Deseret Book, 1998), 161.

5. John J. Collins, *Between Athens and Jerusalem: Jewish Identity in the Hellenistic Diaspora*, 2nd ed. (Grand Rapids, MI: Eerdmans, 2000), 1.

6. Collins, *Between Athens and Jerusalem*, 1.

7. The Maccabean rulers appropriated many Greek cultural traits. They adopted Greek names, their burial monuments and graves "reflect a significant appropriation of Hellenistic forms," their coins begin to have both Greek and Hebrew inscriptions and symbols, and the literature of the time, even if the text berates Hellenism, often reflects strong Greek stylistic influence (e.g., 1 & 2 Maccabees). For a further discussion, see L. Levine, "Hasmonean Jerusalem: A Jewish City in a Hellenistic Orbit," *Judaism* 46, no. 2 (1997): 143–46.

8. See the account in 2 Maccabees 6, where Jews revolt against the edict of Antiochus outlawing the practice of Judaism by openly displaying their loyalty to these four aspects of Judaism. In the decree of Sardis, Jewish citizens are afforded the right to meet together to offer prayers and sacrifices to their God, and market officials are directed to have "suitable food for them brought in" (*Antiquities of the Jews* 14.259–61). Josephus also records Caesar Augustus's decree that Jewish monies sent to the temple are inviolable and that they are exempt from appearing in court on the Sabbath or Sabbath eve (*Antiquities of the Jews* 16.6.1–8). Cicero says that each year Jews from Italy sent gold to

the temple in Jerusalem (*Pro Flacco* 28.66–69; see also Tacitus, *Histories* 5.5). In addition, as we will see, the New Testament shows that for Judaizers, the main areas for concern about letting Gentiles join the church center around circumcision (see Acts 15:1; Galatians 5:1–13) and eating with Gentiles (see Acts 11:3; Galatians 2:11–13). Worship on the Sabbath does not appear to be an issue because the early Christians continued to participate in the synagogue on the Sabbath and then added their service on Sunday. In addition, the early Christians continued to worship at the temple (Acts 21:23–26). For a discussion on pagan attacks on Jewish circumcision, Sabbath observance, and dietary laws, see Louis H. Feldman, *Jew and Gentile in the Ancient World: Attitudes and Interactions from Alexander to Justinian* (Princeton, NJ: Princeton University Press, 1993), 153–70.

9. See James D. G. Dunn, "The Incident at Antioch (Gal. 2:11–18)," *Journal for the Study of the New Testament* 5, no. 3 (1983): 12–25.

10. The reference in Acts 18 aligns well with the account of a Roman writer, Suetonius: "Since the Jews constantly made disturbances at the instigation of Chrestus [probably a misspelling for Christos], he expelled them from Rome" (*Claudius* 25.4).

11. Dunn, "Incident at Antioch," 7–11.

12. For a discussion of early Jewish proselytism, see Feldman, *Jew and Gentile*, 288–341.

13. Tacitus records that proselytes "increase their [i.e., the Jews'] numbers" (*Histories* 5.5).

14. Emile Schürer, *The History of the Jewish People in the Age of Jesus Christ*, 3 vols., rev. & ed. Geza Vermes, Fergus Millar, and Martin Goodman (Edinburgh: T&T Clark, 1986), 3.1:150–76.

15. Unless noted otherwise, all Philo quotations are from *The Works of Philo: Complete and Unabridged; New Updated Version*, trans. C. D. Yonge (Peabody, MA: Hendrickson Publishers, 1993).

16. We find the most detailed description of a conversion to Judaism in a late apocryphal work entitled *Joseph and Aseneth* (third–fourth centuries AD). The impetus for Aseneth's conversion is meeting Joseph and realizing that he is not interested in marrying anyone who does not share his religious beliefs. The account, however, goes to great length to show that Aseneth's conversion is spiritual in nature.

17. The only specific extracanonical evidence for "an organized Jewish proselytizing campaign is found in the policies of the Hasmoneans toward the Idumeans and Itureans in the late second century B.C.E." Collins, *Between Athens and Jerusalem*, 262.

18. There is some debate whether the term *God-fearers* is a technical term for a well-defined class of Gentiles that were connected with the synagogue. The evidence suggests that there were many levels of attachment. For careful discussions on issues, see Feldman, *Jew and Gentile*, 342–82, and Collins, *Between Athens and Jerusalem*, 264–72.

19. An opposing view is found in Dieter Georgi, *Opponents of Paul in Second Corinthians* (Philadelphia: Fortress Press, 1986), 84, 175, n. 1.

20. To the Corinthians, Paul declared, "for in nothing am I behind the very chiefest apostles, though I be nothing" (2 Corinthians 12:11). The question of Paul's apostolic authority is complex. On the one hand, the Biblical text does not give any specific information of when he was called to be an Apostle. In Acts, Luke first calls him an Apostle when he was at Lystra during his first missionary journey (Acts 14:14). On the other hand, the New Testament uses the word apostle (Greek *apostolos*) in different

ways. The basic meaning of *apostolos* is "messenger," and the New Testament uses it in this sense, particularly when talking about messengers who are sent out representing various branches of the church (e.g., Philippians 2:25). Sometimes the New Testament uses it in the sense of a priesthood office that is synonymous with the Twelve (Acts 1:21–26), but sometimes the Twelve and the Apostles seem to be two different groups (1 Corinthians 15:5–7). On one occasion Paul refers to a woman, Junia, who is "of note among the apostles" (Romans 16:7). It seems certain that Paul's opponents in Galatia did not recognize Paul as an Apostle on the same level as Peter and the other Apostles. Paul's point here is that his apostolic authority came directly from Christ himself.

21. Ben Witherington, *Grace in Galatia: A Commentary on Paul's Letter to the Galatians* (Grand Rapids, MI: Eerdmans, 1998), 96.

22. Witherington, *Grace in Galatia*, 116.

23. This is a fact that Paul readily admits in his epistle to the Corinthians. He describes himself as "the least of the apostles, that am not meet to be called an apostle, because I persecuted the church of God" (1 Corinthians 15:9).

24. Paul writes his letters in response to specific events that are taking place in the respective church communities. Scholars have long noted that in Paul's Corinthian epistles he uses slogans from his opponents' rhetoric. For an example, see Denny Burk, "Discerning Corinthian Slogans through Paul's Use of the Diatribe in 1 Corinthians 6:12–20," *Bulletin for Biblical Research* 18, no. 1 (2008): 99–121. It is therefore not unreasonable to assume that he may also have included the stories of his interactions with Peter to correct misinformation that his opponents are disseminating about Paul's relationship with Peter.

25. B. R. Gaventa, "Galatians 1 and 2: Autobiography as Paradigm," *Novum Testamentum* 28, no. 4 (1986): 316–17.

26. For examples of those who argue for two different events, see Witherington, *Grace in Galatia*, 15. See also the discussions in F. F. Bruce, *The Epistle to the Galatians*, The New International Greek Testament Commentary (Grand Rapids, MI: Eerdmans, 1982), 106–27; Joe Morgado Jr., "Paul in Jerusalem: A Comparison of His Visits in Acts and Galatians," *Journal of the Evangelical Theological Society* (March 1994): 55–68. See also Richard Neitzel Holzapfel, Eric D. Huntsman, and Thomas A. Wayment, *Jesus Christ and the World of the New Testament: An Illustrated Reference for Latter-day Saints* (Salt Lake City: Deseret Book, 2006), 216–17.

27. Witherington, *Grace in Galatia*, 14; Richard Lloyd Anderson, *Understanding Paul* (Salt Lake City: Deseret Book, 1983), 156.

28. Witherington, *Grace in Galatia*, 15. See also the discussions in Bruce, *The Epistle to the Galatians*, 106–27; Morgado, "Paul in Jerusalem," 55–68.

29. Hans Dieter Betz, *Galatians*, Hermeneia (Philadelphia: Fortress Press, 1979), 88–89.

30. Gaventa, *Galatians 1 and 2*, 316.

31. For examples of those who see Paul's statement in verse 2 as a reason to separate the two accounts, see Witherington, *Grace in Galatia*, 15; Morgado, "Paul in Jerusalem," 61–62.

32. Bart Ehrman argues that the Cephas in Galatians 2:9 refers to someone other than Peter. "Cephas and Peter," *Journal of Biblical Literature* 109, no. 3 (1990): 463–74. For

a response to his arguments, see Dale C. Allison Jr., "Peter and Cephas: One and the Same," *Journal of Biblical Literature* 111, no. 3 (1992): 489–95.

33. This verse is the genesis for the Collection that Paul encourages the Gentile converts to contribute to in order to help the poor saints in Jerusalem (1 Corinthians 16:1–3; 2 Corinthians 8:1–11; 9:1–12; Romans 15:25–27).

34. James D. G. Dunn, *Unity and Diversity in the New Testament: An Inquiry into the Character of Earliest Christianity*, 3rd ed. (London: SCM, 2006), 255–57; Lawrence H. Schiffman, "At the Crossroads: Tannaitic Perspectives on the Jewish-Christian Schism," in *Jewish and Christian Self-Definition*, vol. 2, *Aspects of Judaism in the Graeco-Roman Period*, ed. E. P. Sanders (London: SCM, 1981), 115–56.

35. Betz, *Galatians*, 108.

36. Tertullian, *Against Marcion*, 1.20, in *Tertullian, Adversus Marcionem*, ed. Ernest Evans (London: Oxford, 1972), 51–53.

37. Dunn, "The Incident at Antioch," 38. Latter-day Saint descriptions of the Jerusalem Conference generally assume that Acts 15:6–35 refers to a single event. For examples, see Robert J. Matthews, "The Jerusalem Council," in *The Apostle Paul: His Life and His Testimony* (Salt Lake City: Deseret Book, 1994), 96–109; Wayment, *From Persecutor to Apostle*, 93–104; Jared Ludlow, "The Book of Acts: A Pattern for Modern Church Growth," in *Shedding Light on the New Testament: Acts–Revelation*, ed. Ray L. Huntington, Frank F. Judd Jr., and David M. Whitchurch (Provo, UT: Religious Studies Center, 2009), 22–24; Richard Neitzel Holzapfel and Thomas A. Wayment, "Unto the Uttermost Part of the Earth," in *The Life and Teachings of the New Testament Apostles: From the Day of Pentecost through the Apocalypse*, ed. Richard Neitzel Holzapfel and Thomas A. Wayment (Salt Lake City: Deseret Book, 2010), 76–78; Frank F. Judd Jr., "The Jerusalem Conference: The First Council of the Christian Church" *Religious Educator* 12, no. 1 (2011): 55–71.

38. For examples of Paul's thanksgiving sections in other epistles, see Romans 1:8; 1 Corinthians 1:4; Philippians 1:3; Colossians 1:3; 1 Thessalonians 1:2; 2 Thessalonians 1:3; 2 Timothy 1:3; Philemon 1:4.

39. See Gaye Strathearn, "Law and Liberty in Galatians 5–6," in *Go Ye into All the World: Messages of the New Testament Apostles* (Salt Lake City: Deseret Book, 2002), 59–62.

40. Bruce R. McConkie, *Doctrinal New Testament Commentary*, 3 vols. (Salt Lake City: Bookcraft, 1979), 2:101.

13

The Case for Petrine Authorship of 1 Peter

Frank F. Judd Jr.

Frank F. Judd Jr. is an associate professor of ancient scripture at
Brigham Young University.

The First Epistle of Peter begins with this declaration: "Peter, an apostle of Jesus Christ, to the strangers scattered throughout Pontus, Galatia, Cappadocia, Asia, and Bithynia" (1 Peter 1:1). During the past couple of centuries, however, some scholars have argued against Petrine authorship of 1 Peter.[1] Yet there are still scholars who hold to the traditional authorship of this epistle.[2] What are the issues involved in this debate? What evidence and reasoning have scholars used to conclude that Peter did or did not write 1 Peter? What are the strengths and weaknesses of these arguments?

The purpose of this paper is multifaceted. First, I will establish the case for Petrine authorship of 1 Peter. Second, I will present and evaluate the most important arguments to the contrary. Third, I will discuss what is known about Greco-Roman scribes, their involvement in the production of New Testament documents, and the implication of scribal activity on the issue of Peter the Apostle being the author of 1 Peter. I will demonstrate that there are reasonable answers to the arguments against Petrine authorship of 1 Peter.[3] Finally, I will conclude by placing the issue of traditional authorship in its proper perspective. While on the one hand it is essential for Latter-day Saints to be informed about the scriptures, one must not lose sight of the fact that it is more important to possess a testimony of the truth of the doctrines taught in a particular book of the Bible than it is to know exactly who wrote it.

The Case for Petrine Authorship

A satisfactory case can be made in favor of Petrine authorship of 1 Peter. There is a correlation between the content of the letter and what is known of the historical figure of Peter. The author of the epistle refers to himself as "Peter, an apostle of Jesus Christ" (1 Peter 1:1) and Peter is unambiguously identified as an Apostle in the Gospels (see Matthew 10:2; Luke 6:13–14), the book of Acts (see Acts 2:37; 5:29), and Paul's Epistle to the Galatians (see Galatians 1:18–19). In addition, the author claims to be "a witness of the sufferings of Christ" (1 Peter 5:1). It should be noted that the word *witness* could be understood two different ways, either an eyewitness or one who testifies.[4] Although there is no scriptural record of Peter being present at the Crucifixion, it is a possibility.[5] John was certainly present when Jesus was crucified (see John 19:25–27), and he and Peter are often mentioned as being together during much of the Passion, including in Gethsemane (see Matthew 26:36–37), during the interrogation before Caiaphas (see John 18:15–16), and at the tomb (see John 20:2–4). Even if Peter was not an eyewitness to the Crucifixion, however, the author's claim to be "a witness of the sufferings of Christ" certainly matches what we know of Peter after the Resurrection, when he boldly testified, or witnessed, concerning the suffering, death, and Resurrection of Jesus the Messiah (see Acts 2:22–36; 3:12–26).

The author of 1 Peter states that he is writing to members of the church who are "scattered throughout Pontus, Galatia, Cappadocia, Asia, and Bithynia" (1 Peter 1:1). Although there is no account of Peter actually visiting those locations in Asia Minor, the book of Acts does indicate that on the day of Pentecost, Peter interacted with Jews "out of every nation under heaven" (Acts 2:5), including those whose homelands were in "Cappadocia, in Pontus, and Asia" (Acts 2:9). On that sacred occasion, the disciples spoke in tongues, Peter addressed the crowds, and "they that gladly received his word were baptized: and the same day there were added unto them about three thousand souls" (Acts 2:41). It is likely that some of those three thousand new converts were from Asia Minor, who then brought the gospel with them when they returned home. This would help explain Peter's personal concern for the Christians living in those areas of Anatolia.

The origin of the letter is stated to be "the church that is at Babylon" (1 Peter 5:13), which is very likely a code name for Rome.[6] Similarly, the book of Revelation also identifies Rome as Babylon, a city with seven hills (Revelation 16:19 and

17:9).[7] Although the book of Acts only contains the narrative of Paul traveling to Rome, many early Christian sources also place Peter in Rome for the last few years of his life as well as for his martyrdom.[8]

The author of the letter also indicates that he has a close relationship with "Marcus my son" (1 Peter 5:13). This may be the same John Mark with whose family Peter had found refuge years earlier. When Peter was miraculously freed from prison in Jerusalem, "he came to the house of Mary the mother of John, whose surname was Mark" (Acts 12:12). John Mark later accompanied Paul and Barnabas on their mission to Cyprus (Acts 12:25; 13:5). A number of early Christian traditions also associate Peter with John Mark during the latter part of the Apostle's ministry in Rome.[9]

The letter makes frequent use of the Old Testament. For example, the author quotes from the books of Leviticus, Isaiah, Psalms, and Proverbs[10] and appeals to the stories of Sarah, Abraham, and Noah.[11] These are the kinds of references one might expect from a man who had been raised in a devout Jewish household of the time period. Josephus, a Jewish historian from the first century AD, interpreted the Torah to instruct parents "to teach reading, in relation to the laws . . . that they know about the exploits of their forebears."[12] Concerning whether this might be done in a particular household, however, Raymond E. Brown has wisely cautioned that it would "depend upon the piety of their parents."[13] Indications are that Peter grew up in an observant family. Years later, when he saw his famous vision on a rooftop in Joppa, Peter declared that he had always lived according to Jewish dietary laws (see Acts 10:13–14).

There are a number of concepts in the letter that are also associated with what we know of Peter from the Gospels and the book of Acts. For instance, the author teaches that God the Father "without respect of persons judgeth according to every man's work" (1 Peter 1:17). Similarly, in the book of Acts, Peter was taught by revelation that "God is no respecter of persons" and that "in every nation he that feareth him, and worketh righteousness, is accepted with him" (Acts 10:34–35). In another example, the author encourages "the elders which are among you" to "feed the flock of God" (1 Peter 5:1–2), which echoes the repeated instruction of the resurrected Jesus to Peter along the shore of the Sea of Galilee: "feed my sheep" (John 21:15–17).[14]

One argument that some scholars have attempted to use against Petrine authorship is the claim that the letter contains ideas that are thought to originate from later periods of time following the death of Peter, which was probably around AD 64.[15] On the contrary, however, there are certain theological perspectives presented in the letter that point to a date of composition within the understood lifetime of Peter. Some of these are similar to what we find in the Pauline epistles, all of which date to before AD 64.[16]

For example, there is what Elliott calls "a vibrant eschatology,"[17] or in other words an expectation of the Second Coming of Christ, which permeates Paul's epistles. The author of 1 Peter testifies that through the Resurrection of Jesus Christ, Christians can have a dynamic hope of eternal life to sustain them through trials so that they might be found worthy "at the appearing of Jesus Christ" (1 Peter 1: 3–7). Paul likewise taught that some people sorrow at the death of loved ones because they lack a testimony "that Jesus died and rose again" and have no "hope" that "the Lord himself shall descend from heaven" (1 Thessalonians 4:13–16).[18]

The epistle also reflects a period in the development of church hierarchy consistent with a composition date before AD 64. The earliest local church leadership was not one bishop[19] presiding over one congregation. Rather the ecclesiastical structure differed from congregation to congregation and only later developed into a mono-episcopacy (or structure of having a single bishop over a single congregation).[20] Rather than addressing one bishop over a single congregation, the author of 1 Peter addresses leaders within the congregation as "elders" and even identifies himself as "also an elder" (1 Peter 5:1).[21] We find this description of church leaders associated with other congregations in Asia Minor—in particular the church at Ephesus. When Paul was traveling to Jerusalem after his third mission, he stopped at Miletus and "he sent to Ephesus, and called the elders of the church" (Acts 20:17).[22] We find further variety in the structure of church hierarchy in Paul's letters as well. For example, in his Epistle to the Philippians, Paul addressed "the bishops and deacons" (Philippians 1:1) instead of one bishop over the Philippian congregation.[23]

Besides the nature of its references to eschatology and ecclesiastical structure, another reason for proposing an early date for 1 Peter concerns its discussion of persecution: "the fiery trial which is to try you" (1 Peter 4:12). The various manifestations of this "fiery trial" mentioned in 1 Peter are described as localized, occasional, and unorganized—primarily having to do with non-Christians speaking evil things against Christians (see 1 Peter 1:6; 2:12, 15; 3:9, 16; 4:12, 16). This is unlike the systematic persecutions ordered by the Emperor Nero in Rome around AD 64–65 and later by others.[24] As Elliott has pointed out, the author makes no connection "between the suffering experienced by the believers and Roman anti-Christian aggression."[25] Though an argument from silence, one would expect some type of reference to these specific persecutions if the letter had been composed during or after their occurrence. This glaring omission may indicate that the letter was more likely to have been written prior to Nero's persecution of Christians and therefore prior to the death of the Apostle Peter.[26]

Additionally, J. N. D. Kelly concluded that 1 Peter does not possess any of the obvious signs of being pseudonymous. This includes an absence of "a self-conscious straining after verisimilitude," meaning a later author obviously attempting to make a document sound like it is from an earlier era, as well as "the barely concealed assumption that the apostolic age lies in the past."[27] Finally, while it is well known that there were debates about whether some documents, such as the book of Revelation, should be included in the canon, there was no such debate about the inclusion of 1 Peter. The acceptance of 1 Peter was early and widespread.[28] While this does not prove authorship, it demonstrates the positive manner in which the early church viewed the epistle's apostolic authority and authenticity.[29] In summary, from the above data, one can see that there are numerous features of 1 Peter that connect it to Peter and are consistent with the conclusion that the letter was written within the lifetime of the Apostle.

Arguments against Petrine Authorship

A number of arguments have been made against the traditional view of Petrine authorship of 1 Peter. We will discuss the most important ones below. First, the epistle employs very sophisticated Greek vocabulary, style, and rhetoric.[30] The claim is that it is highly unlikely that Peter, a first-century Jew from Galilee, would have been familiar and conversant with this level of sophisticated Greek. The book of Acts records that Peter and John were referred to as "unlearned and ignorant men" (Acts 4:13). One must not exaggerate this identification, however, which probably simply means that they were "deficient in formal rabbinic training."[31] So while it is unlikely that Peter received the same level and nature of education as Paul, who was trained under the tutelage of the great Jewish teacher Gamaliel (see Acts 22:3), the real question is the extent to which Peter may have been familiar with the Greek language.

Scholars and archaeologists have debated over the level of Hellenization in Galilee during the first century AD. A number of scholars have postulated that Greco-Roman culture was widespread.[32] Recently, however, Mark Chancey has argued that the archaeological evidence does not support this theory.[33] While the paucity of explicitly Greek or Roman material culture from the first century certainly serves to caution scholars against making exaggerated claims about the level of Hellenistic influence in Galilee during the lifetime of Peter, it is an argument from silence. Ongoing excavations continue to bring to light new evidence to evaluate. The archaeologists who have excavated et-Tell, a possible site of Bethsaida located near Capernaum just east of the River Jordan, have discovered remains of what they conclude were a Hellenistic temple and Roman temple, including a bronze incense shovel and small figurines uncovered nearby.[34] Chancey doubts that these sites were actually pagan cultic installations because no altars, statues, bones of sacrificed animals, or dedicatory inscriptions were discovered within the buildings themselves.[35] Carl Savage, on the other hand, has recently analyzed the pottery and other material culture discovered at et-Tell and concluded that while the dominant population and culture were definitely Jewish during the first century, there also existed "an interplay between local culture and Greco-Roman culture."[36]

In addition to archaeology, other important factors should also be considered. One must not forget that in Capernaum, Peter "was surrounded by Greeks and other gentiles living in the Decapolis as well as by Syro-phoenicians in the Huleh Valley and toward Caesarea Philippi."[37] The Decapolis consisted of ten Hellenistic cities founded sometime after the conquest of Alexander the Great and reestablished as Roman cities after Pompey conquered Judea in the first century BC.[38] In particular, the Decapolis city and port of Hippos were only a few miles south of Capernaum, along the eastern shore of the Sea of Galilee. Archaeologists have uncovered remains of a Roman temple in Hippos from the first century BC, built on the foundations of an earlier Hellenistic temple.[39] The Gospel of Mark says that Jesus, presumably with Peter and the other disciples, visited the region of the Decapolis (see Mark 7:31). The Gospel of Matthew indicates that once his fame began to spread, inhabitants from the Decapolis followed Jesus (see Matthew 4:25).

Even closer to Capernaum, however, was Bethsaida, just east of the River Jordan as it empties into the Sea of Galilee. Whether or not et-Tell is to be identified with the city, Bethsaida was nevertheless the capital of the territory of Gaulanitis, which encompassed such Jewish strongholds as Gamla, as well as a significant Gentile population. By AD 30, Herod Philip had made Bethsaida into a Greek *polis* and renamed it Bethsaida-Julias.[40] The Gospel of John says that Philip, Andrew, and Peter were all originally "of Bethsaida" (John 1:44; see John 12:21). Although Simon is the Greek equivalent of the Hebrew name Simeon, the names Philip and Andrew are both Greek with no Hebrew equivalents—a fact that some scholars interpret as evidence of Greek influence in the area.[41] Jesus visited Bethsaida multiple times with his disciples and performed miracles (see Mark 8:22–26; Luke 9:10–17).[42]

In his study of the fishing industry at the Sea of Galilee, Jerome Murphy-O'Connor has concluded that since eating fish was standard for both the Jewish and non-Jewish population, it was likely that some of those involved in the business of catching, processing, and selling fish would have had some basic understanding of Greek to communicate with those from areas immediately surrounding Galilee to sell their product.[43] The Gospel of John records an instance in which it seems that at least Philip demonstrates the ability to communicate in Greek. When Jesus and his disciples traveled to Jerusalem for Passover, "certain Greeks" (John 12:20) approached Philip, who the Gospel of John reminds us was "of Bethsaida of Galilee" (John 12:21), and asked to see Jesus. Whether they were Gentiles or diaspora Jews, the assumption of the text is that the request "was uttered in Greek."[44] Some scholars have concluded that the implication of the story is that these Greeks approached Philip because he had a Greek name, was from a place influenced by Gentiles (i.e., in Gaulanitis and near the Decapolis), and could therefore understand Greek.[45] While none of these items prove that Peter spoke Greek fluently during his time in Galilee, it at least suggests that having a basic knowledge of the language was possible.

A second argument against Petrine authorship of 1 Peter is related to the first one. When the letter quotes from or alludes to the Old Testament, it does so using language from the Greek Septuagint (LXX), not the traditional Hebrew text or the Aramaic Targums. According to Elliott, the allusions to the Septuagint "indicate a writer thinking in terms of the LXX, not the Hebrew," which is again "difficult to reconcile with an unschooled, Aramaic-speaking fisherman, whose Bible would have been Hebrew and whose language of worship would have been Palestinian Aramaic."[46] In response to this claim, as I have outlined above, it is at least possible that someone like Peter, who lived and worked in general proximity to Gentiles living around Galilee, Gaulanitis, and the Decapolis, could have possessed a basic understanding of the Greek language.

More importantly, however, neither of these first two arguments against Petrine authorship considers implications of the fact that 1 Peter was written many years after Peter left his home in Galilee. For over three decades after the Crucifixion, Peter seems to have had significant interaction with those who spoke Greek. On the day of Pentecost, Peter received an outpouring of the Holy Ghost and manifested the gift of tongues as he "began to speak with other tongues" (Acts 2:4) to diaspora Jews "out of every nation" (Acts 2:5). Even if Peter did not possess a fluency in Greek during the time he grew up in Galilee, the gift of tongues combined with his experiences teaching Gentiles and diaspora Jews over the next thirty years could have helped him develop a general familiarity with the Septuagint.

The New Testament narrates a number of instances in which Peter worked among Hellenistic Jews as well as among Gentiles. In Jerusalem, Peter was faced with the controversy between the "Grecians" (Acts 6:1), or Greek-speaking

Jewish Christians, and the Hebrews. While in Joppa, Peter spoke with the men of Cornelius, a Roman centurion who was stationed in Caesarea Maritima (see Acts 10:1–5,19–23). Peter then traveled to Caesarea and conversed with Cornelius himself (see Acts 10:25–33). Later, Paul reveals that in Antioch the chief Apostle "did eat with the Gentiles" (Galatians 2:12). In addition, as was mentioned above, early Christian tradition indicates that Peter spent the last few years of his life in Rome, where he was eventually martyred.

Thus, as Richard Neitzel Holzapfel and Thomas Wayment have concluded, by the time 1 Peter was written, "Peter had traveled extensively around the eastern Mediterranean and certainly would have become rather proficient in Greek."[47] During that time, according to J. N. D. Kelly, the Septuagint would have been "the Bible for his missionary work abroad."[48] A modern corollary might be the months, not years, diligent Latter-day Saint missionaries immersing themselves in a new language need in order to become familiar with the scriptures in that language. And after decades of evangelizing those who spoke Greek, it is certainly possible that Peter had developed a working knowledge of the Septuagint.

It should be noted that Papias, an early Christian writer from the second century AD, preserves the tradition that John Mark assisted Peter in Rome.[49] Papias, citing an earlier John the Presbyter, states, "Mark, who had been Peter's interpreter, wrote down carefully, but not in order, all that he remembered of the Lord's sayings and doings."[50] What does this mean? The Greek word *hermēneutēs* is usually translated as "interpreter," which could mean that Mark acted as Peter's translator. If, after over thirty years of evangelizing people all over the Mediterranean, Peter was able to communicate in Greek, this understanding may not be accurate. The word *hermēneutēs*, however, can also carry a more general connotation of "one who helps someone to understand thoughts expressed in words."[51] Robert Gundry has concluded that "Peter knew Greek well enough to speak it for himself" and has proposed that the Greek verbal form "favors that Mark became Peter's expositor rather than translator."[52]

It should also be noted that from her detailed analysis of the Greek of 1 Peter, Karen Jobes has detected Semitic influence in the syntax of the epistle and has concluded that the author's native language was Semitic. According to Jobes, this enhances the likelihood of native Semitic speakers being able to write in Greek and be familiar with the Septuagint.[53]

Again, the above items do not prove that Peter was familiar enough with the Greek language that he knew the Septuagint and wrote 1 Peter. But, as Ernest Best has pointed out, even if Peter was primarily comfortable with the Hebrew rather than the Greek, "direct quotations would obviously have been put in the version to which the readers were accustomed, i.e., the LXX, even though the writer himself was accustomed to another version."[54] Paul, who knew both Hebrew and Greek (Acts 21:37–40) and who was trained as a Pharisee under Gamaliel in Jerusalem (see Acts 22:3; Philippians 3:5), used the Septuagint in his letters—the version with which his audience was most familiar.[55] On the other hand, however, it is possible that the use of the Septuagint in 1 Peter may simply reflect the sophistication of the author's scribe and therefore may not actually be evidence against Petrine authorship. The use of scribes will be discussed in more detail below.

A third argument against Petrine authorship of 1 Peter centers on the letter's supposed lack of references to the teachings and ministry of Jesus.[56] This particular argument is very subjective, as are the others. Robert Gundry has identified a number of possible references in 1 Peter to both the teachings as well as the ministry of Jesus.[57] While some scholars find them convincing, others do not.

One example has to do with the counsel concerning persecution. Readers are instructed to "greatly rejoice" though they are experiencing "heaviness through manifold temptations" (1 Peter 1:6). In another passage, readers are again encouraged to "rejoice, inasmuch as ye are partakers of Christ's sufferings" (1 Peter 4:13). This recalls the Sermon on the Mount, where Jesus taught his audience that when people "revile" and "persecute" them, they should "rejoice, and be exceeding glad" (Matthew 5:11–12) because of the heavenly reward they will receive and because they are experiencing the same persecutions as the prophets of old.

In another example, the author discusses the suffering of Jesus:

> Christ also suffered for us, leaving us an example, that ye should follow his steps:
>   Who did no sin, neither was guile found in his mouth:
>   Who, when he was reviled, reviled not again; when he suffered, he threatened not; but committed himself to him that judgeth righteously:
>   Who his own self bare our sins in his own body on the tree, that we, being dead to sins, should live unto righteousness: by whose stripes ye were healed. (1 Peter 2:21–24)

There are scholars who do not find this parallel convincing, because it does not sound like an eyewitness account, but rather it is in the language of the messianic prophecy contained in Isaiah 53.[58] It should be noted that in the book of Acts Peter's preaching consistently emphasizes to his audiences that the Passion of Jesus was in fulfillment of Old Testament prophecy (see Acts 2:22–36; 3:12–18).

Similarly, when the Apostle Paul evangelized Asia Minor and Greece, he also emphasized that the prophets of old prophesied of the death and Resurrection of Jesus (see Acts 13:14–37; 17:1–4).

If one consults a list of the quotations and allusions to Isaiah in the New Testament, it is apparent that while New Testament authors often employed Isaiah 61 when discussing the preaching and ministry of Jesus, Isaiah 53 is often quoted or alluded to in conjunction with the Passion of Christ.[59] A recent study of Isaiah 53 in the New Testament has found that "nearly every NT writer uses at least one allusion with the exception of Jas [James] and Jude."[60] Victor Ludlow concluded that Isaiah 53 was a "favorite chapter" New Testament authors used when teaching about the suffering of Jesus.[61] Thus the author's reference to Isaiah 53 is consistent with Luke's presentation of Peter as well as the practice of other New Testament writers.[62]

A similar type of argument is made against Petrine authorship because of a lack of explicit references to the Apostle Paul. If Peter was indeed writing to disciples in Asia Minor, where Paul had spent so much time, it is argued that "he would have made some reference to his brother apostle's previous work."[63] This criticism, like the one above, is an argument from silence. A letter's authorship and authenticity should not depend upon its containing the types of things that a modern scholar, two thousand years later, wants it to contain.[64] It is possible, however, that Peter and Paul were not on the best of terms with one another, because of the conflict they experienced in Antioch years earlier.[65] On the other hand, the author addresses this letter to those who were living in "Pontus, Galatia, Cappadocia, Asia, and Bithynia" (1 Peter 1:1). Of those five areas, we only have evidence that Paul visited Galatia and Asia.[66] The writer simply may have felt that a reference to Paul would not be meaningful to every recipient of the letter.

The final argument against Petrine authorship that we will consider has to do with 1 Peter's possible connection with the Pauline epistles. It is proposed by some scholars that the author of 1 Peter was familiar with and dependent upon a number of Paul's epistles, and therefore the letter is unlikely to have been written by Peter himself.[67] This argument assumes that by the time he would have had any contact with the epistles of Paul, Peter's own views about the gospel would have been solidified, with the result that he would not likely have been open to new ideas or expressions such as he would have found within the Pauline corpus.

But the stories that the New Testament preserves about Peter paint a different picture of the Apostle. For example, Peter was the first of Jesus' followers to publically declare that Jesus was "the Christ, the Son of the living God" (Matthew 16:16), as well the first disciple to allow Gentiles access to the gospel without keeping the law of Moses (see Acts 10:44–48). As Ernest Best has pointed out concerning this characterization of Peter, "there is no unwillingness in either case to express himself in new ways."[68] Thus there is no reason why Peter could not rely upon his fellow Apostle Paul for new ideas on how to express gospel concepts.[69]

On the other hand, however, it should be remembered that none of the supposed parallels between 1 Peter and Paul's letters is a verbatim quote and there are numerous theological, thematic, and stylistic differences between them, causing John Elliott to conclude that while the writer of 1 Peter may have been familiar with some Pauline material, "it can no longer be claimed that the Petrine author was dependent on Paul for his thoughts and formulations."[70] Concerning these similar ideas, J. N. D. Kelly has concluded, "it is much more likely that 1 Peter and the Pauline letters drew independently on common material than that the former borrowed from the latter."[71]

From the above discussion one can see, as Joseph Fitzmyer has concluded, that "none of the reasons against Petrine authorship has been really convincing."[72] The arguments typically marshaled against Petrine authorship of 1 Peter can be reasonably answered. It is true that the conclusions that one draws with respect to these issues often depends upon one's perspective. The predisposal to accept or to doubt traditional authorship of the books of the Bible certainly affects the conclusions that a scholar draws with respect to these issues. But there is certainly no "smoking gun" argument against Petrine authorship. After weighing the evidence of a relationship between the Apostle Peter and the letter 1 Peter, Ernest Best concluded that a link can be made between them. Admittedly, states Best, there is "nothing which enforces such a connection," but on the other hand, "there is certainly nothing to be detected which is contrary to it."[73] There is, however, one final issue that can give much insight into the authorship of 1 Peter. This will be discussed below.

Scribes and Letter Writing

One of the theories that some scholars have suggested is that Peter used a scribe to compose 1 Peter.[74] The use of scribes is a well-documented phenomenon from the Greco-Roman world in which Peter lived as well as from the New Testament itself.[75] The employment of scribes was not merely a necessity for the illiterate, but a convenience for those who could afford it. There is substantial evidence that Paul, who was well educated and certainly could have written his own epistles, used scribes for the writing process.[76] For example, at the end of his first letter to the Corinthians, Paul wrote: "The salutation of me Paul with mine own hand" (1 Corinthians 16:21).[77] This indicates that Paul dictated the body of this letter to a scribe and then signed the end of the letter in his own handwriting.[78] In one instance among Paul's letters, the scribe actually identifies himself: "I Tertius, who wrote this epistle, salute you in the Lord" (Romans 16:22).

Lincoln Blumell has shown that scribes were primarily used in three different ways: recorder, editor, and substitute author.[79] First, they could be used simply as "recorders" who might either re-copy a first draft of a document into an error-free final copy or write while the author dictated the document. This phenomenon was described by Cicero, a famous Roman statesman from the first century BC, who once lamented to his friend Atticus that he needed to dictate a particular letter to an inexperienced scribe "syllable by syllable" but that his regular scribe, Tiro, "can follow whole sentences."[80]

Second, scribes could be used as "editors" who, depending upon the relationship with the author, might be given more freedom in supplying and correcting the vocabulary and style of the final product. As an example, Cicero often commended his scribe Tiro for his expertise in editing Cicero's grammar. On one occasion, however, Cicero discovered a grammatical error in a letter that Tiro had written to him and genially teased his scribe because of it.[81]

Finally, scribes could be used as "substitute authors" where the original sender only gave basic instruction but left the production of the document completely up to the scribe. On a particular occasion, a decade after he had been exiled from Rome, Cicero was feeling particularly upset that he had not been able to keep current in his correspondence with others. Cicero wrote a letter to his friend Atticus and made the following request: "I should like you to write in my name to Basilus and to anyone else you like, even to Servilius, and say whatever you think fit."[82] Although it was not typical for a writer to give a scribe absolute authority over the content of a letter, this example does illustrate the possible influence a scribe might have over the substance of a document. It should be noted that in the first two examples, authors were expected to review the final product to make sure it accurately represented what they intended to say, but in all cases the sender was considered to be the author of the document, even though a scribe was actually responsible for writing it.[83]

It is possible that Peter also used a scribe when producing 1 Peter. Some scholars have proposed that Peter actually identifies Silvanus[84] as the scribe when he states that he has written this letter "by Silvanus, a faithful brother unto you" (1 Peter 5:12).[85] Others, however, argue that 1 Peter does not identify a scribe because the Greek preposition *dia* ("by") is used here to identify the courier of the letter, basically saying that it was delivered to them by means of Silvanus.[86] It should be noted, however, that not all of Paul's letters identify a scribe either, although it is quite likely that he used one, even for those letters where the use of a scribe is not explicitly mentioned or detected.[87] Thus it is possible that Peter may have also used a scribe but did not identify him by name. In addition, as noted above, early Christian tradition places Peter in Rome with John Mark as a *hermēneutēs*, suggesting Peter's use of disciples in this type of a supporting role.

The possibility that Peter used a scribe when composing 1 Peter presents a number of intriguing implications. First, the use of a scribe, especially one who was well trained, could explain why the Greek of 1 Peter is so sophisticated. Peter may have given the scribe detailed instructions concerning the content of the letter or maybe an initial draft of a letter, but he may also have allowed the scribe considerable freedom to either correct Peter's Greek or even compose the final product using more eloquent Greek than Peter himself would normally have used in everyday speech.

Second, the use of a scribe, especially a Jewish scribe who had been trained in the Greek version of the scriptures, could help explain the frequent quotations from and the allusions to the Septuagint. Third, the use of a scribe, in particular one that would have been exposed to the teachings of Paul, as Paul's former mission companions Silvanus and Mark would have been, could help explain the similarities between some of the expressions in 1 Peter and Paul's epistles. As Blumell concluded, "In most cases, an individual scribe could imprint a distinct literary style on any document he or she wrote, which would greatly affect its form, vocabulary, and perhaps even content."[88]

Latter-day Saint Perspective and Conclusion

The Prophet Joseph Smith stated that "Peter penned the most sublime language of any of the apostles."[89] Some might view this statement as indisputable proof of Petrine authorship of 1 Peter. If one examines the context of this statement, however, it is evident that Joseph Smith was giving a sermon based upon what he read in 2 Peter, not 1 Peter.[90] In addition, this statement does not rule out the possibility that Peter used scribes. If there was anyone who understood the need for secretaries and scribes to help church leaders with their work, it was Joseph Smith, who employed faithful scribes for significant projects throughout his life, including writing the Book of Mormon manuscripts, recording the Joseph Smith Translation, and keeping his own records and journals.

While it has been shown above that a good case can be made for the traditional view of Petrine authorship of 1 Peter and that there are reasonable answers to respond to contrary views, there is no need to be unrealistic or fanatical concerning traditional authorship of the books of the New Testament. Scholarship simply does not possess the tools to either absolutely prove or disprove this issue. One must evaluate what little evidence has been preserved concerning the exact authorship of biblical books. For example, early Christian tradition states that the Gospel of Mark actually originated in the testimony of Peter, and the Gospels of Matthew and John contain evidence that suggest they were at least partially dependent upon previously written sources and were compiled through the help of scribes.[91] In addition, it is possible that Luke or Barnabas, rather than Paul, composed the epistle to the Hebrews.[92]

One of the best statements concerning a balanced Latter-day Saint attitude toward traditional authorship comes from President J. Reuben Clark, a member of the First Presidency for almost thirty years:

> I am not really concerned, and no man of faith should be, about the exact authorship of the books of the Bible. More than one Prophet may well have written parts of books now collected under one heading. I do not know. There may have been "ghost writers" in those days, as now. The Lord gave Aaron to Moses in an equivalent capacity, and spoke to Israel through Moses by the mouth of Aaron. He may have done the same in other cases. If so, what of it?[93]

As Latter-day Saints, we are able to accept the traditional authorship of the books of the Bible as long as that tradition is true—and sometimes we cannot know that with certainty. In addition, Latter-day Saints also appreciate the fact that the exact authorship of a particular biblical book pales in importance compared with the principles of the gospel which that document teaches. Thus the issue of exactly who wrote a book of the Bible should not adversely affect our attitude concerning the inspiration of the doctrines of the gospel of Jesus Christ which are contained in that document. If it turns out that Barnabas or Luke wrote Hebrews instead of Paul, that does not diminish the truth that "faith is the substance of things hoped for, the evidence of things not seen" (Hebrews 11:1). Likewise, if it turns out that Silvanus or Mark or some other scribe(s) received instructions from Peter and then wrote down 1 Peter using their own particular vocabulary and style, that does not tarnish the reality that we are "not redeemed with corruptible things, as silver and gold, . . . but with the precious blood of Christ, as of a lamb without blemish and without spot" (1 Peter 1:18–19).

Notes

1. An important early proponent of this view was F. C. Baur, who in 1835 argued against the authenticity of 1 Peter. See Werner Georg Kümmel, *The New Testament: The History of the Investigation of Its Problems* (Nashville: Abingdon Press, 1972), 130–31.

2. For a brief summary of some of the scholars on the different sides of this issue, I. Howard Marshall, *1 Peter* (Downers Grove, IL: InterVarsity Press, 1991), 21–24, and Birger A. Pearson, "James, 1–2 Peter, Jude," in *The New Testament and Its Modern Interpreters*, ed. Eldon Jay Epp and George W. MacRae (Atlanta: Scholars Press, 1989), 378–79.

3. This paper will only discuss the authorship of 1 Peter. The books of 1 Peter and 2 Peter are quite different with respect to content and style. The authorship of 2 Peter merits its own study and is therefore beyond the scope of this paper. For a conservative assessment of the authorship of 2 Peter, see Michael J. Kruger, "The Authenticity of 2 Peter," *Journal of the Evangelical Theological Society* 4, no. 4 (1999): 645–71.

4. Lewis R. Donelson, *I & II Peter and Jude* (Louisville, KY: Westminster John Knox Press, 2010), 142.

5. There are later apocryphal sources about Peter, some of which claim that he was present at the Crucifixion. The historicity of these documents, however, is suspect. On this, see Bart D. Ehrman, *Peter, Paul, and Mary Magdalene: The Followers of Jesus in History and Legend* (New York: Oxford University Press, 2006), 42–49.

6. On this issue, see Oscar Cullmann, *Peter: Disciple, Apostle, Martyr* (Waco, TX: Baylor University Press, 2011), 84–87.

7. For more information on this identification in the book of Revelation, see Brian K. Blount, *Revelation: A Commentary* (Louisville, KY: Westminster John Knox Press, 2009), 307–36, and Bruce M. Metzger, *Breaking the Code: Understanding the Book of Revelation* (Nashville: Abingdon Press, 1993), 82–88.

8. For references, see Markus Bockmuehl, *Simon Peter in Scripture and Memory: The New Testament Apostle in the Early Church* (Grand Rapids, MI: Baker Academic, 2012), 99–111, and Pheme Perkins, *Peter: Apostle for the Whole Church* (Minneapolis: Fortress Press, 2000), 131–76.

9. See Martin Hengel, *Saint Peter: The Underestimated Apostle* (Grand Rapids, MI: Eerdmans, 2010), 36–48.

10. For example, 1 Peter 1:16 (=Leviticus 11:44–45), 1:24–25 (=Isaiah 40:6–8), 2:6 (=Isaiah 28:16), 2:7 (=Psalm 118:22), 2:8 (=Isaiah 8:14), 2:22 (=Isaiah 53:9), 3:10–12 (=Psalm 34:12–16), 4:18 (=Proverbs 11:31), and 5:5 (=Proverbs 3:34).

11. 1 Peter 3:5–6 (= Sarah and Abraham); 3:18–22 (= Noah).

12. Josephus, *Against Apion* 2.25 (#204). English translation from John M. G. Barclay, *Flavius Josephus: Translation and Commentary*, vol. 10, *Against Apion* (Boston: Brill, 2007), 287.

13. Raymond E. Brown, *An Introduction to the New Testament* (New York: Doubleday, 1997), 68.

14. For other concepts found in 1 Peter and also associated with what we know of Peter from the Gospels and the book of Acts, see Norman Hillyer, *1 and 2 Peter, Jude* (Peabody, MA: Hendrickson, 1992), 1–2, and Alan M. Stibbs and Andrew F. Walls, *The First Epistle General of Peter* (Grand Rapids, MI: Eerdmans, 1981), 34–37.

15. For a summary of some of these claims, see John H. Elliott, *1 Peter* (New York: Doubleday, 2000), 136–38.

16. A convenient chart with the likely dates of Paul's epistles can be found in Thomas A. Wayment, *From Persecutor to Apostle: A Biography of Paul* (Salt Lake City: Deseret Book, 2006), viii–ix.

17. Elliott, *1 Peter*, 119.

18. For other theological perspectives in 1 Peter which point to an early composition date, see Karen H. Jobes, *1 Peter* (Grand Rapids, MI: Baker Books, 2005), 18.

19. The Greek word translated as "bishop" is *episcopos* and means "overseer."

20. On this, see Peter Iver Kaufman, *Church, Book, and Bishop: Conflict and Authority in Early Latin Christianity* (Boulder, CO: Westview Press, 1996), 7–19. For a more comprehensive study, consult Francis A. Sullivan, *From Apostles to Bishops: The Development of the Episcopacy in the Early Christian Church* (Mahwah, NJ: Sullivan Press, 2001), 54–80.

21. Note also that the author of 3 John, presumably John the Apostle, also identifies himself as "the elder" (3 John 1). In addition, modern revelation teaches that "an apostle is an elder" (D&C 20:38).

22. See also 1 Timothy 5:17–22. It should be noted that when Paul addressed the elders from Ephesus, he encouraged them to act as "overseers, to feed the church of God" (Acts 20:28). The word translated as "overseers" comes from *episcopos*, which is the Greek word later translated as "bishop."

23. Contrast, however, Pastoral Epistles that refer to a single bishop who presides over his congregation (1 Timothy 3:1–2 and Titus 1:7). For other relevant New Testament examples, see R. Eduard Schweizer, "Ministry in the Early Church," in *Anchor Bible Dictionary* (New York: Doubleday, 1992), 4:835–42.

24. On these organized persecutions, see Joseph H. Lynch, *Early Christianity: A Brief History* (New York: Oxford University Press, 2010), 82–90.

25. Elliott, *1 Peter*, 119.

26. See the detailed discussions of this topic in Donelson, *I & II Peter and Jude*, 11–13, and Joel B. Green, *1 Peter* (Grand Rapids, MI: Eerdmans, 2007), 8–10.

27. J. N. D. Kelly, *The Epistles of Peter and of Jude* (Peabody, MA: Hendrickson, 1969), 30.

28. Arthur G. Patzia, *The Making of the New Testament: Origin, Collection, Text, and Canon*, 2nd ed. (Downers Grove, IL: InterVarsity Press, 2011), 152–53. See the detailed examination in Elliott, *1 Peter*, 138–49.

29. Larry R. Helyer, *The Life and Witness of Peter* (Downers Grove, IL: InterVarsity Press, 2012), 109.

30. See the extensive discussion in Elliott, *1 Peter*, 41–80.

31. Paul J. Achtemeier, *1 Peter* (Minneapolis: Fortress Press, 1996), 7. See also Helyer, *The Life and Witness of Peter*, 19, and Jobes, *1 Peter*, 326.

32. Note especially, Martin Hengel, *The 'Hellenization' of Judea in the First Century after Christ* (Philadelphia: Trinity Press International, 1989), 30–44.

33. Mark A. Chancey, *Greco-Roman Culture and the Galilee of Jesus* (Cambridge: Cambridge University Press, 2008), 24–42.

34. Fred Strickert, *Philip's City: From Bethsaida to Julias* (Collegeville, MN: Liturgical Press, 2011), 39–40, 181–87; see also Rami Arav, "Bethsaida Excavations: Preliminary Report 1994–1996," in *Bethsaida: A City by the North Shore of the Sea of Galilee*, 4 vols.,

ed. Rami Arav and Richard A. Freund (Kirksville, MO: Truman State University Press, 1999), 2:18–24.

35. Chancey, *Greco-Roman Culture and the Galilee of Jesus*, 90–94.

36. Carl E. Savage, *Biblical Bethsaida: An Archaeological Study of the First Century* (New York: Lexington Books, 2011), 138.

37. Jonathan L. Reed, *Archaeology and the Galilean Jesus: A Re-examination of the Evidence* (Harrisburg, PA: Trinity Press International, 2000), 217–18.

38. Jean-Paul Rey-Coquais, "Decapolis," in *Anchor Bible Dictionary* (New York: Doubleday, 1992), 2:116–21.

39. Arthur Segal and Michael Eisenberg, "Sussita-Hippos of the Decapolis: Town Planning and Architecture of a Roman-Byzantine City," *Near Eastern Archaeology* 70, no. 2 (June 2007): 97, 102.

40. See the discussion in Strickert, *Philip's City*, 113–24, 163–88.

41. For example, see the conclusions of Perkins, *Peter*, 40, and Carsten Peter Thiede, *Simon Peter: From Galilee to Rome* (Cape Town, South Africa: Paternoster Press, 1986), 20–21.

42. Later, Jesus cursed Bethsaida because its inhabitants rejected his miracles (Matthew 11:20–24 and Luke 10:13–15).

43. Jerome Murphy-O'Connor, "Fishers of Fish, Fishers of Men," *Bible Review* 15, no. 3 (1999): 24, 27. For similar conclusions, see also Achtemeier, *1 Peter*, 7.

44. J. Ramsey Michaels, *The Gospel of John* (Grand Rapids, MI: Eerdmans, 2010), 686.

45. See Raymond E. Brown, *The Gospel According to John* (New York: Doubleday, 1966), 1:470, and Francis J. Moloney, *The Gospel of John* (Collegeville, MN: Liturgical Press, 1998), 352.

46. Elliott, *1 Peter*, 120.

47. Richard Neitzel Holzapfel and Thomas A. Wayment, *Making Sense of the New Testament* (Salt Lake City: Deseret Book, 2010), 469.

48. Kelly, *The Epistles of Peter and of Jude*, 31.

49. See Michael F. Bird, "Mark: Interpreter of Peter and Disciple of Paul," in *Paul and the Gospels: Christologies, Conflicts, and Convergences*, ed. Michael F. Bird and Joel Willitts (New York: T&T Clark, 2011), 30–61.

50. Quoted in Eusebius, *Ecclesiastical History* 3.39.15; English translation from G. A. Williamson, trans., *Eusebius: The History of the Church from Christ to Constantine*, rev. ed. (New York: Penguin Books, 1989), 103.

51. Frederick William Danker, *A Greek-English Lexicon of the New Testament and Other Early Christian Literature*, 3rd ed. (Chicago: University of Chicago Press, 2000), 393.

52. Robert H. Gundry, *Mark: A Commentary on His Apology for the Cross* (Grand Rapids, MI: Eerdmans, 1993), 1035–36.

53. See Jobes, *1 Peter*, 327–38, esp. 337.

54. Best, *1 Peter*, 49.

55. Reinhard Feldmeier, *The First Letter of Peter* (Waco, TX: Baylor University Press, 2008), 37.

56. M. Eugene Boring, *1 Peter* (Nashville: Abingdon Press, 1999), 34–36.

57. Robert H. Gundry, "*Verba Christi* in 1 Peter: Their Implications concerning the Authorship of 1 Peter and the Authenticity of the Gospel Tradition," *New Testament Studies* 13 (1967): 336–50.

58. See Best, *1 Peter*, 51.

59. For a convenient chart, see Steve Moyise and Maarten J. J. Menken, eds., *Isaiah in the New Testament* (New York: T&T Clark, 2005), 211–12.

60. Robert John Dixon, *An Examination of the Allusions to Isaiah 52:13–53:12 in the New Testament* (PhD diss., State University of New York at Buffalo, 2008), 225. Dixon's study contains a detailed list of all the New Testament allusions to Isaiah 53 on pp. 221–23.

61. Victor L. Ludlow, "Isaiah as Taught by the New Testament Apostles," in *The New Testament and the Latter-day Saints* (Orem, UT: Randall Book, 1987), 150.

62. For an in-depth study of Isaiah in 1 Peter, see Steve Moyise, "Isaiah in 1 Peter," in *Isaiah in the New Testament*, ed. Steve Moyise and Maarten J. J. Menken (New York: T&T Clark, 2005), 175–88.

63. Best, *1 Peter*, 50.

64. The reference to Paul in 2 Peter 3:15–16 will not be used as evidence in this discussion because many modern scholars deem 2 Peter to be pseudonymous, and the authorship of 2 Peter is beyond the scope of this paper.

65. On this, see Frank F. Judd Jr., "The Jerusalem Conference: The First Council of the Christian Church," *Religious Educator* 12, no. 1 (2011): 66–67.

66. According to the book of Acts, Paul was "forbidden of the Holy Ghost to preach the word in Asia" as well as "Bithynia" (Acts 16:6–7). Later, of course, Paul does preach throughout Asia.

67. See, for example, Boring, *1 Peter*, 31–32, and Peter H. Davids, *The First Epistle of Peter* (Grand Rapids, MI: Eerdmans, 1990), 4–6.

68. Best, *1 Peter*, 50.

69. Notice that arguments against Petrine authorship criticize from both perspectives: either that it cannot have been written by Peter if it does not contain any references to Paul or that it cannot have been written by Peter if it contains too much dependence upon Paul.

70. Elliott, *1 Peter*, 40.

71. Kelly, *The Epistles of Peter and of Jude*, 32.

72. Joseph A. Fitzmyer, *The Jerome Biblical Commentary*, 2 vols. (Englewood Cliffs, NJ: Prentice Hall, 1968), 1:362.

73. Best, *1 Peter*, 54.

74. For a summary of those who have espoused this view, see Elliott, *1 Peter*, 123–24.

75. In particular, see the comprehensive study of Hans-Josef Klauck, *Ancient Letters and the New Testament: A Guide to Context and Exegesis* (Waco, TX: Baylor University Press, 2006).

76. Jerome Murphy-O'Connor, *Paul the Letter-Writer: His World, His Options, His Skills* (Collegeville, MN: Liturgical Press, 1995), 81–93.

77. For similar salutations that indicate Paul's use of scribes, see also Galatians 6:11, 2 Thessalonians 3:17–18, Colossians 4:18, and Philemon 1:19.

78. On Paul's use of scribes, see E. Randolph Richards, *Paul and First-Century Letter Writing: Secretaries, Composition and Collection* (Downers Grove, IL: InterVarsity Press, 2004), 81–93.

79. See Lincoln H. Blumell, "Scribes and Ancient Letters: Implications for the Pauline Epistles," in *How the New Testament Came to Be*, ed. Kent P. Jackson and Frank F. Judd Jr. (Salt Lake City: Deseret Book, 2006), 211–13.

80. Cicero, *Atticus*, 13.25.3. Cited in Blumell, "Scribes and Ancient Letters," 211 and 223 n. 14.

81. Cicero, *Familiares*, 16.17.1. Cited in Richards, *Paul and First-Century Letter Writing*, 75.

82. Cicero, *Atticus*, 11.5. Cited in Blumell, "Scribes and Ancient Letters," 213.

83. See Blumell, "Scribes and Ancient Letters," 212–13, 223–24, esp. n. 21.

84. Silvanus (or Silas) had been the companion of Paul during his second mission. See Acts 15:40–41; 16:19, 25, 29; 17:4, 10, 15; 18:5. Silvanus seems to have been involved in the production of a number of Paul's epistles. See 2 Corinthians 1:19; 1 Thessalonians 1:1; and 2 Thessalonians 1:1.

85. An important proponent of this view was Edward Gordon Selwyn, *The First Epistle of St. Peter* (London: Macmillan, 1946), 9–17.

86. Wayne A. Grudem, *1 Peter: An Introduction and Commentary* (Downers Grove, IL: InterVarsity Press, 1988), 23–25.

87. On this, see Blumell, "Scribes and Ancient Letters," 218–19.

88. Blumell, "Scribes and Ancient Letters," 209.

89. Andrew F. Ehat and Lyndon W. Cook, eds., *The Words of Joseph Smith* (Provo, UT: Religious Studies Center, 1980), 202.

90. William Clayton recorded in his journal: "At 10 Prest. J. preached on 2nd Peter Ch 1." Ehat and Cook, *The Words of Joseph Smith*, 202.

91. See Frank F. Judd Jr., "Who Really Wrote the Gospels? A Study of Traditional Authorship," in *How the New Testament Came to Be*, 123–40.

92. See Terrence L. Szink, "Authorship of the Epistle to the Hebrews," in *How the New Testament Came to Be*, 243–59.

93. J. Reuben Clark Jr., *On the Way to Immortality and Eternal Life* (Salt Lake City: Deseret Book, 1950), 209–10.

14

Make Your Calling and Election Sure

Robert L. Millet

Robert L. Millet is a professor emeritus of ancient scripture at
Brigham Young University.

Joseph Smith the Prophet declared that "Peter penned the most sublime language of any of the apostles."[1] While it is in the first chapter of Peter's second epistle that we encounter the invitation for us to become "partakers of the divine nature" (2 Peter 1:4), both epistles point us powerfully toward that supernal ideal.

Let me first speak of the procedure we will follow in discussing this sacred and sensitive matter. It might be appropriate in a traditional academic conference to spend a significant portion of time reviewing the literature of non-LDS scholars on the writings of 2 Peter, debating the authorship and dating of the epistle, or detailing the various interpretive avenues that New Testament experts from the past have pursued. To be sure, there is much to be learned from scholars and churchmen from other faith traditions regarding the history, language, or culture behind a scriptural text. What follows, however, is a faith-based, Restoration-centered, doctrinal investigation of the subject. We do not turn to Roman Catholic scholars to teach us how to build temples or to Protestant theologians to receive insights into the proper place of covenants and ordinances. When it comes to doctrinal interpretation, our principal and primary source must be the scriptures of the Restoration and the writings and sermons of latter-day apostles and prophets. This is a topic that can only be engaged seriously by a people well acquainted with premortal existence, temples, priesthood keys, sealing powers, and kingdoms of glory hereafter.

To avoid or ignore the distinctive insights provided by modern revelation is foolish at best and spiritually perilous at worst. In a revelation given in March of 1831, the Savior declared, "I have sent *mine everlasting covenant* into the world, *to be a light to the world, and to be a standard for my people,* . . . and to be a messenger before my face to prepare the way before me" (D&C 45:9; emphasis added). In September of that same year, the Lord offered similar counsel: "Behold, I, the Lord, have made my church in these last days like unto a judge sitting on a hill, or in a high place, to judge the nations. For it shall come to pass that *the inhabitants of Zion shall judge all things pertaining to Zion*" (D&C 64:37–38; emphasis added).

Latter-day Saint writers, including general church leaders, have not written of the doctrine of calling and election very often, not because it is a forbidden subject, but rather a sensitive one. Furthermore, because the Brethren have said very little about it publicly, that is not an announcement that we should avoid it like a plague, that the teaching has somehow fallen on hard times, that it has been officially relegated to the category of folklore or pop theology, that it is out of date, or that it is no longer held to be the doctrine of the church. For heaven's sake, this precious truth is found in the standard works, within the New Testament, and the Doctrine and Covenants. And when it comes to relevance or timeliness in the twenty-first century, what could be more everlastingly pertinent than the quest for eternal life and the sweet assurance that one's salvation is secure?

The Sanctification of the Soul

Peter begins with a description of the people of the church of Jesus Christ as the "elect according to the foreknowledge of God," those who have, through the sanctifying blood of the Redeemer, been begotten into what Peter calls a "lively hope," that is, a living hope—a sweet expectation, a sturdy anticipation, a dynamic assurance—of a glorious resurrection. These have placed themselves in a condition to enjoy "an inheritance incorruptible, and undefiled, and that fadeth not away, reserved in heaven for you," those who "are kept by the power of God through faith unto salvation" (1 Peter 1:1–5).

In the second chapter of the first epistle, Peter reminds us that our Lord was guileless, that he never sinned. Thus a significant step toward becoming a partaker of the divine nature is being engaged in the imitation of Christ, the emulation of the sinless Son of Man, following the steps of the prototype or standard for all saved beings (1 Peter 2:21–22).[2] C. S. Lewis observed that "Whatever may have been the powers of unfallen man, it appears that those of redeemed man will be *almost* unlimited. Christ is bringing up human nature with Him. Where He goes, it goes too. It will be made 'like Him.'" Lewis pointed out that divine miracles "anticipate powers which all men will have when they also are 'sons' of God and enter into that 'glorious liberty.'" Christ becomes not a prodigy, but "a pioneer. He is the first of His kind; He will not be the last."[3]

In the fourth chapter, Peter challenges the Saints to gain "the same mind" as Christ (compare 1 Corinthians 2:16). "For you who have suffered in the flesh should cease from sin, that you no longer the rest of your time in the flesh, should live to the lusts of men, but to the will of God" (Joseph Smith Translation, 1 Peter 4:1–2). Peter also reminds the members that because they are living at the end of the age, the final days of the meridian dispensation, they should be sober and watchful. "And above all things have fervent charity among yourselves: for charity preventeth a multitude of sins" (Joseph Smith Translation, 1 Peter 4:8).

In the fifth and final chapter of the first epistle, a passage of profound significance, the members are counseled tenderly: "Humble yourselves therefore under the mighty hand of God, that he may exalt you in due time: casting all your care upon him; for he careth for you" (1 Peter 5:6–7). The New Jerusalem Bible renders this: "Bow down, then, before the power of God now, so that he may raise you up in due time; unload all your burden on to him, since he is concerned about you." Or, as paraphrased in Eugene Peterson's *The Message*: "So be content with who you are, and don't put on airs. God's strong hand is on you; he'll promote you at the right time. Live carefree before God; he is most careful with you."[4]

In the tenth verse of this final chapter, Peter provides a summation of the means by which weak and fallen men and women are made right with God, are made whole, and are established and grounded in the faith: "But the God of all grace, who hath called us unto his eternal glory by Christ Jesus, after that ye have suffered a while, make you perfect, stablish, strengthen, settle you" (1 Peter 5:10).

Like Precious Faith

As we turn our attention to Second Peter, it is fascinating that the senior Apostle begins his letter by addressing himself to *them that have obtained like precious faith with us* through the righteousness of God and our Savior Jesus Christ" (2 Peter 1:1; emphasis added). *Like precious faith.* Those who have come out of the world by covenant, who have been baptized and become members of the household of faith, these have acquired the same kind of faith as the Apostles. There is not one gospel for prophets and another for the rank and file of the church. No, theirs is a like precious faith, the faith that is centered in the Lord Jesus Christ, the faith that trusts totally in, has complete confidence in, and relies wholly upon the Savior. This is the faith that enables one to move steadily through the vicissitudes of life, to make decisions based on gospel priorities, the faith that empowers one to overcome every temptation of the devil (see Alma 37:33), the faith that leads to life and salvation. Such faith brings an actual knowledge that the course one is pursuing in life is according to the divine will,[5] which knowledge is accompanied by "exceeding great and precious promises." And it is by receiving these promises, the peace in this world that is a forerunner of the ultimate peace associated with eternal life in the world to come (D&C 59:23), that the faithful begin to become partakers of the divine nature.

Peter then reports that the fruits that flow from such faith are endowments of the Spirit that represent the Christlike character, the character of one who has begun to enjoy what Paul described as the "fruit of the Spirit" (Galatians 5:22–25). Peter mentions virtue, knowledge, temperance, patience, godliness, brotherly kindness, and charity. A modern revelation teaches that such qualities ought to be found in the hearts and lives of those who aspire to teach the gospel and bring people into the faith (D&C 4:5–6). Respected New Testament scholar N. T. Wright translated this passage: "So, because of this, *you should strain every nerve to supplement your faith with virtue*, and your virtue with knowledge," and so on (The Kingdom New Testament; emphasis added). Perhaps a word or two about each of these qualities or attributes would be helpful.

Virtue is a condition of uprightness, moral excellence, goodness, and a life that demonstrates consistency with truth or with the way things really are (Jacob 4:13; D&C 93:24).

Knowledge is vital because one cannot be saved in ignorance (D&C 131:6) and because a saving conviction is always predicated upon propositions of truth. We cannot live consistent with that which we do not know, nor can we endure faithfully to the end when we do not understand that which requires our lifetime loyalty.

Temperance is self-control. It was Jesus himself who taught, "Blessed are the meek: for they shall inherit the earth" (Matthew 5:5). It is the meek person who is restrained, not alone by social prohibitions but, more importantly, through *temperance*, or self-control.

Patience is that virtue, that Godlike quality that demonstrates one's trust in God's program, trust in the Lord's purposes, and acquiescence to the divine time-table. To have patience is to have hope, to be willing to wait upon the Lord.

Godliness is a quality of a man or woman who has yielded his or her heart unto God (see Helaman 3:35), a believer whose genuine piety is reflected in his or her willing conformity to divine law.

Brotherly kindness is more than nice and attractive; it is a fundamental and vital feature of the outworking of the Spirit of Jesus Christ in our lives. One of the ways we assess our growth unto godliness is the extent to which we have begun to value the children of God, to love our brothers and sisters. Christianity is only partially about individual transformation and personal salvation; it is also concerned with community and corporate growth, how and in what manner we have come to treasure and respect humanity.

Charity, the pure love of Christ, is of course the highest of all spiritual gifts, the grandest of all heavenly endowments, and that "more excellent way" (1 Corinthians 12:31; Ether 12:11). It was Mormon who taught us that true followers of Christ are those who have become by spiritual regeneration the sons and daughters of God, persons who have been lifted, purified, and transformed by this sacred love into the image of Christ. These will see the returning King for who he is, for they will be like him (Moroni 7:47–48).

Truly, as Peter states, a man or woman who possesses these qualities and gifts is neither "barren nor unfruitful in the knowledge of our Lord Jesus Christ," while the person who lacks them is "blind, and cannot see afar off, and hath forgotten that he was purged from his old sins" (2 Peter 1:8–9). That is, the Saint who manifests such attributes is not idle, is not unprofitable; rather, he or she is alive, spiritually productive, contributing regularly and meaningfully to the life of the church of God and the betterment of God's world. On the other hand, one who lacks such qualities is living as though there had been no redemption made (see Moroni 7:38); he or she has a warped perspective on life, views things through the lenses of the natural man, is self-absorbed, is spiritually myopic, and has little sensitivity to sacred things. Such persons cannot see the distant scene.

Note that Peter observes that a member of the church who enjoys this character is fruitful "in the knowledge of our Lord Jesus Christ" (2 Peter 1:8). Such a person is enjoying both the cleansing and enabling powers of the Atonement and is experiencing the enlivening companionship of the Holy Spirit, which is the midwife of such spiritual traits. It is by the blood that we are sanctified from sin and by the medium of the Lord's Spirit that we grow in spiritual graces and in our relationship with God and man. In writing of one who has undergone this mighty change of heart, Elder Parley P. Pratt explained:

> His mind is quickened, his intellectual faculties are aroused to intense activity. He is, as it were, illuminated. He learns more of divine truth in a few days than he could have learned in a lifetime in the best merely human institutions in the world.
>
> His affections are also purified, exalted, and increased in proportion. He loves his Heavenly Father and Jesus Christ with a perfect love. He also loves the members of the church, or the body of Christ, as he loves his own soul; while his bosom swells with the tenderest sympathies and emotions of good will and benevolence for all mankind. He would make any sacrifice that might be expedient to do good. He would lay down his life most cheerfully, without one moment's hesitation or regret, if required of him by the cause of truth.[6]

It was Paul, Peter's apostolic colleague, who wrote so eloquently of the transformation of his own soul following his conversion to Christ and Christianity: "But what things were gain to me [before conversion], those I counted loss for Christ. Yea doubtless, and *I count all things but loss for the excellency of the knowledge of Christ Jesus my Lord*: for whom I have suffered the loss of all things, and do count them but dung, that I may win Christ, and be found in him, not having mine own righteousness, which is of the law, but that which is through the faith of Christ, the righteousness which is of God by faith: *That I may know him*, and the power of his resurrection, and the fellowship of his sufferings, being made conformable unto his death" (Philippians 3:7–10; emphasis added). Indeed, the knowledge that matters, the knowledge that settles and sanctifies the human heart, and the knowledge that prompts purity and motivates one to selfless service, is the knowledge that Jesus Christ is the Son of God and the Savior of all humankind; that through him and him alone, we are able to be delivered from sin and death and hell and endless torment; that there is no weakness he cannot turn to strength, no emptiness he cannot fill, no sickness that the great physician cannot heal. Again quoting Paul, "thanks be to God, [who gives] us the victory through our Lord Jesus Christ" (1 Corinthians 15:57).

Called and Elected

Having spoken of the need to become partakers of the divine nature, the need to acquire the fruit of the Spirit that produces Christlike character, Peter then counsels us: "Wherefore the rather, brethren, give diligence to make your calling and election sure: for if ye do these things ye shall never fall: for so an entrance shall be ministered unto you abundantly into the everlasting kingdom of our Lord and Saviour Jesus Christ" (2 Peter 1:10–11). These are difficult words, particularly as they have been rendered in the King James Version. Alternate translations of "Wherefore the rather, brethren" include: "All the more reason, brethren" (Revised English Bible) or "Be all the more eager to confirm your call and election" (New Revised Standard Version) or "Be all the more eager to make your calling and election sure" (New International Version). That is to say, "Don't be shortsighted or spiritually vacuous, but instead do all within your power to make your calling and election sure."

The words *calling* and *election* are often used interchangeably. In scripture they tend to refer to a duty or an assignment, a responsibility within God's kingdom. Elder Bruce R. McConkie explained:

> To be called is to be a member of the Church and kingdom of God on earth; it is to be numbered with the saints; it is to accept the gospel and receive the everlasting covenant. . . .
>
> It is to be born again; to be a son or a daughter of the Lord Jesus Christ . . . ; it is to have a conditional promise of eternal life; it is to be an inheritor of all of the blessings of the gospel, provided there is continued obedience to the laws and ordinances thereof.
>
> The Lord's calls are the result of foreordination and grow out of faithfulness in the [premortal existence]. . . . That is, the saints were foreordained in the councils of eternity to believe the truth, to be sanctified, and to save their souls; and then in this life they are called to that gospel whereby these eternal promises can be fulfilled. . . . And if by a long course of trial and obedience, while yet in this life, a man proves to the Lord that he has and will abide in the truth, the Lord accepts the exhibited devotion and issues his decree that the promised blessings shall be received. The calling, which up to that time was provisional, is then made sure. The receipt of the promised blessings is no longer conditional; they are guaranteed. Announcement is made that every gospel blessing shall be inherited. . . .
>
> To have one's calling and election made sure is to be sealed up unto eternal life; it is to have the unconditional guarantee of exaltation in the highest heaven of the celestial world; it is to receive the assurance of godhood; it is, in effect, to have the day of judgment advanced.[7]

In other words, the Apostle Peter pointed the minds of the former-day Saints toward their eternal possibilities. He encouraged them, knowing of trying times which lay ahead as they moved toward the end of the age, the end of the dispensation. In the words of Paul, Peter charged them to "press toward the mark for the prize of the high calling of God in Christ Jesus" (Philippians 3:14). Would they make mistakes after receiving the assurance of salvation? Of course they would. Would they sin? Yes, for no person, save the Lord Jesus, has walked this earth and remained free from sin. While the inclination to commit serious sin will generally have been banished from the soul of such a righteous man or woman (see, for example, Mosiah 5:2; Alma 13:12; 19:33), yet the pull of the flesh will remain as long as we reside on a telestial earth.

President Brigham Young asked:

> *Will sin be perfectly destroyed? No, it will not, for it is not so designed in the economy of heaven. . . . Do not suppose that we shall ever in the flesh be free from temptations to sin.* Some suppose that they can in the flesh be sanctified body and spirit and become so pure that they will never again feel the effects of the power of the adversary of truth. Were it possible for a person to attain to this degree of perfection in the flesh, he could not die neither remain in a world where sin predominates. . . . I think we should more or less feel the effects of sin so long as we live, and finally have to pass the ordeals of death.[8]

Consequently, persons who have made their calling and election sure to eternal life are required to be vigilant, humble, and dependent upon the Lord for spiritual protection, and to strive to be true to their covenants until they pass through the veil and are safely dead!

As President Young said on another occasion: "It requires all the atonement of Christ, the mercy of the Father, the pity of angels and the grace of the Lord Jesus Christ to be with us always, and then to do the very best we possibly can, to get rid of this sin within us, so that we may escape from this world into the celestial kingdom."[9]

In a revelation given at the time of the organization of the restored church, we learn, "And we know that justification through the grace of our Lord and Savior Jesus Christ is just and true; and we know also, that sanctification through the grace of our Lord and Savior Jesus Christ is just and true, to all those who love and serve God with all their mights, minds, and strength." Now note this warning: "But *there is a possibility that man may fall from grace* and depart from the living God; therefore *let the church take heed and pray always*, lest they fall into temptation; yea, and even *let those who are sanctified take heed also*" (D&C 20:30–34; emphasis added).

The Presbyterians in Joseph Smith's day taught that one could not fall from grace and that once salvation was received, it could not be lost. The Methodists taught, on the other hand, that one could in fact fall from grace and be renewed and restored. Joseph taught that the fulness of truth took a road between them both—that in general while people could fall from grace and repent, there was a sin, known as the unpardonable sin or sin against the Holy Ghost, against which even the supernal power of Elijah could not seal an individual.[10] The message is clear: every living soul, no matter the spiritual heights to which he or she may have ascended, must endure in faith until the end. Those who have passed the tests of mortality are forgiven of their sins through repentance, just like all of God's children. While much is required of those who have gained the supernal assurance of exaltation (see D&C 82:3), all of humankind are saved by obedience to the laws and ordinances of the gospel (see Articles of Faith 1:3; see also D&C 82:3).[11]

In this context Peter adds that "an entrance shall be ministered unto you abundantly into the everlasting kingdom of our Lord and Saviour Jesus Christ" (2 Peter 1:11). To say this another way, "For if you practice these qualities you will never fall. For in this way there will be richly provided for you an entrance into the eternal kingdom" (English Standard Version). Or, "For in this way, entry into the eternal kingdom of our Lord and Savior Jesus Christ will be richly provided for you" (New Revised Standard Version). Or, "you will receive a rich welcome into the eternal kingdom" (New International Version).

In summary, we are speaking here of what Paul called the "hope of eternal life, which God, that cannot lie, promised before the world began" (Titus 1:2), being made sure, made solid, made secure. We are reminded of the marvelous words of the Prophet Joseph when he taught: "After a person hath faith in Christ, repents of his sins, and is baptized for the remission of his sins and receives the Holy Ghost (by the laying on of hands), . . . then let him continue to humble himself before God, hungering and thirsting after Righteousness, and living by every word of God, and the Lord will soon say unto him, Son, thou shalt be exalted. When the Lord has thoro[ugh]ly proved him, and finds that the man is determined to serve him at all hazards, then the man will find his calling and Election made sure."[12]

The More Sure Word

The senior Apostle then turns himself to testimony. He alludes to the fact that he knows he will soon "put off this my tabernacle, even as our Lord Jesus Christ hath shewed me" (2 Peter 1:14). He then bears witness of the message of the gospel, that Jesus of Nazareth is all that the prophets said he would be, and that he is indeed the Lord of glory: "For we have not followed cunningly devised fables, when we made known unto you the power and coming of our Lord Jesus Christ, but were eyewitnesses of his majesty" (2 Peter 1:16). That is, "We are not making all of this up. This is not some devious and fictitious sham." We "were not following cleverly devised myths. Rather, we were eyewitnesses of his grandeur" (Kingdom New Testament). Peter then makes reference to the transcendent experience he and James and John had enjoyed with the Savior on the Mount of Transfiguration some six months before the Crucifixion: "For [Christ] received from God the Father honour and glory, when there came such a voice to him from the excellent glory, This is my beloved Son, in whom I am well pleased. And this voice which came from heaven we heard, when we were with him in the holy mount" (2 Peter 1:17–18).

Christians have generally viewed the Transfiguration as a display of "a new and greater Moses," a reminder of the baptism of Jesus where that same voice was heard, and a foreshadowing of the glory their Master would receive in the Resurrection.[13] Christian pastor and theologian John MacArthur has written:

> The Jesus who had been living for over thirty years in ordinary human form was now partially seen in the blazing effulgence of God (compare Hebrews 1:1–3). From within himself, in a way that defies full description, much less full explanation, Jesus' divine glory was manifested before Peter, James, and John.
>
> Here is the greatest confirmation of his deity yet in the life of Jesus. Here, more than on any other occasion, Jesus revealed Himself as He truly is, the Son of God. . . . As with the Shekinah manifestations of the Old Testament, God here portrayed Himself to human eyes in a form of light so dazzling and overwhelming that it could barely be withstood.

MacArthur added, "That awesome experience was but a foretaste of the day in which 'the Son of man shall come in the glory of his Father with his angels' (Matthew 16:27)."[14]

Latter-day Saints have received additional insights pertaining to what took place on the mount. We know from modern revelation and prophetic teaching that Peter, James, and John—the meridian First Presidency—were granted a most unusual vision of the future. The Savior declared in August 1831, "Nevertheless, he that endureth in faith and doeth my will, the same shall overcome, and shall receive an inheritance upon the earth when the day of transfiguration shall come"—at the Second Coming, when the earth will be changed, lifted to a terrestrial condition—"when the earth shall be transfigured, even according to the pattern which was shown unto mine apostles upon the mount; of which account the fulness ye have not yet received" (D&C 63:20–21).

Joseph Smith explained, "The Savior, Moses, and Elias gave the keys to Peter, James, and John, on the mount, when they were transfigured before him"—that is, when the three Apostles were also transfigured with their Lord.[15] We would presume that these keys were the same as those conferred upon Joseph Smith and Oliver Cowdery in the Kirtland Temple on April 3, 1836 (D&C 110:11–16). Further, President Joseph Fielding Smith has suggested that it was on the mount that the chief Apostles received what we would know today as the temple endowment.[16]

Finally, James Burgess reported that the Prophet Joseph made the following comments in a sermon in Nauvoo on August 27, 1843: "Men will set up stakes and say thus far will we go and no farther. Did Abraham when [he was] called upon to offer his son? And did the Savior? No. View [the Savior] fulfilling all righteousness again on the banks of Jordan. Also, *on the Mount transfigured before Peter and John, there receiving the fulness of priesthood* or the law of God, setting up no stake but coming right up to the mark in all things."[17] According to Wilford Woodruff's journal, the Prophet said, "If a man gets a fullness of the priesthood of God he has to get it in the same way that Jesus obtained it, and that was by keeping all the commandments and obeying all the ordinances of the house of the Lord."[18]

Peter testified, "We have also a more sure word of prophecy; whereunto ye do well that ye take heed, as unto a light that shineth in a dark place, until the day dawn, and the day star arise in your hearts" (2 Peter 1:19). When the Prophet Joseph Smith was engaged in his inspired translation of the King James Bible, he altered this verse as follows: "We have therefore *a more sure knowledge of the word of prophecy*, to which word of prophecy ye do well that ye take heed" (emphasis added). Now there is no question but that Peter and his apostolic colleagues understood, through supernal and ineffable experience with the Master, "the word of prophecy," what we call the spirit of revelation, and that those within the faith who were less seasoned in utilizing or comprehending the gifts of the Spirit, and particularly the gift of prophecy, were well advised to look to those acknowledged prophets, seers, and revelators as both mentors and interpreters. It seems clear that the Prophet Joseph did not, at this early stage of his spiritual development (between 1832 and 1833),[19] understand the doctrine of calling and election and the more sure word of prophecy. Like all of the Saints of God, the choice seer grew in understanding and experience line upon line, precept upon precept.[20]

In May of 1843, a decade after his inspired translation of 2 Peter, Brother Joseph declared, "The more sure word of prophecy means a man's knowing that he is sealed up unto eternal life, by revelation and the spirit of prophecy, through the power of the Holy Priesthood. It is impossible for a man to be saved in ignorance" (D&C 131:5–6). Also,

> Notwithstanding the apostle exhorts them to add to their faith, virtue, knowledge, temperance, etc., yet he exhorts them to make their calling and election sure. And though they had heard an audible voice from heaven bearing testimony that Jesus was the Son of God, yet he says we have a more sure word or prophecy, whereunto ye do well that ye take heed as unto a light shining in a dark place. Now, wherein could they have a more sure word of prophecy than to hear the voice of God saying, This is my beloved Son?
>
> Now for the secret and grand key. Though they might hear the voice of God and know that Jesus was the Son of God, this would be no evidence that their election and calling was made sure, that they had part with Christ, and were joint heirs with him. They then would want that more sure word of prophecy, that they were sealed in the heavens and had the promise of eternal life in the kingdom of God. Then, having this promise sealed unto them, it was an anchor to the soul, sure and steadfast.

He then added that "this hope and knowledge would support the soul in every hour of trial, trouble and tribulation." The Prophet then made a statement that clarifies and expands upon Peter's words—that having acquired faith, virtue, knowledge, temperance, patience, godliness, brotherly love, and charity we become fruitful "in the knowledge of our Lord Jesus Christ" (2 Peter 1:8): "Then knowledge through our Lord and Savior Jesus Christ is the grand key that unlocks the glories and mysteries of the kingdom of heaven."[21] Knowledge of anything that is "virtuous, lovely, or of good report or praiseworthy" (Articles of Faith 1:13) is worthwhile and commendable, but the knowledge about which Peter and Joseph Smith are speaking is the knowledge that saves, the knowledge that one's course in life is pleasing to God and that one will go on to eternal life and exaltation. Joseph Smith beckons to us: "Then I would exhort you to go on and continue to call upon God until you make your calling and election sure for yourselves, by obtaining this more sure word of prophecy, and wait patiently for the promise until you obtain it."[22]

Conclusion

In reflecting on this glorious doctrine, we might ask, "Is this something we should desire or seek for?" In response, who among us, living in a fallen world filled with disappointment, distress, and hopelessness, does not long to know that our lives are acceptable to God, that we are on course and will one day inherit a better world? As Elder McConkie has written: "Among those who have received the gospel, and who are seeking diligently to live its laws and gain eternal life, there is an instinctive and determined desire to make their calling and election sure. Because they have tasted the good things of God and sipped from the fountain of eternal truth, they now seek the divine presence, where they shall know all things, have all power, all might, and all dominion, and in fact be like Him who is the great Prototype of all saved beings—God our Heavenly and Eternal Father (see D&C 132:20). This is the end objective, the chief goal of all the faithful, and there is nothing greater in all eternity, 'for there is no gift greater than the gift of salvation'" (D&C 6:13).[23]

King Benjamin offered this timeless counsel: "Therefore, I would that ye should be *steadfast and immovable*, always abounding in good works, that Christ, the Lord God Omnipotent, may seal you his, that you may be brought to heaven, that ye may have everlasting salvation and eternal life, through the wisdom, and power, and justice, and mercy of him who created all things, in heaven and in earth, who is God above all" (Mosiah 5:15; emphasis added). Steadfast and immovable—those are the key words, for they are the scriptural description of balance and spiritual stability.

It was while wrestling with his assignment as a new and inexperienced priesthood leader and struggling to know how best to assist those who were in transgression, that Alma the Elder, a good man who "feared that he should do wrong in the sight of God," poured out his heart in prayer to God. Alma was commended for choosing to respond affirmatively to the power and invitation of Abinadi's words, for being willing to repent of his sins, and be a part of the church of Jesus Christ. "Thou art my servant," the Lord stated, "and I covenant with thee that thou shalt have eternal life" (Mosiah 26:13–20). We note that Alma was not seeking to be truer than true when this glorious assurance came to him. He was not on a calling and election crusade. Rather, he was busily engaged in doing his duty, striving with all his heart to bless, lift, and strengthen his brothers and sisters. There's a message there for us.

We must be willing to come to that point of personal commitment where whatever the Lord calls upon us to do, we will do. Such unconditional surrender of self is always prerequisite to gaining the ultimate victory. The Prophet and the early brethren taught that only by being willing to sacrifice all things, including our own life if necessary, can we gain the actual knowledge that our course in life is in harmony with the heavens. Thus "a religion that does not require the sacrifice of all things never has power sufficient to produce the faith necessary unto life and salvation. . . . It was through this sacrifice, and this only, that God has ordained that men should enjoy eternal life; and it is through the medium of the sacrifice of all earthly things that men do actually know that they are doing the things that are well pleasing in the sight of God."[24] In short, the Lord essentially asks us, "Do you want me to give you all that I have?" We of course respond positively. And then the Savior answers, "Then be willing to give me all that you have."

It is worthwhile to read how and why Joseph Smith himself received the assurance of eternal life. The Lord addressed his modern seer: "For I am the Lord thy God, and will be with thee even unto the end of the world, and through all eternity; for verily *I seal upon you your exaltation*, and prepare a throne for you in the kingdom of my Father, with Abraham your father. Behold, *I have seen your sacrifices*, and will forgive all your sins; I have seen your sacrifices in obedience to that which I have told you" (D&C 132:49–50; emphasis added; compare D&C 97:8).

Surely there are few things more important in this life than striving to live in such a manner as to always enjoy companionship with the Holy Ghost. The clearer are our views, the more we will make it a priority never to do anything that would cost us the influence of that Holy Spirit. It is that Spirit that testifies, that confirms, that informs and inspires, and that sanctifies. And it is that Spirit that brings peace (see D&C 6:23). In August of 1831 the Lord counseled the early Saints to "learn that he who doeth the works of righteousness shall receive his reward, even peace in this world, and eternal life in the world to come" (D&C 59:23). In this light, President Marion G. Romney explained, "The fulness of eternal life is not attainable in mortality, but *the peace which is its harbinger and which comes as a result of making one's calling and election sure is attainable in this life*."[25]

Latter-day Saints who have received the ordinances of salvation—including the blessings of the temple—may press forward in the work of the Lord and with quiet dignity and patient maturity seek to be worthy of gaining the certain assurance of salvation before the end of their mortal lives. But should one not formally receive the more sure word of prophecy in this life, he or she has the scriptural promise that faithfully enduring to the end—keeping the covenants and commandments from baptism to the end of their lives (see Mosiah 18:8–9)—leads one to the promise of eternal life, whether that promise be received here or hereafter (see D&C 14:7; 53:7; 2 Nephi 31:20; Mosiah 5:15). "But blessed are they who are faithful and endure, whether in life or in death, for they shall inherit eternal life" (D&C 50:5). God grant that such will be our sweet privilege and our supernal blessing.

Notes

1. William Clayton diary, May 17, 1843.

2. See *Lectures on Faith* (Salt Lake City: Deseret Book, 1985), 75–76, 7:9.

3. C. S. Lewis, *Miracles* (New York: Touchstone, 1996), 178; emphasis added.

4. Eugene H. Peterson, *The Message: The Bible in Contemporary Language* (Colorado Springs, CO: NavPress, 2002), 2216.

5. See *Lectures on Faith*, 67–69, 6:2–7.

6. Parley P. Pratt, *Key to the Science of Theology* (Salt Lake City: Deseret Book, 1985), 59–60.

7. Bruce R. McConkie, *Doctrinal New Testament Commentary*, 3 vols. (Salt Lake City: Bookcraft, 1965–73), 3:326, 327–28, 330–31.

8. Brigham Young, in *Journal of Discourses* (London: Latter-day Saints' Book Depot, 1854–86), 10:173; emphasis added.

9. Young, in *Journal of Discourses*, 11:301.

10. Joseph Smith, *Millennial Star*, February 9, 1861, 88.

11. Citing the Apostle Paul (see Hebrews 10:26) and the Prophet Joseph Smith, Elder McConkie points out that those who have made their calling and election sure who then become guilty of serious sin "must then pay the penalty of their own sins, for the blood of Christ will not cleanse them." More specifically, those who commit adultery or murder break the seal and go to the telestial kingdom, while those who commit the unpardonable sin break the seal and become sons of perdition (*Doctrinal New Testament Commentary* 3:343; *A New Witness for the Articles of Faith* [Salt Lake City: Deseret Book, 1985], 232; Wilford Woodruff Journal, March 10, 1844, 2:363).

12. History, 1838–1856, volume C-1 (2 November 1838–31 July 1842), http://josephsmithpapers.org/paperSummary/history-1838-1856-volume-c-1-2-november-1838-31-july-1842?locale=eng&p=542; http://josephsmithpapers.org/paperSummary/history-1838-1856-volume-c-1-2-november-1838-31-july-1842?locale=eng&p=544.

13. See W. D. Davies and Dale C. Allison, *A Critical and Exegetical Commentary on the Gospel According to Saint Matthew*, 3 vols. (Edinburgh: T&T Clark, 1988–97), 2:687.

14. John MacArthur, *The MacArthur New Testament Commentary—Matthew*, 3 vols. (Chicago: Moody Press, 1985–89), 3:63–64.

15. Andrew F. Ehat and Lyndon W. Cook, *The Words of Joseph Smith: The Contemporary Accounts of the Nauvoo Discourses of the Prophet Joseph* (Provo, UT: Religious Studies Center, 1980), 9.

16. Joseph Fielding Smith, *Doctrines of Salvation*, 3 vols., comp. Bruce R. McConkie (Salt Lake City: Bookcraft, 1954–56), 2:165, 170; see also Bruce R. McConkie, *Doctrinal New Testament Commentary* 1:400.

17. Ehat and Cook, *Words of Joseph Smith*, 246; punctuation supplied.

18. *Words of Joseph Smith*, 307.

19. See Robert J. Matthews, *A Plainer Translation: Joseph Smith's Translation of the Bible, A History and Commentary* (Provo, UT: Brigham Young University Press, 1975), 96.

20. Other examples of alterations in the King James text that indicate that Joseph did not grasp, at the time of the translation, what he would understand and teach in later years, including the JST of Hebrews 11:40 and the JST of Revelation 1:5–6.

21. B. H. Roberts, *The Rise and Fall of Nauvoo* (Salt Lake City: Deseret News, 1900), 214.

22. *Millennial Star*, January 29, 1859, 76.

23. McConkie, *Doctrinal New Testament Commentary* 3:325.

24. *Lectures on Faith*, 69, 6:7.

25. Marion G. Romney, in Conference Report, October 1965; in *Look to God and Live* (Salt Lake City: Deseret Book, 1971), 125–26; emphasis added.

15

"Honor the King"

SUBMISSION TO CIVIL AUTHORITY

Eric-Jon K. Marlowe

Eric-Jon K. Marlowe is an assistant professor of Religious Education at
Brigham Young University–Hawaii.

The Apostle Peter proclaimed, "We ought to obey God rather than men"
(Acts 5:29; see also 4:19–20). Yet Peter also declared, "Submit yourselves
to every ordinance of man for the Lord's sake: whether it be to the king, as
supreme; or unto governors" (1 Peter 2:13–14).[1] Obedience to God's authority and submission to civil authority[2] may seem at odds here. Peter indicates,
however, that submission to civil authority is "for the Lord's sake" (2:13) and
regards it as "the will of God"[3] (2:15). Thus Peter attributes divine will to our
submission to civil authority. As John Elliott explains, it is Peter's reference to
God's will "that serves as our motivation to be subordinate [to civil authority],
and doing what is right."[4] As reaffirmed in our dispensation, "We believe in being subject to kings, presidents, rulers, and magistrates, in obeying, honoring,
and sustaining the law" (Articles of Faith 1:12).

However, history is replete with inefficient, flawed, and even repressive governments. So why does the Lord generally command that we submit to such imperfect authority? In his first epistle, known as 1 Peter, Peter not only affirms
submissiveness to civil authority, but also offers specific rationale for the Lord's
command. Peter's directive regarding civil authority reads:

> Submit yourselves to every ordinance of man for the Lord's sake: whether it be to the king, as supreme;
>
> Or unto governors, as unto them that are sent by him for the punishment of evildoers, and for the praise of them that do well.
>
> For so is the will of God, that with well doing ye may put to silence the ignorance of foolish men:
>
> As free, and not using your liberty for a cloak of maliciousness, but as the servants of God.
>
> Honour all men. Love the brotherhood. Fear God. Honour the king. (1 Peter 2:13–17)

To better understand Peter's directive and its value, the context of 1 Peter will be discussed. Then Peter's specific rationale for submission to civil authority—protection, silencing false accusers, honoring others, and glorifying God—will be considered. Finally, civil involvement and civil disobedience will be discussed in response to Peter's command.

Context of 1 Peter

Peter had been taught firsthand by Jesus not to contend with the Roman demand that subjects serve as porters, but to "go with him twain [two miles]" (Matthew 5:38–44). Peter had also been instructed through his participation in the Savior's miraculous payment of taxes (Matthew 17:24–27), and observed Jesus' response, "Render therefore unto Caesar the things which are Caesar's" (Matthew 22:15–21; see also Mark 12:13–17). After raising his sword against the unjust arrest of Jesus, Peter was restrained and then witnessed Jesus' submission to an unjust trial (see Matthew 26:51–68). It appears Peter was well acquainted with the Lord's desire that his followers comply with civil authority.

Decades later in Rome,[5] Peter writes[6] his first epistle to the church members in Asia Minor[7] (1 Peter 1:1). An important purpose of this letter seems clear: to exhort its readers to stand fast in the face of persecution. Every chapter refers to some kind of suffering (see 1 Peter 1:6–7; 2:19–23; 3:14, 17–18; 4:1, 13–16, 19; 5:1, 9–10). The exact timing of this letter is unclear, but it was probably composed "in the early to mid [AD] 60s, after Peter came to Rome but before Nero began his violent attacks on believers."[8] Tradition indicates that Peter was martyred in Rome under Nero around AD 64–68.[9] If this is the case, the timing of this letter predates the documented state-sponsored persecution of Christians in Asia Minor, and therefore suggests that the suffering Peter addresses is more likely social ostracism and general harassment.[10] It is challenging to imagine Peter advocating such complete allegiance to the emperor and governors, whose duty he describes as punishing evildoers and rewarding good (2:14), if such authority was the main cause of that unjust suffering.

Further supporting trials of social discrimination, most references to suffering in 1 Peter seem to deal with slander (false and damaging accusations, 2:12; 3:16), disassociation from others (4:3–4), or being reviled (abusive criticism, 4:14; 4:16).[11] Of this suffering, Mark Allan Powell suggests:

> The root cause of this abuse seems to be caught up with the letter's identification of its readers as "aliens and exiles" (2:11; see also 1:1, 17). Their conversion to Christ has led them to cut off ties with former associations, and so they have come to be regarded as social misfits or deviants (4:3–4). They may have been viewed as impious, for refusing to give the [Roman] gods their due, as unpatriotic for neglecting to worship the emperor, and as antisocial for avoiding the various rites and festivities that constituted social life in a pagan world.[12]

To be clear, whatever the cause of their suffering, Peter describes it as a "fiery trial" (1 Peter 4:12). And though Rome may not have been the primary cause of their suffering at the time of Peter's first letter, Rome had no particular regard for Christians.[13] It is therefore under the probability of an indifferent government, significant social persecution, and the possibility of Peter's awareness of even greater tribulations to come,[14] that his direction and rationale to church members regarding their relationship to the state will be considered (2:13–17).

Submission to Civil Authority Provides Protection and Order

Referencing 1 Peter 2:13–17, Elder Bruce R. McConkie said, "In Peter's day, and in ours, the saints are subject to two wholly separate and independent systems of direction—the Church . . . and the state which governs in civil affairs. And experience gained through conformity to both systems of government is *essential* to the perfecting of the human soul."[15] Elder McConkie also stated that man's submission to the "laws of the land in which he lives" is "an *essential* part of working out his salvation."[16] And Elder James E. Talmage declared, "Governments are *essential* to human existence . . . and His people are in duty bound to sustain them."[17] So what makes civil authority, these institutions "of men" (2:13), essential to God's plan?

Peter describes that the king (emperor) and governors' purpose is "for the punishment of evildoers, and for the praise of them that do well" (1 Peter 2:14). Rather than its organizational arrangement, Peter extols Roman authority because it punishes delinquents and protects the compliant. In this light, Peter may be understood as saying that civil authority, though a human institution, is to be obeyed because the protection and order it provides is God's will.

Though governments are imperfect and often deficient, the absence of government order is almost always worse. This is a basic argument of such philosophers as Hobbes, Locke, and Rousseau.[18] Without government to restrain people's actions, we would continually be in a state of threat and confusion. Where there are no property rights, no limits on crime, and no restrictions to physical harm, if someone is strong enough (either individually or as a group), they can, without any restraint, remove your agency, pilfer your property, enslave you, or even take your life. The absence of government is not a state of freedom, but rather a state of anarchy and oppression. Almost any form of government is preferable to such conditions.

Elder N. Eldon Tanner quoted the following statement: "In reality the man who defies or flouts the law is like the proverbial fool who saws away the plank on which he sits, and a disrespect or disregard for law is always the first sign of a disintegrating society. Respect for law is the most fundamental of all social virtues, for the alternative to the rule of law is that of violence and anarchy."[19] Consider the descriptions of Ether and Mormon as their people were in the throes of spiraling destruction. Ether explained, "All the people upon the face of the land were shedding blood, and there was none to restrain them" (Ether 13:31). And Mormon exclaimed, "O the depravity of my people! They are without order . . . and I cannot any longer enforce my commands" (Moroni 9:18). As the historian Horneius put it, "Tyranny harasses many, but anarchy overwhelms the whole state."[20] In general, if respect for authority is abandoned, subordination goes with it, and then anarchy and devastation take their place.

In a way, civil authority serves as a check on individual free will. Essentially we set aside our unrestrained individual interest and concede power to others (i.e., civil authority) who enforce and secure for us a degree of protection and order. Elder James E. Faust taught, "We are individuals, but we live in families and communities where order provides a system of harmony that hinges on obedience to principles."[21] A key role of government is to essentially limit individual behavior that harms others.

Finally, it is hard to cultivate human virtues under the constant whimsical threat of someone with a bigger stick. To the degree that governments eliminate or at least reduce such a threat, we are better able to plan, control, and determine the course of our lives.

Submission to Civil Authority Silences False Accusers

Early Christian communities were viewed with suspicion and distrust. Of these rumors, Bible scholar Bart Ehrman explained, "If you can imagine the worst you won't be far off the mark. Christians were thought to meet under the cloak of darkness in order to hide their despicable deeds from the world."[22] Thus, as Terry Ball explains, "Peter was anxious for the Saints to understand that they should live above reproach and thereby give no justification to those looking for excuse to persecute them. He urged the Saints to be honest, law abiding, and obedient to governing entities (see 1 Peter 2:12–14; 4:15). . . . He promises them that with such 'well doing ye may put to silence the ignorance of foolish men' (see 1 Peter 2:15)."[23] Submission to civil authority was then, as it is today, a clear demonstration that our faith is not a threat to social order and that any rumors to the contrary are simply not true.

Members' disregard for civil authority is often seen by those who oppose or persecute the church as justification for their unkindness. Referring to Peter's day (1 Peter 2:13–17), Elder Talmage explained that acts of defiance and indiscretion by church members "furnish excuse, if not reason, for the assaults of persecutors, who . . . denounced [church members] as law-breakers and workers of sedition. Even half-hearted submission [by members] to the civil powers would have been unwise at least, in view of the disfavor with which the Church had come to be regarded by pagan contemporaries."[24] Often it only takes the disregard of a few members for those who are opposed to the church to feel justified in oppressing the entire church. What's more, members' disregard for civil authority can even strengthen the resolve of those who oppose the church.

Speaking collectively of church members in our day, Elder Talmage stated that if they would abide by the law they should be "confident that when the true story of their rise and progress as an established body of religious worshipers is fully known, the loyalty of the Church and the patriotic devotion of its members will be vindicated and extolled by the world in general."[25] Ultimately our lives of "well doing" (1 Peter 2:15) and "good works" (2:12) coupled with loyalty to civil authority (2:13–14) will speak louder than any ignorant or false accusations, as well as help avoid the undue antagonism of others.

Particularly in locations where the church is not well established, Peter's prescription that we submit to civil authority is still one of our best means of silencing false accusations and alleviating others' fears born of ignorance (1 Peter 2:15). In this light, Peter teaches that our conduct, which includes our submission to civil authority, is also a means of defending the gospel. By submitting ourselves to civil authority, we debunk slander and secure for ourselves an honorable reputation. Essentially, our actions will often speak louder than their words.

Submission to Civil Authority Honors Others

Beyond basic protection and silencing false accusations, Peter connects submission to civil authority with honoring "all men" (1 Peter 2:17). We honor and show respect for others by abiding by laws that preserve their rights as well as our own. In a sense it is the Golden Rule (see Matthew 7:12). If I expect certain protections and rights under the law, I must honor the same protections and rights of others by obeying that law. This is well illustrated in the eleventh Article of Faith: We claim the privilege of worshipping Almighty God and show honor to others by allowing them the same privilege, even when we strongly disagree.

Connected to honoring others by submission to the law, Peter warns us against using our fidelity to God as an excuse not to submit to civil authority. Peter acknowledges that we are "free," but that such liberty should not be a "cloak of maliciousness"—a cover-up to less-than-kind treatment of our neighbor (1 Peter 2:16). Commenting on verse 16, Ramsey Michaels explains:

> No matter what the provocation, [Christians, "servants of God" (2:16)] must not lose respect for their fellow citizens or forget the common humanity they all share (see 2:13). The kind of freedom the Christians possessed (i.e., spiritual freedom, new life in Christ) was obviously not something that could be used in Roman society at large as "an excuse to cause trouble" or as a justification for antisocial behavior, but it could be so used *among Christians themselves*. Peter's urgent plea is that his readers never exploit their newly won freedom in this way, deceiving themselves and each other.[26]

Similarly, Elder Talmage explains Peter's caution this way: "The saints rejoiced in their testimony of the truth . . . the truth that was to make them free—and it would have been easy for them to regard all others as inferior to themselves, and to rebel against all authority of man in favor of their allegiance to a higher power. There was constant danger that their zeal would lead them to acts of indiscretion."[27]

Membership in the Lord's church does not afford us "emancipation from moral restraint."[28] We honor others by honoring the law that preserves their basic rights as well as our own. We may be right and have eternal truth on our side, but Peter is clear that it does not afford us the right to defy civil authority or do harm to others.

Submission to Civil Authority Glorifies God

In verse 12 of chapter 2,[29] Peter teaches his readers that "by [their] good works," the Gentiles may "glorify God." It is in this context (2:12) that he teaches submission to civil authority (2:13–17). Simply stated, our compliance to civil authority sets forth an example that can bring glory to God.

Considering the influence of church members within their own countries, Elder Dennis B. Neuenschwander said, "Even though the Church is to 'stand independent above all other creatures' (D&C 78:14), it still must work within the context of law, respect for the society in which it operates, and fidelity to the principles that distinguish it as a religious society. Neither representatives of the Church, nor its members, can [flout] the law and hope to be known as peacemakers or be considered as a valuable, influential, and respected part of society."[30]

Elder Lance B. Wickman said that the "credibility" we gain by honoring the law is "the gateway through which the Church must pass in order to preach the gospel with vigor in any nation."[31] One example of this was the church's desire to have LDS missionaries serve in communist East Germany. President Thomas S. Monson shared that in a meeting with government deputies the nation's chairman Erich Honecker said to him, "We know members of your Church believe in work; you've proven that. We know you believe in the family; you've demonstrated that. We know you are good citizens in whatever country you claim as home; we have observed that. The floor is yours. Make your desires known." After President Monson made his request for missionaries, Chairman Honecker concluded, "We know you. We trust you. We have had experience with you. Your missionary request is approved."[32]

To some degree, our submission to civil authority allows our salt to be savored, and our light to shine (Matthew 5:13–16). Elder L. Tom Perry explained, "in a world of many nations and various laws. . . . as we spread the gospel of Jesus Christ to the four corners of the earth . . . we must respect the governments of each nation we enter. Truly, we believe in obeying, honoring, and sustaining the law of each land."[33]

Civil Involvement

Some may argue that Peter's teaching of submissiveness to civil authority only perpetuates the status quo. However, Peter's apparent silence on engaging and petitioning civil authority should not be interpreted as a declaration of inaction. Peter does tell his readers to be ready to give a defense of the gospel when the occasion presents itself (1 Peter 3:15–16). He also tells them they must show that they are different in a positive way, not just that they no longer practice aspects of pagan life that their neighbors still find appealing (4:3–4).

As members of the church, we are encouraged to participate in political and governmental affairs.[34] Elder L. Tom Perry has said, "As Church members, we live under the banner of many different flags. . . . In those countries that allow us the right to participate in the affairs of government, we should use our free agency and be actively engaged in supporting and defending the principles of truth, right, and freedom."[35] President Gordon B. Hinckley succinctly said, "we desperately need moral men and women who stand on principle, to be involved in the political process. Otherwise, we abdicate power to those whose designs are almost entirely selfish."[36]

Clearly we seek to make our conditions better. However, we recognize that we live in common societies and therefore seek to do so within compliance of the law. Elder N. Eldon Tanner explained, "There are many who question the constitutionality of certain acts passed by their respective governments . . . and they feel to defy and disobey the law. Abraham Lincoln once observed: 'Bad laws, if they exist, should be repealed as soon as possible; still, while they continue in force, they should be religiously observed.' This is the attitude of the Church in regard to law observance."[37] We can and should seek needed change, but we cannot disregard the society in which we live by dismissing civil authority in the process.

Civil Disobedience

Using Peter and others as an example, Bruce R. McConkie stated:

> Obviously . . . situations can arise in which civil power can command an act which so sets at naught the Lord's decrees as to require his saints to follow his law rather than the lesser worldly requirement. When commanded to preach no more in the name of Christ, Peter and John replied: "Whether it be right in the sight of God to hearken unto you more than unto God, judge ye. For we cannot but speak the things which we have seen and heard" (Acts 4:13–21). Similarly, Daniel continued to worship the true God, though the law prohibited prayer to any but Darius (Daniel 6), and the three Hebrew captives [Shadrach, Meshach and Abednego] continued their proper worship though their rebellion against Nebuchadnezzar's law meant the fiery furnace for them. (Daniel 3)[38]

Though there have been exceptions, the bar for any exception seems high. Just because laws may be unjust is not reason enough to renounce civil authority. Peter instructed his readers that "when ye do well, and suffer for it, ye take it patiently, this is acceptable with God" (1 Peter 2:20). And Peter adds that no Christian should provoke suffering from civil authority by breaking the law: "Yet if *any man suffer* as a Christian, let him not be ashamed; but let him glorify God" (4:14–16; emphasis added). Even when we do what we can within the law to improve civil authority, compliance with the command that we submit to such authority can result in our suffering under unjust laws. Elder Talmage explained, "Pending the overruling by Providence in favor of religious liberty, it is the duty of the saints to submit themselves to the laws of their country. . . . The saints have practically demonstrated their acceptance of the doctrine that it is better to suffer evil than to do wrong by purely human opposition to unjust authority."[39]

Furthermore, the Lord explained that "when I give a commandment to any of the sons of men to do a work unto my name, and those sons of men go with all their might and with all they have to perform that work . . . and their enemies come upon them and hinder them from performing that work, behold, it behooveth me to require that work no more at the hands of those sons of men, but to accept of their offerings" (D&C 124:49). President Anthony W. Ivins explained that this verse "reveals to us this great truth, that God does not require at the hands of men the accomplishment of that which is impossible—not impossible to him, but impossible to them. . . . whether it applies to any other [commands] given of the Lord, and which the Church has conscientiously endeavored to carry out and been prevented from doing so by the enactment of civil law which would bring us into direct conflict with the government under which we live—the Lord holds that [command] in abeyance [temporary suspension]."[40] This is not an excuse, but rather the Lord's acknowledgement of our genuine effort, hindered only by civil authority, and affirmation of the importance of abiding by civil law.

Conclusion

Peter clearly supports and gives rationale to our submission to civil authority, but urging subordination is not a call to supernal loyalty or worship. God is sovereign, and Peter appears to use a chiasmus in verse 17 of chapter 2 to emphasize this.

A. Honour all men.

    B. Love the brotherhood.

    B. Fear [revere] God.

A. Honour the king.

Ramsey Michaels explains,

> The double use of "respect"["honour" in the KJV] at the beginning
> and end of the sequence, and the placement of the "brotherhood"
> and "God" side by side in the center gives the whole maxim a chi-
> astic (a-b-b-a) quality, with the obligations of Christian believers to
> God and each other framed by their secondary obligations to fellow
> citizens (including enemies), and to civil rulers. It is the secondary
> obligations that Peter emphasizes by this arrangement but precisely
> with the reminder that they *are* secondary.[41]

In the centuries that follow, Peter's contrast between honor for the emperor and
fear/reverence for God is held up by Christian martyrs—God alone is to be feared
(see Acts 5:29).[42]

It is important to note that Peter does not deal with how we create a civil
society that is more just. Issues of governance can be very complex, and questions
of optimal balance between liberty and order, organizational structure, reach, distribution of power, and so forth, have not been addressed here. Instead, attention
has been given to Peter's rationale for civil authority with the intent that we better
understand, and thus are better enabled to properly abide by this directive. Some
discontent with civil authority seems inevitable; seldom do we always get what we
want. But we need government, and giving up some rights and choosing to abide
by civil authority will inevitably be a necessary aspect of peace in diverse societies.

As in Peter's time, latter-day revelation requires our prudent allegiance to
civil authority. President David O. McKay taught that "three significant words
used in the twelfth Article of Faith express the proper attitude of the membership
of the Church toward law. These words are—obey, honor and sustain.... We obey
law from a sense of right. We honor law because of its necessity and strength to
society. We sustain law by keeping it in good repute."[43] Finally, the Lord has said,
"Let no man break the laws of the land, for he that keepeth the laws of God hath
no need to break the laws of the land. Wherefore, be subject to the powers that be,
until he reigns whose right it is to reign, and subdues all enemies under his feet"
(D&C 58:21–22).

Notes

1. The Savior certainly alluded to abiding by the law of the land (see Matthew 5:38–
44; 17:24–27; 22:15–21), and Paul also declared submission to civil authority (Romans

13:1–7, Timothy 2:1–3; Titus 3:1–3, 8). However, as John H. Elliott explains, 1 Peter 2:13–17 is a clear break from Romans 13:1–7. Peter makes no assertion that civil authorities are "servants" of God representing his authority. Peter's conception of the functions of civil authority is a simple utilitarian one, devoid of divine warrant. Peter's point is not to discourage resistance to authorities established by God, as appears to be the case in Romans 13:2, but to encourage doing what is right as a sign of subordination to God's will and a means to silence detractors. See John H. Elliott, *1 Peter: A New Translation with Introduction and Commentary*, The Anchor Bible 37B (New York: Doubleday, 2000), 493–94.

2. Civil authority (i.e., civil government) here means the person(s) who exercise administrative control over civilian affairs and enforce law and order.

3. Note the phrase "For so is the will of God" in verse 15 may refer to what precedes it in verses 13–14, or it may also refer to what follows—that their good behavior silences the ignorant.

4. Elliott, *1 Peter*, 493. Referring to "for the Lord's sake" (v. 13), Elliott further explains, "The phrase provides the motivation for the imperative" (489). Similarly, Ramsey Michaels explains, "Peter requires cooperation and compliance not because the state requires it, but 'for the sake of the Lord.'" J. Ramsey Michaels, *1 Peter*, Word Biblical Commentary, vol. 49 (Nashville: Thomas Nelson, 1988), 124.

5. Most scholars accept that "Babylon" in 1 Peter 5:13 refers to Rome. Elliott, *1 Peter*, 131–34.

6. In this chapter, the assumption will be that Peter himself, or a secretary/scribe, wrote this epistle. However, there are three general theories of authorship for 1 Peter: (1) it was written by Peter, (2) Peter dictated or conceived the substance of the letter which was written by a secretary/scribe (perhaps Silvanus, see 1 Peter 5:12), or (3) it was pseudonymously written in Peter's name and authority. See Elliott, *1 Peter*, 118–30. John Gee offers support for Peter as author: "Modern scholars have 'arbitrarily' tended to reject Peter as author of the epistle. Historically though, 1 Peter was almost always seen as written by the chief Apostle, Peter. The early Christian author Eusebius cited it as undoubtedly genuine. The epistle was used extensively by Ignatius of Antioch, Clement of Rome, Polycarp of Smyrna, Justin Martyr, Irenaeus of Lyon, and others. Eusebius traced the influence back to Polycarp's use. Presumably Polycarp would not have done this if he had not believed that 1 Peter was authentic, and since he lived only a few years after the letter was written, he was in a good position to know what its origin was." John Gee, "James, First and Second Peter, and Jude: Epistles of Persecution," in *Life and Teachings of the New Testament Apostles: From the Day of Pentecost to the Apocalypse*, ed. Thomas A. Wayment and Richard Neitzel Holzapfel (Salt Lake City: Deseret Book, 2010), 180–82.

7. Modern-day Turkey.

8. Mark Allan Powell, *Introducing the New Testament: A Historical, Literary, and Theological Survey* (Grand Rapids, MI: Baker Academic, 2009) 463–77. John Gee explains a broader window of when this letter could have been written: "An early church tradition has Peter slain at the hands of Nero in Rome, about AD 65. Thus there is about a fifteen-year time period in which the epistle could have been written." Gee, "James, First and Second Peter, and Jude," 180–82. Other scholars, considering 1 Peter to be written pseudonymously, believe it was written near the end of the first century. Bart D. Ehrman,

The New Testament: A Historical Introduction to the Early Christian Writings (London: Oxford University Press, 2004), 434–36. See also Elliott, *1 Peter*, 134–38.

9. Powell, *Introducing the New Testament*, 463–77.

10. Mark Allan Powell explains, "In recent years, however, most scholars have become convinced that the variety of suffering being addressed in 1 Peter is social ostracism and general harassment rather than government-run persecution of the church. As far as we know, Christians in Asia Minor did not endure state-sponsored persecution until the second century. This letter, furthermore, never mentions persecution per se; rather, it speaks of suffering as a common experience that should be regarded as the expected lot of anyone who is a Christian (4:12), anywhere in the world (5:9)." Powell, *Introducing the New Testament*, 463–77.

11. Peter also indicates, at least in the case of some Christian slaves, physical violence (2:19).

12. Powell, *Introducing the New Testament*, 463–77. David Horrell further explains Peter's addressees suffering this way: "One of the things that would have particularly aroused the hostility of their non-Christian neighbours was the Christians' exclusive devotion to the worship of their God alone, and their refusal to honour the various deities of the Greek and Roman pantheon. Since worshipping the gods was thought to be vital to keeping the peace, and to keeping natural and economic disasters at bay, those who refused to do this could be held responsible for bad things that occurred. Moreover, by withdrawing from such religious and social participation, and meeting in what was held to be a secretive and mysterious manner, Christians were felt to be an 'anti-social' people, who—as the Roman historian Tacitus puts it—became known for their 'hatred of the human race.'" David G. Horrell, *1 Peter* (New York: Continuum International, 2008), 55.

13. Ehrman explains that Rome seemed more focused on order than justice: "The provincial [Roman] governors had two main responsibilities: to keep the peace and to collect the taxes. [This was done by] . . . employing whatever means necessary to maintain public order and maximize revenue collection." Ehrman, *The New Testament,* 428. Charles Bigg further explains, "Roman law made no sharp distinction between 'immoral' and 'criminal.' The governour was father as well as magistrate, and his power extended to every action that was *contra bonos mores* [against good morals]." Charles Bigg, *A Critical and Exegetical Commentary on the Epistles of St. Peter and St. Jude*, 2nd ed., The International Critical Commentary (Edinburgh: T&T Clark, 1902), 140.

14. Referring to the fifty-eighth section of the Doctrine and Covenants, Terry Ball explained, "Today we know that the Lord and His prophet were trying to prepare the Saints for the Jackson County persecutions. In the same way, the First Epistle of Peter seems to be trying to prepare the early Saints for the terrible persecutions that they would soon face. For example, in July of AD 64, Nero set fire to Rome and then to absolve himself blamed the Christians for the act. The historian Tacitus described the ruthless persecution that followed." Terry B. Ball, "Peter's Principles: An Approach to the First Epistle of Peter," in *Go Ye into All the World: Messages of the New Testament Apostles* (Salt Lake City: Deseret Book, 2002), 220–29.

15. Bruce R. McConkie, *Doctrinal New Testament Commentary*, 3 vols. (Salt Lake City: Bookcraft, 1965), 3:299.

16. McConkie, *Doctrinal New Testament Commentary*, 3:297.

17. James E. Talmage, *Articles of Faith* (Salt Lake City: Deseret Book, 1915), 381; emphasis added.

18. See Thomas Hobbes, *Leviathan* (1651); John Locke, *Two Treatises of Government*, (1690); Jean-Jacques Rousseau, *The Social Contract* (1762).

19. N. Eldon Tanner, in Conference Report, October 1975, quoting *Case and Comment*, March/April 1965, 20.

20. David Brown, Andrew Robert Fausset, and Robert Jamieson, *A Commentary: Critical, Practical and Explanatory, on the Old and New Testaments* (Toledo, OH: Jerome B. Names, 1884), 420. http://www.ccel.org/ccel/jamieson/jfb http://www.ccel.org/ccel/jamieson/jfb.pdf http://www.ccel.org/ccel/jamieson/jfb.xi.xxi.iii.html.

21. James E. Faust, "Obedience: The Path to Freedom," *Ensign*, May 1999, 45.

22. Ehrman, 429, see also n. 11.

23. Ball, "Peter's Principles: An Approach to the First Epistle of Peter," 220–29.

24. Talmage, *Articles of Faith*, 381.

25. Talmage, *Articles of Faith*, 374.

26. Elliott, *1 Peter*, 129.

27. Talmage, *Articles of Faith*, 381.

28. Bigg, *A Critical and Exegetical Commentary*, 141.

29. In 1 Peter 2:11–12, Peter shifts his message toward the conduct of Christians living in communities where they are falsely accused and subject to suffering. Peter aptly provides his readers instruction on how to act civilly (2:13–17) and domestically (2:18–3:12) in ways that will help disprove and silence slanderous accusations, manifest their honorable character, and demonstrate their fidelity to God. Elliott, *The Anchor Bible*, 484–85.

30. Dennis B. Neuenschwander, *Bridges: Alumni Magazine* (Provo, UT: BYU Kennedy Center for International Studies), Spring 2011, 20–27.

31. Lance B. Wickman, as quoted in Aaron Shill, "Relationships Key to Building Credibility Abroad," *Deseret News*, April 8, 2008. President Gordon B. Hinckley has said, "Wherever we go, we go in the front door. Our representatives honor the laws of the nations to which they go and teach the people to be good citizens." "Gordon B. Hinckley's speech at the National Press Club," *Deseret News*, March 27, 2000.

32. Thomas S. Monson, in Conference Report, April 1989, 69.

33. L. Tom Perry, "The Doctrines and Principles Contained in the Articles of Faith," *Ensign*, November 2013, 48.

34. *Handbook 2: Administering the Church*, "As citizens, Church members are encouraged to participate in political and governmental affairs, including involvement in the political party of their choice. Members are also urged to be actively engaged in worthy causes to improve their communities and make them wholesome places in which to live and rear families" (Salt Lake City: The Church of Jesus Christ of Latter-day Saints, 2010), 21.1.29.

35. L. Tom Perry, in Conference Report, October 1987, 87.

36. Gordon B. Hinckley, *Stand a Little Taller* (Salt Lake City: Deseret Book, 2001), 15. Similarly, Elder M. Russell Ballard declared, "Remember Edmund Burke's statement: 'The only thing necessary for the triumph of evil is for good men to do nothing.' We need to raise our voices with other concerned citizens throughout the world in opposition to current trends." In Conference Report, October 2003, 17.

37. N. Eldon Tanner, in Conference Report, October 1975, 126.

38. Bruce R. McConkie, *Mormon Doctrine*, 2nd ed. (Salt Lake City: Bookcraft, 1966), 437.

39. Talmage, *Articles of Faith*, 383.

40. Anthony W. Ivins, in Conference Report, October 1929, 97; "abeyance" means a state of temporary disuse or suspension.

41. Michaels, *1 Peter*, 123. See also Elliott, *1 Peter*, 497.

42. Elliott, *1 Peter*, 501.

43. David O. McKay, in Conference Report, April 1937, 27–28, as cited in *Latter-day Prophets and the United States Constitution*, ed. Donald Q. Cannon (Provo, UT: Religious Studies Center, 1991), 118.

16

Wondering at His Words
PETER'S INFLUENCE ON THE KNOWLEDGE OF SALVATION FOR THE DEAD

Scott C. Esplin

Scott C. Esplin is an associate professor of Church history and doctrine at
Brigham Young University.

"You do not question what souls these are that suffer here before you?" the
poet Virgil asked Dante as they encountered their first spirits while beginning their descent into the abyss of hell in *The Inferno*. "I wish you to know
before you travel on that these were sinless," Virgil continues. "And still their
merits fail, for they lacked Baptism's grace, which is the door of the true faith
you were born to. Their birth fell before the age of the Christian mysteries, and
so they did not worship God's Trinity in fullest duty. I am one of these," Virgil
lamented. "For such defects are we lost, though spared the fire and suffering
Hell in one affliction only: that without hope we live on in desire."[1]

This fate of souls lacking "Baptism's grace" appears to have troubled Dante, as
it has plagued many others who grapple with the Savior's firm decree to Nicodemus,
"Except a man be born of water and of the Spirit, he cannot enter into the kingdom of God" (John 3:5).[2] Pained by the thought of the "many worthy souls" who
suffer, Dante questioned if anything could be done for those whose "merits fail."
The poet continued, "Instruct me, Master and most noble Sir. . . . Has any, by his
own or another's merit, gone ever from this place to blessedness?' He sensed my inner question and answered it: 'I was still new to this estate of tears when a Mighty

One descended here among us, crowned with the sign of His victorious years,'" Virgil responded. "'He took from us the shade of our first parent, of Abel, his pure son, of ancient Noah, of Moses, the bringer of law, the obedient. Father Abraham, David the King, Israel with his father and his children, Rachel, the holy vessel of His blessing, and many more He chose for elevation among the elect. And before these, you must know, no human soul had ever won salvation.'"[3]

The truth that "a Mighty One descended" to the spirit world to interact with the righteous dead on a mission to save souls does not originate with the late medieval poet Dante. However fragmented his romanticized expression may appear, the motif of Christ reaching beyond the veil is a partially preserved verbalization of earlier Christian teachings, all of which are a heritage of the writings and ministry of the Apostle Peter. In 1 Peter 3:19, he taught that Christ "went and preached unto the spirits in prison." Additionally, Peter both held and conferred priesthood keys relative to salvation. The influence of Peter's participation in the restoration of God's priesthood authority on earth today, coupled with the prompting of prophetic insight brought about by his teachings, have laid the groundwork for Latter-day Saint understanding of salvation for the dead. They remain a modern legacy of Peter, the chief Apostle.

New Testament Teachings on Christ's Ministry in the Spirit World

Christian soteriology, or the study of salvation, is rooted in the teaching of Jesus Christ and the power granted at his hand to perform actions on earth that would impact one's status in heaven. Jesus instructed Nicodemus that being born again, both of water and of Spirit, coupled with belief in him, are required for entrance into God's kingdom and eternal life (see John 3:5, 15–16). Latter-day Saints connect an eternal reward to deeds done while in this life through Christ's declaration "Marvel not at this: for the hour is coming, in the which all that are in the graves shall hear his voice, and shall come forth; they that have *done good*, unto the resurrection of life; and they that have *done evil*, unto the resurrection of damnation" (John 5:28–29; emphasis added).

Called to the apostleship, Peter was charged to "preach the kingdom of God" (Luke 9:2), including the doctrines of faith, repentance, and rebirth (see Acts 2:38; 3:19) necessary for salvation. Boldly declaring his personal witness that Jesus was "the Christ, the Son of the living God" (Matthew 16:16), Peter was promised "the keys of the kingdom," including power that "whatsoever thou shalt bind on earth shall be bound in heaven: and whatsoever thou shalt loose on earth shall be loosed in heaven" (16:19).[4] Six days later, the promise was fulfilled. Matthew records, "Jesus taketh Peter, James, and John his brother, and bringeth them up into an high mountain apart, and was transfigured before them.... And, behold, there appeared unto them Moses and Elias talking with him," the account continues, after which, Peter summarized, "Lord, it is good for us to be here" (17:1–4).[5]

While the New Testament record is unclear regarding all that occurred on the Mount of Transfiguration, Latter-day Saint scripture and prophetic teachings add important insight.[6] The Doctrine and Covenants reveals that we "have not yet received" a full account of what occurred there (D&C 63:20–21). Later, Joseph Smith taught that "the Savior, Moses, and Elias gave the Keys to Peter, James and John on the Mount when they were transfigured before him."[7] From a Latter-day Saint perspective, these keys authorized the Apostles to administer the preaching of the gospel throughout the world and, for the sake of the topic at hand, perform ordinances that would have impact beyond the veil for both the living and the dead. Broadening the benefits of what occurred on the Mount of Transfiguration to those whom Peter would reach because of the experience, one Latter-day Saint scholar wrote, "We are persuaded . . . that the happenings on the Mount of Transfiguration are among the most important in the New Testament."[8] The events matter because Latter-day Saints believe that priesthood authority is essential.

Armed with the teachings of salvation and the power to make its ordinances efficacious beyond the grave, Peter boldly pursued his mission to lead the church and save the children of men following Christ's Resurrection. The book of Acts records Peter's powerful teachings, confident declarations, and prophetic guidance in a nearly two-decade-long Mediterranean ministry. Furthermore, his understanding of Christ's postmortal ministry to the spirits in prison is preserved in the First Epistle General of Peter, likely authored in the early sixties AD to the Saints of Pontus, Galatia, Cappadocia, Asia, and Bithynia (see 1 Peter 1:1).[9] In it, Peter revealed, "For Christ also hath once suffered for sins, the just for the unjust, that he might bring us to God, being put to death in the flesh, but quickened by the Spirit: By which also he went and preached unto the spirits in prison; Which sometime were disobedient, when once the longsuffering of God waited in the days of Noah, while the ark was a preparing, wherein few, that is, eight souls were saved by water" (1 Peter 3:18–20). Speaking of the purposes for his Master's ministry in the spirit world, Peter continued, "For for this cause was the gospel preached also to them that are dead, that they might be judged according to men in the flesh, but live according to God in the spirit" (1 Peter 4:6). In these passages, Peter adds additional insight to Christ's earlier declaration, recorded in the Gospel of John: "Verily, verily, I say unto you, The hour is coming, and now is, when the dead shall hear the voice of the Son of God: and they that hear shall live" (John 5:25).

Taken literally, and when read through the lens of modern revelation (to be discussed later), the passages and the concept they convey appear to be clear: Christ went in spirit to preach to the spirits in prison. The implications of that interpretation, however, have led to a variety of readings, especially when considered without the help of modern scripture. Indeed, "the difficulty does not actually lie in the passage," observed Professor Catherine Thomas, "but in the minds of the interpreters who find a conflict here with their own views of the afterlife and the impossibility of progress or redemption there."[10] For example, writing specifically of 1 Peter 3:19, Martin Luther declared, "That is as strange a text and as dark a saying as any in the New Testament, so that I am not yet sure what St. Peter intended."[11] New Testament scholar Paul Achtemeier summarized, "This verse is one of the shorter, but surely the most problematic, in this letter, if not in the [New Testament] canon as a whole, and eludes any agreement on its precise meaning." Expounding on the problems the passage creates, Achtemeier continues, "There are the questions of the identity of the spirits and the place of and reason for their imprisonment, the direction of Christ's journey (ascent or descent) and the time it occurred, and the content of his proclamation."[12] Importantly, many of these questions are answered in modern revelation sparked by a reading of 1 Peter.

Challenged by the notion of disembodied spirits in prison and post-death repentance, modern scholars have sought for other interpretations to the teachings of Peter regarding Christ's ministry to the disobedient dead. One option ties the preaching to the time of Noah, implying that "Christ preached by the Holy Spirit through the lips of Noah to the wicked generation that lived before the flood." Another applies the passage to speak of the power and reach of Christ, "demonstrating that if the crucified and risen Christ preached to them, evil as they were, then not even death can put the most egregious sinner beyond the reach of Christ's saving power. Such preaching to Noah's generation is thus an example of a larger truth," this reading concludes, "namely, that those who died in the time before Christ, or those who died without the chance for faith in him, are not beyond the reach of his salvation." A third interpretation is that Peter's message was a call to the Saints of his day to stand firm in their "fearless confession" and "have the courage to tell even the most resolute sinners what hope in Christ means," just as Christ did to the wicked from Noah's day. A fourth option links the passage to traditions about Enoch, noting that "Christ in this passage is, like Enoch, announcing to the imprisoned evil angels of the time of Noah their final doom, a doom assured by means of Christ's triumph over them." In this paralleling of Enoch, the message is "not of salvation to the dead but of [Christ's] own triumph, as the result of his death and resurrection, over all rebellious spiritual forces." Summarizing, scholars like Paul Achtemeier note that each line of interpretation is problematic, for one reason or another, and that "one's understanding of the point of the passage will depend in large part on how one resolves those problems on context and meaning."[13]

The content of 1 Peter 4:6 is likewise problematic for modern scholars. In an interpretation that ultimately resonates with modern scripture on the subject, Achtemeier continues, "There is no indication in this verse that Christ was the one doing the preaching; he is more likely to be the subject matter than the agent of the preaching mentioned in the verse." Turning attention on the dead to whom the gospel was preached, some apply the passage to mean that the gospel is preached not to "those who have died physically but to those who were spiritually dead," though again, this reconciliation is problematic, in part because of the context of final judgment implied in 1 Peter 4:5–6. Attempting to reconcile these inconsistencies, Achtemeier notes that "if they had died prior to hearing the gospel, it would have to mean the gospel was preached to them in the realm of the dead, yet any notion of disembodied souls in Hades is a view of the afterlife quite absent from the [New Testament]. Further, it would clearly imply that there is a possibility of repentance and conversion after death, again an idea quite foreign to the [New Testament]."[14] These possibilities run counter to traditional Christian thought. E. M. Blaiklock writes, "It is impossible . . . to support [repentance after this life] by any other passage of Scripture, and the whole weight of the New Testament is against the possibility that any who consciously reject Christ in this life have any opportunity to reconsider their choice in another. Peter himself would repudiate the idea."[15]

Though confusing because of its doctrinal implications for Christianity today, the first-century teaching of Peter that Christ's mission included literal service to those beyond the veil is perpetuated in early Christian thought. Among them, Irenaeus (AD 130–200) declared, "The Lord descended into the regions beneath the earth, preaching His advent there also, and [declaring] the remission of sins received by those who believe in Him."[16] Origen (AD 185–253) likewise taught, "We assert that not only while Jesus was in the body did He win over not a few persons merely . . . but also, that when He became a soul, without the covering of the body, He dwelt among those souls which were without bodily covering, converting such of them as were willing to Himself."[17]

While this was "a teaching of the chief ancient Apostle, held strongly by major Christian teachers for some centuries," the meaning of Peter's teaching is "now largely misunderstood."[18] It was into this void of understanding, "the mystery of this preresurrection ministry of Christ . . . [that] eludes explanation," that the Restoration was born.[19] Importantly, it was Peter and his teachings on Christ's mission to the spirits in prison that sparked Latter-day Saint understanding of salvation for the dead.

Peter's Role in Restoring the Keys of Salvation in the Latter Days

Peter's role in shaping modern understanding of salvation for the dead is rooted in his participation in seminal events of the Restoration. For Joseph Smith, this connection to Peter was personal, as it was with others of his ancient prophetic counterparts. Describing the Prophet's interaction with Peter and other scriptural luminaries, President John Taylor taught, "When Joseph Smith was raised up as a Prophet of God, Mormon, Moroni, Nephi and others of the ancient Prophets who formerly lived on this Continent, and Peter and John and others who lived on the Asiatic Continent, came to him and communicated to him certain principles pertaining to the Gospel of the Son of God. Why? Because they held the keys of the various dispensations, and conferred them upon him, and he upon us."[20]

The earliest recorded reference to Peter in this dispensation comes from an April 1829 revelation to Joseph Smith and Oliver Cowdery when they inquired concerning the fate of John the Beloved, as described in the last chapter of the Gospel of John.[21] Informed that John had tarried on the earth, the account turned to Peter, revealing that he would "minister for [John] and for thy brother James; and unto you three I will give this power and the keys of this ministry until I come" (D&C 7:7). A month later, Peter's possessing the keys of salvation was reiterated in the account of the restoration of the Aaronic Priesthood when John the Baptist appeared, announcing "that he acted under the direction of Peter, James and John, who held the keys of the Priesthood of Melchizedek, which Priesthood, he said, would in due time be conferred" (Joseph Smith—History 1:72).[22]

While no corresponding section exists chronicling the actual conferral of the Melchizedek Priesthood as one does for the Aaronic Priesthood (D&C 13), two later accounts testify to its occurrence. In a September 1830 revelation, the Lord spoke of Joseph Smith's encounter "with Peter, and James, and John, whom I have sent unto you, by whom I have ordained you and confirmed you to be apostles, and especial witnesses of my name, and bear the keys of your ministry and of the same things which I revealed unto them" (D&C 27:12).[23] Continuing, the Lord emphasized the place of priesthood keys prominent in the experience, "Unto whom I have committed the keys of my kingdom, and a dispensation of the gospel for the last times; and for the fulness of times, in the which I will gather together in one all things, both which are in heaven, and which are on earth" (D&C 27:13). More than a decade later, the Prophet himself gave a description of the experience, "And again, what do we hear? . . . The voice of Peter, James, and John in the wilderness between Harmony, Susquehanna county, and Colesville, Broome county, on the Susquehanna river, declaring themselves as possessing the keys of the kingdom, and of the dispensation of the fulness of times!" (D&C 128:20).

In addition to the passing of the keys of salvation, Peter was personally involved in the events that laid the groundwork for the exercising of those keys on behalf of the dead.[24] In his account of the dedication of the Kirtland Temple, the Prophet recorded in his journal, "Presdt Williams also arose and testified that while Presdt Rigdon was making his first prayer an angel entered the window and seated himself between father Smith, and himself, and remained there during his prayer."[25] Truman O. Angell later added, "When the afternoon meeting assembled, Joseph, feeling very much elated, arose the first thing and said the Personage who had appeared in the morning was the Angel Peter come to accept the dedication."[26] President Heber C. Kimball even gave a description of Peter's appearance. "They had a fair view of his person. He was a very tall personage, black eyes, white hair, and stoop shouldered; his garment was whole, extending to near his ankles; on his feet he had sandals. He was sent as a messenger to accept of the dedication."[27] This and other experiences seem to be the basis for John Taylor's praise of the Prophet: "If you were to ask Joseph what sort of a looking man Adam was, he would tell you at once; he would tell you his size and appearance and all about him. You might have asked him what sort of men Peter, James, and John were, and he could have told you. Why? Because he had seen them."[28]

Peter's participation in the restoration of the Melchizedek Priesthood and the dedication of the Kirtland Temple were preparatory to the bestowal of priesthood keys on Joseph Smith and Oliver Cowdery in the Kirtland Temple on April 3, 1836, a week following the building's dedication. While there is no indication that Peter participated with the Savior, Moses, Elias, and Elijah on this occasion, the event certainly mirrored Peter's own receipt of keys on the Mount of Transfiguration eighteen centuries earlier. "The similarity of the events on the Mount of Transfiguration with those of the Kirtland Temple," wrote Robert Matthews, "seems to certify that the main accomplishment of the visitation of the holy beings on the mount was the bestowal of priesthood keys, in order to establish the dispensation of the meridian of time on a solid and complete foundation, with power to preach the gospel, perform the ordinances, call persons to the ministry, seal up the faithful to eternal life, and communicate all the gifts, powers, and graces of the gospel of Jesus Christ."[29] As they had been given to Peter anciently, these powers were likewise given through Peter and others of his ancient prophetic counterparts in the last days.

Shaping Influences of Peter's Writings on Latter-day Understanding of Salvation

While Peter interacted with Joseph Smith and others of the early church in restoring the keys of the Melchizedek Priesthood, the shaping influence of his writings have more recently impacted Latter-day Saint understanding of salvation for the dead. The Prophet Joseph Smith, for his part, had an appreciation for and affinity with the writings of Peter, as he once observed, "Peter penned the most sublime language of any of the Apostles."[30] While Joseph Smith was drawn to the style of writing in 1 and 2 Peter, it was the Prophet's nephew and sixth President of the Church, Joseph F. Smith, for whom Peter's words were the springboard into an understanding of redemption for the dead.

Joseph F. Smith's vision of the redemption of the dead was received on October 3, 1918, a day before the beginning of the eighty-eighth semiannual general conference of the church and a mere six weeks before President Smith's own death.[31] Scholars have carefully analyzed the historical context to Joseph F. Smith's vision, acknowledging the influence of the terrible loss of life associated with both World War I and the worldwide flu epidemic that gripped global society at the time of its reception. In the Great War (1914–18), more than nine million soldiers "and countless legions of civilians perished in the battlefields, battleships, and bombed-out byways," with another twenty-one million wounded.[32] Overshadowing those lost to armed conflict, the worldwide influenza epidemic that erupted on the war's heels claimed between twenty and one hundred million globally from 1918 to 1920, including nearly seven hundred thousand Americans. For the church, the outbreak led to the cancellation of President Smith's public funeral service in November 1918 and the postponement of the April general conference the next year.[33]

Authors have also connected the vision to the personal loss of life in President Smith's own family, stretching back as far as his father, Hyrum Smith, who died when young Joseph was only five years old, and his mother, Mary Fielding Smith, who died when he was thirteen. They have discussed the loss of several of his children, from the passing of his firstborn, Mercy Josephine, who died in 1870 at the age of three, to, most immediately before the revelation, the sudden demise of his firstborn son, forty-five-year-old Apostle Hyrum Mack Smith, who died of complications from a ruptured appendix in January 1918, nine months before the vision.[34] Speaking in a temple meeting just weeks after his son's death, President Smith summarized:

> I ought certainly to have charity for others who suffer and who are tried; for I lost my father when I was but a child; I lost my mother, the sweetest soul that ever lived, when I was only a boy; I have buried one of the loveliest wives that ever blessed the lot of man, and I have buried thirteen of my more than forty children that the Lord gave me. And it has seemed to me that the most promising, the most hopeful, and, if possible, the sweetest and purest and the best have been the earliest called to rest. Surely I have been touched and humbled with all these things and others—the death of my kindred, brothers and sisters, the passing away of men that I loved with all my soul.[35]

Indeed, "death had surrounded him throughout his life," one author wrote, "and the longings these deaths awakened could not be fully soothed in mortality."[36]

Additionally, scholars have examined the proliferation of addresses by President Smith on the topic of life after death in the years leading up to his 1918 vision. Beginning with his April 1916 general conference address entitled "In the Presence of the Divine," and including his February 1918 temple meeting address entitled "The Status of Little Children in the Resurrection," President Smith experienced "an era of unusual spiritual enlightenment in which he delivered to the Church some of the most important and inspiring insights of this dispensation," observed Robert Millet.[37] These experiences, reaching their climax immediately prior to the receiving of the October 1918 vision, may explain President Smith's own words as he addressed the assembled general conference audience in its opening session: "I will not, I dare not, attempt to enter upon many things that are resting upon my mind this morning, and I shall postpone until some future time, the Lord being willing, my attempt to tell you some of the things that are in my mind, and that dwell in my heart. I have not lived alone these five months. I have dwelt in the spirit of prayer, of supplication, of faith and of determination; and I have had my communications with the Spirit of the Lord continuously."[38] These constellations of events and teachings led one commentator to summarize regarding the vision, "The stage was set: preparation of a lifetime and preparation of the moment were recompensed with a heavenly endowment."[39]

While all of these contextual details are important to appreciating Joseph F. Smith's vision, context "does not necessarily imply causality," George Tate, one commentator on Smith's vision, wisely noted. "It is problematic," he continued, "when 'context mistakenly gets treated as the determinant of [something]' rather than as a framework."[40] In this regard, President Smith's declaration on his vision of the redemption of the dead importantly attributes causality to one thing, his pondering on the writings of the Apostle Peter. "On the third of October, in the year nineteen hundred and eighteen, I sat in my room pondering over the scriptures; and reflecting upon the great atoning sacrifice that was made by the Son of God, for the redemption of the world" (D&C 138:1–2), President Smith declared in a message written immediately following the church's October general conference.[41] Turning to the teachings of the chief Apostle, President Smith continued:

> While I was thus engaged, my mind reverted to the writings of the apostle Peter, to the primitive saints scattered abroad throughout Pontus, Galatia, Cappadocia, and other parts of Asia, where the gospel had been preached after the crucifixion of the Lord.
>
> I opened the Bible and read the third and fourth chapters of the first epistle of Peter, and as I read I was greatly impressed, more than I had ever been before, with the following passages:
>
> "For Christ also hath once suffered for sins, the just for the unjust, that he might bring us to God, being put to death in the flesh, but quickened by the Spirit:
>
> "By which also he went and preached unto the spirits in prison;
>
> "Which sometime were disobedient, when once the longsuffering of God waited in the days of Noah, while the ark was a preparing, wherein few, that is, eight souls were saved by water." (1 Peter 3:18–20.)
>
> "For for this cause was the gospel preached also to them that are dead, that they might be judged according to men in the flesh, but live according to God in the spirit." (1 Peter 4:6.) (D&C 138:5–10)

Summarizing the role Peter's writings played as a gateway to the divine, Smith recounted, "As I pondered over these things which are written, the eyes of my understanding were opened, and the Spirit of the Lord rested upon me, and I saw the hosts of the dead, both small and great" (D&C 138:11).

The 1918 vision of President Smith was not the first time he referenced the writings of Peter in public discourse. For example, *Journal of Discourses* contains at least seven different sermons by Joseph F. Smith where he references 1 Peter 3:18–20 or 1 Peter 4:6, the earliest from 1875, more than forty years before the vision.[42] "Jesus himself preached the Gospel to the spirits in prison,"[43] Smith repeatedly emphasized in the addresses, "while his body slept in the tomb," themes that were later expanded upon and clarified in D&C 138.[44] As President of the Church, Smith turned to the text in a 1912 funeral sermon for Sister Mary A. Freeze, a leader in the church's Mutual Improvement Association. On that occasion, he announced:

> I have always believed, and still do believe with all my soul, that such men as Peter and James, and the twelve disciples chosen of the Savior in His time, have been engaged all the centuries that have passed since their martyrdom for the testimony of Jesus Christ, in proclaiming liberty to the captives in the spirit world and in opening their prison doors. I do not believe that they could be employed in any greater work. Their mission is to save men. Their special calling and anointing of the Lord Himself was to save the world, to proclaim liberty to the captives and the opening of the prison doors to those that were bound in chains of darkness, superstition, and ignorance.[45]

Expanding the thought to include those of his own dispensation, Smith continued, "I believe that the disciples who have passed away in this dispensation— Joseph, the Prophet, and his brother Hyrum, and Brigham and Heber, and Willard, and Daniel and John, and Wilford, and all the rest of the prophets that have lived in this dispensation, and that have been intimately associated with the work of redemption and the other ordinances of the Gospel of the Son of God in this world are preaching that same Gospel that they lived and preached here to those who are in darkness in the spirit-world and who had not the knowledge before they went."[46] Both beliefs were confirmed in President Smith's later vision.

The vision of the redemption of the dead, as section 138 has come to be known, answered questions long presented by Peter's earlier writings on the subject while both corroborating and expanding President Smith's earlier teachings. One of the fundamental questions it answers is whom the Savior visited. President Smith noted that he saw assembled "an innumerable company of the spirits of the just, who had been faithful in the testimony of Jesus while they lived in mortality; and who had offered sacrifice in the similitude of the great sacrifice of the Son of God, and had suffered tribulation in their Redeemer's name. All these had departed the mortal life, firm in the hope of a glorious resurrection, through the grace of God the Father and his Only Begotten Son, Jesus Christ" (D&C 138:12–14). The description of a visit to the just and faithful dead who had departed mortality firm in their faith stands in stark contrast to Peter's initial description, which noted that Christ "went and preached unto the spirits in prison; which sometime were

disobedient, when once the longsuffering of God waited in the days of Noah"
(1 Peter 3:19–20).

Peter's version of the visit creates potential questions in the minds of those
who read it literally. Why would Christ choose to visit spirits in prison and,
among them, specifically the disobedient from the days of Noah? Smith's vision
helps with these questions in at least two ways. First, it acknowledges that even
among the most righteous spirits, which included the likes of Adam, Eve, Abel,
Seth, Noah, Shem, Abraham, Isaac, Jacob, Moses, Isaiah, Ezekiel, Daniel, Elias,
Malachi, and "prophets who dwelt among the Nephites" (see D&C 138:38–49),
there was need for deliverance. "The dead had looked upon the long absence of
their spirits from their bodies as a bondage," Smith wrote (D&C 138:50), satisfying in one sense Peter's description that Christ went to the spirits in a prison.
According to this view, spirits must long for "the spirit and the body to be united
never again to be divided, that they might receive a fulness of joy" (D&C 138:17).

Secondly, the vision of the redemption of the dead clarifies that "unto the
wicked [Christ] did not go, and among the ungodly and unrepentant who had
defiled themselves while in the flesh, his voice was not raised" (D&C 138:20).
Wondering at the words of Peter, "wherein he said that the Son of God preached
unto the spirits in prison, who sometime were disobedient, when once the longsuffering of God waited in the days of Noah—and how it was possible for him to
preach to those spirits and perform the necessary labor among them in so short a
time," President Smith learned that rather than ministering "in person among the
wicked and the disobedient who had rejected the truth," the Lord instead "organized his forces and appointed messengers, clothed with power and authority, and
commissioned them to go forth and carry the light of the gospel to them that were
in darkness, even to all the spirits of men; and thus was the gospel preached to the
dead" (D&C 138:28–30). In this way, Christ evidenced a "depth of concern . . . so
great that even the generation that rejected Noah was taught," but did so through
the ministry of faithful Saints commissioned to represent him.[47]

The idea that individuals other than Christ ministered among the wicked in
the spirit world was an important addition to Peter's teachings, clarifying commonly held understandings among Latter-day Saints at the time as well as President
Smith's own earlier teachings. For example, in his classic *Jesus the Christ*, published
a mere three years before the vision was received, James E. Talmage wrote, "While
divested of His body Christ ministered among the departed, both in paradise and
in the prison realm where dwelt in a state of durance the spirits of the disobedient." Commenting specifically on Peter's reference to the disobedient of Noah's
day, Talmage surmised, "We are not to assume from Peter's illustrative mention

of the disobedient antediluvians that they alone were included in the blessed opportunities offered through Christ's ministry in the spirit realm; on the contrary,
we conclude in reason and consistency that all whose wickedness in the flesh had
brought their spirits into the prison house were sharers in the possibilities of expiation, repentance, and release."[48] While the vision clearly states that the latter is true,
namely that spirits in prison have the possibility of "expiation, repentance, and release," the knowledge regarding which individuals deliver the message changes because of Joseph F. Smith's vision.

The vision of the redemption of the dead also expands upon a slight Joseph
Smith Translation change in one of the verses from 1 Peter. While the King
James Version of 1 Peter 4:6 reports, "For this cause *was* the gospel preached also
to them that are dead" (emphasis added), Joseph Smith's translation of the same
verse modifies it to read, "Because of this, *is* the gospel preached to them who
are dead" (Joseph Smith Translation, 1 Peter 4:6; emphasis added). The changing of the preaching to the dead from the past "was" to the present "is" receives
explanation in the latter-day vision. It was "made known that our Redeemer
spent his time during his sojourn in the world of spirits," Joseph F. Smith taught,
"instructing and preparing the faithful spirits of the prophets who had testified
of him in the flesh; That they might carry the message of redemption unto all
the dead, unto whom he could not go personally, because of their rebellion and
transgression, that they through the ministration of his servants might also hear
his words" (D&C 138:36–37). Presumably, the teaching by prophets among the
rebellious occurred after the brief time of preparation conducted by the Savior
and continues today. Transitioning to work in the spirit world during his own
time, President Smith wrote, "I beheld that the faithful elders of this dispensation, when they depart from mortal life, continue their labors in the preaching
of the gospel of repentance and redemption, through the sacrifice of the Only
Begotten Son of God, among those who are in darkness and under the bondage
of sin in the great world of the spirits of the dead" (D&C 138:57).

Finally, the vision of the redemption of the dead clarifies the message taught in
the world of spirits. Earlier, Peter merely declared that the teaching would include
"the gospel" (1 Peter 4:6). To that brief summary, President Smith adds, "These were
taught faith in God, repentance from sin, vicarious baptism for the remission of sins,
the gift of the Holy Ghost by the laying on of hands, And all other principles of the
gospel that were necessary for them to know in order to qualify themselves that they
might be judged according to men in the flesh, but live according to God in the spirit"
(D&C 138:33–34). Therefore, the vision held out hope for redemption on conditions of repentance, even among the dead. "The dead who repent will be redeemed,

through obedience to the ordinances of the house of God," President Smith wrote, concluding the vision. "And after they have paid the penalty of their transgressions, and are washed clean, shall receive a reward according to their works, for they are heirs of salvation" (D&C 138:58–59). In this sense, President Smith's vision adds important insight. Not only is the gospel preached to those who "died in their sins, without a knowledge of the truth" (D&C 138:32). It is also preached to those "in transgression, having rejected the prophets" (D&C 138:32), offering both groups a means for redemption. Commenting on these verses, President James E. Faust noted the careful wording of the passages and their doctrinal implications. "Mercy will not rob justice, and the sealing power of faithful parents will claim wayward children only on the condition of their repentance and Christ's Atonement. Repentant wayward children will enjoy salvation and all the blessings that go with it, but exaltation is much more. It must be fully earned. The question as to who will be exalted must be left to the Lord in His mercy."[49] For this reason, in addition to clarifying misinterpretations of the past, President Smith's message, drawn from the words of Peter, stands as a supreme message of hope.

Conclusion

If Peter was pleased at the dedication of the Kirtland Temple, one can only wonder how he must feel about the influence he has had on the Latter-day Saint understanding of salvation for the dead. Anciently, his teachings influenced early Christian thought regarding a postmortal ministry of Christ in the spirit world. In our day, his restoring of priesthood authority paved the way for these teachings on salvation for the dead to be applied. Furthermore, Peter's sublime words led Joseph F. Smith, one of the greatest doctrinal teachers of this dispensation, to ponder and receive additional light. President Harold B. Lee once remarked, "When I want to seek for a more clear definition of doctrinal subjects, I have usually turned to the writings and sermons of President Joseph F. Smith."[50] Interestingly, when President Smith wanted further light regarding the reach of Christ's Atonement beyond the veil, he turned to the writings of Peter, the chief Apostle. These writings, as well as the humble fisherman who authored them, have guided thinking across dispensations, opening the door for soul-satisfying answers about redemption for the human family. Paying tribute to Peter, Elder Jeffrey R. Holland once aptly wrote, "Through the mighty work of the Melchizedek Priesthood that has gone forth to all the world from that day to this, the 'shadow of Peter' is still passing by and healing them, 'every one.'"[51] Because of his teachings on salvation for the dead, Peter also casts a healing shadow through the veil.

Notes

1. Dante Alighieri, *The Inferno*, trans. John Ciardi (New York: New American Library, 1954), canto IV, lines 31–42; emphasis in original. I am grateful for the excellent article on the redemption of the dead by Catherine Thomas, who begins her examination of the topic with a portion of this selection from *The Inferno*. See M. Catherine Thomas, "Visions of Christ in the Spirit World and the Dead Redeemed," in *Sperry Symposium Classics: The New Testament*, ed. Frank F. Judd Jr. and Gaye Strathearn (Provo, UT: Religious Studies Center; Salt Lake City: Deseret Book, 2006), 354.

2. For a thorough examination of Christian thought regarding the fate of the unevangelized dead, see David L. Paulsen, Roger D. Cook, and Kendel J. Christensen, "The Harrowing of Hell: Salvation for the Dead in Early Christianity," *Journal of the Book of Mormon and Other Restoration Scripture* 19, no. 1 (2010): 56–77. Additional essays by Paulsen and his colleagues expand their analysis to baptism for the dead in early Christianity and the application of the doctrines regarding redemption of the dead in the Restoration. See David L. Paulsen and Brock M. Mason, "Baptism for the Dead in Early Christianity," *Journal of the Book of Mormon and Other Restoration Scripture* 19, no. 2 (2010): 22–49; David L. Paulsen, Kendel J. Christensen, and Martin Pulido, "Redeeming the Dead: Tender Mercies, Turning of Hearts, and Restoration of Authority," *Journal of the Book of Mormon and Other Restoration Scripture* 20, no. 1 (2011): 28–51; and David L. Paulsen, Judson Burton, Kendel J. Christensen, and Martin Pulido, "Redemption of the Dead: Continuing Revelation after Joseph Smith," *Journal of the Book of Mormon and Other Restoration Scripture* 20, no. 2 (2011): 52–69. Importantly, not all Christian readings interpret being born of water and Spirit, described in John 3:5, to be baptism and receiving the Holy Ghost, as Latter-day Saint interpretations generally do. For various interpretations of this passage, see Raymond E. Brown, *The Gospel According to John*, vol. 29 of The Anchor Bible Series (New York: Doubleday, 1966), 138–44.

3. Dante Alighieri, *The Inferno*, canto IV, lines 43–63.

4. For differing interpretations of the concept of binding and loosing, see Shon D. Hopkin's chapter in this volume.

5. Elias identified in Matthew 17:3 was the prophet Elijah.

6. D&C 63:21 notes that in addition to witnessing Christ in a transfigured form as he conversed with Moses and Elijah, Peter and his companions beheld the earth itself in "the pattern" of its future transfigured state. Furthermore, Joseph Fielding Smith offered the opinion that "these three men . . . I believe received their endowments on the mount." Joseph Fielding Smith, *Doctrines of Salvation: Sermons and Writings of Joseph Fielding Smith*, comp. Bruce R. McConkie (Salt Lake City: Bookcraft, 1955), 2:165. Bruce R. McConkie added "that it was while on the mount that they received the more sure word of prophecy, it then being revealed to them that they were sealed up unto eternal life." Bruce R. McConkie, *Doctrinal New Testament Commentary* (Salt Lake City: Bookcraft, 1965), 1:400. For these reasons, "so far as the establishment of the kingdom of God is concerned," Robert Matthews wrote, "the bestowal of keys upon the Twelve appears to be the single most important event in the ministry of the Savior between his baptism and the Garden of Gethsemane." Robert J. Matthews, "Tradition, Testimony, Transfiguration,

and Keys," in *Studies in Scripture*, vol. 5: *The Gospels*, ed. Kent P. Jackson and Robert L. Millet (Salt Lake City: Deseret Book, 1986), 305–6.

7. Manuscript History of the Church, 1838–1856, volume C-1 [2 November 1838–31 July 1842], 11 addenda, josephsmithpapers.org/paperSummary/history-1838-1856-volume-c-1-2-november-1838-31-july-1842?locale=eng&p=546. Of the bestowal of keys, Richard Neitzel Holzapfel notes, "The New Testament implicitly reveals that the promise given by Jesus to Peter about 'the keys of the kingdom,' the power to 'bind [and loose] on earth' (Matthew 16:19), was at some point fulfilled (see Matthew 18:18). The fact that Elijah was known to have the power to 'seal' the heavens (see 1 Kings 17:1) and appeared to Peter, James, and John on the mount between the time of the promise (Matthew 16:19) and Jesus' indication that the Twelve had the power to bind (Matthew 18:18) suggests the setting in Matthew 17 as the most likely time when that power was received under the hands of Elijah, who had held the power before." Richard Neitzel Holzapfel, "The Transfiguration," in *The Life and Teachings of Jesus Christ: From the Transfiguration through the Triumphal Entry*, ed. Richard Neitzel Holzapfel and Thomas A. Wayment (Salt Lake City: Deseret Book, 2006), 68 n. 46.

8. Robert J. Matthews, "Tradition, Testimony, Transfiguration, and Keys," 308.

9. Richard L. Anderson, "Peter's Letters: Progression for the Living and the Dead," *Ensign*, October 1991, 7.

10. Thomas, "Visions of Christ in the Spirit World and the Dead Redeemed," 356. Regarding the differing interpretations of 1 Peter, Richard L. Anderson opined, "The problem is both lack of faith and the rigidity of a traditional faith which insists that at death 'man's destiny is sealed, and the period of grace and repentance has ended.'" Anderson, "Peter's Letters," 10, citing Simon J. Kistemaker, *New Testament Commentary: Exposition of the Epistles of Peter and of the Epistle of Jude* (Grand Rapids, MI: Baker Book House, 1987), 143.

11. Martin Luther, in Paul J. Achtemeier, *1 Peter: A Commentary on First Peter*, in the series *Hermeneia—A Critical and Historical Commentary on the Bible* (Minneapolis: Fortress Press, 1996), 252 n. 146.

12. Achtemeier, *1 Peter*, 252. For a detailed examination of these questions, see 254–62.

13. Achtemeier, *1 Peter*, 244–45. For a full, book-length examination of 1 Peter 3:19, see Bo Reicke, *The Disobedient Spirits and Christian Baptism: A Study of 1 Peter 3:19 and Its Context* (Copenhagen, Denmark: Ejnar Munksgaard, 1946).

14. Achtemeier, *1 Peter*, 289.

15. E. M. Blaiklock, *First Peter* (Waco, TX: Word Books, 1977), 87–88.

16. Irenaeus, "Against Heresies," 4.27.2, in *The Ante-Nicene Fathers*, ed. Alexander Roberts and James Donaldson (Grand Rapids, MI: Eerdmans, 1985), 1:499.

17. Origen, "Against Celsus," 2.43, in *The Ante-Nicene Fathers*, 4:448.

18. Anderson, "Peter's Letters," 10. Catherine Thomas summarized, "For Augustine (AD 354–430), Bede (AD 673–735), Aquinas (AD 1225–74), and others, the difficulties in accepting the plain sense of 1 Peter 3:19 were insuperable." Thomas, "Visions of Christ in the Spirit World and the Dead Redeemed," 359.

19. Blaiklock, *First Peter*, 87.

20. John Taylor, in *Journal of Discourses* (London: Latter-day Saints' Book Depot, 1854–86), 17:374–75.

21. For an examination of this passage, see Frank F. Judd Jr. and Terry L. Szink, "John the Beloved in Latter-day Scripture (D&C 7)," in *The Doctrine and Covenants: Revelations in Context*, ed. Andrew H. Hedges, J. Spencer Fluhman, and Alonzo L. Gaskill (Provo, UT: Religious Studies Center; Salt Lake City: Deseret Book, 2008), 90–107.

22. For a discussion of the documentary evidence regarding priesthood restoration, see Michael Hubbard MacKay et al., eds., *The Joseph Smith Papers: Documents, Volume 1: July 1828–June 1831* (Salt Lake City: The Church Historian's Press, 2009), xxxvii–xxxix; Brian Q. Cannon, "Seventy Contemporaneous Priesthood Restoration Documents," in *Opening the Heavens: Accounts of Divine Manifestations, 1820–1844*, ed. John W. Welch with Erick B. Carlson (Provo, UT: Brigham Young University Press; Salt Lake City: Deseret Book, 2005), 215–63.

23. The first four verses of D&C 27, together with portions of verses 5, 14, and 18, were received in August 1830. Joseph Smith indicated that the remaining portion, including the part referring to Peter, was written the following September. See MacKay et al., *Documents, Volume 1*, 165.

24. For Peter's participation in the dedication of the Kirtland Temple, see Lyndon W. Cook, "The Apostle Peter and the Kirtland Temple," *BYU Studies Quarterly* 15, no. 4 (1975): 550–52.

25. Dean C. Jessee, Mark Ashurst-McGee, and Richard L. Jensen, eds., *Journals, Volume 1: 1832–1839*, vol. 1 of the Journals series of *The Joseph Smith Papers*, ed. Dean C. Jessee, Ronald K. Esplin, and Richard Lyman Bushman (Salt Lake City: Church Historian's Press, 2008), 210–11.

26. Truman O. Angell, "His Journal," in *Our Pioneer Heritage*, comp. Kate B. Carter (Salt Lake City: Daughters of Utah Pioneers, 1967), 10:198.

27. Orson F. Whitney, *The Life of Heber C. Kimball* (Salt Lake City: Bookcraft, 1996), 91.

28. John Taylor, in *Journal of Discourses*, 18:326.

29. Robert J. Matthews, *Behold the Messiah* (Salt Lake City: Bookcraft, 1994), 244.

30. Manuscript History of the Church, 1838–1856, volume D-1, 1552.

31. The fragility of President Smith's health is evident in the journal of Apostle James E. Talmage. Describing the opening session of the October 1918 general conference, Talmage wrote, "To the surprise and joy of the people President Joseph F. Smith was present. He made brief address." James E. Talmage, October 4, 1918, James E. Talmage diary, in James Edward Talmage Collection, L. Tom Perry Special Collections, Harold B. Lee Library, Brigham Young University, Provo, UT. On the subsequent days of the conference, Talmage continued to note both President Smith's presence and, when necessary, his absence. See James E. Talmage, October 5–7, 1918. A month later, on November 13, 1918, Talmage recorded, "President Joseph F. Smith completes his 80th year today. We all regret that he is in a very precarious state of ill health. I called at the Beehive House to express my greetings on his birthday, bearing a note of congratulation and hope as I hesitated to even ask to see him." Two days later, Talmage added, "We cannot be oblivious to the fact that the condition of President Joseph F. Smith grows more serious and alarming every day. I have called daily of late and sometimes several times in a day, and each time I see him I realize that he is weaker than before" (November 15, 1918). The next day, he penned, "President Joseph F. Smith has been in a state of intense suffering.

Added to his former ailments, pleurisy is now developing. The brethren of the Council, by spontaneous and individual effort, continue to exercise their faith in his behalf; but we realize that physically he is near the border of the shadows" (November 16, 1918). The next day, Sunday, Talmage interestingly records, "In the evening the members of our family assembled in a brief and informal though I believe impressive and profitable religious service, in which our united prayers were addressed to the Lord in behalf of President Smith. . . . At this little gathering I read the 'Vision of the Redemption of the Dead' given to President Joseph F. Smith October 3rd, and soon to be published to the Church" (November 17, 1918). Two days later, early in the morning of November 19, 1918, President Smith passed away.

32. Richard E. Bennett, "'And I Saw the Hosts of the Dead, Both Small and Great': Joseph F. Smith, World War I, and His Visions of the Dead," *Religious Educator* 2, no. 1 (2001): 106. The specter of war loomed over the very general conference proceedings that overlapped with the vision's receipt. On the same day that he recorded the events of conference, Talmage skeptically commented in his journal on rumors that the German Chancellor was making overtures for peace. He also recounted special mass meetings held in conjunction with conference to encourage the purchase of Liberty Bonds as well as a vote by church membership sustaining the procurement of additional bonds by the church itself. James E. Talmage, diary, October 5–6, 1918.

33. George S. Tate, "'The Great World of the Spirits of the Dead': Death, the Great War, and the 1918 Influenza Pandemic as Context for Doctrine and Covenants 138," *BYU Studies* 46, no. 1 (2007): 33. On October 10, 1918, James E. Talmage reported in his journal, "Yesterday an order was promulgated by the State Board of Health, effective this morning, directing the suspension of all public gatherings owing to the continued spread of the malady known as the Spanish influenza. The Salt Lake Temple was closed at noon today, and instructions were issued that all the Temples be closed and all Church meetings be suspended. This is probably the first time in the history of the Church that such radical and general action has had to be taken." James E. Talmage, diary, October 10, 1918. Following up in his journal six days later, Talmage continued, "The influenza epidemic is claiming an increasing toll of lives all over the country. Surely a desolating scourge and sickness is sweeping the land. The mandate of the State Board of Health regarding public gatherings in Utah is rigidly enforced. House parties, public funerals, except in the open air, and wedding receptions are specifically forbidden. The exigency seems to fully warrant this drastic action." James E. Talmage, October 16, 1918. Talmage's journal documents well the "unusual circumstances" of President Smith's funeral "entailed by the ban placed upon public assemblies." James E. Talmage, November 22, 1918.

34. Tate, "The Great World of the Spirits of the Dead," 10.

35. Joseph F. Smith, "Status of Children in the Resurrection," *Improvement Era*, May 1918, 568.

36. Tate, "The Great World of the Spirits of the Dead," 12.

37. Robert L. Millet, "Latter-day Insights into the Life Beyond," in *The Capstone of Our Religion: Insights into the Doctrine and Covenants*, ed. Robert L. Millet and Larry E. Dahl (Salt Lake City: Bookcraft, 1989), 206.

38. Joseph F. Smith, in Conference Report, October 1918, 2.

39. Millet, "Latter-day Insights into the Life Beyond," 208.

40. Tate, "The Great World of the Spirits of the Dead," 5, 7.

41. On October 31, 1918, Talmage recorded in his journal, "Attended meeting of the First Presidency and the Twelve. Today President Smith, who is still confined to his home by illness, sent to the Brethren the account of a vision through which, as he states, were revealed to him important facts relating to the work of the disembodied Savior in the realm of departed spirits, and of the missionary work in progress on the other side of the veil. By united action the Council of the Twelve, with the Counselors in the First Presidency, and the Presiding Patriarch accepted and endorsed the revelation as the Word of the Lord. President Smith's signed statement will be published in the next issue (December) of the Improvement Era, which is the organ of the Priesthood quorums of the Church." James E. Talmage, diary, October 31, 1918. For a complete analysis of the recording, dissemination, and eventual canonization of President Smith's vision, see Mary Jane Woodger, "From Obscurity to Scripture: Joseph F. Smith's Vision of the Redemption of the Dead," in *You Shall Have My Word: Exploring the Text of the Doctrine and Covenants*, ed. Scott C. Esplin, Richard O. Cowan, and Rachel Cope (Provo, UT: Religious Studies Center; Salt Lake City: Deseret Book, 2012), 234–54.

42. Joseph F. Smith, in *Journal of Discourses* (London: Latter-day Saints' Book Depot, 1854–86), 18:92, 18:274, 19:264, 20:30, 22:43, 23:171–72, 24:78. Addresses by Joseph F. Smith are also common in *Collected Discourse*, a five-volume compilation of addresses by church leaders from 1886 to 1898, but Smith does not appear to make an explicit reference to the passages from 1 Peter 3 and 4 in any of these sermons. An analysis of Conference Reports from 1897 to 1918 also reveals no explicit reference to the particular verses by President Smith.

43. Joseph F. Smith, in *Journal of Discourses*, 18:92.

44. Joseph F. Smith, in *Journal of Discourses*, 20:30.

45. Joseph F. Smith, "Address of President Joseph F. Smith. Delivered at the Funeral Services of Sister Mary A. Freeze," *Young Woman's Journal*, March 1912, 130.

46. Joseph F. Smith, "Address of President Joseph F. Smith," 130.

47. Anderson, "Peter's Letters," 9.

48. James E. Talmage, *Jesus the Christ* (Salt Lake City: Deseret Book, 1982), 624–25.

49. James E. Faust, in Conference Report, April 2003, 68. On another occasion, citing this passage, President Faust further counseled regarding our obligation towards the dead and their chances for salvation, "It is not likely that you will find any horse thieves in your ancestral line. But if you do, it is important that their temple work be done because we believe in repentance for the dead also." Faust, in Conference Report, October 2003, 59. Recently, Elder David A. Bednar clarified some related misunderstandings regarding repentance by wayward children. See David A. Bednar, "Faithful Parents and Wayward Children: Sustaining Hope While Overcoming Misunderstanding," *Ensign*, March 2014, 28–33; see also D&C 76:73–78.

50. Harold B. Lee, in Conference Report, October 1972, 18.

51. Jeffrey R. Holland, *However Long and Hard the Road* (Salt Lake City: Deseret Book, 1985), 98.

17

Reading 2 Peter as a Farewell Text

John W. Welch and Brent J. Schmidt

John W. Welch is the Robert K. Thomas Professor of Law at Brigham Young University and editor-in-chief of *BYU Studies*. Brent J. Schmidt is a member of the Religious Education faculty at Brigham Young University–Idaho.

Saying good-bye is always hard to do, but especially when the person who is leaving is about to die and there has been a deeply spiritual and personal mentoring relationship between the speaker and the associates being left behind. Such words of departure are unforgettable, searing the memories of the listeners as the speaker pours out his or her deathbed wishes, relives sacred, shared experiences, uses in-group terminology to allude to knowledge that only those people have in common, and leaves exhortations and blessing as well as warnings, counsel, and testimony. Out of such moments have come some of the most sublime passages in scripture, and it is the thesis of this paper that the Second Epistle of Peter can be seen as coming out of such a moment.

Final Moments and Unforgettable Expressions

In ancient times, Moses called together his people, who had followed him for forty years of suffering and learning in the wilderness, as he prepared to leave them and as they prepared to cross over Jordan to enter into the promised land. Out of that final discourse came Deuteronomy 31–33, essentially Moses' last will and testament.[1]

When it came time for Socrates to depart from this life, he said good-bye to the students who had devoted their lives to following him, among whom was his protégé, Plato, and out of those words of farewell came one of the Socratic dialogues, the *Phaedo*, reflecting philosophically on the meaning of death, noble deaths, and life after death.

Likewise, in the Book of Mormon, Lehi gathered his sons and daughters, grandsons and granddaughters around him as he was close to death (2 Nephi 1:4; 4:12), and with all of the tenderness of a deeply concerned prophetic patriarch blessed his posterity, collectively and individually, for ages to come. Out of that setting came 2 Nephi 1–4, a foundational text for the next thousand years of Nephite history and beyond. King Benjamin's masterful address came when he thought he was near to death (Mosiah 1:9; 2:28), although he would live for three more years serving as a co-regent with his newly crowned son Mosiah (Mosiah 6:5). But on that coronation day, anticipating his imminent departure, Benjamin left the world Mosiah 2–5, an incomparable sermon of revelation and reality, assembly and atonement, commandment and covenant.[2]

At the end of the Savior's earthly ministry, on the eve of his arrest and the day before his Crucifixion, Jesus presciently gathered Peter and the other Apostles around him, men who had walked and stood by his side for three astounding years. And out of the dark hours of that Last Supper night came the words of love, assurance, warning, commandment, promise, connectivity, and high priestly blessing in John 13–17. While the Apostle John may not have written these words down until years later, those words were emblazoned in perpetuity not only on his mind, but also, as a result of his making those sacred words publicly known, upon the self-awareness of the early Christian church and, in turn, upon the fundamental definition of what it means to be a Christian.

In recent times, Latter-day Saints will remember the farewell speech of Elder Bruce R. McConkie, unveiling the knowledge and convictions that shaped his life and directed his discipleship of Christ and his apostleship to the world.[3] His powerful parting testimony has several things in common with the impassioned farewell speeches found in the scriptures.

Sometimes these farewell speeches are written by the one who is about to die, but other times they are recorded or composed by one of the closest associates and even the *de facto* or appointed successor. In any case, the words handed down in such farewell texts are unforgettable expressions of love and concern for dear associates. They offer a scintillating review of the most important events and lessons of the past. They disclose eternal truths and solemnly convey urgent and wise instructions. The words spoken on such occasions are remembered and recorded not only to promote the agendas of those who promulgate the words of these departing speakers or to enhance the reputation of any immediate successors (who may even remain anonymous), but most of all to honor, highlight, and perpetuate the teachings of incomparable masters upon their departure from this mortal life. Such texts bear a special seal of veracity, coming as they do when the speaker is facing death and contemplating his or her return to face God. They speak vividly to readers, even centuries later, who can feel in such texts the spirit in which they were delivered, almost as if they were actually there.

Typical Elements in Ancient Farewell Speeches

In approaching 2 Peter as a farewell text, the work of William Kurz is most helpful.[4] This scholar has analyzed twenty-two farewell speeches in the Bible and in classical Greek and Roman literature, identifying twenty elements that appear in these addresses. Farewell speeches rarely include most, let alone all, of these elements, and some features are more clearly present than others. Kurz's twelve biblical texts average about nine elements each, with a high of thirteen (with two possibly implied) and a low of one (with two implied); his ten classical texts average about four elements each, with a high of eleven and a low of one (with three implied).[5] Thus farewell speeches in Israelite or Jewish literature contain more such elements than speeches in Greek and Roman literature. Moreover, in the Greco-Roman literary tradition the dying speaker was usually a philosopher or statesman, whose speeches "are concerned with suicide, the meaning of death, questions about noble deaths, and life after death," whereas this preoccupation with death and dying is absent in the biblical speeches, where the speaker is a man of God and his speech typically focuses on "God's plan, people and covenant, or on theodicy and theological interpretations of history."[6]

Although Kurz did not analyze 2 Peter as one of his twenty-two farewell texts,[7] the list of elements that he has compiled can be applied very naturally to this biblical text, as our study hopes to demonstrate. Here are the twenty characteristics identified by Kurz as constituent elements of typical farewell texts, which we will then compare, side by side, with 2 Peter:

1. *Summons*: The speaker calls together or addresses his successors and followers so they can receive his last instructions.

2. *Invoking own mission as an example*: A description of the speaker's life and calling is followed by a commandment to do as he has done.

3. *Declaration of innocence and discharge of duty*: The speaker declares that he has done his best and fulfilled his obligations. He has accomplished what he intended to do and cannot be held liable for his people's actions in the future.

4. *Reference to impending death*: The announcement of the speaker's impending death does not reveal a fear of death. Rather, the speaker shows courage and an acceptance of his fate. Sometimes he commends his soul to the gods.

5. *Exhortations*: The listeners are encouraged to remember the teachings that the speaker has given before and to obey the commands that he will give during his address. The people are also counseled to have courage during times of trial or difficulty. Exhortations help to solidify the lessons of the past as well as provide comfort for the future.

6. *Warnings and final injunctions*: Warnings about disobedience and its consequences are given. There may also be warnings concerning false teachers who will try to lead the people astray. Commandments or final orders that are designed to aid the people accompany these warnings.

7. *Blessings*: Blessings are usually given in conjunction with the warnings and final orders.

8. *Farewell gestures*: The speaker may make some gesture to bid farewell, but only one of the twelve biblical addresses cited by Kurz mentions a farewell gesture. That instance occurs when Paul kneels down and prays with the disciples at the end of his speech, after which the disciples fall on his neck and kiss him (Acts 20:36–38).

9. *Specific immediate tasks for successors*: Final orders may give specific responsibilities to successors. Jesus, for example, gave final charges to the Apostles at the Last Supper (Luke 22:25–38), and David commanded Solomon to take vengeance on Joab and Shimei (1 Kings 2:5–6, 8–9).

10. *A theological review of history*: A theological review of the past is given, often telling everything from the beginning, emphasizing the guidance, protection, and chastisement of God. Moses, for example, recounted the history of Israel and acknowledged God's hand in its development in Deuteronomy 32.

11. *Revelation of future events*: Often the speaker is aware of future events that could threaten his reputation. Jesus, for instance, predicted both Judas's betrayal and Peter's denial (Luke 22:21, 34).

12. *Promises*: Biblical and Jewish farewell speeches typically promise the prospect of eternal glory. Thus both Jesus (Luke 22) and Mattathias (1 Maccabees 2) promised glory to their followers after teaching them about service, but this element does not appear in the Greco-Roman tradition.

13. *Appoints or refers to a successor*: The appointment of a successor is a very common feature of farewell speeches in the biblical tradition, and this designation

serves to legitimize the authority of the new leader. David's farewell address endorsed Solomon's leadership (1 Kings 2:1–4).

14. *Bewailing the loss*: Often the account describes the mourning of those who loved the speaker.

15. *Future degeneration is to come*: Predictions concerning future heresies and disobedience appear in farewell speeches in the biblical tradition. Such predictions transfer responsibility for adverse developments in the future from the speaker to the coming generations. Moses, for example, declared that Israel would reject the Lord and turn to idolatry.

16. *Covenant renewal (sacrifices)*: The listeners are enjoined to renew their covenant with God. Thus, David's instructions to Solomon ensured the fulfillment of David's covenant with God, and Jesus' actions at the Last Supper signaled a new covenant using bread and wine. The covenant element is unique to the biblical tradition, and in Old Testament times this would generally be accompanied by the making of sacrifices.

17. *Providing for those who will survive*: Since the followers of the aged leader will require guidance and comfort after his death, instructions are given for providing such help. Jesus' command that Peter strengthen the brethren is an example of this element.

18. *Final consolations to the inner circle*: An attempt to comfort the speaker's closest associates is often made. Jesus did this at the Last Supper when he and his most beloved followers were alone.

19. *Didactic speech*: A review of certain principles may be used to help the followers remember what they should do.

20. *Facing death*: This element relates to the leader's approach to death itself. Kurz finds this element expressly present only in the *Phaedo* and by implication in Josephus.

Second Peter as a Farewell Text

The Second Epistle of Peter can well be seen as such a farewell text. Indeed, 2 Peter exemplifies this literary form quite remarkably and informatively. Attentive readers readily notice that 2 Peter skips around from one subject to another. In chapter 1, it seems quite personal and intimate, but in chapter 2, its mood becomes sterner and less personal. The letter as a whole sets out to accomplish several things: it shifts from one objective, such as teaching and promising, to other purposes, such as warning and stigmatizing. It seems to lack a single thesis, and its points surface almost spontaneously without always being tied logically to the subjects that precede or follow them. Thus readers may well wonder what kind of situation holds this composition together. But of all the possible genres that might be used to situate and interpret this epistle, the farewell speech genre can best explain the presence of all of these disparate religious elements and literary features. Indeed, on such an occasion when a speaker or writer is confronting impending death, dear friends come to mind, as do shared experiences, common values, idiosyncratic vocabulary, and concerns about what may happen in the face of serious challenges looming on the horizon. These are the elements that constitute the content of 2 Peter, and analyzing this text through this lens of literary criticism helps readers appreciate the pressing concerns, the sincere messages, and the inspiring coherence of this text, as the following discussion explicates.

1. *Summons*: Simon Peter addresses his dear friends and speaks inclusively to all of them, who together "with *us*" and through "*our* Saviour Jesus Christ" have together obtained the "same" (*isotimon*, a word strongly indicating equality, not just similarity) precious faith as have the Apostles, through their collective righteousness (1:1). He speaks of the divine power that has been given "unto *us*" bestowing upon everyone in the group "all things" that will lead them to life eternal and to godly fulfillment of service to God. He reaches out and calls to his bosom all those in this group who have a testimony of Christ, who has "called" them to "glory and virtue" (1:3). These, his most cherished friends, with whom he expects to share celestial glory in the heavenly assembly, are the ones he addresses and summons to hear his words as he pours out his heart to them. Because these individuals are equal with Peter, they can be his successors and mitigate the succession problem that could arise at his death. Peter extends to his successors the greatest and most precious promises that he previously received as leader of the church (1:4).

2. *Invoking own mission as an example*: Peter's thoughts soon turn to the purposes that he himself has tried to accomplish and to the mission that he hopes he has accomplished. He wants his people to remember the things he has taught them (1:12–13). He implores them to remember that, when he spoke to them, he properly did not follow "cunningly devised fables" or sophistic myths, but rather he and his companions set a solid example in making known to them "the power and coming of our lord Jesus Christ" and that he as an eyewitness fulfilled his mission, testifying of the Lord's majesty (1:16). This was his all-consuming mission, as he had been commissioned by the Lord himself (Matthew 28:19; Luke 24:48; John 21:15–17; Acts 1:8).

3. *Declaration of innocence and discharge of duty*: Just as quickly as he invokes his own life as an example, Peter humbly reflects his own concerns and perhaps even some lingering insecurities, wanting to be sure that the people know that he

was innocent before them and had done everything possible to discharge his obligations and duties towards them. In his opening statement, Peter identified himself as a servant or slave (the Greek here is *doulos*, the usual word in the Roman empire for slave) as well as an Apostle, or "one sent out" (as the Greek word *apostolos* comes from the two words *apo* and *stellō*, to "send out"). In antiquity good slaves were proverbially loyal, especially when they were sent out specifically to accomplish something for their master. If ancient slaves excelled in serving their masters well, they could be freed, which in a gospel context might correspond to the freedom from spiritual death extended by Peter to all who follow the Lord Jesus Christ. Peter overtly and forthrightly declares, "I will not be negligent" but instead will certainly always remind the people of the guiding gospel principles that undergird and fully pervade the life of righteousness (1:12). His innocence is assured in that he has not promoted any false or sophistic teaching (1:16), the "sophists" typically advancing themselves and their supposed learning for money, prestige, and intellectual glory. Obviously, Peter had not promoted any such "error of the wicked" (3:17) but instead the true "knowledge of our Lord and Saviour" (3:18; also 1:5) and true "wisdom" (3:15).

4. *Reference to impending death*: Throughout this letter, Peter's concerns are amplified because he knows, by revelation, that his death is imminent: "Knowing (*eidōs*) that shortly I must put off this my tabernacle, even as our Lord Jesus Christ hath shewed (*edēlōsen*) me" (1:14). As a seer, Peter has seen that his death is at hand. It has been revealed and made plainly evident (*dēlos*) to him, the Greek words here indicating that he has clearly seen what is coming. Thus he turns to teaching, exhorting, and making provision for those who will survive him, assuring them that he will "endeavor . . . after my decease" to leave behind a legacy and, God willing, perhaps even his continued spiritual watchfulness over them, so that they will be able to recall all that he has taught them after his departure and decease (1:15).

5. *Exhortations*: Throughout his missive, Peter's tone is exhortative, often using imperatives, not only inviting but stressing the urgency of following the plan of salvation: "*Add* to your faith" (1:5), "*give diligence* to" (1:10), "*take heed*" (1:19), "*be diligent*" (3:14), "*account* long suffering as salvation" (3:15), "*beware*" (3:17), and "*grow*" (3:18; emphases added). All of these verbs are imperative plurals. Famously, he exhorted them to "add to your faith virtue; and to virtue knowledge; and to knowledge temperance; and to temperance patience; and to patience godliness; and to godliness brotherly kindness; and to brotherly kindness charity" (1:5–7). Filled with charity himself, Peter hoped that these spiritual qualities would "abound" or, translated otherwise, would have an overarching presence (*hyparchonta*, 1:8) in the lives of his adherents.

6. *Warnings and final injunctions*: Knowing of these short-term and long-term predictions, Peter cannot take his leave without issuing stern warnings. He warns them of "the corruption that is in the world through lust" (1:4), of the fact that God's judgment from long ago has not lost its force and effect and "slumbereth not" (2:3), and also that while God knows how to deliver the godly out of temptations, he reserves "the unjust unto the day of judgment to be punished" (2:9). An undercurrent of warning runs throughout much of this text, clear to the end when those who wrest the scriptures are warned that they do this "unto their own destruction" (3:16). And with these perilous times ahead, a few final instructions and injunctions are also in order. Particularly, Peter enjoins the people, "Be mindful of the words which were spoken before by the holy prophets, and of the commandments of us the apostles of the Lord and Savior" (3:2), and "beware lest ye also being led away with the error of the wicked, fall from your own steadfastness" (3:17). Having extra patience is therefore necessary in waiting on the coming of the Lord, for "one day is with the Lord as a thousand years [is to mankind]" (3:8).

7. *Blessings*: Overwhelmed with the spirit of generosity at such a time, Peter begins by pronouncing an abundant blessing upon his people: "Grace and peace be multiplied unto you through the knowledge of God, and of Jesus our Lord" (1:2).

8. *Farewell gestures*: As one might well expect, there would be little role for physical gestures, embraces, or ritual actions in a farewell message that is being sent to people who were not in the immediate presence of the speaker. Nevertheless, one might wonder, when Peter tells his people to be "without spot and blameless" (3:14), if he might have some ritual context in mind, for sacrificial lambs had to be "without spot" (see, for example, Numbers 28:3, 9, 11; 29:17, 26) and without "blemish" (see, for example, Numbers 6:14; 29:2, 8, 13, 20). In at least some ancient farewell addresses, the speaker shook off his garments before the people as a testimony of his innocence and as evidence that he had discharged his duty, so that he could be found without spot and stand blameless before God at the last day.

9. *Specific immediate tasks for successors*: As many farewell discourses draw to a close, their speakers often mention specific tasks that they want to be sure that their followers will not overlook. In Peter's case, he mentions in closing the immediate tasks of remembering "what manner of persons ye ought to be in all holy conversations and godliness, looking and preparing for and hastening under the coming day of God" (3:11–12), of waiting upon the Lord for salvation with long-suffering and patience (3:15), of not "being led away with the error of the wicked"

(3:17), but rather to "grow in grace, and in the knowledge of our Lord and Saviour Jesus Christ" (3:18).

10. *A theological review of history*: Good teachers always draw on personal experiences and ground their conclusions in reliable lessons learned from the past, and on several occasions Peter casts his mind back on his own personal experiences and also the salvation history of Israel. All of these past experiences have theological importance in binding God to mankind and heaven to earth. Peter speaks of the priesthood, which appears to be the idea behind the "divine power" (*theias dynameōs*) unto life and godliness that he says had been given to him and others in this community (1:3). He testified of the voice of God "which came from heaven" and which he heard "when we were with him in the holy mount" (1:18). As he himself had received revelation, so also there had come prophecy "in old time," and "not by the will of man, but holy men of God spake as they were moved by the Holy Ghost" (1:21). But instantly, his mind turns to the fact that "there were false prophets also among the people" in past times (2:1), and that just as surely as in the premortal world "God spared not the angels that sinned, but cast them down to hell" (2:4; see Genesis 6:1–4; 1 Enoch 6–10). He remembered that at the time of the Flood God "saved Noah" (2:5, a theme to which he will return to in 3:6; see Genesis 8:1–19), and in Abraham's day he did not spare the cities of Sodom and Gomorrah (2:6). However, he "rescued Lot," who was bedeviled by the immoral behavior of the lawless (2:7; see Genesis 19:15–22), so still God knows how to spare the righteous and punish the wicked. Using the story of Balaam, who was reprimanded by his own beast of burden (2:15–16; Numbers 22:30), listeners were reminded to not forsake the right way and go astray. Peter extracted these highlights from Old Testament history to help his readers understand God's role in history and to apply gospel principles in their lives. From his reflection on the past, Peter taught principles of humility, repentance, listening to the prophets to avoid destruction, and standing in holy places as elements of righteous living.

11. *Revelation of future events:* Reflecting his thought on the broad sweep of history and truth from the beginning to the end, Peter's attention shifts from the past to making predictions of things to come. He prophesies that "there shall be false teachers among you," and describes them negatively in considerable detail (2:1–3; 2:12–14). These evil spokesmen, Peter says, will bring in heresies (2:1). He predicts that "these, as natural brute beasts, shall be taken and destroyed" (2:12). He also prophesies that "there shall come in the last days scoffers, looking after their own lusts" (3:3) and refuting the promise of the Lord's coming Christ (3:4). He foretells that fire is held in reserve "against the day of judgment and perdition of ungodly men" (3:7).

12. *Promises*: Promises are explicitly given in this parting moment, even "exceeding great and precious promises" (1:4), namely that "if these things be in you, and abound ... ye shall neither be useless [*argous*] or unfruitful" (1:8). Other promises are given: Peter promises his audience that "if you do these things, ye shall never fall" (1:10), and that "an entrance [into the everlasting kingdom of heaven] shall be ministered unto you abundantly" (1:11). Like a light that shines in a dark place, "the day star [shall] arise in your hearts" (1:19). The Lord shall "deliver the godly from temptation" (2:9). Thus people should not doubt "the promise of his coming" (3:4), for "the Lord is not slack concerning his promises and coming" (3:9, Joseph Smith Translation). And indeed, "if we shall endure, we shall be kept according to his promise" (3:13, Joseph Smith Translation), which he has given, that there will be a "new heaven and an earth new" (3:13, quoting Isaiah 65:17; 66:22).

13. *Appoints or refers to a successor*: Although no specific designation of a successor by Peter is found in 2 Peter, he does speak very approvingly of "our beloved brother Paul" (3:14), singling him out in particular. Peter endorses the "wisdom given unto him," that can be found in what Paul has already written to members of the church, as he has spoken in "all his epistles ... of these things" (3:15–16). Paul, having arrived in Rome (Acts 28:16), may have worked there with Peter or with people who had been closest to Peter near his death in Rome.

14. *Bewailing the loss:* There is no sense of sorrow, lamenting, or bewailing the impending death of Peter. Whether or not the people were saddened on this occasion, as they most surely soon would be, Peter shows no remorse or regrets about his decision to return voluntarily to Rome to die. He knew that if he did not submit to the men who opposed him, they would undoubtedly turn on Peter's followers and execute them. Peter, like Jesus and many of the Apostles, went like a lamb to the slaughter, willingly, and without opening his mouth but going forward in faith. Of Kurz's list of twenty characteristics of a farewell speech, this is the one most obviously missing in 2 Peter, but this is understandable because this letter is not a narrative account reporting what was said and what happened just before Peter's death and how the people reacted to it.

15. *Future degeneration is to come*: These warnings, in the mind of the one facing death, became all the more severe looking into the future. Things may be bad at the moment, but Peter is concerned that they may only degenerate and get even worse for the next generation. Peter speaks of this degeneration as he explains that the false teachers will go from bad to worse, becoming not only false and wrong, but presumptuous, self-willed, blasphemers, like "natural brute beasts," indulgent, deceivers, adulterers, beguilers, and covetous. They are catastrophically doomed

"cursed children" (2:10–14). Of them it is said, "It had been better for them not to have known the way of righteousness" and then to have turned against it (2:21).

16. *Covenant renewal (sacrifices)*: Although other farewell speakers will take time at the end of their speech to actually renew covenants with their people, Peter did not enjoy that luxury, at least not within the ambit of this letter. Nevertheless, it seems that Peter was still strengthened by his knowledge of God's covenants, for he speaks often of "remembrance," using either the word *hupomnēsei* or *mnēmēn* (1:12, 13, 15, 3:1, 2). This is reminiscent of the words Paul used in telling the Corinthians to "remember" (*memnēsthe*; 1 Corinthians 11:2) to follow him and the ordinances, and to partake of the sacramental bread and wine in "remembrance" (*anamnēsin*; 11:24–25). Perhaps the allusion to Noah being saved (2:5) refers to the covenant between God and Noah and consequently with all people, and the rescue of Lot (2:7) may have been remembered because it had to do with the covenant God made with Abraham regarding Sodom and Gomorrah (Genesis 18:32; 19:21). Through Peter's statements to "be mindful of the commandment" (3:2) and that "all things continue as they were from the beginning of the creation" (3:4), his followers were effectively reminded to keep their covenants. The term "grace" (*charis*), mentioned in Peter's final verse (3:18), also has covenantal overtones, because it and its Greek cognates generally refer to a reciprocal, albeit asymmetrical, covenant relationship between two willing parties bound to each other.[8]

17. *Providing for those who will survive*: Peter makes no worldly provisions in this epistle for his successors, but he cares fully for their spiritual well-being. Peter made this statement to his readers so that "all should come to repentance" because God "is not willing that any should perish" (3:9). Peter also gives renewed assurances that nothing has changed regarding the promises and covenants of the Lord, that he will come even "as a thief in the night" (3:10; quoting Paul's phrase in 1 Thessalonians 5:2), and, ultimately, that God will provide according to his promise "new heavens and a new earth, wherein dwelleth righteousness" (3:13).

18. *Final consolations to the inner circle*: Likewise, Peter's consolation to his children in the gospel comes in terms of testimonies of reassurance: "We have also a more sure word of prophecy" (1:19; compare D&C 131:5); he calls them his "dearly beloved" (3:1, 14, 17) and assures them that all will be well if "all should come to repentance" (3:9) and that with diligence and endurance "ye may be found of him in peace" (3:14). Christ's Atonement brings about salvation from physical and spiritual death and victory over all one's enemies. This salvation occurs because of the Atonement, which makes eternal life and exaltation possible. Peter testifies that in "the longsuffering of our Lord is salvation" (3:14–15).

Through the gift of the Savior's Atonement, Peter's associates are able to receive consolation at his passing.

19. *Didactic speech*: The exhortations in 2 Peter are given with clear didactic explanations and practical instructions. Peter, always a teacher but now giving his final message, proclaims and expounds the principles of the gospel. He does this in several ways. He shows the progression that builds from faith to virtue, to knowledge, to temperance, to patience, to godliness, to brotherly kindness, and to charity (1:5–7). He explains how Jesus received his majesty, "for he received from God the Father honor and glory, when there came such a voice to him from the excellent glory, 'This is my beloved Son, in whom I am well pleased'" (1:16–17).[9] He teaches the primary principle "that no prophecy of the scripture is of any private interpretation" (1:20, clarified in the Joseph Smith Translation to read "no prophecy of the scriptures is given of any private will of man"). Peter punctuates his warning with the wise adage that "by whom a man is overcome, of the same is he brought into bondage" (2:19). He explicates this point, declaring that it would have been better for rebellious apostates had they not "known the way of righteousness, then, after they had known it, to turn from the holy commandment delivered unto them" (2:21). He buttresses his teaching with the axiom from Proverbs 26:11 that "the dog has turned to his own vomit again; and the sow that was washed to her wallowing in the mire" (2:22). Before concluding, he offers good learning advice when confronted with some things that are "hard to be understood" or that seem counterintuitive to those who are "unlearned and unstable" or untaught or not well grounded; his subjects are counseled not to twist or distort or "wrest" the teachings of inspired leaders (3:16).

20. *Facing death*: Approaching death, Peter does not become sorrowful or morose, as Greek and Roman farewell speakers often did. Instead, he speaks not of death but of the "divine power" that gives "unto us all things that pertain unto life" (1:3). Projecting his faith in the life to come, Peter looks to the day when his people "may be found" by God to be "without spot, and blameless" (3:14), in the presence of his glory in the world to come.[10]

Concluding Observations

First, it seems clear that 2 Peter fits the mold of a farewell speech or text. Seen at the molecular level, nineteen of the individual elements of a classic farewell speech are significantly detectable in 2 Peter, which is considerably stronger than any other instance of this genre previously identified. Moreover, seen at the thematic level, all of the subjects raised sequentially in 2 Peter come into sharper focus and appreciation as one sees these nineteen elements playing their various roles in every section of the text. As a full complement of bright threads woven into the fabric of this text, these correlations corroborate the strength and validity of this reading. Section by section, 2 Peter personally speaks and gives promises to those who are prepared to advance (Kurz, nos. 1, 2, 12; see 2 Peter 1:1–4), didactically articulates and exhorts the Saints to build on the foundations of righteousness (nos. 5, 12, 19; see 2 Peter 1:5–9), and in turn introduces the ultimate goal of true Christians, namely to know with assurance of one's calling and election (nos. 5, 19; see 2 Peter 1:10–11). Peter then bears his personal and covenantal witness, even as he prepares to die (nos. 2, 4, 16, 20; see 2 Peter 1:12–15), that true knowledge has been and is revealed by the voice of God (nos. 2, 3, 10, 19; see 2 Peter 1:16–21). He then warns his readers that false teachers will intrude among them (no. 6; see 2 Peter 2:1–3a), but explains why God willingly delays the looming punishment (no. 6, 10, 11; see 2 Peter 2:3b–9). In considerable detail, he reveals and historically documents the telltale sins and signs of false teachers, and he prophesies about the doom that will befall them (nos. 10, 11, 15, 19; see 2 Peter 2:10–22). Comforting and reassuring his beloved followers, he exhorts them to remember their testimonies and commitments (nos. 5, 6, 16; see 2 Peter 3:1–2) and helps them to understand that just as God willingly delays the punishment of the wicked, he also willingly delays the Second Coming (nos. 11, 17; see 2 Peter 3:3–9). Ending faithfully and positively, he encourages them to prepare for the coming day of the Lord (nos. 9, 17; see 2 Peter 3:10–13), to be patient and understanding, following the wisdom of Paul (nos. 5, 6, 8, 13, 17, 20; see 2 Peter 3:14–16), and finally, assured that they have been taught, he assigns them to be on guard and increase their spirituality (nos. 3, 9; see 2 Peter 3:17–18). Thus not only does the content of this letter clearly communicate important gospel truths, but also these points are conveyed with literary elegance, rhetorical effect, and spiritual power, which one feels by reading this poignant epistle through Peter's eyes, as he sees beyond the veil of mortality and into the realm of God's "glory, both now and for ever" (3:18).

Second, this analysis of 2 Peter as a farewell speech offers a stronger way to read this text than other options that have been proposed. For example, in 1983 (two years before Kurz articulated the profile of the farewell speech), Richard Bauckham proposed that 2 Peter should be seen as belonging to the late Hellenistic genre of testamentary literature.[11] However, more recent commentators on 2 Peter have concluded that 2 Peter fits only loosely into the testamentary category, having little in common with works such as the Testaments of the Twelve Patriarchs or the Testament of Job.[12] As Peter Davids concludes, "Bauckham has not shown that it *obviously* would have been read [as testamentary literature] by *most* readers."[13] Likewise, considering 2 Peter simply to be an "epistle"[14] is not very satisfying, because epistles in antiquity had many uses and were directed to very diverse audiences for different purposes, and thus this designation has not proven to help much in appreciating or interpreting 2 Peter's notable teachings. Certainly, 2 Peter has little in common with other ancient epistles that were commonly exchanged in antiquity between friends (Atticus and Cicero), government leaders (Pliny and Trajan), church officials (Augustine or Jerome and their many associates), or congregations (the Apostle Paul) that were often transmitted around the Mediterranean by networks of loyal slaves. As Davids observes, 2 Peter clearly starts out as a letter, but "after the greeting there are no more letter characteristics." It lacks a thanksgiving section, and in the conclusion "there are no personal greetings or references to the letter carrier. ... Thus, while it was composed to be sent as a letter, the work is not at its core a letter, but more a sermon or speech within a letter structure."[15]

Instead, 2 Peter appears to follow the literary form of a speech. Not only does it contain "deliberative rhetoric with imbedded sections of judicial (1:16–2:10a; 3:1–13) and epideictic rhetoric (2:10b–22),"[16] but it follows the typical elements of a classical speech—namely, after the introductory salutation (which is not normally part of a speech), there is an *exordium* (introductory statement of purpose and call for attention, 1:3–15), a *probatio* (defense of the thesis, 1:16–3:13), which includes a *digressio* (excursus, 2:10b–22) and a *transitio* (resumption after the digression, 3:1–2), concluding with a *peroratio* (recapitulation and final wishes, 3:14–18).[17] Thus behind 2 Peter there indeed stands a speech of some sort, and as the foregoing analysis has shown, that speech was more than just a regular speech. It was a farewell speech,[18] and "there is no reason to suppose that a first century reader would recognize 2 Peter as different in genre from the type of farewell speech found in Acts."[19]

Third, closely related to the question of literary genre is the query "Does this literary analysis shed any light on the perplexing question of the authorship of 2 Peter?" People have puzzled for centuries over the question of the authorship of this book in the New Testament, and scholarship and historical tools have been unable to resolve these issues to everyone's satisfaction.[20] "Both sides on the issue of authorship face problems that are difficult to explain."[21] "There is in the end no conclusive way to respond"[22] to these issues. One cannot prove that Peter did write it, nor that he did not. While this is not the place to discuss the critical arguments concerning the authorship of 2 Peter, seeing it as a farewell speech may make a valuable contribution to this investigation. Seeing 2 Peter this way adds weight to the circumstantial case in favor of its authenticity as Peter's final communication, in several ways:

Literarily, innate elements of the farewell genre make it an unlikely genre to be used by a forger. A forger is unlikely to have sensed from ordinary experience, let alone from the usual awareness of ancient literature, the full profile of farewell speeches manifested in 2 Peter.

Intuitively, if one wanted to write a pious pseudonymous text, which was done often enough in the ancient world, an ordinary letter or a routine narrative would be much safer to pen than a near-death farewell message. Moreover, one might think that a forger would have designed the text to be more like a familiar farewell speech of Socrates or Moses, thus capitalizing on the esteem that would come by association with some other famous person, but this was not done. In addition, a forger intentionally mimicking the farewell speech genre might well have given a more detailed drama of the impending death, but that also was not done.

Socially, parting testimonies were poignant group experiences, making it hard to imagine that such a text could be fabricated. People who were there or knew of the circumstances and who were bonded together in the cause of carrying forward the mission of the Master would have been in a position to repudiate such a text.

Practically, just as Socrates did not write his farewell speech but was fortunate to have Plato, his successor, write down the essence, if not the verbatim speech given by Socrates before he drank the hemlock, Peter too would have been unlikely to sit down at such a time and pen a letter to his friends. The use of a scribe would have been normally expected.

Compositionally, writing a whole letter from scratch in such a moment would normally be too much to expect, and this may explain why Peter drew on the words of Jude on this occasion, as most scholars agree 2 Peter does.[23] Perhaps Peter had even used Jude before in speaking to his people, and thus the incorporation of these already familiar words into his farewell speech would have seemed perfectly appropriate to them.

Personally, since Peter was present at the Last Supper and heard Jesus give his words of farewell before leaving for Gethsemane and Golgotha, and since Peter typically tried to follow his Master's example in as many ways as he could, Peter may well have wanted to follow Jesus' example in this way too, bidding farewell to his followers when the time came time for him to go back into Rome, according to the early Christian tradition, also to be crucified.[24]

In any event, for many reasons, 2 Peter rings true. At such a time, Peter would have wanted, if at all possible, to speak personally and sincerely to all of his followers, seen and unseen, as he said good-bye one last time. He would have been grateful, as we are today, for the scribe who took down Peter's words, as best he could, to memorialize the final message of this indomitable apostolic leader.

Finally, from a distinctively Latter-day Saint point of view, seeing 2 Peter as a farewell text strikes a common chord in the life and ministry of the Prophet Joseph Smith. He was deeply impressed by this letter. Three times in one week in 1843, the Prophet Joseph spoke about the Second Epistle of Peter on Sunday, May 14, in Yelrome, Hancock County; on Wednesday, May 17, in Ramus, Illinois; and on Sunday, May 21, in Nauvoo.[25] During that week, on May 17, the Prophet Joseph said that "Peter penned the most sublime language of any of the apostles,"[26] making it clear that he was thinking of 2 Peter when he made this comment. *A propos* the farewell topic of the present study, it may well be that Joseph's sensitivity to the sublime nature of 2 Peter can be attributed to the fact that Peter was facing death as he fashioned these words, just as Joseph Smith knew, even in 1843, that his time was getting short. As he drew closer to the looming martyrdom, his speeches—in particular his orations about the mission and sealing power of Elijah (August 27, 1843; January 21 and March 10, 1844),[27] and his speeches at the funerals of Elias Higbee (August 13, 1843, quoting 2 Peter 3:10–11),[28] James Adams (October 9, 1843),[29] and King Follett (April 7, 1844),[30] and his discourses about the Resurrection, eternal judgment, and eternal glories (April 6 and June 16, 1844)[31]—focused, like Peter, on such themes as the divine nature, the purpose of existence, facing and overcoming death, the coming of the day of reckoning as a thief in the night, warnings, salvation for the dead, covenants, the sealing power, and eternal life. In the face of death and hell, we find sublimely refined statements and elevated doctrines of eternal life that reach, in the final words of both Peter and of Joseph Smith, beyond this mortal sphere.

Notes

1. See also the farewells of Joshua (Joshua 23–24), of David (1 Kings 2:1–10; 1 Chronicles 28–29), and of Samuel (1 Samuel 12:1–25).

2. For a full discussion, see John W. Welch and Daryl R. Hague, "Benjamin's Sermon as a Traditional Ancient Farewell Address," in *King Benjamin's Speech: "That Ye May Learn Wisdom,"* ed. John W. Welch and Stephen D. Ricks (Provo, UT: FARMS, 1998), 89–118.

3. Bruce R. McConkie, "The Purifying Power of Gethsemane," *Ensign*, May 1985, 9, reprinted in *Ensign*, April 2011, 56–59. In this speech, several elements of the farewell speech genre can be found: a declaration of having discharged his duty, a reference to impending death, a theological review of the past, exhortations, didactic encouragement,

pronouncing of blessings, and frequent reference to the atoning and covenantal sacrifice of the Savior.

4. William S. Kurz, "Luke 22:14–38 and Greco-Roman Biblical Farewell Addresses," *Journal of Biblical Literature* 104 (1985): 251–68; and William S. Kurz, *Farewell Addresses in the New Testament* (Collegeville, MN: Liturgical Press, 1990).

5. Kurz, "Farewell Addresses," 262–63.

6. Kurz, "Farewell Addresses," 261.

7. Some New Testament scholars, including Kurz, have acknowledged that 2 Peter fits into the ancient farewell speech form generally, although it has not been analyzed in detail as such. Kurz describes 2 Peter not as a "farewell speech," but as a "farewell letter" similar to 2 Timothy, because both of these letters exist outside a narrative context, unlike the farewell speeches of Paul in Acts 20 and the words of Jesus in Luke 22 and John 13–17. See Kurz, *Farewell Addresses in the New Testament*, 9.

8. See generally, James R. Harrison, *Paul's Language of Grace in Its Graeco-Roman Context* (Tübingen: Mohr Siebeck, 2003); Gerald W. Peterman, *Paul's Gift from Philippi: Conventions of Gift-Exchange and Christian Giving* (Cambridge: Cambridge University Press, 1997); Brent J. Schmidt, *Obliging Grace* (forthcoming).

9. Literally, the earliest Greek papyrus of 2 Peter 2:17 and *Codex Vaticanus* read "The son mine, the beloved of me, this is, in whom I am well pleased," but most other Greek manuscripts read the same as Matthew 3:17 and 17:5.

10. The benediction at the end of Jude 1:24–25, which was known to Peter as well as to his audience, expresses a similar wish: to be found without fault or blameless (*amōmous*, the same word as in 2 Peter 3:14), which wish in Jude clearly refers to standing "before the presence of [God's] glory" in the world to come.

11. A pseudepigraphical text is one written by one author but attributed to an earlier illustrious individual. Texts that report lengthy deathbed pronouncements naturally seem to be strong candidates to have been written by someone other than the aged decedent. Richard Bauckham, *Jude, 2 Peter* (Waco, TX: Word Books, 1983). Bauckham makes an argument for 2 Peter fitting into the larger testamentary genre throughout his lengthy and learned commentary. See also Scot McKnight, "2 Peter," in *Eerdmans Commentary on the Bible*, ed. James D. G. Dunn and John W. Rogerson (Grand Rapids, MI: Eerdmans, 2003), 1504.

12. Simon J. Kistemaker, *New Testament Commentary: Exposition of the Epistles of Peter and of the Epistle of Jude* (Grand Rapids, MI: Baker Book House, 1987); Peter H. Davids, *The Letters of 2 Peter and Jude* (Grand Rapids, MI: Eerdmans, 2006). Throughout his commentary Davids argues that Bauckham's model of the testamentary genre does not fit 2 Peter or even the testamentary literature that Bauckham uses as models. For these and other testaments, such as the Testaments of Adam, Abraham, Moses, and Solomon, see James H. Charlesworth, *The Old Testament Pseudepigraph*, 2 vols. (New York: Doubleday, 1983), 1:773–995.

13. Peter Davids, *Letters of 2 Peter and Jude* (Grand Rapids, MI:Eerdmans, 2006), 148.

14. Ancient letters include "records of business transactions, official reports of little people to big government, and above all, private letters between individuals." Howard Clark Kee, *The New Testament in Context: Sources and Documents* (Englewood Cliffs, NJ: Prentice-Hall, 1984), 204. See generally, Hans-Josef Klauck, *Ancient Letters and the*

New Testament: A Guide to Content and Exegesis (Waco, TX: Baylor University Press, 2006). "To some extent, the three species of rhetoric—judicial, deliberative, and epideictic—can also be used to classify epistles, . . . [but there is] nothing close to complete conformity." David E. Aune, ed., *The Blackwell Companion to the New Testament* (Oxford: Wiley-Blackwell, 2010), 173.

15. Davids, *Letters of 2 Peter and Jude*, 143.

16. Davids, *Letters of 2 Peter and Jude*, 143; commenting on Duane Frederick Watson, *Invention, Arrangement, and Style: Rhetorical Criticism of Jude and 2 Peter* (Atlanta: Scholars Press, 1988), 85–86.

17. Davids, *Letters of 2 Peter and Jude*, 143–44, drawing on the works of Neyrey, Bauckham, and Watson.

18. "Thus our conclusion is that Bauckham has shown that 2 Peter is a farewell speech." Davids, *Letters of 2 Peter and Jude*, 148.

19. Davids, *Letters of 2 Peter and Jude*, 143.

20. Commentaries on 2 Peter routinely cover the authorship question, often coming to much this same conclusion. See, for example, Daniel Keating, *Catholic Commentary on Sacred Scripture: First and Second Peter, Jude* (Grand Rapids, MI: Baker Academic, 2011), 127–29; Ruth Anne Reese, *Two Horizons New Testament Commentary: 2 Peter and Jude* (Grand Rapids, MI: Eerdmans, 2007), 115–21; Davids, *Letters of 2 Peter and Jude*, 123–30; Kistemaker, *Epistles of Peter*, 213–19; Pheme Perkins, *First and Second Peter, James, and Jude* (Louisville: John Knox, 1995), 159; see generally, F. Lapham, *Peter: The Myth, the Man and the Writings* (London: T&T Clark, 2003), 149–71.

21. Kistemaker, *Epistles of Peter*, 219.

22. Davids, *Letters of 2 Peter and Jude*, 129. "Both sides on the issue of authorship face problems that are difficult to explain."

23. Most scholars agree that 2 Peter is quoting Jude, because this solution can explain the differences between 2 Peter and Jude in several ways. There is a consistency in 2 Peter's editing of Jude: "He adds the point of view that the teachers he opposes were at one time true members of the community; he removes direct references to *1 Enoch* and the *Testament of Moses*; he also simplifies some of Jude's examples by not taking over all three examples that are in some of Jude's groups of three. Finally he drops the ending of Jude (although aspects show up in his own closing) and instead integrates the last part of Jude before the ending of his own apologetic for the capital Parousia." Davids, *Letters of 2 Peter and Jude*, 142.

24. Peter beseeched his executioners to crucify him "with the head downward," to form a likeness of Adam who "fell (was borne) head downwards," who "cast his first state down upon the earth," and thereby revealed a mystery that things "that are above" must be made "as those below, and those that are behind as those that are before," as the mystery of the cross and of the gospel of Jesus Christ inverts the world's expectations in many ways. Acts of Peter, 37–38, in Montague Rhodes James, *The Apocryphal New Testament* (Oxford: Clarendon, 1969), 334–35.

25. Andrew F. Ehat and Lyndon W. Cook, *The Words of Joseph Smith* (Provo, UT: Religious Studies Center, 1980), 200–209.

26. Discourse and Revelation (D&C 131:5–6), William Clayton Journal, May 17, 1843, Church History Library. See also Ehat and Cook, *Words of Joseph Smith*, 202.

27. Ehat and Cook, *Words of Joseph Smith*, 243–48; 317–18; 327–36.
28. Ehat and Cook, *Words of Joseph Smith*, 238–42.
29. Ehat and Cook, *Words of Joseph Smith*, 252–55.
30. Ehat and Cook, *Words of Joseph Smith*, 340–62.
31. Ehat and Cook, *Words of Joseph Smith*, 339–40; 378–83.

18

Peter in the Apocryphal Tradition

Nicholas J. Frederick

Nicholas J. Frederick is an assistant professor of ancient scripture at Brigham Young University.

Students who take New Testament classes studying Acts through Revelation are often perplexed when they realize fully how much Paul's writings dominate class discussions. They study fourteen of Paul's letters (if one counts the Epistle to the Hebrews as part of the Pauline corpus) and only two of Peter's letters. They wonder why Peter, such an integral figure in the Gospels and the head of the church following Jesus' death, could have left such a minute accounting of his post-Ascension activity, especially compared to Paul, a latecomer to the church. At this point, I attempt to assuage some of their frustration by pointing out that Peter, while he may be somewhat underrepresented or marginalized in the New Testament epistles, is actually a popular figure in the noncanonical literature that arises during the second and third centuries of Christianity. Whereas 1 and 2 Peter represent the sum total of Peter's canonical work (with the possible addition of the Gospel of Mark),[1] there are at least fourteen different noncanonical, or apocryphal, works that either claim Petrine authorship or attribute a major role to Peter.[2]

However, there exists an added degree of difficulty when it comes to reading about Peter (or anyone, for that matter) in the apocryphal literature. Readers can study the letters of Paul and find references to his life or gain insights into his temperament and character. They can gain a sense for who the man was and what he believed. This is not necessarily the case with the characterization of Peter presented in the apocryphal literature. If reading Paul's letters allows us to look through a window and see a possible reflection (however darkly) of truth, encountering the apocryphal Peter is like encountering a trick-or-treater on Halloween. While the young boy or girl may be dressed in the disguise of a vampire or a princess, and while he or she may even adopt a personality that matches the costume, observers know that once the disguise is removed someone completely different will be revealed. The vampire or the princess is simply a means of constructing a façade or a persona that fits the current occasion. Likewise, apocryphal narratives may contain a figure who is called "Peter" and who may even act or speak like "Peter," but this figure is no more the historical Peter than the child dressed as a princess is actually a princess. For this reason, it is unwise to read the apocryphal accounts of Peter hoping to find insights or revelations into *who* Peter was. However, studying apocryphal accounts of Peter can be extremely valuable in helping readers understand *what* he was and *how* he was viewed. While there may be little, if any, historical *truth* to the stories contained in the New Testament Apocrypha, they do preserve traditions popular in the early church. The purpose of this paper is to examine the various depictions of Peter, both positive and negative, that arose in the early Christian apocryphal literature as various Christian groups jockeyed for primacy and legitimacy in the early centuries after Christ in order to further understand the role and function of Peter in the early Christian tradition. Additionally, this paper will also argue that, while the apocryphal stories of Peter are valuable for analyzing the early centuries of the Christian church, they should not be viewed as repositories of "plain and precious truths" that somehow escaped the notice of the "great and abominable church" (1 Nephi 13:26). Latter-day Saint readers hoping to uncover new sources of sound doctrine in the extracanonical stories of Peter will find only disappointment.

As a way of illustrating the thorny nature of the Petrine tradition, consider two documents which bear the title *The Apocalypse of Peter*. One of them is extant in Ethiopic and Greek, while the other was written in Coptic and was found with the Nag Hammadi documents in 1945. The Ethiopic/Greek *Apocalypse of Peter* (mid-second century AD) demonstrates a great concern for the fate of the physical body. Peter, while in the presence of the Savior, views a grand vision of hell, witnessing the fate of those who have passed on from this life. This text stresses the positive and eternal nature of the physical body by envisioning a resurrection where the flesh literally returns from the beasts who have eaten it:

On the day of the decision of the judgment of God, all the children of men from the east unto the west shall be gathered before my Father who ever liveth, and he will command *hell* to open its bars of steel and to *give up* all *that is in it*. And the beasts and the fowls shall he command to give back all flesh that they have devoured, since he desires that men should appear (again); for nothing perishes for God, and nothing is impossible with him, since all days are his. (*Apoc. Peter* 4; *NTA* 2:627)[3]

The other text, the *Coptic Apocalypse of Peter* (third century AD) presents an opposite view of the physical body. In this text, Peter and Jesus discuss the true nature of reality and the role of the physical body. In a memorable scene, Peter observes the Crucifixion, which is narrated for him by Jesus. One of the striking images is that Jesus calls his body the "home of demons" and rejoices that his "incorporeal body" has been released from his fleshy prison:

And he [Jesus] said to me, "Be strong, for you are the one to whom these mysteries have been given, to know them through revelation, that he whom they crucified is the first-born, and the home of demons, and the stony vessel in which they dwell, of Elohim, of the cross which is under the Law. But he who stands near him is the living Savior, the first in him whom they seized and released, who stands joyfully looking at those who did him violence, while they are divided among themselves. Therefore he laughs at their lack of perception, knowing that they are born blind. So then the one susceptible to suffering shall come, since the body is the substitute. But what they released was my incorporeal body. But I am intellectual Spirit filled with radiant light." (*Cop. Apoc. Peter* 82.17–83.10; *NHL* 377)

It is unlikely that both these texts were written by Peter, seeing as they promote drastically incongruous views of the physical body. What has likely happened in the case of these two texts is that two competing groups of Christians, each with an explicit, and very different, perspective on the nature of the physical body, have produced texts promoting their viewpoint and putting their words into the mouth of Peter, placing his stamp of validity upon their theological position.[4] In the process, Peter's name and prestige have been appropriated and employed as a mask, allowing for different groups of Christians with competing agendas to argue for their own legitimacy.[5]

Peter as Champion of the Faith (*Pseudo-Clementina*)

The *Pseudo-Clementina* (from the second through the fourth century AD) is the name given to a series of texts that claim to be an account of Clement of Rome and are written in his name.[6] The two primary texts, the *Pseudo-Clementine Homilies* and the *Pseudo-Clementine Recognitions*, are commonly believed to be edited/expanded versions of an original text that is now lost. Because Clement of Rome would become, according to tradition, bishop of Rome, it is not surprising that the *Pseudo-Clementina* contain a repository of traditions regarding Peter, customarily named as the very first bishop of Rome and thus Clement's predecessor. The image of Peter constructed by the *Pseudo-Clementina* is one of a man passionate about Christianity, deeply concerned with the preservation of correct doctrine, unflinching in the face of opposition, and possessor of legitimate authority.

The image of Peter as the staunch defender of truth can be seen in one key theme depicted in the narrative—namely, Peter's disputation with a man named Simon, likely the same Simon who was from Samaria and who had attempted to buy the priesthood from Peter in Acts 8. Simon, readers are told, had gained quite a following through preaching a number of questionable doctrines, such as denial of the Resurrection, existence of a God higher than the creator of the earth, and Simon's own status as the Messiah. Unlike the *Acts of Peter*, where a similar contest between Simon and Peter will be depicted as something akin to a magical duel between the two men, the *Pseudo-Clementina* present Peter as the rational, level-headed speaker of truth who will go to great lengths to preserve truth. Upon his arrival in Caesarea to meet Simon:

> There then Peter entered; and when he had looked on the multitude, every eye in which was fixed upon him in breathless stillness, and on the magician Simon, who stood in the midst, he began to discourse as follows. "Peace be with you all who are ready to commit yourselves to the truth of God, this his great and incomparable gift to our world! He who has sent us, the true prophet of good principle, has commissioned us, by way of salutation and before any instruction, to speak to you of this truth." (Ps.-Clem. Hom. 3.30.1–2; *NTA* 2:514–515)

Simon, bested by Peter after a lengthy debate, hastens away from Caesarea in order to continue spreading his teachings elsewhere. Peter, as the "defender of the faith," continues his pursuit of Simon, saying, "I must hasten after him that his lying assertions may not find a footing and establish themselves everywhere" (*Ps.-Clem. Hom.* 3.59.5; *NTA* 2:517).

Peter encounters Simon again in Berytus (modern-day Beirut), and there readers are granted a further glimpse at the lengths to which Peter will go to preserve truth. Simon, attempting to agitate the townspeople, who have just been through an earthquake, cries out "Flee, ye people, from this man; for he is a magician—you may believe me—and has himself occasioned this earthquake and has caused these diseases to frighten you, as if he himself was a god!" (*Ps.-Clem. Hom.* 7.9.2–3; *NTA* 2:524). Peter's response reveals the high esteem the author of the text has for him: "Peter with a smile and an impressive directness spoke the words: 'Ye men, I admit that, God willing, I am capable of doing what these men here say and in addition am ready, if you will not hear my words, to turn your whole city upside down'" (*Ps.-Clem. Hom.* 8.9.5; *NTA* 2:524). The response of those listening, understandably, was that they "took alarm and readily promised to carry out his commands" (*Ps.-Clem. Hom.* 8.10.1; *NTA* 2:524).

Integral to the struggle between Simon and Peter over correct doctrine is the question of authorized leadership within the church. Over the course of his travels, Peter is constantly authorizing men to assist in leading the church in his absence. Prior to his leaving Caesarea to pursue Simon, Peter calls together his followers and states, "Since now some one must be appointed to fill my place, let us all with one accord pray God to make known the ablest among us who may set himself in the chair of Christ and lead his church in the spirit of godliness ... After these words he laid his hand upon Zacchaeus and said: 'Ruler and Lord of all, Father and God, guard Thou the shepherd with the flock'" (*Ps.-Clem. Hom.* 3.60.1–3.72.1; *NTA* 2:517–520). Prior to his second encounter with Simon in Berytus, Peter "stayed for some days in Tyre and [after he] had instructed all the inhabitants and freed them from numerous sufferings, Peter founded a church and appointed a bishop for them from the number of elders who were accompanying him" (*Ps.-Clem. Hom.* 7.5.3; *NTA* 2:523).

One of the major purposes of the *Pseudo-Clementine* literature is to establish a fixed link between Clement of Rome and Peter, to demonstrate that Clement was simply acting as Peter's authorized representative in his function as bishop of Rome.[7] The transition from Peter to Clement as bishop of Rome is described in a letter included with the *Pseudo-Clementina* known as the *Epistula Clementis* ("Letter of Clement"). This letter, reportedly written by Clement to James the bishop of Jerusalem and brother of Jesus, relays the following account: "In those very days when he [Peter] was about to die, the brethren being assembled together, he suddenly grasped my hand, and standing up said to the congregation: 'Listen to me, brethren and fellow-servants. Since the days of my death are at hand, as I was taught by our Lord and Teacher Jesus Christ who sent me, I appoint to you Clement here as bishop and to him I entrust my teacher's chair'" (*Ep. Clem.* 2.1–2; *NTA* 2:497).

In language echoing Matthew 16, Peter states, "Wherefore I convey to him the authority to bind and to loose, that all that he ordains on earth shall be decreed in heaven" (*Ep. Clem.* 2.4; *NTA* 2:497). Finally, "when he had said this he laid his hands upon me [Clement] publicly, in the presence of all, and constrained me to sit in his chair" (*Ep. Clem.* 19.1; *NTA* 2:502). In this, the "Letter of Clement" clearly hopes to validate the position of the "orthodox" branch of the church and its ecclesiology.[8]

Perhaps more than any other early Christian text, the *Pseudo-Clementina* present readers with the ideal Peter. He has no flaws. He is intelligent, a powerful speaker, tenacious in both his promotion of orthodoxy and his condemnation of heresy, a man who is endowed with divine power and who seeks to bestow that power upon the faithful. He is truly the champion of the orthodox, the defender of the faith. In the *Pseudo-Clementina*, Peter "is remembered as the keystone of the early Christian movement who concerns himself with the unity and purity of the church. His teaching is normative, and he faithfully interprets and passes on the law, fighting the threat of heresy embodied in Simon Magus. For the *Pseudo-Clementina*, Peter is both the repository and embodiment of the apostolic gospel tradition."[9] In many respects, this Peter closely resembles the Peter of the post-Pentecost church described in the book of Acts: outspoken, rational, a master rhetorician, and a possessor of legitimate authority.

Peter as Martyred Miracle Worker (*Acts of Peter*)

The narrative of the *Acts of Peter* (late second century AD) revolves around two dramatic events, both occurring in Rome, the historic site of Peter's episcopacy and martyrdom. The first of these finds Peter in the midst of a competition with the same Simon encountered in the *Pseudo-Clementina*. Peter's contest with Simon takes place in the forum at Rome. In a tale echoing that of Elijah and the priests of Ba'al, Peter is exhorted by onlookers, "Show us, Peter, who is your god, or what is his greatness, which has given you such confidence . . . We have had evidence from Simon, now let us have yours; convince us, both of you, whom we should truly believe" (8.23; *NTA* 2:306). Simon begins by putting a young man to death by whispering in his ear. In response, Peter cries out, "O Lord, in thy power raise up through my voice the man whom Simon killed with his touch!" (8.26; *NTA* 2:308). The boy is instantly restored to life, causing the crowd to cry out, "There is but one God, the one God of Peter" (8.26; *NTA* 2:308). With the situations reversed, Simon is unable to give life to a young man who had recently passed away, and is defeated when Peter touches the boy's side and rouses him with a simple "Stand up" (8.28; *NTA* 2:310). In a last-ditch attempt to win the favor of the Romans, Simon promises to prove the power of his god and astonishes the gathered onlookers by flying in the air around Rome. Unimpressed, Peter cries out, "Make haste, Lord, with thy grace; and let him fall from (this) height, and be crippled, but not die; but let him be disabled and break his leg in three places" (32.3; *NTA* 2:313). Simon instantly falls, his leg broken, and "from that time they all believed in Peter" (32.3; *NTA* 2:313).

In this version of the story, Peter's miraculous deeds led to his death when many of the women he converts refuse to sleep with their husbands due to Peter's promotion of a celibate lifestyle.[10] When Peter hears that these men have conspired to kill him, he attempts to flee from Rome. In a scene Hollywood would later borrow in the 1950s movie *Quo Vadis*, Peter encounters Jesus, and they have the following exchange:

> And when he [Peter] saw him [Jesus], he said: "Lord, whither [goest thou] here [Lat. *Quo vadis, Domine*]?" And the Lord said to him: "I am coming to Rome to be crucified." And Peter said to him: "Lord, art thou being crucified again?" He said unto him: "Yes, Peter, I am being crucified again." And Peter came to himself; and he saw the Lord ascending into heaven; then he returned to Rome rejoicing, and giving praise to the Lord, because he said, "I am being crucified"; [since] this was to happen to Peter. (35.6; *NTA* 2:314)

Peter jubilantly returns to Rome and, upon coming to the place of his execution, requests that he be crucified "head-downwards—in this way and no other" (37.8; *NTA* 2:315). [11] While the explanation often given for this method of execution is that Peter's humility would not allow him to be crucified in the same manner as Jesus, the answer he gives in the *Acts of Peter* describes different reasoning:[12] "For the first man, whose likeness I have in [my] appearance, in falling head-downwards showed a manner of birth that was not so before" (38.9; *NTA* 2:315). In other words, just as Adam came into the world headfirst through the birth canal, so Peter would leave the world headfirst. Having thus rationalized his manner of death, Peter "gave up his spirit to the Lord" (40.11; *NTA* 2:316).

In the final lines of the text, readers are told that the Roman emperor Nero became furious upon hearing of Peter's death, primarily because he had wanted to inflict further suffering upon Peter. His reason for such animosity is due to Peter's impact upon Nero's own household: "But when Nero later discovered that Peter had departed this life, he censured the prefect Agrippa because he had been put to death without his knowledge; for he would have liked to punish him more cruelly and with extra severity; for Peter had made disciples of some of his servants and caused them to leave him; so that he was greatly incensed and for some time would not speak to Agrippa; for he sought to destroy all those brethren who had been made disciples by Peter" (41.12; *NTA* 2:316). Nero's desire to persecute Peter's converts is short lived, however, as he experiences a vision in which he is warned, "Nero, you cannot now persecute or destroy the servants of Christ. Keep your hands away from them!" (41.12; *NTA* 2:317). The result was that "Nero, being greatly alarmed because of this vision, kept away from the disciples from the time that Peter departed from this life" (41.12; *NTA* 2:317). The reality of this tradition, that Peter was both able to carry the Christian message into the imperial household and indirectly bring about a cessation of persecution by Nero, reveals the high estimation of Peter held by the early Christian church, as well as its revisionist historical tendency.[13]

While the veracity of events as relayed in the *Acts of Peter* may be in doubt, the stories themselves tell readers two important ways in which Peter was viewed. First, there is a strong correlation between Jesus and Peter throughout the *Acts of Peter*. By coming to Rome and battling with Simon Magus, Peter demonstrates an ability to perform miraculous deeds not unlike those of Jesus, such as the raising of the young man from the dead. With Jesus now removed to a heavenly sphere, God's power to act on earth now runs through Peter.[14] While meditating upon the cross, Peter sees himself as a "second-Adam," just as Paul did Jesus (see Romans 5 and 1 Corinthians 15). Although he initially leaves, Peter accepts his fate and does not attempt to avoid his execution. Even the comment that "he gave up his spirit to the Lord" echoes the words of Jesus upon the cross: "Father, into thy hands I commend my spirit: and having said thus, he gave up the ghost" (Luke 23:46). Finally, the incident with Nero exhibits that Peter, like Jesus, continued to have an impact upon the nascent Christian church.

Second, Peter's slow but eventual acceptance of his martyrdom would likely have provided an example for those Christians encountering persecution during the second and third centuries of the church. While they, like Peter, may have felt the natural instinct to avoid death, they, like Peter, should embrace the opportunity they had to die for their beliefs: "His change of heart, and his address to the gathered faithful, however, laid down the guidelines for the future. Christians were neither to *seek* martyrdom, nor *avoid* it."[15] Although Jesus provides the ultimate example of accepting one's fate and a willingness to die for what one believes, Peter's example, as a man rather than the son of God, may have proven even more significant, as the early Christians could see in him a figure they could relate to and a behavior they could imitate. To have a hero as revered as Peter accept his fate so calmly and rationally was likely a comfort to a church experiencing persecution, and thus the *Acts of Peter* presented a model to the church of the second century on how to handle similar trials in their own lives, even those resulting in death.[16]

Peter as Antagonist (*Gospel of Thomas* and *Gospel of Mary*)

While some texts, such as the *Acts of Peter* and the *Pseudo-Clementina*, depict a Peter who is the champion of the orthodox tradition and an example for all faithful Christians to follow, other early Christians texts portray a different Peter, namely Peter as an antagonist and opponent of true Christianity. This tradition is most prominent amongst the literature of the Gnostics, a "group" of Christians who taught basically that the acquisition of knowledge was of paramount importance and the primary means of salvation. While much of Gnosticism, including the appropriateness of the term itself, remains the topic of much dispute,[17] what is clear is that by the second and third centuries many Gnostics found themselves labeled as heretics by the "orthodox" church.[18] In response, they produced a series of texts aimed at discrediting the orthodox church and promoting their own beliefs. Peter, as the traditional head of the orthodox church, became the target for much of the Gnostics' animosity.[19] Two texts, the *Gospel of Thomas* (mid-second through early third century AD) and the *Gospel of Mary* (third century AD), both relay rather acerbic disputes between Peter, representing the "orthodox" tradition, and, interestingly enough, Mary Magdalene, representing the "heretical" Gnostic tradition.

The first of these, the *Gospel of Thomas*, is a collection of 114 sayings ascribed to Jesus and likely composed or compiled sometime in the second century.[20] *Thomas* opens by subtly undercutting the authority and competence of Peter as legitimate head of the church. Having assembled his disciples, Jesus asked them to "compare me to someone and tell me whom I am like." Revealing just how little he understands Jesus' true self, Peter responded with "You are like a righteous angel." It is Thomas' answer, "Master, my mouth is wholly incapable of saying whom you are like," that ultimately wins Jesus' favor and introduces three important revelations. When pressed by Peter regarding what Jesus revealed to him, Thomas responds, "If I tell you one of the things which he told me, you will pick up stones and throw them at me; a fire will come out of the stones and burn you up" (13; *NHL* 127). The Peter depicted thus far is an ignorant believer, an individual who hasn't yet reached the point of truly understanding Jesus' message.

This negative portrayal of Peter resurfaces toward the end of the text. The final lines of the *Gospel of Thomas* find Peter harshly demanding that Mary be excused from the group of disciples listening to these secret sayings of the Lord: "Simon Peter said to them, 'Let Mary leave us, for women are not worthy of life.' Jesus said, 'I myself shall lead her in order to make her male, so that she too may become a living spirit resembling you males. For every woman who will make herself male will enter the kingdom of heaven'" (114; *NHL* 138). While Jesus' statement about Mary "making herself male" remains enigmatic,[21] "the rebuke demonstrates that Peter has attempted to limit the circle of disciples,"[22] a statement that would resonate amidst the ongoing dispute between the Gnostics and the orthodox who had likewise attempted to "limit the circle of disciples."

This dispute between Peter and Mary is expanded upon in the *Gospel of Mary*.[23] This text focuses upon Mary, who has apparently been privy to a series of esoteric visions from Jesus. Peter asks her, "Sister, we know that the Savior loved you more than the rest of women. Tell us the words of the Savior which you remember—which you know" (10.1-6; *NHL* 525). Mary's response, "What is hidden from you I will proclaim to you" (10.8-9; *NHL* 525), suggests that she possesses knowledge and information that has been withheld from Jesus' male disciples. Frustrated, Peter responds to Mary's recounting of her vision with "Did he really speak with a woman without our knowledge [and] not openly? Are we to turn about and listen to her? Did he prefer her to us?" (17.18-22; *NHL* 526). Mary, hurt by Peter's disbelief, tearfully answers, "My brother Peter, what do you think? Do you think that I thought this up myself in my heart, or that I am lying about the Savior?" (18.2-5; *NHL* 526). At this point, Levi steps in and rebukes Peter: "Peter, you have always been hot-tempered. Now I see you contending against the woman like the adversaries. But if the Savior made her worthy, who are you indeed to reject her?" (18.7-12; *NHL* 526-27).

The text ends rather abruptly with the declaration that "they began to go forth to proclaim and to preach" (19.1-2; *NHL* 527). As with the *Gospel of Thomas*, readers of the *Gospel of Mary* encounter a Peter who stubbornly refuses to accept that other believers in Jesus could possess knowledge beyond what he himself has and who harshly demands the dismissal of those who don't agree with him, even though he clearly doesn't possess requisite gospel knowledge himself.[24] Taken together, the Gnostic texts represent a challenge to Peter's authority in the early Christian church. Yet, by placing Peter in an antagonistic position, Gnostics have positioned Peter once again as the upholder of the "orthodox" tradition over and against their own tradition. If there is any single individual who personifies firm opposition to alternate viewpoints and beliefs, it is Peter.

Peter as Ignorant Christian (*Apocryphon of James*)

Other texts questioned the legitimacy of the "orthodox" church while remaining much more understated in their negative depiction of Peter. Another Gnostic text found at Nag Hammadi, the *Apocryphon of James* (early third century AD), relays an account of Jesus' appearance to the disciples 550 days after his Resurrection. Upon declaring that no one can enter into heaven without being "filled," Jesus dismisses the disciples save for James and Peter and begins to instruct them privately. Peter is depicted as being rather shortsighted, insisting, "Three times you have told us, 'Become full' but we are full" (3.39–4.2; *NHL* 31). It is James who recognizes that what Jesus is offering goes beyond what they already possess, stating, "Lord, we can obey you if you wish, for we have forsaken our fathers and our mothers and our villages and followed you" (4.23–28; *NHL* 31). Following a lengthy pastiche of esoteric instruction intermixed with parables, a frustrated Peter responds to Jesus with "Sometimes you urge us on to the kingdom of heaven, and then again you turn us back, Lord; sometimes you persuade and draw us to the faith and promise us life, and then again you cast us forth from the kingdom of heaven" (13.28–36; *NHL* 36). After a brief response, Jesus departs "to the place from whence I came" (14.21; *NHL* 36), leaving James and Peter to answer the inquiries of the understandably curious disciples.

What is notable about the *Apocryphon of James* is the subtlety behind its depiction of Peter. While Peter is important enough to be privy to the secret teachings relayed by Jesus, he becomes more or less a passive witness throughout the text. It is James who quickly understands why Jesus has returned, James' questions that prompt much of the dialogue recited by the Savior, and only James who really seems to fully grasp Jesus' meaning. In a statement perhaps indicating that James has effectively supplanted Peter as chief Apostle, it is James who discharges the disciples to various locations while he alone remains in Jerusalem.[25] Peter hears everything James hears, yet fails to make the necessary connections. The positive depiction of James suggests a Jewish-Christian provenance for this text, and it may be that the text was meant to respond to a gradually diminishing role played by the Jewish-Christian members of the increasingly Gentile church.[26] By emphasizing Peter's failure to fully understand Jesus' teachings, the author is implying that the orthodox church itself has meandered off-course and thus missed out on the true message of the gospel. As one scholar observes, "Unlike the more polemical writings, the *Apocryphon of James* seeks to demonstrate that Gnostic revelation is in fact coherent with the publicly known teachings of Jesus. It refers to lists of parables and to other sayings of Jesus throughout. Gnostics interpret the same canonical texts as other Christians do. Peter provides evidence for the authenticity of that interpretation, even if he is not completely enlightened."[27]

While it is unlikely that any of these three texts accurately relay information about what Peter may have said or how he may have felt, they are nonetheless crucial for understanding Peter's role in the apocryphal tradition and in the struggle between competing brands of Christianity. The image of Peter clearly loomed large in the minds of early Christians, who saw in him a figure who would grant validity or legitimacy to their respective belief system through either endorsement or rejection. The prominent role played by Peter in literature seemingly intended to demean or at least tarnish his image suggests an additional insight into the legacy of Peter—he was too big to be ignored, too substantial to be pushed to the side, and too important to be forgotten.

Peter as Witness (*Gospel of Peter*)

The weight of Peter's prestige is most fully reflected in the final text we will examine, a short document known as the *Gospel of Peter*.[28] This Gospel likely dates to the middle of the second century AD[29] and provides an alternate depiction of the Passion narrative. Many elements of the Passion story familiar to readers of the four Gospels can be found in the *Gospel of Peter*, such as the presence of Pilate, Jesus being crucified between two malefactors, the empty tomb, and the role of Mary Magdalene. However, there are a few additions to the story absent from the canonical Gospels, including the curious account of a talking cross:

> And whilst they were relating what they had seen, they saw again three men come out from the sepulchre, and two of them sustaining the other, and a cross following them, and the heads of the two reaching to heaven, but that of him who was led of them by the hand overpassing the heavens. And they heard a voice out of the heavens crying, "hast thou preached to them that sleep?", and from the cross there was heard the answer, "Yea." (10.39–42; *NTA* 1:225)

A further curiosity of the *Gospel of Peter* is the almost complete absence of Peter, who appears only in the closing lines of the Gospel that bears his name: "But I, Simon Peter, and my brother Andrew took our nets and went to the sea" (14.60;

NTA 1:226). The text, then, presents itself as a firsthand account of the Passion written by Peter himself. The attribution of this particular narrative to Peter was likely done not to enhance Christianity's knowledge of Peter, but to grant legitimacy to the theological position taken by the author of the apocryphal text. The bestowal of legitimacy occurs both through the use of Peter's name as well as the usage of the first-person "I." It is Peter's prestige, not Peter's person, that matters to the author. This type of false attribution of authorship was not an uncommon practice in the ancient world, especially where religious literature was concerned: "One particular method of verisimilitude involves the use of first-person narrative, in which an author not only claims to be someone other than who he is, but also narrates events as a personal participant ... The value of the first-person narrative is that it makes the writer an authority not only because of his name but also because of his firsthand experiences."[30] The intended result of this type of practice was that these texts "all function to authenticate the reports in which they are embedded."[31]

So what, then, would the author of the *Gospel of Peter* be attempting to "authenticate" by appropriating Peter's persona? In contrast to the *Apocryphon of James*, at several points in this narrative the author demonstrates a clear anti-Jewish bias. In a scene from the trial of Jesus, the author relates, "But of the Jews none washed their hands, neither Herod nor any one of his judges" (1.1; *NTA* 1:223). Several Jewish groups, including the "scribes," "elders," "priests," "Pharisees," or just simply the "Jews" are portrayed as the prime movers behind Jesus' execution.

Pilate emerges as a sympathetic figure who tries to convince Herod to return the body of Jesus to Joseph for burial.[32] In a telling exchange, the Roman soldiers watching the tomb report to Pilate: "When those who were of the centurion's company saw this, they hastened by night to Pilate, abandoning the sepulchre which they were guarding, and reported everything that they had seen, being full of disquietude and saying, 'In truth he was the Son of God'" (11.45; *NTA* 1:225). Pilate's response is to disavow any responsibility in this miscarriage of justice: "Pilate answered and said, 'I am clean from the blood of the Son of God, upon such a thing have you decided'" (11.46; *NTA* 1:225). Finally, the Jews come to Pilate asking him to maintain secrecy regarding the true nature of Jesus: "Then all came to him, beseeching him and urgently calling upon him to command the centurion and the soldiers to tell no one what they had seen. 'For it is better for us,' they said, 'to make ourselves guilty of the greatest sin before God than to fall into the hands of the people of the Jews and be stoned'" (11:47–48; *NTA* 1:225).

Likely this text was produced in order to explicitly indict the Jews for the crucifixion of Jesus, one of a larger series of texts that emerged in the second and third centuries reflecting anti-Jewish sentiment.[33] By attaching Peter's name to his text and inserting him as an eyewitness, the author immediately gained credence for his theological position. This informs us that Peter's reputation and prestige were imposing in the minds of the early Christians across the board. Quite simply, his name carried weight.[34] However, it is also important to remember that the text likely tells us little of historical truth about Peter himself, and it seems difficult to believe that Peter would share the same level of animosity for Jews expressed in the *Gospel of Peter*.[35] Readers thus would be ill advised to search within the text of the *Gospel of Peter* for any glimpses into who Peter was or what he may have thought, particularly where such a clear agenda is present: "In short, the *Gospel of Peter* has attracted considerable attention in recent years and contains much that is of interest for an understanding of second-century Christianity—but its anemic figure of Peter is little more than a flag of ecclesial convenience adorning its derivative account of the passion."[36]

Apocryphal Accounts and Latter-day Saint Interpretation

Having considered several apocryphal texts involving Peter, it is valuable at this point to discuss just how these types of stories and traditions could be interpreted by Latter-day Saints. As a church, we tend to be sympathetic toward literature such as this, seeing in noncanonical literature such as the Old Testament Pseudepigrapha, the Dead Sea Scrolls, or the New Testament apocrypha a potential reservoir for lost or forgotten truths. There are at least three possible reasons for this common attitude, all relating to the Book of Mormon. First, a crucial part of Nephi's vision of the apostasy of the early Christian church was the role played by an organization termed "the great and abominable church" (1 Nephi 13:6).[37] One of the major offenses committed by the "great and abominable church" is the removal of "plain and precious truths" from the scriptures:

> And after they go forth by the hand of the twelve apostles of the Lamb, from the Jews unto the Gentiles, thou seest the formation of that great and abominable church, which is most abominable above all other churches; for behold, they have taken away from the gospel of the Lamb many parts which are plain and most precious; and also many covenants of the Lord have they taken away.
>
> And all this have they done that they might pervert the right ways of the Lord, that they might blind the eyes and harden the hearts of the children of men.

> Wherefore, thou seest that after the book hath gone forth
> through the hands of the great and abominable church, that there are
> many plain and precious things taken away from the book, which is
> the book of the Lamb of God. (1 Nephi 13:26–28)

It is tempting to see noncanonical literature such as that discussed above as a possible location for discovering these lost "plain and precious" truths. Furthermore,
the fact that Nephi learns that what was lost from the Bible was "plain and precious," including even "many covenants of the Lord," may lead us to believe that
what was lost may in fact be more important than what remained in the extant
Bible we have today.

A second factor comes from the Book of Mormon's discussion of additional
records that exist outside the Bible. Nephi took from Laban a record known as
the plates of brass, containing a record of the history of the Jews, their prophecies,
genealogies, and law. A portion of the Book of Mormon, untranslated, contains
the "sealed" account of the vision of the brother of Jared. Nephi prophesies that
an exchange of "words" will occur among the Jews, Nephites, and lost tribes of
Israel, suggesting that the lost tribes have also kept records of their own: "And
it shall come to pass that the Jews shall have the words of the Nephites, and the
Nephites shall have the words of the Jews; and the Nephites and the Jews shall
have the words of the lost tribes of Israel; and the lost tribes of Israel shall have
the words of the Nephites and the Jews" (2 Nephi 29:13). The Book of Mormon's
promise of multiple legitimate scriptural texts that lay outside the canonized
Bible may prompt Latter-day Saints to accept the pseudepigraphic claims of apocryphal texts more readily than is necessary.

A third factor leading toward sympathetic reception of noncanonical literature is the existence and reality of the Book of Mormon itself.[38] The Book of
Mormon is nonbiblical, yet is a source of true doctrine, the "fulness of the gospel"
(D&C 20:9). Additionally, the circumstances surrounding the discovery of the
gold plates, buried in a hill for over a thousand years, may lead us to view ancient
texts discovered under similar circumstances, such as the Dead Sea Scrolls or the
Nag Hammadi Library, as analogous.

All three of these points are valid, but this validity does not mean that every
noncanonical text carries within it "plain and precious truths" or is a lost record
of God's people.[39] Often these texts may contain words, doctrines, or stories that
parallel the restored gospel, such as the marvelous journey of the young man in the
"Hymn of the Pearl" from the *Acts of Thomas*.[40] But texts such as this are often the
exception rather than the rule, and common themes or doctrines do not necessarily indicate common origins. More accurately, what most apocryphal texts exhibit

is a church deprived of revelation, where individual authors or groups produced "truth" not through divine inspiration but through their own pens. According to Stephen Robinson, "Indeed, the apocrypha do have great value, but not because they teach Mormonism; for by and large they do not. For the most part they are the writing of men but are dressed up to look like scripture. From an LDS point of view, there are often elements of truth in this literature; but always it is truth mixed with falsehood, as the Lord tells us in section 91 of the Doctrine and Covenants."[41] For all we know, the apocryphal documents discussed above could be the product of the entity Nephi termed the "great and abominable church" itself, rather than the source for the "plain and precious truths" the great and abominable church excised. For these reasons, they ought to be explored with caution and a mind toward their original context.

Recent research done by prominent Latter-day Saint scholars has also cautioned against placing too much weight upon the stories preserved in the New Testament apocrypha. In an article investigating the *Gospel of Judas*, John Welch noted, "Filling in the gaps in traditional biblical stories, elevating the interests of one early Christian community over the others, and uncovering new or old secrets with the aim of enlarging the canonical corpus are all hallmarks of the disparate body of literature long referred to as the New Testament Apocrypha, . . . but despite any good intentions, the apocryphal writings are generally wrong-headed and unreliable nonetheless."[42] In an examination of the apocryphal acts of Jesus, John Gee concluded that "Like cream-puffs, most apocryphal accounts of Jesus, though they look enticing, have little nourishment and are usually not as good nor even as sweet as they look, being dusty pastry filled with imitation cream."[43] Finally, Thomas Wayment reminds us that a serious gulf exists between the canonical texts of the New Testament and the apocryphal texts that claim a similar authorship:

> The modern academic mindset has led us to believe that all or at least a significant part of the apocrypha was believed to be historically reliable and that people generally approached them in antiquity as credible sources. This assumption, however, does not hold up after careful scrutiny. The early Church never elevated the apocryphal texts to a status similar or equal to the canonical texts . . . It is safe to say, based on current research, that every apocryphal text that claims to preserve the teachings of a New Testament figure was forged. The same cannot be said of the canonical texts, which indicates that the early Church was quite successful at separating the wheat from the chaff.[44]

This being said, what then can Latter-day Saints learn about Peter from these assorted documents? While it may be tempting to jettison the entire apocryphal tradition about Peter due to the unreliability of the texts themselves, this would be an overreaction. While these texts may be lacking in detailed information regarding the historical Peter, the value of such literature is that it reflects traditions about Peter and captures how the nascent Christian church perceived and understood him in different times and places.[45] Certain texts, such as the *Pseudo-Clementina* and *Acts of Peter*, depict Peter in a variety of positive functions: the leader of the church, the voice of reason, the expounder of doctrine, the healer of the sick, the raiser of the dead, the nemesis of the heretic, the defender of the faith, and the martyr for Christ. Other texts, such as the *Gospel of Peter*, demonstrate just how viable Peter was as a witness, as if placing his name at the end of a text made all that came before valid and legitimate. Still other authors found Peter valuable as an antagonist, the ideal figurehead for the popular Christianity targeted by the authors of texts such as the *Gospel of Mary*, the *Gospel of Thomas*, and the *Apocryphon of James*. But even his antagonists viewed him as the head of the orthodox church and the defender of its tradition.

It becomes quickly apparent that when a group of Christians wanted to present their version of "true" Christianity, they would often employ the figure of Peter in promoting/validating it, either by holding him up as the champion of orthodoxy (i.e. their own doctrine) or by dismissing him as unenlightened or ignorant, opening up space for their own unique teachings and doctrine.[46] This is the crux of the argument: Peter simply could not be ignored or dismissed; his figure loomed large enough that he had to be either embraced or pushed aside. Ultimately, it is Peter's prime position in the midst of these various theological skirmishes that grants modern readers the clearest indication of Peter's legacy. As one scholar has written, "All in all, it is interesting how few of the Petrine texts—like the *Gospel of Peter*, the *Apocalypse of Peter*, or the *Preaching of Peter*—reveal much for Petrine memory, except the *fact* of its importance."[47] While readers of the New Testament apocryphal texts may struggle to discern fact from fiction, history from myth, one thing remains undeniable: Peter mattered. His role was crucial, his position hallowed. Additionally, these traditions about Peter preserved in the New Testament Apocrypha strongly confirm the primacy and authority of Peter in the first-generation church presented in the four canonical Gospels. If the sole purpose served in examining these texts is to remind readers of these points, then they warrant continued study, if only to encounter passages such as the one that closes the *Acts of Peter*. While it is unlikely that Peter ever said these words while hanging upside down on a cross, they stand as a striking testament to the man who was wise enough to answer the Savior's inquiry of "But whom say ye that I am?" with "Thou art the Christ, the Son of the living God" (Matthew 16:15):

> I thank thee, with silence of the voice, with which the spirit within me, that loves thee and speaks to thee and sees thee, makes intercession. Thou art known to the spirit only. Thou art my Father, thou art my Mother, thou my Brother, thou art Friend, thou art Servant, thou art House-keeper; thou art the All, and the All is in thee; thou art Being, and there is nothing that is, except thou. With Him then do you also take refuge, brethren, and learning that in him alone is your real being, you shall obtain those things of which he says to you "What eye has not seen nor ear heard, nor has it entered the heart of man." We ask then, for that which thou hast promised to give us, O Jesus undefiled; we praise thee, we give thanks to thee and confess thee, and being yet men without strength we glorify thee; for that art God alone and no other, to whom be glory both now and for all eternity, Amen. (39:10; *NTA* 2:316)

Notes

1. Some early Christians believed that the source for the Gospel of Mark was Peter, for whom Mark served as translator. See Eusebius, *Historia Ecclesiastica* 3.39.15. Modern scholars are unsure how much validity rests in this tradition and have advanced arguments on both sides of the question. As one scholar writes, "speculation, however intriguing, is not demonstration, and the fairest judgment . . . is the nonprejudicial Scottish legal verdict of 'not proven.'" Joel B. Marcus, *Mark 1–8: A New Translation with Introduction and Commentary* (New York: Doubleday, 1999), 24.

2. This list would include the *Acts of Peter*, the *Apocalypse of Peter*, the *Coptic Apocalypse of Peter*, the *Gospel of Peter*, the *Acts of Peter and the Twelve Apostles*, the *Epistle of Peter*, the *Letter of Peter to Philip*, the *Kerygmata Petrou*, the *Gospel of Thomas*, the *Gospel of Mary*, the *Pseudo-Clementina*, the *Dialogue of the Savior*, the *Pistis-Sophia*, and the *Apocryphon of James*.

3. All quotations and dates for the documents discussed in this paper are from Wilhelm Schneemelcher, ed., *New Testament Apocrypha*, ed., trans. R. McL. Wilson (Westminster: John Knox Press, 1991), hereafter *NTA*; and James M. Robinson, ed., *The Nag Hammadi Library* (San Francisco: Harper & Row, 1977), hereafter *NHL*. Also useful is *The Apocryphal New Testament*, ed. J. K. Elliot (Oxford: Oxford University Press, 1993). These works also contain lengthy bibliographies for those wishing to dig deeper into the respective texts.

4. For more on the relationship between the *Apocalypse of Peter* and the *Coptic Apocalypse of Peter*, see Bart D. Ehrman, *Forgery and Counterforgery: The Use of Literary Deceit in Early Christian Polemics* (Oxford: Oxford University Press, 2013), 450–51.

5. "Various Christian groups validated their teaching by declaring allegiance to a specific apostle or disciple and claiming him . . . as their spiritual founder." Elaine Pagels, *Beyond Belief: The Secret Gospel of Thomas* (New York: Random House, 2003), 65. "With the Fall of Jerusalem, and the dispersion of the Jerusalem church, and as Peter's influence grew apace, . . . it became increasingly important, especially for encratic, legalistic and Gnostic groups, to enlist his support, and claim his authority." F. Lapham, *Peter: The Man, the Myth, and the Writings* (London: T&T Clark International, 2003), 216.

6. For more on the *Pseudo-Clementina*, see Bernard Rehm, *Homilien*, vol. 1 of *Die Pseudoklementinen* (Berlin: Akademie, 1992), GCS 42; and *Rekognitionem*, vol. 2 of *Die Pseudoklementinen* (Berlin: Akademie, 1965), GCS 51. F. Stanley Jones is currently working on a new critical edition and English translation of the Syriac *Pseudo-Clementina* for the series Corpus Christianorum, Series Apocryphorum.

7. "It is by no means difficult, then, to understand the motivation for installing Peter as Rome's first Bishop. Clearly, those churches which could legitimately boast apostolic foundation were in a position to claim superior authority and greater theological credibility." Lapham, *Peter: The Man, the Myth, and the Writings*, 93.

8. The words "orthodox" and "heresy" are loaded terms and ought to be used carefully. They should not be viewed as elevating one church while denigrating another. By "orthodox," I simply mean the church that emerges out of the second and third centuries as the dominant church and thus the definer of "official" church doctrine. By "heresy" I mean any church that stands outside the "orthodox" sphere, which Gnosticism eventually does. Important works on the topic are Walter Bauer, *Orthodoxy and Heresy in Earliest Christianity*, ed. Robert Kraft and Gerhard Krodel (Philadelphia: Fortress Press, 1971); and Bart D. Ehrman, *Lost Christianities* (Oxford: Oxford University Press, 2003). For a contrary opinion, see Andreas J. Kostenberger and Michael J. Kruger, *The Heresy of Orthodoxy* (Wheaton, IL: Crossway, 2010). These labels are scholars' ways of recognizing that the winners write the history, and thus it must be carefully evaluated.

9. Markus Bockmuehl, *Simon Peter in Scripture and Memory* (Grand Rapids, MI: Baker Academic, 2012), 57.

10. Perhaps arising due to the furthered exposure to Hellenism, asceticism, with its denial of the body and sexuality, became a popular idea within parts of the Christian church, in particular many of the so-called "Gnostics." The story of Peter influencing his converts in such a way that they reject their husbands is likely representative of this ascetic tradition. Thus, "the image of Peter as an ascetic who championed celibacy is an alien imposition." Larry R. Helyer, *The Life and Witness of Peter* (Downer's Grove, IL: InterVarsity Press, 2012), 294. The popular stories preserved in the *Acts of Paul and Thecla* attempted to promote a similar viewpoint. For more, see Wayne A. Meeks, *The Moral World of the First Christians* (Philadelphia: Fortress Press, 1986), 105–8; and Robert A. Markus, *The End of Ancient Christianity* (Cambridge: Cambridge University Press, 1997), 21–83.

11. Josephus, *Wars*, 5.11.1, states that during the siege of Titus the Roman soldiers experimented with different methods of crucifixion, which may explain the

upside-down manner of Peter's crucifixion. For early accounts of Peter's death involving upside-down crucifixion, see Tertullian, *De Præscrip. Hær.* 36; Eusebius, *Historia Ecclesiastica.* 3.1. The idea that Peter's choice of upside-down crucifixion was a sign of humility seems to have its origin in a later text known as the "Acts of the Holy Apostles Peter and Paul," which includes the following statement: "And Peter, having come to the cross, said; 'Since my Lord Jesus Christ, who came down from the heaven upon the earth, was raised upon the cross upright, and He has deigned to call to heaven me, who am of the earth, my cross ought to be fixed head downmost, so as to direct my feet towards heaven; for I am not worthy to be crucified like my Lord.' Then, having reversed the cross, they nailed his feet up." Alexander Roberts and James Donaldson, eds., *The Ante-Nicene Father* (Peabody, MA: Hendrickson Publishers, 2004), 8:484.

12.   See also Lapham, *Peter: The Man, the Myth, and the Writings*: "In popular tradition, it was because Peter believed himself to be unworthy of sharing the same form of death as his Lord that he begged his captors to reverse his position on the cross" (65).

13.   The cowed portrayal of Nero depicted by the author of the *Acts of Peter* is likely due to the enmity the early church held for the emperor. It was Nero who initiated persecution of Christians during the 60s AD, and traditionally the deaths of both Peter and Paul are attributed to him. Eusebius records that Nero "gave himself up to unholy practices" but that "To describe the monster of depravity that he became lies outside the scope of the present work." *Hist. Eccl.* 2.25. For Roman accounts of Nero's persecution of the Christians, see Tacitus, *Annals* 15.44; Suetonius, *Nero* 16.

14.   "Stories of Peter besting Simon Magus in a series of miracle-working contests from the *Acts of Peter* illustrated the superiority of the proto-orthodox lineage of the Roman episcopacy over against the various groups of Gnostic contenders." Ehrman, *Forgery and Counterforgery*, 60.

15.   Lapham, *Peter: The Man, the Myth, and the Writings*, 63.

16.   "By concluding with the martyrdom account, the author of *Acts of Peter* has presented a schema in which the controversies stirred up by Simon Magus's false preaching have been overcome. The church has been strengthened by the death of its martyr hero and his companions." Pheme Perkins, *Peter: Apostle for the Whole Church* (Minneapolis: Fortress Press, 2000), 142–43.

17.   See, for example, Karen L. King, *What Is Gnosticism?* (Cambridge, MA: Harvard University Press, 2003); Michael A. Williams, *Rethinking Gnosticism: An Argument for Dismantling a Dubious Category* (Princeton, NJ: Princeton University Press, 1996).

18.   See, for example, Irenaeus, *Adversus Haereses* 1–2; Hippolytus, *Refutation omnium Haeresium* 5.15; Eusebius, *Hist. Eccl.* 4.7.

19.   This is not to say that all Gnostic literature targeted Peter. One short text, the *Letter of Peter to Philip*, preserves a supposed correspondence between a very Gnostically oriented Peter and Philip. In the case of this letter, the author is following the tradition of ascribing certain unusual doctrine and theology to Peter as a means of transforming the unorthodox into the orthodox. However, the *Letter of Peter to Philip* is more the exception than the rule. In addition to the *Gospel of Thomas* and the *Gospel of Mary*, see also the *Dialogue with the Savior,* the *Gospel of the Egyptians*, and the *Pistis Sophia*.

20. For more on the *Gospel of Thomas*, see Marvin W. Meyer, *The Gospel of Thomas: The Hidden Sayings of Jesus* (San Francisco: HarperSanFrancisco, 1992), which includes text, translation, and critical notes.

21. One possible explanation for the rationale behind this phrase is explained by Birger A. Pearson: "A variant on this theme is the notion of maleness as equivalent to perfection, and femaleness as equivalent to imperfection, an idea that goes back to Plato and is given wide expression in the writings of the first-century philosopher Philo of Alexandria." *Ancient Gnosticism: Traditions and Literature* (Minneapolis: Fortress Press, 2007), 265. See also a similar phrase from the *Gospel of Mary:* "Do not weep and do not grieve nor be irresolute, for his grace will be entirely with you and will protect you. But rather let us praise his greatness, for he has prepared us and made us into men." *Gospel of Mary* 9:14–21; *NHL* 525.

22. Perkins, *Peter*, 157,

23. For more on the *Gospel of Mary*, see Christopher Tuckett, *The Gospel of Mary* (Oxford: Oxford University Press, 2007), with text, translation, and commentary.

24. Pheme Perkins identifies an alternate, more positive way of interpreting the "conflict" between Peter and Mary in the Gnostic tradition: "How one treats the conflict between Peter and Mary in *Gospel of Mary* depends on whether one presumes that its author has a hostile Christian majority in view or one assumes that *Gospel of Mary* has formulated a response to the kind of objection raised in Irenaeus about esoteric revelation and the universality of apostolic preaching. In the former case, Peter is the embodiment of orthodox dogmatism. In the latter case, his eventual conversion provides a foundation for a gnostic claim to the inner meaning of Christian teaching." *Gnosticism and the New Testament* (Minneapolis: Fortress Press, 1993), 184–85.

25. "Inasmuch as Peter is also named in the *Apocryphon of James*, it is to assert the superiority of James and of the revelation made to him." John Painter, *Just James: The Brother of Jesus in History and Tradition* (Edinburgh: T&T Clark, 1999), 177.

26. James, as the bishop of Jerusalem, is often portrayed as the standard-bearer for the Jewish-Christian wing of the early Christian church. That Peter would be involved in a text arguing on behalf of Jewish-Christianity is not surprising, as "Peter became a battleground over which the Jewishness of Christianity was fought." Ehrman, *Forgery and Counterforgery*, 332.

27. Perkins, *Peter*, 160.

28. For more on the *Gospel of Peter*, see Paul Foster, *The Gospel of Peter: Introduction, Critical Edition and Commentary* (Leiden, Netherlands: Brill, 2010).

29. This date depends upon the statement made by Serapion regarding his awareness of the "Gospel of Peter" being the same as the extant *Gospel of Peter* discussed here. See Eusebius, *Hist. Eccl.* 6.12.2–6.

30. Ehrman, *Forgery and Counterforgery*, 123. Ehrman adds, "the first-person pronoun (both singular and plural) was widely used in ancient texts, Christian and otherwise, precisely in order to provide authority for the account." *Forgery and Counterforgery*, 270.

31. Ehrman, *Forgery and Counterforgery*, 274.

32. "The tendency to minimize the guilt of Pilate which is found in the *Gospel According to Peter* shows the keen interest with which ancient Christianity regarded

his person. The prominent position occupied by Pontius Pilate in early Christian thought is further evidenced by the *Gospel of Nicodemus*. Into this narrative have been incorporated the so-called *Acts of Pilate*, a supposed official report of the procurator concerning Jesus." Johannes Quasten, *Patrology* (Allen, TX: Christian Classics, 1995), 1:115. For more on the "Acts of Pilate," see Justin Martyr, *First Apology* 35, and Tertullian, *Apology* 21, 24. This exoneration of Pilate extends even further in the Ethiopic church, where Pilate is considered a "saint" and June 25 has been assigned to him and his wife as a feast day.

33. "This appears to be part of an agenda that squarely fastens the blame for Jesus' death on the Jewish leaders under Herod." Helyer, *Life and Witness of Peter*, 291. See also C. H. Turner, "The Gospel of Peter," *Journal of Theological Studies* 14 (1913): 161–87. For discussion of anti-Jewish sentiments within early Christian literature, see Paula Fredriksen and Oded Irshai, "Christian Anti-Judaism: Polemics and Policies," in *The Cambridge History of Judaism Volume IV: The Late Roman-Rabbinic Period*, ed. Steven T. Katz (Cambridge: Cambridge University Press), 977–1034; and L. T. Johnson, "The New Testament's Anti-Jewish Slander and the Convention of Ancient Polemic," *Journal of Biblical Literature* 108 (1989): 419–41.

34. "It is significant that the document does underscore this apostle's specific role as an acknowledged broker of Jesus tradition." Bockmuehl, *Simon Peter in Scripture and Memory*, 52.

35. Although Peter's harsh denouncement of the Jews for their role in Jesus' execution in Acts 2 and 3 comes close, perhaps the anti-Jewish posture of Peter in the *Gospel of Peter* can in part be attributed to Luke's record.

36. Bockmuehl, *Simon Peter in Scripture and Memory*, 52.

37. See Stephen E. Robinson, "Warring against the Saints of God," *Ensign*, January 1988, 34–39.

38. One could include the Book of Moses or the Book of Abraham in this discussion as well.

39. For an exploration of this topic, see Dana M. Pike, "Is the Plan of Salvation Attested in the Dead Sea Scrolls?," in *LDS Perspectives on the Dead Sea Scrolls*, ed. Donald W. Parry and Dana M. Pike (Provo, UT: FARMS, 1997), 73–94.

40. This is certainly one text that resonates with Latter-day Saints due to its elaboration upon the journey of a young man from a premortal state through a mortal and into a postmortal state. See John W. Welch and James V. Garrison, "The 'Hymn of the Pearl': An Ancient Counterpart to 'O My Father,'" *BYU Studies* 36, no. 1 (1996): 127–38.

41. Stephen E. Robinson, "Lying for God: The Uses of Apocrypha," in *Apocryphal Writings and the Latter-day Saints*, ed. C. Wilfred Griggs (Provo, UT: Religious Studies Center, 1986), 148.

42. John W. Welch, "The Apocryphal Judas Revisited," *BYU Studies* 45, no. 2 (2006): 46.

43. John Gee, "The Apocryphal Acts of Jesus," *Interpreter: A Journal of Mormon Scripture*, December 7, 2012, 178.

44. Thomas A. Wayment, "False Gospels: An Approach to Studying the New Testament Apocrypha," in *How the New Testament Came to Be*, ed. Kent P. Jackson and Frank F. Judd Jr. (Provo, UT: Religious Studies Center; Salt Lake City: Deseret Book, 2006), 298–300.

45. "These sources do attest the memory of Peter in the second century, even though there may be few if any biographical or other details of historical interest." Bockmuehl, *Simon Peter in Scripture and Memory*, 54.

46. "It must also be recognized that later writers would want to emphasize different facets of this key figure for their own particular purpose." Lapham, *Peter*, 2.

47. Bockmuehl, *Simon Peter in Scripture and Memory*, 53.

19

Peter and the Restored Priesthood

Steven C. Harper

Steven C. Harper is a historian for the Church History Department who has
contributed to the Joseph Smith Papers Project.

Joseph Knight Sr. steered his wagon from the Susquehanna Valley, where
spring had returned, upstate toward the Whitmers' and the Smiths' houses.
Joseph Smith sat beside him, explaining that the time had come to organize the
Savior's church.[1]

"I will establish my Church," the Lord had told Joseph a year earlier.[2] It had
been an eventful year since. The translation of the Book of Mormon had ended,
and printing had begun. Meanwhile, Joseph and Oliver Cowdery, both mindful of a promise they had received from John the Baptist that they would be ordained to more priesthood, prayed for it until it came. Both Joseph and Oliver
testified that it came, the "reception of the holy Priesthood by the ministering of
angels."[3] According to a secondary account recorded in 1898, Joseph and Oliver
arose from prayer as a heavenly light enveloped them and they saw three angels
standing before them, dressed in white, their faces radiant.[4] "My name is Peter,"
said one who was flanked by companions on each side. "And," he continued,
pointing to the others, "these are James and John. We have come here according
to command from the Almighty to confer upon you the Apostleship to which
we have been ordained."[5]

Joseph remembered the sound of their voices, the wilderness setting, and their declaration that they possessed the keys of the kingdom and of the dispensation of the fulness of times (see D&C 128).[6] Oliver remembered having stood "in the presence of Peter," and how, along with James and John, the resurrected fisherman-Apostle made Apostles of him and Joseph.[7] Neither Joseph nor Oliver is on record saying when this happened. The fragmentary historical record can and has been used to support varied interpretations, all of which necessarily rely on some supposition.[8] Each alternative that deals responsibly with the complexity of the historical record should be considered. None of them, without the addition of conclusive evidence, should be asserted dogmatically.

This chapter is not designed to discover the date on which Peter ordained Joseph Smith, but to explore some implications of that ordination for both Peter and for the Restoration. It will highlight not only contributions Peter made to the Restoration, especially the Melchizedek Priesthood, but also what the Restoration can teach us about Peter, especially the nature of the priesthood he exercised, emphasizing what Peter and Joseph Smith offer us regarding the fulness of priesthood ordinances available in temples.

Restored Knowledge about Peter

As a result of the Restoration, we have knowledge about Peter that significantly expands what is known from the relatively sparse ancient sources. For instance, there is a well-known paronomasia, or play on words, in Matthew 16:18 regarding Peter's name.[9] "Thou art Peter," the Lord says there, "and upon this rock I will build my church." *Petros*, the Greek word the King James translators rendered in English as *Peter*, means "a small rock." The Apostle we call Peter, Jesus called something like Simon the stone. In the King James Version of John 1, recording Jesus' first encounter with Peter, the Savior says to him, "Thou shalt be called Cephas," an Aramaic word meaning "a stone" (John 1:42). In his revision of the Bible, Joseph added *seer*, so that the Joseph Smith Translation of John 1:42 has Jesus renaming Simon, saying, "Thou shalt be called Cephas, which is by interpretation, a seer, or a stone." Given the textual links between Jesus' name for Peter, a seer, a stone, and revelation, we might consider that the wordplay is richer than the King James Translation suggests and that we should regard Peter as a seer, a recipient of revelations, perhaps even by the use of a stone or stones used by other seers.[10]

Another rich insight into Peter's priesthood ministry comes from an early Church minute book, which records Joseph Smith's report of a little-known vision. In February 1834, Joseph Smith organized the Church's first stake, basing the structure on a revelation he'd had about Peter. Joseph gathered twenty-four brethren and promised to "show the order of councils in ancient days as shown to him by vision." He explained that "Jerusalem was the seat of the Church Council in ancient days" and added that "the apostle, Peter, was the president of the Council and held the keys of the Kingdom of God on the earth [and] was appointed to this office by the voice of the Savior and acknowledged in it by the voice of the Church. He had two men appointed as Counsellors with him."[11] A later revelation to Joseph formally linked Peter's roles as seer and president, saying that "the duty of the President of the office of the High Priesthood is to preside over the whole church . . . ; yea, to be a seer, a revelator, a translator, and a prophet, having all the gifts of God which he bestows upon the head of the church" (D&C 107:91–92).

So it was Peter, president of the Church of Jesus Christ, seer, Apostle, keeper of the keys, who returned to earth and bestowed on Joseph Smith the priesthood and keys he had received "under the hand of the Messiah" (see D&C 7, 27, 128).[12] The idea that Peter is alive, that he could appear in the Susquehanna River Valley and bestow priesthood, is a fruit of the Restoration. For believers, the testimony of Joseph and Oliver is evidence of Peter's historicity, and of the Savior's, for Peter appeared to them as a resurrected being in his capacity as an Apostle of the Lord Jesus Christ. To testify of being ordained by Peter in the nineteenth century is to testify of the resurrected Christ *and* of continuity with his original church.

Such a testimony is characteristic of the concrete Restoration. Joseph and Oliver's matter-of-fact story leaves little room to "spiritualize," as Oliver called it, meaning to explain away as figurative or mythical Christianity's bold claims of physical supernaturalism. In contrast to spiritualizing, a corporeal Peter appearing to Joseph and Oliver is what one scholar called "unflinching primitivism." The resulting "resurrection of original structures and practices, is nothing short of the demystification of Christianity itself."[13] To say it another way, "these ordinations by angelic ministrants grounded Joseph Smith's claims to divine authority" even as they testified that the New Testament tells a true story of Jesus' miraculous birth, choosing of twelve Apostles, death, and Resurrection. "Whereas Catholics claim an unbroken line of authority from the days of Peter," wrote philosopher David Paulsen, "Joseph proclaimed that through apostasy the chain had been broken and the authority lost. Whereas Protestants claim that all believers hold priesthood authority, Joseph claimed that God restored divine authority by literal hand-to-head transfer by the very prophets and apostles whose lives and words are recounted in the Bible."[14] So the testimony that Peter appeared at all is a witness that the Restoration was necessary, a witness that the Bible is generally true but insufficient, a witness that Christianity had lost its way and that no Christian in the modern era, however sincere, had authority to act for God until Peter and those acting under his direction restored it.

Peter's Contribution to the Restoration

Peter gave Joseph and Oliver what Joseph (quite early in the historical record) described as "a confirmation and reception of the high Priesthood after the holy order of the son of the living God," "power and ordinence from on high to preach the Gospel in the administration and demonstration of the spirit," and the "Kees of the Kingdom of God."[15] It's not clear whether Joseph used the word *confirmation* here consistently with its later usage to mean the ordinance by which Saints are invited to receive the Holy Ghost and to join the Church, but, if so, then Peter, James, and John not only ordained Joseph and Oliver after their baptisms, but also confirmed them, or at least bestowed the gift of the Holy Ghost.

Joseph's testimony that the ministering angels conferred power to preach the gospel and administer its ordinances helps us understand the nature of priesthood. Whatever understanding of priesthood we have, including the ability to rattle off the fifth Article of Faith, such knowledge is a fruit of what Peter revealed. Before that, it was by no means obvious, or uniform throughout Christendom that, as Joseph taught, "no man can administer salvation through the gospel, to the souls of men, in the name of Jesus Christ, except he is authorized from God, by revelation, or by being ordained by some one whom God hath sent by revelation."[16]

Priesthood keys were not a matter of much interest in Joseph Smith's culture. It is true that even as Joseph Smith led the Church, the Danish sculptor Bertel Thorvaldsen sculpted Peter holding keys, basing his work on the Savior's promise in Matthew 16:19 to give Peter keys of the kingdom of heaven. Catholic and Orthodox traditions value the keys Christ gave to Peter. Iconography from these traditions represents these keys frequently, and theologians have long debated their meaning.[17] But Latter-day Saints have made much of those keys compared to how little they were discussed and valued in the Protestant-dominated period and places of Joseph's ministry.

A revelation given to Joseph in spring 1829 clarified that Jesus gave keys of the apostolic ministry to Peter, James, and John—keys for them to steward until his Second Coming (see D&C 7).[18] Later, after the ancient Apostles had appeared to Joseph, the Lord reminded him about "Peter, and James, and John, whom I have sent unto you, by whom I have ordained you and confirmed you to be apostles, and especial witnesses of my name, and bear the keys of your ministry and of the same things which I revealed unto them" (D&C 27:12). Still later, Joseph reflected on the time he heard "the voice of Peter, James, and John in the wilderness . . . declaring themselves as possessing the keys of the kingdom" (D&C 128:20). In short, as Joseph's contemporary, Latter-day Saint Benjamin Winchester, put it, "Joseph said . . . that the keys of the kingdom had been given to him through the angels, Peter, James, and John," and that he used them to build the Church.[19]

Shortly before his death, Joseph gathered most of the Apostles, the same ones he had endowed, and emphasized to them that if he failed to confer on them the keys and powers he held, "they will be lost from the Earth." He then laid his hands on their heads and confirmed the keys on each of them, saying "thus can this power and these keys be perpetuated in the Earth." The Apostles subsequently testified solemnly "that Joseph Smith did declare that he had conferred upon the Twelve every key and every power that he ever held himself before God."[20]

More than a century later, President Spencer W. Kimball stood with Elder Boyd K. Packer and others in the Church of Our Lady in Copenhagen, Denmark, admiring Thorvaldsen's *Christus* and his sculptures of the Twelve Apostles. "I stood with President Kimball . . . before the statue of Peter," Elder Packer said. "In his hand, depicted in marble, is a set of heavy keys. President Kimball pointed to them and explained what they symbolized."[21] President Kimball then charged Copenhagen stake president Johan Bentine to "tell every prelate in Denmark that they do not hold the keys. I hold the keys!" As the Apostles left the church, President Kimball shook hands with the caretaker, "expressed his appreciation, and explained earnestly, 'These statues are of dead apostles,'" then, pointing to Elders Tanner, Monson, and Packer, added, "You are in the presence of living apostles."[22]

Joseph's Clarification of Peter's Priesthood Keys

Joseph's revelations and teachings not only declare that Peter restored keys, but they tell us how Peter got them and provide some information about their nature. The synoptic Gospels (see Matthew 17, Mark 9, Luke 9) tell the story of Christ's Transfiguration in the presence of Peter, James, and John. According to the account in Matthew, this occurred about a week after the Savior promised to give Peter keys of the kingdom. The Bible does not document the actual event of transmitting keys, but it records the Savior's promise to do so in Matthew 16 and acknowledges in Matthew 18 that the Apostles have the keys. In between is the story of the Savior's Transfiguration, a muddled story as we have it in the New Testament.

In a summer 1831 revelation to Joseph, the Savior explained at least part of the reason for the muddling. He described elements of the Transfiguration experience that are not recorded in the Bible and told Joseph that he had still not received a full account of what happened on the Mount (see D&C 63:20–23). The same revelation promised that those who were faithful would receive more of the mysteries, however, and Joseph apparently did. In an 1841 discourse, Joseph taught that the priesthood is everlasting, then traced how its keys came to him: "The Saviour, Moses, & Elias—gave the Keys to Peter, James & John on the Mount when they were transfigured before him. . . . How have we come at the priesthood in the last days? It came down, down in regular succession. Peter James & John had it given to them & they gave it up [to me]."[23]

Peter, Joseph Smith, and the Fulness of the Priesthood

According to the LDS Bible Dictionary, few biblical events rival the Transfiguration in importance.[24] Peter characterized what he received on the Mount or sometime subsequent to that experience, as a "more sure word of prophecy" (2 Peter 1:19), which Joseph defined, in the context of teaching about temple ordinances, as revealed knowledge of one's election to eternal life. Joseph, in other words, taught that what Peter and the others received on the Mount included "the fulness of preisthood or the law of God."[25] Joseph Fielding Smith took this kind of teaching to mean that "the Savior took the three disciples up on the mount, which is spoken of as the 'Mount of Transfiguration,' he there gave unto them the ordinances that pertain to the house of the Lord and . . . they were endowed."[26]

Early in 1841, Joseph Smith received a revelation in Nauvoo (see D&C 124) that linked the priesthood, its keys, and the ordinances of the temple, much as his September 1832 revelation had done (see D&C 84). Whereas the 1832 revelation called for a temple to be built in Independence, Missouri, for the performance of priesthood ordinances, the 1841 revelation commanded the Saints to build a temple in Nauvoo for the same reason, "for there is not a place found on earth," the revelation said, "that he may come to and restore again that which was lost unto you, or which he hath taken away, even the fulness of the priesthood. . . . Let this house be built unto my name, that I may reveal mine ordinances therein unto my people; for I deign to reveal unto my church . . . all things pertaining to this house, and the priesthood thereof"[27] (D&C 124:28, 40–42).

"It may seem to some, to be a very bold doctrine that we talk of," Joseph wrote to the Saints in September 1842 regarding the idea of priesthood temple ordinances that would endow Saints with power over death, "a power which records

or binds on earth and binds in heaven." Even so, he added, this is what priesthood
had always meant, and what the Lord meant when he told Peter, "I will give unto
thee the keys of the kingdom of heaven: and whatsoever thou shalt bind on earth
shall be bound in heaven; and whatsoever thou shalt loose on earth shall be loosed
in heaven." Obtaining these "powers of the Holy Priesthood," as Joseph called
them, was imperative to saving the human family from sin and death, and he emphasized that such salvation extended to the dead, who could receive priesthood
baptism vicariously (D&C 128:9–11).[28]

At almost the same time that he revealed how the priesthood and its keys
enabled baptism for the dead, Joseph taught about the meaning and significance
of the baptismal covenant generally, once again drawing on Peter. In making the
point that the Apostles fulfilled the Savior's instructions by teaching the law of the
gospel as described in Acts 2, Joseph reportedly said this concerning the matter:

> They were to wait at Jerusalem till they were endowed with power
> from on high and then go and teach all nations whatsoever the Lord
> had commanded them. As Peter held the keys of the kingdom, we
> will examine him first. Now on the day of Pentecost, when there was
> a marvellous display of the gifts, according to the promise in Mark,
> many were pricked in the heart, and said unto Peter, and to the rest
> of the Apostles, men and brethren what shall we do? Peter said unto
> them: Repent, and be baptised every one of you in the name of Jesus
> Christ, for the remission of sins, and ye shall receive the gift of the
> Holy Ghost, &c.—Here one of the witnesses says in so many words,
> repent and be baptised. And we are of the opinion that Peter hav-
> ing been taught by the Lord, and commissioned by the Lord, and
> endowed by the Lord, would be about as correct a counsellor, or
> ambassador as we or they could enquire of to know the right way to
> enter into the kingdom.[29]

It is possible that this editorial's statement that Peter was "endowed by the Lord"
should not be understood to refer to holy ordinances but to a less specific endowment of divine power, but probably not. Joseph had begun endowing Saints via
holy ordinances a few months earlier. And a few months later he said specifically
that "Peter was endowed," meaning the recipient of temple-related ordinances.[30]
Moreover, Joseph's Nauvoo teachings strongly suggested that Peter's more sure
word of prophecy was a kind of knowledge he gained via a process of covenant
making and keeping, mediated by templelike ordinances that led recipients ultimately to certainty of eternal life.

On May 4, 1842, Joseph spent the day with nine Church leaders "giving certain instructions concerning the priesthood." One of the participants, Willard Richards, documented the event in Joseph's journal and elaborated for Joseph's history, saying that Joseph endowed the men, giving them a version of the temple endowment. Teaching "the principles and order of the priesthood, [and] attending to washings & anointings, endowments, and the communication of keys, pertaining to the Aronic Priesthood, and so on to the highe[s]t order of Melchisedec Priesthood," Joseph shared, "all those plans & principles by which any one is enabled to secure the fullness of those blessings which has been prepared for the chu[r]ch of the first-born, and come up, and abide in the prese[n]ce of Eloheim in the eternal worlds."[31]

Willard emphasized that "there was nothing made known to these men but what will be made known to all saints . . . so soon as they are prepared to receive, and a proper place is prepared to communicate them . . . therefore let the saints be diligent in building the Temple."[32] And as the Nauvoo Temple rose, Joseph worked to prepare the Saints for its ordinances, relying heavily on Peter's teachings in 2 Peter 1 to do so.

On Sunday, May 14, 1843, at a settlement of Saints outside Nauvoo, Joseph rose to preach. He said, essentially, that God imparted knowledge by degrees, and then read from 2 Peter 1, emphasizing Peter's admonition to add knowledge to faith. Joseph linked that idea to Peter's more sure word of prophecy in the quest to make one's election to eternal life certain, saying, "Their is some grand secret ther[e] & keys to unlock the subject." Following the text of 2 Peter 1 back to the Mount of Transfiguration, Joseph highlighted Peter's distinction between two revelations he had received. The first was the voice of God declaring the divine sonship of Jesus Christ. "And this voice which came from heaven we heard," Peter wrote, "when we were with him in the holy mount." Then Peter talked about another revelation, saying, "We have also a more sure word of prophecy" (2 Peter 1:16–19). "Now wherein could they have a more sure word of prophecy" Joseph asked provocatively, "than to hear the voice of God saying this is my Beloved Son"? Then Joseph answered his own question: "Now for the Secret & grand Key though they might hear the voice of God & know that Jesus was the Son of God this would be no evidence that their election & Calling was made shure that they had part with Christ & was a Joint heir with him, they then would want that more sure word of Prophecy that they were sealed in the heavens & had the promise of eternal live in the Kingdom of God."[33] Throughout May 1843, Joseph continued preaching 2 Peter 1, restating Peter's admonition for Saints to make eternal life a certainty for them by striving for the revelation of that "Knowledge through our Lord & savior Jesus Christ" and qualifying for the ordinances by which the promise of eternal life would be "sealed unto them."[34]

Joseph visited Saints in Ramus, Illinois, later the same week and told them that "Peter penned the most sublime language of any of the apostles." He preached again on 2 Peter 1, driving home the same temple-centered principles of progressing from one degree of knowledge to another in the quest for eternal life. According to his secretary, William Clayton, Joseph "shewed that knowledge is power & the man who has the most knowledge has the greatest power. Also that salvation means a mans being placed beyond the powers of all his enemies. He said the more sure word of prophecy meant a mans knowing that he is sealed up unto eternal life by revelation & the spirit of prophecy through the power of the Holy priesthood."[35]

Joseph was back in Nauvoo for the Sabbath on May 21, 1843, and he preached the same doctrine there for about two hours.[36] Taking again as his text Peter's teaching about the more sure word of prophecy (2 Peter 1), Joseph explained and elaborated, paraphrasing Peter throughout, especially verses 16–19. He taught that one's calling and election to eternal life could be made sure by seeking and finally obtaining "a promise from God for yourselves that you shall have eternal life."[37] Joseph stressed that Peter was teaching these doctrines to initiated Saints, those "of like precious faith," and that the gist of his teaching was that one must make and keep the gospel covenants, beginning with baptism, until one receives power over death. Howard Coray recorded that Joseph spoke "On Election." He noted that Joseph evoked Peter's testimony of being an eyewitness of the transfigured Lord and also the recipient of a more sure word of prophecy. Then, according to Coray, Joseph asked, "who can explain this[?] no man be [but] he that has obtained these things in the same way that Peter did." As he continued, Joseph said tantalizingly, "these are but hints of those things that were revealed to Peter, and verily brethren there are things in the bosom of the Father, that have been hid from the foundation of the world, that are not Known neither can be except by direct Revelation." Joseph equated such revelation with the kind of knowledge that Peter had exhorted the Saints to add to their faith. Such knowledge, Joseph emphasized, makes one's calling and election sure. "Knowledge is Revelation," Joseph underscored. "Knowledge is the power of God unto Salvation." He explained the kind of knowledge he and Peter had in mind: "It is one thing to receive knowledge by the voice of God, (this is my beloved Son &c.) & another to Know that you yourself will be saved, to have a positive promise of your own[.] Salvation is making your Calling and Election sure. [Namely] the voice of Jesus saying my beloved thou shalt have eternal life. Brethren," Joseph implored, "never cease strug[g]ling until you get this evidence. . . . this more sure word of Prophecy."[38]

Conclusion

Joseph Smith identified with Peter, having received the priesthood and its keys under his hands, having envisioned Peter as he led the church anciently, and sharing the challenge of teaching the Saints that they could and should strive to make and keep the covenants and receive the revelations of eternal life by receiving the fulness of priesthood ordinances. At one point in his historic May 21, 1843, sermon, Joseph appealed to the Apostle, "Oh Peter if they who were of like precious faith with thee were injoined to make their Calling & Election sure, how much more all we."[39]

The Restoration depended on Peter. "The final triumph of Mormonism," wrote Lorenzo Snow, "depends wholly on whether it be a fact that Joseph Smith was authorized of God, through the administration of Peter, James and John, to administer the ordinances of the Gospel."[40] Joseph testified that he was, in fact, so authorized, so ordained. Ten-year-old Angus Cannon heard the Prophet bear that testimony and never forgot it.[41] Adding his witness, Oliver Cowdery testified, "upon this head has Peter James and John laid their hands and confer[r]ed the Holy Melchesdic Priesthood."[42] On another occasion he testified that he had "stood in in the presence of Peter, to receive the Greater [priesthood]" and looked down through time to see its powerful effects.[43] Those effects include the fulness of the priesthood, temple ordinances that endow the faithful with power over sin and death, sealing and repairing relationships, and offering certainty of eternal life.

No wonder the early Saints sang praises to God that identified Joseph Smith as the esteemed latter-day seer who had received priesthood keys from Peter himself. It is a bold doctrine, and beautiful. May we sing, as the early Saints did:

> The Priesthood is again restor'd,
> For this let God be long ador'd.[44]

Notes

1. Joseph Knight, Sr., Reminiscences, n.d., Church History Library, Salt Lake City, 6.

2. Michael Hubbard MacKay, Gerrit J. Dirkmaat, Grant Underwood, Robert J. Woodford, William G. Hartley, eds., *Documents, Volume 1: July 1828–June 1831*, vol. 1 of the Documents series of *The Joseph Smith Papers*, ed. Dean C. Jessee, Ronald K. Esplin, and Richard Lyman Bushman (Salt Lake City: Church Historian's Press, 2013), 17.

3. Karen Lynn Davidson, David J. Whittaker, Mark Ashurst-McGee, and Richard L. Jensen, eds., *Histories, Volume 1: Joseph Smith Histories, 1832–1844*, vol. 1 of the Histories series of *The Joseph Smith Papers*, ed. Dean C. Jessee, Ronald K. Esplin,

and Richard Lyman Bushman (Salt Lake City: Church Historian's Press, 2012), 10. See also Joseph Smith to Oliver Cowdery, Blessing, December 18, 1833, recorded September 1835 in Patriarchal Blessings, Book 1, 12, Church History Library, Salt Lake City.

4. Charles M. Nielsen to Heber J. Grant, February 10, 1898, Church History Library, Salt Lake City. See also Nielsen to Grant, November 14, 1899.

5. Nielsen to Grant, February 10, 1898. See also Nielson to Grant, November 14, 1899.

6. Robin Scott Jensen, Richard E. Turley Jr., and Riley M. Lorimer, eds., *Revelations and Translations, Volume 2: Published Revelations*, vol. 2 of the Revelations and Translations series of *The Joseph Smith Papers*, ed. Dean C. Jessee, Ronald K. Esplin, and Richard Lyman Bushman (Salt Lake City: Church Historian's Press, 2011), 680–90. See also Joseph Smith, "Letter from Joseph Smith," *Times and Seasons*, October 1, 1842, 934–36.

7. Oliver Cowdery to Phineas Young, March 23, 1846, Church History Library, Salt Lake City. See also Oliver Cowdery to Samuel W. Richards, January 13, 1849, *Deseret Evening News*, March 22, 1884, 2.

8. See, most recently, MacKay et al., *Documents, Volume 1*, xxxvii–xxxix, 70–74. See also D&C 27 and 128. Other alternatives are summarized and the historical record set forth in Brian Q. Cannon and BYU Studies Staff, "Priesthood Restoration Documents," *BYU Studies* 35, no. 4 (1995–96): 162–207. See also Larry C. Porter, "Dating the Restoration of the Melchizedek Priesthood," *Ensign*, June 1979, 4–10. See also Richard E. Bennett, "The Circumference of the Apostleship," in *A Firm Foundation: Church Organization and Administration*, ed. David J. Whittaker and Arnold K. Garr (Provo, UT: Religious Studies Center; Salt Lake City: Deseret Book, 2011), 59–81.

9. See Matthew 16:18, footnote *a*.

10. See, for instance, Ether 3:23–24 and D&C 17:1. Regarding revelation as the rock to which Jesus referred, see Joseph Smith, Discourse, January 22, 1843, Nauvoo, Illinois, Wilford Woodruff, Journals, Church History Library, Salt Lake City. See also in Andrew F. Ehat and Lyndon W. Cook, *The Words of Joseph Smith: The Contemporary Accounts of the Nauvoo Discourses of the Prophet Joseph*, Religious Studies Monograph Series, no. 6 (Provo, UT: Religious Studies Center, 1980), 156–59, where Joseph says, "Jesus in his teaching says upon this rock I will build my Church & the gates of hell shall not prevail against it. What rock? Revelation." For a discussion of Joseph Smith's use of seer stones, see Robin Scott Jensen, Robert J. Woodford, and Steven C. Harper, eds., *Manuscript Revelation Books*, facsimile edition, vol. 1 of the Revelations and Translations series of *The Joseph Smith Papers*, ed. Dean C. Jessee, Ronald K. Esplin, and Richard Lyman Bushman (Salt Lake City: Church Historian's Press, 2009), xxi. Also see "Book of Mormon Translation" (accessed December 31, 2013), http://www.lds.org/topics/book-of-mormon-translation?lang=eng.

11. Kirtland Minute Book, February 17–19, Church History Library, Salt Lake City.

12. Patriarchal Blessings, Book 1 (1835), 12, Church History Library, Salt Lake City.

13. Terryl L. Givens, *Viper on the Hearth: Mormons, Myths, and the Construction of Heresy* (New York: Oxford University Press, 1997), 93.

14. David L. Paulsen, "Joseph Smith Challenges the Theological World," *BYU Studies* 44, no. 4, (2005): 184.

15. Davidson et al., *Histories, Volume 1*, 10, original spellings preserved.

16. Joseph Smith to Isaac Galland, March 22, 1839, Liberty, Missouri, *Times and Seasons*, February 1840, 54.

17. George Joyce, "Power of the Keys," in *The Catholic Encyclopedia*, vol. 8 (New York: Robert Appleton Company, 1910), http://www.newadvent.org/cathen/08631b.htm (accessed September 26, 2013). See also John Higgitt, "The Iconography of Saint Peter in Anglo-Saxon England, and Saint Cuthbert's Coffin," in *St. Cuthbert, His Cult and His Community to A.D. 1200*, ed. Gerald Bonner, David Rollason, and Clare Stancliffe (Woodbridge: Boydell and Brewer, 1989), 267–72. For an example of Catholic iconography, see "Saint Peter the Apostle," http://www.aug.edu/augusta/iconography/peter.html (accessed September 26, 2013).

18. John Taylor reportedly said in December 1876, "In speaking with the Prophet Joseph once on this subject, he traced it from the first down to the last, until he got to the Ancient of Days. He wished me to write something for him of this subject, but I found it a very difficult thing to do. He had to correct me several times. We are told that the 'judgment shall sit and the books be opened.' He spoke of the various dispensations and of those holding the keys thereof, and said there would then be a general giving up or accounting for. I wrote that each one holding the keys of the several dispensations would deliver them up to his predecessor, from one to another, until the whole kingdom should be delivered up to the Father, and then God would be 'all in all.' Said he, 'That is not right.' I wrote it again, and again he said it was not right. It is very difficult to find language suitable to convey the meaning of spiritual things. The idea was that they should deliver up or give an account of their administrations, in their several dispensations, but that they would all retain their several positions and Priesthood." *Journal of Discourses*, 26 vols. (London: LDS Booksellers Depot, 1855–86), 18:329–30.

19. Benjamin Winchester, "Primitive Mormonism," *Salt Lake Daily Tribune*, September 22, 1889, 2.

20. Alexander L. Baugh and Richard Neitzel Holzapfel, eds., "'I Roll the Burthen and Responsibility of Leading This Church Off from My Shoulders on to Yours': The 1844/1845 Declaration of the Quorum of the Twelve Regarding Apostolic Succession, *BYU Studies* 49, no. 3 (2010): 18–19.

21. Boyd K. Packer, *The Holy Temple* (Salt Lake City: Deseret Book, 1980), 83.

22. Edward L. Kimball, *Lengthen Your Stride: The Presidency of Spencer W. Kimball* (Salt Lake City: Deseret Book, 2005), 108, 327.

23. Joseph Smith, discourse, May 16, 1841, Nauvoo, Illinois, William Clayton, Notebook, Church History Library, Salt Lake City. Also in Ehat and Cook, *Words of Joseph Smith*, 9.

24. The experience on the Mount of Transfiguration was apparently similar in some ways to Joseph and Oliver's on April 3, 1836. They received keys in the house of the Lord at Kirtland, where Joseph and Oliver were blessed by most if not all of the same ministering angels that appeared to Peter with the Savior on the Mount (see D&C 110 and LDS Bible Dictionary, "Transfiguration, Mount of").

25. Joseph Smith, discourse, August 27, 1843, Nauvoo, Illinois, James Burgess, Journals, 1841–48, vol. 2, Church History Library; original spelling is preserved. Also in Ehat and Cook, *Words of Joseph Smith*, 245–47.

26. Joseph Fielding Smith, *Doctrines of Salvation* 3 vols., comp. Bruce R. McConkie (Salt Lake City: Bookcraft, 1954–56), 2:165.

27. "Extracts from a Revelation given to Joseph Smith, Jr., Jan. 19th 1841," *Times and Seasons*, June 1, 1841, 424–29.

28. Revelation, Joseph Smith to the Church, September 6, 1842, In Hiding (D&C 128), Joseph Smith, Papers, Journals, Book of the Law of the Lord, Church History Library, Salt Lake City, 196–201. Also in Smith, "Letter from Joseph Smith," 934–36.

29. Editorial, "Baptism," *Times and Seasons* 3 (September 1, 1842): 904.

30. Discourse, June 11, 1843, Nauvoo, Illinois, Joseph Smith, Papers, Journals, Church History Library, Salt Lake City.

31. Historian's Office, JS History, draft notes, May 4, 1842, JS History, vol. C-1, 1328–29, *Joseph Smith Papers*; original spelling preserved.

32. Historian's Office, JS History, draft notes, May 4, 1842.

33. Discourse, May 14, 1843, Yelrome, Hancock County, Illinois, Wilford Woodruff, Journal, Church History Library, Salt Lake City. See also Ehat and Cook, *Words of Joseph Smith*, 201.

34. Ehat and Cook, *Words of Joseph Smith*, 201.

35. Discourse and Revelation (D&C 131:5–6), May 17, 1843, Ramus, Illinois, William Clayton, Diary, Church History Library, Salt Lake City. See also Ehat and Cook, *Words of Joseph Smith*, 202.

36. Discourse, May 21, 1843, Nauvoo, Illinois, Levi Richards, Papers, 1837–67, Journal, MS. (MS 1284, box 1, folder 5, vol. 18), Church History Library, Salt Lake City.

37. Discourse, May 21, 1843, Nauvoo, Illinois, James Burgess, Journals, 1841–48, vol. 2, (MS 1858), Church History Library, Salt Lake City. See also Ehat and Cook, *Words of Joseph Smith*, 334.

38. Discourse, May 21, 1843, Nauvoo, Illinois, Howard Coray, in Howard and Martha Coray Notebook, Church History Library, Salt Lake City. See also Ehat and Cook, *Words of Joseph Smith*, 206–8.

39. Discourse, May 21, 1843, Nauvoo, Illinois, Howard Coray, 207–8.

40. Lorenzo Snow, To my family, July 1, 1886, Utah Penitentiary, quoted in full in Dennis B. Horne, *Latter Leaves in the Life of Lorenzo Snow* (Springville, UT: Cedar Fort, 2012), 158–61.

41. "He heard the Prophet Joseph testify regarding the appearance of Peter, James, and John. Though at this time Brother Cannon was a boy of ten years, the words of the Prophet made a deep impression upon him." Statement, Salt Lake Stake, High Priest Quorum Minute Book, 1904–26, series 13, vol. 8A, August 27, 1911, Church History Library, Salt Lake City, 13.

42. David H. Cannon, autobiography, March 13, 1917, 5; photocopy of holography in possession of Richard Lloyd Anderson; original spelling preserved.

43. Oliver Cowdery to Phineas Young, March 23, 1846, Church History Library, Salt Lake City.

44. Emma Smith, *A Collection of Sacred Hymns for the Church of the Latter Day Saints* (Kirtland, OH: Frederick G. Williams and Company, 1835), hymn 72 and hymn 76.

Appendix

Peter, My Brother

Spencer W. Kimball

Spencer W. Kimball was Acting President of the Quorum of the Twelve Apostles
when this was published in *Speeches of the Year*
(Provo, UT: Brigham Young University Press, 1971), 1–8.

*On July 13, 1971, Spencer W. Kimball delivered his seminal address "Peter, My
Brother" at a Brigham Young University devotional. Occasioned by an Easter editorial that President Kimball had read some time earlier, his talk objected to the
frequent use of Peter's apparent failings—particularly his denial of the Savior—in
a way that detracted from the ancient Apostle's stature and subsequent valiance in
spreading and leading the early Christian church. In that regard, much of the talk
must be understood in its original context, in which President Kimball was primarily interested in defending the reputation of Peter by putting his failings into the
larger context of his fervent discipleship and subsequent faithful witness and service.*

*Because this talk is often referred to in discussions about Peter's denial, it is im-
portant to review what Elder Kimball actually did and did not say in it. President
Kimball reviews at least five different reasons for Peter's action. While he acknowledges the possibility that fear or cowardice might have overwhelmed Peter at that
critical moment, President Kimball quickly points out that even if this were the case,
Peter nonetheless provided an important lesson in repenting sincerely and changing
completely (p. 2). Other possible reasons President Kimball reviews include Peter's
acting out of confusion and frustration (p. 3); thinking that circumstances justified*

an outward denial, especially since the Lord had told Peter at Caesarea Philippi that he "should tell no man that he was Jesus the Christ" (p. 3); feeling further frustration because Jesus had prohibited him from trying to stop the Crucifixion (p. 4); and perhaps believing that it was advantageous to the cause for him to avoid being arrested himself so that he could preside over the Church (p. 5).

Nowhere in this address does President Kimball directly suggest that the Savior himself commanded Peter to deny knowing him, although some seem to have deduced that from references to Jesus' directing Peter not to tell anyone that he was the Christ and his prohibiting Peter from trying to keep him from being crucified. In fact, in the end President Kimball simply maintains, "I do not pretend to know what Peter's mental reactions were that night nor what compelled him to say what he did that terrible night." Nevertheless, President Kimball makes it clear that we should be hesitant to judge the chief Apostle and should instead focus on how such experiences focused and refined Peter, seeing them in the greater context of the great things that Peter went on to do after the Savior's Crucifixion and Resurrection. "In light of his proven bravery, courage, great devotion, and limitless love for the Master," President Kimball asks, "could we not give him the benefit of the doubt and at least forgive him as his Savior seems to have done so fully?" (p. 5).

Much referred to and often quoted by many, President Kimball's talk is not always read in its complete form. Accordingly, its full text bears reproduction here for easy and accurate reference (the original pagination, for instance, appears in this text in square brackets at the point of each page break). Further, as a striking portrait of an ancient Apostle by one of his latter-day colleagues, this speech has become a classic as a testimonial of Peter's character and ministry, one that has a natural place in a volume such as this about the chief Apostle.

Today I wish to talk about my brother, my colleague, my fellow Apostle— Simon Barjona or Cephas or Peter the Rock.

Some time ago a newspaper in a distant town carried an Easter Sunday religious editorial by a minister who stated that the presiding authority of the early-day church fell because of self-confidence, indecision, evil companions, failure to pray, lack of humility, and fear of man. He then concluded, "Let us as people, especially those who are Christians and claim to abide by the Word of God, not make the same mistakes and fall as Peter fell."[1]

As I read this, I had some strange emotions. I was shocked, then I was chilled, then my blood changed its temperature and began to boil. I felt I was attacked viciously, for Peter was my brother, my colleague, my example, my prophet, and God's anointed. I whispered to myself, "That is not true. He is maligning my brother."

A Man with Vision

Then I opened my New Testament. I could find no such character as this modern minister described. Instead, I found a man who had grown perfect through his experiences and sufferings—a man with vision, a man of revelations, a man fully trusted by his Lord Jesus Christ.

I remember his sad, triple denial of his acquaintance with the Lord in those terrifying, frustrating moments. I recall his tearful repentance. Many times he was rebuked by the Master, but he learned by experience and never seemed to make the same error twice. I see a lowly fisherman, untaught and untrained, climb gradually under the tutelage of the best Teacher to the high pinnacle of great faith, bold leadership, unwavering testimony, unparalleled courage, and almost limitless understanding. I see the lay disciple become the chief Apostle to preside over the Lord's church and kingdom. I hear him breathing heavily as he laboriously climbs the steep Mount of Transfiguration. Here he sees and hears unspeakable things and has the transcendent experience of being in the presence of his God, Elohim; Jehovah, his Redeemer; and other heavenly beings.

His eyes had seen, his ears had heard, and his heart had understood and accepted the wondrous happenings of the days from the baptism of the Master in the waters of Jordan to the ascension of his Redeemer from the Mount of Olives.

I see this great church president assume leadership of the church. I see the sick and infirm arise and leap to health and normalcy. I hear his powerful sermons. I [2] see him walk steadily, unflinchingly to martyrdom and drink of its bitter cup.

But this sectarian minister belittled him, unmercifully undercut him, and downgraded him.

Much of the criticism of Simon Peter is centered in his denial of his acquaintance with the Master. This has been labeled "cowardice." Are we sure of his motive in that recorded denial? He had already given up his occupation and placed all worldly goods on the altar for the cause. If we admit that he was cowardly and denied the Lord through timidity, we can still find a great lesson. Has anyone more completely overcome mortal selfishness and weakness? Has anyone repented more sincerely? Peter has been accused of being harsh, indiscreet, impetuous, and fearful. If all these were true, then we still ask, Has any man ever more completely triumphed over his weaknesses?

The First Apostle

Good men were among the Lord's followers, yet Cephas was chosen the number one. The Lord knew well the guilelessness of Nathaniel, the tender love of John, the erudition of Nicodemus, and the faithfulness and devotion of James and the other brethren. Christ knew men's inner thoughts and saw their manifestations of faith. In short, he knew men; yet he chose from all of them this great character who possessed the virtues, powers, and leadership needed to give stability to the church and to lead men to accept the gospel and follow truth.

When Christ chose this fisherman for his first and chief Apostle, he was taking no chances. He picked a diamond in the rough—a diamond that would need to be cut, trimmed, and polished by correction, chastisement, and trials—but nevertheless a diamond of real quality. The Savior knew this Apostle could be trusted to receive the keys of the kingdom, the sealing and the loosing power. Like other humans, Peter might make some errors in his developing process, but he would be solid, trustworthy, and dependable as a leader of the kingdom of God. Even with so perfect a teacher, it was difficult to learn the vast gospel plan in three years.

Peter inquired of Jesus:

> Behold, we have forsaken all, and followed thee; what shall we have therefore?
> And Jesus said unto them, Verily I say unto you, That ye which have followed me, in the regeneration when the Son of man shall sit in the throne of his glory, ye also shall sit upon twelve thrones, judging the twelve tribes of Israel. (Matthew 19:27–28)

Is it conceivable that the omniscient Lord would give all these powers and keys to one who was a failure or unworthy?

If Peter was cowardly, how brave he became in so short a time. If he was weak and vacillating, how strong and positive he became in weeks and months. If he was unkind, how tender and sympathetic he became almost immediately. Responsibility as a refiner and a purger usually takes time.

If Peter was frightened in the court when he denied his association with the Lord, how brave he was hours earlier when he drew his sword against an overpowering enemy, the night mob. Later defying the people and state and church officials, he boldly charged, "Him [the Christ] . . . ye have taken, and by wicked hands have crucified and slain" (Acts 2:23). To the astounded populace at the healing of the cripple at the Gate Beautiful, he exclaimed, "Ye men of Israel, . . . the God of our fathers, hath glorified his Son Jesus; whom ye [3] delivered up, and denied him in the presence of Pilate; . . . ye denied the Holy One . . . and killed the Prince of life, whom God hath raised from the dead; whereof we are witnesses" (Acts 3:12–15).

Does this portray cowardice? Quite a bold assertion for a timid one. Remember that Peter never denied the divinity of Christ. He only denied his association or acquaintance with the Christ, which is quite a different matter.

Could it have been confusion and frustration that caused Peter's denial? Could there still have been some lack of understanding concerning the total unfolding of the plan? Being a leader, Peter was a special target of the adversary. As the Lord said,

> Simon, Simon, behold, Satan hath desired to have you, that he may sift you as wheat:
>> But I have prayed for thee, that thy faith fail not. (Luke 22:31–32)

Peter was under fire; all the hosts of hell were against him. The die had been cast for the Savior's Crucifixion. If Satan could destroy Simon now, what a victory he would score. Here was the greatest of all living men. Lucifer wanted to confuse him, frustrate him, limit his prestige, and totally destroy him. However, this was not to be, for he was chosen for and ordained to a high purpose in heaven, as was Abraham.

Peter followed the Savior to his trial and sat in the outer court. What else could he do? He knew that many times the Savior himself had escaped from the crowd by slipping out of their clutches. Would he again do so?

Though the Lord taught of the coming Crucifixion and Resurrection, neither Simon nor anyone else fully comprehended his meaning. Was this so strange? Never before had there been such a person or such an occurrence on the earth. Millions today cannot understand the Resurrection, even though it has been preached for nineteen hundred years as a reality with many infallible proofs. Could these men, then, be criticized for not fully understanding this frustrating situation?

Is it possible that there might have been some other reason for Peter's triple denial?

Could he have felt that circumstances justified expediency? When he bore a strong testimony in Caesarea Philippi, he had been told that "they should tell no man that he was Jesus the Christ" (Matthew 16:20).

When the three Apostles came down from the Mount of Transfiguration, they were again charged implicitly, "Tell the vision to no man, until the Son of man be risen again from the dead" (Matthew 17:9). Could Peter have felt this was not the time to tell of Christ? He had been with his Lord in Nazareth when the Savior was taken by his own people to the brow of the hill, "whereon their city was built, that they might cast him down headlong. But he passing through the midst of them went his way" (Luke 4:29–30). Surely Peter did not think of this escape as cowardice but as wise expediency. Christ's time was not come.

The Approaching Crucifixion

When the Lord had spent some energy in attempting to explain the coming crisis—"how that he must go unto Jerusalem, and suffer many things of the elders and chief priests and scribes, and be killed, and be raised again the third day"—Peter attempted to dissuade the Savior from thinking of such calamity (see Matthew 16:21). He was promptly chastised for suggesting escape from the [4] tragedy. Perhaps he should have understood that it was the Lord's will that the dire happenings occur.

What this meant—that the hour was now come—Peter may not have fully realized, but he was prohibited from resisting the coming Crucifixion by the Redeemer himself. Was he frustrated? Perhaps for the moment, but how many of us in a hostile camp, totally helpless to save, would champion the Lord under such circumstances, especially when previous efforts had been repulsed? Had not Peter single-handedly already raised his sword against "a great multitude with swords and staves" (Matthew 26:47)? Had he not attempted to defend the Lord from all the mob's manhandling and kidnapping, and was he not stopped by his Lord?

The Savior had walked calmly from Gethsemane's garden, seemingly resigned to the inevitable sacrifice of himself. Simon had courageously manifested his willingness to alone fight the great mob to protect his Master. At the risk of death he had struck the contemptible Malthus and sliced off his ear. But this act of bravery and personal disregard was stopped by the Lord, who said to his loyal Apostle:

> Put up again thy sword into his place: for all they that take the sword shall perish with the sword.
>
> Thinkest thou that I cannot now pray to my Father, and he shall presently give me more than twelve legions of angels? (Matthew 26:52–53)

What more could Peter do? How else could he show his loyalty and courage? Could it be that in these last hours Peter realized that he should stop protecting his Lord, that the Crucifixion was inevitable, and that regardless of all his acts, the Lord was moving toward his destiny? I do not know. I only know that this Apostle was brave and fearless.

Events followed each other in rapid succession. At Gethsemane Peter was futilely trying to defend his Lord one hour; in the next he was following the mob. Apparently the Savior was voluntarily suffering men to heap monumental indignities upon him. What should Peter do?

He boldly and meaningfully postulated to the Savior, "Though all men shall be offended because of thee, yet will I never be offended" (Matthew 26:33). To which the Lord replied, "This night, before the cock crow, thou shalt deny me thrice" (Matthew 26:34).

This was a critical moment. Peter's act of protection with his sword slashing had been after this prediction was made. He had tried. He had seen one Apostle betray his Master with a kiss, and his Master had not repulsed him. Peter had been reminded that angels could be summoned if protection was needed; he had been commanded to put away his sword. Even now he did not desert his Master but followed sorrowfully behind the jeering crowd. He would remain to the end. He likely heard every accusation, saw every indignity heaped upon his Lord, felt all the injustice of the mock trial, and noted the perfidy of false witnesses perjuring their souls. He saw them foully expectorate in the face of the Holy One; he saw them buffet, strike, slap, and taunt him. He observed the Lord making no resistance, calling for no protective legions of angels, asking for no mercy. What was Peter to think now?

His Denial

A smart-aleck damsel accused Peter, "Thou also wast with Jesus of Galilee" (Matthew 26:69). What would his further defense of the Lord accomplish in this situation? Would it displease Jesus? Would it only destroy Peter himself without [5] beneficial effect? Would Christ want him to fight now, when he had denied him that privilege earlier that evening?

Then another maid announced to the bystanders and villains, "This fellow was also with Jesus of Nazareth" (Matthew 26:71). Peter replied, "I do not know the man" (Matthew 26:72). And others, recognizing his Galilean accent, declared, "Surely thou also art one of them; for thy speech betrayeth thee" (Matthew 26:73).

What was he to do? Could he do more? What would have been the result had he admitted his connection? Would he have lived to preside over the church? Peter had seen the Savior escape from crowds many times and hide from assassins. Is it conceivable that Peter also saw advisable advantage to the cause in his denial? Had Peter come to fully realize the hidden meaning in the oft-repeated phrase "Mine hour is not yet come" (John 2:4), and did he now understand that "now is the Son of man glorified" (John 13:31)?

I do not pretend to know what Peter's mental reactions were nor what compelled him to say what he did that terrible night. But in light of his proven bravery, courage, great devotion, and limitless love for the Master, could we not give him the benefit of the doubt and at least forgive him as his Savior seems to have done so fully? Almost immediately Christ elevated him to the highest position in his church and endowed him with the complete keys of that kingdom.

Simon Barjona did not have long to consider the matter or change his decisions, for he now heard the cock crow twice and was reminded of Christ's prediction. He was humbled to the dust. Hearing the bird's announcement of the dawn reminded him not only that he had denied the Lord but also that all the Lord had said would be fulfilled, even to the Crucifixion. He went out and wept bitterly. Were his tears for personal repentance only, or were they mingled with sorrowful tears in realization of the fate of his Lord and Master and his own great loss?

Only hours passed until he was among the first at the tomb as the head of the group of believers. Only weeks passed until he was assembling the saints and organizing them into a compact, strong, and unified community. It was not long before he was languishing in prison, being beaten, abused, and "sifted as wheat" as Christ had predicted (see Luke 22:31).

Of Humble Origin

Simon Peter, son of Jonas, began his matchless career under most humble circumstances. A common operator of boats, a fisher of fish, and a man once rated as "ignorant and unlearned," he climbed the ladder of knowledge until he knew, as perhaps no other living person, his Father, Elohim; the Son, Jehovah; and Christ's program and relationship with men. He was spiritual and devout. He came without persuasion, probably walking every step of the length of the major Jordan to hear the powerful sermons of the fearless John the Baptist. Little did he know the great things in store for him. Here he heard the voice of the prophet and may have been baptized by him.

Peter's brother, Andrew, declared, "We have found the Messias, which is, being interpreted, the Christ" (John 1:41). They had undoubtedly heard John the Baptist declare, "Behold the Lamb of God, which taketh away the sin of the world" (John 1:29). But to hear the voice of the living Father, God, now acknowledge Jesus as his Begotten Son must have stirred this humble fisherman to his foundations.

[6] Simon Peter was ill prepared at this time to assume great responsibility, but the Master knew his potential. On the day of his call began the intensive training that was to bring this humble man and his associates to great leadership, immortality, and eternal life.

Simon Peter's education, both secular and spiritual, had been limited, but now he followed the Master Teacher. He heard the Sermon on the Mount; he stood with the Redeemer in the boat and heard the masterful sermons to the congregated people. He sat in the synagogues, listening to the convincing and powerful statements of the Creator. The scriptures were unfolded as they traveled the dusty or rocky paths of Galilee. Surely, his innumerable questions were answered by the Lord as they ate together, slept together, and walked together. The hours were precious as rare jewels. He heard the parables given to the people and learned the rich lessons therein.

Peter heard the constant flow of divinity in the ceaseless unfolding of the way of life. He grasped many lessons readily but had difficulty in understanding the experiences that had never before occurred on earth. He perceived the darkening shadow and the lowering clouds but could not fully comprehend their meaning. No personage in his experience had ever given his life in this manner. No soul on earth had ever been resurrected. It took time for these awesome truths to penetrate his mind. It was hard for him to think of spiritual leadership only. Peter expected Christ to take the sword and redeem Israel. But when Gethsemane was passed, when Golgotha was a hard nightmare, when the Lord had risen and ascended, and when the Comforter had come, the great compelling truth burst forth and was impressed upon his mind. The miscellaneous tiles were now set into a beautiful pattern. The mosaic was a glorious reality; and Peter, James and John and their associates went forth to convert a hard, resisting world.

Peter was full of faith. He never faltered. From the day he forsook his nets and boats, his feet never turned away. Even in his moment of denial, he was as near to his Lord as he could be. Let him who would be critical of this Apostle put himself in the same place—among the bitterest enemies, persecutors, and assassins—with a growing knowledge of the futility of defending his Lord, whose hour had come. He who had forgiven his crucifiers also forgave Peter who had denied him.

Peter was a man of faith. He healed the sick by their merely passing through his shadow. Prison walls could not hold him. Because of him, the dead came back to life. He walked upon the water. Though this was not a total triumph, has any other human soul succeeded? Let him who would scoff at Peter's momentary wavering try such a feat himself.

Simon Peter was humble. He recognized James and John, who were with him on the Holy Mount and who shared with him the sorrows of Gethsemane. Perhaps his first official act, as presiding authority, was to call a conference at which the saints were to have voice in filling the vacancy in the Quorum of the Twelve. A new witness was chosen.

When the lame walked under the administration of Peter and John and when the awestricken multitude gaped and wondered, Peter gave credit to the God of Israel, saying, "Why look ye so earnestly on us, as though by our power or holiness we had made this man to walk?" (Acts 3:12). When Dorcas Tabitha lay dead, there was no display nor ostentation. He simply "put them all forth, and kneeled down, and [7] prayed," and presented the living Tabitha back to her friends (see Acts 9:40–41).

He accepted threats, beatings, and calumny. He defied those who condemned his Lord, saying, "We ought to obey God rather than men" (Acts 5:29).

He charged them with the slaughter of the Redeemer, then stood before them without flinching. He chastised the sorcerer Simon, saying, "Thy money perish with thee" (Acts 8:10). He stood before his brethren and announced a major policy change in the church whereby gentiles might be accepted.

Simon Peter was spiritual and prophetic. He received the revelations concerning the church. Angels accompanied him in and released him from the prison, and a great vision opened the door to millions of honest souls.

His testimony was as the rock, his faith unwavering. The Savior, abandoned by others, asked Peter, "Will ye also go away?" (John 6:67). Peter replied, "Lord, to whom shall we go? thou hast the words of eternal life" (John 6:68). Shortly before the Crucifixion, the Lord asked, "But whom say ye that I am?" (Matthew 16:15). The answer revealed from God expressed the power and character of Peter: "Thou art the Christ, the Son of the living God" (Matthew 16:16). The Savior replied, "Flesh and blood hath not revealed it unto thee, but my Father which is in heaven" (Matthew 16:17). Heavenly messengers he had seen; martyrs he had accompanied; with the Son of God he had lived. The Comforter had come, and never was there faltering or questioning in his mind again.

Peter's Teachings

The teachings of Simon Peter are to all people, even to the latest generation. He bore testimony constantly of the divinity of the Christ. As he had been forgiven of his weaknesses, he now urged all men to forgive. He urged the chaste and virtuous life. He taught honesty and urged that members live in peace with the gentiles. This Apostle taught his people to honor kings, governments, and laws; to endure grief, suffering, and buffeting patiently; and to consider revilement and suffering for the Lord's sake a blessing. Perhaps he had seen much marital unhappiness, for he commanded wives to be subject to and convert their unbelieving husbands through their own goodness and meekness. He commanded the husbands to honor their wives as partners, to love them, to be compassionate to them, and to treasure them. He urged parents to be kind to children and the posterity to honor and obey the parents. He urged employers to be honorable and just with their workers and employees to give service willingly. He urged the clean and constructive life and forbade company with rioters, winebibbers, revelers, banqueters, idolaters, and lustful ones. He urged service in the church, the sober life, a vigilant faith, and works leading toward perfection.

The great leader frequently repeated his testimony as an eyewitness and an ear witness to spectacular and eventful happenings. Foreshadowing the apostasy, he testified that false teachers with damnable heresies would come after his departing to deny the Lord and to make merchandise of the souls of men (see

2 Peter 2:1–3). He placed the divine stamp of approval on the writings of the Old Testament and unfolded the history of the world, which covered the flood, the destruction of Sodom and Gomorrah, and other important events. Again and again, he preached the law of chastity and cleanliness and denounced the evils of sporting, feasting, adultery, incontinence, and covetousness.

[8] As he neared martyrdom, drinking a bitter cup somewhat like his Master and Teacher, he made sure that the world would know his witness and sureness. Sitting figuratively on the brink of his grave, he made a solemn declaration which has been read by countless millions. To the members of the church, he prayed that they might have a "knowledge of God, and of Jesus our Lord" (2 Peter 1:2). He gloried in the "exceeding great and precious promises: that by these ye might be partakers of the divine nature, having escaped the corruption that is in the world through lust" (2 Peter 1:4).

Peter continued:

> Wherefore the rather, brethren, give diligence to make your calling and election sure. . . .
>
> Yea, I think it meet, as long as I am in this tabernacle, to stir you up by putting you in remembrance;
>
> Knowing that shortly I must put off this my tabernacle, even as our Lord Jesus Christ hath shewed me.
>
> Moreover I will endeavour that ye may be able after my decease to have these things always in remembrance.
>
> For we have not followed cunningly devised fables, when we made known unto you the power and coming of our Lord Jesus Christ, but were eyewitnesses of his majesty.
>
> For he received from God the Father honour and glory, when there came such a voice to him from the excellent glory, This is my beloved Son, in whom I am well pleased.
>
> And this voice which came from heaven we heard, when we were with him in the holy mount. (2 Peter 1:10, 13–18)

When his work was done, his testimony borne, his witness delivered, his numbered days run out, Satan who had long desired him was now permitted to take him in martyrdom. His testimony came from his dying lips.

But Simon Peter was not dead. Important changes came to him—the dissolution of his body, but also the resurrection of his soul. With his loyal associates, James and John, Simon Peter returned to the earth, bridging the gap of darkened centuries. Together they appeared on the banks of the Susquehanna River in

Pennsylvania, where Peter delivered to the young prophets the keys of the kingdom, which the Apostles possessed from the Lord Jesus Christ.

The Apostle lives. The weak things of the world confounded the wise. Millions have read his testimony. His powerful witness has stirred multitudes. Through the countless ages of eternity, he will live and extend his influence over the children of this earth. With his brethren, the Twelve, he will judge the nations.

My young brothers and sisters, I hope that you can love and accept the great prophet Peter as I feel in my heart to do. In the name of Jesus Christ, amen.

Note

1. Rev. Dorsey E. Dent, "A Message for This Week."

Index

Italicized numbers refer to images.

A

house of David, key of, 92, 111

house of Israel, covenant with,
229–30, 231

"house of Peter," 41–42

housing complexes, in Capernaum, 39

humility, 11, 269, 382–84

I

iconography, patterns of, on
sarcophagi, 195–200

idolatry, 105

impurity, ritual, 158–62

influenza epidemic, 304, 314 n. 33

innocence, declaration of
in farewell speeches, 320
in 2 Peter, 322–23

interpreters, 116–17

Irenaeus, 172

Isaiah
allusions to, in New
Testament, 256
healing as fulfillment of
prophecy of, 155

J

Jaffa, 194

James. *See also* Apocryphon of James
financial status of, 57 n. 72
as fisherman, 36
at Garden of Gethsemane,
79–80
gives keys to Joseph Smith
and Oliver Cowdery,
361–62, 364–65
keys given to, 112, 298–99,
311 n. 6, 312 n. 7, 365–66

and Mount of Transfiguration
episode, 75–76, 89 n. 35

Paul meets with, 237

separating out of, 88 n. 32

transfiguration of, 24 n. 5,
276–77

Jared, brother of, stones of, 116–17

Jeremiah, 95–96, 121 n. 6

Jerusalem, Paul's second visit to,
237–38

Jerusalem Conference, 220–21,
237–41

"Jesus boat," 35

Jesus Christ. *See also* Atonement;
crucifixion
addresses Peter as "Peter,"
89nn39,42
in Apocrypha, 352
in *Apocryphon of James*,
347
Apostles as witnesses of, 26
n. 19
arrest of, 80–81
clarifies parables, 73–74
clarifies teachings, 87 n. 18
coming unto, 10–11
and commission of Peter, 18
emulation of, 268–69
faith centered in, 269–70
final discourse of, 318
at Garden of Gethsemane,
79–80
grace of, 142–43
healing in name of, 151–53,
165 n. 5
healings performed by,
152–53
holds key of David, 92